◆ ◆ ◆ ◆ ◆ ◆ ◆ ◆ ◆ ◆ ◆ ◆ ◆ ◆ ◆ ◆

GEOGRAPHY AND CONTEMPORARY ISSUES

◆ ◆

GEOGRAPHY AND CONTEMPORARY ISSUES:

with the collaboration of
Shane Davies
Associate Professor of Geography
University of Texas at Austin

STUDIES OF RELEVANT PROBLEMS

◆ ◆

Melvin Albaum

Associate Professor of Geography
University of Colorado

JOHN WILEY & SONS
New York   London   Sydney   Toronto

Library of Congress Cataloging in Publication Data

Albaum, Melvin, 1936-   comp.
   Geography and contemporary issues: studies of relevant problems.

   1. United States—Social conditions—1960-
—Addresses, essays, lectures.   2. United States—
Economic conditions—1961-   —Addresses, essays,
lectures.   I. Title.

HN59.A54   309.1'73'092   72–8011
ISBN 0–471–01879–1
ISBN 0–471–01880–5 (pbk.)

Printed in the United States of America

10 9 8 7 6 5 4 3 2

For My Parents and Jennifer

CONTRIBUTING AUTHORS ❖

John S. Adams
Melvin Albaum
Calvin L. Beale
Alan R. Bird
Stanley D. Brunn
Ian Burton
George W. Carey
James D. Cowhig
Shane Davies
J. Tait Davis
George J. Demko
Donald R. Deskins, Jr.
Reynolds Farley
Gary L. Fowler
Robert Gold
Jacque L. Harper
David Harvey
Keith D. Harries
Wayne L. Hoffman
Helen W. Johnson
John F. Kain

Robert W. Kates
Philip A. Leighton
Mark Lowry II
Peter F. Mason
John L. McCoy
Dennis C. McElrath
Richard L. Morrill
Eugene P. Odom
Joseph J. Persky
Harold M. Rose
William M. Ross
John R. Seeley
Virginia L. Sharp
Joseph Sonnenfeld
Irene B. Tauber
James O. Wheeler
Halliman H. Winsborough
Julian Wolpert
Carl Youngmann
Wilbur Zelinsky

Preface ·

It is dreadfully apparent that man has often forfeited the opportunity to create a balanced system whereby he can coexist with his environment and with his fellow man in a just and orderly fashion. Even with the tremendous advances in technology and science, the abuse of our environment and of fellow men has, nevertheless, resulted in an ecological and social state which may well be taking us to the threshold of disaster. It is equally apparent that there are feasible solutions to many of the problems which confront us and, where solutions do not currently exist, they will have to be found. It may be less apparent, however, that many of the solutions will inherently involve a radical transformation in life styles and values for the various segments of American society, if not the entire world.

During the decade of the 1960's, the American people were confronted with a series of issues and problems which have restructured a large segment of American thinking and policy: the problems of poverty and the poor, the problems of minority groups, the threat of environmental deterioration, the implications of population growth, the multitude of problems associated with cities and urban living, and the shock waves which penetrated into the thoughts of most Americans as a result of violence and conflict. These problems, their causes, and the resultant frustrations did not suddenly emerge in the sixties; they have been developing over several decades. The involvement of the United States in a major conflict in Southeast Asia, coupled with the demands of the civil rights movements and the rise of a "youth culture," which often challenged the values and life-styles of previous generations, asking to be told "like it is," may have been the sparks which ignited much of the impetus and desire for rapid change and the resolution of problems. The numerous studies and reports issued by governmental agencies and private organizations were additional factors drawing attention to the needs and wants of America's people.

Some of the most perceptive and astute Americans have been today's college and university students who have shown a tremendous concern over the mutual problems with which we are confronted and who, often, have been active leaders and participants in programs of amelioration. This volume comes, in part, as a response to this deep concern and interest which our students have shown. It has been assembled to serve several purposes: (1) to illustrate some of the research and study which geographers and scholars in closely related disciplines have been engaged in and which bear social relevance to contemporary issues and problems; (2) to serve as a supplementary or principal text in the study of the social, human, and regional geography of the United States—where all too often these issues are given little treatment in current texts; and, (3) to provoke a greater participation of geography as a research discipline in the study and analysis of contemporary issues, but, perhaps even more important, in the teaching of relevant contemporary issues and problems.

The six topics which this reader treats are rather general. It is extremely difficult to separate the contemporary issues and problems of American society into distinctly separate parts since they are intrinsically interrelated. How can one isolate poverty from the Black ghetto, or the Black ghetto from the problems of the city? How can one isolate the problems of environmental deterioration and stress from the problems of population growth and pressure? While each of the six sections are overlapping phenomena, they are, to some extent, sufficiently distinct so that they can, at least for organizational purposes, be treated under separate headings. Because of the problem of overlapping phenomena, there are several studies included here which could have been placed in more than one section. The arrangement of each section, however, has been made in an effort to offer some continuity to the highly interrelated overall dimension of the issues and problems presented.

Studies often remain scattered in professional journals, discussion papers, government reports, and other sources which vary in their accessibility to students. It is my feeling, and the feeling of others in the profession, that there is much need to bring relevant studies together which can be understood and which have appeal to today's concerned students. I have attempted to assemble articles and original manuscripts on a level which would be suitable for most undergraduate students, both in and out of the discipline. With great difficulty, I have further attempted to avoid those articles which were either too emotional, too general, or were essentially too methodological in nature and which would add little in-depth perspective to the issues being treated here. The articles presented in this reader offer the breadth of the problems at hand and in most, where the case study approach is taken, offer depth both to the problem and the methodology employed. Several of the studies present an overview of the general issue and possible strategies for study and/or solution. However, in keeping with the general purposes of the volume, most of the articles and papers tend to be specific in nature and content. I have not set out to alert the reader to the fact that we are living in a time of "population explosion," "environmental disaster," "urban crisis," etc.; mass media, numerous action groups, and other forms of communication have adequately sounded that alert.

The selection of items which appear in this reader are primarily devoted to the issues and problems of the contemporary United States. The problems of the poor and of poverty, the problems of Black Americans, and the problems of American cities are basically American problems and issues. In areas such as population, environment, and conflict there are obviously greater international ramifications and consequences. However, to treat all of these problems and issues on an international level would have been an almost impossible task and would certainly not have fit into the limitations of a single volume.

It is my sincere hope that this reader will prove itself useful as a principal text in current or newly developing courses on contemporary problems, and as a principal or supplementary text in courses such as the Geography of the United States, Social or Human Geography, and other courses where currently used texts are inadequate in dealing with the issues and problems treated here. It is my further hope and anticipation that this reader will have appeal and usefulness to students of courses in related disciplines.

There are many case studies which should have been included in this reader. Unfortunately, these are either unavailable, are only in the early stages of research and preparation, or nonexistent at this time. Many of the issues and problems presented will have to await future dissemination of research for more complete coverage.

I have avoided the use of introductions to each section, as one often finds in volumes of this type, assuming that the individual reader has already been informed of the impending peril which awaits us and the existence of the issues. Each study represents some aspect of the issues at large and speaks for itself. Furthermore, it is neither the purpose of this volume to dictate strategy for future research, nor to recommend areas which require further research. These should be obvious and are matters which each individual member of the profession should dictate to himself.

There are several individuals who have, in one way or another, assisted with the effort to assemble this reader. My appreciation is extended to Harold Rose and George Demko for their helpful comments; and, to Diana DeAre for her clerical work and general assistance in putting it all together. I would further like to express my appreciation and gratitude to Karen Wiley for her able assistance in proofing the text. The help given by the many authors and publishers, without whose cooperation this volume could not have been assembled, is gratefully acknowledged.

Boulder, Colorado   *Melvin Albaum*

Contents ❖ ❖ ❖ ❖ ❖ ❖ ❖ ❖ ❖ ❖ ❖ ❖ ❖ ❖ ❖

xi

INTRODUCTION

RICHARD L. MORRILL ◆

Geography and the Transformation of Society

Part I

Geographers have long been accustomed to study the transformation of landscape, normally as passive recorders of changes wrought by nature, business, individuals, and nations. We have left to the planners the advocacy of ideal landscapes. Unfortunately, the planner's design bias reveals a fundamental ignorance at times of human social, economic, and spatial behavior. Geographers have no claim to omniscience either, but we have a more interdisciplinary training than others, and ought to be able to evaluate the present landscape and prescribe desirable transformations.

Geographers, like planners, have been insecure. As a discipline deriving its numerical strength from countless state colleges and financial support from military and other governmental sources, it has been truly conservative. We have preferred to refine our understanding of spatial patterns of society as they are, rather than to question the "rightness" of these patterns or the responsibility of society for them. Poverty, injustice, discrimination, hunger, disease, pollution, and overcrowding have been around a long time. It is incredible that geography is only just "discovering" such striking features of the landscape. Even now, who is studying them?

As a conservative discipline, geography looked at such problems as temporary aberrations or as evidence of inherent human inequalities. In this tradition, "landscape transformation" means simply to study the evolutionary change and not to evaluate the causes.

It becomes increasingly evident to the honest man that the persistence of all these problems and their landscape manifestations in the face of increased

◆ SOURCE.   Reprinted by permission of the author and editors from *Antipode: A Radical Journal of Geography*, Vol. 1, 1969, pp. 6–9, and Vol. 2, 1970, pp. 4–10.

wealth, knowledge, and technology means that there must be some fundamental deficiencies in the structures and values of society itself. Within the existing system, the problems are not withering away. It is becoming doubtful, too, whether the increasingly costly "tampering" in the welfare areas will yield the desired results.

For those of us who believe that our institutional (mainly university) role is to help bring about a more just, equal, and peaceful society, a search for more *radical* ways and means to achieve change must be one of our main tasks. I use the word "search" because the old "revolutionary" solutions haven't worked either, but I like the word "radical" because only fundamental changes in society offer effective hope. My own expectation is that the role of geographical expertise will be important, but at a secondary or implementing level, because spatial rearranging, like our present tampering, will not get at basic causes. Still, geographers might be able to suggest spatial arrangements that will make it much easier to achieve desired social transformations.

At this point I'll argue against the "New Left" premise that a revolution is the only route to progress—that is, the idea that the existing system must be destroyed and a new order built. Very probably radical social transformations will be more easily achieved via the existing political structure, and of course would be infinitely less destructive.

In the first place, the dreams of revolution are naive. The power that can and will be brought against revolu-

tion is phenomenal. The means of surveillance is amazingly efficient. No one should imagine that an existing "power structure" will hesitate to destroy utterly those who might attempt to attack it too directly.

Secondly, the New Left vastly exaggerates potential support. The level of disaffection does not even begin to approach the level in any revolution in history. It would be stupid and tragic to sacrifice the black and the intellectual elite in such a futile gesture, especially when the so-called "proletariat" they are wooing would lead the slaughter!

Third, a "revolutionary program" is hopelessly dated and simplistic which imagines that nationalization and "worker control" would usher in a golden age. On the one hand the New Left preaches greater freedom and at the same time is incredibly intolerant of opposing views—even within the narrow spectrum of the far left! A true radical should not want to sacrifice the individual freedom that has taken centuries to achieve for an arbitrary change of ownership and power control.

Fourth, the New Left underestimates the capacity of our society for change and the degree of sympathy and support that can be won from many in the existing "power structure." I might add that while the revolutions of recent centuries have usually resulted in some social improvement, they have been carried out at frightful cost, and have not at all achieved a just society. All revolutions seem to have been betrayed by incompetents who preferred exercising power to executing reform. Furthermore, some of the relatively better societies around, such as Sweden, have never experienced a revolution.

What strategies can I suggest, then, as alternatives to a revolutionary one? The key is to find changes which preserve the obvious forms of the existing society, but which in fact radically transform the substance, changes which do not immediately abolish and replace existing authority but which circumscribe such authority and transfer significant power to those truly dedicated to basic change. Excess concentration of power, even in the hands of "good guys," is by definition, I believe, incompatible with a just and equal society. Also it is urgent to work for quite specific changes aimed at particular deficiencies of society, rather than rely on the "good intentions" and "social awareness" of revolutionaries who could not keep a society functioning. A series of small steps can be effected, with a radical end result, that could not have been accepted initially. In effect, I'm suggesting that "subversion" (to describe the process from the other side) is far more effective than revolution.

Three means for gaining democratic acceptance of truly radical changes are (1) by converting a significant proportion of the intellectual community on humanitarianism and theoretical grounds; and (2) by convincing a sufficient proportion of the business power structure to accept the changes on economic grounds; and (3) by better mobilizing the demands of those who would gain most by radical change—the black, the poor and the elderly.

The first group is increasingly influential—in government, in business, but especially through the mass media. Newscasts and specials on television and magazines such as *Life* and *Look* have been main creators of public opinion against the Vietnam war, for action on pollution and hunger, and for what has been accomplished in racial relations. In a historic context, the changes of the last few years are pretty fantastic. The enlistment of fairly few "natural leaders," who can in turn sway tens of millions, is especially important (an elitist but realistic truth).

The second group—essentially the business world, is neither stupid nor inherently evil. Large businesses, especially, are pragmatic. Most businesses crave stability and fear the destruction of property. Many businesses are potentially vulnerable to the organized sabotage of a fairly small band of discontents. Many businesses could be convinced to accept a dilution of their power and autonomy in return for stability. For example, in many areas, dairy farmers prefer to follow the dictates of the local marketing board's guaranteed price, rather than risk the vagaries of the market.

The third group, those who suffer from injustice and inequity, constitute as much as one-third of the US population (objectively, perhaps, more, but consciously not). Because the specific felt needs of groups vary, it will be difficult to forge unified support. For example, the elderly poor are for a variety of reasons conservative with respect to race relations. Still, alliances are possible of the log rolling type—"you support us and we'll support you."

The validity of these arguments for transformation through non-revolutionary means rests on the discovery of those changes that are acceptable but will bring radical renewal. In any event, it is the only realistic course open.

Part II

"The greatest challenge is to discover whether intelligent life can exist here on earth."—N. Cousins, *Saturday Review*, 1969.

In Part I, a radical but political strategy to transform society was outlined. In Part II, I suggest specific changes which geographers can work toward. There are others certainly. First here is my own:

Declaration of Conscience and Statement of Purpose

The professional geographer's main concerns have been with studying the interrelations of man and environment, patterns of location of man's activities and man himself, and patterns of human variation among regions, cultures and nations.

It would be good to be able to say that we have gone beyond study to enhance and preserve the environment, to effect more satisfying territorial arrangements or to improve international or intercultural understanding. We believe that it is now time to bring to bear the great knowledge we have accumulated on public policy, that we cannot remain aloof as the environment deteriorates, as the imbalances and disorders of urban and rural life are ag-

gravated, as international distrust, ignorance and destruction continue.

Pollution of air and water worsens. Scenic and historic landscapes are ravaged. Wilderness disappears. Economic activities concentrate in the already congested, increasingly dangerous metropolises, at the whim of investors, despite the expressed preference of the majority of the population for non-metropolitan living. While some areas get richer, larger regions stagnate. Even within the prosperous metropolis, many areas decay. Social and geographic polarization of black and white threaten our very survival. Too much geographic research on other countries is oriented to the political and military ends of our own country, rather than the needs of others.

Therefore, we dedicate ourselves to a program of study, education, and action, designed to influence more directly the patterns of our society, to create mechanisms for critical evaluation of public and private proposals, and to make our own positive proposals for improvement. As specialists in environment, location and area studies, we can no longer sit idly by while our world becomes less and less liveable.

I believe that the following principles (in the three facets of geography) should be adopted by the geography profession, and serve as the basis for evaluation of and action toward all decisions of individuals, businesses and governments that affect the human and natural landscape.

1. Further pollution of the natural environment is impermissible, and present pollution must be reduced.

Further encroachment of artificial forms on the remaining wilderness must be resisted with whatever means necessary.

2. The spatial arrangement of human activities must reflect the needs and desires of those occupying areas and society as a whole, not the narrow goals of economic efficiency, nor the interests of just property owners and investors. Jobs should be created where people want to be, not at the whim of investors. Spatial inequality in income, services and justice must be alleviated.

3. Our national relations with other nations and people must be based on serving the creative needs of their people. We must cease economic, political or military interference; and end exploitative economic arrangements.

I shall develop only the second theme, since others are far more competent in the other areas, but there are four general points I would like to make that concern all topics.

First, desired transformations will not occur just because we study "relevant" problems and even find solutions. Obviously, organization, persuasion and action are required. Much can be done through working with existing organizations, such as the ACLU, Sierra Club, or in politics. But geography must have a strong voice of conscience and action itself. The "social action caucus" convened at the 1969 Ann Arbor AAG convention must at the least:

1. communicate findings and recommendations to each other, to public (as via videotapes) and to governments;

2. form regional working committees to investigate, and develop policy and action with respect to existing abuses and problems and all possible threats to people and environment; and

3. perhaps form specific interest committees, for example, concerning the metropolitan black community; the American Indian, the fate of rural society and landscapes; air pollution, surveillance, privacy and remote sensing; academic freedom, tenure and risks of social action research; preservation of wilderness, etc.; with both research and action aims;

4. act to implement findings on specific issues, and to further general principles by education and publicity, and as required, by testifying in hearings, lobbying with other groups, and if necessary, more direct action. A desirable weapon would be a sleek, partly pictorial popular magazine, but that could only come later. In the meantime, good thoughtful articles can be submitted to *Landscape, Transaction* and other magazines.

Second, one can argue I think, that poverty, injustice, and inequality exist because we (as all people) have a frightening capacity for selfishness, greed and aggression. More specifically, the notion that in our "free economy" the price system rationally and fairly allocated resources, land incomes, etc.

is our institutional justification for our selfishness, for the prevalence and persistence of all these problems. In reality, the severe inequality of power of different groups and areas grossly distorts prices and wages—resulting in an absurd degree of income inequality [and much poverty], in undue concentration of investment in already successful metropolises, contrary to the wishes of the majority of the population, in a corollary stagnation and poverty in many areas of the country, and in exploitatively low prices for products imported from weaker countries (and weaker areas of our own country). Inequality in power also results in grotesque misallocation of public resources. Tens of billions of dollars have been spent in the elusive and reckless pursuit of military supremacy, and worse, in the destruction of other peoples and lands. More billions are unnecessarily spent in the chauvinistic diversion of space exploration, conquering nature, because we cannot figure out how to live together decently.

Third, supremacy of economic efficiency criteria continues to further pollution, to ravage remaining wilderness, to aggravate unconscionable concentrations of people and factories in giant metropolises. The solution to the failure of the price system and to excess emphasis on economic efficiency is largely political-economic, but has an important geographic aspect. Since inequality of power is the main villain, equalization of power is the main cure. I believe that the most important institutional change needed for building a more just society (and incidentally,

a means of convergence between capitalism and socialism) is either:

1. that all prices and wages must be set by the equal influence of owners (management, capital), employees, and representatives of the consuming public; or
2. that all prices and wages are most fairly determined by a small group of specialists.

What do the readers think? A simple Marxist-type change in the ownership of business from private to a government (or union) bureaucracy would in all probability decrease production, and would not necessarily bring any improvement in basic conditions. The key is to retain the institution of private property while instituting social control over its exchange and circumscribing its power over people.

The fundamental geographic implication and need is that location and land use decisions (factories, stores, subdivisions, mines, etc.) can no longer be entrusted entirely to the property owners or investors (whether private or government). Those who should have an equal power of decision include, besides the owner, employees and *others who will be affected* by the decision. Sometimes this would be mainly local residents, at other times, the wider society. In most cases why should geographers, as specialists in environment and location, not have a customary role, as *custodians* or watchdogs of the landscape? The responsibility of such a role is enormous, and geographers have not yet achieved the necessary competence. This is why it is so urgent that the "social action" caucus begins now to exercise such a role unofficially, and build up the experience, and reputation.

Fourth, discrimination against minority groups continues to relegate one-seventh of the American population to inferior education and jobs, to locations and areas the white majority doesn't want, and denies them the power to create the landscape they desire. Our bias toward northwest European culture is evidenced by the extreme difference in our economic relations with Canada and Mexico.

The human reaction of fear and discrimination toward those who are different is, I think, more difficult to overcome than economic selfishness and poverty. The evidence of history shows that racial and ethnic differences can be resolved over a long period of intermingling and intermarriage (Sicily, Portugal, Hungary). But our crisis is now, and the perception of difference is greater than the reality.

In the short run (next 5 to 10 years?) equalization in job opportunities and income is the most urgent. Clearly, nothing short of governmental interference (akin to voting registrars) in the actual hiring and firing process of business will end job discrimination. Or perhaps a quota system, both with respect to employment and political representation may be needed for a while. Also, society by now has an obligation to provide decent jobs where the people are (especially on Indian reservations). In the long-run, however, geographers must work toward integra-

tion, including spatial, in order that inter-group conflict may be resolved.

Geographic Strategies for Improving the Arrangement of Human Activities

I argued above that the unhappy state of the landscape, human and natural, is a result of selfishness, inequality of power and income, the excess emphasis on economic efficiency and discrimination. The basic solution is in the politics and economics of income distribution and job provision: for example, urban renewal of slums is of course futile if incomes remain the same. The solution to slums and blight is income improvement so that there is no demand for poor housing.

Still, there are key policies which geographers could work for and contribute expertise to, which will help bring about greater equality and justice. There is severe regional inequality of income and development. Most people *cannot live where they wish,* since job creation is controlled by so few, who obviously are unconcerned with regional disparity or personal choice. We should argue for the principle that the *jobs should go where the people want to be.* This means basically that strict controls must be placed on the growth of the already giant metropolises (the replacement of 30 by 80 story buildings, increasing the already uneconomic and anti-social congestion of New York City, is a horrendous example of how business and government make decisions with the utter disregard of people). The potential new jobs should be shifted instead to create new centers of growth in presently depressed, poor or underdeveloped regions. Geographers should specialize in working out the sizes, arrangements and locations that would permit people to live in the rural, urban or metropolitan setting they desire, while bringing all within easy access of metropolitan services, but especially to bring a wide range of employment opportunities to all regions. Such a scheme could fail unless non-poverty minimum wages were enforced universally, as low-wage industries are but means for owners to take advantage of peoples' desire not to move.

Within the metropolis, inequality is also great. Poverty will be reduced here, too, by shifting decent paying jobs to where the poor are.

The demand that location decisions be subject to far greater social control, with a direct role for geographers, and implementation of the principle that jobs should go where the people want to be, make up one strategy in that part of geography concerned with the arrangement of human activities. Other strategies can be developed; it is mainly necessary to free ourselves from the single criterion of economic efficiency upon which most of our theory is based, and instead focus on maximizing the satisfaction of people.

111111111111111

POVERTY AND THE
POOR IN AMERICA

111111111111111

RICHARD L. MORRILL ◆

Geographical Aspects of Poverty in the United States

"Pastures of plenty" have in the past and still today elude a sizeable proportion of our population. We address ourselves here mainly to a limited question: within the United States, what geographical—that is, environmental, spatial or regional—factors help explain the prevalence and distribution of poverty? At the outset, we can admit that poverty is far more a function of problems of economic and social organization. Still, geography does play a part, and it would be both foolish and perhaps immoral to neglect the study of a problem so real to so many.

Environmental factors of land and climate influence the productivity of an agricultural landscape, which may in turn influence income. Natural resources, of course, are the more obvious geographic key to relative prosperity, but their influence may be exaggerated. Relative location within a national economy, distance to the most "successful" places, and the population den-sity of an area are increasingly important spatial factors. State and local differences in laws and taxation, and sectional variations in social attitudes and practices, are among regional geographic factors. Given the existence of poverty nationally, for economic and social reasons, these geographic factors help to explain the spatial distribution of poverty and to suggest why much poverty is so difficult to end.

It is perhaps not surprising that economists are at times inclined to emphasize geographic reasons for poverty (to avoid admitting that the price system does not allocate value correctly?). Indeed, the theory of regional income convergence suggests that poverty is principally a function of a developmental time lag among regions. Unfortunately, even if all regions were as prosperous as the most successful, a most unlikely prospect, poverty would still be with us.

Poverty in the United States means

◆ **SOURCE.** Reproduced by permission from the *Proceedings* of the Association of American Geographers, Vol. 1, 1969, pp. 117–121.

that the family or individual cannot share in the material and cultural expectations of the middle-class majority. The family income level that signifies poverty thus varies according to family size, region, or rural or urban residence, but a family income below $4000 is a reasonable approximation to a national median for 1968. About one-fifth of the population nationally is not able to enjoy the material fruits of our extraordinary economy, but this proportion varies from about 10% in the richest areas to well over half in the poorest.

Environmental Factors

Variations in land and climate do not take us very far in understanding either the existence or the location of poverty. Highly productive agricultural areas may support a greater population, but not necessarily higher incomes. Poor "stump farmers" or prospectors may be scattered across some mediocre environments but their poverty is for psychological, not physical, reasons. Many Indian reservations are in wretched areas, but social attitudes and politics imprisoned the Indian, not the environment.

Resources can clearly induce economic growth, and may bring high relative incomes, especially to those owning the resources, if the ratio of resources to population is high. Conversely, depletion of resources, or decline in demand and price for a given resource, can induce economic decline, and depress relative incomes. The collapse of demand for anthracite coal and the closing of rail-oriented coal mines after dieselization, or the depletion of some

iron mines, indeed caused areas and places of poverty, since, for a complex of social and economic reasons, part of the population did not leave the declining areas. However, far more commonly it is not the depletion of resources that causes such poverty, but technical improvements in productivity. In fact, most resource-oriented (whether to forest, water, mineral or scenic resources) local economies have fairly severe poverty and unimpressive income levels, owing to the ability to maintain or even increase production with a greatly reduced labor force. The prevalence of poverty in mining and forest areas is thus a function of technologically induced unemployment, together with the relative immobility of the population—not resource problems.

The geographically important result is that poverty is proportionally more severe in such areas, owing to the lack of alternative opportunities, while in most cities technically-caused unemployment is fairly quickly reduced by new demands for labor. Mining and forestry may be all there is to support wide areas of rural America. Unattractiveness of such areas to a diversity of economic activities for which resources are *not* vital is a partial explanation for the spatial pattern of poverty, but the unattractiveness is a function of poor relative location and other factors, not of environment.

Appalachian poverty results from technical change, not the decline of coal. In this particular case the ruggedness of the terrain and the attendant poor accessibility of much of the area does impose an environmental barrier to the attraction of alternate opportunities, in spite of a good location relative to national markets.

Agriculture, of course, supports a far larger proportion of rural America, and an even greater portion of its population, than does forestry or mining. On the average, rural incomes are far below urban incomes, and in fact, the inability of agriculture to provide adequate incomes accounts for the dominant pattern of poverty on the American map, both as a relative proportion of the population of a region, and in absolute numbers.

Low income is common both to the farmer and to the village and small town service populations. Again, the relative poverty of many farming areas is less a function of the natural environment than of prices, relative productivity vis-a-vis urban activities, organizational weakness, the unwarranted popularity of farming, grossly inadequate farm size, preference for the rural life, and above all, the unattractiveness of rural and small-town areas for alternative opportunities. As with forestry and mining, rising productivity reduces demands for labor in farming and the volume of services needed, but again the surplus population, both farmers and small-town people, is unable or unwilling to seek urban opportunities.

If rural poverty is mainly a result of the lack of diversified opportunities, then a geographic process—migration of the surplus population to the cities— is immediately suggested as an answer. The higher ratio of resources to remaining population would presumably improve rural income. Rural-urban migration has truly been gigantic and continuous, but while decline in income

may have been avoided, incomes competitive with urban areas have rarely been achieved, partly because the migration is age-selective, with the most active and productive abandoning the countryside to the old and very young.

Spatial Factors

In an advanced technological society, spatial factors supercede environmental in influencing relative income. The inability of rural areas to attract diversified opportunities is partly spatial. Most economic activities so respond to economies of large scale production and to agglomerative sharing that successful competition requires urban location. Low density areas, and small towns or even small cities in such areas, are in a poor position to compete for activities requiring large markets and labor forces. The fact of greater dispersion then severely limits the activities that may profitably be carried on. The lack of competition for labor weakens its bargaining power; and indeed the dispersion of producers themselves weakens their competitive position vis-a-vis urban activities.

Rural areas and small towns fairly near a metropolis, however, enjoy the possibility of commutation to the city, and thus supplemental income. In addition, relative location near large urban labor markets reduces proportional transport charges and raises effective farm prices.

The partial immobility of the rural population and the inability or unwillingness of many rural residents to seek higher incomes in the cities may be partly spatial, too. Lack of other skills, the security of a home, and other social and personal reasons are perhaps controlling, but familiarity and satisfaction with the known territory, together with fear and uncertainty and ignorance of more distant and different environments are also influential. Distance to possible opportunities, in fact, does hinder migration.

Within the urban realm itself, relative position within the national economy influences income and the degree of poverty. At the risk of over-simplification, let me argue that the relative prosperity of a place is mainly a function of the demand for and hence price of its export industries, and the local productivity of labor in these industries. In general we observe a locational preference of higher paying industries in the largest metropolises and/or in the core economic areas—i.e., the metropolitan Northeast and California. Thus, the smaller the city, and/or the farther from the core markets, the lower the median income and the higher the proportion of poor. The more peripheral are at a disadvantage in transport costs in serving large national markets; the smaller may be at a scale disadvantage.

The diffusion of development out of the northeast core has been gradual. Northern investors did little to diversify the economy of the South; indeed the migration of the textile and furniture industries was partly a seeking of rural, dispersed locations without competitive opportunities, so that incomes could be kept low. The California sub-core developed on the basis of the sheer number of determined migrants. Other metropolitan islands of prosperity have developed on the basis of strong regional control and successful national exports.

Regional Factors

Regional variations in social, political and economic institutions and attitudes influence the spatial distribution of poverty. Thus, states with low minimum wages, and with "right-to-work" laws, in order to attract industry, have markedly lower overall income levels. South Carolina, for example, has a higher proportion of its labor force in manufacturing than does California, but many times the incidence of poverty. It is true that industry in rural and small-town areas provides an alternative to agriculture and forestry, but this has demonstrably failed to create high income levels, given constraints on labor organization. Current programs of bringing industry to the countryside—in order to stem the flow to the cities and to raise incomes—cannot work, since industries will only choose rural locations if wages are low enough to offset the other disadvantages.

Social and economic discrimination against minorities is a major cause of poverty; and the victims are geographically concentrated. In the South generally and in northern and western cities, black Americans have long been relegated to the lowest paying jobs; are the "last hired and first fired." Blacks have jobs and income inferior to whites at the same level of education; and more basically, the education received has been inferior. In the South, personal service remains a major occupation—imprisoning the employee in poverty—owing to the lack of other opportunities.

Discrimination in the South against the black man may result in the largest area and population in poverty, but treatment of the Mexican-American and especially the Indian in the West is, if anything, more cruel. Relegation to reservations tends to prevent the Indian from participation at all in the modern economy, even from competing for the lowliest jobs in the city. As a result income discrepancies between white and non-white are more extreme than in the South.

Poverty is also relatively greater among the elderly, military, and student sub-populations. The elderly are poor because of lack of saving and inflation, but mainly the fact of economic growth (average incomes are much higher than when they were actively earning); thus the only solution is direct transfers of income from those of us working now. Military poverty is simply a result of pay discrimination, where the "employees" are conscripted and not free to organize. Student poverty is temporary, but is worrisome if it prevents the poor from obtaining the skills necessary to rise from poverty. Geographical factors do not cause such forms of poverty, but the impact of such poverty is regionally somewhat concentrated. The elderly form higher ratios in rural areas generally, and in some warm winter climate areas. Military employment is skewed strongly to the South and West.

Poverty in the City

Geographic factors, especially relative location and population density, have been seen to influence the prevalence of poverty, and mainly, of course, (2) a result of relative supply and organizational strength—that is, if there are too many in some occupations and they are unorganized, their employers need not pay competitive wages—and (3) social discrimination against minorities—that is, the groups most looked-down upon by others are relegated to the least competitive occupations. City unemployment, except for temporary adjustments, is in turn a function of excess supply and minority status. Thus raising wages in the weakest occupations could eliminate poverty for those workers, but at the same time could increase unemployment—the solution of which is much more complicated. Upgrading of skill levels will take up much unemployment, but ironically, only the elimination of poverty, the expansion of the demand for goods and services from those now in poverty, will reduce unemployment to minimum levels (c. 1%). This vicious circle of unemployment and poverty will be extremely difficult to break —perhaps through a combination of a temporary guaranteed non-poverty income and investment incentives.

Part of the excess supply, and thus poverty and unemployment, is a result of the *transfer* of rural poverty to the city—that is, people who have been displaced from agriculture and forestry, who lack skills for available urban jobs, and who have come in greater numbers than the city could absorb.

Within the city, the social-geographic process of spatial segregation of

and spatial pattern of poverty, especially within rural portions of our country. The prevalence of poverty even in the richest cities is in part (1) a function of the lower productivity of some occupations, but mainly, of course, (2) the poor and ghettoization of minorities helps maintain poverty. The location of the poor and the creation of slums is a result of the weak bargaining position of the poor. As our cities grew, the more affluent have preferred to shift outward to newer housing and greater space, relegating the poor, who lack choice, to older more central housing and to locations near industries shunned by the wealthier. Since central housing has superior accessibility to employment, loan values and taxes were high, and the houses had to be subdivided and poorly maintained, if the low rent per family were to yield a sufficiently high rent per unit area. Confinement to slum and ghetto created a "culture of poverty" of which we have all read a great deal.

Geography and the Elimination of Poverty

This discussion has tried to show that while geographic factors, especially relative location and density, influence the spatial pattern of poverty, these are not sufficient conditions to account for poverty. Thus the unattractiveness of non-metropolitan areas to a diversity of economic opportunities has resulted in widespread poverty, but *if* farmers were highly organized (made more difficult by spatial dispersion), *if* farm prices were thus stronger, and *if* the excess population all moved to the cities (also made more difficult by spatial isolation), then rural income could be quite competitive with urban.

This geographic analysis leads one to the conclusion that we should encourage strong farm organization, and continued rural depopulation and metropolitanization (hardly the popular cry just now), because the hope of rural economic rebirth is a hoax and delusion. The subsequent transfer of many more millions to the cities places the burden of poverty where it can be more easily tackled, where new jobs are far more easily created. (We suggested earlier that a guaranteed income applied to the city poor, would raise demand and thus increase decent jobs, and then decrease the continued need for such income transfers. In the countryside, however, it could have the undesirable effect of maintaining marginal farms and creating a rural-living parasite class, since the jobs created from the demand for goods would be in cities. Cities could even have labor shortages. Indeed, this is one effect of excessive farm subsidies in Western Europe).

On the other hand, there is increasing evidence of diseconomies in the very large metropolises. Also, rural areas far from a metropolis, even if of high income, will lack many desired services. Finally, we know that many people do not want to leave their home region, although it lacks opportunities. Geographers should play a major role in designing the logical optimum solution to rural poverty; the locating of a set of new metropolises (not towns) scattered over the countryside, which will bring all the rural territory and people within reasonable distance of a metropolis, and which will be able to employ the excess population leaving the countryside (or still living in the countryside, but commuting to the city).

STANLEY D. BRUNN ◆
JAMES O. WHEELER ◆

Spatial Dimensions of Poverty in the United States

Much has been written about the definition, causes, and consequences of poverty in the United States.[1] Defining poverty on the basis of less than a $3000 annual income for a family of four, approximately 35 million, or over 15 percent of Americans, live in poverty. Whereas the majority of poor families live in urban areas, especially in the older inner city, about 40 percent continue to live in rural areas, despite a very considerable rural to urban migration over the last few decades. Certainly a higher proportion of rural than urban families fall below the poverty standard. Roughly three-quarters of the poor are Caucasian, in spite of the popular impression that the majority of the poor is black, although a significantly higher percentage of blacks are considered poor.

Geographers and other social and behavioral scientists as well as urban planners, health practitioners, and legal authorities during the past decade have begun to focus increasingly on the subject of poverty in the United States and the world. Even though poverty is more prevalent in most other countries than in the United States, it exhibits a number of characteristics that need to be understood in the context of this country. Because poverty has a real variability, it is especially important that geographers concentrate on spatial measurement, patterns, and associations of poverty. As noted above, the general literature dealing with the subject of poverty in a broad sense has increased tremendously within the past decade. In geography, now striving to deal increasingly with spatial causes, characteristics, and solutions, there are a number of definite contributions geog-

◆ SOURCE. Reprinted by permission of the authors and the editor from *Geografiska Annaler*, Vol. 53, Series B, 1971, pp. 6–15.

17

raphers can offer. Recently several geographers have argued that research talents should be used more fully in studying poverty.[2]

To date geographers have tackled the subject of poverty specifically in a variety of locations and used a number of different approaches and methods of analysis. Several of these efforts have not been labeled "poverty" studies per se, although they are considered related to levels of "economic health" or "levels of living." It is also recognized that there are numerous studies that have dealt mainly with problems of agriculture, manufacturing, and cities that have included some treatment of poverty conditions.

At an international level Berry and Megee have factor analyzed social, economic, and demographic characteristics of nations.[3] They also derived regional groupings for continents and sub-continents. In the United States the general patterns of income variation have been examined by Scripter, who devotes some attention to areas that have below average incomes.[4] In Canada, Ray has used factor analysis to derive various dimensions that characterize the economic and social diversity within the country.[5] Within the United States, poverty has been treated on a regional basis in the South by Hart and by Romsa, in the Northeast by Lewis, and in Appalachia by Rosing, Wilbanks, and Van Royen and Moryados.[6] On a state and provincial basis, poverty studies have been carried out in Florida by Yeates, in Indiana by Douglas, southern Illinois by Bishop and by Horsley, Louisiana by Louviere, New York by Thompson et al., West Virginia by Goldenberg, and in Ontario by Bell and Stevenson and by

Berry.[7] These studies have been concerned with descriptive as well as quantitative expressions of poverty. It is unfortunate that aspects of poverty in cities in the United States have not been dealt with more than they have. The recent contributions by Bunge, Rose and others are efforts to help fill this present gap in our knowledge.[8]

It is advanced in this study that the subject of the geography of poverty on a national level merits increased attention and that some currently used multivariate techniques can aid in comprehending the areal complexities and variation of poverty. Therefore, the purposes of this study are threefold: (1) to examine the geographic variation in poverty in the light of one commonly used indicator, median family income; (2) to factor analyze a variety of related social, economic, and demographic data on poverty counties to discern both if there are different kinds of poverty and regional variations and groupings of poverty, and (3) to test the relationship between the extracted factors and selected social and political variables. To date there has been no geographic study that has concentrated specifically on poverty counties in the United States using factor analysis to discern if there are kinds of poverty as well as regional order to poverty.

Geographic Approaches to the Study of Poverty

Considering the levels of scale and variety of descriptive and statistical methods available for solving geographic problems, there are at least five overlapping approaches geographers may use in considering the subject of poverty.[9] First, the geographer can utilize the factor analysis model used in this study. A second possible approach would be to concentrate on the geographic causes and symptoms of poverty such as may be revealed in Jim Crowism attitudes,[10] inadequate welfare coverages, high unemployment, and low nutritional levels. A third approach is to study the "culture of poverty" or selected attributes of groups affected by institutional, technological, or societal poverty such as migrant workers, black Americans, American Indians, Appalachian whites, and Spanish Americans.[11] A fourth approach to the study of poverty would focus on the attitudes and images of people, institutions, and the nation toward poverty. These may be reflected in the concern of businessmen to move into the rural South, the federal support for anti-poverty, residential preferences within the city, city-federal cooperation for food distribution services or urban renewal, or even the mental maps people have about poverty-designated areas within the United States.[12] A fifth and final approach would focus on areal changes in poverty or economic health through time.[13] Such analyses may reveal the effects of high rural out-migration, the role of economic diversification in areas such as the South, and the impact urban centers exert on rural poverty areas. In all these approaches geographers can investigate poverty at different scales: city, state, national, or international.

Univariate Analysis: Median Family Income

Geographers are interested both in the location of poverty counties and in the

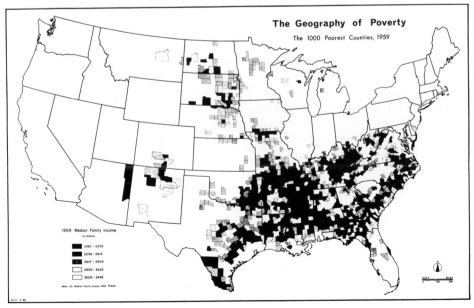

The Geography of Poverty
The 1000 Poorest Counties, 1959

1959 Median Family Income
(in dollars)

1260 – 2255
2256 – 2614
2615 – 2904
2905 – 3228
3229 – 3495

Note: U.S. Median Family Income 1959, $5660

FIGURE 1.

intensity of poverty. Figure 1 illustrates the location and level of poverty of the 1000 poorest counties in the United States in 1959, based on median family income. In view of the fact that most legal and social definitions of poverty on an areal basis refer to some income level, the median family income is used here as a measure for examining the geographic variation of poverty. Even though the data for this map are derived in part from the 1960 census, it should be realized that these census data on a county basis have continued through the 1960's to serve as the basis for a number of federal and state investigations and programs. Furthermore, it is argued that, even though there have been some local changes in the poverty level in the South and other areas since 1960, the areal pattern of poverty counties has remained basically the same as it has for the past several decades.

These 1000 poverty counties cover 18 percent of the total land area, include only 9 percent of the population and altogether accounted for only 4.5 percent of the total national aggregate income in 1959. The percentage of land area in a state in poverty counties varied from highs of 86 percent for Mississippi, 81 percent for Arkansas, and 71 percent for Alabama and Georgia. The states with the largest percentage of their population in poverty counties were Mississippi, 68 percent, and Arkansas, 65 percent. Of all the states these two had the largest proportion of their state income generated in poverty counties, 55 percent.

Some expected patterns are manifested on the map, such as the concentrations in the South, Ozarks, and parts of Appalachia. Poor counties are found in fewer numbers in parts of the Middle West, Great Plains, and Rocky Mountain states. The map reveals further there are definite variations in poverty intensity. For example, most of the counties in Mississippi, southern Alabama, southwest Georgia, and eastern Tennessee, and Kentucky are the poorest. Counties in Nebraska and the Dakotas have higher incomes but are still considerably below the national norm. Some of these very poor counties in these states are Indian reservations. Other noticeable patterns are the contrasts in median family income within Texas, Virginia, Missouri, and Florida. In analyzing geographic patterns of poverty it is worth noting where poverty counties are not found. In the South the metropolitan areas of Atlanta, Birmingham, Jackson, Little Rock, Memphis and cities in the Carolina Research Triangle appear almost as islands of "prosperity" in a sea of poverty. There is an absence of poverty counties in the Carolina piedmont and along the rapidly growing Gulf Coast from Florida to Texas, an area that is associated with "new" urbanization. Figure 1 disguises urban poverty which has definite geographic patterns. Table 1 supports the map by giving the breakdown of the number of poverty counties in each state in each income category. In addition it gives the number of poverty counties and their percent of all counties in the state.

Factor Analytic Approach

The usefulness of factor analysis in regional studies and in regionalization has

TABLE 1. The Geography of Poverty—States > 10 of the 1000 Poorest Counties*

State Class Rank	$1260–2255 1–200	$2256–2614 201–400	$2615–2904 401–600	$2905–3228 601–800	$3229–3425 801–1000	Total Poverty Counties	Total Counties In State	Percent of Poverty Counties
Georgia	28	27	19	21	14	109	159	68
Texas	10	21	20	21	24	96	254	38
Kentucky	28	13	14	13	14	82	120	67
Mississippi	38	16	9	6	4	73	82	89
Tennessee	21	20	12	8	9	70	95	74
Missouri	5	14	18	16	17	70	114	61
Arkansas	19	17	15	10	5	66	75	88
North Carolina	12	18	11	11	5	57	100	57
Alabama	12	10	13	9	6	50	67	75
Virginia	2	5	12	15	15	49	96	51
Louisiana	9	8	9	4	6	36	64	56
South Dakota	1	5	6	11	10	33	67	49
Oklahoma	6	6	6	5	6	29	77	37
Nebraska	0	0	4	10	14	28	93	30
South Carolina	5	9	3	4	6	27	46	58
Florida	1	1	11	6	6	25	67	37
West Virginia	0	6	6	6	5	23	55	42
Iowa	0	1	1	2	8	12	99	12
Minnesota	0	0	0	7	5	12	87	14
North Dakota	1	1	4	2	4	12	53	23

Sources: *County and City Data Book, 1967.*

* Poverty index based on 1959 median family income by county (U.S. median family income, 1959, $5650).

become increasingly appreciated over the past several years.[14] Geographers, especially those interested in urban and economic phenomena, have identified factors, or groupings of variables, mapped and analyzed their spatial variance and related the factors with other conceptually associated variables. In factor analysis, a considerable mass of regional data can be broken down into a manageable and meaningful set of basic factors or dimensions. Points or areas within a region may be strongly associated with one or more factors. For example, one part of a region may be described by a given pattern of relationships among a group of variables, whereas a second portion of the region may have characteristics most related to a different set of connections among variables. Each part of a region can then be understood in terms of where it falls with respect to the several basic components of the data analyzed.[15]

For the 1000 poverty counties in the United States, 24 variables measuring aspects of urban and rural poverty from the 1960 census are correlated and factor analyzed to determine whether or not independent dimensions of poverty can be identified (Table 2). These variables were selected because of their known relationships to poverty, and any one might be separately analyzed as an index of the causes or consequences of poverty. A number of questions come to mind: Is poverty associated only with a single cluster of variables, or are there several groupings of variables representing separate attributes and causes of poverty? How much of the variation among these 1000 counties can be accounted for by the factor analytic

TABLE 2. Variables Used in Factor Analysis

1. Population per square mile, 1960
2. Population change, 1950–1960
3. Percent urban, 1960
4. Percent Negro, 1960
5. Percent foreign stock, 1960
6. Percent over 65 years and older, 1960
7. Median school years completed, 1960
8. Percent completed less than 5 years of school, 1960
9. Percent employment in manufacturing, 1960
10. Percent employed in white collar occupations, 1960
11. Percent of families with incomes under $3,000, income 1959
12. Percent housing units sound, 1960
13. Percent housing units owner occupied, 1960
14. Median value owner occupied housing units, 1960
15. Median gross monthly rent (owner occupied) housing units, 1960
16. Index of home equipment, 1960
17. Value added by manufacture, 1963
18. Percent farms operated by tenants, 1964
19. Proportion of all land in farms, 1964
20. Value of buildings and land per farm, 1964
21. Commercial farms, percent sales under $2500, 1964
22. Average size of farms, 1964
23. Value of farm products sold, average per farm, 1964
24. Farm operator households, percent income from sources other than farm operated, 1964

Source: *County and City Data Book, 1967.*

model? To what extent are there regional differences among the factor scores? To what degree do the poverty dimensions of one state or region overlap with other states or areas? Can economically depressed areas be described by or result from varying combinations of several major factors. Are there significant differences in political preferences among poverty areas, and if so, with which dimensions of poverty are they most strongly connected? These are the basic questions examined in this paper.

Factoring the correlation matrix produces six factors with eigen-values greater than unity. These factors explain 71 percent of the total variance, the first two explaining 25 and 17 percent, respectively (Table 3). Factor I, measuring the socioeconomic dimension of poverty, loads highly on variables such as median school years completed, percentage of sound housing, and an index of home equipment, with high negative loadings on percent completing less than five years schooling, percent annual income less than $3000, and percent Negro (Table 4). Factors II and IV are both measures of rural poverty, the former relating to agricultural

productivity and the latter to agricultural holdings and investment.[16] The rural productivity factor is highly connected with tenant farming, percent of land in farms, and average value of farm products sold; it is loaded negatively on percent in manufacturing, nonfarm employment, and sales less than $2500. Average farm size and value of buildings and land load most highly on Factor IV. Factor III represents a demographic scale, related to population density and change and negatively correlated with percent retired. Factors V and VI, adding a combined value of 10 percent of total variance, are respectively an urban and a manufacturing component of poverty. It is therefore clear that poverty counties in the United States can be described by six separate and independent factors, ranging from urban to rural dimensions.

Figure 2A shows the distribution of states on Factors I and II, derived by taking the average factor score of the counties of each state having 25 or more poverty counties. Thus Nebraska and South Dakota rank highest on both the socioeconomic and agricultural productivity scales, indicating that, of the 1000 poverty counties, those in these two states tend to have the highest socioeconomic composition and the highest levels of farming productivity. In contrast, states of the traditional South (Mississippi, Georgia, South Carolina, Alabama, and Louisiana) rank lowest in socioeconomic status, whereas states peripheral to the traditional South, such as West Virginia, Virginia, Tennessee, and Florida, occupy low positions on the farm productivity scale. In fact, one may note a correspondence between a

TABLE 3.   Variance Explained by Factors

Factors	Percentage Explained	Cumulative Percentage Explained
I. Socioeconomic Status	25.5	25.5
II. Agricultural Productivity	17.4	42.9
III. Demographic	10.7	53.6
IV. Agricultural Holdings	7.8	61.4
V. Urbanization	5.6	67.0
VI. Manufacturing	4.4	71.4

Source: Calculated by Authors.

TABLE 4. Factor Loading Matrix

Variables*	Factor I	Factor II	Factor III	Factor IV	Factor V	Factor VI
1			0.47			
2			0.75			
3					0.80	
4	−0.69					
5	0.40			0.44		
6	0.56		−0.61			
7	0.77					
8	−0.88					
9		−0.55				0.41
10					0.82	
11	−0.67					
12	0.67				0.45	
13	0.72	−0.46				
14			0.61			
15	0.67					
16	0.83					
17						0.82
18	−0.40	0.74				
19		0.77				
20		0.43		0.81		
21		−0.75				
22				0.81		
23		0.61		0.49		
24		−0.74				

Source: Calculated by Authors.

* See Table 2 for variable identification.

state's position on these two major poverty dimensions and its regional location. For example, Southern states are low on the socioeconomic scale and intermediate on the rural productivity dimension. Higher on the socioeconomic continuum but somewhat lower on the productivity scale are states peripheral to the South's poverty core, including parts of Appalachia. The Plains states are associated with relatively high agricultural output and medium to high socioeconomic status.

A somewhat less obvious regional pattern results from plotting the average factor scores for states on the demographic and agricultural holdings scales (Figures 2B). Nevertheless, the states of the South do cluster somewhat above average on the demographic dimension and occupy a medium low position on the agricultural holdings scale. The border states of Tennessee, Kentucky, Arkansas, and West Virginia fall at medium to low points on both scales; and Oklahoma, Missouri, and Texas have the lowest demographic ranks (older population, lower densities, and slower growth or population decline). The greater state to state variations are

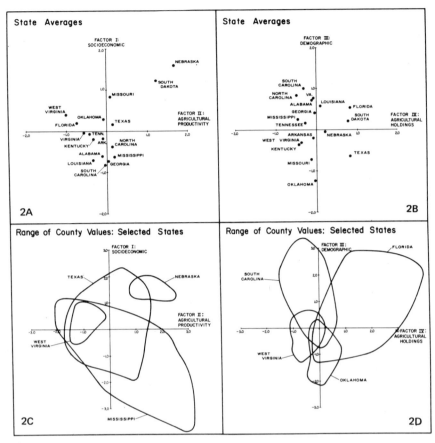

FIGURE 2.   Spatial dimensions of poverty in the United States.

on the demographic dimension rather than the agricultural scale.

The use of state averages somewhat obscures the variety and range of the factor scores among the counties. Figures 2C and 2D illustrate the range of factor scores and the degree of overlap of the poverty dimensions for selected states. For example, Texas in Figure 2C shows considerable county diversity on Factors I and II, overlapping with parts of all the other 16 states having 25 or more poverty counties. Mississippi also displays a wide range among its pov-

erty counties, particularly on the productivity scale, showing that the Delta counties are among the highest in productivity but among the lowest in socioeconomic status. Counties in Nebraska and West Virginia are each rather homogeneous with reference to the first two dimensions of poverty, as are West Virginia and Oklahoma on Factors III and IV. Florida, for example, basically different from Oklahoma on Factors III and IV, nevertheless shares similarities with certain counties of Oklahoma. Thus although the four major poverty dimensions have meaningful state to state variation and show regional patterning, the range of factor scores by state emphasizes in greater detail the degree to which states are similar in the four major independent elements of poverty.

Poverty arises from several different conditions. A region may be sufficiently disadvantaged because of a single poverty dimension. Florida, as an example, has poverty areas related primarily to low agricultural production, whereas the socioeconomic, demographic, and agricultural holdings disadvantages are not as serious. At the other extreme are areas such as Arkansas and Kentucky which are inferior in generating family income as a result of disadvantages in all the major dimensions associated with poverty. The populations of the poorest parts of these states are disadvantaged socioeconomically, tend to be older, and grow more slowly; furthermore farm production is low, the farms themselves tend to be small, and investment in agriculture is meager. Most of the other states described here fall into an intermediate position, having two or three poverty components that present major handicaps.

By examination of the factor scores for a single county, one may likewise discern the components contributing most to its poverty condition. In planning and allocating funds to establish training and educational programs, to make specific improvements in agriculture, or to reverse outmigration and develop industry, one may be guided by a country's factor scores. Although federal spending to alleviate poverty may be in proportion to the intensity of the problem, the specific projects funded ought to vary spatially as the poverty factors, such as identified here, are spatially variable. Poverty, being a general concept made up of several less general components, cannot be successfully attacked by either a shotgun approach or a single project endeavor. Statements such as this have been made before; this analysis both validates such statements and indicates specific guidelines that may be followed in the spatial allocation of funds to reduce poverty. Similarly, these methods of analysis are appropriate for the identification of poverty components in the metropolitan area, where the same kinds of spatial channeling of funds are necessary.

Relation of Poverty to Social and Political Variables

After identifying various kinds of poverty conditions and factors associated with poverty as well as regional variations in poverty in the United States, a further question deserves answering, viz., what is the relationship of these poverty factors to other social and political variables? The factor scores for these 1000 counties from the first four factors were regressed on the following variables; median family income, percent Democratic presidential vote in 1964, the Wallace presidential vote for 1968, a Humphrey-Nixon-Wallace political index for 1968, a hunger index based on the *Hunger U.S.A.* report, and an index based on the 1964 Area Redevelopment Agency (ARA).[17] The regression analysis results reveal several

TABLE 5.   Correlation of Variables with Factor Scores

	Factors			
Variables	I	II	III	IV
Percent Democratic, 1964	.31*	.00	−.17*	.19*
Wallace Vote, 1968	−.39*	−.03	.23*	−.18*
Humphrey, Nixon, Wallace, 1968	.20*	.05	−.23*	.18*
Hunger Index	−.57*	.01	.16*	.05
ARA Counties	−.34*	−.30*	−.16*	−.10*
Median Family Income	.68*	−.02	.35*	.11*

Source: Calculated by Authors.
* Significant at .01 level.

interesting and surprising results about the associations of poverty.

Low but statistically significant correlation coefficients at the .01 level are found between Factors I, III, and IV and the 1964 and 1968 presidential votes (Table 5).[18] These results show that among the nation's poorer counties there is a weak but statistically significant positive relationship between voting Democratic for president in 1964 and socioeconomic and agricultural holdings. There is at the same time a negative correlation with demographic scores. In looking at the 1964 Republican vote, there was a slight tendency for counties with low scores on the socioeconomic and agricultural holdings scale to vote for Goldwater. The same is true of the faster growing poor counties with a more youthful population. The 1968 Wallace vote was very similar among poor counties to the Goldwater pattern.

The hunger index was highly negatively correlated with the socioeconomic factor and positively related to the agricultural productivity factor. Paradoxically, the areas with the highest incidence of hunger in the United States tend to be areas where agricultural production and sales are high, as in the Mississippi Delta and eastern North Carolina. This situation may in part be explained by the high tenancy rate in these areas, the lack of nonfarm employment opportunities, the production of nonfood crops such as cotton and tobacco, and local unwillingness to participate in federal food programs.

The correlations between the factor scores of the first four factors and the ARA classification were low but significant. The coefficients declined in magnitude with the percent of the variance explained by each succeeding factor. Median family income, a commonly used measure of poverty discussed above, is also tested with the factor scores. Income is, as expected, correlated strongly with socioeconomic status among the poverty counties, only weakly correlated with the demographic scale, and uncorrelated with the agricultural dimensions.

In correlating the factor scores with selected social and political variables, it is interesting that there seems to be some relationships between certain derived poverty factors and political performance. The relationships, however, between the factor scores of the hunger index and median income are not entirely what were expected, all of which points out the need for subsequent research at various levels of analysis to clarify the role of specific variables associated with poverty.

Summary

A factor analysis of low income counties in the United States shows that there are several conditions associated with the location and phenomenon of poverty: socioeconomic status, agricultural productivity, demographic composition, agricultural holdings and investment, and the degree of urbanization and manufacturing. These six dimensions of poverty have unequal importance among the poorer regions of the country. Although these components may be more manifestations of poverty than causes, this analysis provides considerable insight into the reasons why areas with diverse attributes may be similar in poverty levels. A particular combination of the derived factors is necessary for an area to have a poverty designation and these combinations, as revealed in Figure 2, have regional variations. People living in certain counties of West Virginia, Mississippi, and Nebraska may be similarly poor, but their poverty has differing facets and arises out of different conditions. Likewise, it is shown that areas spatially separated but falling at similar levels on the poverty dimensions will have like poverty conditions.

It follows directly that efforts to economically elevate poverty areas in the United States should proceed with differing approaches depending on the locality and its particular combination of poverty dimensions. Finally, it is evident that more geographers, whether they take an economic, cultural, political, psychological, or social perspective, should study the spatial dimensions, implications, and policy considerations of poverty at varying areal scales of analysis. The techniques and approach used here have widespread application to varied regional settings and circumstances.

Acknowledgments

The authors acknowledge the assistance of the Institute of Social Science, University of Florida, Gainesville, and the All-University Research Fund of the Michigan State University, East Lansing.

Footnotes

1.   Within the past few years a number of excellent books on poverty in the United States have been published. Some of the more useful ones for geographers include P. Good: *The American Serfs* (New York, Putnam, 1968); L. Ferman, et al., edits.: *Poverty in America; A Book of Readings* (Ann Arbor, University of Michigan Press, 1968); L. Fishman, edit.: *Poverty Amid Affluence* (New Haven, Yale University Press, 1966); M. Harrington: *The Other America* (New York, Macmillan Company 1963); H. H. Meissner, edit.: *Poverty in the Affluent Society* (New York, Harper

and Row, 1966); H. Miller: *Rich Man, Poor Man* (New York, Crowell, 1964). Another useful research source is *Poverty and Human Resources Abstracts* (Ann Arbor, University of Michigan, Institute of Labor and Industrial Relations, 1966); and a number of recent journals devoted to poverty and related subjects such as *Growth and Change; A Journal of Regional Development,* Vol. 1, 1970.

2. For example see R. L. Morrill: "Geographical Aspects of Poverty in the United States," *Proceedings, Association of American Geographers,* Vol. 1, 1969, pp. 84–88; and G. E. Reckord: "The Geography of Poverty in the United States," in *Problems and Trends in American Geography* (edited by Saul B. Cohen; New York, Basic Books, 1967), pp. 92–112.

3. B. J. L. Berry: "An Inductive Approach to the Regionalization of Economic Development," in *Essays on Geography and Economic Development* (edited by N. Ginsburg; University of Chicago, Department of Geography, Research Paper No. 62, 1960), pp. 70–107; M. Megee: "Problems in Regionalizing and Measurement," *Papers, Peace Research Society (International),* Vol. 4, 1966, pp. 7–35; and M. Megee: "Economic Factors and Economic Regionalization in the United States," *Geografiska Annaler,* Vol. 47 B, 1965, pp. 125–137.

4. M. W. Scripter: "Income and Occupations in the United States Counties," *Yearbook, Association of Pacific Coast Geographers,* Vol. 31, 1969, pp. 101–114.

5. D. M. Ray: "The Spatial Structure of Economic and Cultural Differences: A Factorial Ecology of Canada," *Papers, Regional Science Association,* Vol. 23, 1969, pp. 7–23.

6. J. F. Hart: *The Southeastern United States* (Princeton, Van Nostrand, 1967); G. H. Romsa: "A Spatial Analysis of the Dimensions of Economic Health in the Southeastern United States (1950 and 1960)" (Unpublished Ph.D. Dissertation, University of Florida, 1969); G. M. Lewis; "Levels of Living in the Northeastern United States, c. 1960: A New Approach to Regional Geography," *Transactions, Institute of British Geographers* Vol. 45, 1968, pp. 11–37; R. Rosing: "A Regional Approach to Economic Development in Appalachia," (M. A. Thesis, Southern Illinois University, 1968); T. J. Wilbanks: "Socio-cultural Factors and Economic Development in West-Central Appalachia," (M. A. Thesis, Syracuse University, 1967); and W. Van Royen and S. Moryados: "The Economic Geographic Basis of Appalachia's Problems," *Tijdschrift voor Economische en Sociale Geografie,* Vol. 57, 1966, pp. 185–193.

7. M. H. Yeates: "A Multi-variate Analysis of Some Aspects of the Economic Geography of Florida," *Southeastern Geographer,* Vol. 4, 1964, pp. 11–20; R. B. Douglas: "The Regional Delineation and Analysis of Economic Health and Distress in Indiana," (M. A. Thesis, Indiana University, 1967); K. C. Bishop: "Attitudes Toward Economic Development in a Depressed Region: A Case Study of Southern Illinois," (M. A. Thesis, Southern Illinois University, 1968); D. Horsley: "A Comparative Regional Analysis of the Socioeconomic Health of the Middle Mississippi River Valley with Special Reference to Southern Illinois," (M. A. Thesis, Southern Illinois University, 1965); J. J. Louviere: "A Geography of Economic Health in Louisiana, with Special Reference to Underdevelopment in Red River Parish," (M. A. Thesis, University of Nebraska); J. H. Thompson, et al.: "Toward a Geography of Economic Health: The Case of New York State," *Annals, Association of American Geographers,* Vol. 52, 1962, pp. 1–20; D. E. Goldenberg: "Socioeconomic Health in West Virginia," (M. A. Thesis, Pennsylvania State University, 1969); W. H. Bell and D. W. Stevenson: "An Index of Eco-

nomic Health for Ontario Counties and Districts," *Ontario Economic Review*, Vol. 2, 1964; B. J. L. Berry: "Identification of Declining Regions: An Empirical Study of the Dimensions of Rural Poverty," in *Areas of Economic Stress in Canada* (edited by W. D. Wood and R. S. Thoman: Industrial Relations Centre, Kingston, Ontario, 1965), pp. 22–66.

8. W. Bunge: "Field Notes: The First Years of the Detroit Geographical Expedition," (Detroit, Society for Human Exploration, Discussion Paper No. 1, 1969); W. Bunge: *Fitzgerald: The Americanization of A Community* (Cambridge: Shenkman, forthcoming, 1970); H. M. Rose: "Social Processes in the City: Race and Urban Residential Choice," (Washington, D.C.: Association of American Geographers, Commission on College Geography, Resource Paper No. 6, 1969); H. M. Rose: "The Development of an Urban Subsystem: The Case of the Negro Ghetto," *Annals, Association of American Geographers*, Vol. 60, 1970, pp. 1–17; R. A. Winsor: "The Geography of Poverty in Maricopa County, Arizona," (M. A. Thesis, Arizona State University, 1966); G. W. Hartman and J. C. Hook: "Substandard Housing in the United States: A Quantitative Analysis," *Economic Geography*, Vol. 32, 1956, pp. 94–114; and R. J. Fuchs: "Intraurban Variation of Residential Quality," *Economic Geography*, Vol. 36, 1960, pp. 313–325.

9. J. B. Garver, Jr.: "An Approach Toward the Classification of Poverty in the United States," *Annals, Association of American Geographers*, Vol. 59, 1969, pp. 181–182 (abstract). Garver has attempted to classify various types of poverty in the United States based on economic, cultural, and social conditions. He also has performed some regionalizations of these various types.

10. R. Hartshorne: "The Functional Approach to Political Geography," *Annals, As-*

sociation of American Geographers, Vol. 40, 1950, p. 108.

11. L. M. Irelan, et. al.: "Ethnicity, Poverty, and Selected Attributes: A Test of the 'Culture of Poverty' Hypothesis," *Social Forces*, Vol. 47, 1969, pp. 405–411. It is encouraging that geographers and other social and behavioral scientists are currently performing much-needed research on such groups.

12. R. E. Lonsdale: "Barriers to Rural Industrialization in the South," *Proceedings, Association of American Geographers*, Vol. 1, 1969, pp. 84–88; S. D. Brunn and W. L. Hoffman: "The Geography of Federal Grants-in-Aid to States," *Economic Geography*, Vol. 45, 1969, pp. 226–238: H. M. Rose: "Social Processes in the City: Race and Urban Residential Choice," *op. cit.*, (see footnote 8 above); H. M. Rose: "The Development of an Urban Subsystem: The Case of the Negro Ghetto," *op. cit.*, (see footnote 8 above), pp. 1–17; B. J. L. Berry, S. J. Parsons and R. H. Platt: "The Impact of Urban Renewal on Small Business: The Hyde Park-Kenwood Case," (University of Chicago, Center for Urban Studies, 1968); P. R. Gould: "Structuring Information on Spacio-Temporal Preferences," *Journal of Regional Science*, Vol. 7, 1967 supplement, pp. 259–273.

13. G. H. Romsa, *op. cit.*, (see footnote 6 above).

14. "Of the various statistical methods and techniques which have come into prominence in the past few decades, that of factor analysis has had the greatest appeal to regional geographers." See D. Keer: Comments on B. J. L. Berry, *op. cit.*, (see footnote 7 above), p. 97.

15. H. H. Harman: *Modern Factor Analysis* (Chicago, University of Chicago Press, 1960); L. J. King: *Statistical Analysis in Geography* (Englewood Cliffs, Prentice-Hall, 1969).

16. B. J. L. Berry, *op. cit.*, (see footnote 7 above), pp. 22–66. Berry has identified

rural poverty and rural nonfarm poverty as separate dimensions of depressed rural areas.

17. The 1964 county presidential vote and the median income value were taken from the U.S. Department of Commerce, Bureau of the Census, *County and City Data Book 1967* (Washington, D.C., 1967). For the 1968 Wallace variable, a value of one was given to those counties where he was the leading vote-getter and zero to those where such was not the case. In considering the Wallace-Nixon-Humphrey vote, a "conservative-liberal" scale was used to measure the leading candidate in the poverty counties. Values of 1, 2, and 3 were assigned respectively where Wallace, Nixon, and Humphrey captured the most votes. The hunger index was based on the "hunger" map included in the Hunger U.S.A. report: "Citizens Board of Inquiry. *Hunger U.S.A.*," (Boston, 1968). A value of 3 was assigned to those counties the report indicates "extreme hunger," 2 for "emergency hunger" and 1 if the county was not mapped. For the Area Redevelopment Index, a value of one was assigned to those counties that were included under this agency's jurisdiction and zero if those were not. U.S. Department of Agriculture, Resource Development, Economic Research Service, "Median Family Income and Related Data by Counties, Including Rural Farm Income" (Washington, D.C. Statistical Research Bulletin, No. 339, 1964).

18. Low correlation coefficients are not unexpected in view of the large number of observations.

three ••••••••••••••••••••

◆ ALAN R. BIRD
◆ JOHN L. McCOY[1]

White Americans in Rural Poverty

Introduction

Poor rural whites are a major and persistent poverty problem. They have not commonly been the subject of special studies, although they predominate in some wellstudied areas, notably parts of Appalachia.

While many of the problems associated with poverty are regionally concentrated and ethnically linked, most of the rural poor scattered through thousands of villages and farming communities are white. In contrast with nonwhites, white Americans in rural poverty tend to command little public attention. Unlike Negroes, for example, they represent no particular constituency, generally lack unity of purpose and organization, and have no special identification with a social movement aimed at human rights. For these and

other reasons, the white poor, when compared with specific nonwhite minorities, tend to be more unnoticed and relatively isolated from the mainstream of contemporary life.

Approach and Overview

This paper is not a statistical compendium of characteristics of poor rural whites. Rather, it is an attempt to point to the special economic and community circumstances of these people. The purpose is to provide a basis for policy and program improvements that may enrich the lives of all citizens, poor and not-so-poor, white and nonwhite, rural and nonrural.

No definitive answers are presented. The evidence is not available for such conclusions, even though pres-

◆ **SOURCE.** Reprinted from U.S.D.A. Agricultural Economic Report No. 124, November 1967.

32

ent poverty programs often assume such conclusions have been made.

The Problem

Poverty cannot be reduced to the oversimplification of a lack of income alone, although this is obviously the core factor. Regardless of color, residence, or particular beliefs, all poor share a common set of needs tied closely to a severe lack of personal and community resources. Some of the same problems which plague Spanish Americans, Negroes, and Puerto Ricans are the basic concerns of deprived white Americans of Anglo-European origin as well.

Poor rural whites generally have a better chance than poor nonwhites to acquire most available jobs. However, many of those less affected than nonwhites by discriminatory practices have not been placed in full-time jobs or provided with other income opportunities to enable them to escape from poverty.

Most of the rural poor are white, even though the proportion of poor people is higher for nonwhites than whites. For 1964, the Office of Economic Opportunity estimated that of the total of 34.3 million in poverty, 23.7 million were white (14).[2] Using census definitions, rural farm and nonfarm people combined constitute less than one-third of the U.S. population, but account for almost half its poverty. Using the interim definition of poverty as family income of less than $3,000, the 1960 census showed that 46 percent of all families with incomes below this level lived in rural areas (6). (fig. 1). Of all farm families in poverty, 85 percent

were white—a ratio of about four poor whites to every poor nonwhite. When the rural nonfarm population is included, this ratio drops to about 3 to 1 (2).[3]

Where are the poor whites likely to be found? The poverty of white Americans is pervasive and diffuse—thinly scattered over the open country, hamlets, villages, lumbering camps, and mining and farming areas. One such group often associated with poverty conditions is the hired farm working force. In 1965, it was estimated that about 70 percent of this group of 3.1 million workers were whites (1). Of this total work force, only about 15 percent were migratory laborers; and of this sub-group, 78 percent were white, including Spanish Americans. According to 1960 estimates, Spanish Americans made up about 25 percent of the migratory labor force of that year, but only 5 percent of the nonmigratory workers (10).

Successive generations of poor whites, along with recent migrants, live in islands of rural folk culture in some large cities. This element of the rural poverty population is not included in our statistics nor discussed further, although many of the problems of the urban ghetto have resulted, in part, from inmigration of poor, rural people. Depressed areas such as Appalachia, the Ozarks, and sections of the Northern Great Lakes States also account for large numbers. Regional concentration resulting from higher population densities of whites accounts for higher white-nonwhite ratios in the northern States. In the North, about 99 percent of the farm families in poverty are

NUMBER OF RURAL FAMILIES WITH INCOMES UNDER $3,000, 1959

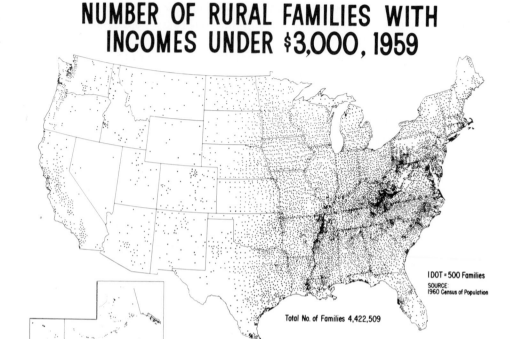

1 DOT = 500 Families
SOURCE:
1960 Census of Population

Total No. of Families 4,422,509

U.S. DEPARTMENT OF AGRICULTURE   NEG. ERS. 2761-64 (4)   ECONOMIC RESEARCH SERVICE

FIGURE 1.

white; in the West, 93 percent; and in the South, where nonwhite population density is higher, the poor farm population is still 73 percent white and this percentage is increasing (3). Because the South is generally lagging in economic development (although it recently has shown a high rate of growth), the limited income opportunities for the white population remain a major problem.

Working Definitions

For conceptual and program purposes, the communities included within our discussion refer to those outside central cities and the urban fringe; that is, all nonmetropolitan territory plus outlying portions of nonmetropolitan areas, as defined by the Bureau of the Census. We have extended our coverage of the rural poverty problem to include such nonmetropolitan areas.[4] In 1960, about 80 percent of the poor families (or 5 million) in this sector were white (2). The proportion of poor nonmetropolitan white families is likely to be at least as high today. This group of white families in nonmetropolitan poverty compares with a U.S. total of 9.65 million white and nonwhite families with reported 1959 net cash incomes of less than $3,000. When we extend our definition of poverty to include poor families with net cash incomes of less than $4,000 (to offset general price increases since 1960) some 85 percent of all poor families (or 7.2 million) in nonmetropolitan territory, i.e., rural farm, rural nonfarm, and nonmetropolitan urban places, were white. About 71 percent of all poor families in central city areas were white.

As we have emphasized, white Americans in poverty continue to be an emerging category of individuals, families, and groups who do not share in the social and economic benefits, including public services and institutions, comparable to those available to the rest of the population. Accordingly, a working definition of poverty can be considered as a relative lack of achievement motivation and/or economic opportunity, including an unawareness of or incapacity to participate in social and economic activities valued by U.S. citizens as necessary to a full life.

Some Illustrative Types of Poverty

Because white Americans in rural and nonmetropolitan poverty are found in a number of different circumstances and scattered communities, we have chosen to represent their predicament by a series of four model situations based on the relative economic status of a county. The four poverty types were classified as follows:

1. the percentage of the total county or regional population that is white;
2. the percentage of the total county or regional population that con-

sists of low-income whites (based on the Council of Economic Advisers interim definition of poverty, although the current OEO definition is also applicable);
3. the ratio of whites in poverty to nonwhites in poverty;
4. the overall economic situation of the area.

It should be pointed out that the type of poverty in a location appears to be correlated both with a general kind of area poverty problem as well as an individual form of poverty status.

The four types do not necessarily reflect exact conditions in any county. There are, for example, a number of economic variants in which a particular county or cluster of counties may not be representative of a given situation, such as pockets of poverty or pockets of affluence within a larger depressed or affluent region. In all of the types, the poor share in a number of common circumstances and social deprivations such as lack of skills, educational underachievement, and lack of adequate community facilities and services. Our approach stresses differences based on location, concentration, and relative economic opportunity (table 1).

TYPE I: A DEPRESSED AREA WITH A MAJORITY OF POOR WHITES[5]

Type I consists of areas in which the vast majority of the people are white and the greater part of this population is poor.[6] Examples which readily come to mind are southern Appalachia, the Ozarks, and the Upper Great Lakes Region (7,11,13). These areas are usu-

TABLE 1.   Poverty types, number of poor rural families, by State, ranking of States in descending order by number of poor rural families, and percentage of State population that was white, 1959

[Poor families are those with net money incomes under $3,000]

States	Suggested poverty types[1]	Ranking by total poor rural families	All poor rural families	Poor rural white families as a percentage of all poor rural families	Percentage of total State population that was white
		Rank	Number	Percent	Percent
Alabama	III, I, IV	7	180,497	64.6	69.9
Arizona		37	23,657	57.8	89.8
Arkansas	I, III	11	148,253	75.7	78.1
California	II, IV	23	103,343	93.7	92.0
Colorado		34	31,910	98.8	97.0
Connecticut	II, IV	42	12,364	98.9	95.6
Delaware	II, IV	45	8,932	74.8	86.1
Florida	III, IV	18	112,039	75.6	82.1
Georgia	III, IV, I	5	187,141	63.3	71.4
Idaho		39	21,094	97.5	98.5
Illinois	II, IV	14	134,958	98.4	89.4
Indiana	II, IV	22	103,594	99.4	94.1
Iowa	II	16	122,508	99.9	99.0
Kansas	IV, II	26	69,918	99.0	95.4
Kentucky	I, II, IV	4	204,997	95.4	92.8
Louisiana	III, IV	15	133,337	55.0	67.9
Maine	II, I	33	32,833	99.0	99.4
Maryland	I, III, IV	28	45,354	76.5	83.0
Massachusetts		38	23,619	97.7	97.6
Michigan	I, IV	20	108,215	97.6	90.6
Minnesota	II, I	17	115,671	99.1	98.8
Mississippi	III, IV	6	187,115	45.6	57.7
Missouri	I, IV, II, III	8	169,102	96.6	90.8
Montana		40	20,500	91.9	96.4
Nebraska	II	27	64,942	97.4	95.4
Nevada		50	3,315	88.2	92.3
New Hampshire ...	II	43	11,283	99.9	99.6
New Jersey	IV, II	35	27,837	88.7	91.3
New Mexico		36	26,743	78.6	92.1
New York	IV, II	21	104,805	97.4	91.1
North Carolina	I, III, IV	1	283,962	65.7	74.6
North Dakota	II, IV	32	35,726	96.9	98.0
Ohio	II, IV	13	138,240	98.4	91.8
Oklahoma	IV	24	98,982	91.6	90.5
Oregon		31	36,502	98.6	97.9
Pennsylvania	I, II, IV	9	168,551	98.5	92.4
Rhode Island		47	4,916	97.2	97.6
South Carolina	III, IV, I	12	141,278	43.9	65.1

TABLE 1. *Continued*

States	Suggested poverty types[1]	Ranking by total poor rural families	All poor rural families	Poor rural white families as a percentage of all poor rural families	Percentage of total State population that was white
		Rank	*Number*	*Percent*	*Percent*
South Dakota	II, IV	29	44,680	94.9	96.0
Tennessee	I, III, IV	3	210,109	87.6	83.5
Texas	III, IV, II, I	2	261,435	81.9	87.4
Utah	II	44	10,397	93.9	98.1
Vermont	II, I	41	15,759	99.8	99.8
Virginia	III, I, IV	10	162,194	71.1	79.2
Washington	II	30	44,199	96.4	96.4
West Virginia	I, IV	19	110,887	95.5	95.1
Wisconsin	II, I	25	98,425	99.0	97.6
Wyoming		46	7,305	95.3	97.8
Alaska		48	4,801	31.4	77.2
Hawaii		49	4,365	26.5	32.0
Total	—	—	4,422,589	83.4	88.6

Source: U.S. Census of Population, 1960. Compiled by the Area Economic Development Branch, RDED, ERS, and the Human Resources Branch, Economic Development Division, ERS.

1. Based on the best estimate of the type of poverty conditions descriptive of the State as a whole. Types overlap State boundaries and are more concretely applicable to counties. Because of insufficient data or sparse rural population, some States have no type listed.

ally isolated and lack the arteries of communication and transportation that are necessary for economic growth (fig. 2). Typical family situations are those with a long history of chronic intergenerational poverty. Families generally have the solidarity of a male head as the chief earner. However, due to a steadily decreasing number of available jobs, stress on the solidarity of the family structure is expected to be great. Families in such extremely impoverished regions have come to be dependent on off-farm income or welfare as their major, if not sole, source of sustenance.

Most of the areas of type I poverty, although rural, are not primarily agricultural. Heavy dependence on declining industries such as mining, and depletion of natural resources, have left most of the available manpower unemployed or underemployed (7,8).

The size of an average "farm" owned by a local resident is often too small to produce income anywhere near adequate without some private or public assistance, including the organization of cooperatives. Often the idea of cooperative organization is unfamiliar to the people in these areas or runs counter to their belief in self reliance. Provincial attitudes and a traditional outlook, including a tendency to prefer the familiar, help to reinforce a low economic status.[7]

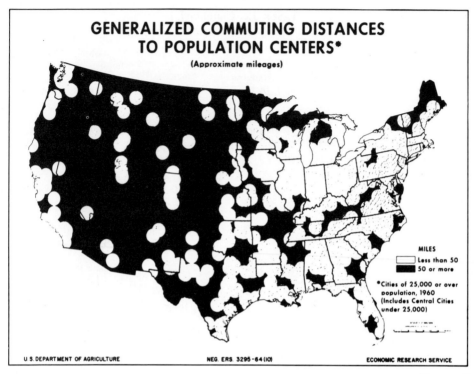

GENERALIZED COMMUTING DISTANCES
TO POPULATION CENTERS*
(Approximate mileages)

MILES
☐ Less than 50
■ 50 or more

*Cities of 25,000 or over
population, 1960
(Includes Central Cities
under 25,000)

U.S. DEPARTMENT OF AGRICULTURE   NEG. ERS. 3295-64 (10)   ECONOMIC RESEARCH SERVICE

FIGURE 2.

Educational achievement levels, as in all poverty situations, are low. Likewise, the quality, staffing, and facilities of educational institutions trail those of nonpoverty locations. The median number of years completed per person may average, at most, about eight; in several counties as high as 70 to 80 percent of the adult population may have less than a seventh-grade education (9).

Youth, in the prime working ages, tends to leave for distant central cities where more opportunities seem available. (Ill-equipped both in basic education and work skills, some may return bitterly disappointed at their lack of success, and prefer to accept their deprivations in the hill country of "home" rather than face seemingly greater hardship in an alien world.) This large exodus of youth places further strain on an already weakened community social system. It serves to further deplete the decaying community of its available talent and its potential leadership, thus aggravating the dependency problems of the aged.

TYPE II: A RELATIVELY AFFLUENT
AREA WITH A POOR WHITE
MINORITY

Type II illustrates situations in which whites in poverty are a distinct economic minority and nearly all residents of the area are white. The highly productive and mechanized farming areas of the Midwest are typical examples. However, since the hired farm working force contains a large number of white laborers, other areas with highly specialized food crops such as Michigan, Washington, and the central valley of California also reflect problems common to type II poverty situations.

In poverty of type II, rural farm residents may still comprise 40 percent of the total population, or even more. Commercial farms with total annual cash sales of $10,000 or more will continue to be a source of declining employment opportunity for the existing labor force (5).

The overall economic status of the area reflects a medium to affluent balanced family income level. The family median income approximates $4,000 (fig. 3). Dependency ratios, i.e., the ratio of persons under 20 years of age and 65 years and over to those 20 through 64 follow the national and State norms. So do other indicators of poverty status. In these areas, the number of poor nonwhites is a distinct minority among the poor.

Education facilities in these areas are superior, on the average, to those in type I (depressed) areas, yet the educational attainment levels of poor whites are very similar to those of poor whites in other rural areas. One of the

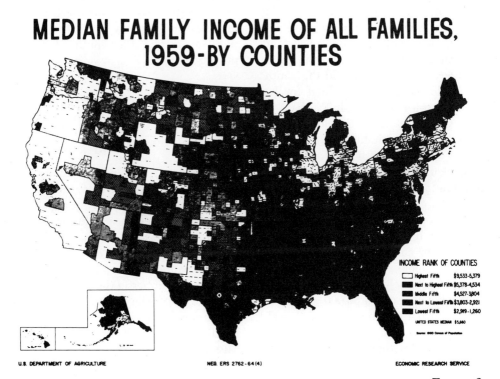

MEDIAN FAMILY INCOME OF ALL FAMILIES, 1959-BY COUNTIES

INCOME RANK OF COUNTIES

- ☐ Highest Fifth $9,533-5,379
- ■ Next to Highest Fifth $5,378-4,534
- ■ Middle Fifth $4,527-3,804
- ■ Next to Lowest Fifth $3,803-2,921
- ■ Lowest Fifth $2,919-1,260

UNITED STATES MEDIAN $5,660

Source: 1960 Census of Population

U.S. DEPARTMENT OF AGRICULTURE   NEG. ERS 2762-64(4)   ECONOMIC RESEARCH SERVICE

FIGURE 3.

notable reasons for this is the higher proportion of children who do not attend kindergarten. Some authorities have argued that this lack of preschool training contributes greatly to low rates of educational attainment and limited achievement values. (Many communities of course, do not have public kindergartens.)

The rural poor are thought to have certain conservative values that tend to isolate them psychologically as well as socially. Thus, remedial programs, such as Head Start, face the difficult challenge of changing values which tend to initiate the poor rural child into the culture of poverty.

Migratory farmworkers who are often employed on large commercial farms in these areas present special problems. Migratory subsistence living consists of one of the most severe and vulnerable aspects of the poverty problem because it tends to hold the youth. The child comes to be valued for his ability to turn out an adult's share of work. Other factors limiting his achievement potential include: Lack of a continuing contact with a community, insufficient medical and health care, and low and irregular school attendance.

The cyclic aspects of poverty are illustrated by the irregular school attendance of children of migrant farmworkers. Some 140,000 children of workers will likely miss school this fall. Of this number, about 50,000 will be on the road from October to May, traveling with a migrant parent from one job to another. Another 90,000 may miss the first few weeks of school because they are still away harvesting (15).

The basic problem appears to be not so much that there are no special programs for this group. Rather, it is a case where the persistence of certain habits, living patterns, and methods of crop production reinforce poverty.

Another characteristic of type II poverty is the relatively frequent dependence of residents upon part-time and seasonal employment. Due to somewhat lower rates of overall outmigration, the percentage of those 65 and over is likely to run higher than the national or regional average.

Development of light industry and strategic and coordinated enlargement of community size are necessary so that the available farm labor force will have adequate access to nonfarm jobs. Lack of developed skills in the clerical and manual occupations will remain a major problem among the youth of white poverty families.

**TYPE III: A RELATIVELY DEPRESSED
AREA WITH A POOR WHITE
MINORITY WITHIN A POOR
NONWHITE MAJORITY**

This model represents situations in which whites are part of the larger majority of the economically deprived, but find themselves a color minority. Illustrative areas are scattered throughout the East South Central and the South Atlantic States. These include a number of counties in the "Deep South" and parts of the Atlantic Seaboard ranging west across the Florida panhandle and the Gulf States beyond the Mississippi.

Agriculture and other rural occupations remain a major source of income and employment, except for some areas with textile and food milling industries. Declining employment on railroads has further complicated the poverty problem. Although the South has shown an increase in economic growth in recent years, especially in light industry and manufacturing, it still contains most of the Nation's rural-farm poverty. For the most part, those who live in poverty work in agriculture. In addition, the increasing reliance on farming methods that use relatively less unskilled labor has decreased these manpower needs, thus further intensifying the underemployment and welfare problems.

One of the most predominant poverty situations in type III concerns small-plot farmers and tenant farmers. In Mississippi, for example, more than 50 percent of the land is in commercial farms with annual cash sales of less than $5,000, including part-time and part-retirement farms (5). Complicating factors include technologically inefficient farm organization as well as a chronic lack of economic and community organization generally.

Outmigration continues to intensify the poverty problem of older whites. Many of the nonwhites continue to leave the areas for employment in northern central cities. Similarly, white youth of prime working ages are also migrating, although at a somewhat lower rate (16). This leaves behind whites in older age groups, who are either out of the labor force or find it relatively difficult to enter new occupations. Males in these groups have limited potential for off-farm job training. When other family members are in-

cluded, the severity of the dependency problem represented by such individuals becomes intensified.

TYPE IV: AREAS RANGING FROM POOR TO AFFLUENT WITH A RELATIVELY BALANCED PROPORTION OF POOR WHITES AND POOR NONWHITES

The poverty situations presented in type IV are most easily discernible as variations of types I and II.

In types I and II, the geographic boundaries are more clearly distinguishable than in type IV. Examples of type IV areas include:

1. places where the ratio of whites and nonwhites in poverty is about the same, but population density varies; and
2. locations which range in overall economic status from poverty to affluence.

Situations which are similar to type I are depressed areas that lack racial homogeneity. Situations like type II are further removed from general poverty, but lack a color majority.

Areas where representative cases are found occur in States adjacent to the South as well as in selected areas with the South; in areas of continuing agricultural prosperity which have made successful adjustments to technology; and in areas which depend primarily on the hired farm labor force to harvest specialty fruit and vegetable crops. In addition, we may expect problem situations to occur in areas undergoing change from a predominantly agricultural economy to one of light industry. Demographic characteristics will reflect a high rate of change from rural farm to nonfarm and urban residence. Finally, areas surrounding large central cities or where a suburban fringe extends into a rural farming community may also constitute type IV poverty.

These situations suggest fairly rapid social and technological changes. Such circumstances present special problems for poor whites, especially those who are more likely to be in recent migratory status, and others who are more likely to feel the effects of rapidly changing social and economic conditions. Adjustment problems tend to intensify as a result of greater proximity to others of higher status, as well as increased contact with nonwhites of similar status.

Perhaps some of the greatest adjustment problems will occur among low-income whites in type IV situations. In type I, poverty is more of a pervasive problem, and therefore, may have certain "soothing" advantages of similarity among the families in the area. In type II, some possible residual advantages may accrue to low-income whites from being in a more affluent area. In type III, low-income whites may be thought to gain some reassurance from a traditional pattern of living commonly referred to as "discrimination." However, the climate of opinion represented in this situation helps to reinforce and continue the poverty status of the whites as well. In type IV, greater competition for a relatively limited number of available jobs, readjustment of attitudes of the white migrant toward the low-income nonwhite,

and increased interracial contact in general, might be points of interpersonal conflict with severe economic implications.

Some Associated Aspects of Economic Separation

Some elements of the foreclosure of opportunity for poor rural whites which have been mentioned may be less strikingly obvious than for other particularly disadvantaged ethnic groups. Yet the persistence of such problems among the white population is forceful evidence as to the intractability of their causes.

Both low income and lack of personal assets tend to separate poor whites from their fellow citizens. The causes may be one or many—personal, community, industry or program-related. Direct personal causes may include a failure to recognize and realize potential economic opportunities, overinvestment in an uncertain enterprise, ill health, accidents, and mental breakdown.

Irrespective of the causes, the conditions of economic separation tend to predispose the poor to still further separation from American life—social, psychological, and cultural—which confirm their disadvantaged status. Assuming that low-income families wish to participate, many low-income families, including some not considered poor, are effectively excluded from PTA meetings and numerous other community activities, including those which are church-affiliated, because they work irregular or unusual hours, or lack clothes or social attributes necessary for successful community activity.

An example of these difficulties is the small dairy farmer who obtained a janitor's job. He quickly found the need to sell his cows and rent out his cropland since his employers and associates objected to his presence when he was "smelling of cows." It is, of course, also important to point out that many wealthy people may be excluded from community participation by schedule conflicts, simple lack of interest, and for other reasons. However, these families may yet enjoy many of the benefits of community activities and successfully substitute cash for other contributions-in-kind.

It may be thought that poor families in a predominantly affluent community can enjoy many benefits of life in such a community, irrespective of their financial status. Yet special and severe psychological problems have been reported. For example, the children of such poor families, sensitive to their differences—either real or attributed—may find it difficult to participate fully in school activities, even school lunch programs.

On the other hand, in a community where rural poverty is the norm, the social withdrawal of families may be compounded by the isolation of that community from the rest of the State and the Nation. Community activities may be quite visible (perhaps more so than in a wealthy suburb), but the question is whether such activities tend to develop relations with other communities or intensify isolation. Are the activities centered on upgrading education, for example?

The very existence of low-income status sets in train further economic and other forces to perpetuate the condition. In seeking remedies for poverty, this paper tends to place greater stress on factors that perpetuate the condition and common measures devised to alleviate it.

We suggest that:

1. The problems of escape from poverty may be more uniform than the means of entry; and
2. Avoiding further complication of these problems may necessitate looking at problems of escape from poverty (for white and nonwhite) in a more general context of widening opportunities for the poor and not-so-poor to participate more fully in the larger world of economic and social activities.

Further Examples of Economic and Social Separation

THE CASE OF THE SMALL FARMER

This is mainly a problem of rural whites. Under present economic conditions, the small farmer does not have sufficient resources to enable him and his family to earn an income from farming alone that would place him, and allow him to remain, above the poverty line. For the farmer with a small acreage, the price support programs and farm income support programs can usually make only a limited contribution to his income.

However, in the overall adjustment sense, it could be argued that the major regressive factors affecting the small farmer are his present location and his ownership of insufficient resources. The white farmer is more likely to own land than the nonwhite. Hence, his family has an additional incentive to remain on the farm. The prospects for such a family obtaining significant increases in income and significant benefits from additional community services and facilities hinge on the ability and willingness of the family members to gain access to these opportunities throughout the year. Poor farmers, like other rural people, need to be within convenient commuting time of a town or group of communities that have a sufficient range of employment and training opportunities. Opinions differ on what size such towns must be. And current data are insufficient for definitive judgment.

However, with some major new technology or resource discovery, it is apparent that, for the same area, the feasible number of towns in sparsely populated parts, as in the western Corn Belt and the Great Plains, is impressively less than elsewhere in the Nation (fig. 2). Even with use of new transportation modes and revision of present transportation systems (and, perhaps, even subsidization of transportation costs for poor farm families in sparsely populated areas) many families of such isolated small farmers may need to relocate in or near distant cities. Present programs provide no explicit help or guidance to enable or expedite such relocation decisions.

This is not to say that relocation has not occurred. Indeed, some investigators point out that most of the exodus from farming has occurred, perhaps ironically, during the periods of relatively high price supports. Even further, price supports and other farm income maintenance programs may have been important indirect causes of this farm exodus. Because of them, wealthier neighbors on larger farms could compete intensively to bid up the sale price of smaller neighboring farms or of their "allotment" acres. (And, of course, these small farms have a relatively higher price because of the conventional, perhaps historic, value of "fixed improvements.")

A small farmer has limited and insufficient programs he can turn to —even though his expected income may still fall short of the conventional poverty line in the foreseeable future. He has least access to programs to upgrade his income from farming and may be effectively excluded from some alternative programs. For example, homeownership may prevent him from access to special housing funds for low-income people, unless he chooses to repair and renovate the home rather than relocate.

In sparsely populated areas, and in other areas such as the Ozarks, Appalachia, the Southeast, and the Delta, small farmers apparently share other disadvantages that subject them to continued poverty. And white families, because of their relatively higher representation as farmowners, are more chronically vulnerable to these disadvantages. For example, educational services and facilities, as suggested previously, are likely to be below national norms in school size as well as range and quality of course offerings. Where vocational education is available, it is more likely to be limited to areas of declining opportunity for rural youth. Employment services are also likely to be limited, particularly in their ability to refer applicants between the two sectors of farm and nonfarm work. Public transportation services are apt to be quite limited, and, in fact, may not exist without special subsidies. Beyond that, technological changes may further reduce the income expectations of areas with many small farms, as has happened in the cotton-producing areas of the South. Such a similar impact on many adjoining farms further restricts the ability of these residents to support adequate community facilities and services.

RURAL NONFARM FAMILIES

Rural nonfarm poor families face similarly reduced opportunities for escaping from poverty. In sparsely settled areas, farm enlargement and mechanization and increasing patronage by farmers of distant service centers, tend to make superfluous many businesses located in small towns. Yet these victims of major structural changes in the economy of the Nation have no identifiable programs to enable them to anticipate liquidation by relocating for more profitable businesses or occupations. Poor rural businessmen (most are white) do not have the equivalent of the relocation assistance available to victims of urban renewal, although their disadvantageous circumstances may be quite validly compared with

those of the businessmen in an urban slum. Indeed, the rural businessman may have substantially less insurance against losses caused by community changes than his urban counterpart.

Communication with Poor Whites

One major problem facing most poverty program leaders is capturing the attention and cooperation of those whom the programs are specifically designed to serve. Along with the usual basic inadequacies in community organization and services, there exist prominent barriers to communication—often a spirit of disinterest or suspicion. The poor, too, have their pride. A certain distaste in having to take something for nothing may predispose many among them to shun or to give only token recognition to the common efforts of professional philanthropy. Such problems are a general manifestation of most of the poor, regardless of color.

Special Problems of Poor Rural Whites Associated with Recent Programs

Recent programs to aid the poor and to upgrade poor areas involve a parallel danger that they will actually reduce opportunities for some whites to escape from rural poverty. Disadvantages to whites not previously cited, result from two emerging situations: (1) Antipoverty, civil rights, and related activities tend to be identified, particularly in the

South, as programs for Negroes rather than for disadvantaged people generally. (2) Emphasis on the poor, as they are identified through an arbitrary, discrete criterion such as income level, tends to increase the chances of ignoring the very real problems of those just beyond arbitrary poverty lines. These borderline cases are the most likely alternative candidates for the apparently limited job, training, and other community opportunities in a depressed rural area. Situations described in types III and IV should reflect a below-average ratio of poor white participation.

Examples of serious difficulties imposed by the erroneous identification of antipoverty programs as programs for Negroes only are: (1) Closing of public schools in response to integration requirements, and (2) underrepresentation of poor whites in antipoverty activities that require participation by the poor.

The following circumstances highlight the great difficulty of increasing the participation of poor rural whites in antipoverty programs:

1. By contrast, even in affluent urban communities without significant ethnic problems, the proportionate number of well-educated citizens participating in meetings addressed to major problems, such as juvenile delinquency and zoning, is quite low indeed.
2. Poor rural communities where greater participation of low-income whites is currently expected are areas disadvantaged by relatively poor educational systems,

lack of sufficient numbers of local jobs, little previous involvement with public programs, and relatively little experience and instruction in community activities.
3. Perhaps most crucially, residents of such poor communities are likely to be least informed on possible benefits from further participation in community activities, and their participation may entail relatively major short-term personal and family sacrifices.

Summary Suggestions, Explorations, and Implications

Poor rural whites are a major and persistent poverty problem; they have apparently received insufficient attention —considering the size, distribution, and special characteristics of their population. In lieu of conclusions concerning these people, it is suggested that (1) whites in poverty, as with other disadvantaged subgroups, tend to be separated from major national markets (particularly labor markets) and the generally accepted American ways of life; (2) emergence of many special programs to cater to "target groups" on the basis of economic and social need, together with increasingly exclusive definitions of these groups, tend to accentuate this separation; (3) such separation may work particularly to the detriment of poor rural whites, and those with incomes just above arbitrary poverty lines; (4) major new programs or major reorientations of present programs, including consolidation of these programs, may be needed to remedy this situation; (5) this needed new program emphasis should be toward unified efforts that provide continuing opportunities for all citizens, rather than further polarization and fragmentation of "special groups"; and (6) this new emphasis will likely involve development of programs for all nonmetropolitan territory that strengthen the effectiveness of programs in census-defined rural areas.

As a guide to the development of consolidated programs, we have sketched four area types of poverty as follows:

    I.—Depressed area with a majority of whites in poverty;

    II.—Relatively affluent area with a minority of whites in poverty;

    III.—Relatively depressed area with a poor white minority within a majority of nonwhites in poverty;

    IV.—Area ranging from poor to affluent with balanced proportions of poor whites and poor nonwhites.

These types apply to rural and nonmetropolitan areas as defined by the census. This extended application recognizes the increasing emphasis on multicounty units as a basis for coordinated programming.

It has been suggested that a combination of circumstances places poor rural whites at a particular disadvantage and tends to insure their continued poverty status. Among these are:

1. A tendency, considered acute in the South (types III and IV), to identify poverty, by-and-large, as a nonwhite problem, and for the white community to consider programs in these areas to be aimed almost exclusively at the Negro community;

2. Trends of increasing competition among whites and nonwhites for the few available income opportunities in depressed areas (types III and IV);

3. Emphasis on expected social participation of all age groups as a qualifying condition for program benefits—a practice that apparently exceeds performance expectations in nonpoverty areas;

4. Communication barriers among the poor, and between the poor and nonpoor program personnel. This includes lack of feeling of common identity and hence a chronic need for improved social and economic organization;

5. A higher incidence of small farmers among the white population in locations that preclude access to economic opportunities, and a lack of remedial programs to alleviate their "boxed-in" condition.

Over and above these special conditions, poor rural whites are, of course, thought to share with other poor critical inadequacies in schooling (particularly in the early years), health, income maintenance payments (particularly for the aged), and in overall access to community services and facilities.

It is thought that further inquiries now underway and those that may take place in the future will confirm the above special disadvantages of rural whites. If so, urgent needs include:

1. Design and implementation of a national program for income and employment opportunities, particularly nonfarm jobs, so that significant amounts of new industry are concentrated in hitherto depressed areas and regions, consistent with the location of natural resources. Such a new concentration of industry implies the need to encourage systematic inmigration of key personnel with above-average income and educational levels and to establish in cooperation with them communities that are attractive places both to work and live.

2. Establishment of qualifying conditions for program participation by the poor that preclude the erroneous identification of anti-poverty and welfare programs as Negro programs.

3. Provision of incentive or compensation payments for owners of rural property and businesses, so that they may be able to relocate on a par with disadvantaged urban property owners in response to disadvantageous changes in community economic conditions.

4. Increased emphasis on education and training programs for all children, especially those of preschool and elementary age, as well as exceptional children, including the gifted and retarded. Since a great part of the poverty problem has its roots in "cultural retardation" and functional illiteracy, a basic remedial education program is of paramount importance. In addition to these needs, occupational training should place increasingly greater emphasis on nonfarm occupations and professions. Finally, a complementary need is the establishment of special adult education and training centers in strategic locations.

5. Continued improvements in collecting timely and relevant data, and in their analysis and interpretation to enable community leaders, program managers, and others to develop more effective programs, and better implement existing programs.

Literature Cited

1. Bowles, Gladys K. 1966. *The Hired Farm Working Force of 1965.* U.S. Dept. Agr., Agr. Econ. Rpt. 98, Sept.
2. Bureau of the Census. 1963. *1960 Census of Population Supplementary Reports, Families.* U.S. Dept. Commerce PC (2)–4A.
3. ———. 1964. *1960 Census of Population Supplementary Reports, Low Income Families: 1960.* PC (S1)–43, Feb.
4. ———. 1962. County and City Data Book 1962. U.S. Dept. Commerce.
5. ———. 1962. United States Census of Agriculture 1959. *Economic Class of Farm.* U.S. Dept. Commerce.
6. Cohen, Wilbur J., and Eugenia Sullivan. 1964. *Poverty in the United States. Health, Education and Wel-*

fare Indicators. U.S. Dept. Health, Ed. and Welfare, Feb.

7. Coltrane, R. I., and E. L. Baum. 1965. *An Economic Survey of the Appalachian Region.* U.S. Dept. Agr. Econ. Rpt. 69, Apr.

8. Economic Research Service. 1966. *Rural People in the American Economy.* U.S. Dept. Agr., Agr. Econ. Rpt. 101.

9. ————. 1960. U.S. Counties Ranked According to a Five Factor Index of the Relative Poverty Status of Their Rural Population. Unpublished data. U.S. Dept. Agr., Econ. Devl. Div., Econ. Res. Serv.

10. Friend, Reed E., and Samuel Baum. 1963. *Economic, Social, and Demographic Characteristics of Spanish-American Wage Workers on U.S. Farms.* U.S. Dept. Agr., Agr. Econ. Rpt. 27, Mar.

11. Jordan, Max F., and Lloyd Bender. 1966. *An Economic Survey of the Ozark Region.* U.S. Dept. Agr., Agr. Econ. Rpt. 97.

12. Leonard, Olen E., and Helen W. Johnson. 1967. *Low-Income Families in the Spanish-Surname Population of the Southwest.* U.S. Dept. Agr., Agr. Econ. Rpt. 112.

13. Loomis, R. A., and M. E. Wirth. 1967. *An Economic Survey of the Northern Lake States Region.* U.S. Dept. Agr., Agr. Econ. Rpt. 108.

14. Office of Economic Opportunity. 1965. *Dimensions of Poverty in 1964.* Oct.

15. Rapton, Avra. 1967. *Domestic Migratory Farmworkers—Personal and Economic Characteristics.* U.S. Dept. Agr., Agr. Econ. Rpt. 108.

16. U.S. Department of Labor. 1967. Manpower Report of the President. Apr.

Footnotes

1. The authors wish to thank Helen Johnson, John H. Southern, Calvin L. Beale, Robert B. Glasgow, John M. Zimmer, and other colleagues for their help. This report is part of continuing research in cooperation with the Office of Economic Opportunity.

2. Italic numbers in parentheses refer to items in the Literature Cited.

3. Ordinarily, Americans with Spanish surnames are included within the census of the white population. Hence, the above estimates include this subgroup. However, we have excluded further specific treatment of problems associated with them, since they are treated in a separate paper. The largest concentration of Spanish-surname people consists of 3.5 million in five Southwestern States (Arizona, California, Colorado, New Mexico, and Texas). Although predominantly rural only a few decades ago, this Southwestern group was nearly 80 percent urban by 1960 (*12*).

4. For at least two reasons, these nonmetropolitan communities are considered to be the most fruitful units of analyses for program improvements: (1) From 1950 to 1960, the established trend was for counties with no town of at least 10,000 to suffer the least percentage increase in nonfarm employment, relatively high rates of out-migration, and special difficulties due to population sparsity in providing adequate public services and facilities at per capita costs comparable to other areas. Partial recognition of this spill-over of problems to towns larger than 2,500 has occurred in recent legislation. For example, under P.L. 89–240, the Farmers Home Administration is now authorized to help finance housing and community water and sewer systems in towns of up to 5,500, instead of 2,500 as before. (2) There is increasing, if not universal, recognition of the need for joint planning of antipoverty and development

programs on a multicounty basis to reinforce activities at county, State, and regional levels. The President has directed all Federal agencies to recognize such multicounty·units adopted by the States to the maximum feasible extent. Multicounty planning and related action programs can provide improved mobilization of the resources of both traditionally defined rural areas and neighboring small communities. Despite the general problems of rural areas cited above, the Annual and Final Report of the Area Redevelopment Administration (Dec. 1965) reveals that more than half (65,000 out of 117,875) of the reported jobs created by that agency from May 1, 1961 to August 31, 1965 were in rural areas as defined by the Census Bureau. Already of course, the likely fruitfulness of working with these consolidated communities is formally recognized by many State development groups, in the Appalachian Redevelopment Act of 1965 (P.L. 89–4),

authorizing local development districts, and in the Public Works and Economic Development Act of 1965 (P.L. 89–136), authorizing multicounty economic development districts. Related examples are OEO's multicounty Community Action Agencies and Resource Conservation and Development Districts and Rural Renewal Areas served by the U.S. Department of Agriculture.

5. Generalizations were drawn from a number of sources and reports other than those listed.

6. For suggested types corresponding to various States, see table 1.

7. We do not intend to suggest here, or elsewhere, that poor rural whites have a monopoly on such characteristics. On the contrary, there are reasons to expect that provincialism, for example, is at least as much a characteristic of many residents of large cities.

◆ **four**

HELEN W. JOHNSON ◆

Rural Indian Americans in Poverty

Introduction

Most Indian Americans are rural residents, and they are poor. They are not attuned to the modern technological economy of America, nor are they certain in what direction their future lies—within the larger society or separate from it; on the reservation or away from it; as Indians or as Indian Americans. Somewhere between these polar points, a way will doubtless be found.

The story of why rural Indians today are in poverty has roots in their history, in the development of the industrialized American economy, and in the difficult process of assimilation of a minority culture by the dominant one in every society. There is considerable documentation of the history of this minority group vis-à-vis the U.S. Government in the long contention over land, tribal rights, relocation of living space, and redirection of occupational activity. All of these past events have a bearing on the size and vigor of the Indian population, their attitudes and present outlook, and the eventual resolution of their problems. This history will not be recounted here since its major impacts are already well-known to the American public.[1]

The critical element in the history of the U.S. economy which helps to explain the current distress of rural Indians is the development of an urbanized, technical society—a society for which rural Indians are not prepared. Nothing in their history or experience has contributed to making possible successful adjustment in a nonfarm economy—educationally, occupationally, or socially. Rural in orientation and largely separated from the rapid urbanization of the last few decades, Indians have been out of touch

◆ **SOURCE.** Reprinted from U.S.D.A. Agricultural Economic Report, No. 167, September 1969.

51

with industrial and technological developments now predominant in our national economy.

The cultural hiatus between Indian Americans and the society around them is equally severe in its implications for rural Indian disadvantage. Acculturation of a minority population is always a long and tortuous process. A minority group confronted with the loss of its own cultural heritage as the price of assimilation finds itself resisting new ways as long as possible. At some point in time, a choice is made—to give up the old familiar values and patterns of living, to adopt the ways of the alien culture, or to effect some combination of the old and the new. Meanwhile, there is a drawing apart of the two cultures on both sides. The dominant society, not really understanding the dilemma, often manifests impatience and prejudice, or at the very least, lack of empathy. Until the gap between the two cultures is closed, the minority group suffers not only economic and social discrimination, but malaise of spirit.

Indian experience with American culture has been no exception. Rural Indians today are mostly poor, ill at ease, and largely unacculturated. They are in limbo, not at home in either world. The way to achieve an intermediate position between the familiar culture and the dominant but alien one is not at all clear. Some first steps, however, are quite apparent and apply to people in poverty wherever they are and of whatever cultural origin. Alleviation of poverty status, improvement of educational and employment opportunity, and wider participation in the society at large constitute high-priority needs for all people in distress. Rural Indians are among the most deprived groups in America today. The pages that follow will give some measure of the depth of their disadvantage.

Rural Indians in the 1960's

DEMOGRAPHIC CHARACTERISTICS

In 1960, there were 552,000 Indians in the United States, including 28,000 Aleuts and Eskimos in Alaska (app. table 1).[2] Indians constituted the smallest of three minority ethnic groups, or less than 1 percent of the U.S. total population. The Spanish-surname population, by contrast, was about 2 percent of the total and Negroes were 11 percent. Indians were, however, the most rural of these groups,—about 70 percent of them were classified in the 1960 Census as living in rural areas, compared with 21 percent of the Spanish-surname people and 27 percent of the Negro population. More than half the rural Indians (55 percent) were rural nonfarm residents.

A majority of Indians were located in 27 States, their number in these States ranging from 2,500 in Florida to 83,000 in Arizona (fig. 1 and app. table 1). More than two-fifths of the total U.S. Indian population lived in Arizona, Oklahoma, New Mexico, and California. If Alaskan Natives are added to the four-State total, the proportion located in the West rises to more than one-half. In a majority of

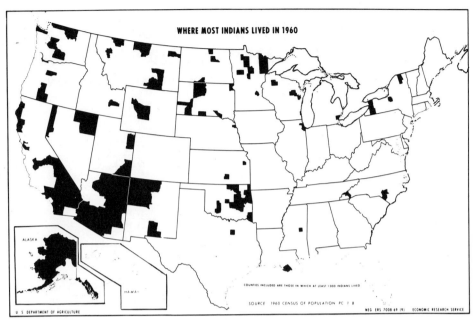

WHERE MOST INDIANS LIVED IN 1960

ALASKA

HAWAII

COUNTIES INCLUDED ARE THOSE IN WHICH AT LEAST 1 000 INDIANS LIVED

SOURCE 1960 CENSUS OF POPULATION PC 1 B

U S DEPARTMENT OF AGRICULTURE

NEG ERS 7008 69 (9) ECONOMIC RESEARCH SERVICE

FIGURE 1.

the 27 States, more than half the Indians lived on reservations. In all but one State, about 30 to 96 percent of the Indian population was rural; in Illinois the rural proportion was only 7 percent.

The Indian population as a whole is very young (fig. 2). The median age of rural Indians in 1960 was 17.7 years, compared with 27.3 for the total rural population. More than 60 percent of the rural Indian population was under 25 years of age (app. table 2). In the total rural population, the figure was 48 percent. This high proportion of young people among rural Indians is especially significant for future population growth when viewed together with the high birth rate of Indians. Rural Indians have one of the highest

birth rates of any minority ethnic group in the United States. While life expectancy at birth for Indians was below that of the United States as a whole in 1964, it had increased 12.5 years since 1940. For Indians, the 1964 figure was 63.5 years, and for the United States, 70.2 years.[3]

As would be expected in a population with these demographic characteristics, the average size of Indian families is large. Two out of three rural Indian families have four persons or more, compared with one out of two in the total rural population (app. table 3). Small, two-person families are only about half as frequent among rural Indians as in the total rural population. More than one-fourth of Indian families have seven members or

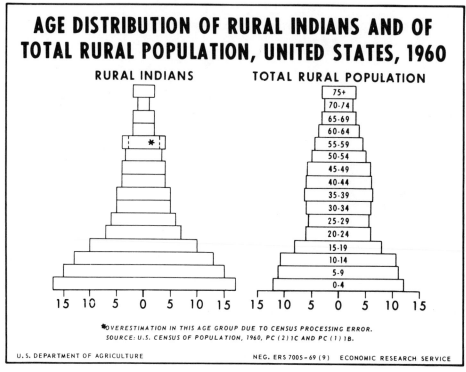

AGE DISTRIBUTION OF RURAL INDIANS AND OF TOTAL RURAL POPULATION, UNITED STATES, 1960

RURAL INDIANS   TOTAL RURAL POPULATION

*OVERESTIMATION IN THIS AGE GROUP DUE TO CENSUS PROCESSING ERROR.
SOURCE: U.S. CENSUS OF POPULATION, 1960, PC (2)1C AND PC (1)1B.

U.S. DEPARTMENT OF AGRICULTURE   NEG. ERS 7005–69 (9)   ECONOMIC RESEARCH SERVICE

FIGURE 2.

more; in the rural population, the proportion is only 9 percent. The large size of Indian families reflects in part the age structure of the population and in part its high birth rate.

FAMILY INCOME

More than three out of five rural Indian families had less than $3,000 income in 1959, nearly twice the proportion in the total rural population (fig. 3). Family income below the $1,000 level was three times as prevalent among the rural Indian population as among the total rural population. At the other end of the scale, less than 3 percent of rural Indian families had

incomes of $10,000 or more, whereas nearly 12 percent of families in the total rural population reported that level of income (app. table 4). The high proportion of rural Indians in a low-income position points to especially serious deprivation when the large average size of families is considered.

The income of rural Indian families is not only low, but is derived largely from sources unproductive for the Indian families and for the national economy. Many families are receiving public assistance from Federal or State funds. Many reservation Indians also obtain some income from leases of land, but these rents are generally low because much of the land is of poor

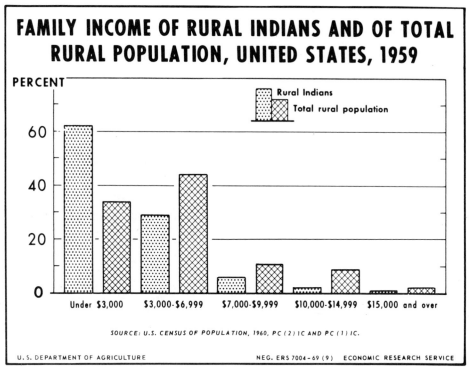

FAMILY INCOME OF RURAL INDIANS AND OF TOTAL RURAL POPULATION, UNITED STATES, 1959

PERCENT

Rural Indians
Total rural population

60

40

20

0

Under $3,000 $3,000-$6,999 $7,000-$9,999 $10,000-$14,999 $15,000 and over

SOURCE: U.S. CENSUS OF POPULATION, 1960, PC (2) 1C AND PC (1) 1C.

U.S. DEPARTMENT OF AGRICULTURE   NEG. ERS 7004-69 (9)   ECONOMIC RESEARCH SERVICE

FIGURE 3.

quality. Moreover, the share of income each family receives has greatly diminished over the years due to the fragmentation of property rights through generations of inheritance in large families. Income derived from employment available on and near reservations is relatively limited because of prevailing low wage rates and the seasonal or sporadic nature of the jobs. Income from all sources, therefore, still leaves most rural Indian families in poverty.

EDUCATION

The educational attainment level in the rural Indian population 14 years old and over in 1960 was low (fig. 4).

Fourteen percent of rural Indians had received no schooling at all, compared with only 2 percent of the total rural population. Only about one-third of the rural Indians had gone to high school and 3 percent to college. In the total rural population, comparable figures were 45 percent for high school attendance and 10 percent for college.

Possession of functional literacy is said to require at least 5 years of schooling—a level that 27 percent of rural Indians 14 and over in 1960 had not attained (app. table 5).

In terms of median years of school completed by Indians 14 years old and over, there was wide variation among the States in which most of them lived.

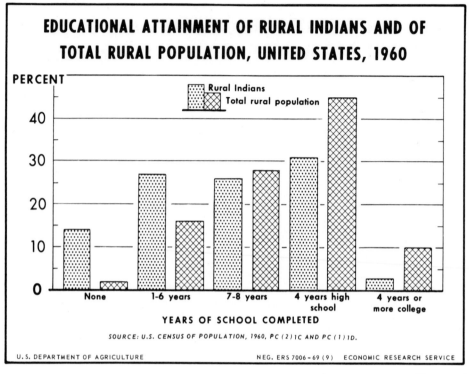

FIGURE 4.

In all States except Kansas, where the figure was 11 years, the medians were below the national average of 10.6 years in 1960. The median in Louisiana was only 3.9 years, while in the rest of the States the range was from 5.2 years in Mississippi to 9.7 in California.

The Federal Government, through the Bureau of Indian Affairs (BIA), provides educational services for children who live in isolated areas not served by public schools or who have other special needs. During the 1967/ 68 school year, 51,595 Indian youths attended 226 Bureau schools in 17 States. An additional 4,200 lived in Bureau dormitories and attended public schools. Also, about 8,500 Indian students, ages 6 through 18, were enrolled in mission and other private schools (app. table 10).

During the last 10 years, the Indian high school dropout rate has fallen from an estimated 60 percent to slightly more than 42 percent. This rate was still higher than the national figure of 26 percent, but represented a net gain of about 7 percent on the general population. The educational achievement of Indian students as measured by standardized tests, lags behind the national norms, the deficit by grade 12 typically being as much as 2½ years.

Indian children, like other minority groups, face special problems that complicate their educational experiences. More than half of them must learn English as a second language. They encounter many new concepts, values, and attitudes when they enter school. A large proportion have grown up in geographic and social isolation and have had little experience with the majority culture. Efforts are being made to meet their special needs through such programs as TESL (Teaching English as a Second Language), and through expanded staff services, improved curriculum offerings, school year and summer enrichment experiences, kindergarten programs, increased parental and community involvement in school affairs, and improvement of educational staff.[4]

HEALTH

Since 1955, on about 250 reservations in 23 Federal Indian Reservation States and in several hundred villages in Alaska, the Indian population has received health protection from the Public Health Service (PHS) of the U.S. Department of Health, Education, and Welfare. The service population, estimated to be 381,000 in 1965, comprises potential beneficiaries who depend in varying degrees on PHS for essential health services. These beneficiaries include some small groups for whom sanitation facilities projects are authorized, but who do not receive medical services from the Indian Health Service (in PHS). The stated goal of the Public Health Service is to "elevate the health status of Indians and Alaskan Natives (Indians, Aleuts, and Eskimos) to the highest possible level."[5]

Some aspects of Indian health have shown marked improvement in the past 10 to 15 years, but stubborn problems remain. Provision of adequate health services and facilities is complicated by the heterogeneity of the Indian tribal population and its dispersion over a very large geographic area, frequently in out-of-the-way places. Reaching these people with health assistance is difficult because of language barriers, the Indians' frequent lack of knowledge that help is available, and their high degree of social as well as physical isolation. Some of the most acute problems in safeguarding and improving the health of Indians are rooted in the environmental hazards under which they live. These include substandard, overcrowded housing; lack of adequate sanitation facilities and safe water supplies; insufficient understanding of proper hygienic practices; and often a pervading atmosphere of despair and frustration, which introduces a sense of hopelessness about improved health and well-being. In addition, there are diet deficiencies which contribute to physical and spiritual debilitation.

In an attempt to remedy the most serious problems, the Public Health Service has instituted programs to increase the number and kind of health services, to make them more accessible, and to raise their acceptance level. To supplement their own hospitals and health centers and to stretch resources, the Public Health Service has contractual arrangements with hundreds of private health practitioners, community general hospitals, State and local tuberculosis and mental hospitals, and a few nursing homes. In the PHS program to improve sanitation, Indians themselves have participated in planning and constructing facilities and have contributed more than one-third of the total program effort since 1959 by donating labor, materials, and money. There are also training programs being carried on for Indian personnel in all phases of the health field.

Considerable progress has been made in reducing mortality from communicable diseases and in lowering infant mortality rates. The most outstanding success has been in decreasing the number of deaths from tuberculosis, a disease very widespread in the Indian population. The rate had declined to 21 deaths per 100,000 population by 1964, a drop of 61 percent in 10 years (app. table 6). Infant mortality rates decreased 45 percent during 1954–64. However, compared with the general population the progress has been relative. These 1964 rates, for example, are roughly comparable to those in the total population some 15 or 20 years ago and are thus still much higher than rates among non-Indians.

"Unfinished business" in the Indian health field is enormous. Life expectancy among Indians is considerably below that of the general population; infant and maternal mortality rates remain high; and environmental changes needed to bring about substantial improvement in health are far from accomplished. Unmet needs of varying dimensions cover the entire health spectrum, including not only facilities and services, but educational and environmental improvement.

OCCUPATIONAL DISTRIBUTION

There are striking similarities between the occupational patterns of rural Indians and rural people as a whole. Both populations are overwhelmingly in nonfarm occupations—63 percent for employed rural Indians and 76 percent for the total employed rural population, according to the 1960 Census of Population (app. table 7). About 38 percent of both groups were in blue-collar occupations, and a slightly larger percentage of rural Indians than total rural population were in service work (13 and 9 percent, respectively). In white-collar occupations, however, the proportion of all rural people was twice as high as for rural Indians—28 percent, compared with 12 percent (fig. 5). This undoubtedly reflects a relative lack of nonfarm job opportunities and a lower level of educational attainment among rural Indians. The predominance of rural Indian workers in lower paid occupations also helps to account for their generally low level of income.

Rural Nonreservation Indian Groups

The foregoing discussion dealt primarily with the rural Indian population living on reservations, plus Alaskan Natives. It has been estimated in the Economic Research Service that there were more than 100,000 rural Indians living off of reservations in 1960 (app. table 8).[6] They were located in the rural areas of 20 States in every part of the country, from Maine to Califor-

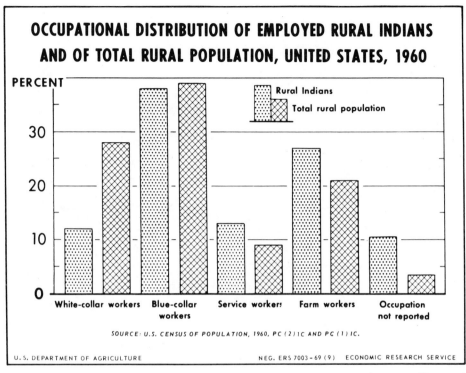

OCCUPATIONAL DISTRIBUTION OF EMPLOYED RURAL INDIANS AND OF TOTAL RURAL POPULATION, UNITED STATES, 1960

PERCENT

Rural Indians

Total rural population

30

20

10

0

White-collar workers Blue-collar workers Service workers Farm workers Occupation not reported

SOURCE: U.S. CENSUS OF POPULATION, 1960, PC (2) 1C AND PC (1) 1C.

U. S. DEPARTMENT OF AGRICULTURE   NEG. ERS 7003-69 (9)   ECONOMIC RESEARCH SERVICE

FIGURE 5.

nia (fig. 6). More than 60 percent lived in Oklahoma and North Carolina. Estimates on the size of these rural nonreservation Indian groups include only the counties that had at least 100 rural Indians.

Information is limited about rural Indians who live off of reservations. They do not receive Federal support as Indians, nor do they receive the BIA or PHS services that reservation Indians do. Some nonreservation Indians never have received such services. Their status and characteristics vary widely in the different parts of the country, making it difficult to generalize about them. Some have re-

mained separate populations and have tried to retain their Indian culture and traditions. Others have become triracial through generations of intermarriage with Negroes and whites. With the termination of reservation status for many Indians and their dispersal through the general population, it is impossible to state precisely the socioeconomic conditions under which rural nonreservation Indians live. Detailed information on local circumstances is essential for better understanding.

It is believed from available evidence that many of these Indian groups are in poverty, in poor health, in poor housing. Educational levels are gen-

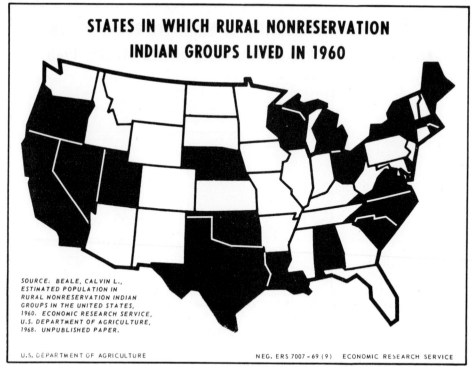

FIGURE 6.

erally low, and both unemployment and underemployment are widespread. For example, those who are trying to make a living in tobacco farming, as in North Carolina and Virginia, are small-scale owners, tenants, or hired workers. Operating on a poor land base and threatened by increasing mechanization in tobacco production, they face further deterioration in an already low level of living unless alternative employment becomes available. Some Indians—in Wisconsin, for example—are part-time, noncommercial farmers who depend primarily on timber and sawmill operations for income. Their economic situation is better than that of most rural

nonreservation Indians but still below acceptable standards. Some nonfarm Indians are employed in construction and industrial enterprises, such as steel workers in New York State and cotton mill workers in the South. Some rural Indians are seasonally employed in tourist trade in the recreation areas of a number of States. Many engage in hunting, fishing, and trapping. However, some communities of rural Indians are heavily dependent on public welfare. By and large, the scattered evidence suggests that the sources of livelihood open to rural nonreservation Indians are precarious, and their socioeconomic status is below an acceptable level.

Case Studies in Oklahoma

As part of a study of rural poverty conducted by the Economic Research Service in the Ozarks Region in 1966, 37 nonreservation Indian families in two counties in Oklahoma were interviewed. While this number is too small to permit much generalization, there are common threads that run through the stories of these families that shed some light on their situation. It is believed that the families in the survey are reasonably typical of rural families in parts of the Ozarks Region.

Findings revealed that the income of these Indian families was universally low, much of the financial support coming from public assistance. Most of the families were very large. While the parents had had little or no education, the children still at home were attending school. However, few of those who had left home had completed more than about 8 years of schooling. Housing was usually crowded and of poor quality; plumbing facilities and sewage disposal were found to be inadequate or nonexistent. Unemployment and underemployment were widespread. Most families had some indebtedness, chiefly for medical or dental services; few carried health or life insurance. A number of them maintained home garden plots, but few families produced any meat or poultry for home consumption.

The obvious conclusion is that these rural Indian families are destitute. Their opportunities to get out of poverty appear to be extremely limited in their present location and with the educational and skill levels they now have.

Programs designed to alleviate the poverty of these rural Indian families would encompass essentially the same objectives as those for other rural poor: namely, to increase incomes and job opportunities; to provide better housing and health services; and to make available improved education and vocational training.

Whither Indian Youth?

Rural Indian young people today stand at a fork in the road, uncertain which direction to go. Poised between the world of their ancestors and the alien world of the larger society, they lack a clear guidepost pointing the way to social and economic opportunity. Reluctant to depart from the Indian environment of known culture and tradition, and fearful of the unfamiliar ways of another culture, these youths are following as yet uncharted paths.

The plight of Indian youth and their elders is neither new nor unique. For many decades, Indian Americans have been confronted with the choice of remaining in reservation status under paternalistic protection or breaking away to the unknown hazards of "becoming Americanized" in the larger society. Their dilemma has been aggravated by the vacillating posture of U.S. Indian policy which at times has urged them to make their way by developing industry on the reservation, and at other times has encouraged them to abandon reservation life and become assimilated into American society. Neither of these alternatives has worked very well. Indian Americans are still at the cross-roads.

Sociologically, Indian youth symbolize a "lost generation." Like second-generation immigrants of yesterday, they are in a sense "cultural hybrids" or "marginal men"—caught between two worlds, at home in neither. As with other minority groups, they find themselves trying to cope with two quite different sets of expectations and values. They are being asked to give up one cluster of cultural traits before another one has been acquired. This situation creates uncertainty and inner conflict, a feeling of loss of identity and selfhood, a strong sense of alienation. Whether the individual blames society for his alienation or feels responsible for his own estrangement, the resulting disenchantment is equally destructive.

Alienation is often found among minority cultural groups and among people who have long suffered poverty and deprivation. Indian Americans fit into both of these categories. More than most minority ethnic groups they have known discrimination and dependence on outside society due to prolonged reservation status. This situation has effectively maintained a chasm between them and the dominant, non-Indian population. Most rural Indians have been in poverty for a very long time. The generally poor land base they started with has steadily become poorer, and the land they control is far less extensive than it once was. Commercial farming and cattle ranching are no longer feasible as a livelihood for most Indians, and they have not been prepared for alternative occupations. Nor do job opportunities exist on or

near most reservations. With this kind of history and heritage, the door is closed to the great majority of Indian young people to build fruitful lives on the reservation.

In addition to lack of economic opportunity, social disorganization affects Indian youth adversely. Pressures of poverty and unemployment, as well as tensions between the Indian and non-Indian cultures, have torn at the roots of traditional family ties. The prevalence of divorce, separation, and unwed mothers signals a weakening of family strength, one indication being the disproportionate number of foster children from broken Indian homes. An official of the National Committee on Indian Health testified recently that in North and South Dakota, 17 times as many Indian as white children are placed in foster homes.[7] The most startling evidence of social disorganization, however, is the prevalence of suicide among the young. For example, the suicide rate among Indians 15 to 24 years old is four times that of the same age group in the general population.[8]

Disorientation, anxiety, and isolation among Indian youth are thought to lead early in life to excessive drinking, accidents, and fatalities. Alcoholism, widespread among adults also, has long been a health and environmental problem among reservation Indians. It is often attributed to prohibition restrictions on some reservations and to a desire for release from the emptiness of reservation life. One reservation doctor is quoted as saying that the primary disease of the alcoholic is not alcoholism but rather "a disturbed relationship with his fellows and with society in general, a relationship that finds its overt pathology in the uncontrolled use of alcohol, and the diseases and accidents which go along with such use."[9] Young people are widely exposed to the pattern of heavy drinking on the part of their elders. Confronted also by what they regard as excessive restrictions by tribal authorities, many young people seek greater independence of action apart from reservation life.

One alternative open to Indian youth is acculturation to the larger society. This society's sophisticated, technological economy is changing rapidly and growing ever more complex, and calls for skills beyond those which most young Indians possess. They do not acquire from their own culture many of the concepts deeply embedded in today's world of work. For example, Indian cultural traits do not typically embrace the ideas of working on a fixed time schedule, of competing rather than sharing, of "saving for a rainy day." Work habits taken almost for granted by modern business and industry are not a part of the orientation Indian youth acquire from their own society. Nor, because of both their rural and reservation residence, have they had available adequate educational preparation or vocational training, guidance, and counseling which would teach them the work habits and attitudes required where the jobs are. This "preparation gap" grows ever wider as the American economy becomes more complicated, more bureaucratic, and more specialized in the skills required to run it.

Thus we return to the question, Whither Indian youth? Some leaders urge Indian young people to obtain all the education they can and then take the plunge into the world outside of the reservation. Many have done this. Some have succeeded; others have returned to reservation life after varying periods of time spent in unsuccessfully searching for adjustment outside. Some have returned to their reservations in the hope of sharing with families and tribal members what they have learned from pursuing higher education. There are those who feel that economic opportunity can be developed on the reservation if industry can be attracted to available sites, where partial support of training is usually provided by the Bureau of Indian Affairs for the local labor force.

On many reservations, this approach has worked in a variety of enterprises. One industrial plant with almost all Navajo Indian personnel is the largest nongovernment employer in New Mexico. However, some reservations have been unable to combine successfully the ingredients for industrial development.

An answer to the question about the road Indian youth might take is not easy to find. In the end, Indian young people will decide for themselves between life on the reservation or off, toward separatism, or toward integration. But a few beginning steps appear to be in order regardless of the decision made. Greater social and economic opportunity could be opened to all Indian Americans to raise their levels of income and provide improved housing, health facilities, and other services, the requisites of a better life for the rural poor of every cultural origin.

A favorable home environment would get Indian youth off to a better start no matter where they seek fulfillment of their goals. For these young people, more relevant education and vocational training, improved employment counseling and placement, and greater patience and understanding from the larger society will aid their transition to productive lives in a new setting.

A Few Forward Steps

Although most rural Indians are indeed in poverty and in physical and social isolation, some hopeful developments are emerging. There is scattered evidence of local decision-making among reservation Indians concerning steps they can take themselves to improve their situation. In some places, voter registration drives have been conducted, Head Start programs have been established, and Indian adults have participated in Work-Incentive, Job Corps, and special Community Action programs.[10] One writer quotes a North Dakota Indian as saying, "The Indian is in a period of transition and is just beginning to catch on to political maneuvering."[11] Another observer of the Indian situation says that "the Indian is capable of change . . . has changed in the past, and will adapt to technocracy and urbanism when he wants to. He will act now when he has to, though not always knowing why."[12] Changes in habits and attitudes take time, but a beginning has been made. Successful adjustment has been demonstrated by the many Indians who have risen to prominence in various fields,

including government, business, and the arts. Local efforts to attract business and industry to reservations have also paid off in some areas.

As for Indian youth, more of them each year are enrolled in school—a majority in public schools—more are going on to college or to technical schools, and scholarship assistance is more widely available than formerly for pursuing higher education. Indian languages and lore are being introduced into the curriculums of some Indian schools. Young people who go to large cities such as Chicago and Los Angeles are finding church-supported centers to aid them in finding housing, jobs, and friends.[13] Several nationwide organizations are attempting to coordinate programs of this kind and to articulate the needs and desires of Indians of all ages. Inadequate as these efforts are relative to the dimensions of need, they are nevertheless "a few forward steps."

Conclusion

Rural Indian Americans comprise a relatively small but exceptionally needy minority group. They are not only poor in material goods, they are widely impoverished in spirit. This is due to a prolonged period of dependence on society at large, as well as profound disturbance about the future. More than a century of social isolation in separate enclaves has taken its toll on initiative, creativity, and independent thought and action. The way ahead, especially for the present generation of Indian youth, abounds in difficult questions, with few positive answers to the problem of accommodating Indian culture to the surrounding society.

Although the present size of the Indian population is not known, estimates range from 600,000 to 800,000. Even accepting the latter figure as approximately correct, the Indian population in need represents a relatively small proportion of the total rural poor. Considering the depth of distress of rural Indians, the task of ameliorating the poverty of the great majority of them would not be an insuperable undertaking for an affluent country like the United States. Material poverty can be lifted primarily with money and jobs. It has been estimated that "the basic economic problems of the Indian communities could be solved by the provision of 40,000 jobs. This would seem a small demand for a nation where civilian employment has increased an average of 723,000 each year from 1955 to 1965, and where the last five years the average increase has been almost 1.5 million per year."[14]

Poverty of spirit can perhaps be lifted by releasing the energies and talents of Indians in local decision-making and by developing creative public and private relationships to work out feasible solutions to difficult problems. Some new kind of Indian-Government partnership to guide the future course of Indian communities, whether on or off reservation lands, appears to be desirable.

It is important not only to recognize the need for Indian leadership and full participation in policy making, but also to identify specific Indian wants and desires. To remedy the unusual situation of prolonged dependent status in American society requires extraordinary effort and understanding on the part of the non-Indian population. As a recent task force report of the Chamber of Commerce of the United States said, "Indian spokesmen have stated Indian wants. They want to retain their culture. They want to be consulted and to have a real voice in decisions relating to themselves. They want to retain their reservation lands. And Indians want to enter modern economic life and enjoy its advantages. The Task Force supports these legitimate aspirations of Indian Americans. The Task Force further believes the public has a special and continuing national responsibility to see that the opportunities and rewards of society are fully extended to these citizens."[15]

Genuine acculturation of the Indian people can be promoted only when they play their full part in the life of the larger society. When rural Indian Americans come to feel they have not only a real stake in the future of America, but a responsibility, and the ability, to contribute to it, they will then be able to lift themselves out of poverty of spirit. Meanwhile, the rest of society can help by finding a way to remove the conditions that produce material poverty. Achieving these twin objectives will then lend credence to the phrase Indian *Americans*.

TABLE 1. Indian population in selected States, by urban or rural residence, and in United States, 1960

State	Total	Urban	Rural	Percentage rural
	Number	Number	Number	Percent
Alaska	42,522[1]	5,425	37,097[1]	87.3
Arizona	83,387	8,300	75,087	90.0
California	39,014	20,619	18,395	47.1
Colorado	4,288	1,792	2,496	58.2
Florida	2,504	1,024	1,480	59.1
Idaho	5,231	689	4,542	86.8
Illinois	4,704	4,380	324	6.9
Kansas	5,069	3,564	1,505	29.7
Louisiana	3,587	745	2,842	79.2
Michigan	9,701	5,007	4,694	48.3
Minnesota	15,496	4,798	10,698	69.0
Mississippi	3,119	170	2,949	94.6
Montana	21,181	2,572	18,609	87.9
Nebraska	5,545	1,971	3,574	64.5
Nevada	6,681	1,678	5,003	74.9
New Mexico	56,255	8,960	47,295	84.1
New York	16,491	8,852	7,639	46.3
North Carolina	38,129	1,698	36,431	95.5
North Dakota	11,736	1,174	10,562	90.0
Oklahoma	64,689	23,917	40,772	63.0
Oregon	8,026	2,580	5,446	67.9
South Dakota	25,794	4,558	21,236	82.3
Texas	5,750	4,101	1,649	28.7
Utah	6,961	1,643	5,318	76.4
Washington	21,076	7,025	14,051	66.6
Wisconsin	14,297	3,996	10,301	72.0
Wyoming	4,020	422	3,598	89.5
Total, 27 States	525,253	—	—	74.9
Total, United States	551,669	—	—	—

Source: U.S. Census of Population, 1960 PC(2) 1C, Nonwhite Population by Race. (Includes States with 2,500 or more total Indian population.) PC(1) 1B, United States Summary, General Population Characteristics (table 56).

1. Includes Aleuts and Eskimos. Residence distribution partly estimated.

TABLE 2.   Age distribution of rural Indians and total rural population, United States, 1960

Age	Rural Indians		U.S. rural population	
	Total	Percentage of total	Total	Percentage of total
	Number	*Percent*	*Number*	*Percent*
Years:				
Under 5	64,340	16.9	6,260,791	11.6
5 to 9	56,988	15.0	6,083,155	11.3
10 to 14	48,481	12.7	5,725,977	10.6
15 to 19	37,080	9.8	4,487,549	8.3
20 to 24	25,934	6.8	3,076,511	5.7
25 to 29	21,829	5.7	3,023,849	5.6
30 to 34	20,161	5.3	3,306,444	6.1
35 to 39	18,550	4.9	3,436,986	6.4
40 to 44	15,825	4.2	3,275,216	6.1
45 to 49	15,378	4.0	3,122,993	5.8
50 to 54	13,120	3.5	2,754,841	5.1
55 to 59	15,046	4.0[1]	2,415,273	4.5
60 to 64	8,500	2.2	2,051,452	3.8
65 to 69	7,309	1.9	1,855,498	3.4
70 to 74	5,139	1.4	1,424,809	2.6
75 and over	6,626	1.7	1,753,081	3.3
Total, all ages	380,306	100.0	54,054,425	100.0[2]
	Years		*Years*	
Median age	17.7	—	27.3	—

Source: U.S. Census of Population, 1960, PC(2) 1C and PC(1) 1B.

1. Overestimation in this group due to Census processing error.
2. Percentages are based on unrounded data and may not total 100.

TABLE 3.   Size of family for rural Indians and total rural population, United States, 1960

Size of family	Rural Indians		U.S. rural population	
	Families	Percentage of total	Families	Percentage of total
	Number	*Percent*	*Number*	*Percent*
2 persons	10,878	16.9	4,033,744	30.6
3 persons	10,091	15.7	2,673,386	20.3
4 persons	9,325	14.5	2,522,948	19.1
5 persons	8,915	13.8	1,757,769	13.3
6 persons	7,515	11.7	1,035,401	7.9
7 or more persons	17,637	27.4	1,165,107	8.8
All families	64,361	100.0	13,188,355	100.0

Source: 1960 Census of Population, PC(2) 1C and PC(1) 1D.

TABLE 4.   Distribution of family income for rural Indians and total rural population, United States, 1960

Income	Rural Indians		U.S. rural population	
	Families	Percentage of total	Families	Percentage of total
	Number	*Percent*	*Number*	*Percent*
Under $1,000	18,025	28.0	1,310,295	9.9
$ 1,000 to $2,999	22,085	34.3	3,112,294	23.6
$ 3,000 to $4,999	12,391	19.2	3,154,303	23.9
$ 5,000 to $6,999	6,557	10.2	2,670,812	20.3
$ 7,000 to $9,999	3,659	5.7	1,422,191	10.8
$10,000 to $14,999	1,290	2.0	1,198,998	9.1
$15,000 and over	354	0.6	319,458	2.4
Total families	64,361	100.0	13,188,351	100.0

Source: 1960 Census of Population, PC(2) 1C and PC(1) 1C.

TABLE 5. Years of school completed by persons 14 years old and over in the rural Indian and total rural population, United States, 1960

Years of school completed	Rural Indians		Total rural population	
	Total	Percentage of total	Total	Percentage of total
	Number	*Percent*	*Number*	*Percent*
No school years completed	29,550	13.5	788,380	2.1
Elementary school:				
1 to 4 years	29,020	13.3	2,626,000	7.1
5 to 6 years	29,343	13.4	3,123,443	8.5
7 years	21,480	9.8	3,026,772	8.2
8 years	34,585	15.8	7,165,249	19.4
High school:				
1 to 3 years	47,403	21.7	8,446,084	22.9
4 years	20,819	9.5	8,061,562	21.8
College:				
1 to 3 years	5,106	2.3	2,276,682	6.2
4 years or more	1,599	.7	1,436,057	3.9
Total	218,905	100.0	36,950,229	100.0

Source: U.S. Census of Population, 1960, PC(2) 1C and PC(1) 1D.

TABLE 6.   Selected vital statistics, Indians and total U.S. population, 1964 and 1954

Vital statistics	Indians	United States (all races)
	Number	Number
Infant deaths per 1,000 live births:		
1964	35.9	24.8
1954	65.0	26.6
Maternal deaths per 10,000 live births:		
1964	6.3	3.4
1954	18.4	5.2
Deaths per 100,000 population, by specific cause—		
Tuberculosis:		
1964	21.3	4.3
1954	54.0	10.2
Gastritis, enteritis, etc.		
1964	19.3	4.3
1954	56.0	4.9
Morbidity per 100,000 population, by specified cause[1]—		
Tuberculosis:		
1964	184.1	26.6
1954	571.0	62.4
Dysentery:		
1964	417.5	8.5
1963	428.1	8.4
23 Federal Indian Reservation States—Birth rate (registered live births per 1,000 population):		
1964	43.1	21.0
	Years	Years
Average age of death, 1964	43.8	63.6
Life expectancy at birth, 1964	63.5	70.2
Median age of population	17.3	29.5
	Percent	Percent
Percentage of population under 20 years	55.2	38.5

Source: Indian Health Highlights, 1966 edition U.S. Dept. Health, Educ., and Welfare, Pub. Health Serv., pp. xvi, 7.

1. Cases reported per 100,000 population.

TABLE 7. Occupational distribution of employed rural Indians and total rural population, United States, 1960

Occupational category	Rural Indians		Total rural population	
	Total	Percentage of total	Total	Percentage of total
	Number	Percent	Number	Percent
White-collar workers ...	7,892	12.0	4,752,562	27.6
Blue-collar workers	25,241	38.3	6,707,235	38.9
Service workers	8,382	12.7	1,566,678	9.1
Farmworkers	17,506	26.5	3,604,185	20.9
Occupation not reported	6,939	10.5	618,197	3.6
Total employed	65,960	100.0	17,248,857	100.0

Source: U.S. Census of Population, 1960, PC(2) 1C and PC(1) 1C.

Note: White-collar workers: Professional and technical; managers, officials, and proprietors; clerical; and sales. Blue-collar workers: Craftsmen and foremen; operatives, and nonfarm laborers. Service workers: Private household and service. Farmworkers: Farmers and farm managers, farm laborers, and foremen.

TABLE 8. Estimated population of rural "nonreservation" Indian groups, by State, 1960

State[1]	Number	State[1]	Number
Oklahoma	37,730	Nebraska	1,000
North Carolina	31,345	Alabama	755
California	13,995	Delaware	540
New York	6,950	South Carolina	535
Oregon	2,955	Massachusetts	425
Louisiana	2,470	Texas	370
Wisconsin	2,400	Rhode Island	300
Michigan	1,715	Ohio	130
Maine	1,435	Nevada	100
Virginia	1,131	Utah	100
		Total	106,380

Source: Beale, Calvin L., Estimated Population in Rural Nonreservation Indian Groups in the United States, 1960, Econ. Res. Serv., U.S. Dept. Agr., 1968. Unpublished paper.

1. States that had counties in which at least 100 rural Indians lived.

TABLE 9.   Estimated Indian population resident on, or adjacent to, Federal reservations, by State, September 1968

State	Estimated population	State	Estimated population
Alaska[1]	55,400	Nebraska	2,500
Arizona	105,900	Nevada	4,400
California	6,600	New Mexico	74,500
Colorado	1,600	North Carolina	4,600
Florida	1,200	North Dakota	13,600
Idaho	5,100	Oklahoma[2]	72,400
Iowa	500	Oregon	2,800
Kansas	1,000	South Dakota	30,000
Louisiana	300	Utah	5,700
Michigan	1,000	Washington	16,000
Minnesota	10,400	Wisconsin	6,500
Mississippi	3,200	Wyoming	4,100
Montana	23,100		
		Total	452,000

Source: Estimates of the Indian Population Served by the Bureau of Indian Affairs: September 1968, Office of Program Coordination, Bureau of Indian Affairs, U.S. Dept. of the Interior, March 1969, table 1.

1. Includes Aleuts and Eskimos.
2. Includes former reservation areas in Oklahoma.

TABLE 10. Enrollment of Indians, ages 6 through 18, by type of school, selected years, 1952–68

Year	Total enrollment	Public schools		Federal (BIA) schools		Other schools	
		Enrollment	Percentage of total	Enrollment	Percentage of total	Enrollment	Percentage of total
	Number	*Number*	*Percent*	*Number*	*Percent*	*Number*	*Percent*
1952	99,441	52,960	53.3	36,414	36.6	10,067	10.1
1954	104,470	58,855	56.3	35,586	34.1	10,029	9.6
1956	122,855	71,956	58.6	39,676	32.2	11,223	9.1
1958	129,760	78,822	60.7	39,677	30.6	11,261	8.7
1960	133,316	84,650	63.5	37,377	28.0	11,289	8.5
1962	117,562	69,651	59.2	38,887	33.1	9,024	7.7
1964	132,654	79,286	59.8	44,132	33.3	9,236	7.0
1966	141,694	86,827	61.3	46,154	32.6	8,713	6.1
1968	142,630	87,361	61.2	46,725	32.8	8,544	6.0

Source: Annual School Census of Indian Children, Bureau of Indian Affairs, U.S. Dept. of the Interior, 1952–1968.

Note: In 1961, the Bureau dropped from its school census Indian children living in the States of California, Idaho, Michigan, Minnesota, Nebraska, Oregon, Texas, Washington, and Wisconsin, where educational responsibility for Indians had previously been assumed by the States. It is estimated there were at least 115,000 Indian children in public schools in 1968.

Footnotes

1. Brandon, William, The American Heritage Book of Indians, Dell Publ. Co., New York, 1964. See also, "Indian, North American," Encyclopaedia Britannica, Vol. 12, 1957 edition and references cited therein, p. 209.
2. U.S. Census of Population, 1960, PC (2)1C, Nonwhite Population by Race, Subject Reports.
3. Indian Health Highlights, Public Health Serv., U.S. Dept. Health, Education, and Welfare, 1966, p. xiv.
4. Statement supplied by Bureau of Indian Affairs.
5. Ibid., pp. xi-xii and p. 1.
6. Beale, Calvin L., Estimated Population in Rural Nonreservation Indian Groups in the United States, 1960, Econ. Res. Serv., U.S. Dept. Agr., 1968. Unpublished paper.
7. Statements of William Byler and Dr. Daniel J. O'Connell in hearings before the Subcommittee on Indian Education of the Committee on Labor and Public Welfare, U.S. Senate, Wash., D.C., Oct. 1, 1968.
8. Indian Health Highlights, op. cit., p. 19.
9. Olson, Cal, "The Indian in North Dakota," The Fargo Forum and Moorhead News, Fargo, N.D., Jan. 19, 1966, p. 8.
10. Manpower Report of the President, U.S. Dept. Labor, Jan. 1969, pp. 107–108.
11. Olson, Cal, op. cit.
12. Lynn, Paul Ross, A Study of Developmental Problems of American Indian Children and Youth. Report prepared for United Church of Christ, Mar. 1964, p. 2.
13. Hoffman, James W., "A Comeback for the Vanishing American?" Presbyterian Life, Feb. 1, 1969.
14. Nader, Ralph, "Lo, the Poor Indian," The New Republic, Mar. 30, 1968, quoting Professor Gary Orfield of the Univ. of Virginia, p. 15.

15. Chamber of Commerce of the United States, Rural Poverty and Regional Progress in an Urban Society, Task Force on Economic Growth and Opportunity, Fourth Report, 1969.

Bibliography

1. Beale, Calvin L. 1968. Estimated Population in Rural Nonreservation Indian Groups in the United States, 1960. Econ. Res. Serv., U.S. Dept. of Agr. Unpublished paper. March.

2. Bennett, Robert L. 1967. American Indians—A Special Minority. Remarks before the Institute of Race Relations, Fisk University, Nashville, Tenn. Bureau of Indian Affairs, U.S. Dept. of the Interior. June 29.

3. Brand, David. 1969. Red Power— Young Indians Borrow Tactics From Blacks As They Fight Poverty. The Wall Street Journal. April 30.

4. Brandon, William. 1964. The American Heritage Book of Indians. Dell Publ. Co., N.Y.

5. Brophy, William A. and Aberle, Sophie D. 1967. The Indian: America's Unfinished Business. Report of the Commission on the Rights, Liberties, and Responsibilities of the American Indian. Univ. of Okla. Press, Norman, Okla. Nov.

6. Byler, William and O'Connell, Daniel J. 1968. Hearings before the Subcommittee on Indian Education of the Committee on Labor and Public Welfare, U.S. Senate, Washington, D.C. Oct. 1.

7. Chamber of Commerce of the United States. 1969. Rural Poverty and Regional Progress in an Urban Society. Task Force on Economic Growth and Opportunity, Fourth Report.

8. Cohen, Warren H. and Mause, Philip J. 1968. The Indian: The Forgotten American. Harvard Law Review, 81(8):1818–1858. June.

9. Congressional Record. 1969. Education Problems of Indians. 67: S4071. April 25.

10. Encyclopaedia Britannica 1957. Indian, North American, Vol. 12.

11. Farb, Peter. 1968. The American Indian, A Portrait in Limbo. Sat. Review. Oct. 12.

12. Greider, William. 1969. Wounded Knee Still Festers. Washington Post. Feb. 23.

13. Hoffman, James W. 1969. A Comeback for the Vanishing American? Presbyterian Life. Jan. 15, Feb. 1 and 15, and March 1.

14. Josephson, Eric and Mary, ed. 1968. Man Alone—Alienation in Modern Society. Dell Publ. Co. Sept.

15. Koenig, Samuel. 1957. Man and Society. Barnes and Noble, Inc., New York.

16. Lynn, Paul Ross. 1964. A Study of Developmental Problems of American Indian Children and Youth. Report prepared for United Church of Christ, Dept. of Church in Town and Country. March.

17. Nader, Ralph. 1968. Lo, the Poor Indian. The New Republic. March 30.

18. Olson, Cal. 1966. The Indian in North Dakota. The Fargo Forum and Moorhead News. Jan. 16–20.

19. Parmee, Edward A. 1968. Formal Education and Culture Change: A Modern Apache Indian Community and Government Education Programs. The Univ. of Ariz. Press, Tucson.

20. Reifel, Ben. 1958. Indians of the Missouri Basin—Cultural Factors in Their Social and Economic Adjustment. Paper presented at the M.B.I.A.C. Meeting, Aberdeen, S.D., May 14–15.

21. Sorkin, Alan L. 1969. American Indians Industrialize to Combat Poverty. Monthly Labor Review. March.

22. Taviss, Irene. 1969. Changes in the Form of Alienation: The 1900's vs. the 1950's. Amer. Soc. Rev. 34(1): 46–57. Feb.

23. U.S. Bureau of the Census. 1960. Census of Population, PC(1)B; PC(2)1C, Nonwhite Population by Race, Subject Reports.

24. U.S. Department of Agriculture. 1966. Rural People in the American Economy. Agr. Econ. Rept. No. 101, Econ. Res. Serv. Oct.

25. U.S. Department of Health, Education, and Welfare. 1966. Indian Health Highlights. Public Health Service.

26. U.S. Department of the Interior. 1968. Statistics Concerning Indian Education. Bureau of Indian Affairs, Div. of Education.

27. U.S. Department of Labor. 1969. Manpower Report of the President. Jan.

five ◆ ◆ ◆ ◆ ◆ ◆ ◆ ◆ ◆ ◆ ◆ ◆ ◆ ◆ ◆ ◆ ◆ ◆ ◆

◆ MARK LOWRY II

Race and Socioeconomic Well-Being: A Geographical Analysis of the Mississippi Case

The racially discordant nature of socioeconomic conditions in the United States is well recognized. Much social strife and public concern are directly and indirectly attributable to the discriminatory nature of our society. Geographers are showing increased interest in contemporary social problems, but in view of their magnitude, the geographical literature on these problems is relatively sparse.

The theme of racial diversity is not new in geography. For several decades geographers have been producing substantial material on the distribution and migration of different racial groups in the United States.[1] Recently segregation in and around urban areas and the racial ghettos have been receiving more attention.[2] Two studies by George W. Carey and his co-workers—one on Manhattan's population and housing patterns and the other on educational and demographic factors in Washington, D.C.[3]—treat phenomena similar to those studied here. However, the present study covers the entire rural state of Mississippi. It is not intended as a commentary on the methods and substance of other works; rather it is offered as a contribution to the growing body of geographical literature on contemporary socioeconomic conditions in the United States.

The study grew initially from impressions gained during 1967 and 1968, when the writer traveled the length and breadth of Mississippi. One of the most striking observations was that although the contrast between living conditions

◆ SOURCE. Reprinted by permission from the *Geographical Review*, Vol. 60, 1970, pp. 511–528, copyrighted by the American Geographical Society of New York.

of Negroes and whites was often stark, it was by no means equally pronounced in all parts of the state. At one extreme abject Negro poverty exists alongside white affluence; at the other extreme living conditions are about equal. This variation in racial disparity can also be seen in the degree of racial integration in schools and employment, in racial attitudes, and in many other facets of everyday life. The geographical significance is that the living conditions vary from place to place in a meaningful pattern. The complex array of factors bearing on the situation was overwhelming in the field. However, it seemed that the degree of socioeconomic disparity between races was related spatially to at least three major elements—the degree of urbanization, the economic activities of the people, and the proportion of Negroes in the population. Taken separately and out of context, any one of these elements cannot explain much and is likely to be misleading, but considered against the background of what we know about the plural society of the South, they take on greater meaning. The purpose of this study is to test the validity of the observations made in the field and to consider some of their implications.

Mississippi is an ideal area for this study. The population is 42.3 percent Negro (1960); the socioeconomic disparities between the races are great; and the discriminatory aspect of our society has been most intense in the area.[4] Furthermore, the effects of conditions in Mississippi have not been confined within the political boundaries of that state or to the South. As geographers and sociologists have demon-

strated, migrants have been moving from Mississippi to the North and West for many decades.[5] These migrant streams hold clues to racially discordant socioeconomic conditions. For example, northward streams are predominantly Negro, reflecting, in part, the attempt to escape conditions in the South. Thus much of the nation is affected by conditions and events in Mississippi.

The term "socioeconomic well-being" as used here expresses the degree of prosperity or welfare of people with respect to their material needs. It reflects much of what one could see in the way of living conditions if one traveled around the state. The concepts of poverty, economic health, and economic development are related to socioeconomic well-being, but as they have been applied by geographers[6] they are less directly focused on the people, which is where the emphasis of this study lies. Although other socially determined characteristics, such as some demographic features and health, are closely related to socioeconomic well-being, they have been excluded from this study, not as irrelevant, but in the interest of simplicity.

In order to compare the races with respect to their patterns of socioeconomic well-being, the population has been divided first into its white and Negro components and then into its farm and nonfarm components. Quantitative indexes of socioeconomic well-being are derived for the total population and for each population component. Quantitative measures are derived for well-being gaps between the white and Negro indexes. Statistical and cartographic analyses reveal significant differences among these indexes, and further analysis shows that this approach to the geographical study of racial disparities is useful.

Socioeconomic Well-Being Indexes

To derive composite indexes of socioeconomic well-being, the basic variables used refer to material possessions. The method of derivation is to average the standard scores[7] of all basic variables, and the areal unit is the county.[8] This equal weighting eliminates biases resulting from differences in the magnitude of the variable values. Since an index of the consumption of goods and services by farm people is not strictly comparable with that for the nonfarm population, two kinds of indexes were calculated, one for the total population (SEWTP), the other for the farm population (SEWTF) (Table 1). However, these two indexes cannot be calculated separately for the white and Negro components of the population, because the variables are not tabulated by race, and closely correlated indicators must be used as surrogates.

In the Mississippi case, certain indexes of income and education, which are available by race, are good indicators of socioeconomic well-being. SEWTP has a .81 correlation with median school years completed by persons twenty-five years of age and older

TABLE 1.   Variables Used to Derive Socioeconomic Well-Being Indexes

Variables for total population SEWTP	Variables for total farm population SEWTF
Dwelling units (%)	*Farmhouses (%)*
with one or more automobiles available	with piped water
with two or more automobiles available	with automobiles[a]
with one or more air-conditioning units available	with telephone[a]
with two or more air-conditioning units available	with home food freezer[a]
with exclusive use of bathtub or shower	with hot and cold piped water indoors
with clothes dryer	with exclusive use of flush toilet
with clothes washing machine	with exclusive use of bathtub or shower
with exclusive use of flush toilet	in sound structural condition
with hot and cold piped water indoors	not dilapidated
with home food freezer	with bathtub or shower
with one or more radios	
with two or more radios	
with telephone available	
with one or more television sets	
with two or more television sets	

Source: United States Census of Housing, 1960.
[a] United States Census of Agriculture, 1964.

TABLE 2. Socioeconomic Well-Being Indexes

Name	Description	Name	Description
SESTP	Socioeconomic well-being of total population	SESTW	Socioeconomic well-being of total white population
SESTU	Socioeconomic well-being of total nonfarm population	SESWU	Socioeconomic well-being of white nonfarm population
SESTF	Socioeconomic well-being of total farm population	SESWF	Socioeconomic well-being of white farm population
SESTN	Socioeconomic well-being of total Negro population	SESTG	Socioeconomic well-being gap, total population
SESNU	Socioeconomic well-being of Negro nonfarm population	SESUG	Socioeconomic well-being gap, nonfarm population
SESNF	Socioeconomic well-being of Negro farm population	SESFG	Socioeconomic well-being gap, farm population

and a .89 correlation with median family income.[9] SEWTF has a .83 correlation with median farm family income and a .73 correlation with median school years completed by farm population twenty-five years of age and older. Therefore the three specific indicators used to derive indexes for the total population and for all population components considered are average number of years of school completed by persons age twenty-five and over, average income of persons age fourteen and over, and occupation of employed persons (Table 2).[10]

The method of deriving the indexes of socioeconomic well-being has been published in a Bureau of the Census Working Paper.[11] The publication provides three tables, one for each of the indicators used in this study. Each table contains scores ranging from 0 to 100, which are equated with the corresponding values of the appropriate indicator. Three scores are obtained by checking a county's values for income, education, and occupation against the three tables.

The average of the three scores is the socioeconomic well-being index for the county. Racial gaps, an innovation of this study, are derived by subtracting Negro indexes from corresponding white indexes.

Factor analysis (Table 3) and

TABLE 3. Factor Loadings of Socioeconomic Well-Being Indexes

Factor 1 44.92% of variation		Factor 2 36.20% of variation	
SESTN	.9620	SESTW	.9584
SESTP	.9486	SESWU	.9506
SESTF	.8849	SESTG	.9331
SESNU	.8576	SESFG	.8702
SESTU	.8255	SESUG	.8250
SEWTP	.7812	SESWF	.7065
SEWTF	.7597	SEWTP	.2649
SESNF	.7256	SESTU	.2342
SESWF	.3922	SESTP	.2067
SESTW	.2390	SESNU	.1959
SESWU	.0424	SESTN	.1068
SESFG	−.1086	SEWTF	−.2411
SESTG	−.3170	SESTF	−.2430
SESUG	−.4743	SESNF	−.3222

maps (Figs. 2–5) are employed to identify and measure correspondence in place-to-place variation of each of the indexes.[12] Since the information desired from the maps is relative spatial variation, the indexes are mapped in standardized form. In all cases means and standard deviations are listed on the maps to permit more detailed analysis.

Factor 1 reveals three groups of indexes, each identified by its similar loadings. The first group includes all the indexes for Negroes and for the total population, but no indexes for whites. The middle group is composed of the white indexes exclusively. This grouping suggests that spatial patterns of socioeconomic well-being for the total population are similar to patterns of Negro socioeconomic well-being. On the other hand, white socioeconomic well-being varies from place to place in patterns considerably different from the Negro and total-population patterns.

The maps confirm the factor-analysis finding. Figures 2 and 3 portray generally below-average levels for the total population and for Negroes in the Yazoo Basin and along the Bluff Hills in the western part of the state (Fig. 1), but there are some notable exceptions, especially in the cases of total- and nonfarm-population maps in both figures. Above average levels show more scattered patterns. On the nonfarm-population maps, most of the more urbanized counties are in the two highest categories. Maps of total population in both figures reflect the same kind of urban influence, though it is not as pronounced for the total Negro population. The farm-population maps do not reflect an urban influence. High levels for the farm population in both figures are found in the Pine Hills and the coastal counties. The Negro farm-population map shows additional high-level counties in the north-central and northeastern areas.

By contrast, the patterns for whites (Fig. 4), though they reflect considerable influence of urbanization, exhibit regional orientations that differ from those for the total population and for Negroes. High levels are found in counties along the Mississippi River, in the hills south of the Yazoo Basin, in the Black Belt, and in the coastal area. The total- and nonfarm-population maps show additional high-level counties in the southern part of the Yazoo Basin. Below-average counties on all three maps are in the northeast and north-central areas and are scattered southward through the center of the state into the Pine Hills. On the nonfarm-population map low levels extend to the coast, and the farm-population map shows several low-level counties in the Yazoo Basin.

Factor 2 (Table 3) also reveals three groups of indexes. The first group, all with strong positive loadings, comprises the six white and gap indexes. White well-being and socioeconomic well-being gaps vary similarly from place to place. The gap is wide in most of the Yazoo Basin, in the Bluff Hills, and in the Black Belt (Fig. 5); the rest of the state exhibits gaps ranging generally from average to relatively narrow, though there are some exceptions.

Why do gap indexes correspond so closely with white indexes? The answer lies in the concept of the socioeconomic well-being gap. There are great differ-

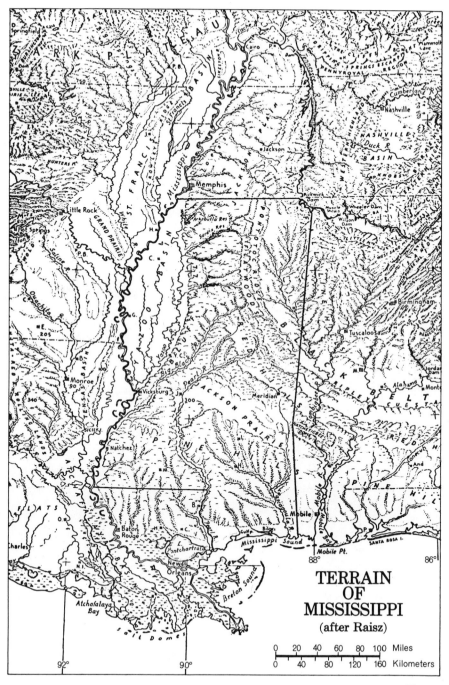

TERRAIN
OF
MISSISSIPPI
(after Raisz)

| 0 | 20 | 40 | 60 | 80 | 100 | Miles |
| 0 | 40 | 80 | 120 | 160 | | Kilometers |

FIGURE 1.

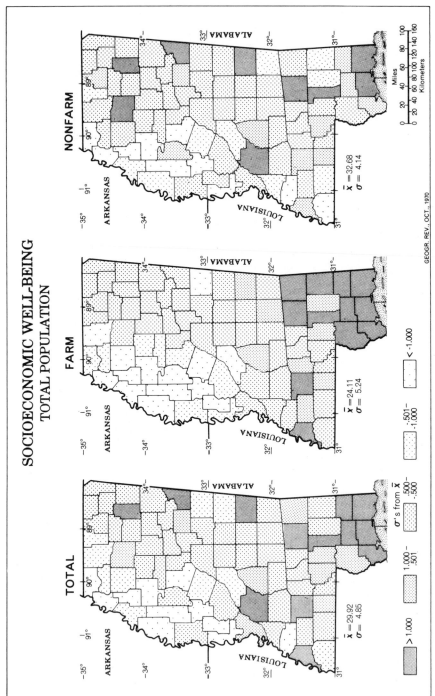

SOCIOECONOMIC WELL-BEING
TOTAL POPULATION

TOTAL

FARM

NONFARM

$\bar{x}$ = 29.92
σ = 4.85

$\bar{x}$ = 24.11
σ = 5.24

$\bar{x}$ = 32.68
σ = 4.14

σ's from $\bar{x}$

> 1.000

1.000 –
.501

.500 –
.500

–.501 –
–1.000

< –1.000

Miles
0 20 40 60 80 100
0 20 40 60 80 100 120 140 160
Kilometers

GEOGR. REV., OCT., 1970

FIGURE 2.

SOCIOECONOMIC WELL-BEING
NEGRO POPULATION

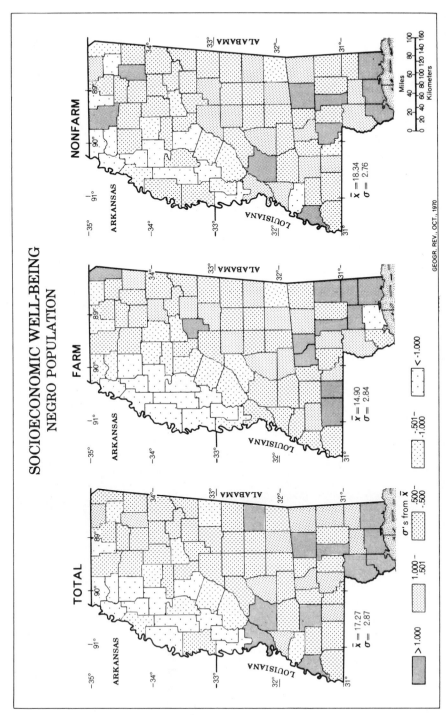

FIGURE 3.

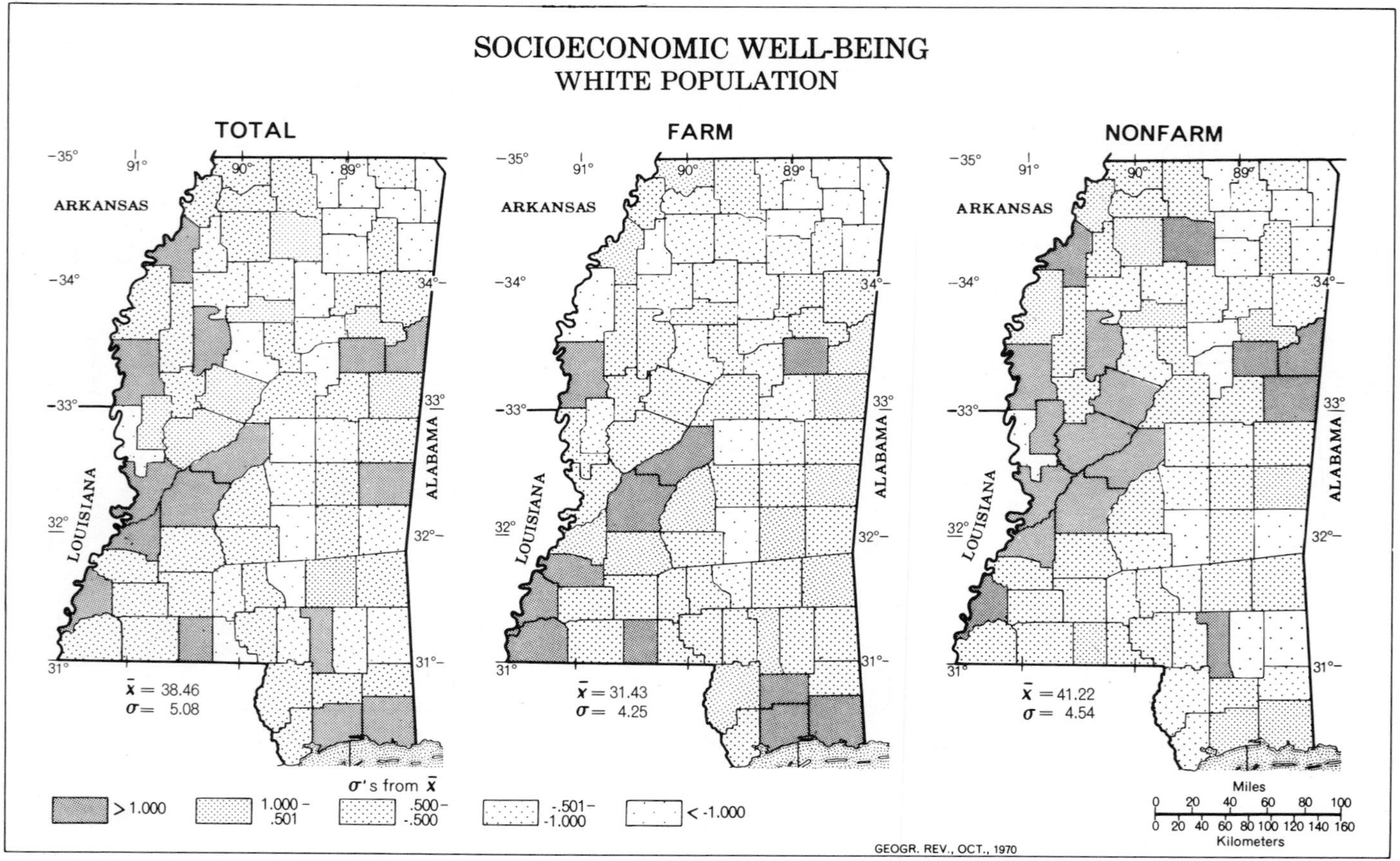

SOCIOECONOMIC WELL-BEING
WHITE POPULATION

TOTAL

FARM

NONFARM

σ's from x̄

> 1.000

1.000 –
.501

.500 –
-.500

-.501 –
-1.000

< -1.000

TOTAL
x̄ = 38.46
σ = 5.08

FARM
x̄ = 31.43
σ = 4.25

NONFARM
x̄ = 41.22
σ = 4.54

GEOGR. REV., OCT., 1970

FIGURE 4.

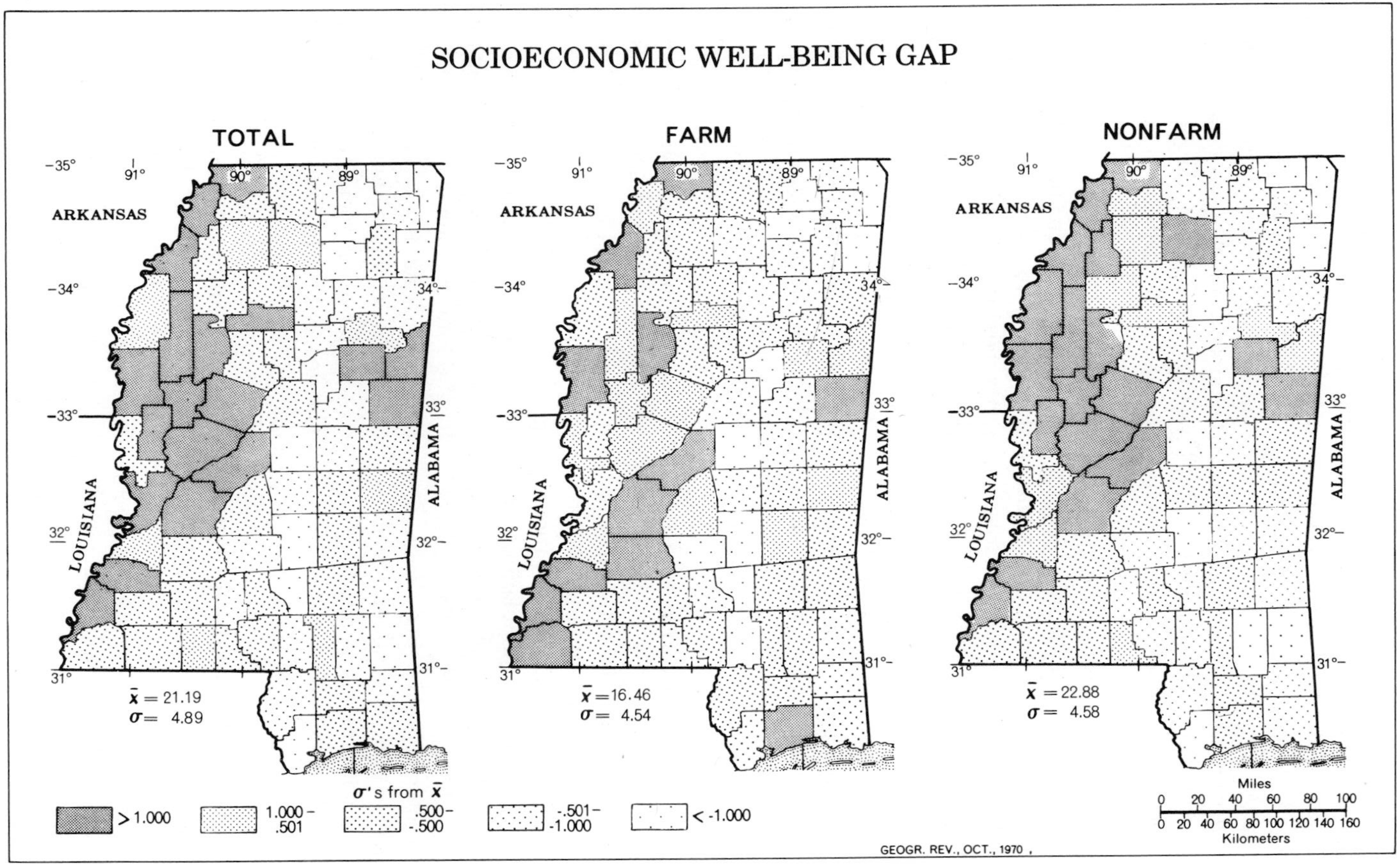
SOCIOECONOMIC WELL-BEING GAP
TOTAL
FARM
NONFARM
ARKANSAS
LOUISIANA
ALABAMA
-35°
-34°
-33°
32°
31°
91°
90°
89°
34°
33°
32°
31°
$\bar{x}$ = 21.19
σ = 4.89
$\bar{x}$ = 16.46
σ = 4.54
$\bar{x}$ = 22.88
σ = 4.58
σ's from $\bar{x}$
> 1.000
1.000 - .501
.500 - -.500
-.501 - -1.000
< -1.000
Miles
0 20 40 60 80 100
0 20 40 60 80 100 120 140 160
Kilometers
GEOGR. REV., OCT., 1970 ,

FIGURE 5.

ences between average levels for Negroes and whites. In all cases—farm,
nonfarm, and both combined—average
white levels are more than twice as high
as average Negro levels, so that average
gaps are greater than the average Negro
levels. Accordingly, all standard deviations for white indexes are much
larger than those for Negro indexes. It
follows that white indexes have greater
place-to-place variations than Negro indexes have. County values for white
indexes range widely around relatively
high averages, while county values for
Negro indexes cluster closely around
relatively low averages. Therefore,
when a Negro index is subtracted from
a white index to obtain a gap index,
spatial variations in the white index
dominate the gap pattern.

A Preliminary Analysis

The following analysis considers the
three major types of independent variables: degree of urbanization, proportion of Negroes in the population, and
an array of economic phenomena
(Table 5). Each of the twelve indexes
of socioeconomic well-being (Table 2)
is treated as the dependent variable,
and the significance is pointed up by
the disparate results among the twelve
analyses. By its very nature, this section does not seek to fix cause or to
explain (the word is used here in the
purely statistical meaning) the patterns
of socioeconomic well-being. To establish cause in any degree would require a
comprehensive historical study,[13] and
the present study has no time element
in its quantitative analyses. It simply

seeks significant relationships from
which generalizations can be drawn and
on which further research can be based.

Table 4 displays four groups of
indexes and correlation coefficients.
The first group shows a strong negative
relationship between the percentage of
Negroes in the population and the socioeconomic well-being of the total population. This is not surprising, since
Negro levels are far below white levels
throughout the state, and where Negroes comprise a high percentage of
the population they naturally lower
the index for the total population (Figs.
2 and 6). The second and third groups
of coefficients show that racial composition has a strong negative relationship with Negro socioeconomic well-
being and a positive relationship with
white socioeconomic well-being. That
is, where Negroes comprise high percentages of the population, Negro levels
are usually low, and white levels are
relatively high (Figs. 3, 4, and 6). It
follows that socioeconomic well-being
gaps are wide where Negro percentages
are high and narrow where Negroes
are a small minority. This is confirmed
by the fourth group of coefficients and
by Figures 5 and 6.

Urbanization generally has a positive influence on socioeconomic levels.
The degree of urbanization is positively
related to all indexes, except to the
Negro farm index. White farm people
fare better in more urbanized counties
than in rural counties, but Negro farm
people do not. It is significant that urbanization increases the socioeconomic
well-being gaps between the races; for
whites are more able than Negroes to
take advantage of opportunities of-

TABLE 4. Correlations of Population Variables and Socioeconomic Well-Being Indexes[a]

	% Negro in total population	% Negro in nonfarm population	% Negro in farm population	% Urban in total population
SESTP	−.64			.64
SESTU		−.61		.61
SESTF			−.79	.18
SESTN	−.56			.53
SESNU		−.40		.55
SESNF			−.56	−.06
SESTW	.38			.71
SESWU		.48		.60
SESWF			.21	.45
SESTG	.72			.43
SESUG		.72		.27
SESFG			.57	.45

Source: Population variables from Bureau of the Census publications.

[a] Pearson's product moment correlation coefficients.

fered by urbanization. These findings suggest that Negroes and whites as well as farm and nonfarm population components are integrated into the economic system in different ways. This seems obvious for the farm and nonfarm components, but it is not so obvious for the racial components. If the observation is true, the patterns of socioeconomic well-being should be related to different sets of economic phenomena.

A series of multiple correlation analyses supports this supposition. Table 5 shows the results of twelve separate analyses, one for each index of socioeconomic well-being. The same fourteen independent economic variables were used in each analysis. Twenty-six economic variables were considered for these analyses, but because of high correlations (± .7 and larger) between some pairs of variables, nine were eliminated, and three

others were dropped because they made no contribution to the statistical explanation. Although not all possible independent economic variables were included, the fourteen chosen adequately represent the kinds of economic phenomena most closely related to socioeconomic well-being in Mississippi. A different small set of independent variables explains statistically a large percentage of the variation (R^2) in each index.

Some notable comparisons emphasize the differences. Total Negro socioeconomic well-being (SESTN) is largely explained statistically by secondary and tertiary activities and by certain aspects of cotton farming; total white socioeconomic well-being (SESTW) is explained statistically by tertiary activities, manufacturing productivity, and matters associated with farm management and Negro farm op-

TABLE 5. Multiple Correlation Analysis: BETA, R and R^2

Independent economic variables*	Beta coefficients†					
	SESFG	SESUG	SESTG	SESWF	SESWU	SESTW
Labor force in tertiary activities (%)	.47	.28	.37	.41	.58	.68
Negro farm operators as % of all farm operators	.67	.78	.73	.79	.58	.60
Average size of farms	.43		.21	.34		
Farms in cotton (%)				−.68		
Labor force in secondary activities (%)	.25			.31		
Value of farm land and buildings	.33	.18	.25	.40		
Per capita value of farm products sold, total population						
Per capita value added by manufacturing						.27
Per capita value of farm products sold, farm population	−.24			−.20		
Labor force working outside county of residence (%)					−.30	
Farms operated by managers (%)						
Poultry farms (%)						.15
Cash grain farms (%)		.22				
Livestock farms, other than poultry or dairying (%)						
R‡	.87	.89	.93	.91	.88	.93
R^2§	.76	.78	.86	.83	.77	.87

TABLE 5. (Continued)

Independent economic variables*	Beta coefficients†					
	SESNF	SESNU	SESTN	SESTF	SESTU	SESTP
Labor force in tertiary activities (%)		.35	.62		.62	.76
Negro farm operators as % of all farm operators				−.35	−.37	−.18
Average size of farms						.25
Farms in cotton (%)	−.74		−.27	−.67		
Labor force in secondary activities (%)	.17		.31			
Value of farm land and buildings				.18		
Per capita value of farm products sold, total population		−.44				
Per capita value added by manufacturing		.21		.15	.28	.20
Per capita value of farm products sold, farm population						
Labor force working outside county of residence (%)	.14					
Farms operated by managers (%)						
Poultry farms (%)		.19				
Cash grain farms (%)						
Livestock farms, other than poultry or dairying (%)	−.20					
R‡	.82	.84	.91	.95	.86	.96
R²§	.67	.70	.82	.90	.75	.91

* Calculated from Bureau of the Census publications.

† The BETA coefficient is a measure of the individual importance of the independent variables. The rank order and relative magnitude, regardless of sign, indicate the relative importance. The sign of the BETA coefficient indicates a positive or negative association between the dependent and independent variables in simple correlation. All multiple correlations are statistically significant beyond the .001 point (Croxton and others, *op. cit.* [see text footnote 7], pp. 732–734).

‡ R (the coefficient of multiple correlation) has no sign, "since the association may be positive with one but negative with the other independent variable. If we were able to include all pertinent independent variables, R would be 1.0, and we could make perfect estimates" of the dependent variable on the basis of the independent variables (*ibid.*, pp. 557–558).

§ "R² (the coefficient of multiple determination) states the proportion of total variation (of the dependent variable) . . . which has been explained by reference to the independent variables" (*ibid.*, p. 534).

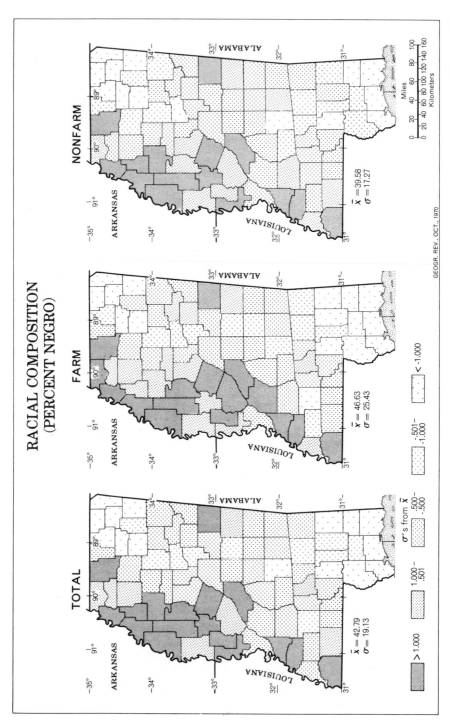

RACIAL COMPOSITION
(PERCENT NEGRO)

TOTAL

FARM

NONFARM

$\bar{x} = 42.79$
$\sigma = 19.13$

$\bar{x} = 46.63$
$\sigma = 25.43$

$\bar{x} = 39.58$
$\sigma = 17.27$

σ's from $\bar{x}$

> 1.000

1.000 – .501

.500 – .500

.501 – 1.000

< -1.000

Miles
0   20   40   60   80   100
0 20 40 60 80 100 120 140 160
Kilometers

GEOGR. REV., OCT., 1970

FIGURE 6.

erators. The most striking contrast, however, is between the socioeconomic well-being of the white and Negro farm populations (SESWF and SESNF). Negro farm levels are explained statistically by aspects of cotton and livestock farming, secondary activities, and intensity of labor commuting. This small range of independent variables reflects the limited economic diversity of the Negro farm population. On the other hand, white levels are explained statistically by a much greater range of phenomena, including secondary and tertiary activities, matters associated with Negro farm operators, farm size, farm property value, farm productivity, and cotton farming. This situation is related to the earlier finding that white farmers benefit from urbanization and that Negro farmers do not. The socioeconomic well-being gap is largely explained statistically by tertiary activities and matters associated with Negro farm operators, farm size, and farm property value.

A Comment on the Analysis

Although this study is limited, the findings are significant. Since whites and Negroes exhibit different patterns of socioeconomic well-being, geographical investigation can reveal much more when the racial patterns are studied. Furthermore, to analyze geographically the socioeconomic well-being gap between the races, separate indexes must be derived for each race. The social significance of race cannot be realized by studying the characteristics of the total population, because the total, although it exhibits important spatial patterns and relationships of its own, conceals important racial differences.

In seeking to understand the socioeconomic well-being gap, one must be mindful of the nature of plural society and of the historical processes that have perpetuated pluralism. As we have seen, the pattern of the gap reflects many things other than the racial composition of the population. Although this study does not attempt to establish why the relationship exists between the gap and the racial composition, the explanation is probably largely concealed in the historical processes that produced the present racial pattern and in the forces that have maintained the pattern for more than a century. For we know that the densities of both races have changed considerably but that the pattern of racial composition has not changed significantly.[14]

To any individual or agency concerned with socioeconomic conditions, particularly in Mississippi, these findings could be helpful. First, the maps show areas with varying degrees of socioeconomic problems and racial disparity. Second, a set of economic phenomena closely related to the socioeconomic well-being of each race and the racial gap is revealed. A researcher might do well to start his investigation with these sets of phenomena. The differences among them lead one to suspect that solutions to socioeconomic problems of one race are likely to differ somewhat from solutions to socioeconomic problems of the other.

Footnotes

Grateful acknowledgment is made to the staff and graduate students of the Department of Geography, Syracuse University, for useful ideas and suggestions, and to many friends in Mississippi whose understanding and assistance made the field research much easier than it might have been.

1. C. Warren Thornthwaite: Internal Migration in the United States (Philadelphia, 1934); Richard Hartshorne: Racial Maps of the United States, Geogr. Rev., Vol. 28, 1938, pp. 276–288; Wesley C. Calef and Howard J. Nelson: Distribution of Negro Population in the United States, ibid., Vol. 46, 1956, pp. 82–97; John Fraser Hart: The Changing Distribution of the American Negro, Annals Assn. of Amer. Geogrs., Vol. 50, 1960, pp. 242–266; Karl E. Taeuber and Alma F. Taeuber: The Changing Character of Negro Migration, Amer. Journ. of Sociology, Vol. 70, 1964–1965, pp. 429–441; "New Maps of United States Minority Populations as of 1960," GE-50, Nos. 14–16, U.S. Bureau of the Census, Washington, D. C., 1967.

2. William H. Pease and Jane H. Pease: Organized Negro Communities: A North American Experiment, Journ. of Negro Hist., Vol. 47, 1962, pp. 19–34; Harold M. Rose: Metropolitan Miami's Changing Negro Population, 1950–1960, Econ. Geography, Vol. 40, 1964, pp. 221–238; Karl E. Taeuber: Negro Residential Segregation: Trends and Measurements, Social Problems, Vol. 12, 1964, pp. 42–50; Pierce F. Lewis: Impact of Negro Migration on the Electoral Geography of Flint, Michigan, 1932–1962; A Cartographic Analysis, Annals Assn. of Amer. Geogrs., Vol. 55, 1965, pp. 1–25; Richard L. Morrill: The Negro Ghetto: Problems and Alternatives, Geogr. Rev., Vol. 55, 1965, pp. 339–361; Harold M. Rose: The All-Negro Town: Its Evolution and Function, ibid., pp. 362–381; Leo

F. Schnore and Philip C. Evenson: Segregation in Southern Cities, Amer. Journ. of Sociology, Vol. 72, 1966–1967, pp. 58–67; Paul S. Salter and Robert C. Mings: A Geographic Aspect of the 1968 Miami Racial Disturbance: A Preliminary Investigation, Professional Geographer, Vol. 21, 1969, pp. 79–86.

3. George W. Carey: The Regional Interpretation of Manhattan Population and Housing Patterns through Factor Analysis, Geogr. Rev., Vol. 56, 1966, pp. 551–569; George W. Carey, Lenore Macomber, and Michael Greenberg: Educational and Demographic Factors in the Urban Geography of Washington, D.C., ibid., Vol. 58, 1968, pp. 515–537.

4. See, for example, Allison Davis, Burleigh B. Gardner, and Mary R. Gardner: Deep South: A Social Anthropological Study of Caste and Class (Chicago, 1965); Frank Ellis Smith: Look Away from Dixie (Baton Rouge, 1965); Charles Spurgeon Johnson: Shadow of the Plantation (Chicago, 1966); idem: Growing Up in the Black Belt (New York, 1967); James Wesley Silver: Mississippi: The Closed Society (2nd edit.; New York, 1966); Comer Vann Woodward: The Strange Career of Jim Crow (2nd edit.; New York, 1966); Pierre Louis Van den Berghe: Race and Racism (New York, 1967); Leon Friedman: Southern Justice (New York, 1967).

5. See, for example, Thornthwaite, op. cit. [see footnote 1 above], p. 12; Donald J. Bogue: The Geography of Recent Population Trends in the United States, Annals Assn. of Amer. Geogrs., Vol. 44, 1954, pp. 124–134; Calef and Nelson, op. cit. [see footnote 1 above]; Wilbur Zelinsky: Changes in the Geographic Patterns of Rural Population in the United States, 1790–1960, Geogr. Rev., Vol. 52, 1962, pp. 492–524.

6. See, for example, Brian J. L. Berry: Basic Patterns of Economic Development,

in Atlas of Economic Development (edited by Norton Ginsburg; Chicago, 1961) pp. 110–119; John H. Thompson, Sidney C. Sufrin, Peter R. Gould, and Marion A. Buck: Toward a Geography of Economic Health: The Case of New York State, *Annals Assn. of Amer. Geogrs.*, Vol. 52, 1962, pp. 1–20; John B. Garver, Jr.: An Approach toward the Classification of Poverty in the United States (paper delivered at the annual meeting of the Association of American Geographers, Washington, D. C., August, 1968); *idem:* The Geography of Poverty in New York State: A Selective Analysis, *in* "Proceedings of the Ninth Annual Meeting of the New York–New Jersey Division of the Association of American Geographers Held in Albany, N. Y., October 11–12, 1968," 1969, pp. 151–162.

7. $Z = (x - \bar{x})/\sigma$, where $Z =$ standard score, $x =$ variable value, $\bar{x} =$ average value of variable, and $\sigma =$ standard deviation of the variable (Frederick Emory Croxton and others: Applied General Statistics [3rd edit.; Englewood Cliffs, N.J., 1967], pp. 219–220).

8. The eighty-two counties used as observation units in this study are adequate for the mapping methods and statistical techniques used. See Laurence G. Wolf: The American County: A Problem in Scale, *Annals Assn. of Amer. Geogrs.*, Vol. 48, 1958, pp. 297–298; John C. Weaver: The County as a Spatial Average in Agricultural Geography, *Geogr. Rev.*, Vol. 46, 1956, pp. 536–565.

9. All simple correlation coefficients are Pearson's product moment correlation coefficients (Linton C. Freeman: Elementary Applied Statistics for Students in Behavioral Science [New York, 1965], p. 89).

10. The indicators are from published and unpublished 1960 United States Bureau of the Census sources. Correlation analysis further validates substitution of indicators for evidence variables. The cor-

relation between SEWTP and SESTP is .88, and that between SEWTF and SESTF is .87. It is assumed that similar high correlations would exist for all the population components considered, if evidence were available for the other variables.

11. "Methodology and Scores of Socioeconomic Status," *U. S. Bur. of the Census Working Paper No. 15*, Washington, D. C., 1963. Individual county indexes based on the three indicators were calculated and published by E. S. Bryant (Socioeconomic Status Indexes for Mississippi Counties, *Mississippi Agric. Exper. Station Bull. 724*, 1966), who willingly consented to my use of them (personal interview, June, 1967). I computed the racial gap indexes and standardized all indexes for analysis in this study. The Bureau of the Census used the same three basic indicators, at a different level of aggregation and scale, to derive socioeconomic characteristics for a sample of the national population in 1960 ("Socioeconomic Characteristics of the Population, 1960," *U. S. Bur. of the Census Tech. Studies, Current Population Reports P-23, No. 12*, Washington, D. C., 1964).

12. Factor loadings in Table 3 constitute a summary resolution of a correlation matrix. In general the loadings are interpreted as follows. Factor loadings range from 1.0 to −1.0. The sum of the squares of a particular variable's loadings on all factors cannot exceed 1.0. Therefore, if a variable has a large loading on one factor, it will not be as significantly represented on the other factor. Two or more variables with similar large loadings on a particular factor can be taken as having a large degree of common variation, and the correspondence will be reflected on the maps. See Benjamin Fruchter: Introduction to Factor Analysis (New York and London, 1954); Mary Megee: Factor Analysis in Hypothesis Testing and Decision Making, *Professional Geographer,* Vol. 16, No. 4,

1964, pp. 24–27. The choropleth technique of mapping has been applied. See Arthur H. Robinson: Elements of Cartography (2nd edit.; New York and London, 1960), pp. 171–177.

13.   Preston E. James: Introduction: The Field of Geography, *in* American Geography: Inventory & Prospect (edited by Preston E. James and Clarence F. Jones; Syracuse, N. Y., 1954), pp. 3–18; Emrys Jones: Cause and Effect in Human Geog-raphy, *Annals Assn. of Amer. Geogrs.*, Vol. 46, 1956, pp. 369–377; Robert Morrison MacIver: Social Causation (New York, 1964).

14.   See, for example, Charles O. Paullin: Atlas of the Historical Geography of the United States (edited by John K. Wright), *Carnegie Instn. Publ. No. 401*, 1932, p. 48 and plates 67–70; Charles Sackett Sydnor: Slavery in Mississippi (Baton Rouge, 1966).

GARY L. FOWLER ◆
SHANE DAVIES ◆
MELVIN ALBAUM ◆

The Residential Location of Disadvantaged Urban Migrants: White Migrants to Indianapolis

Disadvantaged migrants to large metropolitan areas are the link between conditions of rural poverty in their areas of origin and urban poverty in the centers to which they move.[1] Although large numbers of blacks from the South have traditionally dominated this movement, other non-white minorities and whites from depressed areas, such as Appalachia, are among the most disadvantaged of the migrants. The residential site selection of disadvantaged migrants condition their urban adjustment. Most are restricted to poverty areas in the central city.[2] Whereas factors of racial segregation are assumed to explain the location of blacks, aggregative forces such as regional cultural similarities and feedback in the social communication network, are important to the urban settlement patterns of disadvantaged whites. The hillbilly ghettos and kin-based neighborhoods of Appalachian migrants have served as the most pervasive model for the whites.[3]

The relationship between the residential location decision of disadvantaged urban migrants and the geographical pattern of their urban settlement is the concern of this paper. The conceptual framework of the decision-making process is developed from contemporary behavioral theories of migration and intra-urban mobility, and recent surveys of lower class migrants to selected cities. The general-

◆ SOURCE. Printed by permission of authors.

95

izations are then applied to the residential location of a sample of recent disadvantaged migrants to Indianapolis, Indiana. The urban migration of disadvantaged individuals is a general phenomenon, and Indianapolis exemplifies most of the characteristics of medium-sized northern metropolitan centers that have traditionally received large numbers of such migrants.

Residential Location of the Disadvantaged Migrant

The objective of a household's migration is to maximize the perceived utility gained by moving to another location. The decision to migrate includes both a change in place of employment and residence.[4] Job-related constraints, which include the geographical distribution of employment opportunities, the education and skill level of the migrant, and expected future income are important to the selection of a new place of employment. In peasant societies, however, there is a strong, customary bias against mobility. If migration does occur, the kinship network is important in preserving the social unit. Ethnic patterns are transferred from rural to urban areas and communities are reinforced where migrants experience segregation. This type of culturally patterned behavior is analogous to the migration of the disadvantaged. As their primary source of job information the disadvantaged urban migrants depend upon social communication networks composed of friends and relatives who have previously migrated.

This source is also a principal factor in their choice of housing location.[5] Because of the reliance upon friends and relatives as the mode-of-entry into the city, cultural and kinship constraints are added to those which initially control their choice of residential location, such as income, race, life-cycle characteristics of the family, and environmental characteristics of the housing space.

The ecological characteristics of the subregions within which the migrants settle particularly reflect these cultural constraints, as well as their special housing needs. In Chicago, Freedman found migrants concentrated in low-rent areas characterized by mobile living arrangements (small, furnished apartments; hotel rooms; and rooming houses) and a social environment in which secondary relationships, with considerable freedom from social controls, were more important than "neighboring" and primary social relationships.[6] The migrants were segregated by functional as well as cultural roles within these areas. Compared to the situation of blacks, white migrants are faced with a less depressing neighborhood environment and considerably more economic opportunity and housing choice.[7] However, they tend to regard the neighborhoods in which they initially locate as temporary, in anticipation of further geographic mobility within the metropolitan area, or a return home. Many who remain later move into stable working class neighborhoods within the central city.

In order to find a place to live, disadvantaged migrants presumably follow a decision-making process analogous to the relocation decision in intra-urban migration.[8] Two decisions are usually made: (1) the choice of an initial residence, and (2) the location of the first permanent residence. The majority of disadvantaged migrants initially stay with relatives and friends until such time that suitable employment is obtained and a permanent residence located. This may vary from one to three weeks, to several months in the case of blacks.[9] The subregions of a city which satisfy the aspirations of the disadvantaged migrant define the set of places in the urban residential structure within which the location decision is formulated. The constraints upon the migrant, however, suggest that the search behavior followed is biased and spatially restricted. The migrants' image of the city is based upon limited information from indirect and infrequent contacts. The majority of the disadvantaged migrants move directly to the city from their place of birth, after a short period of preparation to migrate, and their previous contacts are from visiting friends and relatives who live in the city, and talking with previous migrants who return home to visit. Consequently, the urban awareness of the prospective migrant is developed from indirect contacts mediated by friends and relatives.

Because of the importance of friends and relatives as channels of information, the configuration of the migrants' search space is expected to approximate their social communication network. According to Brown and Moore:[10]

. . . *locations of vacancies discovered through interpersonal communication will be spatially, socially, and economically biased by the configuration of the intended migrant household's acquaintance circle and the awareness spaces of the acquaintances contained within that circle.*

Relatives and friends introduce cultural constraints in the new migrant's location decision that may subsume economic and social factors that otherwise would be directly relevant and helpful to him. They also contribute significantly to building and maintaining place-based communities in the urban area which have large numbers of the members of the social communication network in close geographical proximity to one another.

The attenuating influence of race affects the residential location decision.[11] The residential location of black migrants is the result of both socioeconomic and attitudinal factors, whereas the location of white migrants stems from socioeconomic factors alone. Socioeconomic segregation is the spatial condition enforced by group disparities in income class and family size. Its visual result is the centralized poverty pockets in which poor people, regardless of race, are compelled to live. Residential segregation of the population by socioeconomic status is indigenous to all metropolitan areas and is readily reflected in the distribution of housing quality. Attitudinal segregation is the residue left after the effects of the socioeconomic variables have been removed. This type of segregation, which is attributed to racial prejudice, is specifically relevant to residential segregation of blacks.

The disadvantaged white migrant does not suffer the discriminatory influence of race in the residential location decision. The urban settlement patterns, therefore, will be developed with greater sensitivity to the influences of cultural or ethnic similarities among the migrants, and feedback in the social communication network. The clustered residential settlements of Appalachian migrant "hillbilly ghettos" is one pattern that may result.[12] The importance of kinship, kin-based communities, and ties with the "home" area are dominant characteristics of their behavior since group membership is important as a guide to an unfamiliar environment. Where cultural constraints are strong and meaningful, and kin and friends are useful as a proxy for experience, a clustered residential pattern is expected.

Reduction in cultural constraints, a change in the nature of the individual's use of the social communication network, or its distribution in the urban area, may result in a more dispersed pattern of residential location. Cultural constraints are reduced if migrants are from the same region within which the city is located. Further, those who are more familiar with an urban center through direct experience may be less influenced by friends and relatives in the location decision. This suggests that proximity to an urban center, and frequent visits to it would increase the migrant's opportunity for finding a suitable residential location in the city. A concomitant increase in the size and

spatial extent of the social communication network would facilitate the development of a more dispersed settlement pattern for the disadvantaged migrants.

Disadvantaged Migrants in Indianapolis

There are eleven neighborhoods within the Indianapolis poverty area.[13] The poorest of these, which are to the north and east of Monument Circle, primarily house the central city's black population. Those to the immediate south of the Circle house poor whites, many of whom are from Southern Appalachia. The residential choice of low-income whites is restricted by socioeconomic segregation to specific areas of older housing within the poverty areas. The predominantly white areas are less impoverished than the black ghettos, and whites are the least-impoverished group within the black areas.[14]

The majority of the people experiencing employment difficulties are located in the inner city poverty areas.[15] In order to assist the hard core unemployed in job placement, the Indianapolis Employment Security Division (IESD) opened Employment Outreach Centers in each poverty target neighborhood in 1966. The data used in this study are from the records of personal information on job seekers who filed Employment Security ES 511 Y job application forms in each center between August, 1966 and August, 1968 (Table 1). Of a total 4,840 applications, there were 146 cases of whites who established residence in Indianapolis

TABLE 1. Distribution of Job Applicants to IESD Outreach Centers by Race, Sex and Mobility Status, August, 1966, to August, 1968

| Mobility Status | Percentage Distribution | | | |
| | White | | Black | |
	Male	Female	Male	Female
Recent Migrants	23.3	23.2	07.9	14.3
Indigenous to ISMSA	76.7	76.8	92.1	85.7
Sample Size	318	311	1638	2553

Source: Calculated from IESD ES 511 Y Job Application Forms.

during this period. These are defined as disadvantaged urban migrants.[16]

Patterns of Migration

The immigration field of the disadvantaged whites is concentrated in the Midwest and the Border South (Figure 1).[17] The largest proportion are from small towns in Indiana, Kentucky, and Tennessee.[18] At greater distances, the migrants are from larger metropolitan centers, such as Chicago, Cleveland and New York City. Approximately three-quarters of the migrants moved directly to Indianapolis. Those who reached the city in a sequence of moves

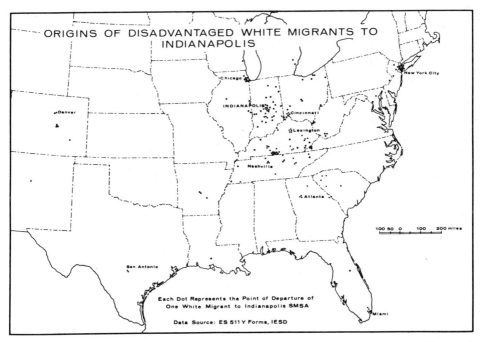

ORIGINS OF DISADVANTAGED WHITE MIGRANTS TO INDIANAPOLIS

Each Dot Represents the Point of Departure of One White Migrant to Indianapolis SMSA

Data Source: ES 511 Y Forms, IESD

FIGURE 1.

generally resided in an intermediate location for less than a year, some returning to their area of origin before moving to Indianapolis. Stage migration is not characteristic of the movement of disadvantaged whites to Indianapolis.

The size of the sample and geographical dispersal blurs the relationships between migration differentials and the spatial characteristics of the field. However, there are three general types of disadvantaged whites who migrate to Indianapolis. The first is a relatively young, married male from a small town in Kentucky or Tennessee. The second migrant type is a poorly educated woman, often a household head, who migrates with her family. She, too, is generally from a small town in Kentucky or Tennessee. The third

type is generally from a large urban center. This migrant is younger, better educated, and more often single.

Residential Location Patterns

Upon entering Indianapolis, the majority of the disadvantaged white migrants reside in white poverty neighborhoods, particularly Southeast, Broadway, Tech, and Park (Figure 2 and Table 2). With the exception of Broadway, which is predominantly black, whites are at least 80 percent of the total population in each neighborhood. Broadway and Park are transitional areas. Both experienced large-scale incursions of black residents and a white exodus during the 1960's as the frontiers of the ghettos expanded

TABLE 2.   Selected Socioeconomic Characteristics of the Indianapolis Poverty Area Neighborhoods Preferred by Disadvantaged White Migrants

Poverty Area Neighborhood[a]	Total Population 1965	Percentage Change 1960–1965	Level of Poverty 1959[b]
	Non-White		
Broadway	14,491	31.9	31.7
Park	2,786	02.4	27.8[c]
Tech	1,235	09.6	20.5[c]
Southeast	752	− 05.3	20.0[c]
	White		
Broadway	13,111	− 13.4	22.6
Park	11,723	− 17.3	27.8[c]
Tech	23,456	05.7	20.5[c]
Southeast	17,596	06.6	20.0[c]

Source: Community Service Council of Metropolitan Indianapolis, *Social Characteristics Analysis of Eleven Selected Target Areas in Indianapolis* (Indianapolis: Community Service Council, July, 1966).

[a] See Figure 2
[b] Percentage of families with total incomes of $3,000 or less
[c] Not available by race

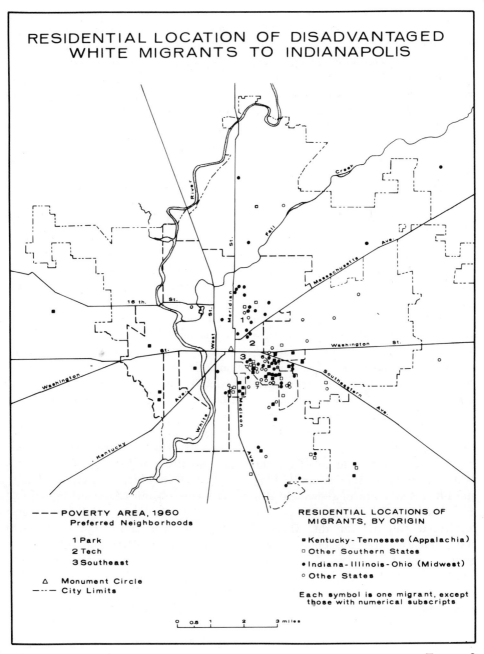

RESIDENTIAL LOCATION OF DISADVANTAGED
WHITE MIGRANTS TO INDIANAPOLIS

——— POVERTY AREA, 1960
    Preferred Neighborhoods

    1 Park
    2 Tech
    3 Southeast

△ Monument Circle
—·—— City Limits

0   0.5   1   2   3 miles

RESIDENTIAL LOCATIONS OF
MIGRANTS, BY ORIGIN

▪ Kentucky - Tennessee (Appalachia)
□ Other Southern States
● Indiana - Illinois - Ohio (Midwest)
○ Other States

Each symbol is one migrant, except
    those with numerical subscripts

FIGURE 2.

throughout the poverty areas north of Monument Circle. The migrants prefer the predominantly white neighborhoods of stable racial composition. The level of poverty in these areas is not as severe as in the ghetto neighborhoods. However, the effect of the tight housing market is as severe for disadvantaged whites as for blacks.[19]

When segregated by state or region of origin, the residential location of the migrants form different patterns. The clustered pattern common to Southern Appalachian migrants is dominant in the Southeast neighborhood, where most are located within a few blocks of each other. Southeast has been a traditional port-of-entry for southern migrants to Indianapolis. The residential location pattern for the Appalachian migrants from Kentucky and Tennessee is interpreted as a product of strong sociocultural controls over the location decision. Constraints of kinship and the aggregative affects of social communication networks upon Appalachian migrants may be more important to these people.

The location of migrants from the Midwest (Indiana, Illinois, and Ohio) and other states are more widely dispersed among the poverty areas. The residential patterns for the Midwest and, similarly, the metropolitan migrants, may be explained by their familiarity with Indianapolis and other urban places. Proximity to Indianapolis and the probability that the migrant's contact field is more varied and extensive is a sufficient condition to create the greater residential dispersal of Midwest migrants. Membership in the cultural tradition of the region in which the city is located is also an influential factor. The metropolitan migrants come to Indianapolis with a background of urban experience. Familiarity with an analogous environment may reduce the uncertainty of moving to the city, even though the migrant from Cleveland or Chicago may have no more direct contact with it than one from Scottsville, Kentucky.

Job Duration and Wage Rates of Migrants

When comparing the job duration and wage rates of similar Midwest and Appalachian migrant groups it appears that the buffer effect produced by the Appalachian kinship group on the disadvantaged migrants from Kentucky and Tennessee seriously retards their effective entry into the metropolitan job market.[20] Although the disparity in job duration is not apparent, there is a noticeable difference in wage earning capacity. The Midwest migrant generally obtains a higher wage rate than his Appalachian white counterpart of similar socioeconomic characteristics (Table 3). These findings tentatively suggest that the absorption of the Appalachian migrant by relatives and friends may have a detrimental effect on his ability to obtain a suitable job. The kinship groups, although providing temporary aid, may retard the migrant's assimilation into the Indianapolis job market. Further, for both migrant groups, geographical mobility did not necessarily result in an immediate improvement in job stability and wage rate.

TABLE 3. Cumulative Percent Distribution by Job Duration and Wage Rates of Appalachian and Midwest Migrants in Indianapolis

	Job Duration (Months)				
	0–1	1–3	4–6	7–9	10–15
Appalachian	21	57	78	92	100
Midwest	40	65	85	90	100
	Hourly Wage Rate					
	1.25	1.26–1.45	1.46–1.65	1.66–1.85	1.86–2.05	2.06–2.65
Appalachian	7	20	53	73	86	100
Midwest	4	4	17	34	55	100

Source: ES 511 Y Job Application Forms.

Conclusions

The residential location decisions of the disadvantaged migrant are constrained by his relationship to a particular social communication network, and its distribution in the city. As in Indianapolis, the geographical distribution of the migrant's residences may vary from the highly clustered pattern of the Appalachian group to the more dispersed pattern of those whose experiences and resources increased the range of vacancies available to them. The strong influence of kin and friends may also restrict the range of suitable job opportunities and residential locations available to the rural Appalachian migrant.

Footnotes

1. See: Woo Sik Kee; "The Causes of Urban Poverty," *The Journal of Human Resources,* Vol. 4 (1969), pp. 97–98; John F. Kain and Joseph J. Persky, "The North's Stake in Southern Rural Poverty," in *Rural Poverty in the United States,* a Report by the President's National Advisory Commission on Rural Poverty (Washington, D.C.: U.S. Government Printing Office, 1968), pp. 288–306; and Niles M. Hansen, *Rural Poverty and the Urban Crisis* (Bloomington, Indiana: Indiana University Press, 1970), pp. 150, 238–70. According to the Manpower Administration, a disadvantaged individual is a member of a poor family (for example, a family of five with a total annual income of $3,800 or less) who is unemployed, underemployed or hindered from seeking work; and who is either (1) a school dropout, (2) a member of a minority, (3) 22 years of age or less, (4) 45 years of age or older, or (5) physically handicapped (U.S. Department of Labor, Manpower Administration, *Definition of the Term Disadvantaged Individual* [Washington D.C., U.S. Department of Labor, Order No. 2–68, 1968]).

2. Lee Rainwater, "Social and Cultural Problems of Migrants to Cities," in *Rural Poverty in the United States,* a Report by the President's National Commission on Rural Poverty (Washington, D.C.: U.S. Government Printing Office, 1968), pp. 248–249, 251–255; and M. M. Webber, "The Post-City Age," *Daedalus,* Vol. 97 (Fall, 1968), pp. 1101–1104.

3. James S. Brown, Harry K. Schwarzweller, and Joseph J. Mangalam, "Kentucky Mountain Migration and the Stem

Family: an American Variation on a Theme by LePlay," *Rural Sociology*, Vol. 28 (March, 1963), pp. 48–69. An overview of this sociological tradition is by Lewis M. Killian, *White Southerners* (New York: Random House, 1970), pp. 91–119.

4. Cf. James M. Beshers, *Population Processes in Social Systems* (New York: the Free Press, 1967), pp. 136–140.

5. See the review of earlier studies by Leonard Blumberg and Robert R. Bell, "Urban Migration and Kinship Ties," *Social Problems*, Vol. 6 (1959), pp. 328–333; and John B. Lansing and Eva Mueller, *The Geographic Mobility of Labor* (Ann Arbor: Survey Research Center, Institute for Social Research, the University of Michigan, 1967), pp. 132–135, 216–230. Lansing and Mueller found that 69 percent of their national sample moved to labor markets in which they had relatives and friends. The proportion was higher for blue-collar workers, and for those from depressed (redevelopment) areas.

6. Ronald Freedman, "Cityward Migration, Urban Ecology, and Social Theory," in Ernest W. Burgess and Donald J. Bogue, *Contributions to Urban Sociology* (Chicago: University of Chicago Press, 1964), pp. 178–200. His data are for 1935–40.

7. Rainwater, *loc. cit.;* and Wilfred G. Marston, "Socioeconomic Differentiation within Negro Areas of American Cities," *Social Forces*, Vol. 48 (1969), pp. 165–176.

8. As described by Lawrence A. Brown and Eric G. Moore, "The Intra-Urban Migration Process; a Perspective," *Geografiska Annaler*, Vol. 52B (1970), pp. 1–13. The second phase, or relocation decision, is relevant here, as the decision to migrate is assumed to have been made. Recent studies including relevant data for the disadvantaged are: Gene Petersen and Laure M. Sharp, *Southern Migrants to Cleveland. Work and Social Adjustment of Recent Inmigrants Living in Low-Income Neighbor-*

hoods (Washington, D.C.: Bureau of Social Science Research, Ind., July, 1969); John D. Photiadis, *Social and Sociopsychological Characteristics of West Virginians in their Own State and in Cleveland, Ohio* (Morgantown, W. Va.: Appalachian Center, West Virginia University, 1970); Eldon D. Smith, "Migration Adjustment Experiences of Rural Migrant Workers in Indianapolis" (Ph.D. dissertation, University of Wisconsin, 1953); Charles Tilly, *Migration to an American City* (Newark: University of Delaware, Agricultural Experiment Station and Division of Urban Affairs, 1965); and *Final Report. A Study of Economic Consequences of Rural to Urban Migration,* prepared by Daniel O. Price (TRACOR Project 253–006; Austin, Texas; TRACOR, December, 1969).

9. Cf. Petersen and Sharp, *op. cit.,* pp. 197–206. Relatives were most important. For example, 58 percent of white males and 72 percent of white females; 87 percent of black males and 85 percent of black females spent the first night in Cleveland with relatives.

10. Brown and Moore, *op. cit.,* p. 9.

11. Anthony H. Pascal, *The Economics of Housing Segregation* (Santa Monica, California: The RAND Corp., 1967), pp. 1–8, Chapter VI, and Chapter VIII; Gary Becker, *The Economics of Discrimination* (Chicago: University of Chicago Press, 1957), pp. 56–62; Karl E. and Alma F. Taeuber, *Negroes in Cities* (Chicago: Aldine Press, 1965), Chapter VIII; Anthony Downs, "The Future of American Ghettos," *Daedalus*, Vol. 97 (Fall, 1968), pp. 1331–1378.

12. Cf. Brown, Schwarzweller, and Mangalam, *loc. cit.;* and Harry K. Schwarzweller and John F. Seggar, "Kinship Involvement: A Factor in the Adjustment of Rural Migrants," *Journal of Marriage and the Family*, Vol. 29 (1967), pp. 662–671.

13. See Figure 2. The poverty area is delimited from the Office of Economic Op-

portunity maps, and the neighborhoods are after the Community Service Council of Metropolitan Indianapolis, *Social Characteristics Analysis of Eleven Selected Poverty Target Areas in Indianapolis, Indiana* (Indianapolis: Community Service Council, July 22, 1966).

14. In Martindale, for example, 45.0 percent of the black families had incomes of $3,000 or less (1959) compared with 22.2 percent of whites; and in Haughville the statistics were 19.3 and 28.9 percent. Martindale was 98.1 percent black by 1965 whereas Haughville was 68.6 percent white.

15. *See:* Indianapolis Employment Security Division, *Labor Force Status in Three Indianapolis Neighborhoods: Broadway, Hillside, and Methodist, Summer, 1968* (Indianapolis: IESD, January, 1969). Whereas the seasonal adjusted employment rate for the ISMSA was 2.6 percent in July, 1968, the black unemployment rate for the three neighborhoods was 12.3 percent and the white 9.3 percent.

16. The ES 511 Y forms do not provide information on the net income from all sources received by all members of the job applicant's family. However, the applicants do conform to all other constraints in the Manpower Administration's definition of the term, disadvantaged individual.

17. The migration data are from the education and work history sections of the ES 511 Y forms. A migrant's origin is defined by the location of the high school attended, and the year left. This is a surrogate for the time and place he entered, or tried to enter, the labor force. Migration sequences are identified from the work history section by changes in the individual's place of employment.

18. Indianapolis, however, is not a primary destination for Appalachian migrants from Kentucky, Tennessee, and West Virginia. The majority of them who move north prefer cities in Southern Ohio, such as Cincinnati, Hamilton, Dayton, Columbus, and Cleveland; cf. George A. Hillery, James S. Brown, and Gordon F. De Jong, "Migration Systems of the Southern Appalachians: Some Demographic Observations," *Rural Sociology,* Vol. 30 (1965), pp. 33–48.

19. The demolition of occupied housing units through freeway construction, urban renewal, Indiana University downtown expansion, other publicly supported programs and old age, fire and the merging process tightened the housing market in poverty areas. Public demolitions alone removed 7,600 housing units between 1960 and 1967. Within this tightened housing market the disadvantaged white migrant is one of the weakest competitors for available housing units. Thus, his dependency on kin and friends is intensified. Metropolitan Planning Department, *Metropolitan Indianapolis Housing Study. Summary Report,* prepared by Hammer, Greene, Siler Associates (Indianapolis: Metropolitan Planning Department, October, 1968).

20. Smith, *op. cit.,* 81–89; and his "Nonfarm Employment Information for Rural People," *Journal of Farm Economics,* Vol. 38 (1956), pp. 813–827.

seven ◆ ◆ ◆ ◆ ◆ ◆ ◆ ◆ ◆ ◆ ◆ ◆ ◆ ◆ ◆ ◆ ◆

◆ SHANE DAVIES

◆ MELVIN ALBAUM

The Mobility Problems of the Poor in Indianapolis

Reverse commuters are those individuals whose journey to work entails a trip from a central city residence to a job located in the suburbs. Barriers resulting from an increasing distance between low income, inner city residents and decentralizing work place locations have created a reverse commuter problem. Interrelationships between metropolitan changes in job locations and residences, and deficiencies in public transit systems have been found to adversely affect the employment opportunities of the inner city poor.[1] Together with poor educational attainment, skill deficiencies, low motivation and discriminatory hiring practices, the reverse commuter transit problem has been offered as an additional causal factor behind the high unemployment levels of low income, inner city groups.[2]

This paper focuses upon the reverse commuter transit problem in Indianapolis where central city unemployment is a major problem.[3] The Indianapolis Manpower Coordinating Committee found that, ". . . many of the unemployed and underemployed groups could qualify for current job openings if they had transportation available on either a personal or public basis. The locations of many major industrial plants are far removed from the target areas [poverty pockets] and many of them have no adequate public transportation facilities."[4] The major complaints recorded by the Transportation

◆ SOURCE. Reprinted by permission of the authors and the editor from Antipode Monographs in Social Georgraphy, No. 1, *Geographical Perspectives on American Poverty*, 1972, pp. 67–87.

106

Task Force Committee of Indianapolis were inadequate service to a specific location, lack of night and early morning service, the inconvenience of downtown transfers and inadequate protection.[5]

This paper first investigates relationships among residential segregation, decentralizing job opportunities and deficiencies in public transit and the job distribution of low skilled motorized and non-motorized workers in Indianapolis. A second objective is to examine how effective the Indianapolis Public Transit System is in serving the employment needs of the disadvantaged. The third objective is to suggest how present transit services can be restructured or supplemented to provide solutions to the reverse commuter transit problem. Ultimate solutions to the problems of central city dwellers will depend upon the effectiveness of long-range programs for education and health, residential desegregation, and elimination of discriminatory hiring practices. In the meantime, short-term programs can be designed to supplement these long-term goals. The major objective of this paper is to outline in detail one such short-run strategy. This strategy is designed to link ghetto dwellers with suburban job locations.

Data Source

Eleven poverty pockets are delineated around Monument Circle on the bases of housing quality, unemployment, income, health and welfare measures (Fig. 1).[6] The Indianapolis Employ-

ment Security Division (IESD) located an Employment Outreach Center in each of these eleven target areas for the purpose of job placement.

A complete record of personal information was taken on 4,840 job seekers who filed Employment Security 511Y (ES-511Y) job application forms in each of the Outreach Centers between August 1967 and October 1968. This is the target population used in this study. Social data registered for this population includes race,[7] age, education, marital status, sex, household size, recentness of residence, work experience and present residence. The economic data records the applicant's mode of transit for the journey to work; his labor force status; whether a school dropout in the past six months, six to twelve months, or over twelve months; the location, wage rate and period worked for each of his last three jobs; and, finally his occupational code.

The individuals who make up the sampled population can generally be considered "disadvantaged persons" as the term is used in connection with all programs under the jurisdiction of the Manpower Administration.[8] A disadvantaged person is defined as one who is unemployed, underemployed or hindered from seeking work; and who is either (1) a school dropout, (2) a member of a minority group, (3) under 22 years of age, (4) 45 or more years old, or (5) physically handicapped.

The remaining data on the spatial distribution of low skilled basic entry jobs are obtained from the Closed Job Order files of the IESD's Commercial and Professional and Industrial Sector.

Indianapolis Target Areas and Inner Loop Freeway Plan

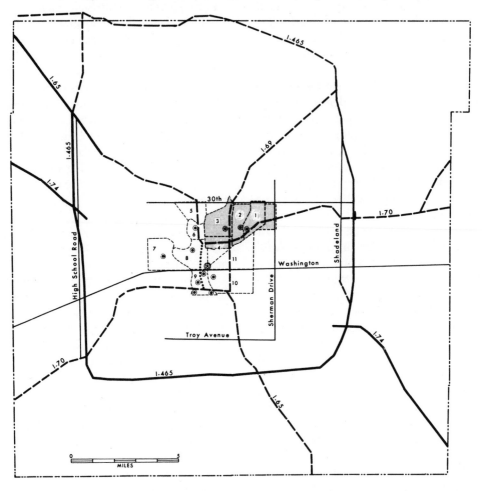

	Completed Freeway	◉	Monument Circle
	Proposed Freeway	◎	Outreach Station
	Proposed One-Way Freeway		Target (Poverty) Area

Model Cities Area

Base Map furnished by Metropolitan Planning Department, Marion County, Indiana

FIGURE 1.

Residential Segregation

Indianapolis exhibits two residential processes common to U.S. cities today: the exodus of middle and upper income whites to the suburbs and the influx of a poor, principally black population to areas in the central city.[9] Low income white and black inner city residents, through socioeconomic and attitudinal segregation, are residentially confined to specific areas of older housing in the city. Restrictive forms of residential zoning ordinances, house purchasing covenants and white hostility to black residential encroachment create segregated black housing patterns in Indianapolis (Fig. 2).[10] The housing market accessible to blacks has been tightened through the construction of the inner loop freeway system, Indiana University expansion and urban renewal which together dislocated 7,800 families between 1964 and 1970.[11] Black relocation into white neighborhoods distant from all-black areas has been less than one percent of all black residential moves during this period.[12] While these forces restricted the development of new black housing units, black income rose and the total population of young black adults sharply increased. As a consequence, there exists a repressed net demand for 5,000 standard housing units. Black persons per household increased from an estimated figure of 3.54 for 1960, to 3.63 for 1967. During the same time period white household size decreased from 3.18 to 3.00 persons per household.[13]

In these low income areas the "extended" rather than the "nuclear" family of the suburbs is found. Close-knit neighborhoods centered around local stores, church, tavern and pool hall are evident. The carless poor satisfy the majority of their social needs within the narrow confines of these poverty pockets. They generate shorter work, shopping and recreational trips than suburbanites and their limited movement has been found to reduce their motivation to seek improved positions of employment.[14]

The exodus of middle and upper income whites to the suburbs is primarily a result of the flight from the external diseconomies associated with the low wealth, higher expenditures and higher property taxes of central city jurisdictions. This movement has made inaccessible what was previously an important, if menial, source of basic entry jobs for black female domestics and male yard workers. Further, the shopping malls which are accompanying this outward movement, are finding it difficult to obtain the required low skilled help. This difficulty can be partially attributed to either the lack of transit or inadequate transit schedules. These factors contribute to the high degree of female and teenage unemployment found in the poverty pockets. It could be argued that the outward movement of whites, when correlated with the economic decentralization of jobs, would improve the black's chance of bidding more competitively for the remaining central city employment. However, since the central city is becoming more demanding in skill levels, this constitutes a negligible short-term benefit.[15]

Black Residential Areas in Indianapolis

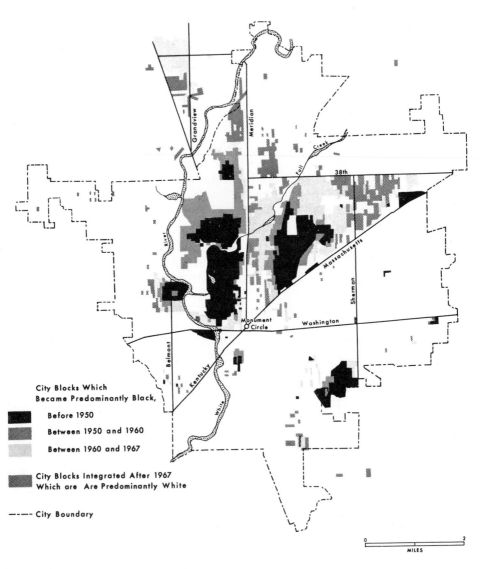

City Blocks Which
Became Predominantly Black,

■ Before 1950

▦ Between 1950 and 1960

░ Between 1960 and 1967

▦ City Blocks Integrated After 1967
Which are Are Predominantly White

----- City Boundary

0   2
MILES

Source: Indiana Civil Rights Commision, 1967

FIGURE 2.

Suburbanization of Employment

The movement of jobs to suburban locations in Indianapolis has been considerable. Forty-three percent of the metropolitan area's jobs in 1967 were located in outlying areas as compared to only 32 percent in 1961. The downtown proportion of overall employment fell from 33 percent to 25 percent, registering the only negative change. This decline occurred even though the total number of jobs increased by 61,000.[16]

A further study examined 922 affiliated members of the Chamber of Commerce between 1947 and 1968 for shifts in the location of their industrial activities. Two hundred and twenty-eight firms are found to have changed their residential location during this period. These decentralizing firms generated 11,304 job opportunities. Only 440 jobs were generated by the 17 firms which moved in toward the central city. These firms require a small and professional work force. The average outward distance moved for all firms exceeded three miles. Manufacturing firms, a main supplier of low skilled basic entry jobs, moved on the average 3.9 miles in an outward direction in this period.[17]

The hard core unemployed in this study are presently capable of filling only the lowest skilled occupations. It is therefore more important to analyze employment shifts differentiated by skill levels rather than undifferentiated job changes at the aggregate level. In rather similar investigations Hamilton, Kain and Persky utilized aggregate job

statistics with no distinction by type, which raises questions as to the validity and usefulness of their results for developing transit policy for the disadvantaged.[18] Only by ascertaining the geographic distribution of basic entry jobs for the ISMSA can the spatial barrier affecting the placement of low skilled inner city residents be readily assessed. The spatial distribution of low skilled manufacturing, clerical, sales and service jobs provides an insight into those locations most suitable for the placement of the hard core unemployed.

Of the low skilled job opportunities, clerical jobs which the inner city residents are least capable of filling are located nearest to their place of residence as well as being the most accessible by public transit. Clerical and sales jobs require far higher entry qualifications than manufacturing, and are the least accessible to the disadvantaged.[19] Clerical positions peak in the 0–10 minute zone, drop sharply, and then gradually decline outwards, whereas manufacturing demand retains a fairly constant level out to the peripheral time zones (Fig. 3).

Two spatially opposed processes, residential nucleation and industrial dispersion, interact to increase the distance between the disadvantaged's place of residence and his prospective places of work. This contributes to the job seeker's sense of geographic isolation and job inaccessibility. The problem is further aggravated by the present national trend toward white collar employment and the movement away from skilled and semiskilled jobs. If present trends continue, the work-residence

The Distribution of Low Skilled Clerical, Manufacturing, Service, Sales and Miscellaneous Jobs Over Public Transit Time Zones in Marion County: 1968

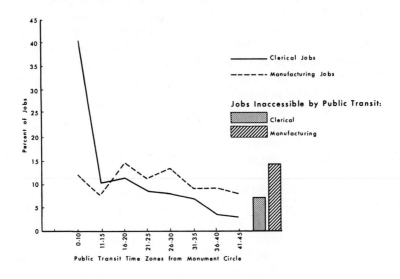

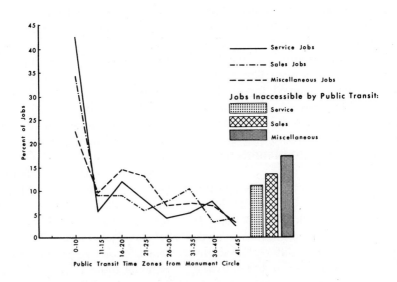

Data furnished by Indianapolis Employment Security Division

FIGURE 3.

spatial separation will increase and further constrain the potential catchment area of low skilled employment opportunities for the non-motorized hard core unemployed.

This spatial barrier has two consequences for the supply side of the labor market. First, the channels of labor market information are no longer effective because of the increased physical distance. Second, those inner city unemployed who do succeed in finding employment in peripheral job locations are adversely affected by lack of transportation, inadequate routing of public transit and excessive costs in time and money.

The shift of manufacturing from the central city to peripheral areas isolated from the public transit system indicates the apparent assumption on the part of industrial employers that automobiles are generally available to their labor force. Since automobiles are becoming more important for the work trip, the non-motorized job seeker is becoming increasingly handicapped.[20] Therefore, carless job seekers are particularly dependent on the spatial distribution of the facilities of the Indianapolis Transit System (ITS). Increasing or decreasing the geographic bounds of this network increases or decreases the disadvantaged job seeker's market for basic entry jobs.

Public Transit

The hard core unemployed lack automobiles for driving to work. Eighty-two percent of the 4,840 job applicants depend on public transit for the work trip (Table 1). Moreover, 87 percent are black, of which 84.4 percent depend on the bus system. The high proportion of the hard core unemployed lacking cars suggests that automobile ownership is a variable related to the acquisition of some suitable form of employment. It is a factor necessary for obtaining job interviews and crucial to the retention of a job. These "captive riders" are forced to find employment either in the immediate vicinity of their homes or are dependent upon job opportunities along the routes of the Indianapolis Transit System.

Public transit in this study refers to bus travel; Indianapolis has no commuter rail facilities. The inner city poverty pockets are particularly well serviced by CBD oriented lines. However, the utility of these lines is considerably lessened by the lack of crosstown and outward-bound buses serving peripheral work place locations. Except for one east-west crosstown route, all 26 public transit routes are radial in character and converge on the CBD. This deficiency in crosstown transport forces the disadvantaged to journey downtown prior to any outward movement. Slow bus speeds and the necessity of downtown transfers extends the length of many peripheral journeys beyond profitable limits. The prolonged length of time between buses and the lack of late and early morning services to coincide with shift times are major complaints of industries in the ISMSA.[21]

Present trends indicate that bus travel in Indianapolis will continue to

TABLE 1. Distribution of IESD Job Applicants by Age, Race, Sex and Mode of Transit for the Journey to Work, August 1967–August 1968

| Age of Worker and Method of Transportation | Percentage Distribution | | | |
| | White | | Black | |
	Male	Female	Male	Female
Workers Commuting By Auto				
All Age Groups, Sample Size	124	58	376	276
Distribution by Age				
Under 21	40%	12%	29%	18%
21–30	32	41	41	34
31–45	18	27	20	39
46–60	10	17	9	9
61 and over	0	1	1	0
Workers Commuting By Public Transportation				
All Age Groups, Sample Size	194	253	1262	2277
Distribution by Age				
Under 21	50%	29%	51%	38%
21–30	23	27	30	29
31–45	16	22	12	24
46–60	9	17	5	8
61 and over	2	5	2	1

Source: Indianapolis Employment Security Division ES-511Y forms, 1968.

decline, and eventually offer a more restricted route distribution for its patrons. The increases in car ownership and transit operating costs do not show signs of changing direction in the foreseeable future. Inner city residents who work at downtown locations will probably continue to receive good service if the route structure of the ITS does not change from its current orientation. Those who wish to obtain access to suburban industrial parks, recreational facilities and rural areas will encounter increased difficulties.

Mobility Characteristics of the Disadvantaged

No significant trip length disparities with regard to sex or race are found among reverse commuter groups commuting to work by bus; the mean trip length is 2.2 miles (Table 2).[22] This implies that inner city residents of both races might proportionately benefit from improved transit facilities. Though low income whites experience less discrimination in housing and jobs, they record equally restricted work-trip dis-

TABLE 2.   Journey to Work Trip Length Differences of Low Income Inner City Residents by Race, Sex and Transit Mode

	Treatment Group		DF	Estimate of Variance	F Ratio
	White Males Car	Black Males Car			
Sample Size	131	145	1	5.404	1.920
Mean	3.040	3.321	274	2.814	
Standard Dev.	1.729	1.630			
Decision: $F_{05} = 1.920$ 3.84 accept null hypothesis					
	White Males Bus	Black Males Bus			
Sample Size	153	149	1	0.001	0.004
Mean	2.234	2.230	300	2.571	
Standard Dev.	1.672	1.529			
Decision: $F_{05} = 1.0$ accept null hypothesis					
	White Females Bus	Black Females Bus			
Sample Size	136	151	1	0.776	0.3499
Mean	2.248	2.352	285	2.218	
Standard Dev.	1.583	1.400			
Decision: $F_{05} = 1.0$ accept null hypothesis					
	Black Males Bus	Black Males Car			
Sample Size	149	145	1	87.377	35.003
Mean	2.230	3.321	292	2.496	
Standard Dev.	1.529	1.630			
Decision: $F_{05} = 35.0037$ 3.84 reject null hypothesis					
	White Males Bus	Black Males Car			
Sample Size	153	131	1	45.932	15.924
Mean	2.234	2.040	282	2.884	
Standard Dev.	1.672	1.729			
Decision: Since $F_{05} = 15.924$ 3.84 reject null hypothesis					

Source: Indianapolis Employment Security Division ES-511Y forms, 1968.

tances. It might be stressed, however, that greater attention should be focused on black neighborhoods, since the data reflect a more acute unemployment problem in this social group.

No journey-to-work trip length differences are observed between disadvantaged male car users by race. The mean work trip is 3.32 miles for black males, 3.04 miles for the white males. Disparities exist between the trip lengths of car and bus users, both within and between racial groups. The work trip length of black male car owners averages 1.1 miles greater than trips of bus users. A similar relationship exists for white male car owners (Fig. 4).

The reverse commuter work trip patterns of disadvantaged inner city residents are not very extensive regardless of the vehicular mode available, especially when these patterns are compared with trip lengths of suburban-CBD oriented commuters. Suburban commuters have longer work trips than inner city residents when their journeys are measured in miles, but shorter when measured in time.[23] The disparity is due to the difference between car and bus travel.

The shorter work trip of the disadvantaged workers reflects a more confined catchment area of job opportunities. This distorted labor shed of employment opportunities is strongly influenced by the hard core unemployed's misconception of distance and his inability to efficiently overcome the barriers to movement facing him in a complex urban environment. This restricted territorial boundary may also be the result of budgetary constraints

and the lag in acquiring job information. The results of the preceding analysis suggest that while relatively few disadvantaged persons have automobiles for the work trip, improved spatial mobility exists for those who do.

Job Duration and Wage Rate Characteristics

A series of cumulative frequency curves were constructed to test the hypothesis that variations in job duration exist between inner city groups when stratified by age, sex, education and mode of transit available for the journey to work. The overall findings indicate that inner city car users are more likely than bus users to hold jobs for a greater length of time. Comparison of the distributions show that car users are skewed toward the higher job retention periods of around 9 months as opposed to 3 months for bus users. This inequality is decidedly pronounced in the 22–29 years of age category.

It was also hypothesized that the disadvantaged, inner city residents who have a car available for the journey to work, when classified by race, age, sex and educational level, receive a higher wage rate than individuals whose mode of transit is by bus. The findings suggest that improved accessibility permits car users to obtain jobs which generally pay higher wages.[24] The mean for bus users occurs in the $1.46–1.65 wage earning category as opposed to $1.86–2.05 for auto users (Fig. 5).

The higher wage rates, longer job duration and wider employment area for motorized workers are presented as

Home Based Work-Trip Length Distribution
of Males by Race and Transit Mode

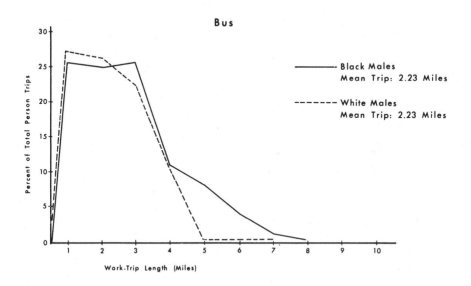

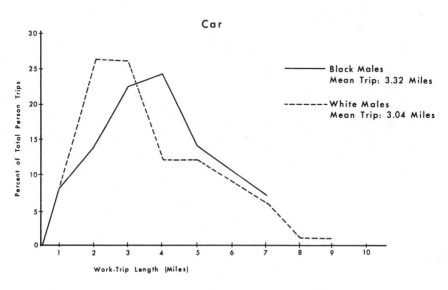

Data furnished by Indianapolis Employment Security Division

FIGURE 4.

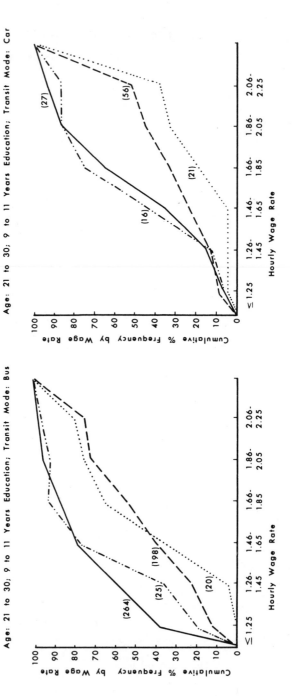

Wage Distribution for Inner City Residents of Marion County by Race, Sex, Age, Education and Transit Mode: 1968

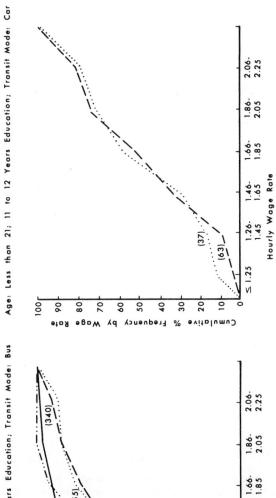

Black Females — Black Males

White Females · · · · · White Males

Numbers in parentheses indicate sample size.

Age: Less than 21; 9 to 11 Years Education; Transit Mode: Bus

Age: Less than 21; 11 to 12 Years Education; Transit Mode: Car

Hourly Wage Rate

Cumulative % Frequency by Wage Rate

Data furnished by Indianapolis Employment Security Division

FIGURE 5.

evidence to improve channels of access for carless, unemployed job seekers. Provided transit and suitable job opportunities are available to the disadvantaged, the suburban industrial job frequently offers more lucrative opportunities for the inner city resident to upgrade his standard of living.

Transit Design

The solution advocated for Indianapolis is the restructuring of the existing bus system by the adoption of new transit routes to link central city poverty pockets and areas of suburban employment (Fig. 6). The nature of these bus lines contrasts with the present radially oriented transit system centered on the CBD. The routes are constructed to cross both low income black and white poverty areas with frequent stops for passenger loading. Once outside the poverty pockets, the buses show a direct path towards the areas of suburban manufacturing and commercial development.

Indianapolis Transit System provides a functional operating base and experienced administrative and managerial personnel. With the aid of federal subsidies, its equipment, maintenance facilities and work force can be adapted to the new reverse commuter transit routes. These bus lines will not directly generate new positions of employment, but they will aid in alleviating the present inner city unemployment problem by providing the opportunity for the hard core unemployed to seek and retain a position of employment in locations previously in-

accessible or difficult to reach. Since a high proportion of the unemployed in the sample are below age 30, programs designed to improve workplace accessibility for the job seekers offer the potential for long-range effects and short-term alleviation for older individuals.

Several factors are important in deciding upon the spatial pattern of these new transit routes. (1) To offset expenses, there must be adequate density along the routes to generate sufficient patronage. (2) The bus routes must run as near as possible to customers oriented on a block basis. (3) The routes should be kept reasonably direct, yet provide adequate coverage of the poverty pockets and areas of industrial and commercial activity. (4) The schedules must be dependable, well-maintained and reasonably attractive to the potential rider.

The three bus lines are designed to aid inner city residents in the following order of priority. First, those hard core unemployed residing in the poverty neighborhoods will have an opportunity to obtain and then retain a position of employment in peripheral areas. Second, those temporarily unemployed will be able to resume a position of employment. Third, carless residents already employed will have the option of choosing an alternative job location. And finally, car users who are already employed along the new routes will be provided an opportunity to change to a bus mode for their journey to work.

Rather than present a definitive justification of the new transit routes, some of the major traveller and community benefits are identified.[25] The

The Three Proposed Transit Routes

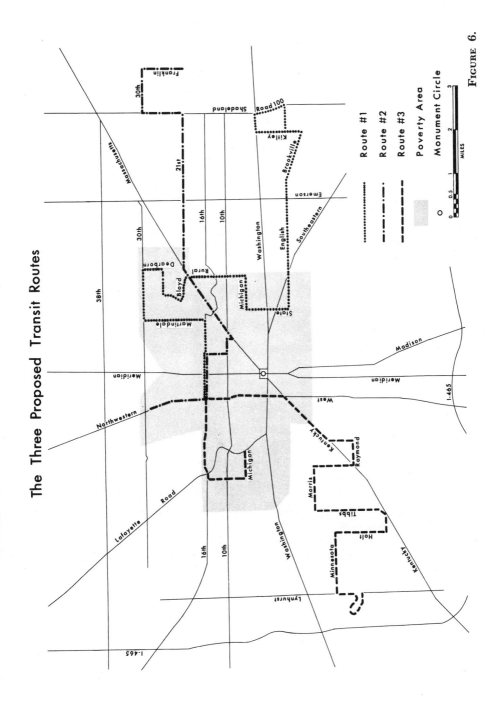

Route #1
Route #2
Route #3

Poverty Area

Monument Circle

MILES

FIGURE 6.

new services offer a significant time savings in the work trip for the residents of the transit areas. Since travel costs are a function of time consumed en route plus fares paid, then a travel time reduction will result in decreased travel costs and thus provide a traveler benefit. Those presently using automobiles who resort to bus travel will find costs savings through reduced operating, parking, vehicle ownership and accident expenses. This cost reduction, however, must be balanced against the increased costs of bus travel time and the intangible cost associated with the loss of privacy.

The routes will encourage the central city job seeker to widen his range of job search by applying for what were previously inaccessible suburban jobs. The disadvantaged resident is now able to compete with the suburbanite for outlying jobs. The improved employment opportunities generated by the transit line may reduce the normal time it takes the job seeker to find employment. Few benefits would be realized, however, if jobs attained through the routes only lasted a few weeks. Likewise, no resultant overall unemployment reduction would develop if only one unemployed person merely outcompeted another for a scarce job. Substantial benefits would result if these routes allowed individuals previously unemployed to obtain higher paying positions for a more sustained length of time.

The improvement in the labor catchment area for firms will shorten the time span industries experience in filling job vacancies. The further possibility of a decrease in absenteeism and tardiness could contribute to a reduced industrial turnover rate. Employers who are presently reluctant to hire workers without the means of transport for the journey to work will be able to relax this restriction. Individuals will be able to utilize the transit routes until they join car pools or have sufficient capital to purchase their own mode of transport.

If the results of this experiment prove beneficial, the Indianapolis Transit System could bolster its declining patronage by reorienting some of its routes along the crosstown paths projected in this design. At the same time, it would provide a vital "life-line" to the hard core unemployed residents in downtown ghetto areas. Even if the routes do not prove to be self-sufficient, it may be possible to argue that they generate enough community benefits to warrant their subsidization.

The major benefits accruing to the community on the implementation of transit routes are the decline in unemployment and resultant relief to overburdened welfare services. The employment gains that accrue to welfare recipients will reduce their need and the public cost in welfare payments. Through decreasing inner city unemployment and poverty, the routes incur a reduction in the required subsidies for other social costs such as crime, health and substandard housing. Further, it will decrease unemployment compensation paid by Indianapolis employers.

After initiating the project, a benefit-cost analysis would assess whether additional public transit linking poverty pockets to peripheral areas of low skilled job demand significantly contributes to a reduction in the unemployment levels and related social ills in the city's low income neighborhoods. This analysis could determine whether total benefits from the project (traveler and community benefits) are in excess of total costs. The results will suggest a future course of action. The alternatives facing the city will be either to retain the service, to drop it, to subsidize it by local funding or to initiate some new policy. The overall analysis will determine the relationship that exists between the transit facilities available to project area residents, and their levels of unemployment. The short-run strategy will be evaluated by the traveler and community benefits generated when balanced against the cost of the transit system.

Conclusions

The preceding research has documented that work-residence spatial disparities constrain the employment opportunities of inner city residents. The primary contributing forces to this problem, restrictive residential patterns and economic decentralization, show relatively few signs of changing.

The radial orientation of bus routes and the lack of crosstown connections reduces the effectiveness of the Indianapolis Transit System for the carless disadvantaged. These "captive riders" are forced to find employment opportunities either within walking distance of their homes or along the routes of the transit system. An increase or decrease in the spatial configuration of the transit network affects the disadvantaged residents' market for low skilled job opportunities.

The residence and work place locations of low skilled labor are not presently subject to substantial change, but it is possible to change the transportation linking them. The short-run strategy of redistributing transit routes offers potential benefits to the city and the unemployed central city resident. This short-term goal will alleviate the effects of the in-out transit problem until more comprehensive long-term goals are initiated.

It is not argued that deficient access is the most urgent problem of residents in poverty areas. Rather, it is argued that a remedy for mobility deficiencies is an important step in a series of ameliorative policies destined to upgrade the living standard of the disadvantaged. The contention is that an investment in this essential facet of urban life will contribute to the mitigation of inner city deprivation.

Footnotes

1. *Conference on Poverty and Transportation, June 7, 1968: Summary and Conclusions and Papers Presented,* American Academy of Arts and Sciences, Brookline, Mass., sponsored by the Dept. of Housing and Urban Development and the Dept. of Transportation, Washington, D.C.; John F. Kain, "Housing Segregation, Negro Employment and Metropolitan Decentralization," *The Quarterly Journal of Economics,* 82 (May, 1968), pp. 175–197. Joseph D. Mooney, "Housing Segregation, Negro Employment and Metropolitan Decentralization: An Alternative Perspective," *The*

Quarterly Journal of Economics, 83 (May, 1969), pp. 299–311.

2. In the Indianapolis Standard Metropolitan Area generally tight labor market conditions have alleviated some of these unemployment problems. Normally restrictive hiring criteria of employers have been somewhat relaxed by the high overall demand for labor. Increases in consumer demand and higher production goals have created an urgency to fill job vacancies. This has produced a greater probability that unskilled workers in the lower preference ranks will be hired.

Yet even under these improved labor market conditions, severe levels of unemployment still exist within the central city of Indianapolis. A household survey conducted by the Indianapolis Employment Security Division and designed to ascertain the labor force status of residents 16 years of age and older in three of the city's low income areas—Broadway (3), Methodist (16) and Hillside (1)—found that whereas the seasonal adjusted employment rate for the ISMSA was 2.6 percent in July 1968, the average rate for the three neighborhoods was 11.7 percent (12.3 percent for blacks and 9.3 percent for whites). The unemployment rate for youths 16 to 21 years old was 23.5 percent (33.7 percent when summer job seekers were included). Indianapolis Employment Security Division, *Labor Force Status in Three Indianapolis Neighborhoods: Broadway, Hillside and Methodist, Summer, 1968,* Report by the Research and Statistics Dept. January, 1969.

3. Christopher S. Davies, "The Reverse Commuter Transit Problem in Indianapolis" (unpublished Ph.D. dissertation, Dept. of Geography, Indiana University, 1970).

4. Indianapolis Manpower Coordinating Committee, *The Indianapolis Area Cooperative Manpower Plan, Fiscal Year 1968,* June 16, 1967, p. 9.

5. Indianapolis Transporation Task Force Committee, *Indianapolis Personnel Association Survey,* July, 1969.

6. Community Service Council of Metropolitan Indianapolis, *Social Characteristics Analysis of Eleven Selected Poverty Target Areas in Indianapolis, Indiana,* July 22, 1966.

7. "Recording Race, Color and National Origin on Local Office Records," Memorandum No. 601, Indianapolis Employment Division, July 19, 1967.

8. U.S. Dept. of Labor, Manpower Administration, *Definition of the Term Disadvantaged Individual,* Washington, 1968, Order No. 2–68.

9. Davies, *op. cit.,* pp. 13–30; see also Karl E. and Alma F. Taeuber, *Negroes in Cities* (Chicago: Aldine Press, 1965), p. 30; Anthony H. Pascal, *The Economics of Housing Segregation* (Santa Monica, Calif.: The Rand Corp., 1967), pp. 30–56; Anthony Downs, "The Future of the American Ghettos," *Daedalus,* 82 (Fall, 1968), pp. 1331–1378.

10. Emma Lou Thornbrough, *Since Emancipation,* Indianapolis, Indiana Division American Negro Emancipation Authority, 1963.

11. Community Service Council, *Study of Relocation Problems,* Indianapolis, September 1964, pp. 1–16.

12. Metropolitan Planning Commission, *Metropolitan Indianapolis Housing Study, Summary Report,* p. 26; see also, Indianapolis Regional Transportation and Development Study (IRTADS), *A Transportation and Land Development Plan for the Indianapolis Region, A Summary Report,* Barton-Aschman Associates, Supervising Consultant, Chicago, October, 1968; and Greater Indianapolis Progress Committee, "Study of Housing Conditions for Urban Renewal and of Low Income Housing," 1966 (mimeo).

13. Metropolitan Planning Department, Marion County, *Preliminary Projection of*

Housing Needs, '67–'85, Technical Work Paper No. 1, prepared by Hammer, Greene, Siler Associates, March, 1968.

14.   Gordon Fellman and Roger Rosenblatt, "The Social Costs of an Urban Highway," *Conference on Poverty and Transportation, June 7, 1968.*

15.   Kain, *op. cit.,* p. 194.

16.   Indianapolis Employment Security Division, *Covered Employment: Marion County, September, 1967,* Research and Statistic Dept., Indianapolis May, 1967.

17.   Davies, *op. cit.,* pp. 34–38.

18.   W. F. Hamilton, "Transportation Innovations and Job Accessibility," *Conference on Transportation and Poverty,* pp. 5–8; A. H. Pascal, *The Economics of Housing Segregation,* Chapter VI; Kain, *op. cit.,* pp. 175–197.

19.   Georgia Institute of Technology, *Methods of Job Development for the Hard Core Unemployed,* Industrial Management Center, Atlanta, Ga., January, 1969. The graphs represent 3,280 Clerical, 810 Sales, 1900 Manufacturing, 890 Miscellaneous, and 2475 Service basic entry jobs.

20.   U.S. Dept. of Commerce, *Special Report on Household Ownership and Purchases of Automobiles and Selected Household Durables, 1960 to 1967,* No. 18, August, 1967, p. 65.

21.   Indianapolis Regional Transportation and Development Study, *Transit Inventory,* Job 4210, March 1966.

22.   A disproportional stratified random sample is obtained from the population previously classified by race, sex and transit mode. Straight-line linear distance between the resident's exact home address and work location is measured on a map of scale $1'' = 4,000'$.

23.   Donald R. Deskins, "Residence-Work Place Interaction Vectors for the Detroit Metropolitan Area 1953 to 1965," *Interaction Patterns and the Spatial Form of the Ghetto,* Special Publication No. 3, Dept. of Geography, Northwestern University, Evanston, Ill., Feb., 1970.

24.   David P. Taylor, "Discrimination and Occupational Wage Differences in the Market for Unskilled Labor," *Industrial Labor Relations Review* (April, 1968), pp. 375–390.

25.   Community benefits are those that accrue to the community as a whole other than traveller benefits—that is, income benefits through reduced unemployment and welfare expenditures. A traveller benefit is a time or cost savings which accrues to the reverse commuter. An employee solely dependent on the bus for gaining initial entry into the job market derives an income benefit. An individual using the bus as an alternative mode of transport to work can be considered to derive a traveller or community benefit. Dan G. Harvey, John L. Crain, Albert E. Moon, *Traveler and Community Benefits from the Proposed Los Angeles Rapid Transit System* (Menlo Park, Calif.: Stanford Research Institute, 1969), pp. 8–31; Edward Kalacheck, "Benefits of Improving Public Transportation Between the Central City and Suburban Work Sites: Preliminary Report on a Case Study," St. Louis: Washington Institution for Urban and Regional Studies, 1969 (mimeo); D.A. Quarmby, "Choice of Travel Mode for the Journey to Work," Dept. of Management Studies, University of Leeds, April, 1967, pp. 37–38 (mimeo); John L. Crain, *Appendix C: Benefit-Cost Model Service Development Grant Program,* Menlo Park, Calif. (Stanford Research Institute, 1969).

22222222222

BLACK AMERICA AND THE BLACK GHETTO

22222222222

◆ eight

JAMES D. COWHIG ◆

The Negro Population of the United States, March, 1967

Differences in the geographic distributions of the population of the United States have important consequences for the Nation's welfare. Equally—if not more—important in their consequences are differences in age distribution and in family size, composition, and income.

In 1967 the white population of the United States stood at 172 million; the Negro population at 22 million, not including persons in the armed services or in institutions.[1] Between 1960 and 1967 the white population rose 11 percent; the Negro population, 12 percent. Negroes were about 11 percent of the total population.

Place of Residence

The population of the United States is predominantly urban, though where people live within metropolitan areas differs by race. In March 1967 about 55 of every 100 Negroes lived in the central cities of metropolitan areas; 13 of every 100 lived in other parts of metropolitan areas, including suburban areas. In marked contrast, only 27 of every 100 white persons lived in central cities; 37 of every 100 lived in the largely suburban areas outside central cities but within metropolitan areas. The concentration of Negroes in central cities and of white persons in other parts of metropolitan areas had increased since the 1960 Census. As a result, Negroes accounted for 25 percent of all persons living in central cities but for only 4 percent of persons living in metropolitan areas outside central cities. The proportion of both races living outside metropolitan areas dropped between 1960 and 1967, as the number and pro-

◆ SOURCE. Reprinted from *Welfare in Review,* Vol. 7, January–February 1969, pp. 14–16.

portion of persons counted as urban residents continued to rise.

About 4 percent of all Negroes had migrated (moved from one county to another) between 1960 and (March) 1967, and 45 percent of all who had migrated had left the South. Nevertheless, a majority (54 percent) of all U.S. Negroes still lived in the South in 1967.

Age and Sex

In 1967 the Negro population of the United States was much younger than the white population, as shown by the fact that the median age for white persons was 29.0 years and for Negroes, 21.2 years. Well over half (55 percent) of the Negro population was under 25 years old; only 45 percent of the white population was that young.

Negro and white populations differ in sex ratios (the number of males per 100 females). The ratio for Negroes is lower, at birth and at all ages. For both Negroes and white persons, females outnumber males at ages above 13. At ages 25–34, for instance, there are about 96 white men for every 100 white women, as compared with 86 Negro men for every 100 Negro women.

However, part of the differences in sex ratios is due to exclusion of most persons in the armed forces and inmates of institutions from the Current Population Survey (CPS). Inmates of institutions, particularly among nonwhite persons, are predominantly men. Also, the CPS probably underenumerates young Negro men.[2]

Differences in sex ratios are not due to differences in mortality. Even though mortality rates for Negroes are higher than rates for white persons in each age-sex category, the effect of differences in mortality is to increase rather than to decrease sex ratios. Both Negro and white men die at earlier average ages than women.

Family Characteristics

In March 1967 the average Negro family had 4.38 members; the average white family, 3.62 members. One in four of all Negro families was headed by a woman; one in 11 of all white families had a woman as its head. For both races the proportion of families headed by women had risen since 1960: by 22 percent (Negro) and 8 percent (white). Thus, in 1967 a disproportionately high number of Negro families (1.1 million) were without a man at the head and were, therefore, subject to a higher than usual risk of economic dependency. The total of 5.2 million families headed by women included the majority of the 1.3 million families receiving assistance under the aid to families with dependent children (AFDC) program.

Among persons who had ever been married, rates of separation or divorce were substantially higher for Negroes than for white persons. About 3 percent of white men and women who had ever been married were separated or divorced in 1967; among Negroes, 8 percent of the men and 13 percent of the women who had ever been married were separated or divorced. (No information is available on the proportion of married persons who had been divorced and remarried.)

TABLE 1. Age Distribution and Sex Ratios of Negro and White Persons in the Population, United States, 1967

Age	Negro	White	Males per 100 females	
			Negro	White
Total (00's)	21,631	172,198	91.9	94.7
Percent	100.0	100.0	—	—
Under 5 years	13.4	9.5	101.4	104.8
5–13 years	22.8	18.2	99.8	104.1
14–19 years	12.1	10.0	96.9	99.2
20–24 years	7.0	6.9	84.4	84.9
25–34 years	11.2	11.4	86.3	95.6
35–44 years	10.9	12.3	84.3	96.1
45–54 years	9.5	11.6	87.4	94.4
55–64 years	6.8	9.2	88.0	91.0
65 years and over	6.3	10.0	80.2	75.4
Median age	21.2	29.0		

Source: U.S. Bureau of the Census, *Current Population Reports,* "Negro Population: March 1967," Series P-20, No. 175, Table 3.

Median family income in 1966 was $7,722 for white persons and $4,463 for Negroes. The ratio of Negro to white median family income was .58 and ranged from about .74 in the North Central region to .51 in the South. Because the average Negro family has more members than the average white family, per capita median family income was about $2,100 for white and about $1,000 for Negro families; the ratio of Negro to white per capita family income was .48.

Education

Among persons 25–34 years old, almost all of whom had completed formal education, the median years of schooling completed was 12.5 for white persons and 12.1 for Negroes: half of both white persons and Negroes 25–34 years old had completed high school. However, the rates of completion of college were substantially higher for white persons 25–34 years old (15 percent) than for Negroes (6 percent) in the same age group.

The educational attainment of persons 25–34 years old was different from that of older persons; the median years of school completed by persons 35 years old and over was 11.7 for white persons and 8.4 for Negroes. The educational gap, therefore, was greater between Negroes above and below 35 years of age than between white persons above and below that age.

Implications

What do these social and demographic characteristics mean? What consequences might they have for research in-

TABLE 2.   Selected Social and Economic Characteristics of Negro and White Families and Persons, United States, March 1967

Characteristic	Negro	White
Percent living in:		
Metropolitan areas	67.9	64.2
Central cities	54.5	27.1
Outside central cities	13.4	37.1
Nonmetropolitan areas	32.1	35.8
Percent of families with woman as head:		
1960	21.7	8.1
1964	25.0	9.1
Percent ever-married persons 14 years old and over separated or divorced:		
Men	8.2	3.0
Women	13.1	2.9
Ratio of Negro to white median family incomes:		
Total	.58	—
Northeast	.67	—
North Central	.74	—
West	.72	—
South	.51	—
Median years of school completed by age:		
25–34 years old	12.1	12.5
35 years and over	8.4	11.7

Source: U.S. Bureau of the Census, *Current Population Reports,* "Negro Population: March 1967," Series P-20, No. 175, October 23, 1968, Tables A, 1, and 2.

volving comparisons of different population groups? Several conclusions seem reasonable.

Whatever problems are associated with providing education and jobs are proportionately more serious for Negroes than for white persons because large proportions of Negroes are approaching school age or the age when most people are employed full-time. In contrast, the social and economic adjustments coincident with retirement at age 65 are faced by proportionately fewer Negroes (6 percent) than white persons (10 percent). These conclusions are derived solely from data on age distribution and say nothing about the significance of racial discrimination or segregation for Negroes living in central cities, entering school, or seeking jobs. Even if there were no other differences between white persons and Negroes, the younger age of the Negro population would mean higher rates of family formation and higher rates of events related to age: school enrollment, unemployment, delinquency, and fertility. The use of rates unadjusted for age differences may be proper for a general description of population differences, but more specific descriptions require more refined measures.

To illustrate: AFDC rates are usually computed as the proportion of children in the total population under 18 years of age whose circumstances make them recipients of assistance. But the risk of economic dependency is comparatively high among families headed by women, with low incomes, and with more children than average. These characteristics are more common in Negro than in white families. Recipient rates based on more nearly complete data reflecting exposure to risk might be different from rates based on age alone. Thus, both of the following statements could be true: "AFDC recipient rates are higher among Negroes than among white persons"; and "When the sex of the head of the family, the number of children in the family, the family income, and the age of the head of the family are considered, there are no racial differences in recipient rates."

Comparisons are further complicated by the fact that in most surveys, enumeration of the sample population is incomplete and persons in certain age groups are missed more often than others.[2] The combined effects of a close relation between a specific characteristic and age and the underenumeration of persons in specific age groups may make estimates of incidence and prevalence very difficult. On the one hand, underestimates of the total population inflate rates because the denominator of the rate is too low; for example, crime rates based on the

number of persons 20–29 years old would be inflated, particularly for Negroes. On the other hand, if a specific characteristic, say being unemployed, is much more prevalent among those missed than among those counted in surveys, unemployment estimates will be low. It cannot be assumed that the effects of underenumeration will be uniform.

To the extent that Negro women actually outnumber Negro men at the young adult ages, Negro women have comparatively fewer opportunities for marriage with Negro men than white women have with white men. This fact, together with the higher rate of separation and divorce among Negroes, may lead to one-parent families, particularly to families headed by women, and to higher risks of economic dependency.

The wide differences in education between Negroes over 35 and those under that age reflect different experience in different environments. These differences may or may not be what is meant by the "generation gap," but there can be no argument that these differences exist and, indeed, are inevitable.

Perhaps the most important meaning for research is that, in accounting for differences observed in population groups, the possibility that these differences are due solely or largely to variations in demographic characteristics should be ruled out before less obvious explanations are used. This is particularly important in research dealing with low-income population groups where economic conditions limit choice and where the sheer matter of surviving to the next higher age may be of much more immediate concern than among middle- and high-income groups.

Footnotes

1. Unless otherwise noted, all information in this article was derived from tables shown in Current Population Reports, "Negro Population: March 1967," U.S. Bureau of the Census, Series P-20, No. 175, October 23, 1968. The data were taken from the March 1967 Current Pop-

ulation Survey (CPS) from a national sample of about 50,000 households. The survey excludes members of the armed forces (except those living off post or with their families on post) and inmates of institutions.

2. Jacob Siegel has estimated that the 1965 CPS omitted one in four of non-white men 30–39 years old. See: *Social Statistics and the City,* Joint Center for Urban Studies of the Massachusetts Institute of Technology and Harvard University, 1968, p. 31.

HAROLD M. ROSE ♦

The Development of an Urban Subsystem: The Case of the Negro Ghetto

The internal development of individual urban places has not traditionally been one of central focus in geography. This probably stems in part from the over-riding emphasis on regions in general and the urban geographer's concern with the interrelationships among individual urban nodes. American geographers have only recently turned their attention to the internal structure of urban areas, no doubt an outgrowth of general interest in central place theory. Increasing interest in urban subsystems has resulted in a concomitant interest in the spatial structure of these systems. This paper attempts to provide insights on the spatial dynamics of a single sub-system within the metropolitan system, the Negro ghetto.

The Negro ghetto, as a universal and viable urban subsystem within the American urban system, has evolved with the rise of the Negro population in northern urban centers beginning with the decade prior to World War I.[1] The almost continuous flow of Negroes from both the rural and urban South to the North and West has permitted and promoted the development of Negro ghettos in all of the nation's major population centers. By 1960 more than thirty percent of the nation's Negro population resided in twenty metropolitan areas. Whereas the Negro ghetto is found in nearly all 200 metropolitan areas in the United States, the basic concern of this study is with the processes responsible for its change in scale in northern urban centers. The previous legality of a system of racial

♦ **SOURCE.** Reproduced by permission from the *Annals* of the Association of American Geographers, Vol. 60, 1970, pp. 1–17.

separation in the American South served as an exogenous factor, overriding all others, in the promotion and maintenance of residential clusters based on race. For a brief period there existed laws which were specifically designed to maintain residential segregation based on race. The Supreme Court outlawed attempts to maintain a legal system of residential separation in 1917, in the case of Buchanan *versus* Warley.[2] Such a legalized role-prescription tends to reduce the fruitfulness of a behaviorally oriented study, and thereby accounts for the limiting of this investigation to northern cities.

To date, only Morrill's pioneer work might be described as a spatial behavioral approach to the study of the changing state of the ghetto.[3] The model he assembled was employed to replicate the process of ghetto development in Seattle. Other researchers are beginning to show increasing concern for the general problem, with emphasis on the spatial dimension. Beauchamp recently suggested the use of Markov Chain Analysis as a means of specifying or identifying territorial units as ghetto or non-ghetto by investigating the dynamic changes taking place in the racial composition of areas.[4]

The process of the changing ghetto state has been described elsewhere as a diffusion process.[5] Diffusion models have attracted the interest of a small number of geographers who have employed them as a means of describing the spatial spread of an innovation. The more notable of these are associated with the work of Hägerstrand. The suitability of diffusion models as a means of describing the spread of the ghetto, however, is questionable. It appears that the spread of the ghetto is a phenomenon of a different type. More specifically, it appears that the spread of the Negro ghetto is a function of white adjustment to a perceived threat. The distinction between adjustment and diffusion was recently reviewed by Carlsson.[6] He averred that motivation and values transcend knowledge, in importance, in explaining certain types of behavioral change.[7] If the diffusion thesis is accepted as a means of explaining rather than describing the expansion of the Negro ghetto, then it must be assumed that each metropolitan system operates as a closed system. Since this is not the case, the adjustment hypothesis which Carlsson supports is undeniably more appealing than the diffusion hypothesis as a means of explaining the spread of the ghetto. Admittedly, whites must first be aware of the presence of Negroes if a change in their normative mobility pattern is to occur, but awareness here promotes the kind of behavior which has also become accepted as normative. Thus, the necessary adjustment is made as a means of maintaining the steady state condition. The kind of behavior inferred here was described by Zelinsky as social avoidance.[8] Morrill, who previously described the ghetto development process in terms of diffusion, now describes processes of this general type, which are interactional in nature, as quasi-diffusionary.[9]

Intra-Urban Population Mobility

The spatial mobility of the American population, both in terms of long distance moves and intraurban shifts, was intensified during the decade of the 1950's. As major metropolitan systems were the target of most long distance moves, these moves resulted in the rapid dispersion of population into what was previously part of the rural countryside. The latter phenomenon has attracted the attention of researchers from a vast array of disciplines, geographers included. Geographers have also focused particular interest on the centrifugal flow of population, as this flow has had the most obvious impact on the form and areal magnitude of urban systems. But to consider the latter and ignore the role of the centripetal movement weakens the analysis of population shifts within the system and of the ensuing patterns which evolve.

Movements toward the periphery of the urban system, both from within the system and from without, have been principally responsible for the increase in the size of individual metropolitan aggregates. At the same time many central cities within metropolitan systems have suffered absolute losses in their populations. Thus, the centripetal flow into the central cities of metropolitan systems has seldom been sufficiently large to offset the counter flow. The most rapid and easily observed flow into the nation's larger central cities is that of Negro in-migration, a phenomenon which has had far-reaching effects on the color composition of metropolitan areas.[10] By the mid-sixties there was official evidence that this process was continuing. The city of Cleveland, Ohio, undertook a special census on April 1, 1965. The results showed that the city had lost 91,436 white residents during the five years

that had elapsed since the last census, while gaining an additional 26,244 Negro residents.[11] The Negro proportion of Cleveland's population rose by five percentage points during that period, from twenty-nine to thirty-four percent. Since the census was confined to the political city of Cleveland, it is impossible to determine the extent to which Negroes entered the stream of movers destined for suburbia.

In response to the changing magnitude and composition of metropolitan populations, a network of transport links has evolved to facilitate the spatial redistribution of the population. Where an individual chooses to locate himself within the urban system is a function of occupational status, income, place of employment, and social taste. The operation or interaction of these factors has produced a strongly segmented pattern of urban occupance. A change in an individual's socioeconomic status frequently results in relocation within the metropolitan system. As the nation's occupational structure is being rapidly altered in the direction of a larger proportion of white collar workers, especially technical and professional workers, with a concomitant alteration in the income structure, spatial mobility is further accelerated. Changes of this nature tend to produce shifts in territorial status assignment in urban space. Davis, in a recent study, described the magnitude of territorial shifts in the location of middle class housing areas in a selected group of American cities.[12] With the redistribution of the population towards the periphery, there has subsequently been an outward shift of the inner boundary of the zone of middle class housing. As a consequence, these shifts frequently create gray areas which act as zones of transition or buffers between middle and lower class occupance. It is within these gray areas, with their high vacancy rates, that most of the centrifugal Negro flow is destined. The growing intensity of mobility within the metropolitan system has affected all segments of the population, although somewhat differentially. The pattern of movement of whites and nonwhites in urban space is akin to the pattern of inter-regional movement within the nation as a whole. In both instances nonwhite moves are characterized by short distance, whereas whites are more frequently engaged in long distance moves.

The nature of population movement within the urban system is highly related to the magnitude and form of the set of urban subsystems which evolve. The Negro ghetto which comprises one such subsystem or social area is directly related to this process. Since spatial mobility is related both to age and income, one would expect to observe the evolution of a series of patterns which reflect the economic health of a specific metropolitan system, the nature of its economic base, and its subsequent ability to attract population through the process of internal migration; the latter phenomenon has the effect of altering the age distribution of the population. If ability to purchase was the single most significant variable influencing the distribution of population in metropolitan space, it should be easy to predict the kind of sorting-out which eventually occurs. Although this can be done in a rather general man-

ner, purchasing ability alone is far from adequate in explaining the development of the ghetto.[13] The relative stability of the Negro's economic position vis-a-vis the white's during the last several years may have reduced or severely limited the ability of individual Negroes to cross critical rent isolines. On the other hand, the brisk hiring of Negroes to salaried positions by an increasing number of firms pledged to the goal of equality of opportunity, could have the effect of increasing the length of the individual move. It is impossible at this time to specify with any degree of precision the effect of either factor upon the pattern of Negro movement, even though they both may be significant.

TERRITORIALITY

The existence and persistence of the Negro ghetto as a spatially based social community may best be explained within the framework of the social assignment of territory. Once a slice of physical space is identified as the territorial realm of a specific social group, any attempt to alter this assignment results in group conflict, both overt and covert. Stea recently described this behavior in the following way: "We have reason to believe that 'territorial behavior,' the desire both to possess and occupy positions of space, is as pervasive among men as among their animal forbears."[14] Weber attributed this kind of behavior simply to working class groups for whom physical space is an extension of one's ego.[15]

Human ecologists have employed terms such as invasion and succession to describe the process of residential change in which members of competing groups struggle for territory. Henderson recently questioned the employment of the term invasion to describe the process of Negro entry into areas bordering on the ghetto.[16] Admittedly the term invasion appears to be appropriate only within the context of territorial conflict. Viewed outside this context, the term does not appear to be meaningful. A further point, no doubt the one which concerned Henderson, is that the term invasion not only reflects the white resident's perception of events, but the perception of the researcher as well. It has been said, "When our own tribe engages in this behavior we call it nationalism or aggression."[17] From another vantage point, it would appear that the term retreat describes the process more accurately. Since both terms, invasion and retreat, refer to territorial conflict, no major point is settled by substituting one for the other. Nevertheless, it should be kept in mind that the nature of the behavior which occurs within this context does so within the context of a fear-safety syndrome.

The territorial acquisition by advancing Negro populations cannot always be viewed as a gain in this game of psychological warfare, for once the territory is transferred from one group to the other, it is perceived by the white population as having been contaminated and, therefore, undesirable. The formalization or codification of this attitude is associated with the Federal Housing Administration's policy of promoting racial homogeneity in neighborhoods during the period 1935–1950.[18] Hoyt's classic study on the growth of

residential neighborhoods strongly supported this position, and possibly served to support and justify the government's position.[19] Thus, the whole notion of stable property values revolves around the transfer of the status designation from a group to the territory occupied by the group. More recently Bailey observed in one case that unstable property values were associated with those zones located in the shadow of the ghetto rather than in the ghetto itself.[20] However, it is the slack demand for housing in a racially changing neighborhood that is likely to drive down housing values. The unwillingness of whites to compete with nonwhites for housing in a common housing market, coupled with vacancy rates which frequently exceed Negro demand, could eventually lead to a lessening of values. Thus, land abandoned by whites on the margins of the Negro ghetto at some single point in time is almost never known to be retrieved by such residents.

The behavior described above is rapidly leading to the development in the United States of central cities within which territorial dominance is being relinquished to the Negro population. This fact has undoubtedly had much to do with the increasing demand by Negroes for black power, and logically so. If one inherits a piece of turf it is only natural for him to seek control of the area of occupance. Thus, both the critics and supporters of black power have traditional white behavior and the public decisions stemming therefrom for its overt crystallization. Grier recently noted that it was not until President Kennedy signed his executive order of 1962, which treated the problem of discrimination in housing, had the federal government ever gone on record as opposing discrimination in housing.[21] Yet even today, as the nation's ghettos continue to expand, public policy abets their existence and expansion.

The Model

The previous description of a set of general processes goes far in explaining the continuous expansion of the Negro ghetto. The processes described reflect the values of society and, as Pahl recently pointed out, residential patterns are a reflection of the functioning of a social system.[22] It is possible within the framework of systems analysis to devise a model which replicates the total process of metropolitan systems development, but such an understanding exceeds the skills of a single researcher or the knowledge and focus of a single academic discipline. However, a single researcher might attempt to develop a simple model which replicates some aspect of the development of the metropolitan system. A model of this nature, although promoting keener insights into an understanding of processes operative at the micro-level, is characterized by serious shortcomings as it basically reflects the operation of endogenous processes. Nevertheless, the advantages emanating from the development of such models outweigh the previously specified shortcomings.

COMPONENTS OF THE MODEL

A model of ghetto development is of the type described by Chorley and Haggett as normative.[23] An effective model describing ghetto development should include at least three basic components: (1) a demographic component, (2) a producer component, and (3) a consumer component. The data employed to describe these components serve as input for the model. The demographic component is employed to determine housing demand, the producer component to determine availability, and the consumer component to determine allocation. The operation of and subsequent interaction associated with these components permits the model to be placed in the category of behavioral models. The demographic and producer components are generated deterministically, whereas the consumer component is generated probabilistically. Thus, the spread of the ghetto is described in an indeterminate manner. The weakness of the simulation lies primarily in the gross assumption employed in the producer component and secondarily in the projections derived from the operation of the demographic components, both of which acutely affect the emerging pattern of ghetto development.

THE DEMOGRAPHIC COMPONENT

Gross changes in the magnitude of the ghetto are associated basically with the changing demographic character of the Negro population. The demographic characteristics of the white population residing in ghetto space will likewise influence the pattern or form of the ghetto at any point in time. The competition for housing and its subsequent allocation is largely influenced by the demographic characteristics of both the white and Negro populations. In order to better understand the role of population dynamics on ghetto development, interest is focused on the population occupying what is here identified as "ghetto space."[24] Ghetto space in the city selected for testing the model, Milwaukee, Wisconsin, spreads out over a twelve square mile area extending north and west from the central business district. The area in 1960 contained approximately 217,000 persons of which only twenty percent was nonwhite. Nested within ghetto space was a much smaller area, approximately four square miles in extent, which had already become identified as the ghetto. This smaller area included 92,000 persons of whom approximately sixty-eight percent were nonwhite. Thus, the area identified as the Negro ghetto was slightly more than two-thirds Negro and included many blocks which did not contain a single Negro household. In identifying the twelve square mile area as ghetto space, an assumption is posited that the spread of the Negro population will be largely confined to this area in the city of Milwaukee during the current decade and no doubt the decade which follows. By adopting this assumption it is clear that the model being developed here is a strict segregation model.

The principal reason for incorporating a demographic component in the model is to arrive at a reasonable estimate of housing demand. Demand is generated through the employment of an appropriate set of age-specific rates. Age-specific birth and death rates, by color, were applied to the population at one year intervals for a ten year period. This procedure permitted the recording of year by year changes in the population resulting from an excess of births over deaths. Since in-migration is also an important aspect of population change in the Negro population, a migration factor was included. Migration was not thought to contribute significantly to net changes within the white population residing in ghetto space and was omitted as a growth producing factor.

A major weakness of the above described procedure is that it allows a piling up of population in census tracts. This condition is an outgrowth of the absence of a mechanism which would generate data on white out-movement at the tract level. The application of age-specific intracounty mobility rates could be applied to the white population as a means of generating a more accurate measure of the population actually in residence in a census tract at any given point in time. The employment of a correction factor of this type possesses the added advantage of enabling one to compare the actual rate of white movement from tracts with the expected rate; the expected rate would represent the number of movers generated through the use of intracounty mobility rates.

THE PRODUCER COMPONENT

The producer component is employed to create housing vacancies which might allow a Negro household to establish residence in a given block located in ghetto space. As few new housing units are constructed in older neighborhoods, residential space is essentially made available by white abandonment. It is generally agreed that there exists some level of tolerance beyond which whites will no longer continue to share a common residential space with Negroes. On the other hand, there is no general agreement on what whites perceive to be an acceptable residential mix. Nevertheless, a curve in which the leaving rate of whites is a function of the increase in the proportion of Negro households in a block may be described intuitively. Although it would be more logical to describe the leaving process as indeterminate rather than determinate, there is an absence of sufficient data upon which a stochastic process might be based. As the general leaving process becomes better understood, it may be described stochastically.

A shortcoming of the producer component based on assumed white leaving-rates is that it produces an excessive number of vacancies in those parts of the ghetto space which are somewhat remote from the main body of the ghetto. The social distance effect is not as pervasive over space as the vacancy-creating mechanism suggests. Some constraints should be placed upon the territorial limits of ghetto space that would be open to Negro occupancy during any given time interval, under conditions of strict segregation (in order to effect a more realistic description of the actual process). The problem by nature suggests that ghetto space should be made available incrementally. These increments, which are unlikely to fall within the sphere of Negro residential search behavior

during the initial time period, should not be influenced by the vacancy creating mechanism. The creation of vacancies on the periphery of ghetto space results in a series of random residential assignments which leads to a more dispersed settlement pattern than that which actually occurs. This suggests that interaction along what is perceived as the ghetto edge during any single time period is far more pervasive in its impact upon the actual ghetto form than interaction about individual clusters, which might evolve under conditions of random residential assignment if the total ghetto is available for entry throughout a ten-year time interval.

CONSUMER COMPONENT

The consumer component of the model is a residential assignment mechanism. The housing demand of the Negro population during any one-year period is derived by means of determining the number of households formed during the interval. Household formation is deduced by applying an appropriate set of age-specific marriage rates to that segment of the population classified as single. In a situation where in-migration is responsible for a significant proportion of the increase in the local population, it is difficult to choose the most appropriate marriage rates to be employed. In this case the rates characterizing the North Central region were employed. It is suspected that the employment of such rates under conditions of heavy in-migration is likely to produce a larger than actual number of marriages. The existence of a sizeable number of single persons in a new environment is thought to have a depressing effect on the formation of new households.

Negro household assignments were made annually on the basis of the group's known propensity to purchase (or rent) housing in specific price categories. In order to generate household assignments, every block in ghetto space was assigned a probability of receiving a Negro home seeker. The highest probabilities were assigned to those blocks in which the median rent was in the $60–69 range, as blocks characterized by such rents housed the largest percentage of the Negro population in 1960. An assignment could not be made in a block wherein an appropriate number of vacancies did not exist.

The model oversimplifies the process of housing competition in ghetto space in not permitting whites and Negroes to compete for housing in a common market. Obviously, whites continue to seek housing in ghetto space until some critical threshold level is attained. Data on white entry into census tracts in ghetto space which had a minimum of forty percent Negro occupancy by 1960, confirms that whites continue to seek housing in close physical proximity to Negroes until Negro occupancy attains a level of approximately thirty percent. And even then about one-fifth of the housing seekers continue to be white, but falling off sharply thereafter. In the one census tract in ghetto space which exceeded seventy percent Negro occupance in 1958, there was only a negligible number of white entrants; less than two percent. Thus, the exodus of whites at the tract level takes place within a very

short period of time, seemingly as a function of the Negro build up in contiguous space. This fact implies an initial saturation at the block level, proceeding outward from blocks with an already heavy Negro concentration (Fig. 1). Changes in Negro-white relations during the past few years may have altered the expected behavior in contiguous physical space.

The continual expansion of the ghetto is essentially dependent upon the collective behavior of individual residents of ghetto space, white and black. A strict segregation model, such as that developed here, is an attempt to add to an understanding of the operation of the residential market existing within ghetto space. Although knowledge of the behavior of individuals based on race aids in this understanding, it is by no means the only force operating to promote the expected pattern of residential behavior. The operation of exogenous forces are more unpredictable, but critically affect the ensuing pattern of racial residential development. In order to better understand the operation of the internal variables it is necessary to gain insights into the residential search behavior of prospective Negro home seekers as well as white propensity for residential desegregation. Morrill's ghetto residential assignment model was basically governed by the former consideration, whereas the model developed here emphasizes the latter as a means of shedding light on the dual problem.

Whereas Negroes move more often than whites, the lengths of the moves are usually shorter. A sample of Negro movers occupying units on the edge

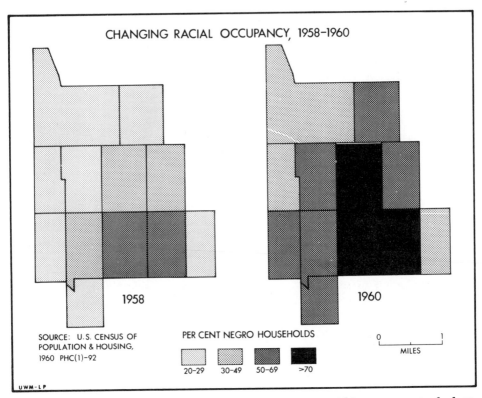

FIGURE 1. The changing intensity of Negro occupance within a segment of ghetto space over a two-year interval is graphically demonstrated. It is evident that the rate of change is essentially linked to the intensity of Negro occupance in contiguous units in the previous time period.

of the ghetto in 1950 exemplifies the pattern of intraurban movement attributed to Negro home seekers. Only four percent of the Negro movers selected housing located more than ten blocks beyond the original ghetto neighborhood, thirty-nine percent selected housing within five blocks of the ghetto, while forty-one percent acquired housing within the same neighborhood (Fig. 2).[25] A similar pattern apparently continued to persist as is evidenced by the number of Negro households occupying units located on

the fringe of the ghetto in 1960. It seems safe to say that whites and Negroes seldom compete for housing in a common market over an extended period of time. Wolf, in analyzing the concept of the tipping point in neighborhood change, was concerned with the following question as one of those critical to an understanding of the tipping point: Does the tipping mechanism refer to the point at which whites begin to leave, or the point at which whites refuse to enter?[26] The answer is yet unclear, but it is apparent that both factors are at

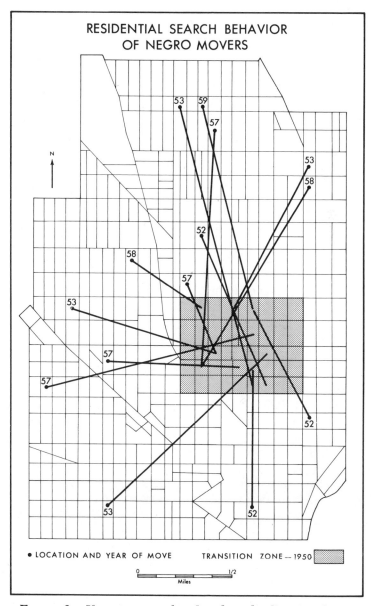

FIGURE 2. Vectors are employed to show the direction, distance, and time of move of a sample of Negro movers who were residents of the ghetto edge in 1950. None of the sample movers chose to settle beyond the confines of ghetto space.

work. The model developed here is based on the former question, and some of its weaknesses undoubtedly stem from an initial ignorance of the latter question. An examination of the success of the model will demonstrate this more effectively.

EVALUATION OF THE MODEL

Once a model of the type described above has been assembled, it can be treated in one of two ways. It may simply be judged on the basis of the logic employed in its construction or it might be made operational as a means of actually testing its validity. The latter course of action has been chosen in this instance. The construct described here is recursive, and is designed to generate changes in the spatial pattern of Negro occupance over a ten-year period. An evaluation of the results of such a model is no mean task. The first problem is selecting the most appropriate method of evaluation. Opinion relative to this matter is mixed. Some researchers have employed various statistical techniques as a means of evaluating the goodness of fit between the simulated pattern and the actual pattern. Others have been content to evaluate the results empirically. Because of the nature of the data and the lack of precise information which can be employed to describe the actual pattern, an empirical analysis will be conducted. The lack of precise information in this case stems from the fact that the model which utilizes census data as input has been calibrated by employing the results of the 1960 census. The yearly changes in the spatial pattern

of residential occupance occurring after the base year can only be crudely evaluated at this time. Only after the results of the 1970 census are available can the model output be subjected to a more rigorous analysis.

A second question concerns the appropriate spatial unit to be employed in the evaluation. Data have been assembled at the block level, for it is generally assumed that race as a factor in the promotion of residential mobility has its most pervasive impact at this level. Yet the prevalence of other forces located within what Wolpert identified as the action space of the individual must not be overlooked.[27] Any meaningful analysis on a block-by-block basis would strongly suggest the use of statistical rather than empirical treatment. Even then, the results of statistical tests applied to the aggregation of blocks constituting ghetto space could prove misleading. In order to eliminate a modicum of the chaos which might arise in this type of analysis, a subaggregation of blocks has been chosen for investigation. These subaggregations may be considered housing market areas.

Only two of the housing market areas in ghetto space have been chosen for intensive observation. One of these is situated on the western edge of the ghetto, and the other is situated several blocks to the north of the original Negro core. Considering the characteristics of these areas at the beginning of the period, they may be described as a declining blue collar housing area and a stable housing area of skilled and semi-skilled workers, respectively. These two prospective appendages of the ghetto are identified, respectively, as the West Central housing market area and the Keefe-Capitol-Congress housing market area.

These two housing market areas contained approximately 7,500 housing units in 1960, a number sufficient to satisfy approximately one-half of the anticipated Negro housing demand during the following ten years. The quality of housing in the two market areas differs significantly, with the quality in the West Central market being generally lower than that which Negroes had previously inherited on the northern margins of the ghetto. Thus, given a choice of housing available in close proximity to the existing ghetto boundaries, the Keefe-Capitol-Congress market area, with its more attractive housing, should prove to be the major target area for Negro occupance during the ensuing ten-year period.

The Keefe-Capitol-Congress area is in many ways similar in housing quality and population characteristics to the Baxter area of Detroit, an area whose pattern of racial change was recently described by Wolf.[28] The Keefe-Capitol-Congress area includes the only sizable volume of single family detached structures in close proximity to the ghetto.

In 1960 the total number of Negro households situated in these two housing market areas numbered less than 150, with the great majority of these located in blocks contiguous to the ghetto. The northern and western margins of the market areas were beyond the distance which most Negro movers travel to seek housing accommodations. This being the case, one would normally expect a block by block filling in, proceeding from areas heavily built up with Negro households to those without Negro households in the initial time period. As a means of comparing the actual process of racial change with the results generated by the simulation model, it was necessary to devise a sampling frame. The question of the type of sample to be employed had to be confronted. Because of the nature of the question to which answers are being sought, it was finally decided that two different sampling techniques would be employed. As a means of gaining insights into the general pattern of household mobility in the two market areas, a stratified random sample stratified by block was employed. In order to reveal more clearly the changes in the pattern of racial occupance, a quadrat or cluster sample was also introduced. The latter technique allowed observation of all changes taking place within a micro-housing environment through time.

The results of the stratified random sample demonstrate that the West-Central housing market area is far less stable than its northern counterpart. Samples drawn from the two census tracts which largely comprise the west central market showed that sixty percent of the 1960 residents in the tract nearest the ghetto, and fifty-two percent of the residents of the tract more distant from the ghetto, were no longer residents of this housing market area by 1965. Likewise, Negro householders served as the basic replacement population in the eastern half of the housing market area, which in 1965 possessed a vacancy rate of twenty percent. The western segment of this market, although exhibiting signs of instability, was not yet receiving large numbers of Negro householders. Negroes at this date constituted fewer than ten percent of the housing market entrants. The fact that five years had elapsed and Negro entrance into the western segment of the market was minimal, strongly supports the contention that Negroes do not search for housing far beyond the margins of already heavily built up Negro areas. The vacancy rate in the western segment of this housing market area was considerably less than that which characterized the east.

In the Keefe-Capitol-Congress housing market, residential mobility was less than half that which characterized the West-Central market. In the northern segment of this market only twenty percent of the original residents had abandoned the area by 1965. The higher level of stability in this housing market was no doubt influenced by its greater physical attractiveness, its higher incidence of owner occupancy and the prevalence of older families. The latter factor is only a temporary contributing factor which will have the opposite impact on stability at a later time. As was true in the eastern half of the West-Central housing area, Negro families represented the chief replacement households in the southern half of the Keefe-Capitol-Congress area. Only about one-third of the replacement households in the northern segment of the market were Negro. The peripheral segment of each of these housing market areas received a smaller number of Negro households during the five-year interval than did those

segments of the market contiguous to the ghetto.

A number of blocks were selected at random within the two housing areas in which to observe the pattern of residential mobility of the universe of occupants located within those blocks. The city directory was employed as the basic source of information on the moves of individual occupants of the sample blocks on a year by year basis. It is often possible to determine the race of entering households on the basis of name, place of previous residence, and occupation data, all of which can be derived from the city directory. Although this technique is not without its shortcomings, it does enable one to arrive at crude index of racial change within a local housing environment.

Twenty-one sample blocks, or in this case quadrats, as the block configuration employed here is the census block rather than the linear block, were selected for intensive investigation (Fig. 3). Eleven of these quadrats are located in the Keefe-Capitol-Congress housing market area, and the remaining ten are in the West-Central housing market area. The sample blocks in the West-Central area are characterized by rental levels which were prevalent in areas already heavily Negro in 1960. The median rental levels of the sample blocks in the northern market were generally higher than those occupied by the Negro population in the initial year. Thus, the probability of a Negro household receiving an assignment in the latter market area is less than that of receiving such an assignment in the former area.

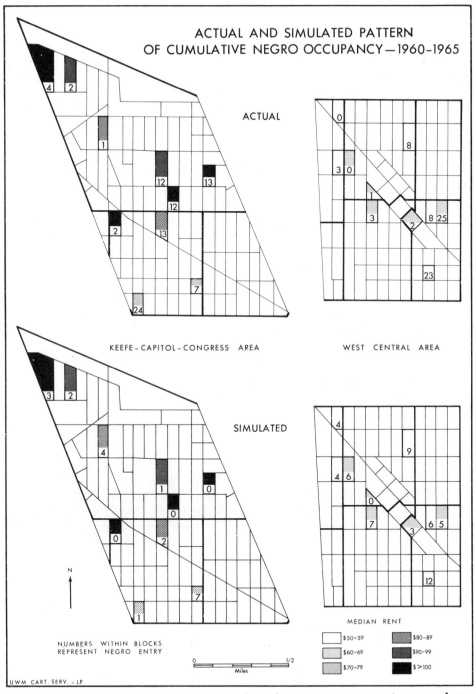

FIGURE 3. The actual and simulated number of Negro movers entering two ghetto fringe housing market areas is shown above. Visual variations in the goodness of fit can be observed within the set of sample blocks.

A sequential running of the model over a five-year period allowed comparison of the simulated pattern of Negro entry in the sample blocks with the observed actual pattern. In all but one of the sample blocks in the Keefe-Capitol-Congress area, the model underpredicted the number of entrants. The basic flaw leading to underprediction in these blocks is the lack of an owner-occupancy mechanism in the model. These are blocks in which most homes are owner occupied structures. This results in high median rental values being assigned them, thereby reducing the probability of a Negro occupant receiving an assignment. In actuality, this area is one in which Negro home purchases have been rather substantial, as Negroes constituted the principal entrants by 1965. A combination of distance and high rents led to a nearly congruent relationship between the actual and simulated pattern in the northernmost blocks in the housing market area.

In the West-Central housing market area the model tended to underpredict in those blocks nearest the ghetto edge and to overpredict in those blocks farther removed. In only three of the sample blocks was there any real similarity between the actual and simulated pattern of Negro entries. Overprediction near the margins of the ghetto suggests that the vacancy creating mechanism in the model requires modification as a means of improving its sensitivity to the presence of small numbers of Negro households within blocks. This lack of sensitivity results in too little concentration along the ghetto edge and too much dispersion in the outer areas of ghetto space, especially when blocks in the outer areas possess similar rental characteristics to those in the ghetto. This weakness was apparent in the overall simulation pattern characterizing ghetto space, as well as in individual housing market areas (Figs. 4 and 5).

A total view of the ghetto configuration is described in Figure 4. Figure 5 reveals the simulated state of the ghetto in 1968. The overall weakness of the model can best be detected by viewing the excessive dispersion of the Negro population along the western edge of ghetto space and the current under concentration along the northern margin of the ghetto (Fig. 5). Several nonresidential blocks within the interior of the ghetto are shown on these maps, without shading. Maps of the type represented by Figures 4 and 5 can be produced for each year, over the ten-year period, from computer output generated by the model.

In evaluating the model it is apparent that the model's performance in the Keefe-Capitol-Congress housing market surpassed its performance in the West-Central market. This fact partially reflects the lack of constraints other than housing costs, to access to all housing in ghetto space. The sequential opening of segments of ghetto space within a time frame should result in a general improvement in the level of model performance. This further indicates that the ghetto resident is engaged in a series of short distance moves, seldom exceeding a ten-block distance and most frequently confined to distances of less than six blocks. This practice permits whites to continue to

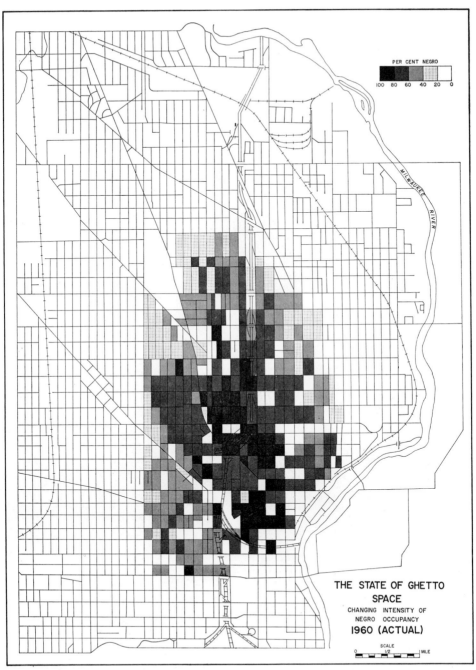

FIGURE 4. The actual intensity of Negro occupancy within the context of ghetto space, as of 1960, is revealed above. The non-shaded blocks within the interior of the ghetto represent non-residential blocks, or blocks with a minimal number of housing units.

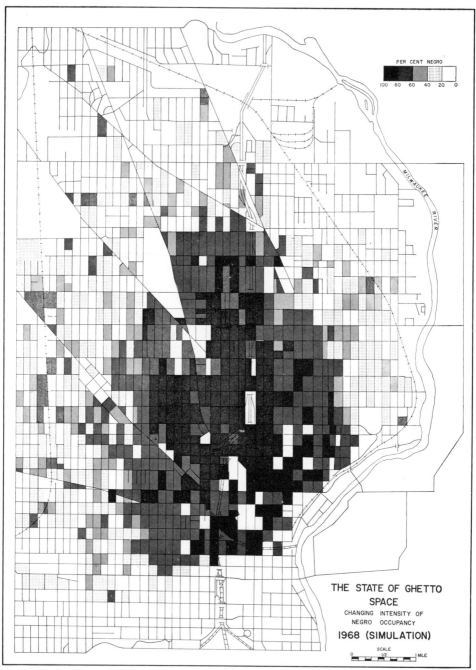

PER CENT NEGRO

100 80 60 40 20 0

MILWAUKEE RIVER

THE STATE OF GHETTO
SPACE
CHANGING INTENSITY OF
NEGRO OCCUPANCY
1968 (SIMULATION)

SCALE
0   1/2   MILE

FIGURE 5. The simulated pattern of Negro residential expansion through an eight-year period can be observed above. The simulation is subject to maximum error along the eastern and western edges of the simulated zones of intensive Negro occupance.

compete for housing only a short distance from the margin of the ghetto, as the slow process of filling-in occurs along the ghetto edge.

THE VALIDITY OF THE CONCEPTUAL MODEL

The previous discussion which dealt with the behavior of whites and non-whites in a common housing market was an attempt to demonstrate the soundness of the use of the previously specified components as input in a ghetto developer model. As the behavior of the individual decision maker operating within a common market is based on a host of factors, it is an inconceivable task to disaggregate all factors impinging on one's decision to move. Nevertheless, the role of the racial composition of the population in housing sub-markets has been employed as the principal factor generating a reduction of white demand and a corresponding intensification of Negro demand in such areas. The question which arises here concerns the validity of the assumptions employed as the basis for model calibration. Since the model described here is a strict segregation model, employing the terminology of Thompson, it may be considered by many to be a distortion of the real-world process of residential household allocation.[29] Admittedly, it is an oversimplification of the process, but it generally appears to provide a closer approximation of racial residential patterns than an open system operating without social constraints.

Unless there is a radical departure in the behavior of individual house-holders, both white and black, as well as the innumerable exogenous forces whose impact is heavily felt in influencing the racial makeup of residential space, the strict segregation model will be effective in simulating the pattern of ghetto development for some time to come. Ghetto maintenance is strongly rooted in the nation's institutional mores. Whereas some question the wisdom of maintaining the ghetto intact, especially after a series of very hot summers, it appears that many professionals and a much larger segment of the lay population feel either that the task of breaking it up is an impossible one or that its maintenance is desirable. The recent flurry of open occupancy laws, at both the state and national level, do not alter this fact.

It appears that many social scientists, regardless of their basic motivations, currently support what Downs describes as a ghetto enrichment strategy.[30] Piven and Cloward, writing recently, strongly suggest that efforts at integration have worked against the Negro's acquisition of adequate housing.[31] This same type of reasoning was recently but somewhat more subtly stated by Spengler, who tends to emphasize the role of a satisfactory social environment.[32] Keller, a planner and strong advocate of the promotion of homogeneous communities, denied that one must favor complete segregation, but admitted that one should use caution in mixing neighborhoods in light of the evidence assembled.[33]

Thus, those in the ghetto who strongly advocate the development of black power and likewise opt for an enrichment strategy, and who consequently tend to be generally opposed to dispersion, seem to have strong professional backing. Downs, unlike Piven and Cloward, in evaluating the enrichment strategy, expressed uncertainty about its potential for success. Yet Grier has openly stated that public policy in the United States should be aimed at allowing the Negro to enter the mainstream of American life and not to solidify the structure of the ghetto.[34] After reviewing the evidence there appears to be strong support for the conceptual validity of something approaching a strict segregation model.

Depending upon the direction and impact of public policy on individual residential location choices, an alternative model might be developed. Such a model might generate specific levels of ghetto escapement on the basis of changing patterns of behavior, growing out of modified economic policies and social relations. But even if all future housing demands on the part of a rapidly growing urban black population are satisfied outside of the ghetto, the ghetto configuration will continue to generate conditions which may be thought to be inimical to the best interests of the nation. There is little question that the phenomenon treated here is complex and transcends the more simplistic problem of understanding housing markets. The ghetto is not simply a spatial configuration, but a social and ideological configuration that has spatial expression.

Models of the type described here might be employed with some modifications to aid the planning process, if the ghetto enrichment strategy is chosen. Similarly, with additional modifica-

tions, such models might be employed as an aid in predicting the location and intensity of certain types of economic and social problems. If one opts for a strategy of dispersal, the strict segregation model will no longer represent a conceptually valid construct. An open system model might be developed which could generally be described as a "ghetto destroyer" model. At the moment there exists no body of information which might serve as a foundation for the development of a model of this type. Furthermore, such a model could only be employed to generate residential spatial patterns which do not currently exist on any meaningful scale. Yet, these currently non-existent patterns could become a reality by altering human behavior as a result of major decisions emanating from both the public and private sectors of the economy.

Summary and Conclusions

An attempt has been made here to describe the basic behavior of individuals which gives rise to residential ghettos in northern metropolitan systems. After gaining limited insights into the behavioral dimension, a model was developed using these basic insights as input. The model, described as a ghetto-developer model, was employed to predict the future state of the ghetto. The state of the ghetto reflects the intensity of the spatial concentration of the Negro population within a contiguous area. Although models of this type can never be expected to duplicate the existing pattern, they can replicate in a general way the real-world process, which leads to the development of spatial patterns that bear varying degrees of similarity to the actual pattern. Whereas models of this type have some predictive value, the real merit derived from them is the gaining of additional understanding of the processes one is attempting to simulate.

The ghetto-developer model was run using data from Milwaukee, Wisconsin. The results provided evidence of deficiency in some of the basic assumptions incorporated in the model, both in terms of the aggregate simulated ghetto spatial pattern, as well as the resulting pattern occurring within individual housing market areas. The employment of the model to generate ghetto expansion in a series of urban systems should permit one to ascertain if a general set of assumptions might be employed to describe fairly accurately the process of ghetto formation.

Models of the type described above are attempts to replicate an actual ongoing process. The initiation of strategies designed to alter the existing process would tend to invalidate the model. At the same time, models may be developed based on the behavior necessary to modify the existing residential spatial pattern. Models of this type could very well serve as planning models, providing that in this case there is a national opting for an alternative strategy. The strict segregation model currently generates a spatial pattern that approaches the actual pattern, even though, in reality, ghetto escapements occur. But the extent of such occurrences are not sufficiently significant to alter the spatial configuration of the ghetto.

Footnotes

1. A. Meier and E. M. Rudwick, *From Plantation to Ghetto* (New York: Hill and Wang, 1966), pp. 191–92.
2. R. L. Rice, "Residential Segregation by Law," *The Journal of Southern History*, Vol. 34 (1968), pp. 194–99.
3. R. L. Morrill, "The Negro Ghetto: Problems and Alternatives," *The Geographical Review*, Vol. 55 (1965), pp. 339–61.
4. A. Beauchamp, "Processual Indices of Segregation: Some Preliminary Comments," *Behavioral Science*, Vol. 11 (1966), pp. 190–92.
5. Morrill, *op. cit.*, footnote 3, p. 348; R. L. Morrill, *Migration and the Spread and Growth of Urban Settlement* (Lund, Sweden: C. W. K. Gleerup, 1965), p. 186.
6. G. Carlsson, "Decline of Fertility: Innovation or Adjustment Process," *Population Studies*, Vol. 20 (November 1966), pp. 149–50.
7. Carlsson, *op. cit.*, footnote 6, p. 150.
8. W. Zelinsky, *A Prologue to Population Geography* (New York: Prentice-Hall, 1965), pp. 45–46.
9. R. L. Morrill, "Waves of Spatial Diffusion," *Journal of Regional Science*, Vol. 8 (Summer, 1968), p. 2.
10. See H. Sharp and L. F. Schnore, "The Changing Color Composition of Metropolitan Areas," *Land Economics*, Vol. 38 (1962), pp. 169–85.
11. Special Census of Cleveland, Ohio, April, 1965, *Current Population Reports*, Series p-28, No. 1390 (1965).
12. J. T. Davis, "Middle Class Housing in the Central City," *Economic Geography*, Vol. 41 (1965), pp. 238–51.
13. For a methodological discussion of this point see K. E. Taeuber and A. F. Taeuber, *Negroes in Cities* (Chicago: Aldine Publishing Co., 1965), pp. 78–95.
14. D. Stea, "Space, Territory and Human Movements," *Landscape*, Vol. 15 (1965), p. 13.

15.   M. M. Weber, "Culture, Territoriality and the Elastic Mile," *The Regional Science Association Papers,* Vol. 13 (1964), pp. 61–63.

16.   G. C. Henderson, "Negroes Into Americans: A Dialectical Development," *Journal of Human Relations,* Vol. 14 (1966), p. 537.

17.   Stea, *op. cit.,* footnote 14, p. 13.

18.   E. Grier and G. C. Grier, "Equality and Beyond: Housing Segregation in the Great Society," *Daedalus,* Vol. 95 (1966), p. 82.

19.   H. Hoyt, *The Structure and Growth of Residential Neighborhoods in American Cities* (Washington, D.C.: Government Printing Office, 1939), pp. 62 and 71.

20.   M. J. Bailey, "Effects of Race and Other Demographic Factors on the Values of Single-Family Homes," *Land Economics,* Vol. 42 (1966), pp. 214–18.

21.   G. C. Grier, "The Negro Ghettos and Federal Housing Policy," *Law and Contemporary Problems* (Summer, 1967), p. 555.

22.   R. E. Pahl, "Sociological Models in Geography," in R. J. Chorley and P. Haggett (Eds.), *Models in Geography* (London: Methuen and Co., Ltd., 1967), p. 239.

23.   Chorley and Haggett, *op. cit.,* footnote 22, p. 25.

24.   Ghetto space represents the area presently identified as the ghetto as well as that expanse of contiguous territory thought to be sufficiently adequate to house the net increase of Negro households over a ten year period.

25.   The zone of transition shown on Figure 2 is areally coincidental with what has been described above as the same neighborhood.

26.   E. P. Wolf, "The Tipping Point in Racially Changing Neighborhoods," *Journal of American Institute of Planners,* Vol. 29 (1963), p. 219.

27.   J. Wolpert, "Behavioral Aspects of the Decision to Migrate," *The Regional Science Association Papers,* Vol. 15 (1965), p. 163.

28.   E. P. Wolf, "The Baxter Area: A New Trend in Neighborhood Changes?" *Phylon,* Vol. 26 (1965), pp. 347–48.

29.   W. R. Thompson, *A Preface to Urban Economics* (Baltimore: The Johns Hopkins Press, 1965), pp. 309–13.

30.   A. Downs, "The Future of American Ghettos," *Daedalus,* Vol. 97 (1968), pp. 1346–47.

31.   F. F. Piven and R. Cloward, "The Case Against Urban Desegregation," *Social Work,* Vol. 12 (1967), p. 12.

32.   J. J. Spengler, "Population Pressure, Housing Habitat," *Law and Contemporary Problems,* Vol. 32 (1967), p. 172.

33.   S. Keller, "Social Class in Physical Planning," *International Social Science Journal,* Vol. 18 (1966), pp. 506–507.

34.   Grier, *op. cit.,* footnote 21, p. 560.

◆ **ten**

DONALD R. DESKINS, JR. ◆

Residence-Workplace Interaction Vectors for the Detroit Metropolitan Area: 1953 to 1965

Introduction

The inhabitants of Negro ghettos in the United States are confronted with a myriad of problems, many of which have been and are continuing to be rigorously examined.[1] The great volume of literature addressed to the problems facing urban Negroes is not only evidence of their immediacy but is also an expression of the level of concern for these issues shown by many social scientists. This is a concern that continues to produce a staggering quantity of output, yet substantively there remain many insights to be gained. Nearly every literate person in the United States is or should be cognizant that residential separation of Negroes exists in some form in all urban areas. For those who are not aware of this fact, a cursory glance at the daily newspaper sufficiently reveals the intensity of this institutionalized phenomenon. Ironically, much of the scholarly literature addressed to this issue provides insights no greater than those in the news media.

However, some researchers—not nearly enough—have placed emphasis on the effects that residential segregation have on the degree of spatial inter-

◆ **SOURCE.** This paper was originally read at a Colloquium on *Interaction Patterns and the Spatial Form of the Ghetto*, sponsored by the Center for Urban Affairs, the Transportation Center, and the Department of Geography, Northwestern University, and published in Special Publication No. 3, Department of Geography, Northwestern University, February 1970.

157

action exercised by urban Negroes. Clearly, the exploratory inquiries by John F. Kain and more recently those of James O. Wheeler have this focus.[2]

Kain is perhaps the first social scientist to examine the linkage between discrimination in housing and the distribution and level of Negro employment. However, he does not have the distinction of being the first scholar to deal with these topics individually.[3] Since his initial paper, "The Effects of the Ghetto on the Distribution and Level of Non-White Employment in Urban Areas," Kain has frequently commented on the effects that residential segregation has on journey-to-work for both Negro and white workers.[4] The recurring thesis in his research is expressed in the following hypothesis:

> *Racial segregation in the housing market affects the distributions of Negro employment in such a manner that residentially Negro workers are centrally located near the CBD, as they usually tend to be in most U.S. cities, so that Negro workers commute less far on the average than they would if housing were not segregated.*[5]

This suggestive hypothesis requires rigorous testing since it implies that Negro workers are not allowed to commute as far as white workers; therefore their residence-workplace interaction is less than that exercised by their white counterparts. Acknowledging the necessity to test this proposition, Kain attempted to fit a series of multiple regression models to sets of data for the Detroit and Chicago metropolitan areas, respectively. In the

models selected, percent of total Negro employment in each workplace zone served as the dependent variable. A series of proxy variables representing the factors causing Negroes to be vastly underrepresented at workplaces distant from the CBD served as independent variables.[6] The resulting coefficients were sufficient to support the above stated hypothesis. In both Chicago and Detroit Negro residence-workplace interaction was found to be less than that of whites.

Wheeler also found Pittsburgh's and Tulsa's Negro workers to be highly concentrated residentially. The journey-to-work observed by Wheeler in Pittsburgh corroborates Kain's finding.[7] However, in Tulsa the inverse was true; the average Negro journey-to-work was greater than that exercised by whites.[8] Needless to say, the wide variance in the respective Pittsburgh and Tulsa findings provides ample grounds for examining the residence-workplace relationship further. In particular, what seems to be implied is that workplaces for Negroes are more concentrated than for whites.

Study Purpose

It is then the purpose of this paper to examine the residence-workplace interaction patterns for both Negro and white occupational groups in the Detroit metropolitan area in two time periods. This is done to determine: (1) if Kain's hypothesis on Negro residence-workplace interaction can be supported temporally and (2) if there are variations among the residence-workplace interaction patterns of the occupational groups comprising the Negro and white labor force components.

Neither of the above mentioned points received detailed treatment by Wheeler or Kain. In their respective studies, both authors confined their analyses to a single time period. Although both authors did comment on the occupational groups comprising the total Negro and white work force, neither author pursued this analysis to the extent that definitive statements could be made on the orientation of a single occupational group's interaction. Nevertheless, Wheeler in his Pittsburgh study did report the average distance traveled to work by race and occupation. He did not, however, emphasize the direction and pattern of interaction by occupational category.[9]

Data and Analytical Procedure

The vectors central to this analysis are calculated in a rather straightforward manner. Before a detailed discussion of the procedure employed in determining vectors is pursued, comments on the study area as well as the data utilized are in order.

This study is focused upon the longitudinal residence-workplace interaction of workers in the Detroit metropolitan area. The Detroit metropolitan area as defined here does not precisely conform to traditional census definitions. Within the study area is the central city —Detroit—and the contiguous urban-

ized area. Consequently, its boundary has been adjusted so that it follows that of the nearest political units of uniform size, in this instance townships (Figure 1). By so doing, an area is delineated which has historical continuity, thus eliminating some of the data management and analytical problems which would arise if the study area boundary were not held constant. The respective boundaries within which the two samples were drawn generally coincide and encompass approximately a 700-square mile area with an estimated 1965 total population of three and one-half million. One fifth of these people are Negroes, mostly residing in the core city of Detroit (Table 1).

Success in deriving residence-workplace interaction patterns is largely contingent upon the availability of rather specific data on individual employed members of the labor force residing within the study area. For each worker it is necessary to have information on race, occupation, residential location, and work location—both accompanied by coordinates. For this study these data were obtained from two sources. The first data set used in the analysis was drawn from the *Detroit Metropolitan Area Traffic Study: Internal Trip Survey*.[10] These data, collected in 1953, are components of the identical set used by Kain.[11] The second data set was collected in 1965 and is the basis for the report: *Community Support for Public Schools in a Large Metropolitan Area*.[12] Both data sets were assembled by probability sample survey techniques and

FIGURE 1.

TABLE 1. Population, Detroit Metropolitan Area: 1950–1965

	Metropolitan Area			City of Detroit			% Area's Negro Pop.
Year	Total	Negro	% Negro	Total	Negro	% Negro	
1950	2,746,989	340,627	12.4	1,845,321	300,506	16.3	88.2
1953	2,968,875E	415,643E	14.0	1,848,675E	364,179E	19.7	87.6
1960	3,338,190	534,411	16.0	1,670,144	482,229	28.9	90.2
1965	3,496,346E	629,324E	18.0	1,533,487E	543,099E	35.4	86.3

E = Estimate
Source: Detroit Regional Transportation and Land Use Study, "A Profile of Southeastern Michigan—Talus Data," pp. 6–15.
"Detroit Metropolitan Area Traffic Study, Part I: Data Summary and Interpretation," pp. 126–42.
U. S. Bureau of the Census, *U.S. Census of Population: 1960, Vol. 1,* Characteristics of the Population, Part A, *Number of Inhabitants,* (1960) Table 7.
U.S. Bureau of the Census, *U.S. Census of Population: 1950, Vol. 1, Number of Inhabitants,* (1952) Table 6.

are representative of the respective universes from which they were drawn, even though the sample sizes vary.[13] In 1953 a stratified sampling frame was employed which sampled the workers in incorporated areas at 4% and workers from the remaining area at 10%, resulting in 42,000 observations. The 1965 sample is much smaller with only 640 observations, the result of a sampling frame where the working population residing in the metropolitan area was sampled at a rate of less than 1%. Since both samples were drawn on a probability basis, where each worker in the study area had an equal chance of being selected, both samples are presumed representative of their respective universes. Although the time interval between the collection of the data sets exceeds a little more than a decade, these data are compatible for comparative analysis because identical information was elicited in both samples. The results of both samples by race and occupational group are illustrated in Figure 2 as a percentage of the total labor force.

ANALYTICAL PROCEDURE

Paired locational coordinates for each worker selected, one for residence and the other for workplace, are the basic data input for determining residence-workplace interaction vectors. Once these data are separated into nine major occupational groups by race for each period,[14] the mean center and standard distance are calculated for each group in a manner similar to that described by Roberto Bachi.[15] Bachi's standard distance equation not only yields the mean center for each distribution measured; it also provides a statistic describing the degree of disper-

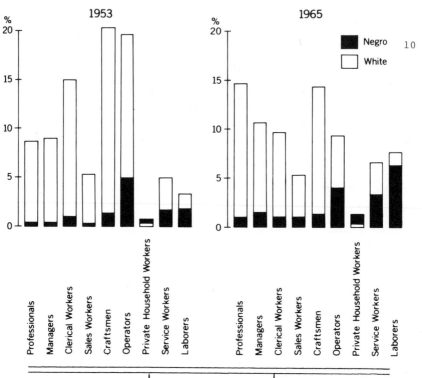

Occupational Groups as a Percentage of the Total Labor Force
Detroit Metropolitan Area, 1953 and 1965

Occupation	1953		1965	
	White	Negro	White	Negro
Professionals	8.66	.37	14.84	1.09
Managers	9.08	.35	10.63	1.56
Clerical Workers	15.13	1.02	9.69	1.09
Sales Workers	5.17	.17	5.31	1.09
Craftsmen	20.85	1.43	14.22	1.75
Operatives	19.79	4.97	9.38	3.91
Private Household Workers	.36	.72	.31	1.25
Service Workers	4.93	1.73	6.88	3.28
Laborers	3.41	1.86	7.81	6.41
Total	100.00		100.00	

Source: Calculated from "The Detroit Metropolitan Area
          Traffic Study," and "Community Support for Pub-
          lic Schools in a Large Megropolitan Area" data.

FIGURE 2.

sion. Once calculated, the paired mean centers, one for residence and the other for workplace, are plotted and connected yielding a residence-workplace interaction vector for each occupation by race. The vectors are in fact a graphic representation of the average distance, which has a definite directional orientation, between residence and workplace (Figure 3).

The differences in length and direction among vectors can be better illustrated by adjusting all Negro and white vectors to the mean residential centers for all Negroes and all white workers respectively (Figure 4). By following this procedure the metropolitan area's composite home-workplace interaction pattern by occupation and race is produced. It should be noted, however, that the adjustment of vectors to the respective population mean centers does not affect the length nor the direction of each vector.

Interaction Patterns

The most obvious generalization resulting from an examination of the interaction patterns for the two periods considered in this study is that Negro and white interaction patterns are quite separate. It appears that the vectors cluster by race and not by occupation. Evidence to support this generalization can be obtained by examining the interaction patterns illustrated in Figure 4. By construction, it is quite easy to fit a line which discriminates between the respective Negro and white interaction patterns for both decades. In addition to the separate interaction fields, re-

vealed by race, there has been considerable change in the distance as well as the direction of the vectors by occupational category.

1953

In 1953, seven of nine white occupational groups traveled longer distances to work. Only in cases of clerical workers and laborers did Negroes travel further than whites (Table 2). In each of these latter two cases the differences in distance never exceeded $\frac{1}{5}$ of a mile. The general directional orientation of white travel to work was from their residences located in the suburbs to a work destination located in the central city. It is not easy to generalize about the orientation of the Negro journey-to-work because their trips follow nearly all points of the compass except to the north where the suburbs are located. Private household workers are the only Negro group which has its journey-to-work oriented towards the suburbs.

1965

A decade later, eight of the nine Negro occupational groups' average vector lengths were greater than those of the white workers. White operatives is the only group which travels further than its Negro counterpart. The direction of Negro interaction vectors continue to follow all points of the compass. The white pattern also continues to be oriented towards the CBD (Table 3). The one exception to this generalization is that of the white service workers, who as a group travel towards the suburbs.

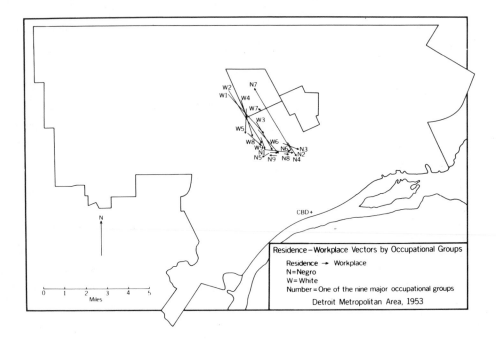

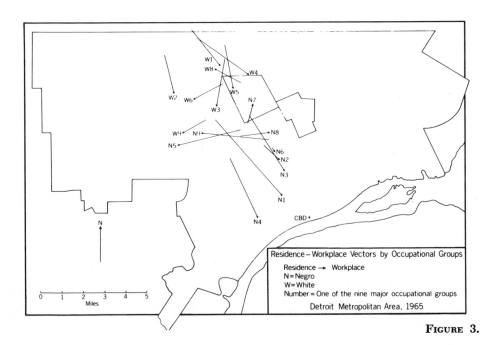

FIGURE 3.

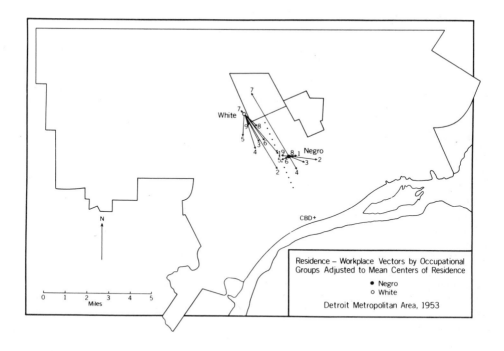

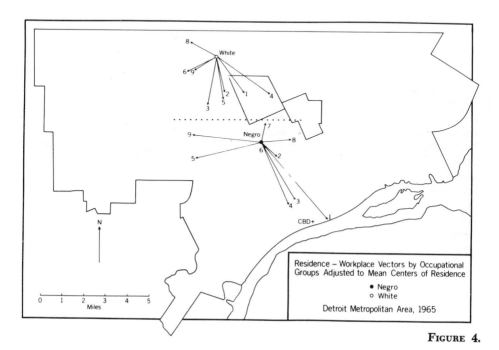

FIGURE 4.

TABLE 2.   Residence-Workplace Interaction Vectors, 1953 (Distance in Miles)

Occupation	Vector Length	Standard Distance Residence	Standard Distance Workplace
Negro			
Professionals	0.3	4.7	5.3
Managers	1.3	4.4	4.0
Clerical Workers	0.7	4.9	5.4
Sales Workers	0.7	3.0	3.7
Craftsmen	0.4	5.0	5.6
Operatives	0.1	4.0	5.1
Private Household Workers	3.3	4.5	6.6
Service Workers	0.1	4.6	5.2
Laborers	0.4	5.2	5.9
White			
Professionals	2.3	8.4	7.0
Managers	2.8	8.5	7.3
Clerical Workers	0.6	7.7	6.4
Sales Workers	1.8	8.9	7.8
Craftsmen	1.1	9.0	7.5
Operatives	1.5	8.1	6.5
Private Household Workers	0.2	13.0	13.0
Service Workers	0.9	7.9	7.3
Laborers	0.2	8.9	7.7
Difference			
Professionals	−2.0	−3.7	−1.7
Managers	−1.5	−4.1	−3.3
Clerical Workers	0.1	−2.8	−1.0
Sales Workers	−1.1	−5.9	−4.1
Craftsmen	−0.7	−4.0	−1.9
Operatives	−1.4	−4.1	−1.4
Private Household Workers	−3.1	−8.5	−6.4
Service Workers	−0.8	−3.3	−2.1
Laborers	0.2	−3.7	−1.8

Source: Calculated from "The Detroit Metropolitan Area Traffic Study," and "Community Support for Public Schools in a Large Metropolitan Area" data.

TABLE 3. Residence-Workplace Interaction Vectors, 1965 (Distance in Miles)

Occupation	Vector Length	Standard Distance Residence	Standard Distance Workplace
Negro			
Professionals	4.7	3.7	3.2
Managers	3.1	2.4	2.2
Clerical Workers	3.0	2.7	3.8
Sales Workers	3.0	2.7	4.1
Craftsmen	3.1	1.6	5.6
Operatives	0.3	4.2	7.0
Private Household Workers	1.0	3.1	6.4
Service Workers	1.4	4.1	6.7
Laborers	3.1	3.4	7.0
White			
Professionals	2.1	8.8	8.2
Managers	1.7	7.6	8.4
Clerical Workers	2.2	8.5	8.4
Sales Workers	2.9	7.4	6.3
Craftsmen	2.0	8.3	9.0
Operatives	1.4	8.6	9.3
Private Household Workers	N.A.	N.A.	N.A.
Service Workers	1.3	7.7	8.7
Laborers	1.2	8.4	8.6
Difference			
Professionals	2.6	−5.1	−5.0
Managers	1.4	−5.2	−6.2
Clerical Workers	0.8	−5.8	−4.6
Sales Workers	0.1	−4.7	−2.2
Craftsmen	1.1	−6.7	−3.4
Operatives	−1.1	−4.4	−2.3
Private Household Workers	N.A.	N.A.	N.A.
Service Workers	0.1	−3.6	−2.0
Laborers	1.9	−5.0	−1.6

Source: Calculated from "The Detroit Metropolitan Area Traffic Study," and "Community Support for Public Schools in a Large Metropolitan Area" data.

CHANGE

The most obvious change in residence-workplace interaction patterns to occur since 1953 is the change in the average distances that Negro and white groups travel. In 1953 whites as a group on their journey-to-work traveled greater distances to work than did Negroes. A decade later the inverse of this relationship was true when Negroes on the average were found to travel greater distances to work than whites (Figure 5). The results graphed on Figure 2 clearly indicate that Kain's hypothesis does not hold temporally for the Detroit metropolitan area since the data examined only confirm this hypothesis for 1953. Clearly a discussion of the change in the relationship between Negro and white residence-workplace interaction revealed by the 1965 analysis is in order.

First of all, the relative residential location of Negroes in the study area has not substantially changed during the twelve-year period under investigation. Although the distance of the residential mean centers of all Negro workers from the CBD showed an increase of 1.1 miles, Negroes remain highly segregated and their relationship to the residential locations of white workers remains relatively the same.[16] During the same period the distance of the white residential mean center from the CBD increased by 2.8 miles, still maintaining a relative location which placed their residences near the suburbs (Table 4). The increase in distance from the CBD of the residential mean centers of the Negro and white groups is only a function of an expanding

metropolitan area not indicative of change in the relative relationships between Negro and white residential locations.

The discussion of the relationship between the residential location of Negro and white groups alone is not sufficient to explain why Negroes in 1965 travel greater distances to work than whites, the inverse of the relationship that existed a decade ago. A reason can be found in discussing the location of workplace. In 1953 the majority of the metropolitan work opportunities were located in the central city. This situation generated interaction patterns which resulted in the vast majority of white workers traveling from their residential location near the city limits or in the suburbs to the central city. In the case of Negroes, their residential locations, due to residential segregation, was confined to the inner city, which was also the central location for most of the metropolitan area's work opportunities. Consequently, Negro interaction between residence and workplace covered comparatively shorter distances than white interaction.

In twelve years, the residential situation of Negroes shows little change; however, the shifts in workplace location are quite discernible. During this period many of the firms that had previously been located in the central city relocated in the suburbs.[17] The decentralization of workplace in conjunction with continued residential segregation of Negro workers are the primary reasons causing Negro workers in 1965 to travel greater distances to work than whites. This relationship between residence and workplace for Negroes and

Residence–Workplace Interaction Vectors and Standard Distances for
Residence and Workplace by Occupational Group
Detroit Metropolitan Area, 1953 and 1965

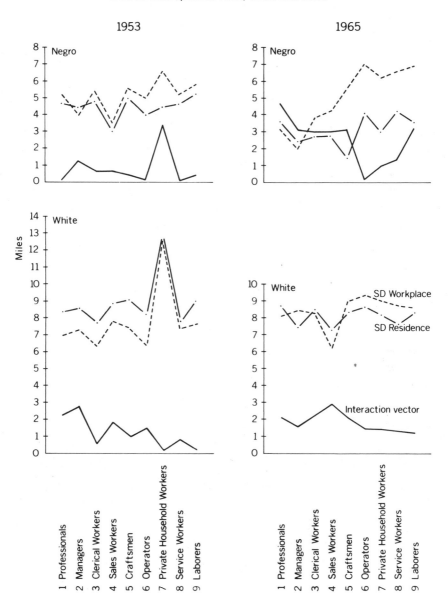

Source: Collected from "The Detroit Metropolitan Area Traffic Study" and "Community Support
for Public Schools in a Large Metropolitan Area" data.

FIGURE 5.

TABLE 4. Distance to CBD from Mean Centers of Residence and Workplace
(Distance in Miles)

| | 1953 | | | | | |
| | Negro | | White | | Difference | |
Occupation	Resi-dence	Work-place	Resi-dence	Work-place	Resi-dence	Work-place
Professionals	3.2	3.1	6.5	4.2	−3.3	−1.1
Managers	3.4	2.8	6.7	3.8	−3.3	−1.0
Clerical Workers	3.3	2.8	4.7	3.2	−1.4	−0.4
Sales Workers	3.3	2.7	6.0	4.3	−2.7	−1.6
Craftsmen	3.3	3.3	5.5	4.6	−2.2	−1.3
Operatives	2.9	2.9	4.3	3.0	−1.4	−0.1
Private Household Workers	2.9	6.3	5.1	5.2	−2.2	1.1
Service Workers	2.8	2.7	4.6	3.9	−1.8	−1.2
Laborers	2.9	3.2	4.1	3.5	−1.2	−0.3
All Workers	3.0	3.1	5.6	4.0	−2.6	−0.9
	1965					
Professionals	6.1	1.4	9.8	8.0	−3.7	−6.6
Managers	3.8	2.9	9.7	8.3	−5.9	−5.4
Clerical Workers	5.3	2.3	8.0	6.5	−2.7	−4.2
Sales Workers	4.3	2.2	9.6	7.0	−5.3	−4.8
Craftsmen	5.0	6.8	8.6	6.7	−3.6	0.1
Operatives	3.6	3.2	7.1	7.4	−3.5	−4.2
Private Household Workers	5.1	5.8	N.A.	N.A.	N.A.	N.A.
Service Workers	4.8	4.2	6.8	7.9	−2.0	−3.7
Laborers	3.9	6.2	6.4	6.8	−2.5	−0.6
All Workers	4.1	4.5	8.4	7.0	−4.3	−2.5
	Change 1953–1965					
					Difference in Negro–White Change	
Professionals	+2.9	−1.7	+3.3	+3.8	−0.4	−5.5
Managers	+0.4	+0.1	+3.0	+4.5	−2.6	−4.4
Clerical Workers	+2.0	−0.5	+3.3	+3.3	−1.3	−3.8
Sales Workers	+1.0	−0.5	+3.6	+2.7	−2.6	−3.2
Craftsmen	+1.7	+3.5	+3.1	+2.1	−1.4	+1.4
Operatives	+0.7	+0.3	+2.8	+4.4	−2.1	−4.3
Private Household Workers	+2.2	−0.5	N.A.	N.A.	N.A.	N.A.
Service Workers	+2.0	+1.5	+2.2	+4.0	−0.2	−2.5
Laborers	+1.0	+3.0	+2.3	+3.3	−1.3	−0.3
All Workers	+1.1	+1.4	+2.8	+3.0	−1.7	−1.6

Source: Calculated from "The Detroit Metropolitan Area Traffic Study," and "Community Support for Public Schools in a Large Metropolitan Area" data.

whites is illustrated on Figure 6 where diagrams are employed to portray the relationship of residence and workplace using the respective mean centers of residence and workplace for both Negroes and whites and their respective standard distances as radii. By so doing a graphic illustration of the relationship between residence and workplace and the change is illustrated.

Although the change in distance traveled to work for Negroes can be explained as a function of continued residential segregation and decentralization of workplace, there are several other interesting factors worth mentioning. For example, there are several factors which have contributed to the increase in residence-workplace vector of Negro professionals. In 1953 professional Negro interaction distance on the average was three-tenths of a mile. The shortness of this interaction vector is due to the fact that the market for services rendered by professional Negroes was restricted to the ghetto. It is a commonly known fact that Negro doctors, lawyers, etc., until recently were forced to practice in their own community. The combination of the constraints on the opportunity to render services and residential segregation accounted for the spatially restricted interaction experienced by professional Negroes. In 1965, approximately a decade later, Negro professional interaction distance has increased so that professional Negroes traveled a distance to work which exceeded that of all other Negro and white groups. Explanation of this change in vector distance which had increased to 4.7 miles is primarily due to the factors of in-

creased employment as well as wider housing opportunities. Professional Negroes residentially have shifted to the northwestern section of the city; to an area recently vacated by elements of the white middle class that have fled to the suburbs. The housing, most of which abuts the northern city limits in the vicinity of Eightmile Road, is generally sound but pre-World War II in vintage. Consequently, this group of Negroes is located further from the CBD than any other Negro group.

Today professional Negroes perform services for the larger community to a far greater degree than they did in the past. Even though opportunities have expanded, most professional Negroes are employed in the public sector or at large firms headquartered in the CBD. The concentration of professional job opportunities in the CBD, along with wider but still restricted housing opportunities, accounts for the increase in length of the Negro professionals' residence-workplace vector between 1953 and 1965. The same reasons help explain the shifts in the other occupational categories, particularly the white collar occupations: managers, clerical workers and sales workers. Similar factors have contributed to shifts in the interaction of blue collar workers, however in these instances the workplace is decentralized and Negro interaction is towards the suburbs.

Conclusions

On the basis of results extracted from the data examined for the two periods covered in this study, Kain's hypothesis

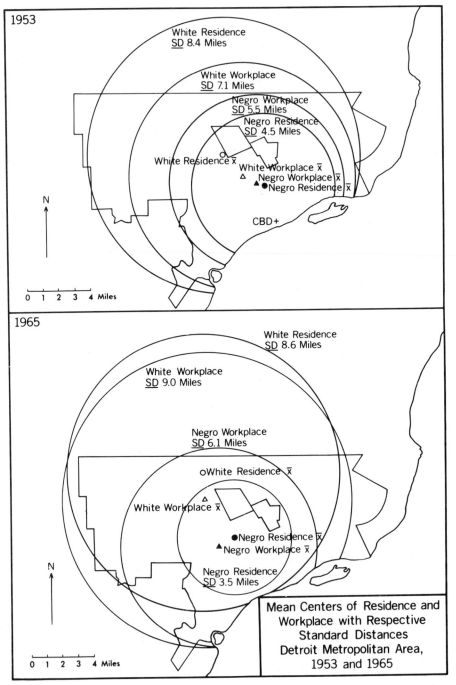

1953

White Residence
SD 8.4 Miles

White Workplace
SD 7.1 Miles

Negro Workplace
SD 5.5 Miles

Negro Residence
SD 4.5 Miles

White Residence x̄   ○

White Workplace x̄
△ Negro Workplace x̄
●Negro Residence x̄

CBD+

N

0 1 2 3   4 Miles

1965

White Residence
SD 8.6 Miles

White Workplace
SD 9.0 Miles

Negro Workplace
SD 6.1 Miles

○White Residence x̄

△
White Workplace x̄

●Negro Residence x̄
▲Negro Workplace x̄

Negro Residence
SD 3.5 Miles

N

0 1 2 3   4 Miles

Mean Centers of Residence and
Workplace with Respective
Standard Distances
Detroit Metropolitan Area,
1953 and 1965

FIGURE 6.

does not hold temporally and therefore has to be rejected. In 1953 evidence to support Kain's notion is quite precise. Due to a combination of factors: (1) the continuation of residential segregation, (2) the decentralization of workplace, and (3) a broadening of the range of job opportunities, the hypothesis was not supported by the 1965 data. It is quite obvious that residential segregation plays a dominant role in shaping the residence-workplace interaction of both Negro and white workers in large metropolitan areas. In the Detroit case, these factors resulted collectively in a complete reversal of the interaction patterns between the white and Negro group respectively. The change in these interaction patterns have implications for policy planning, particularly in the area of mass transit planning focused to meet the travel needs of urbanites. Much of the demand ascertained in transportation studies is usually presented in an aggregate form. By so doing the particular transportation needs of minority groups are generally averaged or smoothed to the degree that these needs which are peculiar to minority groups are not adequately identified and therefore never met. In order to meet the needs of minority groups, transportation planning decisions must be based on analyses that treat the needs of minority groups apart from those of the larger society. It is apparent that the analysis used in this study, although far from utopian, is at least focused on the differences in residence-workplace interaction between Negroes and white workers. If the additional factors of the differentials in Negro and white income as well as

automobile ownership[18] are considered, then the need is further emphasized for transportation policy planning based upon analysis of the components of the work force rather than on the work force aggregate.

Footnotes

1. There are two recent excellent works documenting the comprehensive nature of research addressed to the problems facing Negroes in the United States. The first is an annotated bibliography and the second is a survey of the research conducted on this topic. These works respectively are: Elizabeth W. Miller, *The Negro in America: A Bibliography,* (Cambridge, Massachusetts: Harvard University), and John P. Davis, ed., *The American Negro Reference Book,* (Englewood Cliffs, N.J.: Prentice-Hall, 1966). Earlier documentation of problems facing Negroes is found in T. J. Woofter, Jr., *Negro Problems in Cities,* (Garden City: Doubleday, Doran, 1928). For definitive treatments of residential segregation and related processes, see Otis Dudley Duncan and Beverly Duncan, *The Negro Population of Chicago,* (Chicago: University of Chicago Press, 1957), and Karl E. Taeuber and Alma F. Taeuber, *Negroes in Cities,* (Chicago: Aldine, 1965).

2. John F. Kain, "The Effect of the Ghetto on the Distribution and Level of Nonwhite Employment in Urban Areas," paper presented at the Annual Meeting of the American Statistical Association, Chicago, December 27–30, 1964; "Race and the Urban Transportation Problem," in J. R. Meyer, J. F. Kain and M. Wohl, *The Urban Transportation Problem,* (Cambridge, Massachusetts: Harvard University Press, 1966), pp. 114–167; John F. Kain, "Housing Segregation, Negro Employment and Metropolitan Decentralization," *Quar-*

terly Journal of Economics, 82, (May, 1968), pp. 175–197; James O. Wheeler, "Work-trip Length and the Ghetto," *Land Economics,* 44 (February, 1968), pp. 107–112; James O. Wheeler, "Transportation Problems in Negro Ghettos," *Sociology and Social Research,* 53 (January, 1969), pp. 171–179; and James O. Wheeler, "Some Effects of Occupational Status on Work-trips," *Journal of Regional Science,* 9, (April, 1969), pp. 69–77.

3. Following are a few selected recent works on residential segregation and housing: Davis McEntire, *Residence and Race,* (Berkeley: University of California Press, 1960); Luigi Laurenti, *Property Values and Race,* (Berkeley: University of California Press, 1960); Nathan Grazer and Davis McEntire, *Studies in Housing and Minority Groups,* (Berkeley: University of California Press, 1960).

4. Kain, "The Effect of the Ghetto on the Distribution and Level of Nonwhite Employment in Urban Areas," p. 1; Meyer, Kain and Wohl, *The Urban Transportation Problem,* p. 145, and Kain, "Housing Segregation, Negro Employment and Metropolitan Decentralization," p. 117.

5. This hypothesis is central to the thesis developed in all Kain's works that are cited in Footnote 4.

6. Kain, "Housing Segregation, Negro Employment and Metropolitan Decentralization," pp. 178–180.

7. Wheeler, "Work-Trip Length and the Ghetto," p. 107.

8. Wheeler, "Transportation Problems in Negro Ghettos," p. 176.

9. Wheeler, "Work-Trip Length and the Ghetto," p. 108.

10. Detroit Metropolitan Area Traffic Study, *Part I: Data Summary and Interpretation,* (Lansing, Michigan: Speaker—Hines and Thomas, 1955).

11. Kain, "Housing Segregation, Negro Employment, and Metropolitan Decentralization," p. 176.

12. Ralph V. Smith, Stanley E. Flory, Rashid L. Bashshur and Gary W. Shannon, *Community Support for the Public Schools in a Large Metropolitan Area,* (Ypsilanti, Michigan: Eastern Michigan University, 1968).

13. C. A. Moser, *Survey Methods in Social Investigation,* (London: Heinemann, 1966), p. 116.

14. U.S. Bureau of the Census, *1960 Census of Population, Classified Index of Occupations and Industries,* (Washington, D.C.: Government Printing Office, 1960), pp. XV–XX.

15. Roberto Bachi, "Standard Distance Measures and Related Methods for Spatial Analysis," *Regional Science Association Papers,* 10, (1963), pp. 83–132. The program used to calculate mean centers and standard distances was developed by Waldo R. Tobler, Department of Geography, University of Michigan.

16. Taeuber and Taeuber, *Negroes in Cities,* p. 39, and Albert J. Mayer and Thomas F. Hoult, *Race and Residence in Detroit,* (Detroit: Institute for Urban Studies, Wayne State University, 1962), p. 13.

17. *The Changing Pattern of Manufacturing Plants and Employments: 1950–1960 in the Detroit Region,* (Detroit: Detroit Metropolitan Area Planning Commission, 1961), and Robert B. Smock, The Inner-City Worker, (Dearborn: Center for Urban Studies, The University of Michigan, Dearborn Campus, 1967), p. 5.

18. There are numerous works focused upon the Negro and white differentials in income. Herman P. Miller, *Rich Man—Poor Man,* (New York: Thomas Y. Crowell, 1964), is representative of this work. The literature on differentials in automobile ownership is not as broad, however. John B. Lansing and Gary Hendricks, *Automobile Ownership and Residential Density,* (Ann Arbor, Michigan: Survey Research Center, The University of Michigan, 1967), provides an adequate springboard for this type of inquiry.

♦ ♦ ♦ ♦ ♦ ♦ ♦ ♦ ♦ ♦ ♦ ♦ ♦ ♦ ♦ ♦ ♦ ♦ ♦ eleven

REYNOLDS FARLEY ♦

The Changing Distribution of Negroes within Metropolitan Areas: The Emergence of Black Suburbs

Introduction

After World War II, many studies claimed that new life-styles were developing within suburbia. These life-styles demanded that suburbanites be very friendly to their neighbors, spend much time on child-rearing activities, and participate in many community endeavors. Some sociologists argued that the major reason for the development of these new social patterns was that suburbs contained a young, middle-class, native American population which shared common values, unlike central cities which contained a heterogeneous population (Fava 1956; Martin 1956; Riesman 1957; Whyte 1957).

Long ago some authors had shown there was a variety of types of communities in the suburban territory surrounding central cities (Douglas 1925; Harris 1943), but further research was required to challenge the myth of suburban homogeneity. Schnore (1957, 1965) pointed out the differences in ethnic composition and socioeconomic status which could be found within the nation's suburbs. Further study found that suburban living did not completely

♦ SOURCE. Reprinted from the *American Journal of Sociology*, Vol. 75, 1970, pp. 512–529, with permission of the author and the University of Chicago Press, copyrighted 1970, by the University of Chicago, all rights reserved.

175

change working-class life-styles and that middle- and working-class residents could be found within the same suburb (Dobriner 1963). The similarity of cities and suburbs was demonstrated by another investigation which showed that patterns of residential segregation common to central cities were also found in suburbs (Lieberson 1962).

Recently much publicity has been given to the idea that central cities are coming to contain a principally black population while the surrounding suburbs are residential areas for whites. President Johnson's Commission on Civil Disorders stated succinctly in warning that if present trends continue there will be "a white society principally located in suburbs, in smaller central cities and in the peripheral parts of large cities and a Negro society largely concentrated within large cities" (U.S., National Advisory Commission on Civil Disorders 1968, p. 407).

This paper examines the hypothesis that cities and suburbs are coming to have racially dissimilar populations. First, historical trends in racial composition are reviewed. Second, data are examined to study the rapidity of black population growth in suburbia in recent years. Third, the socioeconomic characteristics of blacks in suburbia and those moving into suburbia are analyzed. Finally, the types of suburbs which have experienced Negro population growth are described.

Historical Trends

Changes since 1900 in the racial composition of central cities and the sub-

urban area that surrounds them can be determined from census data. Figure 1 shows the proportion of the total population which was Negro in central cities and suburban rings for dates between 1900 and 1968. These figures are based on information for all the 212 Standard Metropolitan Statistical Areas (SMSA) defined in 1960. The suburban ring includes, at each date, the area which was outside the central city but within the counties comprising the SMSA in 1960. Data are shown separately for SMSAs in the North and West and for those in the South.

Central cities outside the South contained relatively few blacks prior to World War I; thereafter a cessation of European immigration combined with an influx of blacks gradually changed the racial composition of these cities. As recently as 1940, however, the proportion black was no greater than 6 percent. During and after World War II, the in-migration of Negroes continued, and, in many cities, the white population decreased. As a consequence, the proportion black in these cities went up and by the late 1960s reached 18 percent.

Very different trends characterize southern central cities. Prior to the Civil War the number of blacks in many southern cities actually decreased (Wade 1964, pp. 325–30), but after Emancipation freed men left their plantations and between 1860 and 1870 the proportion black in southern cities rose (Farley 1968, p. 274). However, there was little change in the racial composition of these cities after 1870. While their black populations grew the cities annexed outlying territory, and their white populations have grown at about the same rate, effecting no substantial change in their color composition. Since 1950 there has been a slight rise in the proportion black in the southern cities. If these cities, in the future, find it difficult to annex outlying areas which have rapidly growing white population, their color composition will change.

There have always been some blacks in the suburban rings which surround northern and western cities. The proportion black in these areas remained approximately 3 percent for many decades. As white suburban communities were growing, Negro suburban communities were expanding at a correspondingly rapid rate. Some of these black suburbs date from the early years of this century and have histories similar to those of white suburbs. For instance, just before 1900, a tract west of Saint Louis, Missouri, was subdivided, and lots were sold to Negroes. This suburb, called Kinloch, grew slowly for some decades but was incorporated in 1939, and by 1960 it had a population of 6,500, all but two of whom were black (Kramer and Walter 1967; U.S., Bureau of the Census 1961a, table 25). In the Chicago area, a Negro realtor secured land west of the city prior to World War I and sold homesites to blacks. This suburb, Robbins, was incorporated in 1917 and has continued to grow, reaching a population of 7,500 in 1960 (Rose 1965, p. 369; U.S., Bureau of the Census 1961b, table 25). Near Cincinnati, Ohio, the black suburb of Lincoln Heights developed during the 1920s and by 1960 had 7,800 residents (Rose 1965, p. 369; U.S., Bureau of the Census 1961g, table 22).

Suburban rings surrounding southern cities have undergone great change in racial composition. Early in this century, when these suburban rings contained extensive rural areas, at least one-third of the population was black. Gradually but consistently this proportion decreased, for, as southern cities grew, suburbs developed and whites moved into outlying areas. In some suburban rings whites displaced blacks (Heberle 1948, p. 34); in other suburban rings the black population continued to grow but at a slower rate than the white population. Nevertheless, black suburbs have sprung up near some major cities. For example, after World War II a suburban development for Negroes was built near Miami, Florida, and by 1960 this suburb, Richmond Heights, contained some of the nicer homes available to Miami blacks (U.S., Bureau of the Census 1962a, tables 37–40; Rose 1965, p. 370). In the 1950s, after an expressway cut through the black ghetto of Shreveport, Louisiana, many inexpensive homes were put up in an area to the north of the city. In 1960 North Shreveport had a black population of 8,000 (U.S., Bureau of the Census 1961c, table 22; 1961f, table 37).

Recent Trends

It has been almost a decade since the last national census was conducted, so it is difficult to know exactly what population changes have occurred since 1960. However, the Census Bureau's monthly Current Population Survey, which now involves a national sample of 50,000 housing units, provides increasingly detailed information about blacks. Table 1 indicates the Negro and white populations of central cities and suburban rings in 1960 and 1968 and growth rates for the intervening period. It must be remembered that these data were obtained by sampling the population and that between 1968 and 1970 many central cities may annex outlying territory. Hence, growth rates for the 1960–1970 period may differ from those for the 1960–1968 span contained in Table 1.

Since 1960 there has been continued growth of the black population in the nation's central cities both within and outside the South, although growth rates for the 1960s are lower than those of the 1950s (U.S., Bureau of the Census 1963a, table 1; 1969a, pp. 2–6). The white population of central cities, with the exception of western cities, has decreased, and this too continues a trend which developed in the World War II era.

The black population in suburban rings has grown quite rapidly. In the suburban rings of the North and West, the black population has increased since 1960, not only more rapidly than it did during the 1950s but more rapidly than the white population. This has produced a slight change in the racial composition of these suburban rings as indicated by Figure 1. Within southern suburban rings, the white population increased at a higher rate than the black, but the Negro population has grown more rapidly during this decade than during the last.

Despite the suburbanization of blacks, the data in Table 1 show that central cities are becoming more racially differentiated from their suburban

rings. The proportion of population which is black is rising more rapidly in central cities than in suburban rings. This finding lends credence to the view of the Commission on Civil Disorders, but two facts should not be overlooked.

First, at present blacks are a minority in most central cities. In 1965 only one of the nation's thirty largest cities, Washington, D.C., had a black majority; and in only four others (Atlanta, Georgia; Memphis, Tennessee; New Orleans, Louisiana; and Newark, New Jersey) did blacks comprise as much as 40 percent of the population (U.S., Bureau of the Census 1967a, p. 11). In the future some large cities in both the North and the South will have black majorities, but these cities will be the exceptions rather than the rule. If the growth rates from central cities which obtained between 1960 and 1966 continue to 1980, the proportion of population in central cities which is nonwhite will rise from 22 percent in 1966 to 32 percent in 1980. (This projection is based on figures from U.S., Bureau of the Census 1967b, table A. For a more elaborate set of projections, see Hodge and Hauser 1968, p. 26.) Since 1960 the rate of natural increase among blacks has decreased for fertility rates have fallen (U.S., Bureau of the Census 1969d, tables 2 and 3), and by 1967 only a little more than one million blacks remained on the nation's farms (U.S., Bureau of the Census 1969e, table 3). The black population is simply not growing rapidly enough, nor are there sufficient numbers of rural Negroes to radically change the racial composition of most central cities even if whites continue to move away.

Second, suburban rings do con-

TABLE 1. Change of Negro and White Populations in Central Cities and Suburban Areas, 1960–1968*

	Negro Population			White Population		
	1960	1968	Average Annual Change (%)	1960	1968	Average Annual Change (%)
	(in Millions)			(in Millions)		
Total population of United States	18.4	22.0	+2.2	158.7	174.0	+1.2
Northeast and North Central:						
Central cities	5.0	6.8	+3.8	28.6	26.4	−1.0
Suburban rings	0.9	1.2	+3.6	31.5	37.7	+2.2
South:						
Central cities	3.7	4.1	+1.3	11.1	10.8	−0.3
Suburban rings	1.4	1.6	+1.7	10.1	14.2	+4.3
West:						
Central cities	0.7	0.9	+3.2	8.0	8.2	+0.3
Suburban rings	0.3	0.5	+6.4	10.3	14.0	+3.8

Source: U.S., Bureau of the Census 1969a, pp. 2 and 6.

* Standard metropolitan statistical areas as defined in 1960 were used in this analysis. The suburban ring includes that area outside the central city but within the standard metropolitan statistical area.

tain Negroes, and some suburban black communities, both in the North and the South, have grown in the recent past. A Census Bureau study indicates that within suburban rings the black population increased much more rapidly between 1966 and 1968 than between 1960 and 1966, although sampling variability may affect this finding (U.S., Bureau of the Census 1969a, p. 3).

Aggregate figures obtained from national samples of the population give no indication of which specific suburban communities have growing black populations. In both Illinois and New York, however, a number of communities have requested the Census Bureau to conduct special enumerations since 1960 because certain state appropria-

tions are based upon the population of local areas as officially enumerated. This provides an incentive for growing suburbs to request special censuses, and in both the Chicago and New York metropolitan areas many of these have been conducted. This permits us to investigate racial change in the suburbs near the nation's two largest cities, New York and Chicago.

NEGROES IN THE CHICAGO
SUBURBAN AREA

A total of seventy-six places within Cook County but outside the city of Chicago, that is, suburban cities, towns, and villages, were covered by special census enumerations between 1964 and 1968. These places, in 1960, contained about five-eighths of the suburban population of Cook County (U.S., Bureau of the Census 1961d, table 7).

Chicago's suburban population increased rapidly after 1960. Among the places covered by special censuses, the total population went up from about one million in 1960 to one and one-third million at the special census dates (U.S., Bureau of the Census 1968a, table A-1; 1968b, table 1; 1968c, table 1; 1969b, table 1; 1969c, table 1). The nonwhite population increased at a higher rate than the white, affecting a small change in the proportion nonwhite in these suburbs, a rise from 2.2 percent in 1960 to 2.6 percent when the special enumerations were carried out (U.S., Bureau of the Census 1961b, tables 21 and 22; 1965, table 1; 1966a, table 1; 1967c, table 1; 1968a, table 1; 1968b, table 1; 1968c, table 1; 1969b, table 1; 1969c, table 1).

A closer examination of these data reveals that little integration has occurred. Rather than being distributed throughout the suburbs, the growth of black population has concentrated in three areas; one in Maywood, one in and around Harvey, and a third area of Chicago Heights and East Chicago Heights.

Between 1960 and 1965 the black population of Maywood doubled, increasing from 5,000 to 10,000. This is an older suburb which was settled after the Civil War and grew rapidly when rail lines linked it to Chicago (Kitagawa and Taeuber 1963, p. 194). Maywood did not participate in the post-World War II boom; in fact, its peak growth followed World War I. It is a suburb of older, relatively less expensive homes

(U.S., Bureau of the Census 1962b, tables 17 and 21). Maywood has experienced population replacement since 1950, for as its white population declined, its Negro population grew, while its total population has remained about constant.

The black population of Harvey, another old suburb, and the nearby but newer suburb of Markham increased. Harvey was founded in the 1890s but has continued to grow, and in recent years manufacturing firms have located in this area (U.S., Bureau of the Census 1966b, table 4). In 1960 the majority of blacks in Harvey lived in older homes, but one-third lived in houses which had been erected after World War II (U.S., Bureau of the Census, 1962b, table 37). Since 1960 there has been a modest building boom in this suburb, and new construction as well as the conversion of older homes from white to Negro occupancy account for the growth of black population. Markham is a post-World War II suburb. In recent years many new single-family homes have been built, and both the white and Negro populations have increased (U.S., Bureau of the Census 1966c, table B-6; 1965, table 1).

The third suburban area which had a growing black population included a section of Chicago Heights and the village of East Chicago Heights. Steel and chemical plants have been in this area since the 1890s. During World War I blacks began moving into Chicago Heights, and their members rose during World War II (Kitagawa and Taeuber 1963, p. 176). A pattern of intracommunity segregation emerged; and an area separated from the rest of the suburb by a major rail line contained the black population (U.S., Bureau of the Census 1962c, table P-1). Bordering Chicago Heights is an area of older, low-quality homes. In 1960, 60 percent of them lacked indoor toilets and half were in deteriorating or dilapidated condition (U.S., Bureau of the Census 1962b, table 37). This is the suburb of East Chicago Heights. During 1964 a public housing project was started, and this along with other new construction explains the rise of black population.

NEGROES IN THE NEW YORK SUBURBAN AREA

New York City's suburban ring, in 1960, included four counties. Those closer to the city are Nassau which lies immediately east of New York on Long Island and Westchester which is located just north of the city. The outer counties are Suffolk on Long Island and Rockland which is northwest of the city and across the Hudson River. Between 1965 and 1968 the population of this entire area was enumerated by special census except for some small enclaves. These special census data make it possible to determine the number and age of recent migrants to the suburban ring. Table 2 shows the color composition of each county, the net number of migrants and net migration rates specific for age and color. Data are shown for two sections of Suffolk County, for an area nearer the central city which was enumerated in 1967, and for an area further from the city which was counted one year later.

The figures in Table 2 indicate,

first, that the Negro population of the suburban ring has grown since 1960; by the mid-1960s there were at least 175,000 blacks in these suburbs. In each suburban area, except the outer towns of Suffolk County, the Negro population increased more rapidly than the white, producing a small rise in the proportion black within the New York suburban ring.

Second, Negro population growth has occurred not only because of natural increase but also because blacks are migrating into these suburbs. Examination of the migration rates reveals that the highest rates were for the age groups 20–34 and 0–4 in 1960. This indicates that black families headed by young adults along with their young children are moving into the suburban ring.

Third, there are racial differences in growth rates and migration patterns. Population growth has been very slow in the suburban counties closer to New York. These counties attracted whites who were in the early stages of family formation but lost about an equal number of teenagers and older whites, so their net migration rates for whites were near zero. The outer counties, Suffolk and Rockland, have grown rapidly and attracted whites of all ages. Black population growth has occurred in all counties, but the largest increases in numbers occurred within the suburban areas nearer New York City.

Long Island will be considered first in investigating which suburbs have growing black populations. Although there are few incorporated cities on Long Island, census tracts—that is, geographical areas containing about 5,000 people—were defined for the entire

TABLE 2. Population Composition and Migration Information for Places within New York Suburban Ring Enumerated since 1960*

	Population Data					Migration Data						
	Population (in Thousands)		Racial Composition (%)		Net Migrants	Migration Rates Per 100 Persons Present in 1960						
	1960	Later	1960	Later		Total	0–9	10–19	20–34	35–49	50+	
Nassau County, Area Enumerated in 1965†												
Whites	1,211	1,292	97.4	96.2	+ 9,246	+ 1	+ 6	−16	+ 19	0	− 6	
Nonwhites	32	50	2.6	3.8	+ 7,664	+ 20	+ 25	+ 38	+ 9	+ 11	− 7	
Entirety of Rockland County, Enumerated in 1966												
Whites	118	172	95.5	97.4	+ 35,102	+ 30	+ 62	+ 8	+ 70	+ 20	+ 5	
Nonwhites	6	8	4.5	4.6	+ 1,367	+ 24	+ 30	+ 29	+ 41	+ 10	+ 1	
Suffolk County, Area Enumerated in 1968‡												
Whites	147	296	97.2	97.4	+ 95,684	+ 65	+ 67	+ 67	+ 127	+ 42	+ 25	
Nonwhites	4	8	2.8	2.6	+ 2,201	+ 48	+ 59	+ 46	+ 88	+ 27	+ 9	
Suffolk County, Area Enumerated in 1967‡												
Whites	252	342	94.7	92.9	+ 48,955	+ 19	+ 22	+ 1	+ 50	+ 11	+ 9	
Nonwhites	14	24	5.3	7.1	+ 6,090	+ 42	+ 54	+ 47	+ 70	+ 21	+ 10	
Entirety of Westchester County, Enumerated in 1965												
Whites	743	775	92.4	91.4	+ 172	0	+ 4	− 5	+ 11	+ 3	− 8	
Nonwhites	61	73	7.6	8.6	+ 6,977	+ 11	+ 18	+ 27	+ 16	+ 4	− 5	
Mount Vernon City, Enumerated in 1965												
Whites	61	53	80.1	72.6	− 8,543	− 14	− 25	− 14	− 18	− 6	− 15	
Nonwhites	15	20	19.9	27.4	+ 3,244	+ 22	+ 17	+ 27	+ 33	+ 17	+ 2	

| | Population Data | | | | Migration Data | | | | | | | |
| | Population (in Thousands) | | Racial Composition (%) | | Net Migrants | Total | Migration Rates Per 100 Persons Present in 1960 | | | | |
	1960	Later	1960	Later			0–9	10–19	20–34	35–49	50+
New Rochelle City, Enumerated in 1965											
Whites	66	65	86.4	86.4	− 3,480	− 5	− 5	− 5	− 1	− 1	− 12
Nonwhites	10	10	13.6	13.6	− 698	− 7	−10	+ 8	− 8	−10	− 10
White Plains City, Enumerated in 1965											
Whites	44	43	88.1	86.4	− 1,953	− 4	− 4	− 9	+ 1	0	− 9
Nonwhites	6	7	11.9	13.6	+ 376	+ 6	− 3	+28	+13	+ 1	− 10
Yonkers City, Enumerated in 1965											
Whites	183	191	95.8	94.5	− 250	0	− 5	+ 4	+ 5	+ 4	− 6
Nonwhites	8	11	4.2	5.5	+ 1,732	+22	+21	+18	+30	+16	− 12
Balance of Westchester County, Enumerated in 1965											
Whites	389	423	94.8	94.4	+14,398	+ 4	+12	−11	+29	+ 4	− 6
Nonwhites	21	25	5.2	5.6	+ 2,323	+10	+32	+18	+11	0	− 8

Sources: U.S., Bureau of the Census 1962*d*, table P-1; 1966*d*, table 2; 1966*e*, table 2; 1966*f*, table 2; 1966*g*, table 2; 1967*e*, table 2; 1967*f*, table 2; 1968*h*, table 2; 1968*i*, table 2.

* Data in this table refer to nonwhites. The proportion of nonwhites who were Negroes ranged from 93 percent in Nassau County in 1960 to 99 percent in Mount Vernon in 1965. This suburban ring contains six large mental hospitals and one prison. To eliminate changes in the number of inmates, data for census tracts containing these institutions were not used in these computations. Migration estimates refer to age groups alive in 1960. No estimates were made of the migration of people who were born since 1960.

† Hempstead, North Hempstead, and Oyster Bay towns were enumerated in 1965. These towns contained 96 percent of the total Nassau County population in 1960.

‡ Brookhaven and Smithtown towns were enumerated in 1968. These towns contained 24 percent of Suffolk County's population in 1960. Babylon and Huntington towns were enumerated in 1967. They contained 40 percent of Suffolk County's population in 1960.

area in 1960, and special census tabulations have been presented for these same areas. Twenty-two census tracts on Long Island had increases of 250 or more blacks between 1960 and the special census date. They can be divided into two groups.

One group, located principally within the county near New York, gained Negroes and lost whites while the total population remained about constant. The homes in these census tracts were older than was typical for Long Island (U.S., Bureau of the Census 1962*d*, table H-1). Population replacement occurred in these suburbs. The second group of tracts, most of them within Suffolk County, gained large numbers of both Negroes and whites. Many new homes must have been built to accommodate these population increases, although it is impossible to determine from special census data the number of new homes or the race of their occupants. The Census of 1970 will reveal more about these suburban areas which gained both whites and Negroes and will indicate whether blacks have occupied new homes or have replaced whites in older homes.

Most of the recent growth of black population within Westchester County has taken place within four suburbs. Mount Vernon, New Rochelle, White Plains, and Yonkers are large and older suburbs. World War I interrupted their period of most rapid growth. While the number of blacks in each of these suburbs increased, their patterns of demographic change were quite different. These same patterns of change undoubtedly are occurring in central cities and suburbs throughout the nation.

Table 2 presents data for each of these suburbs.

Mount Vernon exemplifies a common pattern of change. This suburb lost whites and gained Negroes while its total population slowly declined. By 1965, one quarter of the population was black. The tracks of the New York, New Haven and Hartford Railroad bisect Mount Vernon. In 1960 the area south of the railroad was racially mixed, but since then whites have moved away and Negroes moved in. If the patterns of racial change observed in large cities in the 1940s and 1950s (Duncan and Duncan 1957, chap. 6; Taeuber and Taeuber 1965*a*, chap. 5) are duplicated in Mount Vernon, whites will continue to leave and the southern half will soon be a black ghetto of 30,000. North of the rail line there has been little population change. The area was 98 percent white in 1960 and 97 percent white in 1965 (U.S., Bureau of the Census 1962*d*, table P-1; 1966*d*, table 2).

Yonkers illustrates a second pattern of change. This suburb attracted relatively many blacks, but among whites in-migration has been matched by out-migration. An area of older homes near the center of Yonkers has lost white and gained black population. In the northern extremities of this suburb, new construction has taken place, and the increase in white population in one area offsets a loss in another area. If no vacant land for new construction remains, the color composition of this suburb will change as more blacks move into older residential areas.

Other types of change, reflecting urban renewal activities, occurred within New Rochelle and White Plains.

New Rochelle's population and racial composition remained stable after 1960. An urban renewal project was begun in New Rochelle which led to an out-migration of both blacks and whites sufficient in size to offset the effects of natural increase (U.S., Department of Housing and Urban Development 1967, p. 44).

Since 1960, the white population of White Plains decreased while its black population grew slowly. This suburb has many of the same characteristics as Mount Vernon and Yonkers, and one might expect its black population to increase rapidly. However, an urban renewal project was started which will raze the homes of 400 white and 400 Negro families (U.S., Department of Housing and Urban Development 1967, p. 44). This involves only about 3 percent of the white but 21 percent of the Negro population (U.S., Bureau of the Census 1961e, table 21). If the displaced black families relocate outside this suburb, the process of racial succession will be slowed.

Rockland County had a sparse population in 1960, so census tracts in this county included very extensive land areas. The black population in a number of tracts went up, but more detailed information is needed to ascertain which particular areas have attracted black residents.

The Characteristics of Suburban In-Migrants

Data from the special censuses conducted in the New York and Chicago suburban rings indicate there is a grow-ing black suburban population and suggest that young black families are moving into suburbia. However, the socioeconomic selectivity of these suburban in-migrants or the status of blacks in suburbia, compared to that of blacks in central cities, is not revealed by these special censuses.

Whites who live in suburbs, particularly suburbs near the large central cities, are typically better educated, hold more prestigious jobs, and have larger incomes than central city whites (Duncan and Riess 1956, pp. 127–133; Schnore 1965, p. 245; U.S., Bureau of the Census 1963a, tables 3, 6a and 8). One of the reasons for this is the selectivity of migrants who move into suburbs. The Taeubers investigated metropolitan migration patterns for whites for the period 1955–1960 and discovered that suburban rings attracted large streams of high-status migrants from their central cities. In addition, there was a sizable stream of intermetropolitan migrants, many of whom moved directly into suburbs when they came into a new area (Taeuber and Taeuber 1964a, pp. 718–729).

The most recent data showing the socioeconomic characteristics of suburban blacks pertain to 1960, and the latest period for which figures are available about the characteristics of migrants is 1955–1960. To describe the Negro suburban population, the ten metropolitan areas whose suburban rings had the largest black populations in 1960 were selected. Table 3 summarizes some of the information which was examined. It shows, first, the total number of nonwhites, age five and over, in each area in 1960 by their place of residence in 1955. This indicates the size of migration streams. The table also shows the proportion of men in each migration category who held white collar or craftsman jobs, which allows us to study the characteristics of migrants and compare them to those of nonmigrants.

Central city blacks rather than suburban blacks had the higher socioeconomic status. Both in the South and in the North, men in the cities held proportionately more of the prestigious jobs than did men in suburbia. Only in Newark was there a reversal of this pattern. A comparison of differences in educational attainment (data not shown) revealed a similar finding. In each of these areas, save Newark, the proportion of blacks who were high school graduates was higher in the central city than in the suburban ring.

This finding—that unlike whites suburban blacks in 1960 were often lower in social status than those in the city—is further substantiated by the figures below which refer to all SMSAs which had populations of 250,000 or more in 1960 (U.S., Bureau of the Census 1963a, tables 3, 6a, and 8).

The causes of this unusual pattern of city-suburban differentiation are difficult to specify. In the South, suburban rings still contain some blacks who are farmers, and this tends to lower average socioeconomic status in southern suburban rings. Within the North it was thought that city-suburban differences in age composition might account for this finding. However, after age differences were taken into account by a standardization procedure, suburban blacks still did not match central city blacks in social status. (For further discussion, see Schnore 1965, pp. 242–252.)

Metropolitan migration patterns among blacks are similar to those of whites, even though there are important differences in the volume of migration. In eight of the ten metropolitan areas for which data are presented in Table 3, the largest stream of blacks moving into suburban rings were people leaving the central city. In each area except Birmingham, these city-to-suburb movers were higher in socioeconomic status than either the blacks who remained in the central city or the other blacks who lived in the suburban ring.

The suburbs attracted two other, but typically smaller, streams of migrants. Among Negroes, as among whites, there was a stream of higher

	Whites (%)		Nonwhites (%)	
	Cities	Suburban Rings	Cities	Suburban Rings
Proportion of adults with some college education	18	21	10	9
Proportion of families with incomes of $10,000 or more	19	23	6	7
Proportion of employed men with white-collar jobs	31	30	14	11

TABLE 3. Distribution of Nonwhite Population in 1960 by Place of Residence in 1955 and Proportion of Employed Males Working at White Collar or Craftsmen Jobs*

	New York		Philadelphia		Newark		Birmingham		Chicago	
	N (thousands)	White Collar, Crafts (%)	N (thousands)	White Collar, Crafts (%)	N (thousands)	White Collar, Crafts (%)	N (thousands)	White Collar, Crafts (%)	N (thousands)	White Collar, Crafts (%)
Central city residents:*										
Total†	1,000	34	464	30	118	21	117	19	707	27
Residents, both 1955 and 1960	875	35	420	31	94	22	108	20	587	30
In-migrants from the suburban ring	5	35	4	44	4	23	3	17	6	32
In-migrants from other SMSAs	30	43	12	38	6	26	2	23	24	26
In-migrants from nonmetropolitan areas	29	29	11	21	8	17	4	15	31	22
Suburban ring residents:*										
Total	129	30	126	26	77	30	73	14	71	27
Residents, both 1955 and 1960	86	29	104	25	61	30	64	14	48	25
In-migrants from the central city	14	42	7	41	4	43	5	18	9	40
In-migrants from other SMSAs	8	33	6	33	5	45	1	26	4	37
In-migrants from nonmetropolitan areas	10	29	4	20	2	11	2	11	5	20

TABLE 3. (Continued)

	Saint Louis		Detroit		Washington		Miami		Pittsburgh	
	N (thousands)	White Collar, Crafts (%)	N (thousands)	White Collar, Crafts (%)	N (thousands)	White Collar, Crafts (%)	N (thousands)	White Collar, Crafts (%)	N (thousands)	White Collar, Crafts (%)
Central city residents:										
Total	183	23	418	26	362	36	56	16	89	23
Residents, both 1955 and 1960	163	24	375	26	304	37	42	17	81	24
In-migrants from the suburban ring	2	24	10	27	5	36	1	19	2	23
In-migrants from other SMSAs	3	35	11	41	15	47	3	18	2	34
In-migrants from nonmetropolitan areas	6	21	9	22	17	27	6	14	2	28
Suburban ring residents:										
Total	69	20	68	24	68	29	61	16	54	20
Residents, both 1955 and 1960	61	20	52	23	50	27	40	16	48	20
In-migrants from the central city ..	3	30	8	28	5	47	10	21	2	32
In-migrants from other SMSAs	2	30	3	38	3	48	3	25	2	47
In-migrants from nonmetropolitan areas	2	14	2	30	4	17	5	14	1	26

Source: U.S., Bureau of the Census 1963b, table 4.

* These figures refer to nonwhites. In each of the cities and suburban rings Negroes comprised between 93 and 99 percent of the nonwhite population.

† The total population exceeds the sum of the residents in the listed areas because it includes people who were abroad in 1955 and people who did not report their 1955 place of residence.

status intermetropolitan migrants who moved directly into the suburban ring between 1955 and 1960. (For further description of these higher status intermetropolitan nonwhite migrants, see Taeuber and Taeuber 1965b, pp. 429–441.) There was also a stream of young migrants from nonmetropolitan areas who were low in socioeconomic status. Many of these migrants may have left southern rural areas or small towns for the economic opportunities of large metropolitan areas.

Table 3 shows these central cities attracted two streams of migrants which were of approximately equal size. One stream came from other metropolitan areas and was high in socioeconomic status. The second stream came from nonmetropolitan areas, and few of the men held white collar or craftsmen jobs. In addition, the central cities attracted migrants from suburbia, and these ring-to-city movers were generally high in socioeconomic status. This is similar to the Taeubers's finding that, between 1955 and 1960, cities and their suburbs exchanged relatively high-status white population (Taeuber and Taeuber 1964a). Unlike the situation for whites, however, among Negroes the number of city-to-ring movers did not always greatly exceed the number of ring-to-city movers. In some areas, New York and Miami, for instance, the number moving from the city to the ring exceeded the number moving in the other direction, but in other areas, such as Detroit, Michigan, ring-to-city movers were more numerous.

The data presented in this paper clearly indicate that between 1955 and 1960 suburban rings attracted higher status black residents from their central cities and also attracted a sizable share of the higher status intermetropolitan migrants. The growth of the Negro suburban population has increased since 1960, and the migrants to suburbia during this decade are probably of higher status as were the migrants during the last decade. This migration may already be of sufficient size to establish a pattern of city-suburban socioeconomic differences among blacks, similar to that observed among whites. For instance, in 1959 median family income among blacks in the suburban rings was far below that of blacks in central cities, but by 1967 it was higher in the suburban rings (U.S., Bureau of the Census 1969a, p. 37). Among young adult blacks, educational attainment levels in 1960 were lower in the suburban rings than in the cities, but by 1968 this was reversed, probably reflecting the migration to the suburbs of well-educated young Negroes (U.S., Bureau of the Census 1969a, p. 23). It is likely that the Census of 1970 will find that suburban blacks are higher in socioeconomic status than those in central cities.

The Process of Suburbanization

The demographic data indicate that suburban rings are attracting black migrants and that, while all economic levels are represented, the migrants to suburbia tend to be higher in socioeconomic status. It appears that three types of suburban areas have gained black population. First, particularly in the North, there are older, densely settled suburbs often containing or near employment centers. Such places as Maywood, Yonkers, and East Cleveland, Ohio, have experienced population replacement—that is, decreases in white population but growth of black —and in the future more suburbs will undergo similar change. Studies of residential change have found that the first Negroes to move into a white neighborhood are those who are financially able to purchase better housing than that which is generally available to blacks (Taeuber and Taeuber 1965a, pp. 154–166; Duncan and Duncan 1957, pp. 215–236). Such older suburbs contain housing units which are better than those blacks can occupy in the ghettoes. On the other hand, because of the age of the homes and the small lots on which they were built, homes in these suburbs may not appeal to whites who move out from the central city. The causes of racial change in any particular older suburb may be idiosyncratic, but proximity to employment is probably an important factor.

The second type of area with growing black population is the new suburban development. Some are built exclusively for Negroes. Richmond Heights, Florida, which was described previously, is one example; in recent years Hollydale has been built near Cincinnati (Rose 1965, p. 380), and new homes have gone up in Inkster, a Detroit suburb with a large black population (U.S., Bureau of the Census 1966c, table B-6). In addition, it is possible that a small number of blacks are moving into new and integrated suburban developments.

A third type of area with a growing Negro population is to be found in the suburban rings of many large cities. Areas lacking adequate sewer and water facilities, containing dilapidated homes of low value, and having exclusively black populations could be located in 1960 in suburban areas. They have grown partly because of natural increase, partly because some public housing has been erected (between 1959 and 1966, seventy-five public housing units were authorized in Robbins, 216 in East Chicago Heights, and 150 in Kinloch [U.S., Bureau of the Census 1966c, table B-7; 1968d, table 8]), and partly because low-income blacks may find inexpensive housing close to their jobs in these suburbs.

Expansion of the black suburban population will depend upon many factors; three of the most important are discussed here. First is the rate at which the economic status of blacks improves. In recent years the income of Negroes has gone up much faster than have prices. For instance, median family income of blacks increased about 6 percent each year from 1960 to 1967 while the cost of living went up by less than 2 percent annually (U.S., Bureau of the Census 1967d, table G; 1968e, table 3; 1968g, table 505). Negroes now have more money to spend for shelter and consumer goods. The migration of blacks to suburbia reflects such economic gains, and if incomes continue to go up more rapidly than the cost of living, more blacks will be able to afford better housing.

The second factor is the rate at which new housing is constructed and the housing policies which will be favored by the federal government. At present, a little over 1.5 million housing units are built annually (U.S., Bureau of the Census 1969f, table 1). The President's Committee on Urban Housing estimated that 2.7 million new housing units were needed each year to provide for the growing population and to replace substandard housing (U.S., President's Committee on Urban Housing 1967, p. 7). The Kerner Commission Report recommended numerous programs to encourage building new homes for low- and moderate-income families outside central city ghettoes (U.S., National Advisory Commission on Civil Disorders 1968, pp. 467–482). If there is a great volume of new construction, and if clusters of low and moderately priced homes are spread throughout suburbia and are open to Negro occupancy, there may be a rise in the black suburban population.

The third factor is the rapidity with which suburban housing becomes available to blacks. Since 1960 the incomes of Negroes have increased more rapidly than those of whites (U.S., Bureau of the Census 1968f, p. 6). If this continues, more Negroes will be able to compete with whites for suburban housing. Perhaps when the federal open occupancy law becomes fully effective, discrimination will be reduced, and more suburbs will include blacks in their population. This is an optimistic view. Racial policies in the new suburb of Levittown, New Jersey, were described by Gans (1967, pp. 22, 371–378). Despite a state open occupancy law, the developers announced plans to sell only to whites and turned away black customers. Negroes were eventually accepted after a suit proceeded through the courts for two years. Even after this, special policies were instituted to screen Negro buyers and place them in isolated areas. If this is duplicated in other suburbs, blacks who desire to move into the suburbs will still face immense difficulties regardless of their financial means.

The Consequences of Suburbanization

The suburbanization of blacks does not herald a basic change in the patterns of racial segregation within metropolitan areas. Cities and their suburban rings are becoming more dissimilar in racial composition, and the out-migration of some blacks from the city will not alter this process. It will do no more than slow the growth of the black population of some cities while adding still greater diversity to the already heterogeneous population of suburbia.

It does indicate that Negroes, similar to European ethnic groups, are becoming more decentralized throughout the metropolitan area after they have been in the city for some time and improved their economic status (Cressey 1938, pp. 59–69; Taeuber and Taeuber 1966, pp. 130–136; Schnore 1965, pp. 126–133). However, improvements in economic status brought about not only the residential decentralization of European immigrant groups but also reductions in their residential segregation (Lieberson 1963, chaps. 3 and 4). Negroes have deviated widely from this pattern for, despite economic gains and some decentralization of predominately black residential areas, the residential segregation of Negroes has persisted (Taeuber and Taeuber 1964b, pp. 374–382). Even during the prosperous period from the end of World War II to the present, there is no evidence that the residential segregation of blacks decreased (Taeuber and Taeuber 1965a, chap. 3; Clemence 1967, pp. 562–568; Farley and Taeuber 1968, p. 983). It is possible that the suburbanization of blacks will alter this pattern, and a future census may reveal integrated suburban neighborhoods. In the meantime, we can be certain that the residential segregation patterns of central cities are reappearing within the suburbs.

Footnotes

1.   This is a revised version of a paper which was delivered at the Annual Meetings of the Population Association of America, Atlantic City, New Jersey, April 11, 1969. Beverly Duncan, James Palmore, and Karl Taeuber provided helpful comments and suggestions.

References

Clemence, Theodore G. 1967. "Residential Segregation in the Mid-Sixties." *Demography* 4:562–568.

Cressey, Paul Frederick. 1938. "Population Succession in Chicago: 1898–1930." *American Journal of Sociology* 44 (July):59–69.

Dobriner, William. 1963. *Class in Suburbia*. Englewood Cliffs, N.J.: Prentice-Hall.

Douglas, Harlan Paul. 1925. *The Suburban Trend*. New York: Century.

Duncan, Otis Dudley, and Beverly Duncan. 1957. *The Negro Population of Chicago*. Chicago: University of Chicago Press.

Duncan, Otis Dudley, and Albert J. Reiss, Jr. 1956. *Social Characteristics of Urban and Rural Communities, 1950*. New York: Wiley.

Farley, Reynolds. 1968. "The Urbanization of Negroes in the United States." *Journal of Social History* 2 (Spring):241–258.

Farley, Reynolds, and Karl E. Taeuber. 1968. "Population Trends and Residential Segregation Since 1960." *Science* 156 (March 1): 953–956.

Fava, Sylvia. 1956. "Suburbanization as a Way of Life." *American Sociological Review* 21 (February):34–43.

Gans, Herbert J. 1967. *The Levittowners*. New York: Pantheon.

Harris, Chauncy D. 1943. "Suburbs." *American Journal of Sociology* 47 (May):1–13.

Heberle, Rudolph. 1948. "Social Consequences of the Industrialization of Southern Cities." *Social Forces* 27 (October):29–37.

Hodge, Patricia Leavy, and Philip M. Hauser. 1968. *The Challenge of America's Metropolitan Population Outlook, 1960–1985*. New York: Praeger.

Kitagawa, Evelyn M., and Karl E. Taeuber. 1963. *Local Community Fact Book, Chicago Metropolitan Area: 1960*. Chicago: Chicago Community Inventory.

Kramer, John, and Ingo Walter. 1967. "An Analysis of the Social Structure of an All Negro City." Mimeographed. Saint Louis: University of Missouri.

Lieberson, Stanley. 1962. "Suburbs and Ethnic Residential Patterns." *American*

Journal of Sociology 67 (May):673–681.

———. 1963. *Ethnic Patterns in American Cities.* New York: Free Press.

Martin, Walter. 1956. "The Structuring of Social Relationships Engendered by Suburban Residence." *American Sociological Review* 21 (August):446–453.

Riesman, David. 1957. "The Suburban Dislocation." *Annals of the American Academy of Political and Social Science* 312 (November): 123–147.

Rose, Harold M. 1965. "The All Negro Town: Its Evolution and Function." *Geographical Review* 55 (July):362–381.

Schnore, Leo. 1957. "Satellites and Suburbs." *Social Forces* 36 (December): 121–127.

———. 1965. *The Urban Scene.* New York: Free Press.

Taeuber, Karl E., and Alma F. Taeuber. 1964a. "White Migration and Socio-Economic Differences between Cities and Suburbs." *American Sociological Review* 29 (October):718–729.

———. 1964b. "The Negro as an Immigrant Group: Recent Trends in Racial and Ethnic Segregation in Chicago." *American Journal of Sociology* 69 (January):374–382.

———. 1965a. *Negroes in Cities.* Chicago: Aldine.

———. 1965b. "The Changing Character of Negro Migration." *American Journal of Sociology* 70 (January):429–441.

———. 1966. "The Negro Population in the United States." In *The American Negro Reference Book*, edited by John P. Davis. Englewood Cliffs, N.J.: Prentice-Hall.

U.S., Bureau of the Census. 1961a. *Census of Population: 1960.* PC(1)-27B.

———. 1961b. *Census of Population: 1960,* PC(1)-15B.

———. 1961c. *Census of Population: 1960,* PC(1)-20B.

———. 1961d. *Census of Population: 1960,* PC(1)-15A.

———. 1961e. *Census of Population: 1960,* PC(1)-34B.

———. 1961f. *Census of Housing: 1960,* HC(1)-20.

———. 1961g. *Census of Population: 1960,* PC(1)-37B.

———. 1962a. *Census of Housing: 1960,* HC(1)-11.

———. 1962b. *Census of Housing: 1960,* HC(1)-15.

———. 1962c. *Censuses of Population and Housing: 1960,* PHC(1)-26.

———. 1962d. *Censuses of Population and Housing: 1960,* PHC(1)-104, pt. 2.

———. 1963a. *Census of Population: 1960,* PC(3)-1D.

———. 1963b. *Census of Population: 1960,* PC(2)-2C.

———. 1965. "Summary of Special Censuses Conducted by the Bureau of the Census between Jan. 1 and Dec. 31, 1964." *Current Population Reports,* ser. P-28, no. 1388.

———. 1966a. "Summary of Special Censuses Conducted by the Bureau of the Census between Jan. 1 and Dec. 31, 1965." *Current Population Reports,* Ser. P-28, no. 1420.

———. 1966b. *Census of Manufacturers: 1960,* MC63(3)-14.

———. 1966c. *Housing Construction Statistics: 1889–1964.*

———. 1966d. "Special Census of Westchester County, New York: April 6, 1965." *Current Population Reports,* ser. P-28, no. 1394.

———. 1966e. "Special Census of Oyster Bay Town, New York: April 26, 1965." *Current Population Reports,* ser. P-28, no. 1395.

————. 1966f. "Special Census of Hempstead Town, New York: March 15, 1965." *Current Population Reports*, ser. P-28, no. 1396.

————. 1966g. "Special Census of Rockland County, New York: April 28, 1966." *Current Population Reports*, ser. P-28, no. 1428.

————. 1967a. "Social and Economic Conditions of Negroes in the United States." *Current Population Reports*, ser. P-23, no. 24.

————. 1967b. "Population of the United States by Metropolitan and Non-Metropolitan Residence: April 1966 and 1960." *Current Population Reports*, ser. P-20, no. 167.

————. 1967c. "Summary of Special Censuses Conducted by the Bureau of the Census between January 1 and December 31, 1966." *Current Population Reports*, ser. P-28, no. 1447.

————. 1967d. "Income in 1966 of Families and Persons in the United States." *Current Population Reports*, ser. P-60, no. 53.

————. 1967e. "Special Census of Huntington Town, New York: May 13, 1967." *Current Population Reports*, ser. P-28, no. 1454.

————. 1967f. "Special Census of Babylon Town, New York: May 6, 1967." *Current Population Reports*, ser. P-28, no. 1456.

————. 1968a. "Summary of Special Censuses Conducted by the Bureau of the Census between January 1 and December 31, 1967." *Current Population Reports*, ser. P-28, no. 1466.

————. 1968b. "Summary of Special Censuses Conducted by the Bureau of the Census between January 1 and March 31, 1968." *Current Population Reports*, ser. P-28, no. 1468.

————. 1968c. "Summary of Special Censuses Conducted by the Bureau of the Census between April 1 and June 30, 1968." *Current Population Reports*, ser. P-28, no. 1474.

————. 1968d. "Housing Authorized by Building Permits and Public Contracts: 1967." *Construction Reports*, C40/C42-67-13.

————. 1968e. "Family Income Advances, Poverty Reduced in 1967." *Current Population Reports*, ser. P-60, no. 55.

————. 1968f. "Recent Trends in Social and Economic Conditions of Negroes in the United States." *Current Population Reports*, ser. P-23, no. 26.

————. 1968g. *Statistical Abstract of the United States: 1968.*

————. 1968h. "Special Census of Brookhaven Town, New York: May 6, 1968." *Current Population Reports*, ser. P-38, no. 1471.

————. 1968i. "Special Census of Smithtown, New York: May 6, 1968." *Current Population Reports*, ser. P-28, no. 1473.

————. 1969a. "Trends in Social and Economic Conditions in Metropolitan Areas." *Current Population Reports*, ser. P-23, no. 27.

————. 1969b. "Summary of Special Censuses Conducted by the Bureau of the Census between July 1 and September 30, 1968." *Current Population Reports*, ser. P-28, no. 1480.

————. 1969c. "Summary of Special Censuses Conducted by the Bureau of the Census between October 1 and December 31, 1968." *Current Population Reports*, ser. P-28, no. 1484.

————. 1969d. "Estimates of the Population of the United States and Components of Change: 1940 to 1969." *Current Population Reports*, ser. P-25, no. 418.

————. 1969e. "Farm Population of the

United States: 1967." *Current Population Reports,* ser. P-27, no. 39.

————. 1969*f.* "Housing Authorized by Building Permits and Public Contracts." *Construction Reports,* C42-69-4.

U.S., Department of Housing and Urban Development. 1967. *Urban Renewal Project Characteristics: June 30, 1966.*

U.S., National Advisory Commission on Civil Disorders. 1968. *Report of the National Advisory Commission on Civil Disorders.*

U.S., President's Committee on Urban Housing. 1967. *The Report of the President's Committee on Urban Housing: Technical Studies,* vol. 1.

Wade, Richard C. 1964. *Slavery in Cities.* New York: Oxford University Press.

Whyte, William. 1957. *The Organization Man.* Garden City, N.Y.: Doubleday.

twelve ◆ ◆ ◆ ◆ ◆ ◆ ◆ ◆ ◆ ◆ ◆ ◆ ◆ ◆ ◆

◆ JAMES O. WHEELER
◆ STANLEY D. BRUNN

Negro Migration into Rural Southwestern Michigan

One of the dominant migration streams of the twentieth century in the United States is the flood of rural Negroes from the South to metropolitan areas in the North and, to a smaller extent, in the West.[1] But despite the magnitude of the urbanward flow, there has been almost no Negro migration to rural areas of the North. The lack of rural settlement by Negroes is attributable partly to the decreasing number of persons engaged in agriculture, especially small-scale operators, to the growing expense of entering farming, and to differences in agricultural practices.[2] In addition, industrial employment is limited in most rural areas, which have had a labor surplus since the rise of urbanization; and even when employment opportunities ex-

isted, the dominance of the whites in the rural North has kept Negroes from settling there.[3]

Recent Negro migration into rural southwestern Michigan suggests the beginning of a trend that may become increasingly common in the North. The general pattern of Negro migration from rural South to urban North seems to be taking on an added dimension. A segment of the Negro population, which is to a large extent blocked from city to suburbs migration, is skipping the suburban stage.[4] Instead, some Negroes are moving into small, formerly agricultural, communities and are buying homes from the whites who are leaving. Apparently only the difficulty of gaining a foothold and finding employment is preventing an even greater

◆ SOURCE. Reprinted by permission from the *Geographical Review*, Vol. 58, 1968. pp. 214–230, copyrighted by the American Geographical Society of New York.

number of Negroes from settling in small rural villages and towns. Although some retired Negroes have migrated into rural southwestern Michigan, the majority there consists of Negro families who are attempting to escape the problems of ghetto living and enjoy the attractions of a comparatively quiet and peaceful rural community.

The migration patterns and distribution of the American Negro have been examined by geographers as well as by sociologists, demographers, and others.[5] A study by Hartshorne in 1938 examined the proportional distribution of Negroes in the United States.[6] His map (1930) revealed that no county in the North Central States had more than 10 percent Negro population. Later, Calef and Nelson, using 1940 and 1950 census data, published several maps of Negro population distribution.[7] Commenting on the distribution of rural Negroes, they noted that "Western Michigan . . . shows the unusual pattern of a widely scattered rural Negro population in a northern state."[8] More recently, Hart has traced the historical changes in Negro population.[9] The Negro concentration in rural southwestern Michigan appears on several of his maps, and other maps reveal the recency of the in-migration. In another study Hart examined an area in Lake County, Michigan, used by Northern Negroes as a rural retreat, a retirement and summer-resort center.[10] Most recently, Rose, in describing the development of several all-Negro towns in the United States, was able to enumerate only eight such towns of more than 1000 population in the North, all

of which are near a metropolitan area.[11]

Purpose and Method

The present study examines the conditions and characteristics underlying the spatial distribution of Negroes in southwestern Michigan. Specifically, it traces the migration of Negroes into the area, analyzes their demographic composition, and compares their social and economic ties with those of the white population. Such questions as the following are explored: What has been the basis for the recent migration? Where are the migrants from? How do their shopping and work trips compare with those of whites living in the same community?

In addition to basic census data, a sample of four communities is used (Fig. 1): Parkville (population, 100), Vandalia (357), Covert (600), and Dowagiac (7208).[12] These communities were selected because of differences in population size, observed Negro concentrations, and scattered location. Household interviews were conducted with both whites and Negroes during the summer and fall of 1966. Interviews were attempted at each residence in all the communities except Dowagiac, where the Negroes are segregated in the southwestern part. The sample of white interviews obtained in Dowagiac cannot be considered representative, since the houses were in or near the Negro section of the town. More than 350 interviews were obtained, of which 228 were with Negroes. Nearly

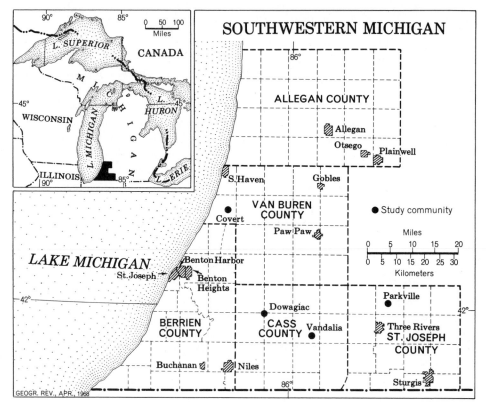

FIGURE 1. Location map, showing study communities.

200 interviews were conducted in Dowagiac, about 70 each in Vandalia and Covert, and 26 in Parkville.

Northward Movement of Negroes

The Negro population in the United States in 1960 was about nineteen million, or about 10.5 percent of the total population. Some 60 percent of the Negroes lived in the South, 40 percent in the North and West. If the rapid out-migration to northern and western states continues, these percentages may be reversed by 1980 or 1990, and by 2000 most large cities may have a Negro majority.[13] In 1910 about 27 percent of the Negro population was considered urban; by 1960 the same percentage was classified as rural. The spatial distribution of Negroes in the South today is largely a result of natural increase, whereas the patterns in the North and West are attributable primarily to in-migration.

Negro migration from the South did not really accelerate until the 1920's. It slowed somewhat during the depression of the 1930's, but since then it has been increasing rapidly. In Michigan

TABLE 1. Negroes in North Central States Leading in Negro Population, 1910–1960

State	1910	1920	1930	1940	1950	1960	% Negro 1960
Illinois	109,049	182,274	328,972	387,446	645,980	1,037,470	10.3
Michigan	17,115	60,082	169,453	208,345	442,296	717,581	9.2
Ohio	111,452	186,187	309,304	339,461	513,072	786,097	8.1
Indiana	60,320	80,810	111,982	121,916	174,168	269,275	5.8

Source: United States Census of Population: 1960, Vol. 1, Parts 15, 16, 24, and 37 (U. S. Bureau of the Census, Washington, D. C., 1963).

the number of Negroes jumped from 17,000 in 1910 to 717,581 in 1960 (Table 1). The increments in other North Central States, though smaller, are also remarkable.

The leading North Central States in Negro population are Illinois, Ohio, Michigan, and Indiana, but there is considerable variation among and within these states. The areal pattern of Negro population by nonmetropolitan counties reveals particularly strong concentrations in southwestern Michigan, in the area south of Chicago, in southern Illinois, and in southern Ohio (Fig. 2). The concentration in southern Illinois represents a northward extension of Southern Negro populations.[14] Concentrations similar to those in southwestern Michigan and Kankakee County, Illinois, are found around the suburban areas of Cleveland and Detroit. In Wisconsin, Minnesota, and

Iowa no nonmetropolitan county has more than 1 percent of its population classed as Negro.[15]

Before the mass out-migration, most of the Negroes that left the South had been engaged in agriculture; few lived, or were employed, in urban areas. The switch from the plight of a poor rural tenant in the South to the anticipated "better life" of an urban-industrial laborer in the North has meant a marked change during the past half century in the residence and occupation patterns of the American Negro. The Northern urban Negro, as well as the Southern Negro (who is rapidly becoming urbanized in the South also), has lost much of the rural identity of his forefathers. Most of the Negroes in Illinois, Michigan, Ohio, and Indiana are classed as urban residents and live in the central city or in Negro settlements on its periphery[16] (Table 2).

TABLE 2. Negro Population by Rural–Urban Classes, 1960

State	Urban	Rural: Places of 1000 to 2500	Other Rural	% Rural
Illinois	1,013,199	3,668	20,603	2.3
Michigan	686,591	1,879	29,111	4.3
Ohio	751,479	2,578	32,040	4.4
Indiana	260,864	727	7,684	3.1

Source: See footnote to Table 1.

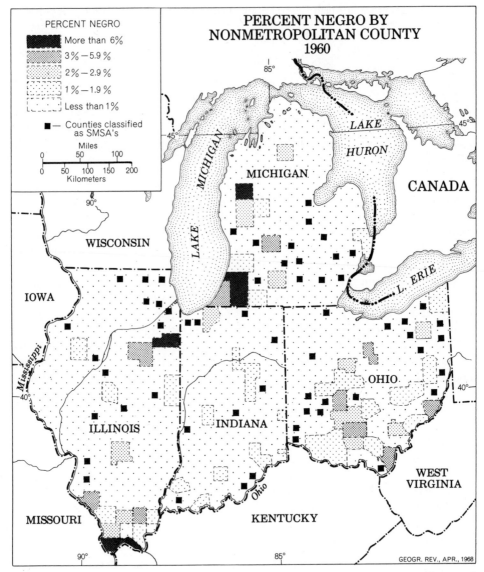

PERCENT NEGRO BY
NONMETROPOLITAN COUNTY
1960

PERCENT NEGRO
More than 6%
3% – 5.9%
2% – 2.9%
1% – 1.9%
Less than 1%
■ — Counties classified
as SMSA's

Miles
0   50   100
0   50 100 150 200
Kilometers

GEOGR. REV., APR., 1968

FIGURE 2.

Few Negroes have succeeded in becoming integrated into the suburbs, owing to the social, economic, and legal barriers established by the middle-class white community.[17]

Negroes in Southwestern Michigan

Southwestern Michigan has a tradition of Negro settlement dating from the Underground Railroad in the early 1840's. One line, operated by early Quaker settlers, moved runaway slaves out of Kentucky into Cass County, Michigan. Another, called the Illinois Line, helped slaves escape into Michigan from as far away as Mississippi. Initially they simply passed through Cass County on their way to Canada. But

as time passed, the slaves enjoyed greater immunity from the dangers of pursuit and recapture, and many of them finding occupation . . . remained here with friends, thinking that they would be nearly as safe as in Canada. Some of the fugitives who had settled down in Cass County owned small tracts of ground, for which they were about equally indebted to their own industry, and the generosity of their white friends.

By 1847 there were about fifty runaway slaves residing in Penn and Calvin Townships in Cass County.[18] The initial Negro settlement, about five miles south of Vandalia in and around the hamlet of Calvin Center, now consists of only a dozen houses.[19] This settlement formed the nucleus of a Negro colony that has survived to the present.

The wave of Southern Negroes into the urban-industrial market of the North at the beginning of the century brought some Negroes into Benton Harbor (population, 19,136) and South Haven (6149). As the influx continued, especially after World War II, Negro settlement focused on the village of Covert and the nearby rural areas, both in Van Buren County and in adjacent townships of Allegan County (Fig. 4). Covert itself, an unincorporated settlement eight miles south of South Haven, is presently 80 percent Negro and has some of the characteristics of a rural slum. Although the commercial businesses appear relatively viable (Fig. 5), in most of the residential areas the houses are run-down and the streets unpaved.

Negro settlement also increased gradually in Cass County before World War II, and after the war a noticeable Negro population appeared in Vandalia, in Dowagiac, and, to a smaller extent, in Cassopolis. The community with the largest proportion of Negroes is Vandalia, shown by the interviews to be 75 percent Negro. Two groups of Negroes reside here: those who have lived in and around Vandalia for most of their lives; and those who have recently migrated from larger places. Despite the increasing Negro population in Vandalia, the total population —about 360—has not changed much in the past generation. The rather constant population total and the lack of recently constructed houses indicate that the Negro influx has been roughly proportionate to the white exodus.

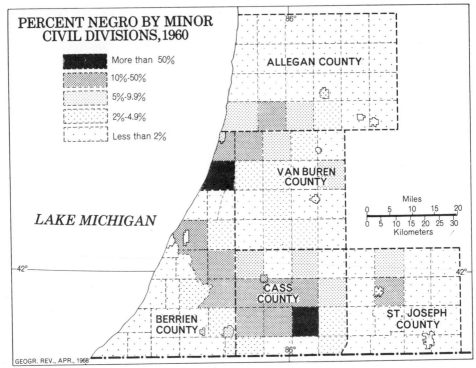

PERCENT NEGRO BY MINOR
CIVIL DIVISIONS, 1960

More than 50%

10%-50%

5%-9.9%

2%-4.9%

Less than 2%

ALLEGAN COUNTY

VAN BUREN
COUNTY

LAKE MICHIGAN

Miles
0   5   10   15   20
0 5 10 15 20 25 30
Kilometers

CASS
COUNTY

BERRIEN
COUNTY

ST. JOSEPH
COUNTY

GEOGR. REV., APR., 1968

FIGURE 3.

FIGURE 4. Cement-block home of rural
Negro family in Lee Township, Allegan
County.

FIGURE 5. Negro-owned grocery in
Covert, featuring chicken necks, eggs,
and watermelons.

FIGURE 6. One of the better-kept Negro houses in Vandalia.

FIGURE 7. A group of abandoned stores in Vandalia.

In contrast with Covert, most of the houses in Vandalia are reasonably sound (Fig. 6), though there are some abandoned, dilapidated structures. The number of commercial establishments has decreased noticeably during the past several years. The main street (Highway 60) and adjacent side streets show abandoned businesses, such as service stations, groceries, restaurants, and apparel shops, that were once the backbone of this agricultural trade center (Fig. 7). About a mile south of Vandalia, a Negro resort community has developed around Paradise Lake, which brings the area into greater contact with the Chicago Negroes who frequent it.

A dispersed Negro settlement developed in a rural area a mile north of Parkville immediately before World War II. A Chicago land company bought farmland cheaply, platted it into five- to twenty-acre plots, and sold it to Negroes.[20] Most of the houses, hastily constructed at the time, are abandoned. A growing Negro minority is now found in Three Rivers, and also in the hamlet of Parkville, where interviews indicated that nearly 40 percent of the residents are Negro.

More than a dozen townships in a largely rural five-county area of southwestern Michigan now have a Negro population greater than 10 percent. Two townships, Calvin and Covert, have 66 and 52 percent respectively. A total of twenty-eight townships and other minor civil divisions have more than 5 percent Negro. The largest absolute concentrations are in Benton Township and the cities of Benton Harbor, Niles, and Dowagiac. Several formerly all-white hamlets and villages have acquired Negro families in the last few years, an indication of a continuing spread of Negro settlement in rural southwestern Michigan. No other part of Michigan outside the metropolitan areas has so large a Negro component except Lake County, studied by Hart,[21] and adjoining Newaygo County.

Migration Patterns

The great majority of Negro adults living in the rural communities of southwestern Michigan were born and grew up in the South; only about 20 percent were raised in southwestern Michigan. In the four communities examined, the proportion of Negro adults raised in the South ranges from one-half (Vandalia) to two-thirds (Dowagiac). One-third of the Negroes raised in the South are from Mississippi, and nearly one-fifth are from Tennessee. Others came largely from Alabama, Arkansas, Missouri, and Georgia. These migration patterns are somewhat similar to those of other Northern Negroes[22] in the North Central States.[23] Of the communities studied, Vandalia has the highest percentage (30) of adult Negroes who were raised in southwestern Michigan, and Covert has the lowest (10). The percentages decrease with distance from the area of initial Negro settlement in Cass County.

Only about 6 percent of the Negro families have moved into southwestern Michigan directly from the South. Rather, they were attracted at first to the larger northern cities, principally Chicago; but becoming dissatisfied with ghetto living, especially when raising a family, they turned to the small communities near Chicago where housing opportunities existed. About half of the Negro families moved directly from Chicago into one of the four Michigan communities studied. Others moved into one of these villages from the southwestern Michigan community in which they had initially settled. There is also a considerable amount of intra-community migration.

Negro migration into southwestern

Michigan from Chicago and other urban centers of the Middle West began primarily after World War II and has continued at a slowly increasing rate. The flow of migrants is restricted by the availability of existing housing, since the Negroes move into houses that were formerly (and in some cases are still) owned by whites. One measure of the recency of migration is the average number of years Negro families have lived in their present houses. In the communities examined, the mean is less for Negroes than for whites—just over ten years in Dowagiac and eight years in Covert. In Vandalia some 37 percent of the Negroes have lived there for more than ten years, as compared with more than 50 percent of the whites; 46 percent of the Negroes have lived there for five years or less, as compared with about 25 percent of the whites. For Covert and Dowagiac the percentages are about the same, for both Negroes and whites. In Vandalia 9 percent, and in Dowagiac 7 percent, of the Negro families have occupied the same houses for thirty years or more, but no Negro family in Covert has lived in its present house as long as that. Thus in these communities there has been a relatively long tradition of a Negro minority, which recently has been considerably enlarged.

More whites than Negroes own their houses, a larger number of Negroes than of whites are buying houses, and a slightly higher percentage of whites than of Negroes are renting. Whites who own their houses have generally lived in the community for some time and have not left simply because they do own their property, have lived most of their lives there, and either are planning to retire or have already done so. A much smaller number of whites are renters, many of whom would like to move elsewhere. The vacant and abandoned houses, especially in Vandalia, are largely the former homes of whites. Some whites cannot afford even the moderate cost of houses in these small communities. About one-third of the Negro families are buying, versus less than a fifth of the whites, a reflection of the shorter period of residence of the Negroes and the realization of many whites of the lack of any future for the community.

The same contrasts are noticeable in length of time in the present job. Whites have worked in their present jobs for an average of about nine years, as compared with six years for Negroes. The lower mean for Negroes is attributable to their more recent arrival in the communities, to their relatively lower job skills and the accompanying instability of employment, and to the fact that only the most entrenched whites have remained in Vandalia and Covert as the Negroes have become a more dominant segment of the population.

Among the reasons given by Negroes for moving to the small communities of southwestern Michigan were greater personal freedom, dislike of large cities, an improved environment for raising a family, a quiet and peaceful "country life," nearness to friends and relatives, cheaper housing, less crowded schools, larger house and yard, advantages for retirement, and the opportunities for fishing and gardening. Disadvantages mentioned were the great distance to work and the lack of jobs, public transit, and city services, of recreational facilities, and of suitable activities for teen-agers.

Many whites perceived a different set of problems associated with living in the small communities. Some did not like the changing character of the town, the noise and the fast automobiles, the uncooperative community attitude of certain residents, the "ghost town" environment, and, as some frankly stated, "the colored people." Other whites, however, spoke of the friendliness of the town and listed complaints similar to those of the Negroes.

The question whether the community is growing, declining, or stable also brought contrasting replies from Negroes and whites (Table 3). About three-quarters of the Negroes interviewed felt that their community was growing; the proportion of whites, however, was much smaller—as low as 6 percent in Vandalia. Few Negroes viewed their community as declining, but in Vandalia, where there is a larger proportion of "established" Negro families, the response exceeded 20 percent. In addition to the greater tendency for whites to view the community as declining, a higher percentage of whites than of Negroes seemed uncertain about their community's future, perceiving no recent trend of growth or decline.

Most Negroes reported having heard about housing availability in the community through friends and relatives. The great majority of Negro households have relatives living in the same community or nearby. Moreover,

TABLE 3.   Percentages Reporting
Community Growing,
Declining, or Stable

Community	Growing	Declining	Stable
Dowagiac			
Negro	78.8	5.9	15.2
White[a]	66.6	8.6	24.6
Covert			
Negro	78.2	2.1	19.5
White	31.2	31.2	37.6
Vandalia			
Negro	46.9	21.9	31.3
White	5.9	35.3	58.8
Parkville[b]			
Negro	80.0	10.0	10.0
White	35.7	7.1	57.2

[a] White population sampled in Dowagiac is not representative of white population of town.
[b] Based on a small number of households.

except in Dowagiac, a larger proportion of Negro than of white households have more than 60 percent of their friends residing in the same community.

Demographic Structure

Other Negro-white contrasts are revealed by age structure (Table 4). For example, in both Vandalia and Covert there are more retired whites than retired Negroes. Nevertheless, a surprisingly large proportion of the Negroes of the four communities are also retired, one-quarter of the Negro households in Covert and Vandalia having at least one member retired. Although nearly 11 percent of the Negroes in Covert,

and 12 percent in Vandalia, are of retirement age, the percentages for whites are about 17 and 29 respectively. However, many of the elderly Negroes are recent migrants who have sought out a peaceful retirement community. In Vandalia they are not only those who have moved away from Chicago but also Negro families from the nearby countryside. A few Negro families were encountered who, though not yet having any member at retirement age, had migrated to establish a base for their retirement. They live in the community either permanently or for only part of the year (summer vacations and weekends). The larger proportion of retired whites, by contrast, have lived in the community for many years and feel that they have no other place to go.

There is a noticeable lack of younger white children and young white adults in Covert and Vandalia, but white and Negro teen-agers are about equally represented. Some of the white families with teen-age children were established before the greatest Negro influx took place and have adjusted to their changing community. Some white families with children are very poor and seem to be economically below the general Negro level. Adults over twenty-six years of age constitute 63 and 58 percent of the whites in Vandalia and Covert respectively; the corresponding figures for Negroes are 50 and 44 percent. The age structure of the Negro population of Dowagiac differs somewhat from that of Covert and Vandalia, notably in having fewer adults of retirement age and more children of preschool age. Nearly 60 per-

TABLE 4.   Age Structure of Population Interviewed (In Percentages)

Community	Born before 1900	1900–1920	1920–1940	1940–1950	1950–1960	After 1960
Dowagiac						
Negro	4.0	17.7	18.8	15.7	30.9	12.9
White[a]	12.3	17.2	23.1	13.5	21.2	12.7
Covert						
Negro	10.9	15.6	17.5	7.6	31.3	17.1
White	16.6	21.7	20.0	6.6	31.7	3.4
Vandalia						
Negro	11.9	13.8	24.4	9.4	21.1	19.4
White	29.4	13.7	19.6	3.9	23.5	9.8
Parkville[b]						
Negro	14.3	34.3	20.0	2.8	20.0	8.6
White	11.1	9.3	33.3	5.6	25.9	14.8

[a] White population sampled in Dowagiac is not representative of white population of town.
[b] Based on small population totals.

cent of the Dowagiac Negro population is less than twenty-six years of age.

There is a definite contrast in the sex ratios for the whites and Negroes sampled. Although there is generally an almost even balance between men and women among the whites, there are many more Negro women than men. The proportion of Negro females is 53 percent in Dowagiac, 55 percent in Covert, 58 percent in Vandalia, and 63 percent in the small Parkville sample. However, such an imbalance in favor of the female is not unusual in Negro neighborhoods.[24]

Economic Ties

Negroes and whites living in the same community, and within the same lower ranks of the urban hierarchy, show different patterns of travel to work and to shop. The most noticeable contrasts are in trips to work: Negroes have to travel farther than whites. Although there is less difference in the use of the urban hierarchy for shopping, Negroes are again somewhat more mobile than whites, both for lower-order goods such as gasoline and groceries and for higher-order goods such as clothing. Part of the greater shopping mobility of Negroes is related to their combining shopping and work trips. In communities where Negroes own businesses, a strong local Negro clientele is served. However, few Negroes seem to travel long distances merely to patronize Negro-owned establishments, partly because these generally provide only lower-order goods and services.

In Covert there is relatively little difference in Negro and white travel for groceries, despite the fact that the two grocery stores in Covert are Negro-owned. About one-quarter of the households purchase some groceries in Covert, and nearly half go to South Haven. In Vandalia, on the other hand, the white-owned grocery attracts 22 percent of the whites interviewed but only 7 percent of the Negroes. Dowagiac is a larger community, with greater shopping opportunities. All the whites who responded to the questionnaire reported shopping for groceries in Dowagiac alone, but nearly 10 percent of the Negroes go elsewhere.

The purchase of clothing shows an even greater contrast in Negro-white shopping behavior. In Dowagiac more than three-quarters of the white households interviewed indicated that they bought their clothes in the town, but more than half of the Negroes reported buying clothes in some other community, a quarter of the households mentioning South Bend. A much larger proportion of Negroes than of whites shop for clothing in Chicago, during vacations and visits with friends and relatives.

Newspaper subscriptions by city of publication also reveal differences in Negro-white preferences. Metropolitan newspapers enable Negroes to maintain closer contact with events in Chicago, with which they are often more concerned than with the local news in the community newspapers. The Cassopolis newspaper, the chief community paper serving Vandalia, is taken by more than 30 percent of the Vandalia whites who subscribe to a newspaper, but by only 11 percent of Negro subscribers; however, the most popular

paper in Vandalia among both whites and Negroes is the *South Bend Tribune*. In Dowagiac, among those subscribing to some newspaper, the local paper is somewhat more popular with whites than with Negroes. In Covert the Benton Harbor and South Haven newspapers account for 95 percent of the subscriptions by whites but for only 70 percent of Negro subscriptions. About one-quarter of Covert's Negro families take a Chicago paper. In sum, the Negro families of southwestern Michigan are less likely to subscribe to a local newspaper, preferring to obtain news from a paper published in a large city.

Negro migration to the small communities of southwestern Michigan is not principally a response to job opportunities. Place of residence is determined by availability of housing—an availability more selective for Negroes than for whites. Since the small communities to which the Negro has moved cannot normally provide many additional jobs, he is often forced to travel a considerable distance to reach his place of work. Although some Negro migration within the region reflects an attempt to reside closer to work, most Negroes prefer to live in a community with friends and relatives where they can own their houses, even though this means greater effort to get to work. Some Negro breadwinners, in fact, live in Chicago during the week and return to their families on weekends.

Whether measured by distance or by travel time, Negroes · average a longer work trip than whites (Table 5). The differences are greatest for the smallest communities, which are lacking in employment opportunities. For example, a survey of twenty workers in the hamlet of Parkville showed that Negroes drive an average of twenty miles (twenty-eight minutes) to work, whites less than six miles (thirteen minutes). Negroes in Vandalia travel an average of ten miles farther than whites, and the trips require an average of fifteen minutes more. In Covert, which has slightly more employment, the Negro-white contrast is smaller—four highway miles and ten minutes. Since most whites and Negroes interviewed in Dowagiac also work in that town, Negro and white work-trip averages are more nearly the same.

Although more Negroes than

TABLE 5. Employment Characteristics of White-Negro Work Force

Community	Mean miles travelled to work	Mean minutes travelled to work	Mean years at present job
Dowagiac			
Negro	8.9	18.2	5.2
White[a]	7.1	17.1	8.8
Covert			
Negro	10.2	21.2	7.6
White	6.2	10.6	10.6
Vandalia			
Negro	19.8	32.7	4.4
White	9.8	17.3	8.2
Parkville[b]			
Negro	20.6	28.0	1.5
White	5.7	12.5	13.6

[a] White population sampled in Dowagiac is not representative of white population of town.
[b] Based on small work-force totals.

whites interviewed were unemployed, the percentages for unemployment were relatively low. Of the whites interviewed, most work in the town in which they live. Two-thirds of the white living in Dowagiac and Covert, and about half of the white workers in Vandalia and Parkville, work in their respective communities (though in the last two the number of white workers is not large). The proportions for Negroes are smaller in Covert (less than a fifth) and Vandalia (less than a tenth); Dowagiac has just over a half, and no Parkville Negroes work within the hamlet.

Certain communities draw a disproportionate share of Negro workers, largely to factory jobs. When factory employment is not available in the community of residence, Negroes are willing to travel relatively long distances to factories in other towns. For example, 16 percent of the Negro workers interviewed in Dowagiac travel the twenty miles to Buchanan (1960 population, 5341), but only 4 percent of the whites. More than 40 percent of Covert's Negro workers work in South Haven, as compared with 13 percent of the white workers. The Indiana towns of Mishawaka, Elkhart, and South Bend provide nearly 40 percent of the employment for Negro workers living in Vandalia, but just over 20 percent for whites.

Urban–Rural Migration as an Alternative to Ghetto Life

Negro migration into southwestern Michigan may be an indicator of a future trend associated with metropolitan environments. As the population of central cities becomes increasingly Negro, and the growing suburbs remain predominantly white, Negroes may move from the ghettos into a third zone, beyond the suburbs. This phenomenon could become common before the end of the century. If metropolitan decentralization of industry continues, job opportunities may increase in this quasi-urban zone; and with urban renewal and the return of some whites to the central city, some Negroes may be displaced to smaller centers on the urban periphery.

Although not a satisfactory long-run solution to the problems of ghetto life, a metropolitan spatial structure with a mixture of Negroes and whites in the rural-urban fringe may represent some improvement in the short run. A recent Gallup Poll[25] indicated that seven out of ten whites in the North believed Negro families have a better life in smaller cities and towns, but only one out of three Negroes agreed.

Experiments have been carried out in the past to create new Negro settlements.[26] Several Negro communities were established in southern Ontario about the time of the Civil War, and some in Nova Scotia after the War of 1812. Recently there have been organized moves to settle Negroes in new communities in the South. Negroes in Mississippi, backed by the Delta Ministry, a civil-rights arm of the National Council of Churches, have bought a tract of land south of Greenville, where it is planned to build houses for thirty families and to coax some industry into the community.[27] Whether or not new Negro communities in the North are at present a realistic short-term alternative to ghetto living is a complex question, and the example of southwestern Michigan does not provide an unambiguous answer. The answer seems to depend, in its final evaluation, on the degree to which such migration would allow the American Negro to participate in the social mobility available to white citizens.

Footnotes

The authors would like to thank the following individuals for assistance at various stages of this study: Mr. Bruce Bullis, Mr. David G. Dickason, Dr. F. Stanley Moore, and Dr. Henry A. Raup, Western Michigan University; Dr. John A. Jakle, University of Illinois; Mr. Robert B. South, University of Maryland; and Mr. Hans J. Stolle, University of Waterloo.

1. In spite of the slowly falling legal barriers and a rise in socioeconomic status for some Negroes, it is often as difficult for Southern Negroes to "escape" rural poverty as for Northern Negroes to "escape" the urban ghettos. For recent studies of the urban ghetto see Karl E. Taeuber and Alma F. Taeuber: Negroes in Cities (Chicago, 1965); and Richard L. Morrill: The Negro Ghetto: Problems and Alternatives, Geogr. Rev., Vol. 55, 1965, pp. 339–361.
2. In a chapter entitled "The Negro in American Agriculture" in "The American Negro Reference Book" (edited by John P. Davis; Englewood Cliffs, N.J., 1966; pp. 161–204 [Chap. 3]), Calvin L. Beale makes no mention of rural Negroes outside the South.
3. An interesting case was reported on the NBC Huntley-Brinkley Report on De-

cember 22, 1966. An Armour meat-packing plant was recently built in Worthington, Minnesota, a community of 9000 people, and forty-four Negro families in which there were Armour workers transferred to Worthington. Their integration into the community has been notably peaceful.

4. The same trend is currently observable in the white population. The Taeubers have concluded that "Negro migration should increasingly manifest patterns similar to those found among the white population" (Karl E. Taeuber and Alma F. Taeuber: The Changing Character of Negro Migration, *Amer. Journ. of Sociol.*, Vol. 70, 1964–1965, pp. 429–441; reference on p. 440). By leapfrogging the suburbs some Negroes are attempting to obtain the benefits of suburban living and minimize the doom of ghetto life.

5. An excellent survey of research on the American Negro is Davis, *op. cit.* [see footnote 2 above].

6. Richard Hartshorne: Racial Maps of the United States, *Geogr. Rev.*, Vol. 28, 1938, pp. 276–288. See Figure 1 (p. 277).

7. Wesley C. Calef and Howard J. Nelson: Distribution of Negro Population in the United States, *Geogr. Rev.*, Vol. 46, 1956, pp. 82–97.

8. *Ibid.*, p. 85.

9. John Fraser Hart: The Changing Distribution of the American Negro, *Annals Assn. of Amer. Geogrs.*, Vol. 50, 1960, pp. 242–266.

10. John Fraser Hart: A Rural Retreat for Northern Negroes, *Geogr. Rev.*, Vol. 50, 1960, pp. 147–168.

11. Harold M. Rose: The All-Negro Town: Its Evolution and Function, *Geogr. Rev.*, Vol. 55, 1965, pp. 362–381.

12. Figures for Vandalia and Dowagiac are from the United States Census of Population: 1960, Vol. 1, Part A (U. S. Bureau of the Census, Washington, D. C., 1961), p. 14–16. The population of Park-

ville is an estimate based on interviews, and the Covert population is an estimate from the "Rand McNally Commercial Atlas and Marketing Guide" (98th edit.; Chicago, New York, San Francisco, 1967), p. 244.

13. "Negroes Nearing a Majority in Major Northern Cities," *Congressional Quart. Weekly Rept.*, Vol. 24, 1966, pp. 1860–1863.

14. Hart, A Rural Retreat for Northern Negroes [see footnote 10 above], p. 147, footnote 1.

15. However, certain counties in northern Minnesota and northern Wisconsin have higher nonwhite percentages, due to Indian population.

16. Rose, *op. cit.* [see footnote 11 above].

17. Leo F. Schnore: Social Class Segregation among Nonwhites in Metropolitan Centers, *Demography*, Vol. 2, 1965, pp. 126–133; and Karl E. Taeuber; Negro Residential Segregation: Trends and Measurements, *Social Problems*, Vol. 12, 1964, pp. 42–50.

18. "History of Cass County" (Chicago, 1882), pp. 109–110. See also John C. Dancy: The Negro People in Michigan, *Michigan Hist. Mag.*, Vol. 24, 1940, pp. 221–240.

19. Another preponderantly Negro settlement in Cass County is the hamlet of Brownsville, consisting of only about a dozen houses. Possibly the most hidden hamlet in southwestern Michigan, Brownsville is tucked away between Vandalia and Calvin Center just off Route 326 on Crooked Creek Road.

20. Interview with Mrs. Joseph H. Garman, Wateredge Centennial Farm, just south of Parkville.

21. Hart, A Rural Retreat for Northern Negroes [see footnote 10 above]. In Ionia County two townships, Berlin and Easton, are listed in the census with 16.4 and 15.6 percent Negro respectively, but the Negro

population in Berlin consists of patients at the Ionia State Hospital and in Easton of inmates of the Ionia State Prison and Reformatory.

22.   The use of the phrase "other Northern Negroes" is meant to indicate that the adult Negroes of southwestern Michigan who had been raised in the South had already been living in the North as urban Negroes before they migrated to this rural part of Michigan. Other Negroes grew up in the area, as a result of in-migration either by parents in the 1940's or by ancestors as early as the nineteenth century.

23.   Hart, The Changing Distribution of the American Negro [see footnote 9 above], p. 265.

24.   See Jeanne L. Noble: The American Negro Women, in The American Negro Reference Book [see footnote 2 above], pp. 522–547 (Chap. 13).

25.   Press release Aug. 17, 1966.

26.   William H. Pease and Jane H. Pease: Organized Negro Communities: A North American Experiment, *Journ. of Negro History*, Vol. 47, 1962, pp. 19–34.

27.   "Hardship and Heartbreak in Freedom City," *National Observer*, Dec. 26, 1966, p. 6.

• • • • • • • • • • • • • • • • • thirteen

JOHN F. KAIN ◆
JOSEPH J. PERSKY ◆

Alternatives to the Gilded Ghetto

Nothing less than a complete change in the structure of the metropolis will solve the problem of the ghetto. It is therefore ironic that current programs which ostensibly are concerned with the welfare of urban Negroes are willing to accept, and are even based on, the permanence of central ghettos. Thus, under every heading of social welfare legislation—education, income transfer, employment, and housing— we find programs that can only serve to strengthen the ghetto and the serious problems that it generates. In particular, these programs concentrate on beautifying the fundamentally ugly structure of the current metropolis and not on providing individuals with the tools necessary to break out of that structure. The shame of the situation is that viable alternatives *do* exist.

Thus, in approaching the problems of Negro employment, first steps could be an improved information system at the disposal of Negro job seekers, strong training programs linked to job placement in industry, and improved transit access between central ghettos and outlying employment areas. Besides the direct effects of such programs on unemployment and incomes, they have the added advantage of encouraging the dispersion of the ghetto and not its further concentration. For example, Negroes employed in suburban areas distant from the ghetto have strong incentives to reduce the time and cost of commuting by seeking out residences near their work places. Frequent informal contact with white coworkers will both increase their information about housing in predominantly white residential areas and help to break down the mutual distrust that is usually associated with the process of integration.

◆ SOURCE.   Reprinted in modified version from *The Public Interest*, No. 14, 1969, pp. 74–87, with permission from the authors and editor. Copyright National Affairs Inc., 1969.

213

Prospects of housing desegregation would be much enhanced by major changes in urban renewal and housing programs. Current schemes accept and reinforce some of the worst aspects of the housing market. Thus, even the best urban renewal projects involve the government in drastically reducing the supply (and thereby increasing the cost) of low income housing—all this at great expense to the taxpayer. At best there is an implicit acceptance of the alleged desire of the poor to remain in central city slums. At worst, current programs could be viewed as a concerted effort to maintain the ghetto. The same observation can be made about public housing programs. The Commission on Civil Rights in its report on school segregation concluded that government policies for low cost housing were "further reinforcing the trend toward racial and economic separation in metropolitan areas."

An alternative approach would aim at drastically expanding the supply of low income housing *outside* the ghetto. Given the high costs of reclaiming land in central areas, subsidies equivalent to existing urban renewal expenditures for use anywhere in the metropolitan area would lead to the construction of many more units. The new mix by type and location would be likely to favor small, single-family homes and garden apartments on the urban periphery. Some over-building would be desirable, the object being the creation of a glut in the low income suburban housing market. It is hard to imagine a situation that would make developers and renters less sensitive to skin color.

These measures would be greatly reinforced by programs that increase the effective demand of Negroes for housing. Rent subsidies to individuals are highly desirable, because they represent the transfer of purchasing power that can be used anywhere in the metropolitan area. Other income transfer programs not specifically tied to housing would have similar advantages in improving the prospects of ghetto dispersal. Vigorous enforcement of open housing statutes would aid the performance of the "impersonal" market, perhaps most importantly by providing developers, lenders, and realtors with an excuse to act in their own self-interest.

Suburbanization of the Negro

Even in the face of continuing practices of residential segregation, the suburbanization of the Negro can still continue apace. It is important to realize that the presence of Negroes in the suburbs does not necessarily imply Negro integration into white residential neighborhoods. Suburbanization of the Negro and housing integration are not synonymous. Many of the disadvantages of massive, central ghettos would be overcome if they were replaced or even augmented by smaller, dispersed Negro *communities.* Such a pattern would remove the limitations on Negro employment opportunities attributable to the geography of the ghetto. Similarly, the reduced pressure on central city housing markets would improve the prospects for the renewal of middle-income neighborhoods through the operations of the private market. Once the peripheral growth of central city ghettos is checked, the demands for costly investment in specialized, long-distance transport facilities serving central employment areas would be reduced. In addition programs designed to reduce *de facto* school segregation by means of redistributing, bussing, and similar measures would be much more feasible.

Although such a segregated pattern does not represent the authors' idea of a more open society, it could still prove a valuable first step toward the goal. Most groups attempting to integrate suburban neighborhoods have placed great stress on achieving and maintaining some preconceived interracial balance. Because integration is the goal, they feel the need to proceed slowly and make elaborate precautions to avoid "tipping" the neighborhood. The result has been a small, black trickle into all-white suburbs. But if the immediate goal is seen as destroying the ghetto, different strategies should be employed. "Tipping," rather than something to be carefully avoided, might be viewed as a tactic for opening large amounts of suburban housing. If enough suburban neighborhoods are "tipped," the danger of any one of them becoming a massive ghetto would be small.

Education is still another tool that can be used to weaken the ties of the ghetto. Formal schooling plays a particularly important role in preparing individuals to participate in the complex urban society of today. It greatly enhances their ability to compete in the job market with the promise of higher incomes. As a result, large scale programs of compensatory education can make important contributions to a strategy of weakening and eventually abolishing the Negro ghetto. Nevertheless, the important gains of such compensatory programs must be continually weighed against the more general advantages of school desegregation. Where real alternatives exist in the short run, programs consistent with this latter objective should always be chosen. It is important to note that truly effective programs of compensatory education are likely to be extremely expensive and that strategies involving significant amounts of desegregation may achieve the same educational objectives at much lower costs.

Bussing of Negro students may be such a program. Like better access to suburban employment for ghetto job seekers, bussing would weaken the geographic dominance of the ghetto. Just as the informal experience of integration on the job is an important element in changing racial attitudes, integration in the classroom is a powerful learning experience. Insofar as the resistance of suburban communities to accepting low income residents and students is the result of a narrow cost-minimization calculus that attempts to avoid providing public services and in particular education, substantial state and federal subsidies for the education of low income students can prove an effective carrot. Title I programs of the Elementary and Secondary Education Act of 1965 and grants to areas containing large federal installations are precedents. Subsidies should be large enough to cover more than the marginal cost of educating students from low income families, and should make it *profitable* for communities and school districts to accept such students. The experience of the MET-CO program in Boston strongly suggests that suburban communities can be induced to accept ghetto school children if external sources of financing are available.

Because the above proposals would still leave unanswered some immediate needs of ghetto residents, a strong argument can be made for direct income transfers. Although certain constraints on the use of funds, for example rent supplements, might be maintained, the emphasis should be on providing resources to individuals and not on freezing them into geographic areas. The extent to which welfare schemes are currently tied to particular neighborhoods or communities should be determined, and these programs should be altered so as to remove such limitations on mobility. Keeping in mind the crucial links between the ghetto and the rural South, it is essential that the Southern Negro share in these income transfers.

The Ghetto and the Nation

Although there are major benefits to be gained by both the Negro community and the metropolis at large through a dispersal of the central ghetto, these benefits cannot be realized and are likely to be hindered by programs aimed at making the ghetto a more livable place. In addition to the important objections discussed so far, there is the very real possibility that such programs will run afoul of major migration links

with the Negro population of the South. A striking example of this problem can be seen in the issue of ghetto job creation, one of the most popular proposals to improve the ghetto.

Although ghetto job creation, like other "gilding" programs, might initially reduce Negro unemployment, it must eventually affect the system that binds the Northern ghetto to the rural and urban areas of the South. This system will react to any sudden changes in employment and income opportunities in Northern ghettos. If there are no offsetting improvements in the South, the result will be increased rates of migration into still restricted ghetto areas. While we need to know much more than we now do about the elasticity of migration to various economic improvements, the direction of the effect is clear. Indeed it is possible that more than one migrant would appear in the ghetto for every job created. Even at lower levels of sensitivity, a strong wave of in-migration could prove extremely harmful to many other programs. The South in 1960 still accounted for about 60 per cent of the country's Negro population, more than half of which live in nonmetropolitan areas. In particular, the number of *potential* migrants from the rural South has not declined greatly in recent years.

Although the differential in white and Negro migration is clearly related to differential economic opportunity, the over-all level of Southern out-migration must be ascribed to the underdeveloped nature of the region. A more rapid pace of Southern economic development could change these historic patterns of Negro migration. Tentative research findings indicate that both manufacturing growth and urbanization in the South reduce Negro out-migration. Although the holding effect of these changes is not so strong for Negroes as for whites, the difference between the two responses can be substantially narrowed. If development took place at a higher rate, the job market would tighten and thus encourage Negroes to stay. Moreover, the *quid pro quo* for large scale subsidies for Southern development might be strong commitments to hire Negro applicants. A serious program of Southern development is worthwhile in its own right as a cure to a century of imbalance in the distribution of economic activity in the nation. From the narrow viewpoint of the North, however, the economic development of the South can play a crucial role in providing leverage in the handling of metropolitan problems.

Belated recognition of the problems created for Northern metropolitan areas by these large-scale streams of rural migration have led in recent months to a large number of proposals to encourage development in rural areas. Not surprisingly the Department of Agriculture has been quick to seize the opportunities provided. A "rural renaissance" has been its response. Full-page advertisements headed, "To save our cities, We must have rural-urban balance," have appeared in a large number of magazines under the aegis of the National Rural Electric Cooperative Association. These proposals invariably fail to recognize that Negro migration from the rural South differs in important respects from rural-urban

migration and has different consequences. Failing as they do to distinguish between beneficial and potentially disruptive migration, these proposals for large-scale programs to keep people on the farms, everywhere, are likely to lead to great waste and inefficiency, while failing to come to grips with the problem that motivated the original concern.

Improving Skills

A second important approach to easing the pressure on the ghetto is to improve the educational and skill level of incoming migrants. An investment in the under-utilized human resource represented by the Southern white and Negro will pay off in either an expanded Southern economy or a Northern metropolitan job market. Indeed, it is just this flexibility that makes programs oriented to individuals so attractive in comparison to programs oriented to geography. To the extent that a potential migrant can gain skills in demand, his integration into the metropolis, North or South, is that much eased. In light of these benefits, progress in Southern schools has been pitifully slow. Southern Negro achievement levels are the lowest for any group in the country. Southern states with small tax bases and high fertility rates have found it expedient in the past to spend as little as possible on Negro education. Much of the rationalization for this policy is based on the fact that a large proportion of Southern Negroes will migrate and thus deprive the area of whatever educational investment is made in them. This fact undoubtedly has led to some underinvestment in the education of Southern whites as well, but the brunt has been borne by the Negro community.

Clearly it is to the advantage of those areas that are likely to receive these migrants to guarantee their ability to cope with an urban environment. This would be in sharp contrast to migrants who move to the ghetto dependent on the social services of the community and unable to venture into the larger world of the metropolis. Nor are the impacts of inadequate Southern education limited to the first generation of Negro migrants. Parents ill-equipped to adjust to complex urban patterns are likely to provide the support necessary for preparing children to cope with a hostile environment. The pattern can be clearly seen in the second generation's reaction to life in the ghetto. It is the children of migrants and not the migrants themselves who seem most prone to riot in the city.

Thus, education of potential migrants is of great importance to both the North and South. The value of the investment is compounded by the extent to which the over-all level of Negro opportunity is expanded. In the North, this is dependent on a weakening of the constricting ties of the ghetto. In the South it depends on economic development per se.

Concluding Thoughts

This article has considered alternative strategies for the urban ghetto in light of the strong economic and social link of that community to the metropolis in which it is imbedded and to the nation as a whole. In particular the analysis has centered on the likely repercussions of "gilding programs."

Included prominently among these programs are a variety of proposals designed to attract industry to metropolitan ghettos. There have also been numerous proposals for massive expenditures on compensatory education, housing, welfare, and the like. Model cities programs must be included under this rubric. All such proposals aim at raising the employment, incomes, and well-being of ghetto residents, *within* the existing framework of racial discrimination.

Much of the political appeal of these programs lies in their ability to attract support from a wide spectrum ranging from white separatists, to liberals, to advocates of black power. However, there is an overriding objection to this approach. "Gilding" programs must accept as given a continued growth of Negro ghettos, ghettos which are directly or indirectly responsible for the failure of urban renewal, the crisis in central city finance, urban transportation problems, Negro unemployment, and the inadequacy of metropolitan school systems. Ghetto gilding programs, apart from being objectionable on moral grounds, accept a very large cost in terms of economic inefficiency, while making the solution of many social problems inordinately difficult.

A final objection is that such programs may not work at all, if pursued in isolation. The ultimate result of efforts to increase Negro incomes or reduce

Negro unemployment in central city ghettos may be simply to induce a much higher rate of migration of Negroes from Southern rural areas. This will accelerate the already rapid growth of black ghettos, complicating the already impressive list of urban problems.

Recognition of the migration link between Northern ghettos and Southern rural areas has led in recent months to proposals to subsidize economic development, educational opportunities, and living standards in rural areas. It is important to clarify the valuable, but limited, contributions well-designed programs of this kind can make to the problems of the metropolitan ghetto. Anti-migration and migrant improvement programs cannot in themselves improve conditions in Northern ghettos. They cannot overcome the prejudice, discrimination, low incomes, and lack of education that are the underlying "causes" of ghetto unrest. At best they are complementary to programs intended to deal directly with ghetto problems. Their greatest value would be in permitting an aggressive assault on the problems of the ghetto—their role is that of a counterweight which permits meaningful and large-scale programs within *metropolitan* areas.

What form should this larger effort take? It would seem that ghetto dispersal is the only strategy that promises a long-run solution. In support of this contention we have identified three important arguments:

1. None of the other programs will reduce the distortions of metropolitan growth and loss of efficiency that result from the continued rapid expansion of "massive" Negro ghettos in metropolitan areas.
2. Ghetto dispersal programs would generally lower the costs of achieving many objectives that are posited by ghetto improvement or gilding schemes.
3. As between ghetto gilding and ghetto dispersal strategies, only the latter is consistent with stated goals of American society.

The conclusion is straightforward. Where alternatives exist, and it has been a major effort of this article to show that they do exist, considerable weight must be placed on their differential impact on the ghetto. Programs that tend to strengthen this segregated pattern should generally be rejected in favor of programs that achieve the same objectives while weakening the ghetto. Such a strategy is not only consistent with the nation's long-run goals, but will often be substantially cheaper in the short run.

333333333333

URBAN LIFE
AND HOUSING

333333333333

• • • • • • • • • • • • • • • fourteen

DENNIS C. McELRATH ◆

Urban Differentiation: Problems and Prospects

Cities are focal points for a great variety of America's ills. City people daily clog highways, befoul air, pollute water, challenge sewer systems, make streets hazardous and public spaces lethal. Their sick, indigent, deviants, and aged make demands; their slums spread; their race relations sicken our conscience; their children run amuck; and their girls go bad.

Most of these problems, however, though identified with urban America, are not unique to this growing sector of society. It is patently impractical, undesirable, and almost meaningless in a complex society undergoing rapid and widespread change to separate the city, with its problems and prospects, from the larger society. Cities today are part-societies where everyday activities are linked to greater polities, economics,

and extended networks of kin and friend. Much current discussion of urban affairs nevertheless treats this portion of society without reference to the whole. It is a curious abstraction to view both social order and its concomitant problems within the community as static or discrete, since all activities in an urban society are interwoven to form a large fabric whose pattern, like an "op" painting, constantly vibrates, restructures, moves unceasingly, and never settles down. The fascination of urban sociology lies in defining and understanding this constantly changing organization of thousands of disparate yet widely interdependent acts performed daily by all the people of the city and all those linked to it by interdependence or interaction. A profoundly important

◆ SOURCE. Reprinted with permission from a symposium "Urban Problems and Prospects" appearing in *Law and Contemporary Problems*, Vol. 30, No. 1, Winter 1965, published by the Duke University School of Law, Durham, N.C. Copyright, 1965, Duke University.

223

perspective may be thus gained for evaluating, formulating, and implementing enlightened public policy.

Such a perspective is not easy to acquire. No neat theory of urban social organization exists today even though the current renascence in urban studies and its attendant affluence has greatly increased research, writing, and systematic thinking in this area. What is being formed, instead, are sets of related ideas which are grounded in careful observations and which hang together well enough to be termed theoretical frames of reference. Basically, the framework for analysis of urban problems and prospects which is used here relates broad changes occurring in the larger society to the activities and opportunities of people settled in local areas of the city. This patterned sifting and sorting of people into local areas is part of the present transformation of urban communities, and a source of many current difficulties.

Of the several recent and significant influences, industrialization and urbanization are the two major changes most instrumental in transforming society through healing or eliminating old divisions within it and yielding new ones. Industrialization has destroyed the traditional skill hierarchy, supplanting a set of distinctions based on an equation of age and seniority with skill, and substituting for it a new hierarchical division topped, for the moment, by those who possess highly specific technical skills. This current division apparently operates in all advanced industrial countries.[1]

An additional and serendipitous result of the new industrialization is the greatly diminished relevance of sex as a basis for limiting access to resources and rewards in the community. Recent expansion of the tertiary sector of industries and the dramatic enlargement in size and scale of many enterprises has widened the opportunity for gainful employment of women outside the household. It has yielded thereby a viable alternative to a style of life which centered on household, children, family, and kin. This new division, moreover, stemming from changes in the mode and scale of production, does not rest on the possession of certain types of skills but rather on opting one style of life over another. The distinction here, therefore, is between "urbanism" as characterized by small families and women working; and "familism," a life style associated with larger families and women at home.[2]

As Durkheim, among others, points out, the process of industrialization thus erases older distinctions based on an age-graded, sex-selective division of labor.[3] These older, ascriptive molds for the allocation of tasks and resources fall into disrepute only to be replaced by other sets of constraints, based on achieved skills and the exercise of a choice of life style. The newer constraints are buttressed by and defended in terms of the prevailing morality of "a career open to talents" and "the maximization of personal choice."

Viewed simply as the process of concentrating a large proportion of the population in a relatively few locations, urbanization inevitably produces new divisions within the community. The spatial consolidation of peoples destroys the internal homogeneity of the community because, in effect, it can be accomplished only by a major spatial redistribution of the population. This redistributive process yields two analytically distinct divisions within the urban community.

The first may be termed "migration status" and is based upon the extent to which movement from a place of origin to an urban center represents a movement across important *social boundaries*. Thus the experience of Whyte's organization man in going from one suburb to another across the country is not a movement over social boundaries. Whyte's organization man is not a stranger to the suburb: he is merely an urban man on the move. On the other hand, a strip miner's migration from Appalachia to Chicago traverses fewer miles, yet it crosses a much wider social gap. The miner is a newcomer to the city, and his choices are constrained not merely by his redundant skills or an option to a particular style of life but also by *the novelty and alienness of a complex urban world.*

Ethnic heterogeneity within the urban community is another consequence of the redistribution of people associated with urbanization. To the extent that cities draw upon populations with different physical or cultural backgrounds their composition is altered; and the urban community is divided by social visibilities.[4]

Both migration status and ethnic status are byproducts of the current pattern of urbanization in America. In its present form, this pattern results in the accumulation of substantial urban populations, each with distinct migration experiences and a variety of social

visibilities. Like the divisions engendered by industrialization, these divisions also operate so as to limit access of individuals to the resources and rewards of the community. Unlike the constraints based on acquired skills and choice of life style, however, limitations arising from these sources are not directly legitimized by the prevailing public morality. But their indirect support is revealed by a close scrutiny of the "melting pot" ideology which indicates a widespread acceptance of the view that inequity is just and legitimate as long as cultural pluralism and inappropriate ruralism persists. In addition, the continuing American dilemma in race relations exposes the persistence of an indirect buttressing of inequity based on physical visibility.

Urbanization and industrialization, then, yield four basic dimensions of social differentiation along which the rewards and resources of urban communities are distributed. In the city the range of opportunities available to an individual or family is subject to the multiple constraints of economic status (based on skills); family status (based on life style option); migration status (based on migration experience); and ethnic status (based on social visibility).

Allocation of resources in terms of each of these status dimensions is, to some extent, legitimized by prevailing norms. In addition, all four statuses act in concert to delimit the range of opportunities open to urbanites. This is especially applicable in the case of housing opportunities. A long list of studies conducted in cities and metropolitan areas throughout the United

States attests to the fact that all of these dimensions operate both separately and in combination to structure the pattern of residential settlement in American cities.[5] This accumulated evidence indicates that local areas contain distinctive types of populations occupying different constellations of statuses and, as a consequence, have markedly different needs, demands, information, facilities, and modes of action.

Sets of relatively discrete problems are associated with the operation of each of these dimensions. Economic status distinguishes local area populations in terms of the prevalent level of skills and other resources. Thus when localities are arrayed along this dimension they vary in concomitant needs and demands associated with occupational and educational achievements. At the lower levels of economic status, where localities contain substantial proportions of unskilled and uneducated workers, most of these problems resolve into the absolute constriction of life chances arising from poverty and ignorance. At somewhat higher statuses, lack of specific skills, skill redundancy, precarious employment, and highly unstable and insecure career trajectories are major issues. Above this lie the worries of the middle class: a scattering of problems concerned with extended educational training prior to employment, early plateauing of career trajectories, all the insecurities of white collar employment, and prolonged retirement and widowhood.

Important differences in concerns are observed as well between local areas arranged by family status. In urban localities where most people dwell in apartments, where wives work, families are small, and where there are many single people either just beginning their careers or retired from them, there exists some concern for the maintenance and improvement of the urban ambient. Occasionally worry is expressed about maintaining safe public spaces or preserving lively neighborhoods. For the most part, the world of the urban man is a world of career and consumption not oriented to the locality, where personal problems have more to do with economic status, ethnicity, and migrancy than with life style.[6] The public problems of these areas, however, are great. For the most part they revolve around decay and sterile renewal, a shrinking tax base, and the creation of a residential scene which perhaps only few people want and within which even the committed urbanite finds it difficult to persist.[7]

A quite different picture is observed, however, in familistic areas characterized by high fertility and women at home. Here, among the mortgaged single family dwellings of suburbia and in the familistic areas of the central city there exists a much greater concern for and involvement in the local area. Children blaze paths of interaction, bind local knots of interdependence, and magnify the importance of schools, neighborhood, and local community. In these areas current problems derive from the rearing of children and, often, the rapid, recent creation of vast horizontal neighborhoods.[8]

Ethnic status designates localities in terms of the presence of culturally and physically visible minorities. These areas are focal points associated with problems of shedding social visibilities and assimilation into the larger community. In the case of the culturally visible this process is generally a matter of three or four generations in America.[9] With the physically visible, the rate of assimilation is appreciably slower, for their stigmata may be erased only through amalgamation or by *defining the differences as socially meaningless* in the acquisition of benefits of the community. This process, requiring dramatic normative and attitudinal changes is, to be sure, lengthy and its results often volatile.[10]

Finally, migration status identifies a set of local problems arising from the absence of urban skills and magnified by local reactions to newcomers.[11] Historically, the difficulties which beset migrants were empirically and socially confused with ethnic status. It is now clear that the necessary skills, resources, and even motives for action in a large scale urban society are qualitatively distinct from the requirements of the little communities of the hinterland and foreland. The problems of the migrants arise from the inappropriate responses to an urban world. Even when the experience of migration is less dramatic, constraints arise from the alienness of the new environment and the severing of old ties, modes of action, connections, and amenities. For migrants, then, basic problems involve the acquisition of urban skills and the establishment of new and meaningful relations with the alien community.

Each of these dimensions identifies sets of personal and social concerns which are problematic in our time.

Only a few of these are isolated above; but even this listing indicates how the significance and relevance of urban problems systematically varies from one locality in the city to another, in accordance with the relative standing of the population of each along four basic dimensions of social differentiation.

These are not isolated findings gleaned from occasional samples or a few scattered studies: the evidence is garnered from a large number of separate investigations which span the nation and several decades, and it is consistent evidence. From Providence to San Diego, all four dimensions differentiate between populations and define the problems of each.[12] Within any community a greater understanding of the assets and activities of local area residents is gained by taking into account their standing along each of these dimensions and, more importantly, by considering the configuration of their standings. Their resources are limited not only by the prevalence of migrants, ethnics, an urban life style, or semi-skilled workers, but also by the combined influence of all of these limits.

This is critical to the present discussion because many of the enduring problems which presently plague cities arise from compounding inequity and constraint in localities within the community. Residents of an urban ghetto are disproportionately disadvantaged by the accumulation of limits stemming from low economic status, high levels of ethnicity, migrancy, and an urban life style. It is, however, not only a compounding of effects among the spatially isolated disadvantaged which is problem generating; difficulties also arise because these status dimensions are frequently crystallized among the advantaged as well.

The combined assets of localities which contain a high proportion of skilled, white, Protestant, long-term urbanites when conjoined with an option to familism usually involves an alignment with the amenities of suburbia. Not only does this result in the oft decried drainage of tax support from the central city but also in the removal of a significant sector of the population from a daily confrontation with the problems of the urban core. The highly disadvantaged who are entrapped in localities suffering from compounded deprivations thus become invisible to their opposites in suburbia.[13] The compounding of extremes of deprivation on the one hand, and of advantage on the other, thus presents problems in addition to those which are directly associated with each dimension of differentiation.

Status crystallization at the extremes of each dimension, conjoined with residential segregation, is not, however, the usual condition in cities. Most localities beyond a minimum level of economic status vary widely in life style. Ethnicity and migrancy are often compounded in the extreme as, for example, in urban areas settled by Negroes from the rural South who are generally of low economic status. But this does not always obtain: "hillbillies" are unskilled, rural-to-urban migrants. However, they are not physically visible, while most Negroes in Chicago are visible; but these latter are often urban men—not migrants—and occasionally

highly skilled. In fact, in almost every city studied, it is not possible to predict accurately where a locality stands along any one continuum from a knowledge of its standing along another. Each of the four dimensions is, except possibly at the extremes, quite independent of all of the others.[14] This independence of the different ways of distributing resources within the community means that each local area is characterized by a fairly distinct status profile and, in turn, by a particular constellation of relevant problems and concerns. This metropolitan mosaic contains few concerns which are shared by all segments of the community. What is highly problematic in one locality is viewed with passive disinterest in another across the tracks or out among the trees of suburbia. But now, by careful analysis of mass data, we can begin to isolate these different types of localities and mixtures of interests and perhaps even begin to mobilize personal and community resources in terms of their needs.

The community, however, is not static and the divisions which now separate localities are being altered by advancing industrialization and urbanization. If present trends continue, it is likely that several of these dimensions will cease to affect large segments of the community and, more importantly, that the range of variation of localities along each will shift radically. First, the general rise in economic status of most localities in metropolitan areas, as observed in the last two censuses, is considered likely to continue. This change has resulted in a general upward shift for most localities and a marked increase in the proportion of highly advantaged localities. But the proportion of highly disadvantaged localities at the lowest levels of economic status has not altered greatly.

It is difficult to tell at this time if this upward increase in the average economic status will continue to be accompanied by a widening of the range of inequity. Perhaps present efforts to raise the skills and education of the most disadvantaged will result in the upward progression of the *average* economic status, accompanied by a shrinking range of inequity or, at the least, a fairly constant range.

The proportion of familistic localities has increased in nearly all metropolitan areas each decade since 1940. In addition, it has been observed that this life style is by far the most prevalent in (1) those areas of the nation which have experienced the greatest growth (the Southwest and Far West); (2) those sections of all metropolitan areas which have experienced greatest growth (the suburbs and fringe areas); and (3) among those economic groupings which have most increased in status (upper and middle class).[15] It is likely that, given this strong thrust, this style of life will continue to be chosen by an increasingly large proportion of the total society. Further, with increasing economic status, it is probable that urban life style, at least in its present form, will be increasingly limited to those entrapped in the central city and unable to move.

The extreme form of migration status—the result of a radical shift from peasant to urban life—is likely to disappear in the next few decades. This will be due to both a diminution in the rate of rural to urban migration (we are running out of farmers) and the continued extension of urban forms throughout America and the continued increase in the intensity of involvement of all people in urban life. This long-term trend in the urbanization of American society is not likely to cease. Less extreme forms of migration status associated with movement that does not cross steep social boundaries will, however, probably persist since there is no evidence that the rate of long distance or short distance residential movement is likely to diminish. Changes in communications technology may, however, alter the social significance of this movement.

Proximate changes in ethnic status are difficult to assess in the light of recent changes in immigration policies which will affect the volume of immigration and the distribution of physical and cultural visibilities, as well as the distribution of skills among immigrants. Recent fluctuations in the migration patterns of Puerto Ricans also make projections with respect to this large minority difficult. Finally, current changes in norms and attitudes surrounding race relations will have a profound effect on the relevance of physical visibility to the distribution of resources within the community and concomitant problems. It is likely, however, that Negroes will continue to migrate to the urban North and West; that they will suffer inequities based on race alone; and that in many instances these will be compounded with disadvantages which stem from migrancy and low economic status.

In sum, the twin processes of urbanization and industrialization have yielded a fourfold division within the urban community. Each of these separately and in concert produce many current problems. The future course of these processes may heal some divisions and, possibly, bring about new ones.

Footnotes

1. See Seymour Martin Lipset & Reinhard Bendix, Social Mobility in Industrial Society (1959); Neil J. Smelser, The Sociology of Economic Life (1963); and Wilbert E. Moore & Bert F. Hoselitz (Eds.), Industrialization and Society (in collaboration with UNESCO) (1963), for general discussions of this process and significant consequences.
2. See Eshref Shevky & Marilyn Williams, The Social Areas of Los Angeles (1949); and Eshref Shevky & Wendell Bell, Social Area Analysis: Theory, Illustrative Application and Computational Procedures (1955), for an insightful synopsis of this transformation.
3. Emile Durkheim, The Division of Labor in Society cc. 3–8 (1949).
4. W. L. Warner & Leo Srole, The Social Systems of American Ethnic Groups (1945); Nathan Glazer and Daniel Patrick Moynihan, Beyond the Melting Pot: The Negroes, Puerto Ricans, Jews, Italians, and Irish in New York City (1963); Oscar Handlin, The Newcomers (1963).
5. Cf. Warner & Srole, op. cit. supra note 4, and other volumes of the Yankee City series for careful observations on the role of migrancy, ethnicity and class on patterns of settlement completed some twenty years ago. Recent materials include: Beverly Duncan & Philip Hauser, Housing a Metropolis—Chicago (1960); Stanley Lieberson, Ethnic Patterns in American Cities: A Comparative Study Using Data

from Ten Urban Centers (1963); Anderson & Bean, The Shevky-Bell Social Areas: Confirmation of Results and a Reinterpretation, 40 Social Forces 119 (1961); Anderson & Egeland, Spatial Aspects of Social Area Analysis, 26 Am. Socio. Rev. 392 (1961); Bell, The Social Areas of the San Francisco Bay Region, 18 Am. Socio. Rev. 39 (1953); Bell, Economic, Family, and Ethnic Status: An Empirical Test, 20 Am. Socio. Rev. 45 (1955); Bell, The Utility of the Shevky Typology for the Design of Urban Subarea Field Studies, 47 J. Soc. Psy. 71–83 (1958); Bell, Social Areas: Typology of Urban Neighborhoods, in Marvin Sussman (Ed.), Community Structure and Analysis (1959); John C. Bollens, Explaining the Metropolitan Community (1961); Goldstein & Mayer, Population Decline and the Social and Demographic Structure of an American City, 29 Am. Socio. Rev. 48 (1964); Greer, Urbanism Reconsidered, 21 Am. Socio. Rev. 19 (1956); Kahl, A Comparison of Indexes of Socio-Economic Status, 20 Am. Socio. Rev. 317 (1955); Walter C. Kaufman, A Factor-Analytic Test of Revisions in the Shevky-Bell Typology for Chicago and San Francisco, 1950 (unpublished Ph.D. thesis in Northwestern University Library, 1961); McElrath, The Social Areas of Rome: A Comparative Analysis, 27 Am. Socio. Rev. 376 (1962); Mack & McElrath, Urban Social Differentiation and the Allocation of Resources, 352 Annals 25–32 (1964); Schmid, MacCannell & Van Arsdol, Jr., The Ecology of the American City: Further Comparison and Validation of Generalizations, 23 Am. Socio. Rev. 392 (1958); Robert C. Tryon, Identification of Social Areas by Cluster Analysis (1955); Van Arsdol, Jr., Schmid & Camilleri, A Deviant Case of Shevky's Dimensions of Urban Structure, Research Studies of the State College of Washington (June 1957); Van Arsdol, Jr., Schmid & Camilleri, The Generality of Urban Social Area Indexes,

23 Am. Socio. Rev. 277 (1958); an Arsdol, Jr., Schmid & Camilleri, *An Application of the Shevky Social Area Indexes to a Model of Urban Society,* 37 Social Forces 26 (1958).
6. Cf. Bell, *Social Choice, Life Styles and Suburban Residence,* in William M. Dobriner (Ed.), The Suburban Community 225–47 (1958).
7. For a lively presentation of this polemic, see Jane Jacobs, The Death and Life of Great American Cities (1961); as well as The Editors of Fortune, The Exploding Metropolis (1961).
8. See especially Mowrer, *The Family in Suburbia,* in Dobriner, *op. cit. supra* note 6, at 147–164, as well as several other chapters in this volume.
9. Warner & Srole, *op. cit. supra* note 4, and Lieberson, *op. cit. supra* note 5, are especially pertinent.

10. See works cited *supra* note 4.
11. *Ibid.*
12. Shevky & Williams, *op. cit. supra* note 2; Shevky & Bell, *op. cit. supra* note 2; and the last eighteen items of note 5 *supra,* are pertinent, along with several pieces in George A. Theodorson (Ed.), Studies in Human Ecology, esp. Part II (1961); Marvin B. Sussman (Ed.), Community Structure and Analysis (1959); as well as the excellent discussion in Scott Greer, The Emerging City: Myth and Reality (1962).
13. Cf. Michael Harrington, The Other America: Poverty in the United States (1962).
14. Cf. the several articles by Van Arsdol and others, *supra* note 5; and also Ralph Ellison, The Invisible Man (1952).
15. Dennis McElrath, The New Urbanization and Trip Generation [forthcoming].

fifteen ••••••••••••••••••

• JOHN R. SEELEY

The Slum: Its Nature, Use, and Users

To cling to a dream or a vision may be heroic—or merely pathetic. Slum-clearance, slum renewal, or, more grandiosely, the extirpation of the slum, is for many planners just such a dream: brightly imagined, cherished, fought for, often seeming—but for stupidity here or cupidity or malice there—at very fingertip's reach. To ask how realistic this orientation is, what is possible at what costs and to whose benefit, is almost as idle-seeming an enterprise to many as it would be to raise doubts about the sanctity of American motherhood or the soundness of the American home. If a direct challenge to the orthodox view seems too bold, let us tease at the fabric of the dream only a little, to see how it appears—and perhaps still shimmers—in the cooler light of moderately disinterested curiosity as against the warm glow of programmatic commitment.

I

The very notion of a "slum" depends on a number of more primitive notions. We must invoke at least—(and I believe only)—the notions of

Space
Population
A *value-position* defining "goods" and "ills"
Dispersion in the distribution of any good (or ill) among the population so that, in that respect, all men are not equal
Correlation[1] among goods (or ills) so that one good tends to be attended by another, rather than offset by an ill
Concentration (in space) of those who have the most (and also those who have the least) of what there is to get.

◆ SOURCE. Reprinted by permission of the *Journal of the American Institute of Planners*, Vol. 25, 1959, pp. 7–14.

232

Any alteration in any of the realities that lie behind these six terms changes what "the slum problem" is; the elimination of any corresponding reality eliminates slums; and anything short of that guarantees the slum's survival. It cannot be overemphasized that no change in the plane of living—as for example, the doubling of all real incomes—would remove the problem. It is not a matter of absolutes. In a society where nearly everyone walks, the man with a horse is a rich man, and the man without is a poor man; in a society where nearly everyone has (or could have) a car, the man who can only afford a bicycle is *by that much* disadvantaged, and, potentially, a slum dweller. The criteria for what is a slum —as a social *fact*—are subjective and relative: for one brand of mystic this world is a slum (relative to the next) and for another there *is* no slum, because the proper objects of desire are as available in one area as another.

Since, for the planner, space is an eternal datum and population is also given, at least in the moderately long run, any attempt to "deal with" the slum must turn on affecting in some way one of the other factors. Since, commonly, the value-position from which goods or ills are to be defined is uncritically received from the culture or projected by the individual planner, this too appears as something given— although this unexamined acceptance undoubtedly leads to much of the defeat and frustration which the planner encounters and manufactures. We shall have to return to this question of values later, but for the moment we may ask, what is possible if indeed a single value-scheme—the value-scheme of middle-class materialism—is applicable? The answer, if the analysis is correct so far, is obvious: we can attempt an attack on any one or on all of the remaining factors: dispersion, correlation, and concentration. These are discussed in decreasing order of difficulty.

To attempt to diminish the dispersion in the distribution of any one good —say, money—is actually a matter of high politics rather than "planning" in the customary sense. Two courses are classically open politically: the periodic redistribution of goods gained; and the blocking of opportunities to gain them. An example of the first is the combination of income taxation or succession-duties with "equalizing" distribution of the proceeds—as, for instance, by differential "social security benefits." An example of the second—insofar as it is effective at all—lies in antitrust or anti-monopoly proceedings, more particularly in the form which they have taken in recent years, that is, the prevention of particularly blatant potential concentrations before they actually occur. Not only is this whole route attended by vexing ethical and political problems, but also limits are set for it by the culture and, in the ultimate analysis, by economics itself. We may or may not be anywhere near those limits in North America, but it is obvious that dispersion-reduction beyond a certain point may, in fact, reduce the total of what there is to distribute—may, in fact, reduce it to the point where the least advantaged are in absolute, though not relative, terms more disadvantaged than before. We may discover limits and optimum points by trial-and-error or experiment in the course of history, but this clearly falls outside the planning procedure. This leaves us with correlation and concentration to examine.

An attack upon the correlation of goods with goods and ills with ills, in the life of any person or group, is notoriously difficult. Nothing multiplies like misfortune or succeeds like success. As the work of Bradley Buell[2] so unequivocally demonstrated for the whole range of problems with which social work deals, disaster is so wedded to further disaster in the lives of families that the combined case-load of innumerable separate agencies in a city is very largely represented by only a small core of "multi-problem families," families in which economic dependency may be the child of poor nutrition and poor physical health and the father of overcrowding and desperate family relations and poor mental health—and so, in a new and horrible incest, in turn the father of its own father, more economic dependency . . . and so on. And what Buell finds for social work problems is not restricted to that field. Within single problem-fields themselves, diseases tend to follow diseases in the field of medicine, just as one bungled social relation generally follows another, as students of society observe, and one psychological catastrophe is the ancestor of the next in the case history of almost any psychiatric patient. Every social agency, every "caretaker institution,"[3] is concerned to break up or diminish these correlations or to palliate their effects; but the whole apparatus can deal with only the few,

worst cases; and nothing short of a society quite different from any yet seriously contemplated is likely to make sensible inroads upon the fact of correlation itself. In any case, this too falls outside the domain of local, or even regional, planning. So we are left with geographic concentration as our last point, seemingly, of promising attack. And it is at this point, if I am not mistaken, that the weight of the planners' planning has so far largely fallen.

The problem of "deconcentration" may be seen as the problem of moving from the present state of a heterogeneity of neighborhoods each homogeneous within itself to a homogeneity of neighborhoods each heterogeneous within itself. Upon succeeding, we should no longer be able to write of *The Gold Coast and the Slum*[4] but only, perhaps, of the gold coast within the slum and the slum within the gold coast. It is hard to doubt that—if we are willing to pay the price—here we *can* be successful. And it is equally hard to doubt that some increases in positive goods and some diminutions in positive evils would follow upon such a geographic transfer of the "variance" in fortune from the "between communities" label to the "within communities" one.

No one, perhaps, has put the case for the positive benefits so well as Catherine Bauer who brings knowledge, experience, vision, and passion to her task.[5] She argues, in reality, from the full depth of her feelings, but, in form at least, from primitive democratic principles against the one-class, one-occupation, one-economic-level community and for the broad-spectrum neighborhood where a child may at least encounter the aged, the ethnically strange, the poorer, the richer, the better, the worse, the different, and, therefore, the educative and exciting. The essence of her argument, I think, is that since the efficacy of our type of democracy depends on the achievement of consensus even in a highly differentiated society, whatever militates against "understanding" diminishes the national welfare. This is a telling point, especially if lack of direct exposure does militate against "understanding," and if increased exposure promotes it.

Another argument for "deconcentration" can be made, I believe, on negative grounds; and for some it may have considerable force. The argument is that the very concentration of evils or ills is itself an additional ill or evil—quite separate from the mere sum of the evils concentrated. I think this is a valid point. Anyone who has watched a child checking quite equably his separate bruises and scratches before bedtime, only to be suddenly overborne emotionally as their totality dawns upon him, will know what is meant at an individual level.[6] The pervasive air of squalor of a Tobacco Road or any of its innumerable counterparts is, I think, differentiable from the separately existent miseries that otherwise go to make it up.

However, even at this level of analysis, things are not so simple as they seem. If it is true that the concentration of the defeated and despairing casts a pall, a psychological smog, of defeatism and despair, it is also true that "misery loves company" and that support to bear the hurt comes chiefly from the hurt. Beyond this, awareness of one's disabilities and disasters is heightened if they must be borne in the presence of the able and successful; and this awareness—unless it can lead to a remedy—is itself an additional, and perhaps disabling, disaster. It is also to be noted that to the extent that compresent misery adds to misery at one end of the scale, the "slum," compresent abundance adds to the sense of abundance and security at the other end, the elite community or "gold coast." Thus, at the very least, "deconcentration" is not likely to be an unmixed good to anyone or even a mixed good to everyone.

Things are much less simple again if we are willing to be realistic and to recall for re-examination one of the premises accepted for the sake of argument earlier: that the question may properly be examined at all in the light of the planner's value-system, or the one he assumes to represent the society at large. The first possibility we shall not even examine; few would argue seriously that an urban plan should rest ultimately purely on the private preferences of the urban planner who plans to please himself. The second is worth some study.

It is a persistent illusion characterizing, I believe, only the middle-class meliorist, and only the middle-class meliorist in America—where it is least true!—that there is some particular case-applicable value-system that may be ascribed to the society at large. I do not doubt that *at a very high level of abstraction* consensus around value-statements can be obtained: America believes in justice; it simply divides on segregation. America believes in due process; it divides, however, on the propriety of what happens at many a Congressional investigation. What is at issue regarding the slum is a case and not an abstraction, and around it Americans divide, not simply in terms of slum-dwellers versus non-slum-dwellers, but within as well as between both groups.

It must be recognized at the outset, I believe, that the slum is almost as much a "social necessity" for some sizable segment of the elite as is, say, an adequate, centralized, and appropriately located medical center. I do not mean this only in the relative trivial sense, referred to earlier, in which those who enjoy the greater proportion of social goods also desire protection against the debris entailed in their production. I mean it in the quite literal sense that, like the supermarket in its locus, or the central business district in its locus, the slum provides on an appropriate site a set of services called out by, produced for, delivered to, and paid for by the selfsame elite whose wives are likely to adorn with their names the letterheads of committees to wipe out or "clean up" the slum. Many of the services provided by the slum are not within the monetary reach of slum people: the bulk of the bootlegging, the call-girl services, a great part of what some feel able to call "vice," the greater part of the gambling, and the whole set of connections that connect the underworld with the overworld serve the latter rather than the former, and are as much a response to effective (that is, money-backed) de-

mand as is the price of a share of A. T. & T. or General Motors.

Given this "effective demand," taking it for granted that such demand will indeed call out "supply" somewhere, the question for the planner—at least in the moderately long run—must not be *whether?* but *where?* To the degree that the services are highly specialized, as many of them are,[7] there seems no economically appropriate locus for them too far from the core of the central city proper. To the degree that the services are not so specialized, they will generally have already found their way —by a combination of economic logic with police pressure—to the ring of satellite municipalities immediately outside the city itself.

If these services, and a whole chain of other "opportunities" that the slum presents, were solely of interest and profit to an elite group who already had most of what there was to get, a case might be made out for the abolition of the slum (if possible) as being in the public interest. (There is a sense in which this is true just as, no doubt, sinlessness or prohibition are in the public interest.) But this view of a one-sided exploitative interest in the maintenance of the slum by *outside* landlords or "service" users simply will not fit the facts. The facts are that the slum-dwellers also have sizable investments, of interest, of sentiment, and of opportunity, both in the site of these services and its appurtenances and in the way of life that goes on there.

Slums differ, of course, and I have lived intensively only in one, Back-of-the-Yards, Chicago, in the early forties, and, together with others,[8] have studied another, "Relocation Area A" in Indianapolis. I do not intend to give in detail any account of the former, especially as the main features of a somewhat similar area were sketched in William Foote Whyte's *Street Corner Society*.[9] Something of the intensity, excitement, rewardingness, and color of the slum that I experienced is missing from his account of his slum, either because his *was* different or because sociological reporting militates against vibrancy of description (or, perhaps, because we cut into the material of our participant-observer experience in different ways). In any case, I would have to say, for what it is worth, that no society I have lived in before or since, seemed to me to present to so many of its members so many possibilities and actualities of fulfillment of a number at least of basic human demands: for an outlet for aggressiveness, for adventure, for a sense of effectiveness, for deep feelings of belonging without undue sacrifice of uniqueness or identity, for sex satisfaction, for strong if not fierce loyalties, for a sense of independence from the pervasive, omnicompetent, omniscient, authority-in-general, which at that time still overwhelmed the middle-class child to a greater degree than it now does. These things had their prices, of course—not all values can be simultaneously maximized. But few of the inhabitants whom I reciprocally took "slumming" into middle-class life understood it, or, where they did, were at all envious of it. And, be it asserted, this was not a matter of "ignorance" or incapacity to "appreciate finer things."

It was merely an inability to see one moderately coherent and sense-making satisfaction-system which they didn't know, as preferable to the quite coherent and sense-making satisfaction-system they did know. This is not analogous to Beethoven versus boogie-woogie, but more nearly to the choice between English and French as a vehicle of expression. (I will not even say which is which.)

Possibly I can give a clearer impression of the variety of dwellers in one slum and the variety of uses they make of it by quoting at length from the published report of the Indianapolis area that we studied. Section II of this paper is accordingly taken from that report.[10]

II. Types of Slum-Dwellers

There are always, of course, innumerable ways of classifying a population so immensely various as that of the slum, or, perhaps, of any urban area. We were struck again and again (both when we examined the way in which these people thought about themselves and when we examined behavior objectively) by two major differences: the difference between necessity and opportunity, and the difference between permanence and change.

Quit obviously, for many the slum constitutes a set of opportunities for behavior which they want (at least at the conscious level) to indulge in or to be permitted. For others, equally obviously, the slum constitutes a set of necessities to which, despite their wants, they have been reduced.

Similarly—though changes are *possible*—some are in the slum and feel they are in the slum on a temporary basis only, and others are there and feel they are there to stay. These distinctions establish four major types:

1. The "permanent necessitarians"
2. The "temporary necessitarians"
3. The "permanent opportunists"
4. The "temporary opportunists"

The meaning of these terms[11] will become clear as we proceed. Schematically, these might be represented as follows:

TABLE 1.   **Principal Slum Types: Area "A"**

	Relation	
Time	Necessity	Opportunity
Permanent	1	3
Temporary	2	4

Within each of these primary types, the data cast up a dozen or more fairly obvious subtypes whose characteristics are worth recording. The chart below (Table 2), which locates some twelve of these, fills in some details for the chart above (Table 1) and gives an orderly way of arranging what is to follow in this section.

THE PERMANENT NECESSITARIANS

Those in the slum permanently and by necessity evidently include at least three subtypes: the "indolent," the "adjusted poor," and the "social outcasts." In Area "A," these three subtypes seem to constitute the greater part of that "hard and unmovable core," which in turn constitutes about half of the population still living in Redevelopment Commission property. These are the people who feel they "cannot" leave the area, and who will or can do nothing to find alternative housing.

TABLE 2.   **Types and Subtypes of Slum-Dwellers: Area "A"**

Likeliest term of involvement	Primary reason for slum involvement	
	Necessity	Opportunity
Permanent	1.	3.
	a. The indolent	a. Fugitives
	b. The "adjusted" poor	b. Unfindables
	c. Social outcasts	c. "Models"
		d. "Sporting Crowd"
Temporary	2.	4.
	a. The respectable poor	a. Beginners
	b. The "trapped"	b. "Climbers"
		c. "Entrepreneurs"

The "indolent" are those whose most striking characteristic[12] is a general apathy or immobility. Whether from inherent characteristics, disease, maleducation, malnutrition, the experience of perennial defeat, religiously founded "resignation," or mere valuation of other things—these are the do-nothings, those who "have no get up and go," those whose immobility is grounded now in their very physique or character.

Whatever the cause for the "indolence," and no matter what miracles feeding, better care, or therapy (physical or psychological) could accomplish for such people in the very long run, at least in the short run no plan looking to them for even moderate effort or initiative is a feasible one. "Care" and "custody" are the only public-policy alternatives to neglect;[13] rehabilitation, if possible at all, would be a long, hard, slow process of uncertain outcome or economy.

The "*adjusted poor*" represent similarly, though likely less immovably, a population living in the slum by necessity but adapted by deep-seated habit (and now almost by preference) to its ways. This group represents the concentration in the area of the destitute, or nearly destitute, whose adaptation consists in "acceptance" of the nearly unfit-for-human-habitation shacks and shanties, holes and cellars of the area—provided only they be available at "that low rent." Among them are many of those who value independence fiercely enough that they would rather cling to this most marginal physical existence in independence than accept relative comfort in dependency—even supposing they could have the latter. (At least this is their first and habitual reaction. Some few who were persuaded later to move into Lockefield Gardens are now glad they made the exchange of relative independence for relative comfort.) In this group are many of the very old, the "single" women with many dependents, and other persons prevented in one way or another from working continuously enough or at pay high enough to qualify for a more respectable poverty. Many, if not most of these, are still in the area in Redevelopment Commission property, "unable to move" and unlikely, in the absence of harder necessity than they yet know, to do so.

The last subgroup among the "permanent necessitarians" are the "*social outcasts.*"[14] Police evidence, tradition, and common gossip have it that these people were relatively prominent in Area "A" at one time, but left when redevelopment became imminent or even earlier. These people included the "winoes," the drug addicts, peddlers and pushers, the "hustlers," prostitutes and pimps, and others whose marginal, counter-legal, or "shady" activities both excluded them from better-organized neighborhoods and made the slum a more receptive or less rejecting habitat.

In any case, by 1955 these had largely disappeared from the area. By that date, all that was left of this group seemed to be those living in common-law relationships, a handful of "winoes," and a few others living habitually in unconventional ways, for whom the slum provided escape, refuge, sympathy, tolerance, and even some stimulation by the very fact of their being together.

THE TEMPORARY NECESSITARIANS

The *"respectable poor,"* who are in the slum by necessity but whose residence there is or may be more temporary, usually spend a good part of their lives in it—now in and now out, although mostly in. Though slum-dwellers, and often as poor financially as the "adjusted poor," these people are unadjusted or unreconciled to the slum in the sense that all their values and identifications and most of their associations are outside it. They pay their bills, mind their own business, remain well inside the law, hold the aspirations and, within their means, practice the lifeways of a socially higher class, most of whose members far outrank them economically.

Some of these wind up in public housing, but more often than not they resist such a solution, hoping that "things will take a turn for the better," a turn that will permit them to live more nearly where they feel they belong and how they feel they should. For many of these, redevelopment provided either the money (if they owned their homes) or the incentive or both that made that "turn for the better" reality rather than wish.

The *"trapped"* are people who, having bought a home (or had one left to them by a parent or relative) at a time when the area was not so run down, one day find themselves living right in the middle of a slum. Blight filters insensibly in and around them, destroying the value of their property. Though many remain, through a program such as redevelopment many more are induced finally to get out.

THE PERMANENT OPPORTUNISTS

Those who are in the slum to stay, primarily because of the opportunities it affords, are the fugitives, the unfindables, the "models" and the "sporting crowd."

The *fugitives* are really of two types: those whose encounters with the law or the credit agency have led them into a life of subterfuge and flight, more or less permanent; and those whose nature or experience has decided them to flee the exigencies of rigorous competition in a better area in their own business or profession.

The former, probably not numerous, are really using the possibility of anonymity which the slum offers. To them it offers literal sanctuary or asylum, a cover or protection from the too-pressing inquiries of the more respectable world. These people, poorly circumstanced for the most part, had also left Area "A" in large numbers before our study began.

The latter, seeking escape from the status struggles of the world outside, or looking for a more easily maintained economic niche, occupied some of the best property within the area, and when catapulted out by redevelopment, found successful ways to maintain themselves and even to enhance their position outside the area. Many of them were merchants, doctors, lawyers, or other professionals who had served that part of the population that was later to migrate to the "better neighborhoods" with them. (They resembled the "climbers" discussed below, except that they did not want or expect to escape from their refuge in the slums.)

Somewhat like the first group of fugitives are the *"unfindables."* By definition, we had no contact with them, although we did have contact with those who had had contact. From their descriptions, there is suggested the presence in the population (before the advent of redevelopment) of a sizable "floating population," who could not readily be located, rarely got counted in any census, and lived a shadowy kind of existence both in terms of location and social identity. These were not so much people in flight as people whose individualism of outlook and whose detachment from urban ways led them to seek no clear social identity (or to operate under many). Some could be found by laboriously following a chain of vague touch-and-go relationships, some only by sorting out and tracing down a variety of "names" and nicknames under which each had serially or simultaneously lived. Most could not be found at all—with our resources or the census-taker's. These, too, had mostly disappeared from the area by the time we came, although some were left, and the memory of others was still green.

The *"models"* constitute a rare but interesting type. These are people who have somehow become, or conceived of themselves as, social or religious missionaries. They are people who stay in the slum (actually, or as they interpret their own behavior) primarily in order to "furnish an example" or "bring a message" to "the others," the "less cultured," or the "unsaved." Some of them are people who were first among "the trapped," but who have adapted further by finding a satisfying permanent life

in the slum; the satisfaction consists in bringing culture or religious light to "those still less fortunate." Some of them patently find some martyr-like satisfaction in such "service," but others more soberly find genuine relatedness and utility in this adaptation.

Some of these remained in Area "A"; some went early. Those who went seemed shortly to find themselves cast in the same role in their new neighborhoods.

Finally among the (relatively) permanent opportunists are the members of the *"sporting crowd."* This term, in local use, evidently connotes a range of characters noted primarily for their jollity and informality—perhaps a certain breezy offhandedness is their distinguishing characteristic—rather than for any necessary preference for illegal or marginal activities as such. They live in the slum for a complex of reasons. First, living in the slum leaves them more money to spend on "other things"; second, having spent a large share of their incomes on those "other things," what is left is only enough for slum rents; third, the slum is the place to meet others similarly situated; fourth, the slum itself provides (or, rather, in the case of Area "A," did provide once) facilities for their pursuits, such as taverns, bookmaking and other betting facilities, and so on. Marginal to this type are those who have been described to us as ranging from "the roughnecks who make it unsafe for others to be in the area" to the less violent types who just create nuisances, which, as one woman explains, ". . . cause you to be afraid to have a friend visit, because you never know whether someone is going to walk in on you without any clothes on." The informality, rather than roughness or nudity as such, is the hallmark of this group.

These, too, by now have mostly fled the area.

THE TEMPORARY OPPORTUNISTS

It remains to describe the temporary opportunists, a most important group both because of their numbers and because the slum of these people is a way —perhaps the only way—to the pursuit of those things that American culture has taught them are worth pursuing: "self-improvement," independence, property, a savings account, and so on. It may be only for this group that the general reader will feel fully sympathetic, and it may be only here that he will ask himself, "How are these people to get where we want them to get, if we systematically destroy the slums which are the traditional, if unspoken-of, way of getting there?" The question is a good one, and the study leaves its answering to the wisdom of the agencies, public and private, charged or self-charged with such responsibility.

We find that in this group there are three subtypes: the "beginners," the "climbers," and the "entrepreneurs."

The *"beginners"* are mostly the unattached immigrants to the city who have neither helpful kin nor access to powerful agencies of assimilation, such as churches and ethnic associations. The slum is simply their "area of first settlement" where they rest on arrival in the city not for "the pause that refreshes" so much as for the pause that instructs, the pause that permits

them a precarious period in which to "get oriented," find a first job, and learn the elements of urban living. Many of these are young married couples, some with first children, trying to learn simultaneously to be citizens, husbands and wives, and parents in the urban manner. Their slim resources, financial, educational, and psychological, necessitate a place to stay that will not strain these resources much further; the slum furnishes an opportunity to rest, to gather fresh forces, and to prepare for moving on as soon as may be—if disease, misfortune, or the fortune of more children does not exert more "drag" than can be overcome. From this source the city replenishes its labor force at the lower economic levels, and its "respectable poor" and other types at the lower social rungs.

The *"climbers"* are somewhat similar to the beginners except that they may have been in the city for some time and that their plans are somewhat more long-term and ambitious. These are the ones who live in the slum in what amounts to a period of apprenticeship, self-denial and self-sacrifice with a view to accumulating enough goods, money, and know-how to leap later into a much "better" area, a considerably higher standard of living, and a much more "respectable" way of life. They are "saving"—out of the very stuff of their own lives—the material and nonmaterial means of achieving better housing, greater status, "success," and homeownership.

For many of these, the period of stay becomes protracted because the dream tends to become embellished even as savings accumulate, and the time to move seems always "a little later, when we have a little more." Redevelopment, for many of these, helped toward a settlement with reality by putting period to an unduly prolonged stay in the slums or overextended plans; for a few, it cut off the possibility of any great "improvement" at all, insofar as it caught them in the initial phases of their plans. Some of those thus "caught" simply moved into neighboring slums to begin again. Some abandoned plans for ownership and became renters outside the area.

Last are the *"entrepreneurs,"* a special class of climbers, oriented similarly to the climbers, mostly more ambitious, but saving out of businesslike enterprises—rather than their own miseries —the wherewithal to escape misery in due time. Beginning usually as people of small financial means, they establish a small business or, more frequently, make the slum itself their business. They somehow (frequently by a kind of financial skin-of-your-teeth operation) get hold of a duplex or house that can be "subdivided." That part of it in which they do not themselves reside must, if possible, pay the costs of the whole, and moreover, yield "a little something" so that more property can be bought as time goes by. Often they purchase property, first, in the slum and, later, in better neighborhoods. In the case of at least one person in the area, a drug store was eventually purchased out of the money thus saved by living in the slums.

This kind of person lives a large part of his life in the slum, but usually leaves about the time he reaches fifty. He may by then own enough slum property to live very comfortably in a better neighborhood; or he may, out of his small-scale slum business operation, develop a larger business in a different area, becoming thus an undifferentiable element of the respectable business community.

III

If the earlier part of this paper made— or even labored—the point that in no way within reach of local planning could the slum be "wiped out," and if the second part drew attention via a particular case to the general situation of a vast variety of people coexisting in the slum's complex fastnesses, what, it may be asked, happens when planned steps are nevertheless taken to "do something" about an area, in this case to "redevelop" it. No general answer can be given—it depends on the steps and the people—except that the greater part of what happens is a redistribution of phenomena in space. We say "the greater part of what happens" because, as is evident from the original report,[15] this is not all that happens: in the very act of relocation *some* "positive" potentialities that were formerly only latent are released or actualized. As far as the redistribution in space is concerned, it is hard to say whether it should be viewed as "deconcentration": it is rather like a resifting and resorting, a speeding up of the city's "natural" ecological processes, with results both "good" and "bad," certainly unintended as well as intended. In this process, opportunities are created for some and destroyed for others, or very often for the same person; certainly, lifelong adjustments or habituations, comfortable and uncomfortable, productive and nonproductive, are overset, disturbed, interrupted, or destroyed. Moreover, in most cases one population is advantaged and another further disadvantaged, and it is not at all clear that the balance is tipped in favor of those who initially had least—perhaps, rather, the contrary.

Footnotes

1. "Positive correlation," of course.
2. See Bradley Buell, *Community Planning for Human Services* (New York: Columbia University Press, 1952).
3. To use the phrase of Erich Lindemann.
4. See Harvey Zorbaugh, *The Gold Coast and the Slum* (Chicago: University of Chicago Press, 1937).
5. See, e.g., Catherine Bauer, "Good Neighborhoods," *The Annals of the American Academy of Political and Social Science*, Vol. 242 (1945), pp. 104–115.
6. Cf. Bruno Bettelheim, *Love is Not Enough* (Glencoe: Free Press, 1950).
7. Compare, for instance, the (twelve at least) institutionalized sets of provisions for sex satisfaction demanded and supplied in a large mid-Western metropolis simply out of the changes to be rung on gender, race, and activity as against passivity. Omitting further variations and refinements, and using an obvious code, we have: (*MNA–MNP*), (*MNA–MWP*), (*MNP–MWA*), (*MWA–MWP*), (*FNA–FNP*), (*FNA–FWP*), (*FNP–FWA*), (*FWA–FWP*), (*MN–FN*), (*MN–FW*), (*MW–FN*) and (*MW–FW*).

8. Mr. Donald A. Saltzman and Dr. B. H. Junker.
9. Second edition (Chicago: University of Chicago Press, 1958).
10. *Redevelopment: Some Human Gains and Losses* (Indianapolis: Community Surveys, 1956), pp. 48–59. Field work by Mr. Donald A. Saltzman and others; report by Mr. Saltzman, Dr. B. H. Junker, and the author in collaboration.
11. The distinction—like other human distinctions—must not be "overworked." The difference between necessity and opportunity is largely subjective—a necessity welcomed with joy is often regarded as an opportunity; an opportunity accepted only with regret may be construed as a necessity. Even "permanent" and "temporary" refer largely subjectively to expectations and intentions, though they also partly (on that account) refer objectively to probabilities of later behavior.
12. It should not be overlooked that we have classified only by the most obvious characteristic. Many people have several characteristics, e.g., one could find examples of the "indolent-adjusted poor" or the "adjusted poor and trapped."
13. "Neglect," as used here, means "leaving them alone" or "not interfering" with the "natural" process by which these people are able to get along and to subsist.
14. They are so classified although some of them belong no doubt among the permanent opportunists (those who feel they *chose* the slum as a place of operation rather than that they were excluded from better areas) and some (those few who find their way to "respectable" roles) among the "temporary necessitarians." The peculiar arrow in Chart 2 symbolizes this difficulty of classification.
15. *Ibid.*, pp. 67–143.

sixteen

J. TAIT DAVIS ◆

Middle-Class Housing in the Central City

The years between 1945 and 1960 constitute a significant period in the shaping of American urban patterns. Accelerating urban growth rates and spreading suburbanization have dramatically altered pre-war concepts about urban shapes, sizes, and interrelationships. By 1960 many master plans for metropolitan regions attested to a felt need for urban designs which could accommodate post-war changes and the individual aspirations which prompted them. Of the several changes experienced by urban regions between 1945 and 1960, one is of particular significance to our conception of the city as a place to live. This one is related to the growing differences between the central city and its suburban fringes. The resolution of these differences is an essential prerequisite to the continued social and economic viability of our metropolitan complexes.

It is a well-documented fact that the major portion of urban population growth since World War II has been associated with the suburban areas of large metropolitan regions. Newcomers to the urban scene have tended to locate there. Many residents of the central city have migrated to this periphery, drawn by real and imagined advantages of suburban living, and driven by real and imagined changes in the character of the central city itself. Within the central city the population has tended to become polarized, divided into the exclusive categories of the very rich and the very poor. This polarization phenomenon suggests that middle income groups, with their mediating, leavening potential, are being phased out of the central city and dispersed throughout suburbia.

The central question addressed in this paper is this: To what extent do

◆ SOURCE. Reprinted by permission from *Economic Geography*, Vol. 41, July 1965, pp. 238–251.

246 URBAN LIFE AND HOUSING ♦♦♦♦♦♦♦♦♦♦♦♦♦♦♦♦♦♦♦♦♦♦♦♦♦

observed changes in the areas of central city housing available to families of the middle income class support a conclusion that the middle class is being squeezed out of the central city? In the process of finding an answer to this question some light might be shed upon the differences that may be observed among several central cities in the spatial importance of middle-class housing.

Preliminary Considerations

The selection of a time period for a comparative study of changes in the middle-class housing patterns must, of necessity, take into account the kinds of data which are available to support such an investigation. The most available and the most detailed information on housing values is provided by the U.S. Census of Housing, Block Statistics. Use of the block data unit reduces a choice of years to those for which block statistics are available. Of these, the years 1950 and 1960 approximate the post-war period of dramatic change in urban patterns; these two years have been used here.

The present study is an outgrowth of a survey made of the Washington, D.C., metropolitan region with respect to housing availability and population distribution changes in the 1945–1960 period. The procedures used for other cities were tested and somewhat refined by reference to the Washington area. An additional 12 cities were selected, quite arbitrarily, with a view to providing a range of city sizes in different regional contexts. Each of the cities

is a central city of a Standard Metropolitan Statistical Area (SMSA) and was a central city for a Standard Metropolitan Area (SMA) in 1950. The cities selected and certain characteristics relevant to an interpretation of subsequent maps are set out in Table 1.

The problem of specifically defining a middle class is not easily resolved. In this case it seemed appropriate to define a middle class in terms of income, particularly a range of incomes about a "middle" income. The appropriateness of income as a measure of the middle class in this case stems from the importance of income as an indicator of ability to pay for a given quality of housing. It must be recognized that several other factors besides income enter into an evaluation of an individual's "ability to pay." These include such criteria as occupation, age, marital status, and attitudes towards home ownership. Nevertheless, there is considerable precedent for assuming a predominant influence of income upon housing choice.

The middle class has been defined in terms of a range of incomes about the median income of all families in the SMA or SMSA as reported by the U.S. Census. A range of $1000 above and below the median income has been employed throughout to define the middle class.

A feature of this method for delimiting the middle class is the fact that it is based on local income criteria. There is, for the cities studied here, a considerable variation in median income of families: for example, the median figure for Washington, D.C., SMSA in 1960 was $7577; for Atlanta

TABLE 1. Characteristics of Housing 1950 and 1960, Selected Central Cities

City	Year	Total dwelling/ housing units	Percent owner occupied	Percent renter occupied	Percent white	Percent non-white	Average value current dollars	Average rent dollars/ month	Percent vacant
Atlanta	1950	94,530	39.1	58.9	66.9	33.1	8,739	32	2.0
	1960	154,264	43.1	51.6	67.1	32.9	14,800	59	5.3
Boston	1950	222,079	24.4	73.8	94.8	5.2	9,573	38	1.8
	1960	238,816	25.7	68.4	90.4	9.6	13,700	63	6.0
Cincinnati	1950	162,591	37.1	60.7	85.2	14.8	12,970	34	2.2
	1960	171,679	38.1	56.1	79.9	20.1	16,800	61	5.8
Denver	1950	133,690	50.4	47.1	96.4	3.6	10,371	43	2.6
	1960	174,124	50.9	44.2	93.8	6.2	14,900	71	4.9
Houston	1950	191,681	47.3	47.1	80.3	19.7	9,215	48	5.7
	1960	313,097	54.5	35.7	78.7	21.3	12,800	64	9.8
Miami	1950	87,532	43.3	46.3	88.7	11.3	10,818	60	10.4
	1960	120,069	38.1	51.8	82.3	17.7	14,600	74	10.1
Milwaukee	1950	188,926	42.3	56.0	97.4	2.6	11,014	46	1.7
	1960	241,593	46.3	49.3	93.1	6.9	15,400	74	4.4
Minneapolis	1950	161,974	51.7	46.7	98.5	1.5	10,399	41	1.7
	1960	173,155	50.9	45.1	97.3	2.7	14,800	71	4.0
St. Paul	1950	93,359	55.1	43.6	98.1	1.9	9,956	40	1.2
	1960	102,326	58.4	38.4	97.4	2.6	14,800	66	3.2
San Diego	1950	110,005	44.1	51.2	95.6	4.4	10,630	44	4.8
	1960	192,269	48.1	53.2	93.6	6.4	17,600	80	8.7
Seattle	1950	160,872	54.3	41.8	95.2	4.8	10,070	43	3.9
	1960	215,981	53.3	39.6	92.8	7.2	15,300	69	7.1
Pittsburgh	1950	193,889	41.8	56.7	89.2	10.8	9,258	41	1.6
	1960	196,168	46.9	49.2	84.4	15.6	12,500	65	3.9
Washington	1950	229,738	31.5	66.1	72.1	27.9	15,978	57	2.4
	1960	262,641	28.8	67.2	55.8	44.2	18,100	82	4.0

Source: United States Censuses of Housing 1950 and 1960.

SMSA the median was $5758 in the same year. The fact that prices and market values of housing are largely determined in local real estate markets suggests that the middle-class classification should consider local criteria.

The middle class is defined as those families in the SMA or SMSA with incomes within a range of $1000 of the median income.

Identification of Middle-Class Housing Areas

The relationship between income and housing value is not subject to a consensus. As noted above, there are other factors considered important as indications of an individual's ability to pay for housing. There are, however, some factors frequently employed as "rules-of-thumb" to describe this relationship. An example of this is provided by Andrews, who, in discussing housing, employs "a generous multiplier of two and one-half times income" to determine the top new home price which could be afforded by families at or near the top of the lower-middle-income group.[1]

In practice the relationship between income and housing value is wrapped up in home mortgage considerations. Each mortgage involves special consideration of individual situations. Gallion, in presenting an example of the application of two "rules of thumb," indicates a much lower ratio between value and income than the 2.50 suggested by Andrews. The "rules of thumb" he considers are: (1) that shelter costs ought not exceed one-fifth

of the income of a family of moderate means, and (2) that costs of shelter and utilities should approximate one-quarter of annual income. His example yields a value/income ratio of 1.76 or 1.87 depending upon which of the "rules of thumb" is employed.[2]

The Federal Housing Administration (F.H.A.), with a nationwide interest in home financing, provides information from which some indication of a value income ratio might be derived. In Tables 2 and 3 the median F.H.A. estimated value, the median annual effective income, and the ratio between them is set out for selected years. There are dangers attendant upon computing a ratio from medians, but the values of the ratio are useful in

TABLE 2. Median F.H.A. Estimated Values and Median Annual Effective Income, New Home Transactions, for Selected Years 1946 to 1962

Year	F.H.A. estimated value	Annual effective income	Value/ income ratio
1962 ...	$15,151	$7,289	2.07
1961 ...	14,918	7,328	2.03
1960 ...	14,607	7,168	2.03
1959 ...	14,329	6,912	2.07
1958 ...	14,207	6,803	2.08
1957 ...	14,261	6,632	2.15
1956 ...	13,203	6,054	2.18
1955 ...	11,742	5,484	2.14
1954 ...	10,678	5,139	2.08
1952 ...	10,022	4,811	2.08
1950 ...	8,286	3,861	2.15
1946 ...	6,558	3,313	1.98

Source: Derived from materials provided by Federal Housing Administration Division of Research and Statistics.

TABLE 3. Median F.H.A. Estimated Values and Median Effective Income, Not-New Home Transactions, for Selected Years 1946 to 1962

Year	F.H.A. estimated value	Annual effective income	Value/ income ratio
1962 ...	$14,082	$7,135	1.97
1961 ...	13,474	6,971	1.93
1960 ...	13,043	6,784	1.92
1959 ...	12,914	6,575	1.96
1958 ...	12,778	6,502	1.96
1957 ...	12,572	6,296	1.90
1956 ...	12,261	6,033	2.03
1955 ...	11,555	5,669	2.04
1954 ...	11,549	5,696	2.03
1952 ...	10,289	4,938	2.08
1950 ...	8,865	4,274	2.07
1946 ...	5,934	3,101	1.91

Source: Same as Table 2.

indicating trends in the magnitude of the ratio.

The trend in the value/income ratios since 1950 suggests that a higher multiplier is appropriate for 1950 than for 1960 (2.15 compared to 2.03). The larger ratio is about 6 per cent greater than the smaller.

Both the 1950 and 1960 Censuses of Housing provide information on value/income ratios for metropolitan areas and urban places. The value/income ratio is defined as "the quotient of the value of owner occupied dwelling unit divided by the total income in 1949 of the primary family or the primary individual" (1950 definition). The 1960 definition is similar except that midpoints of value and income categories were used to compute the ratios rather than the actual values employed in 1950.

The modal categories of the value/income ratio and the mid-points of the categories in which the median housing (dwelling) unit falls are set out in Table 4 for the cities used in this study. The differences between 1950 and 1960 are striking. Considering the median

TABLE 4. Modal and Median Values of the Value/Income ratio for 12 Cities, 1950 and 1960

City	1950		1960	
	Mode	Median	Mode	Median
Atlanta	2.5	2.5	0.8	1.7
Boston	3.0+	2.5	0.8	2.2
Cincinnati	3.0+	3.0+	0.8	2.2
Denver	3.0+	2.5	0.8	1.7
Houston	2.5	2.5	0.8	1.7
Miami	3.0+	3.0+	0.8	2.2
Milwaukee	3.0+	2.5	0.8	2.2
Minneapolis–St. Paul	2.5	2.5	0.8	1.7
Pittsburgh	2.5	2.5	0.8	1.7
San Diego	3.0+	2.5	1.7	2.2
Seattle	2.5	2.5	0.8	1.7
Washington	3.0+	3.0+	0.8	2.2

Source: Derived from U.S. Censuses of Housing, 1950 and 1960.

category, a majority of cities in 1950 displayed ratios between 2.0 and 2.9; in 1960 the ratios for six cities were between 2.0 and 2.4, and six were between 1.5 and 1.9.[3]

Altogether, the 1950 data suggest that a ratio of 2.50 is reasonably representative; for 1960 a ratio in the vicinity of 2.00 seems representative of actualities.

The magnitudes of the census value/income ratios differ from those derived from F.H.A. data, but the trend is similar. It appears desirable to use a larger multiplying ratio to determine housing values for 1950 than for those of 1960. This has been done for the present study.

The considerations of the previous paragraphs notwithstanding, the final choice of a multiplying ratio remains somewhat subjective. For 1960 deter-

minations a value/income ratio of 2.0 has been assumed; for 1950 determinations a ratio of 2.5 has been assumed. The middle-class income categories and related housing values are listed in Table 5. These form the basis for delimiting the middle-class housing areas on the maps.

For each of the cities considered two maps were prepared: one for 1950, and one for 1960. The base map is, in each case, the central city as defined in 1950. Several of the cities analyzed annexed portions of adjacent areas between 1950 and 1960. But because block data for such additions were not available in the 1950 census, comparisons made here refer to the areas included within the central city of 1950.

Each of the maps is a value contour map of the central city and is based on data from a random sample of blocks

TABLE 5.   Middle-Class Income Ranges and Related Values for Middle-Class Housing in 12 Metropolitan Areas, 1950 and 1960, in Hundreds of Dollars

	1950 SMA		1960 SMSA	
City	Income range	Housing value	Income range	Housing value
Atlanta	19–39	48– 98	48–68	96–136
Boston	25–45	63–113	57–77	114–154
Cincinnati	23–43	58–108	53–73	106–146
Denver	25–45	63–113	56–76	112–152
Houston	25–45	63–113	50–70	100–140
Miami	21–41	53–103	43–63	86–126
Milwaukee	29–49	73–123	60–80	120–160
Minneapolis–St. Paul	28–48	70–120	48–68	96–136
Pittsburgh	23–43	58–108	50–70	100–140
San Diego	25–45	63–113	45–65	90–130
Seattle	28–48	70–120	59–79	118–158
Washington	33–53	83–133	66–86	132–172

within census tracts. A minimum sample of 15 per cent of the blocks within census tracts was used. Overall, the sample ranges between 15 per cent and 25 per cent of all blocks in any central city.

The value contours based on these samples were checked in each map by at least one value profile based on all blocks intersected by a traverse line. These traverses suggest that the random sampling procedure used provides a reasonable approximation of the value configurations of these cities. It should be noted here that in the case of central cities which are greatly fragmented by physical features, such as San Diego, a larger sample size seemed necessary.

Amount of Change in Middle-Class Housing Area

Changes in the area of the central city occupied by middle-class housing vary considerably among the several cities. It must be recognized that changes in areas of middle-class housing cannot be equated directly to changes in the number of middle-class housing units.

Different building densities and housing standards make such an assumption risky. However, the amount of surface area occupied by middle-class housing and changes in this area over a decade of active urban development are suggestive of trends affecting a substantial portion of the central city's land-use structure.

Between 1950 and 1960 there was an average decrease in the middle-class housing area of 21 per cent. Actual changes ranged from 51 per cent to 12 per cent of the 1950 area (Table 6) with an average deviation from the mean of 9 per cent.

Employment of an elementary linkage analysis served to identify three groups of cities on the basis of percentage change in middle-class housing area[4] (Table 7). These three groups represent substantial, minor, and average changes in the areas of the central cities occupied by middle-class housing. It seems possible that these differences in the degree of change in middle-class housing areas might be associated with overall rates of growth of the metropolitan areas of which these central cities formed a part.

TABLE 6. Percentage Change in Middle-Class Housing Areas of Selected Central Cities, 1950–1960

City	Percentage change	City	Percentage change
Atlanta	− 30	Milwaukee	− 25
Boston	− 31	Minneapolis–St. Paul	− 32
Cincinnati	0	Pittsburgh	− 25
Denver	− 29	San Diego	− 33
Houston	− 51	Seattle	+ 12
Miami	− 4	Washington, D.C.	− 4

TABLE 7. City Groups Based on Percentage Change in Middle-Class Housing Areas

Group	Percentage change		
	Low	High	Average
I. Atlanta, Boston, Denver, Minneapolis– St. Paul, San Diego, Houston	−29	−51	−34
II. Miami, Cincinnati, Seattle, Washington	− 4	+12	+ 1
III. Milwaukee, Pittsburgh	−25		−25

Rates of Growth of Metropolitan Areas, 1950 to 1960

It might be expected that some of the differences in the residential structure among the cities could be accounted for by their different rates of growth. It seems reasonable to postulate that rapidly growing urban regions have the greatest amount of new construction and, concurrently, afford the greatest suburban migration opportunities for middle class families. It also seems possible that pressures on central city middle-class areas would be greatest in rapidly growing urban areas.

The percentage increase in population between 1950 and 1960 is indicated in Table 8 for each city. Elementary linkage analysis suggested four groups of cities on the basis of their population growth between 1950 and 1960 (Table 9).

It can be seen that the groups based on percentage change of population do not correspond with the groups based on changes of the middle-class housing areas of central cities. For example, San Diego and Miami, both with large and similar population increments, have experienced considerably different degrees of change in middle-class housing areas. As a matter of interest, a Spearman correlation coefficient between percentage change in population and percentage change in housing area was computed. A low coefficient ($r = -.29$) indicates the extent of the differences revealed be-

TABLE 8. Population Growth of Selected Metropolitan Areas in the United States, 1950–1960

City	Percentage increase	City	Percentage increase
Atlanta	+40	Milwaukee	+25
Boston	+ 7	Minneapolis–St. Paul	+29
Cincinnati	+18	Pittsburgh	+ 9
Denver	+52	San Diego	+86
Houston	+54	Seattle	+33
Miami	+89	Washington, D.C.	+37

Source: Urban Land News and Trends in City Development. Urban Land Institute, February, 1961.

TABLE 9. City Groups Based on Population Change, 1950–1960

Group	Percentage change		
	Low	High	Average
A. Atlanta, Cincinnati, Milwaukee, Minneapolis– St. Paul, Seattle, Washington	18	40	30
B. Boston, Pittsburgh	7	9	8
C. Denver, Houston	52	54	53
D. Miami, San Diego	86	89	88

tween the two groups and suggests that in these cities some factors other than population growth are associated with the observed changes in middle-class housing areas.

Patterns of Middle-Class Housing Areas

Change in the area of the central city occupied by middle-class housing has produced some interesting patterns. Previous studies of the residential structuring of American cities have been made by many individuals. Perhaps the best known of these are the contributions of Burgess,[5] Hoyt,[6] and McKenzie.[7] From their work a number of conceptions can be drawn to serve as a point to begin evaluating the patterns of middle-class housing observed in the limited sample of cities considered here. In particular, the concepts of concentricity, sector clustering, and randomness, as applied to the spatial distribution of residential types, seem relevant here.

In their work, Burgess, Hoyt, and McKenzie have made use of the Central Business District (CBD) as a base or reference point for characterizations of

the urban structure. In the case of the cities studied here, this basic orientation of housing areas seems too obvious to require mention. In most cases housing areas do appear to be oriented about the CBD in some fashion. In at least two cases, however, this basic orientation is not obvious.

Studies of the CBD by Murphy[8] and others have demonstrated that the CBD does not always occupy the geographic center of the urban complex. It is postulated here that the eccentricity of the location of the CBD, with respect to the geographic center of the central city has significant effects upon the patterns of residential types that evolve. Of the cities considered here, fully half do not have their CBD at the approximate geographic center of the central city.

Two types of cities can be identified on the basis of the relative location of the CBD—cities with a centrally located CBD, and those with an eccentrically located CBD. Atlanta, Pittsburgh and St. Paul are examples of the first type; examples of the second type are Miami, Seattle, and Boston. For the purposes of this classification, the CBD identifications used in the 1954 and 1958 Censuses of Business have been employed. The residential pat-

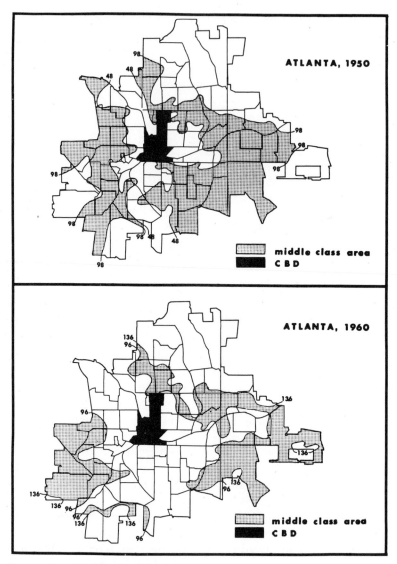

FIGURE 1.   Middle-class housing areas, Atlanta, Georgia, 1950 and 1960 (value in hundreds of dollars).

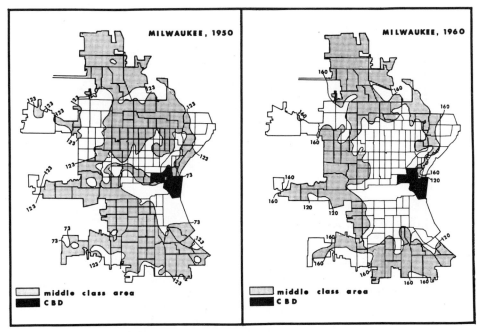

FIGURE 2.   Middle-class housing areas, Milwaukee, Wisconsin, 1950 and 1960 (value in hundreds of dollars).

terning associated with each of these two basic types appears to be different.

Where the CBD is centrally located, a concentric zonation of residential types is observable in most cases. This zonation is reminiscent of Burgess' concentric zonation of low-, middle-, and high-class areas which extend outward from the CBD. Five of six cities with a central CBD display this pattern. The one exception is Houston, where a pronounced sector development prevails. In this city the middle-class housing area abuts the CBD to the northwest and southeast. Atlanta is illustrative of the prevailing pattern in cities with a centrally located CBD (Fig. 1).

Where the CBD is eccentrically lo-

cated, a variety of housing value patterns may be observed. Milwaukee is basically a truncated concentric zonation (Fig. 2). Miami, Cincinnati, and Boston are best described as sector clusterings, analogous to those described by Hoyt. Washington, San Diego, and Seattle defy any characterization other than random. An example of each of these latter patterns is presented in Figures 3 and 4.

The three cities with random patterns of housing values are extremely compartmentalized by physical features. San Diego and Seattle have large marine intrusions dividing parts of the central city. Rock Creek and the Anacostia River separate portions of Washington. In each of these cities areas of

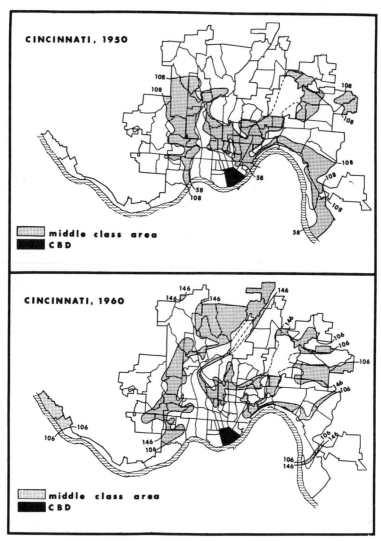

FIGURE 3. Middle-class housing areas, Cincinnati, Ohio, 1950 and 1960 (value in hundreds of dollars).

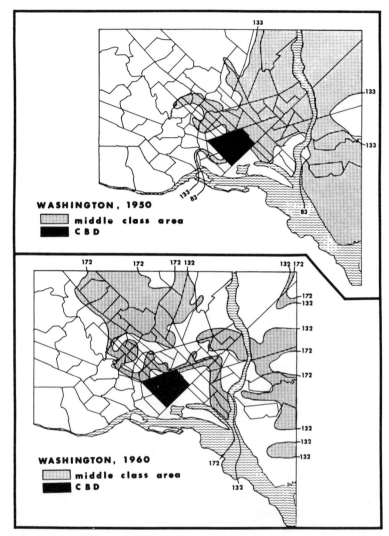

FIGURE 4.   Middle-class housing areas, Washington, D.C., 1950 and 1960 (values in hundreds of dollars).

high-value housing may be observed adjacent to one or more of the major physical features of the city site. Middle-class housing areas tend to occupy the interstices between areas of higher value housing.

A detailed study of the relationships between housing values and physical features of the urban site has been made only in the case of Washington. In this city there is a sharp value divide along Rock Creek Valley (Fig. 5). A comparison of 1950 values with those of 1960 suggests that this value divide has remained stable throughout the time period under study.

Not all major physical features are associated with higher value housing. Note values adjacent to the Potomac River and Palisades and those adjacent to the ravine occupied by Glover Archbold Park in 1950 and 1960. For several possible reasons certain major physical features in Washington have become associated with high-value housing.

In Washington housing values appear randomly oriented with reference to the CBD. Hence, the distribution of middle-class housing is also random with reference to the CBD. However, housing values do appear to be arranged in value plateaus stepping down from high points adjacent to selected physical features. This circumstance suggests that physical features regarded as desirable by the community have replaced the CBD as the points about which housing values and housing-type areas are oriented.

An interesting feature of the housing patterns in most of the cities considered here is the frequent absence of

a transitional zone between the different types of housing. In more cases than not, housing values represent plateaus separated from each other by sharp value escarpments (Fig. 5). This feature is most pronounced in 1960 for the boundary between middle-class housing and higher value housing. More evidence of a transition zone can be found in the case of the boundary between middle-class and lower-class housing areas. Increasing the value of the isoline representing the upper extent of middle-class housing by several hundreds of dollars did not materially alter its location. Value traverses reinforce a conclusion that the boundary between middle-class housing areas and higher-class areas tends to be sharp and narrow.

This phenomenon suggests a possible major factor in the general displacement of middle-class housing in the central city. The large value differential between the present upper limit of value for middle-class housing and the lower limit of value for higher-class housing suggests that traditional concepts of filtering of housing from high- to low-income groups cannot operate in most of these cities. The absence of housing filtered down from above adds to the pressures for migration of the middle class from the central city. Andrews has noted some deficiencies in the filtering process, and the evidence of the cities considered here reinforces a conclusion that the filtering process in central city areas has not operated to replace middle-class housing that has been passed on to lower income groups.[9]

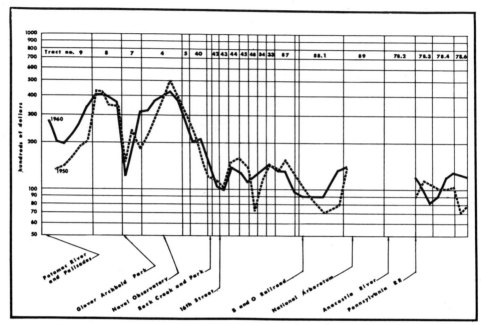

FIGURE 5.   Profile of housing values, Washington, D.C., 1950 and 1960.

Changes in Middle-Class Housing Areas

It is difficult to generalize about the patterns of change in middle-class housing areas. Any generalization made here, of course, would be subjective. Nevertheless, there are some observations that should be made for the possible implication on concepts of invasion and succession theories of neighborhood development. These concepts suggest that an alien type makes entry into a homogeneous neighborhood, establishes itself, and attracts like fellows, the eventual result being that the pre-existing neighborhood type is completely displaced by the invader.

The essence of the house filtering process described in most texts on urban real estate associates obsolescence of housing in an area with declines in housing values. As housing values decline, the area becomes more accessible to lower income groups which move in and eventually replace the pre-existing population. In this sequence of change, the filtering process may be viewed as preliminary to the invasion of a neighborhood by a lower income group. As applied to middle-class area changes, the invasion-succession hypothesis appears inadequate to account for all the differences observed between 1950 and 1960.

In general, middle-class housing areas in 1960 were also middle-class housing areas in 1950. In relatively few instances was a middle-class area identified in the latter year that was not so classified in the earlier. Deletions from the middle-class areas have not been compensated in these cities by depreciation of higher value residential areas.

In some cities, small pockets of 1960 middle-class area were observed in areas that were higher class in 1950. In others, the higher-class areas themselves appear to have expanded into what was middle-class area in 1950. The process of urban renewal has changed low- and middle-class areas into high value neighborhoods in such places as Washington, D.C.

The greatest change in middle-class housing areas seems attributable to expansion of lower value housing areas in the hearts of central cities. This pattern of change is paralleled by increasing concentrations of relatively low income families in central city areas. A polarization of housing values into the relatively high and the relatively low is a feature of most of the cities studied, although the degree of this polarization differs markedly from one place to another.

In general, the middle-class housing area has been displaced outwards from the CBD. In its wake lower-class housing has expanded, but not uniformly. Contiguous areas of middle-class housing identified in 1950 have tended to become fragmented by intrusions and exclaves of lower-class housing in 1960. Some expansion and higher value exclaves were also evident, but the overall dominant factor appears to be expansion of lower-class housing.

In this process there have been significant losses of central city area available to the middle class. One may assume that these losses have become part of a general suburban migration.

The probability and possibility of middle-class expansion into higher value areas of the central city appears to be limited, and this limit seems to have been reached in the cities considered here sometime between 1950 and 1960. The boundary between the middle-class housing and the higher-class housing experienced little change over this decade in several instances. The higher value housing areas seem able to preserve themselves from invasions of lower income groups and to constitute a relatively stable part of the central city residential structure.

Summary and Conclusions

A study of these 12 cities indicates that there was, on the average, a substantial decrease between 1950 and 1960 in the area of the central city occupied by middle-class housing.

The boundary between middle-class housing and higher-class housing appears, in many instances, to be stabilized and abrupt, reducing the opportunities for a filtering process to make housing available to the middle class in central cities.

The location of the CBD, centrally or noncentrally within the central city, appears to be closely related to the development of concentric or sector clusters of housing values within the central city.

The nature of changes between 1950 and 1960 has been to reduce the extent to which this type shares in the land available within the central city. Housing areas lost to lower income groups are not being replaced, and there is not much likelihood that they will be. To an increasing extent, it would appear that the central city is being compartmentalized into extremes of high and low housing values. The mediating and leavening role of the middle class in all aspects of central city life, to the extent that this can be measured by the area of the central city occupied by middle-class housing, seems likely to continue to dwindle. So-called "natural" processes of housing value changes (filtering, for example) are unlikely prospects to alter this trend.

Assuming an indefinite continuation of present trends, the middle class will be squeezed out of some cities within the next decade; in others, the process, operating more slowly, would take 30 to 50 years. A more likely assumption is that the trend will accelerate in the absence of a concerted effort to reverse present development trends.

Acknowledgments

The writer would like to express his sincere appreciation to the several members of a graduate seminar whose assistance, more rather than less voluntary, in the collection, tabulation, and plotting of housing values greatly facilitated the progress of this study.

Footnotes

1. R. B. Andrews: Urban Growth and Development (New York, 1962), p. 183.
2. Arthur B. Gallion and Simon Eisner: The Urban Pattern (New York, 1950), pp. 207–221.
3. The categories of value/income ratios (defined by the U.S. Census) were different in each year. For 1950 they were 1.0; 1.0 to 1.4; 1.5 to 1.9; 2.0 to 2.9; 3.0+. For 1960: 1.5; 1.5 to 1.9; 2.0 to 2.4; 2.5 to 2.9; 3.0 to 3.9; 4.0+.
4. Louis L. McQuitty: Elementary Linkage Analysis for Isolating Orthogonal and Oblique Types and Typal Relevancies, *Educational and Psychological Measurement,* Vol. 17, 1958, pp. 207–229.
5. Ernest W. Burgess: The Growth of the City, *in* R. E. Park and others, edits.: The City (Chicago, 1925).
6. Homer Hoyt: The Structure and Growth of Residential Neighborhoods in American Cities (Federal Housing Administration, 1939).
7. R. D. McKenzie: The Metropolitan Community (New York, 1933).
8. Raymond E. Murphy and J. E. Vance, Jr.: A Comparative Study of Nine Central Business Districts, *Econ. Geogr.,* Vol. 30, 1954, pp. 301–336.
9. Andrews, *op. cit.,* pp. 183–196.

seventeen ◆ ◆ ◆ ◆ ◆ ◆ ◆ ◆ ◆ ◆ ◆ ◆ ◆

◆ STANLEY D. BRUNN
◆ WAYNE L. HOFFMAN

The Spatial Response of Negroes and Whites Toward Open Housing: The Flint Referendum

The social, economic, and political controversy surrounding the issue of open housing has been heightened in the past few years by the passage of civil rights legislation affecting minority groups, by the judicial decisions rendered by the United States Supreme Court and lower courts, and by the election to public offices of individuals with certain persuasions.[1] The responses toward open housing, other than in a legal framework, have been reflected in various ways. For example, there have been the reactions of real estate developers who have tied Negro presence and ownership to declining land values, the appearance of "block-busters," community zoning ordinances as well as the financial investment of groups into integrated housing ventures, the establishment and enforcement of "fair housing" codes, and the election of public officials with favorable stances on open housing and similar legislation. In spite of some obstacles and apparent setbacks, attitudes with respect to residential integration have been gaining increasing acceptance in the South as well as in the North.[2] The overriding importance of this residential issue is linked closely with other civil rights programs such as school desegregation, busing pupils for "neighborhood balance," desegregation of public facilities such as playgrounds, voter registration, and equal job opportunity.

Prior to the congressional passage

◆ SOURCE. Reproduced by permission from the *Annals* of the Association of American Geographers, Vol. 60, 1970, pp. 18–36.

of the open housing bill in April, and the Supreme Court's judgment in June, 1968, voters in several states and cities had expressed their views about open housing.[3] The federal ruling stated that discrimination based on race in the sale or rental of housing was illegal.[4] It is worth noting from a historical perspective that from 1935 to 1950 the federal government aided residential discrimination against Negroes in various financial and construction policies. During this period the government encouraged neighborhood homogeneity, which meant the exclusion of Negroes.[5] Such programs and policies thereby helped promote white dominance in the suburbs and public housing concentrations for Negroes in the central cities. Prior to the 1968 federal ruling on open housing, this topic had been a hotly contested issue in several northern industrial cities, one of which was Flint, Michigan. This was the first city to have a referendum on open housing approved by its voters, and this was only after the city council had approved it by a narrow five to four margin.[6]

Brink and Harris stated that probably no civil rights measure other than possibly that on intermarriage has had such a profound emotional effect on white urban Americans.[7] The emotional response evoked questions of whether open housing invades the sanctity of the home, the inherent "right" to private property, and the basic freedom to make individual decisions. In addition this issue arouses a number of less subtle but evident white responses toward Negroes such as stereotyping physical characteristics, social values, economic spirit and, above all, their

association with declining land values once they appear in white neighborhoods. For the Negro the equal response to purchase or rent a residence is viewed as a basic inalienable right.[8] Their frustration to achieve this goal leads to despair and may manifest itself in the form of peaceful or violent non-cooperation with the white power structure.

Open housing for all citizens has become a more acute need in recent years from the civil rights point of view and from the short and long term consequences of *de facto* segregation policies in our cities. This has become a problem in the northern as well as the southern cities.[9] At the very root of the open housing question lie such issues as the survival of the commercial core in the cities, the employment and education opportunities and facilities for minority groups in the inner city, and the necessity for coordinated decisions rendered by representatives from the varying social and economic strata in the city.[10] Today there are few major cities where Negroes do not comprise a sizeable segment of the urban population and where housing for them is not a major problem. By restricting complete freedom in the sale or rental of residence many urban planners have concluded that policies of housing apartheid will lead eventually to increased ghetto expansion and a host of related social, economic, and political problems.[11] Some of the planning schemes designed to "solve" Negro housing problems, such as urban renewal, have not always been popular with Negroes. Frequently these programs have stressed commercial development in former residential areas which has meant that the residential space available for immediate Negro occupancy has been reduced. This results in increased crowding in already overcrowded facilities.[12] It is not difficult to imagine how feelings of separateness have developed among the black residents in our cities especially when urban housing problems are considered. Recent investigations by Farley and Taeuber into population increases and densities for Negroes and whites in our major cities have demonstrated that there is more residential segregation today between the inner city and the suburbs than in 1960.[13] Furthermore, they indicate the separateness is increasing.

For many central city Negroes not only has the finding of adequate and sufficient housing become a major problem but so has locating a permanent source of employment. Discrimination in housing does reduce the job opportunities for those in the middle as well as the lower stratum. For many Negroes their place of employment is not in the central city but in the suburbs. This means their journey-to-work in terms of distance, time, and cost is placing them far from their residences.[14] Some central city ghetto Negroes have solved their residence problems by leapfrogging the suburbs to settle in small rural towns beyond the white suburban ring.[15] There can be no doubt but that *de facto* segregation policies associated with housing, schooling, and employment have contributed substantially to the separation of the white and Negro populations, the former being allowed the freedom of selection and mobility

and the latter being denied the same privileges.

In a consideration of an open housing issue there are a number of facets that make the issue worthy of a political and social geographic investigation, and that have some utility in city planning. For example, what is the areal extent of the white and Negro populations? What are the spatial facets important in ghetto expansion? What effect does urban renewal have on the Negro migration? Do views of whites and blacks toward open housing, as reflected in a referendum, vary over space? What social and economic characteristics are associated with the vote in the ghetto, the suburbs, and the transitional zone? And what effect does distance from the ghetto have on the voting pattern for the whites?

The February 20, 1968, referendum in Flint, Michigan, was used to test and analyze several of the above spatial aspects related to open housing. This achieved national attention because it was the first time the residents of a major city had approved an open housing referendum. The final vote was indeed very close: 20,170 for the issue and 20,140 against.[16] Flint is similar to other large northern industrial centers such as Cleveland, Detroit, Gary, and Chicago which also have large Negro populations. In Flint about seventeen percent of the city was Negro in 1960, and it was estimated to be about twenty percent in 1968. Most Negroes reside in two main concentrations that are surrounded by the white population.[17] In using Flint as a case study the purposes of this investigation are threefold: (1) to determine the white and

Negro reactions toward open housing as measured by the vote; (2) to examine the geographic variation with respect to income, education, and housing values for Negroes and whites; and (3) to investigate the effects distance from the center of the ghetto and from the ghetto periphery have on the voting behavior of the whites. The social, economic, and distance indicators and the open housing vote were incorporated into simple and stepwise multiple regression models. Separate models were used to investigate the behavior of the blacks and the whites. In addition to the statistical results various maps and tables are incorporated into the analysis.

Survey of Literature

There is a wealth of literature by political scientists, sociologists, psychologists, public administrators, economists, and some geographers that has bearing on this problem. For example, there are studies concerned with policy making, voting behavior, Negro-white relations, ghetto characteristics, Negro "invasion," real estate values, housing conditions, and attitudes toward issues such as open housing. However, it is not the purpose of this study to present a review and summarize all these topics but rather to concentrate on urban voting patterns and especially those related to nonpartisan referendums and on the attitudes of whites and Negroes toward open housing.

A notable trend in social and political geography in recent years has been the concern with voting behavior and patterns. Although most of the voting studies have been concerned with political parties in states or countries there have been several that have dealt with cities such as those by Clodfelter, Van Duzer, Kasperson, Lewis, Roberts and Rumage, Rowley, Simmons, and Cox.[18] To date there has been only one geographic study that has considered aspects of urban nonpartisan referendums, even though the research possibilities for future studies are great.[19] In the main the urban investigations by political scientists and sociologists have dealt with both partisan and nonpartisan issues. They have been concerned with the administering of elections, the policy-making mechanisms at various levels, the salient differences in central city and suburban behavior, the growing political power of the suburbs, and the role of religion, party, class, and race in given elections.[20]

With regard to housing there have been several studies by geographers concerned with topics related to its quality, density, and composition in different cities and parts of a city.[21] There have been no studies that have dealt with such social issues as open housing or about the variation in attitudes toward this or similar programs. The urban sociologists have done a great deal of work on such topics as varying attitudes within urban areas, social distances between groups, residential patterns for ethnic groups, Negro population changes, urban discrimination indices, and the movement of Negroes into white areas.[22] Of particular relevance to this study are those that have investigated the opinions and attitudes of both Negroes and whites prior to, during, and after Negroes have moved into predominantly all-white neighborhoods.[23] Also, the contributions of urban economists and real estate and appraisal experts demonstrate a concern for a number of facets related to open housing that may be associated with how people vote on open housing referendums. Their concern has been mainly with the changes in property values, taxation discrimination, and land use changes as a result of the invasion of Negroes into transitional areas and exclusive white residential areas.[24] The significant findings of these studies and others help form a basis from which to postulate research hypotheses that can be used to analyze the voting patterns for the open housing referendum in Flint.

Hypotheses

From the literature of various associated studies by geographers, sociologists, political scientists, and others several hypotheses relating to the geographic distribution of the open housing referendum are advanced. Separate hypotheses are postulated for the white and the Negro populations.

First, in relation to the white sector a positive relationship is predicted between the affirmative vote and median income, median education level, and the median value of owner occupied dwellings. The correlation between education and racial attitudes is particularly well documented by Lipset and Allport; both devote ample attention to this relationship.[25] Their findings substantiate the expected relationship.

Allport, for example, stated ". . . that general education to an appreciable degree helps raise the level of tolerance."[26] Median income plays a key role according to Lipset; he concluded that for many underlying reasons the wealthier are more tolerant where issues of civil liberties and race relations are concerned.[27] This notion was corroborated further by Brink and Harris, who found in their survey research that affluent whites are much more favorably inclined toward the Negro than their low income counterpart.[28] The role of the median value of owner occupied dwellings, although not dealt with specifically in the literature on attitude formation, seems to be directly related to the above statements. It is assumed that the better educated and wealthier classes would occupy, with only slight exceptions, the homes of higher median value.

For the white population it is also hypothesized that physical proximity to Negroes will play an important role in their voting decision process. Various studies have demonstrated that social distance between groups has affected white's voting behavior for minority group leaders.[29] The elements of social distance can be related in an urban setting to physical distance between groups (ethnic, racial, social, or occupational classes) which likewise would undoubtedly affect voting patterns.[30] The result may be "block" voting by whites, blacks, or other major groups which exhibit strong feelings of unity. In Kramer's study of the southern edge of the black belt in Chicago he found that when interviewing whites the physical distance from Negroes did play

TABLE 1.   Spontaneous Expressions of Anti-Negro Sentiment: After Kramer

	Zone 1	Zone 2	Zone 3	Zone 4	Zone 5
Percent Spontaneously Expressing Anti-Negro Sentiment	64	43	27	14	4
Number Interviewed	118	115	121	123	142

Source: Brink and Harris, *op. cit.*, footnote 7, p. 232.

a definite role in the attitude formation and in the amount of racial friction.[31] After marking off five zones, with number one being at the point of contact with the expanding Negro ghetto and number five three miles away, he interviewed white respondents for spontaneous expressions of black hostility (Table 1). A similar finding was reported by Winder; he found that low income whites in the same zone with Negroes showed more prejudice than those in an intermediate zone. The difference was attributed to competition for low income housing.[32] The concept of distance and its effect on the voting behavior is tested in this study by incorporating two spatial variables into the framework of the regression model. They are straight line distance from the center of the ghetto and straight line distance from the closest Negro precinct. It is postulated that a positive relationship exists between the favorable vote for open housing and distance from the ghetto and nearest Negro precinct.[33]

For the Negro, racial concern and pride, plus an awareness of the inherent advantages of open housing, are expected to override major internal differences. Survey research has indicated that Negroes of all income classes do desire to live in integrated neighborhoods (Table 2).[34] It has been demonstrated by Horton and Thompson, Wilson, and Wilson and Banfield that some of the socially and economically deprived groups vote negatively on nonpartisan issues.[35] Wilson and Banfield in their research on Negroes mention that they, as distinct from some other minority groups, have a greater "public regardingness" on certain issues and vote in a positive manner. Even though most Negroes in Flint live in relatively low valued housing areas, and have lower education levels than their white counterparts, they are expected to support strongly this particularly nonpartisan issue. It is postulated, therefore, that for Negroes there is a negative relationship between the favorable open housing vote and median income, median education, and median housing values. These assumptions are strengthened by recent research in Columbus, Ohio, where in another nonpartisan referendum, viz., one dealing with urban renewal, rather large negative correlation values appeared between such variables as education, income, and the vote when the Negro community was isolated for analysis.[36] The effect of distance and the vote was also tested for the black area in Flint. It is

TABLE 2.   Negro Attitudes Toward Desired Housing and Neighborhood: After Brink and Harris

Question: In living in a neighborhood, if you could find the housing you want and like, would you rather live in a neighborhood with Negro families, or in a neighborhood that had both whites and Negroes?

	Negroes		Whites and Negroes		Not Sure	
	1966 %	1963 %	1966 %	1963 %	1966 %	1963 %
Total all interviews	17	20	68	64	15	16
Total non-South	8	11	79	75	13	14
Non-South						
Low Income	10	19	79	75	11	6
Lower Middle Income	7	11	78	75	15	14
Middle and Upper						
Income	6	12	80	69	14	19
Total South	26	27	57	55	17	18
South						
Urban	22	26	58	57	20	17
Non-Urban	29	33	56	50	15	17
Middle and Upper						
Income	17	6	70	69	13	25
Age						
Under 35 years	12		75		13	
35–49 years	17		67		16	
50 years and over	21		63		16	
Civil rights pace too slow	13		75		12	
Negro community leaders	10		59		31	

Source: Brink and Harris, *op. cit.*, footnote 7, p. 232.

TABLE 3.   Predicted Direction of Relationships

	Median income	Median education	Median housing value	Distance center of ghetto	Distance nearest Negro precinct
Negroes	−	−	−	−	−
Whites	+	+	+	+	+

Source: Calculated by authors.

− = negative relationship.

+ = positive relationship.

interesting to speculate here on the influence of the white proximity to the Negro. If, as Kramer contended, white hostility increases with proximity to Negroes, could it also be assumed that Negro hostility increases with proximity to whites in transitional areas? Unfortunately little work has been done in this area to formulate a sound hypothesis. A negative relationship is expected between the positive vote and distance from the center of the ghetto (Table 3).

Research Design

Through the use of simple and stepwise regression models, map comparisons, and profiles the above hypotheses are tested. It is felt that through the marriage of such traditional geographic techniques as mapping and construction of profiles in conjunction with the somewhat more recent statistical manipulations of data a higher level and more meaningful analysis is obtained.

In this study there are, however, two inherent difficulties that merit brief consideration. The first is aimed at reconciling variations in the sizes of reporting units, whereas the second is concerned with justifying differences between the 1960 population characteristics from the census and the 1968 voting data. Urban voting returns are given usually on a ward and precinct basis, whereas population characteristics from the census sources are provided for blocks and census tracts. The problem, then, is to "fit" one reporting unit to the other. In this study Flint's 122 precincts were assigned, through the use of an overlay pro-

cedure, either entirely or partially to one of the city's forty-one census tracts (Fig. 1).[37] It is worth noting at this juncture that, as aggregate data are used, the problem of ecological correlation arises. Therefore, the findings of this study are linked to areal units and cannot be attributed to the voting behavior of individual residents of Flint.[38] Had survey data been available on income, age, occupation, political orientation, participation rates, open housing views, and attitudes of the blacks towards whites and vice versa, they would have provided a basis for examining individual attitudes through the city.[39]

As noted in the formulation of the hypotheses, the white and Negro populations have been divided for purposes of examining inter- and intra-variation. This is necessary in order to insure a meaningful interpretation of the voting behavior since, for example, the Negro poor are not expected to vote in similar fashion to their white counterparts. An initial regression analysis was made with no division between the groups; however, it revealed the weight of the Negro vote adversely affected the correlations and interpretations for such variables as the vote for open housing and median income and median education. Once the division of the populations into two groups was accomplished a more realistic picture of the relationships emerged. The division of the precincts into the black or white group was based on the percentage of Negroes residing in a particular precinct according to the 1960 census. Any unit with ten percent or more Negro population, which in this case was thirty-

PRECINCTS and WARDS

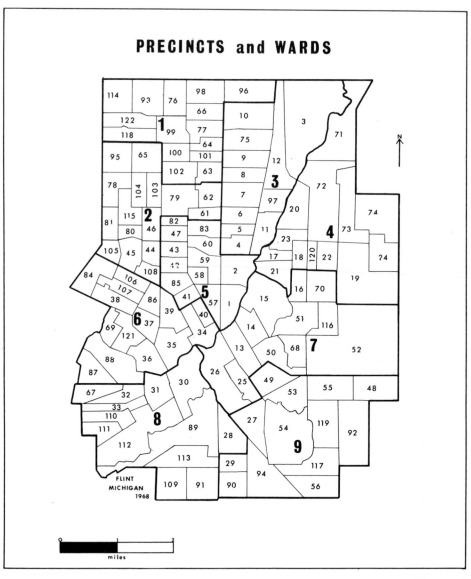

FLINT
MICHIGAN
1968

miles

FIGURE 1.

nine precincts, was included in the Negro sector, whereas those with fewer than ten percent Negro population, eighty-three precincts, were included in the white group. The decision to use ten percent as a basis for dividing the two groups was based on similar usage by Morrill, and by Smith, as indicating meaningful threshold levels for Negro expansion.[40] Once any unit reaches ten percent Negro population, it seems to indicate a swing toward eventual complete Negro dominance. With increases in the Negro population since 1960, many of those precincts which had almost ten percent then undoubtedly had much greater percentages in 1968 (Fig. 2). This difference from the time of the census and the vote for open housing in 1968 presents difficulties in providing a meaningful interpretation of the white and Negro voting behavior, especially for those precincts in the transitional zones. It is suggested that the areas of Flint that overwhelmingly supported open housing may represent a rather accurate picture of the major Negro concentrations in 1968 (Fig. 3).[41]

Analysis

A visual comparison of the voting map and the map of Negro population suggests immediately that the Negro precincts supported open housing and the white precincts did not (Figs. 3 and 2). However, in view of the fact that only a small percent of the population is Negro, it is evident that a considerable amount of white support was necessary for passage of this issue. A good part of this support came from such organizations as the National Association for the Advancement of Colored People, Urban League, UAW-CIO labor organization, Council of Churches, American

TABLE 4. Characteristics of Selected Precincts in Flint

Precinct number	Percent favorable vote	Median income	Median years education	Median housing value	Percent Negro	Distance center of ghetto	Distance nearest Negro precinct
2	92	$4342	9.1	$ 9,280	82	.4 mi.	0.00 mi.
18	31	$5437	9.8	$ 8,600	0	1.0 mi.	.53 mi.
43	56	$7158	12.3	$13,200	0	1.5 mi.	.82 mi.
53	98	$5167	9.3	$ 8,900	96	0.0 mi.	0.00 mi.
63	72	$6390	10.3	$11,500	0	1.1 mi.	.24 mi.
71	17	$5831	10.2	$ 9,700	0	2.1 mi.	1.00 mi.
112	48	$7005	12.1	$12,600	0	2.7 mi.	.75 mi.
117	33	$7265	11.9	$13,600	10	1.6 mi.	0.00 mi.

Sources: United States Bureau of the Census, *United States Censuses of Population and Housing: 1960, Census Tracts,* Final Report PHC (1)-47, Flint, Michigan (Washington, D.C.: Government Printing Office, 1962).

Distances calculated by authors. The voting data were obtained from *The Flint Journal,* February 21, 1968, p. 17.

NEGRO DISTRIBUTION

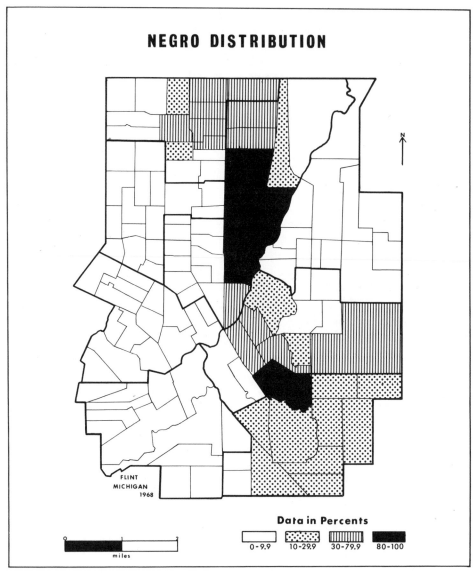

FLINT
MICHIGAN
1968

Data in Percents

0 - 9.9 | 10 - 29.9 | 30 - 79.9 | 80 - 100

miles

FIGURE 2.

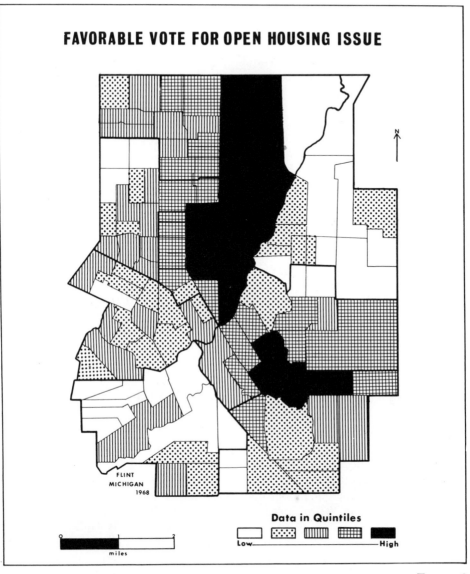

FAVORABLE VOTE FOR OPEN HOUSING ISSUE

FLINT
MICHIGAN
1968

Data in Quintiles

Low ——————————————— High

miles

FIGURE 3.

Civil Liberties Union, League of Women Voters, and two other local organizations known as HOME (Housing Opportunities Made Equal) and the Friends of Fair Housing. The variations of the vote and the social and economic characteristics of the population are illustrated for a sample of eight precincts in Table 4.

Within the city there were entire wards, such as 4, 6, and 8, where not one precinct yielded one-half or more of its vote in favor of open housing. This concentrated opposition is not surprising for Wards 4 and 8 when the voting pattern is compared with that of median income (Fig. 4). It is observed readily that these white areas are comprised with few exceptions of the income levels in the middle or lower segments.[42] The visual correlation of the vote and median income does not materialize in Ward 6 or in parts of Ward 2. In fact in such precincts as numbers 38, 80, 81, 106, and 107, which are some of the wealthiest in Flint, there was very little support for this issue. We can only speculate at this juncture why this pattern occurred. First, it is noted that the "white precincts" that did support the referendum are located in proximity to the Negro area. As stated previously some of these transitional "white precincts" would have to be classed as "black precincts" today. When such an explanation is offered, it is easier to interpret the patterns in Ward 5 which generally supported the issue and the reaction of certain precincts in the contiguous Wards 2 and 6.

The profiles produce another view of the distribution of the vote (Fig. 5). They were drawn from the northwest corner of the city to the southeast corner and from the northeast to the southwest corner. The profiles are very similar with only slight deviations. The outlying white dominated areas simply did not support the open housing referendum. In fact as one moves from the ghetto, where the blacks voted overwhelmingly in favor of open housing, to the city fringe, racial attitudes in the form of a positive vote for the issue appear either to harden or at best to remain constant. Therefore, empirical observation suggests that a spatial element, as hypothesized above, is not strongly present in this referendum.

By carrying the investigation of the white population a step further through the vehicle of simple correlation, measured relationships were produced which can be used to confirm or reject the empirical observations. An examination of the simple correlations shed considerable light on the voting behavior (Table 5). The virtual absence of any significant correlation between the vote and median income ($-.06$), median education ($-.08$), and median value of owner occupied dwellings ($+.04$) confirms the empirical observations and, therefore, leads to a rejection of the research hypotheses for the whites. Thus, it would appear that on the basis of the categories for white and black precincts the general behavior of white residents with high as well as low incomes and those with few and many years of schooling do not fit into one homogeneous voting pattern. There are examples of some low income precincts, which are probably predominantly Negro today, and some high income precincts which supported

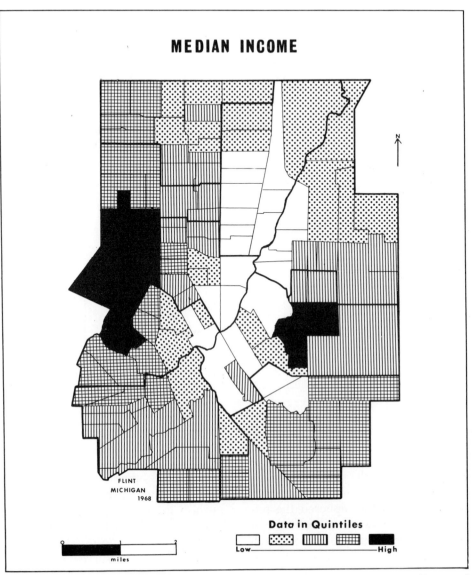

MEDIAN INCOME

FLINT
MICHIGAN
1968

Data in Quintiles

Low ——————————————— High

miles

FIGURE 4.

PROFILES OF FAVORABLE VOTE

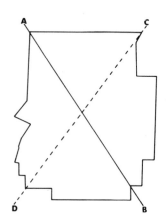

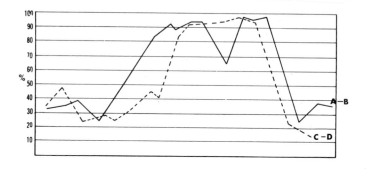

FIGURE 5.

open housing. On the other hand there are precincts of low, middle, and high median incomes that opposed the referendum. These variations in behavior are not in accord with previous research on the attitudes of white people and their support for social welfare measures. It may be that the explosive and emotional nature of this issue to many white people of differing incomes makes it different from other nonpartisan issues such as those dealing with education bonds or library construction funds. Two factors may account par-

tially for this apparent anomalous pattern of white behavior. One is that much of the previous research on attitudes involving racial feelings has been of the survey nature.[43] In forming opinions for these surveys the white residents of the more educated and affluent areas of cities may perceive that it is "unfashionable" or unwise to exhibit their true feelings to a stranger conducting the interviews. Therefore, as a recent study on opinions about open housing has demonstrated, very few of the respondents strongly ap-

TABLE 5. Correlation Coefficients for White and Negro Sectors

Variable	White sector	Negro sector
X1 Median Income	−.06	−.49*
X2 Median Years Completed	−.08	−.53*
X3 Median Value of House	.04	−.40*
X4 Distance from Center of Ghetto	−.36*	−.56*
X5 Distance from Nearest Negro Precinct	−.30*	**

Source: Calculated by authors.
* Significant at .01 level.
** Omitted from regression analysis as all Negro precincts have at least ten percent Negro population, as defined for purposes of this study.

proved or opposed open housing. Most of the people were unwilling or unable to state their preferences on the open housing question frankly.[44] Abrams has stated that when a person finds his moral and property rights in conflict, as in open housing, the person will usually vote his property rights against his moral scruples.[45] Therefore, once inside a voting booth where no one can hold him accountable for his attitudes, the individual may vent his true feelings and cast a vote which has little bearing on his educational achievement or philosophical commitments.

When measuring the effects of proximity of the whites to the Negro population, both relationships, straight line distance to the ghetto center (−.36), and straight line distance to the nearest black precinct (−.30),

were statistically significant. This suggests that the transitional areas voted in favor of open housing and those in the fringes voted against the measure. The increases in Negro population in the transitional areas between 1960 and 1968 account in part for this deviation. It can be stated, however, that the correlation values do indicate that the spatial element as presented by Kramer in Chicago was not reflected in the attitudes of the whites in terms of this vote.

For the Negro sector a visual correlation of the maps of the vote and the Negro population demonstrates the great similarity in the two patterns (Figs. 3 and 2). Some of the areas with a very high favorable vote for open housing reflect Negro expansion since 1960 especially in the Buick district. The vote for open housing carried heavily in all those Negro precincts except where from ten to 29.9 percent of the population was black. Here the support on occasion fell below fifty percent. As might be expected there is also an excellent visual fit between the areas of low median income and the favorable vote (Fig. 4). In northern cities such as Flint the Negro occupies the lowest rungs of the economic ladder and it is in these areas of lowest average incomes that a very high percent of their vote was in favor of open housing.

When the hypotheses were tested statistically for the Negro sector the simple correlations support the empirical contentions (Table 4). Very high and statistically significant relationships were observed for all variables. As postulated these were negative correlations. That is, there were inverse relationships between the positive vote and median income, median education level, and median value of owner occupied dwellings. These research hypotheses were accepted. Furthermore, the negative relationships between the vote and distance from the ghetto were confirmed.

At this juncture it seems appropriate to examine the validity of the variables utilized in the regression model and to determine to what extent they together helped explain the total open housing vote. Individually some played a much more important part than others. In order to determine what percent of the total variation was accounted for by all the variables together, the stepwise multiple regression model was used. In this model the variables are selected one by one in order of the amount they explained of the total variance. For the white sector, distance from the ghetto proved to be the most important variable in explaining the vote (Table 6). This was followed by the median value of owner

occupied dwellings, median income, distance from the nearest black precinct, and median education level. When all these variables were considered together in the model, thirty-two percent of the total variation was explained. Although this is a statistically significant figure it does not account for a large portion of the variance. It is suggested that additional studies on nonpartisan referendums incorporate other variables, use other sources of data, hopefully survey data, and employ more sophisticated models such as factor analysis. Some indices that might have a bearing on the voting behavior are the ethnic population, age, dominant religion, owner versus rented residences, and years residence in the same dwelling.

For the Negro area the explained variance is slightly higher, forty-six percent. The distance from the center of the ghetto proved to be the most important variable in the stepwise regression model, the same index as in the white sector. Others that were important were median education level,

TABLE 6.   Coefficients of Multiple Correlation and Multiple Determination: Stepwise Regression Model

White sector			Negro sector		
Variable	R	R^2	Variable	R	R^2
Distance from Center of Ghetto	−.36	13%	Distance from Center of Ghetto	−.56	31%
Median Value of House	.43	19%	Median Years Completed	.67	46%
Median Income	.55	30%	Median Value of House	.68	46%
Distance from Nearest Negro Precinct	.56	32%	Median Income	.68*	46%
Median Years Completed	.56*	32%			

Source: Calculated by authors.

* Significant at .01 level.

median value of owner occupied homes, and median income. Variables that merit inclusion in future ecological studies where Negro voting behavior is measured are indicators of unemployment, welfare coverage, household characteristics, family size, and major occupations.

An additional factor that should be considered in this analysis is the voter participation or turnout on this crucial issue. An examination of the percent of eligible voters in each precinct reveals the turnout varied widely in the wards and precincts. The largest number of precincts with low turnouts were in Wards 4 and 9 and fewer precincts in Wards 5, 6, and 7. In these particular precincts fewer than forty percent of the registered voters cast ballots on this referendum. In several only thirty-four percent voted. By contrast the precincts in Wards 2, 3, and parts of 6, 7, and 9 were considerably above the city average of fifty-one percent. A number of these had over sixty percent of the eligible voters vote on the referendum. The highest turnouts were in several precincts in Ward 9 where seventy-four percent of the voters voted. The highest turnouts in the city were in the very low income Negro areas and upper middle and high income white areas. In general these areas had over fifty-five percent of the eligible voters cast ballots. These two groups occasionally vote in like manner on nonpartisan issues, according to Wilson and Banfield.[46] However, on this issue a homogeneous voting pattern is not apparent. As has been mentioned the low income black areas voted heavily in favor of open housing. The white

behavior did not fit into a homogeneous pattern. The high income precincts in Wards 2 and 6 did not support open housing although adjacent precincts with slightly lower incomes did. By contrast the high income areas in Ward 7 did tend to favor the referendum. In general the low income and middle income white areas, especially in Wards 4, 6, and 8 did not support open housing nor did they have exceptionally high turnouts, generally less than fifty percent. It seems that the slim margin of victory for this issue is attributed to the high turnout and overwhelming support in the Negro areas and the small margins of support in several upper middle and high income white precincts. It is probably individuals in these income groupings who comprised the various civic organizations that favored passage of this issue.

Summary and Conclusions

This study has been concerned with investigating some of the reasons behind the geographic variation in the attitudes of the residents of Flint, Michigan, toward open housing. These variations in attitudes are analyzed by a consideration of the recent referendum dealing with this issue. An examination of the maps, profiles, and correlation values revealed there were measurable differences between the Negro and white behavior. In the case of the Negroes, they turned out in large numbers and voted almost solidly for this measure. The behavior of the whites was not unanimously against open housing as support from various upper middle and high income precincts was necessary for its passage. When the whites were considered as one group, their behavior did not seem related to expected measures of income or education. It is worthy of note that the white turnout varied considerably, with the lowest turnouts in the low income and highest in the upper middle and high income precincts. Also the distances of whites from the center and edge of the ghettoes did not affect the voting pattern noticeably on this particular issue. This study has demonstrated that there needs to be a great deal more geographic research performed on black and white voting behavior on nonpartisan issues before we can attach meaningful results to differences in income, education, race, and various spatial measures.

Whether the findings for Flint on this or similar issues are indicative of the political behavior in other cities merits further research. For example, what meaningful geographic patterns are characteristic of votes for such issues as urban renewal, school bonds, fluoridation, public works, or welfare levies? Are there similar voting patterns on these issues for the central cities, the suburbs, or the lower, middle, and upper income areas? What effects do age groups, sex ratios, race, occupation status, and home owners *versus* renters have on voting behavior? Does affiliation with a national political party exhibit a positive or negative relationship with certain urban social referendums? Is there a national or regional voting model that can be formulated through other techniques such as factor analysis, or predicted from simulation runs? What effect do other geographic elements such as psychological barriers, stress points, territoriality, and gerrymandering have on attitude formation and expression in voting for or against particular issues?[47] The answers to these questions are dependent on future research on urban voting behavior in which geographers include other variables and use other models or techniques, as well as keep abreast of related research in fields such as political science, sociology, and psychology. It is in this manner that the contribution of social and political geographers will not only aid in the gradual construction of significant urban models for the social sciences but likewise lead perhaps to the formulation of urban policies.[48]

Footnotes

1. For several authoritative and well documented statements on ghetto development, open housing schemes, and related urban residential problems, see: M. Grodzins, "The New Shame of the Cities," *Confluence*, Vol. 7 (1958), pp. 29–46; F. S. Horne, "Interracial Housing in the United States," *Phylon*, Vol. 19 (1958), pp. 13–20; R. C. Weaver, "Non-White Population Movements and Urban Ghettoes," *Phylon*, Vol. 29 (1959), pp. 235–41; R. C. Morrill, "The Negro Ghetto: Problems and Alternatives," *Geographical Review*, Vol. 55 (1965), pp. 339–61; L. M. Friedman, "Government and Slum Housing: Some General Considerations," *Law and Contemporary Problems*, Vol. 32 (1967), pp. 357–70; W. M. Young, "The Case for Urban Integration," *Social Work*, Vol. 12 (1967), pp. 12–17; *Report of the National Advisory Commission on Civil Disorders*

(Washington, D.C.: Government Printing Office, 1968); and D. Ward, "The Emergence of Central Immigrant Ghettoes in American Cities: 1840–1920," *Annals*, Association of American Geographers, Vol. 58 (1968), pp. 343–59.

2. P. S. Sheatsley, "White Attitudes Toward the Negro," *Daedalus* (Winter, 1966), pp. 217–38. In addition, the Columbia Broadcasting System reported in its program "Of Black America" on September 2, 1968, that in its analysis of a national poll taken in May and June that forty-eight percent of the whites interviewed said they would object to Negroes coming into all white housing areas.

3. Prior to Flint the issue was subject to a vote by the electorate in Berkeley, California (in 1963); the state of California with its controversial Proposition 14 (in 1964); Seattle and Tacoma, Washington; Akron and Springfield, Ohio; Jackson and Flint, Michigan; and Columbia, Missouri. "Flint Recount," *Trends in Housing*, Vol. 12 (April, 1968), p. 7.

4. "Open-Housing Law Highlights 20 Year Civil Rights Effort," *Congressional Quarterly*, April 19, 1968, pp. 888–902.

5. The federal government's position and role in encouraging residential segregation is covered in: E. and G. Grier, "Equality and Beyond: Housing Segregation and the Great Society," *Daedalus* (Winter, 1966), pp. 77–106.

6. *The Flint Journal*, February 21, 1968, p. 17. It is worthy of note that since the Flint referendum the electorate in five other cities have approved fair housing ordinances. Four are in Michigan (Birmingham, Plymouth, Pontiac, and Saginaw), and the other in Illinois (Normal). "Referenda Approvals," *Trends in Housing*, Vol. 12 (May–July, 1968), p. 8. In the same issue the National Committee Against Discrimination in Housing reported there were 229 state and local fair housing laws: twenty-three states, the District of Colum-

bia, and 205 local ordinances. If the Supreme Court had not rendered its decision in June there would have been similar referendums in other cities.

7. W. Brink and L. Harris, *Black and White. A Study of U. S. Racial Attitudes Today* (New York: Simon and Schuster, 1966), pp. 40–41.

8. Myrdal has commented on the awareness of all Americans with regard to the basic rights expressed in the American Creed; G. Myrdal, *The American Dilemma. Vol. 1. The Negro in a White Dilemma* (New York: McGraw-Hill, Paperback Edition, 1964; originally published in 1944), p. 4.

9. Abrams in his discussion of the housing problems Negroes entail stated: "The big city has thus been performing its historic role as refuge for minorities, while the Northern and Western suburbs have become the new Mason-Dixon lines of America. . ."; C. Abrams, "The Housing Problem and the Negro," *Daedalus* (Winter, 1966), p. 68.

10. J. Meltzer and J. Whitley, "Social and Physical Planning for the Urban Slum," in B. J. L. Berry and J. Meltzer, *Goals for Urban America* (Englewood Cliffs, N.J.: Prentice-Hall, Inc., 1967), pp. 133–52.

11. Brink and Harris, *op. cit.*, footnote 7, pp. 131–32 and 136.

12. In fact in the United States from sixty to seventy-two percent of those displaced by urban renewal have been Negroes and only a small number of new houses constructed on the sites are open to them. It is therefore not surprising that urban renewal has been labeled "Negro removal" by civil rights groups. See Abrams, *op. cit.*, footnote 9, pp. 64–76. Two examples that illustrate this situation are: E. P. Wolf and C. N. Lebeaux, "On the Destruction of Poor Neighborhoods by Urban Renewal," *Social Problems*, Vol. 15 (1965), pp. 3–8, and F. J. Davis, "The

Effects of a Freeway Displacement on Racial Housing Segregation in a Northern City," *Phylon,* Vol. 26 (1965), pp. 209–15.

13. R. Farley and K. E. Taeuber, "Population Trends and Residential Segregation since 1960," *Science,* Vol. 159 (1968), pp. 953–56.

14. J. O. Wheeler, "Work-Trip Length and the Ghetto," *Land Economics,* Vol. 44 (1968), pp. 107–12.

15. J. O. Wheeler and S. D. Brunn, "Negro Migration into Rural Southwestern Michigan," *Geographical Review,* Vol. 58 (1968), pp. 214–30.

16. *The Flint Journal,* March 6, 1968, p. 1.

17. P. F. Lewis, "Impact of Negro Migration on the Electoral Geography of Flint, Michigan, 1932–1962: A Cartographic Analysis," *Annals,* Association of American Geographers, Vol. 55 (1965), pp. 1–25. The two Negro neighborhoods, Thread Lake in the east central part of Flint, and the Buick one in the north central part, exhibit some differences in socioeconomic status, income, age, occupation, and general housing conditions. The Thread Lake is older and has higher income Negroes with more improved housing than the ghetto associated with the Buick factory.

18. Examples of voting studies by geographers on partisan elections in cities include: C. Clodfelter, "Political Regions of the City: An Analysis of Voting in Cincinnati" (unpublished Master's thesis, Department of Geography, Clark University, 1961); E. F. Van Duzer, "An Analysis of the Differences in Republican Presidential Vote in Cities and Their Suburbs" (unpublished Ph.D. dissertation, Department of Geography, University of Iowa, 1962); R. E. Kasperson, "Toward a Geography of Urban Politics: Chicago, A Case Study," *Economic Geography,* Vol. 41 (1965), pp. 95–107; Lewis, *op. cit.,* footnote 17; M. C. Roberts and K. W. Rumage, "The Spatial

Variations in Urban Left Wing Voting in England and Wales in 1951," *Annals,* Association of American Geographers, Vol. 55 (1965), pp. 161–78; G. Rowley, "The Greater London Council Elections of 1964: Some Geographical Considerations," *Tijdschrift voor economische en sociale geografie,* Vol. 56 (1965), pp. 113–14; J. W. Simmons, "Voting Behavior and Socio-Economic Characteristics: The Middlesex East Federal Election, 1965," *Canadian Journal of Economic and Political Science,* Vol. 33 (1967), pp. 389–400; and K. R. Cox, "Suburbia and Voting Behavior in the London Metropolitan Area," *Annals,* Association of American Geographers, Vol. 58 (1968), pp. 111–27.

19. The only example of a nonpartisan urban referendum analyzed by a geographer is: W. L. Hoffman, "A Statistical and Cartographic Analysis of the 1954 and 1964 Urban Renewal Referendums for Columbus, Ohio" (unpublished M. A. thesis, Department of Geography, Ohio State University, 1966). Two other recent theses that are concerned with urban renewal aspects are: F. Bean, "Political Regionalism in an Urban Setting: Pittsburgh, Pennsylvania, 1948–1964" (unpublished M. A. thesis, Department of Geography, University of Pittsburgh, 1966), and R. Davis, "A Geographic Analysis of Political Socialization in the Phoenix Area" (unpublished M. A. thesis, Department of Geography, Arizona State University, 1967).

20. For examples of urban voting studies by political scientists and sociologists see: C. R. Adrian, "A Typology of Nonpartisan Elections," *Western Political Quarterly,* Vol. 12 (1959), pp. 449–58; O. Gantz, "Protestant and Catholic Voting in a Metropolitan Area," *Public Opinion Quarterly,* Vol. 23 (1959), pp. 73–82; W. C. Kaufman and S. Greer, "Voting in a Metropolitan Community: An Application of Social Area Analysis," *Social Forces,*

Vol. 38 (1960), pp. 196–210; J. W. Vander Zanden, "Voting in Segregationist Referenda," *Public Opinion Quarterly*, Vol. 25 (1961), pp. 92–105; C. Gilbert, "Some Aspects of Nonpartisan Elections in Large Cities," *Midwest Journal of Political Science*, Vol. 6 (1962), pp. 345–62; J. E. Horton and W. E. Thompson, "Powerlessness and Political Negativism: A Study of Defeated Local Referendums," *American Journal of Sociology*, Vol. 67 (1962), pp. 485–93; N. I. Lustig, "The Relationships Between Demographic Characteristics and Pro-Integration Vote of White Precincts in a Metropolitan Southern County," *Social Forces*, Vol. 40 (1962), pp. 205–08; J. A. Norton, "Referenda Voting in a Metropolitan Area," *Western Political Quarterly*, Vol. 16 (1963), pp. 195–214; M. Pinard, "Structural Attachments and Political Support in Urban Politics: The Case of Fluoridation Referendums," *American Journal of Sociology*, Vol. 68 (1963), pp. 513–26; R. Salisbury and G. Black, "Class and Party in Partisan and Non-Partisan Elections: The Case of Des Moines," *American Political Science Review*, Vol. 57 (1963), pp. 584–92; J. Q. Wilson, "Planning and Politics: Citizen Participation in Urban Renewal," *Journal of the American Institute of Planners*, Vol. 29 (1963), pp. 242–49; A. Boskoff and H. Zeigler, *Voting Patterns in a Local Election* (New York, J. P. Lippencott, 1964); W. Erbe, "Social Involvement and Political Activity: A Replication and Elaboration," *American Sociological Review*, Vol. 29 (1964), pp. 198–215; M. K. Jennings and L. H. Zeigler, "A Moderate Victory in a Southern Congressional District," *Public Opinion Quarterly*, Vol. 28 (1964), pp. 595–603; F. M. Wirt, "The Political Sociology of American Suburbia: A Reinterpretation," *Journal of Politics*, Vol. 27 (1965), pp. 647–66; M. Kent Jennings and H. Zeigler, "Class, Party, and Race in Four Types of Elections: The Case of Atlanta," *Journal of Politics*, Vol. 28

(1966), pp. 391–407; G. Pomper, "Ethnic and Group Behavior in Nonpartisan Municipal Elections," *Public Opinion Quarterly*, Vol. 30 (1966); pp. 79–97; D. M. Olson, "The Structure of Electoral Politics," *Journal of Politics*, Vol. 29 (1967), pp. 352–67; J. Zikmund, "A Comparison of the Political Attitude and Activity Patterns in Central Cities and Suburbs," *Public Opinion Quarterly*, Vol. 31 (1967), pp. 69–75; "Suburban Voting in Presidential Elections, 1948–1964," *Midwest Journal of Political Science*, Vol. 12 (1968), pp. 239–58; and B. W. Hawkins, "Fringe-City Life-Style Distance and Fringe Support of Political Integration," *American Journal of Sociology*, Vol. 74 (1968), pp. 248–55.
21. Studies by geographers on housing and the residential structure of cities include: G. W. Hartman and J. C. Hook, "Substandard Urban Housing in the United States: A Quantitative Analysis," *Economic Geography*, Vol. 32 (1956), pp. 95–114; P. Camu, "Types de Maisons dans la Region Suburbaine de Montreal," *The Canadian Geographer*, Vol. 9 (1957), pp. 21–29; E. Jones, "The Delimitation of Some Urban Landscape Features in Belfast," *The Scottish Geographer*, Vol. 74 (1958), pp. 150–66; R. J. Fuchs, "Intraurban Variations in Residential Quality," *Economic Geography*, Vol. 36 (1960), pp. 313–25; K. E. Corey, "A Geographic Analysis of an Urban Renewal Area: A Case Study of the Avondale I-Corryville Conservation Project (Ohio R-6), Cincinnati, Ohio" (unpublished Master's thesis, Department of Geography, University of Cincinnati, 1962); J. T. Davis, "Middle Class Housing in the Central City," *Economic Geography*, Vol. 41 (1965), pp. 238–51; J. Forrest, "Residential Renewal in New Zealand," *Proceedings*, Fourth New Zealand Geography Conference (New Zealand Geography Society, Dunedin), 1965, pp. 151–59; Morrill, *op. cit.*, footnote 1; G. W. Carey, "The

Regional Interpretation of Manhattan Population and Housing Patterns Through Factor Analysis," *Geographical Review,* Vol. 56 (1966), pp. 551–69; L. S. Bourne, *Private Redevelopment of the Central City* (Chicago: The Department of Geography, University of Chicago, 1967); "Market, Location, and Site Selection in Apartment Construction," *The Canadian Geographer,* Vol. 12 (1968), 211–26; and J. W. Simmons, "Changing Residence in the City: A Review of Intraurban Mobility," *Geographical Review,* Vol. 58 (1968), pp. 622–51.

22. O. D. Duncan and B. Duncan, "Residential Distribution and Occupational Stratification," *American Journal of Sociology,* Vol. 60 (1955), pp. 493–503; D. O. Cowgill, "Trends in Residential Segregation of Non-Whites in American Cities, 1940–1950," *American Sociological Review,* Vol. 21 (1956), pp. 43–47 and his "Segregation Scores for Metropolitan Areas," *American Sociological Review,* Vol. 27 (1962), pp. 400–02; S. Lieberson, "Suburbs and Ethnic Residential Patterns," *American Journal of Sociology,* Vol. 67 (1962), pp. 673–81; L. F. Schnore and H. Sharp, "Racial Changes in Metropolitan Areas: 1950–1960," *Social Forces,* Vol. 41 (1963), pp. 247–52; J. M. Beshers, et al, "Ethnic Composition—Segregation, Assimilation, and Stratification," *Social Forces,* Vol. 42 (1964), pp. 482–89; K. Taeuber, "Negro Residential Segregation: Trends and Measurement," *Social Problems,* Vol. 12 (1964), pp. 42–50; T. R. Dye, "City-Suburban Social Distance and Public Policy," *Social Forces,* Vol. 44 (1965), pp. 100–06; O. R. Galle and K. E. Taeuber, "Metropolitan Migration and Intervening Opportunities," *American Sociological Review,* Vol. 31 (1966), pp. 5–13; H. M. Bahr and J. P. Gibbs, "Racial Differentiation in American Metropolitan Areas," *Social Forces,* Vol. 45 (1967), pp. 521–32; B. C. Straits, "Residential Movement Among Negroes and Whites in Chicago," *Social Science Quarterly,* Vol. 49 (1968), pp. 573–92.

23. For example, see the following studies: A. E. Winder, "White Attitudes Toward Negro-white Integration in an Area of Changing Racial Composition," *American Psychologist,* Vol. 7 (1952), pp. 330–31; A. M. Rose, et al, "Neighborhood Reactions to Isolated Negro Residents: An Alternative to Invasion and Succession," *American Sociological Review,* Vol. 18 (1953), pp. 497–507; O. D. and R. Duncan, *The Negro Population of Chicago: A Study of Residential Succession* (Chicago: University of Chicago Press, 1957); M. Grodzins, "Metropolitan Segregation," *Scientific American,* Vol. 197 (1957), pp. 33–41; E. P. Wolf, "The Invasion-Succession Sequence as a Self-Fulfilling Prophecy," *Journal of Social Issues,* Vol. 13 (1957), pp. 7–20; S. L. Clark and J. H. Kirk, "Characteristics of Minority Group Families Who Have Tried To Move into White Neighborhoods," *American Journal of Economics and Sociology,* Vol. 18 (1959), pp. 243–48; C. L. Hunt, "Negro-White Perceptions of Interracial Housing," *Journal of Social Issues,* Vol. 15 (1959), pp. 24–29; M. Rubin, "The Negro Wish to Move: The Boston Case," *Journal of Social Issues,* Vol. 15 (1959), pp. 4–13; B. Smith, Jr., "The Differential Residential Segregation of Working-Class Negroes in New Haven," *American Sociological Review,* Vol. 24 (1959), pp. 529–33; "The Reshuffling Phenomenon: A Pattern of Residence of Unsegregated Negroes," *American Sociological Review,* Vol. 24 (1959), pp. 77–79; D. McEntire, *Residence and Race: Final and Comprehensive Report to the Commission on Race and Housing* (Berkeley: University of California Press, 1960); N. Glazer and D. McEntire (Eds.), *Studies in Housing and Minority Groups* (Berkeley: University of California Press, 1960); C. Rapkin and

W. G. Grigsby, *The Demand for Housing in a Racially Mixed Area: A Study of the Nature of Neighborhood Change* (Berkeley: University of California Press, 1960); H. B. C. Spiegel, " 'Tenants' Intergroup Attitudes in a Public Housing Project with Declining White Population," *Phylon,* Vol. 21 (1960), pp. 30–39; E. K. Ward and E. P. Wolf, "Factors Affecting Racial Change in Two Middle Class Income Housing Areas," *Phylon,* Vol. 21 (1960), pp. 225–33; E. Works, "Residence in Integrated and Segregated Housing and Improvement in Self-Concept of Negroes," *Sociology and Social Research,* Vol. 46 (1962), pp. 294–301; J. B. McKee, "Changing Patterns of Race and Housing: A Toledo Study," *Social Forces,* Vol. 41 (1963), pp. 253–60; L. K. Northwood and E. A. T. Barth, *Urban Desegregation: Negro Pioneers and Their White Neighbors* (Seattle: University of Washington Press, 1965); B. Meer and E. Freeman, "The Impact of Negro Neighbors on White Home Owners," *Social Forces,* Vol. 45 (1966), pp. 11–19; S. Pruitt, "Ethnic and Racial Composition of Selected Cleveland Neighborhoods," *Social Science,* Vol. 43 (1968), pp. 171–74.

24. Several examples of relevant studies include: L. Rodwin, "The Theory of Residential Growth and Structure," *Appraisal Journal,* Vol. 18 (1950), pp. 295–317; L. Laurenti, *Property Values and Race. Studies in Seven Cities* (Berkeley: University of California Press, 1960); E. Palmore and J. Howe, "Residential Integration and Property Values," *Social Problems,* Vol. 10 (1962), pp. 52–55; E. Palmore, "Integration and Property Values in Washington, D.C.," *Phylon,* Vol. 27 (1966), pp. 15–19; J. W. Hannaford, "An Economic Theory on Housing Segregation," *Proceedings,* Indiana Academy of Science, Third Series, Vol. 2 (1967), pp. 112–19; C. K. Edgley, W. G. Steglich, and W. J. Cartwright, "Rent Subsidy and Housing Satisfaction," *American Journal of Economics and Sociology,* Vol. 27 (1968), pp. 113–24; W. S. Hendon, "Discrimination Against Negro Homeowners in Property Tax Assessments," *American Journal of Economics and Sociology,* Vol. 27 (1968), pp. 125–32.

25. S. M. Lipset, *Political Man: The Social Bases for Politics* (New York: Doubleday and Company, Inc., 1963), pp. 101–03 and 318–22; G. W. Allport, *The Nature of Prejudice* (New York: Doubleday and Company, 1958), pp. 405–07. In addition in Casstevens study on the Berkeley fair housing referendum in 1963 he found that persons with a postgraduate training and in professional or semi-professional occupations supported the measure: T. W. Casstevens, *Politics, Housing and Race Relations: The Defeat of Berkeley's Fair Housing Ordinance* (Berkeley: University of California, Institute of Governmental Studies, 1965), pp. 90–94. See also R. E. Wolfinger and F. I. Greenstein, "The Repeal of Fair Housing in California: An Analysis of Referendum Voting," *American Political Science Review,* Vol. 62 (1968), pp. 753–69. This recent study demonstrates, likewise, that the voting differences on Proposition 14 or the Rumford Act were attributed to educational and regional differences.

26. Allport, *op. cit.,* footnote 25, p. 406.

27. Lipset, *op. cit.,* footnote 25, p. 318.

28. Brink and Harris, *op. cit.,* footnote 7, p. 136. Although a number of social scientists have demonstrated that the degree of prejudice declines with increased social and economic status, there are studies which have demonstrated that greater prejudice may be more characteristic of the higher rather than the lower social and economic groups. Thus, the attitudes and feelings of whites in different social classes toward Negroes have not been conclusive or consistent with research investigations in various places. See, for example: H. G.

Erskine, "The Polls: Race Relations," *Public Opinion Quarterly*, Vol. 26 (1962), pp. 137–48; H. H. Hyman and P. B. Sheatsley, "Attitudes Toward Desegregation," *Scientific American*, Vol. 211 (1964), pp. 16–23; Sheatsley, *op. cit.*, footnote 2; C. H. Stember, *Education and Attitude Change* (New York: Institute of Human Relations Press, 1961).

29. As an example, see A. D. Kirsh, *Social Distance in Voting Behavior Related to N Variables* (Lafayette, Indiana: Purdue University, Division of Educational Reference, Studies in Higher Education No. 86, 1967).

30. Duncan and Duncan, *op. cit.*, footnote 22, p. 502. They stated that there is ". . . strong support for the proposition that spatial distances between occupational groups are closely related to social distances. . . ."

31. B. M. Kramer, "Residential Contact as a Determinant of Attitudes Toward Negroes" (unpublished paper, Harvard College Library, 1950). His work is described and referenced in Allport, *op. cit.*, footnote 25.

32. Winder, *op. cit.*, footnote 23.

33. The physical and social distances between the city and its suburbs and the effects on contrasting political behavior are mentioned by Norton, *op. cit.*, footnote 20; Dye, *op. cit.*, footnote 20; and by Zikmund, *op. cit.*, footnote 20. The significance of "social distance" in urban social geography is stated amply in: R. E. Pahl, "Trends in Social Geography," in R. J. Chorley and P. Haggett (Eds.), *Frontiers in Geographical Teaching* (London: Methuen and Co., Ltd., 1965), p. 95.

34. Brink and Harris, *op. cit.*, footnote 7, p. 10. A 1969 poll of black Americans conducted by the Gallup Organization for *Newsweek* revealed similar results: seventy-four percent of those interviewed said they would rather live in an integrated neighborhood; "Report from Black America," *Newsweek*, June 30, 1969, p. 20. Several other recent survey studies that consider Negro attitudes are N. S. Caplan and J. M. Paige, "A Study of Ghetto Rioters," *Scientific American*, Vol. 219, No. 2 (1968), pp. 15–21; E. F. Cataldo, K. M. Johnson, and L. A. Kellstedt, "Political Attitudes of the Urban Poor: Some Implications for Policy Makers," *Abstracts*, American Political Science Association, 64th Annual Meeting, Washington, D.C., 1968; W. McCord and J. Howard, "Negro Opinions in Three Riot Cities," *American Behavioral Scientist*, Vol. 2, No. 4 (1968), pp. 24–26; D. O. Sears and T. M. Tomlinson, "Riot Ideology in Los Angeles: A Study of Negro Attitudes," *Social Science Quarterly*, Vol. 49 (1968), pp. 485–503; and L. M. Irelan, O. C. Moles, and R. M. O'Shea, "Ethnicity, Poverty, and Selected Attitudes: A Test of the 'Culture of Poverty' Hypothesis," *Social Forces*, Vol. 47 (1969), pp. 405–11.

35. Horton and Thompson, *op. cit.*, footnote 20; Wilson, *op. cit.*, footnote 20; and J. Q. Wilson and E. C. Banfield, "Public Regardingness as a Value Premise in Voting Behavior," *American Political Science Review*, Vol. 53 (1964), pp. 876–87.

36. Hoffman, *op. cit.*, footnote 19.

37. For a concise and clear explanation of the use of overlays in electoral analyses, see Lewis, *op. cit.*, footnote 17.

38. For a discussion on the limitations of the application of ecological correlations to individual attributes, see: W. S. Robinson, "Ecological Correlations and the Behavior of Individuals," *American Sociological Review*, Vol. 15 (1956), 351–57.

39. For a recent exchange on the merits of survey data as opposed to ecological data in geography see: R. E. Kasperson, "On Suburbia and Voting Behavior," *Annals*, Association of American Geographers, Vol. 59 (1969), pp. 406–07, and K. R. Cox, "Comments in Reply to Kasperson and Taylor," *Annals*, Association of Ameri-

can Geographers, Vol. 59 (1969), p. 413.

40. Morrill, *op. cit.*, footnote 1; and B. Smith, *op. cit.*, footnote 23.

41. The authors acknowledge gratefully the assistance provided by Mr. Henry Horton of the Model Cities Program, Mr. Donald Johnson of the Department of Community Development, Mr. William Chase of *The Flint Journal*, and Mrs. Richard F. Beardsley for knowledge of recent changes and developments in the population of Flint as well as local accounts of the open housing referendum.

42. A further indication of the attitudes of the white population towards the various emotions and views attached to open housing is the vote of the 1968 American Independent Party candidate, George C. Wallace. He campaigned in Flint in hopes of receiving a sizeable segment of the labor vote. He received eleven percent of the presidential vote here with the remainder going mostly to the Democratic Party candidate, Hubert H. Humphrey, fifty-four percent. The Republican candidate, Richard M. Nixon, received thirty-four percent, and the remaining one percent went to several minor candidates. Most of the vote for Wallace was in Ward 4 where he received from twenty to thirty-three percent of the vote in the same precincts that voted heavily against open housing. Similar precincts in Wards 8 and 9 that voted down the open housing referendum also gave the former Alabama governor from twenty to thirty-four percent of their vote. However, in other areas of Flint where the residents voted against the open housing referendum, Wallace received less than ten percent. Therefore, it does seem that the lower income white residents of Flint in Ward 4 and parts of other wards reflected similar attitudes in their votes against open housing and for George Wallace.

43. The recent study by H. Hahn, "Northern Referenda on Fair Housing: The Response of White Votes," *Western Political Quarterly*, Vol. 21 (1968), pp. 483–95, reveals the attitudes of a small sample of Detroit's residents for support of the 1964 Home Owners Ordinance, government activity and desegregation of schools, and neighborhood integration. Hahn finds no consistent attitude among whites of varying socio-economic status for these three measures.

44. G. H. DeFriese and W. S. Ford, Jr., "Open Occupancy—What Whites Say, What They Do," *Transaction*, Vol. 5 (April, 1968), pp. 53–56.

45. Abrams, *op. cit.*, footnote 9, p. 72.

46. Wilson and Banfield, *op. cit.*, footnote 35.

47. The significance of stress points in cities is mentioned in two recent geography studies: G. W. Carey, L. Macomber, and M. Greenberg. "Educational and Demographic Factors in the Urban Geography of Washington, D.C.," *Geographical Review*, Vol. 58 (1968), 515–37, and P. S. Salter and R. C. Mings, "Some Geographic Aspects of the 1968 Miami Racial Disturbance: A Preliminary Examination," *Professional Geographer*, Vol. 21 (1969), pp. 79–86.

48. The case for the development and utilization of various models in social geography is stated by: D. Timms, "Quantitative Techniques in Urban Social Geography," in Chorley and Haggett, *op. cit.*, footnote 33, pp. 239–65, and R. E. Pahl, "Sociological Models in Geography," in R. J. Chorley and P. Haggett (Eds.), *Models in Geography* (London: Methuen and Co., Ltd., 1967), pp. 217–42.

eighteen ◆ ◆ ◆ ◆ ◆ ◆ ◆ ◆ ◆ ◆ ◆ ◆ ◆ ◆

◆ HAROLD M. ROSE

The Structure of Retail Trade in a Racially Changing Trade Area

During the period following World War II a revolution occurred in the pattern of retail location in U.S. cities. The decline of the central business district and the subsequent rise of regional shopping centers, have often been topics of in-depth research by retail location analysts. A lesser concern of researchers has been the future of unplanned shopping districts in the older neighborhoods of central cities. Of the limited attention devoted to these areas, one recent study described them this way: "Many are Sick, Many are Dying . . . What can be Done?"[10]

The most frequent death of unplanned centers is taking place within areas undergoing racial change. This has prompted a spate of statements which indicate major commercial institutions are not serving the needs of ghetto populations, and anger in the black community is frequently an outgrowth of dissatisfaction with ghetto merchants.[17] The complexity of these and other forces operating in metropolitan areas has dictated that a closer look be given at the role of race on retail structure in racially changing trade areas.

In this study race will be viewed as a social characteristic. That it is an important factor affecting retail structure was pointed out by Rolph[16] more than a generation ago. Further, Bucklin[7] has found that race, like distance, is a variable which affects one's choice of a place to shop. Yet, to date only Pred[15] among American geographers has sought to investigate this phenomenon.

The specific objective of this study is to attempt to relate changes in retail structure to the entry of Negroes into a given trade area during the period

◆ SOURCE. Reprinted by permission from *Geographical Analysis*, Vol. 2, 1970, pp. 135–148. Copyright 1970, by the Ohio State University Press, Columbus, Ohio, all rights reserved.

1950–1965. The problem of isolating changes emanating from a changing racial composition in a retail sub-system is difficult, since numerous other forces are at work which prompt change in the character and structure of a retail trade area. The problem is further compounded by the fact that retail trade areas of the type that are becoming predominantly Negro have been going through states of decline for some time, a trend which is only incidentally related to the racial character of the market. This factor was mentioned by writers assessing the possibility of commercial redevelopment along the riot ravaged commercial strips of Detroit.[18]

The Study Area

The area selected for this investigation lies approximately two and one-half miles northwest of the central business district in the city of Milwaukee, Wisconsin (Figure 1). It is a rectangular area embracing less than two square miles, and in both 1950 and 1960 it contained approximately 42,000 persons. The study area does not represent a precisely delineated trade area, but a series of contiguous neighborhoods. One assumes that the residents of the area will seek to satisfy as many of their basic retail needs as is possible from the set of commercial outlets found in close proximity to their places of residence, although there is growing evidence[13] that residents of low income areas possess a keen awareness of price differences in stores located beyond the margins of the local neighborhood, a factor

which would have a demonstrated impact upon shopping patterns.

The vast majority of retail outlets in the area under investigation are situated along four major arterials which transect the district. Two of these, North Avenue and Center Street, run east-west, while the other two, Fond du Lac Avenue and Teutonia Avenue, run to the northwest. Since many of the retail outlets which have evolved along these roads cater to the local residential market, they are more than simple string streets or ribbon developments. The retail character of the area is best reflected in the small, unplanned shopping centers found nested along stretches of the arterials. In 1950 there were seven unplanned shopping centers located along various stretches of the transecting roads. The seven individual centers were spaced at approximately one-quarter mile intervals. The spaces separating these centers were also largely commercial, generally performing urban arterial functions, although along some stretches residential land uses tended to predominate. The unplanned centers included approximately one-half of the retail establishments located along these radials. This ratio coincides with Boal and Johnson's[6] assessment of the higher importance of hierarchic functions along commercial ribbons situated in the older parts of the city. Among the seven centers or districts, there were present in the initial period a small shopping goods center, a community center, and five neighborhood centers (Figure 2).

Since the principal objective of this study is to consider the impact of the

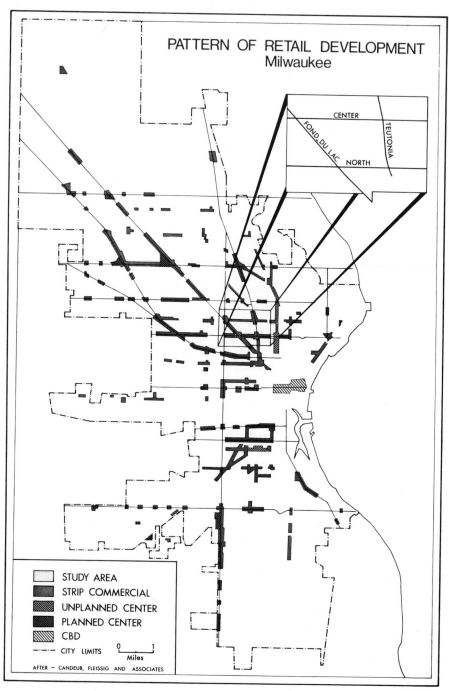

PATTERN OF RETAIL DEVELOPMENT
Milwaukee

CENTER

FOND DU LAC

TEUTONIA

NORTH

STUDY AREA
STRIP COMMERCIAL
UNPLANNED CENTER
PLANNED CENTER
CBD
CITY LIMITS

0
Miles

AFTER — CANDEUB, FLEISSIG AND ASSOCIATES

FIGURE 1.

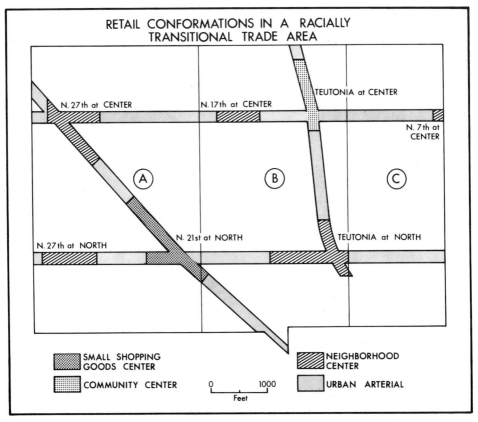

RETAIL CONFORMATIONS IN A RACIALLY
TRANSITIONAL TRADE AREA

N. 27th at CENTER   N.17th at CENTER   TEUTONIA at CENTER

N. 7th at CENTER

Ⓐ   Ⓑ   Ⓒ

N. 27th at NORTH   N. 21st at NORTH   TEUTONIA at NORTH

SMALL SHOPPING GOODS CENTER   NEIGHBORHOOD CENTER

COMMUNITY CENTER   0   1000   URBAN ARTERIAL

Feet

FIGURE 2.

changing racial composition of the trade area on retail structure, it is useful to subdivide the trade area into smaller segments in line with the community area designations developed for Milwaukee by Tien.[19] The study area embraces two complete community areas and parts of a third. These areas are designated as community areas A, B, and C in Figure 2. Only a fraction of the community area C is included within the trade area, but in the initial time period it was this segment of the community that contained the only sizable number of Negro consumers in

the entire market area. As recently as 1950, Negroes constituted only about seven per cent of the population in the total market area, but almost 30 per cent within community area C.

The racial composition of the population within the trade area moved from a Negro share of approximately seven per cent in 1950 to 49 per cent in 1960. If racial composition does in fact produce a significant impact on the number of operating establishments, then the racial threshold reflecting the decision of an existing operator to relocate or terminate his operation was not reached prior to 1955. This view is supported by the fact that there was only a four per cent decline in the number of establishments within the area during the initial five-year interval. Berry[5] recently demonstrated the catalytic effect of racial turnover on the retail structure in several community areas in Chicago, but like others, he has pointed out the difficulty of separating race from income.

Markov Analysis and Retail Change

To answer the question, "what effect does the spatial development of the Negro ghetto in major central cities have on the retail structure of business clusters situated within its area," it was necessary to search for a method or technique which is sensitive to processes having an impact on retail character. Berry and his colleagues have developed models to describe changes in a given aspect of retail character as a function of certain status variables measured at some specified point in time. But these models have been found to be inadequate for predicting retail change in small unit areas[4] and also, they do not include social variables among the independent variables. In areas undergoing racial change the models were least able to predict satisfactory results.[3]

Certain features of Markov Chain models appear to offer more satisfactory alternatives for predicting changes of the type with which this study is concerned. Markov Chain models have found only limited use among geogra-

phers, although their utility has been demonstrated by both Marble[14] and Clark.[9] These models are used here to describe the changes of commercial structures from one retail category to another over time.

A five year interval was selected as an appropriate time period for describing shifts in retail character. Transition probability matrices were constructed which described shifts among some twelve retail categories for the set of commercial structures located along each ribbon.

These matrices demonstrate the stability or lack of stability of the various retail types. They likewise reflect the suitability, in terms of rents or character of physical facilities, which might readily allow shifts in retail types to occur. The existence of zeros in cells indicates that it is not possible for a unit in the ith state to transfer to the jth state; for example, a unit which housed an automotive service in the initial time period cannot house a clothing store at the next time period.

Depending upon one's objectives, Markov models can be employed in a number of ways. Both Marble and Clark focused their attentions solely on the transition matrix as a clue to expected behavior. Other researchers have utilized the matrix of transition probabilities to predict future outcomes. In this case, the matrix of transition probabilities is multiplied by a vector describing each category's share of the set of businesses in the present time period as a means of predicting future shares.

A matrix of transition probabilities was constructed for each of the commercial ribbons in the study area for the times 1955, 1960, and 1965. In each instance, the matrix reflects shifts in states over the preceding five years. The construction of a series of transition matrices (1950–1955, 1955–1960, 1960–1965) reflects a desire to illustrate the impact of changes taking place during the immediate past period on retail stability. A conventional Markov Chain analysis which might use only the initial transition probability matrix (1950–1955) to predict future changes would not get at this principal concern. Besides, in anticipating the impact of racial composition upon the structure of retail trade, it appears logical to expect that the dispersion of the Negro population within the trade area over subsequent five-year intervals, would distort the predicted results associated with a given transition matrix. This logic is based on recognized subcultural differences reflected in differential propensities to consume specific items[1, 2, 8] and the traditional behavior of white entrepreneurs engaged in the provision of social services. Eventually, the transition matrices should begin to reflect the changing racial composition of the population although the role of race cannot be precisely specified. Galloway,[12] using a Markov model, encountered a similar problem in attempting to partition the role of specified variables in explaining differences in the propensity for poverty on the basis of race.

The retail structure along all commercial ribbons in the study area during the period 1950–1955 can be described as stable. Some of the more important conditions leading to the retail stability were residential stability, limited change in the income characteristics of the local consumer population, and the absence of attractive alternative retail locations. These conditions are essentially related to the sub-system itself.

Tables 1 and 2, examples of the matrices of transition probabilities, demonstrate the stability that characterized retail activity in the trade area during the initial interval. Although conditions along only two arteries are shown, there was little variability within the whole area during the interval. The rate and character of change along these two arteries in the following two five-year periods, however, is quite disparate. Teutonia Avenue (Table 2) lies along the main axis of ghetto development, whereas North Avenue (Table 1) is situated at a right angle to this major direction of ghetto spread. The physical orientation of these axes accounts for far reaching changes in the later time periods.

The entries along the main diagonals of the matrices give the probabilities of remaining in the same state over the one time interval and are called the *retention probabilities*. It is clear from observing these matrices that the structures housing certain retail categories are often ill-suited to house other categories. The nature of the structures which house categories S_9–S_{11} seem to permit most readily changes of state among categories.

The development of a set of transition probability matrices for each ribbon permits one to begin to look for causal factors which would explain the differential shifts in the retail character along these ribbons. The transition

TABLE 1. Transition Probabilities for the North Avenue Businesses

1950 Retail Category	1955 S_1	S_2	S_3	S_4	S_5	S_6	S_7	S_8	S_9	S_{10}	S_{11}	S_{12}
Professional S_1	1.00											
Personal S_2		.80		.05							.15	.17
Financial S_3			.57	.13						.13		.05
Eating & Drinking S_4				.95								.04
Groc. & Rel. Goods S_5		.08			.84			.04				
Clothing S_6		.10				.60			.20			.10
Auto Sales & Serv. S_7				.04			.78		.04			.04
Multifunctionals S_8								1.00				
Specialty S_9		.06							.75	.06	.06	.06
Household Furnish. & Related Goods S_{10}										1.00		
Miscellaneous S_{11}		.07			.07					.13	.60	.13
Vacancy S_{12}												1.00

TABLE 2. Transition Probabilities for the Teutonia Avenue Businesses

1950 Retail Category		1955										
	S_1	S_2	S_3	S_4	S_5	S_6	S_7	S_8	S_9	S_{10}	S_{11}	S_{12}
S_1 Professional	1.00											
S_2 Personal		.75							.25			
S_3 Financial			1.00									
S_4 Eating & Drinking				.95							.05	
S_5 Groc. & Rel. Goods					.80				.10	.10		
S_6 Clothing						1.00						
S_7 Auto Sales & Serv.							.91			.09		
S_8 Multifunctionals								1.00				
S_9 Specialty				.07				.08	.50	.08	.17	.17
S_{10} Household Furnish. & Related Goods										.85	.07	.09
S_{11} Miscellaneous									.09	.18	.63	
S_{12} Vacancy												1.00

TABLE 3. Predicted Percentage Retail Mix 1960, as Function of Processes Operating 1950–55

Retail Category	North Avenue		Teutonia Avenue	
	Observed	Predicted*	Observed	Predicted*
S_1 Professional	0.6	0.0	2.1	0.0
S_2 Personal	10.4	10.9	5.3	4.5
S_3 Financial	1.2	4.7	3.2	2.0
S_4 Eating & Drinking	15.3	15.3	20.2	20.2
S_5 Groceries	9.2	9.9	6.6	9.9
S_6 Clothing	3.1	9.5	4.3	10.0
S_7 Auto Sales & Serv.	9.8	10.6	8.5	10.7
S_8 Multifunctionals	4.9	6.3	3.2	4.0
S_9 Specialty	7.9	9.0	5.3	8.6
S_{10} Household Furnish.	11.0	11.7	10.6	17.5
S_{11} Miscellaneous	14.1	12.3	8.5	10.7
S_{12} Vacancy	12.8	11.6	22.3	0.0

* Product of 1955 state vector and transition probability matrix for 1950–55.

matrix has been employed as a predictive device in order to test for the homogeneity of processes occurring through time (Table 3).

Along both sample ribbons, the differences between the observed and predicted shares of S_4 (Eating and Drinking) and S_2 (Personal Services) are minor. Some other differences are, in part, a function of the original retail character of the ribbons themselves. The predictive ability of the model is less satisfactory for Teutonia than for North Avenue. While a general decline in retail functions can be detected along both ribbons, the more serious decline along Teutonia is probably related to the facts that it contained fewer establishments originally, had less retail diversity, and greater residential instability during this interval.

The matrices describing shifts in the retail mix during each successive five-year interval show a general decline in the retention probabilities among states. This condition, no doubt, is basically related to the economic decline of old neighborhoods. But variations in the sensitivity of some retail categories reflect changing social characteristics.

In the transition probability matrices for those ribbons which cut across the principal axis of ghetto development, such as North Avenue and Center Street, the impact of changing racial character is less evident. Changes taking place along one stretch of the axis are masked by entry decisions occurring elsewhere on the street, since the racial factor has a less pervasive impact along the total length of the ribbon in any given year.

Neighborhood Shopping Centers

As a means of highlighting the role of the racial composition of the trade area on retail structure, a set of transition probability matrices has been developed for the two retail conformations situated along North Avenue. Both of the conformations represent neighborhood retail centers. Since the retail changes there were minor during 1950–55, attention is focused on structural changes that took place during the 1955–1960 and 1960–1965 periods.

By 1960, the racial composition of the trade area upon which the center at 14th and North Avenue depended had become predominantly Negro. At the same time, Negro entry into the trade area served by the center at 27th and North Avenue was only nominal. Through analysis it can be demonstrated that retail entrants in the former center reflected the changing racial composition of the population while the latter center has been seemingly unaffected. Assuming that the same set of processes determined the nature of retail entry during the 1960–1965 interval as during the previous five-year interval, a first-order Markov Chain analysis should produce a close approximation of the retail structure of these centers in 1965 (Table 4).

In both instances a general economic decline affected the predictive power of the analysis. Overprediction of shares was common for both centers. But for the 14th St. center, the analysis seriously underpredicted the proportion of retail outlets providing personal services and eating and drinking accommodations. These two categories are those which Negro businessmen are known to have a high propensity for entry. These same two categories were overpredicted for the 27th St. center. It is apparent that the process of economic decline continued within both centers and actually accelerated during the most recent period at the 27th St. center. It is likewise obvious that social factors influenced the decision of retail entrants, especially in the other center.

The retail mix of neighborhood centers characteristically reflects the

TABLE 4. **Retail Composition of Two Neighborhood Retail Centers 1965**

Retail Category	N. Ave. at 14th St.		N. Ave. at N. 27th St.	
	Observed	Predicted	Observed	Predicted
		Percentages		
Professional	3.3	3.2	2.5	0.0
Personal	26.6	16.6	12.8	16.1
Financial	9.9	3.2	10.2	1.2
Eating & Drinking	16.6	6.4	25.6	28.2
Groceries	10.0	17.2	0.0	2.0
Clothing	0.0	3.2	0.0	2.4
Automotive	6.6	5.6	0.0	0.0
Multifunctional	0.0	0.0	5.1	7.6
Specialty	10.0	9.6	7.6	10.0
Household	6.6	11.2	17.9	13.3
Miscellaneous	6.6	6.4	7.6	5.1
Vacant	13.3	19.3	10.2	2.5

cultural taste of the trade area's residents, and a structure once initiated affects the future use of existing retail outlets. Ethnic propensities were apparent in the retail character of the two neighborhood shopping centers during the initial time period. In 1950 the center at 14th and North Avenue still served a sizable Jewish population, a fact that was evident in the number of grocery and related activities occupying units there. Similarly, the *gemuetlichkeit* of the German neighborhood was expressed by the importance of the German owned drinking establishments occupying space in the center at 27th and North Avenue. The Negro population, representing the most recent entrant into the area, is in effect responsible for the superimposition of a new retail structure upon the remnants of a decaying structure. Although the social and economic factors cannot always be easily separated, while operating together they each yield outcomes which are more readily related to one than to the other.

Obviously, it is difficult to ascertain the effects of racial composition on the retention probabilities of the derived matrices, but the probability of entry is more clearly associated with the racial composition of the trade area. Thus, the land uses Pred[15] described as being more characteristic of Negro commercial development appear to be widespread, showing up in commercial developments serving a Negro population in cities throughout the nation.

Once the process of racial change is complete, there is generally less retail diversity to be found within neighborhood centers than previously (Figure 3). While both centers in Figure 3 were on the decline, the center serving a predominantly white clientele provided only one less function in 1965 than it had in 1950. The center serving a predominantly Negro population, although suffering a smaller absolute decline in number of stores, provided nine fewer functions in 1965 than it had in 1950. It is evident that both of the described commercial ribbons will eventually house businesses that cater to a predominantly Negro population; it is also obvious that the probability analysis is better suited to analyze the change in retail structure which is related to race on a center-by-center basis.

Summary and Conclusions

It is apparent that competition for business space in older areas is on the decline, thereby permitting the easy entry of a multiplicity of low-order businesses. This deterioration in demand subsequently leads to the evolution of commercial blight. When one considers the relative location of commercial ribbons transecting ghetto areas one cannot be certain of the role which race plays in this situation. Yet it is apparent that race tends to serve as a catalyst which accelerates the commercial transition.

Through the use of a simplified Markov Chain analysis it was found that one could predict rather accurately the retail mix along a commercial ribbon prior to Negro entry. After Negro entry, the matrices of transition probabilities demonstrated the operation of a set of forces that were not previously discer-

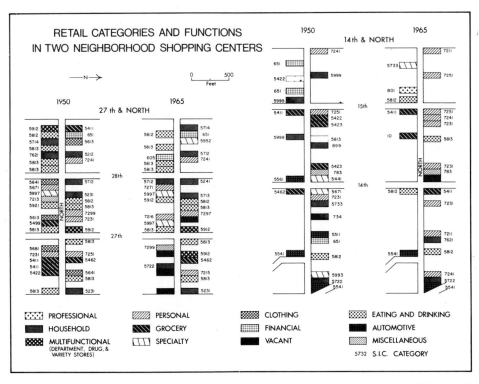

FIGURE 3.

nible. The major drawback of Markov Chain analysis in this kind of study is that it does not permit one to identify precisely the roles of specific change-producing variables. Improvements in this respect might be obtained either by increasing the number of retail categories or reducing the length of the time interval upon which the matrix of transition probabilities is based, or both.

In the evolution of the Negro business street, the dropping out of goods-supplying units is frequently observed, and this permits an increase in the relative importance of suppliers of social services. The Negro business operator

along the arteries is principally engaged in operating units in this latter category. With the declining relative importance of goods outlets along commercial ribbons in Negro residential areas, the neighborhood center diminishes in importance as a source of convenience goods. At the same time, the neighborhood center becomes essentially a place for obtaining social services. This phenomenon more and more draws convenience goods shoppers into the shopping goods center, a situation that is somewhat unique.

The continuous expansion of the ghetto as an urban sub-system also means the continuous spread of com-

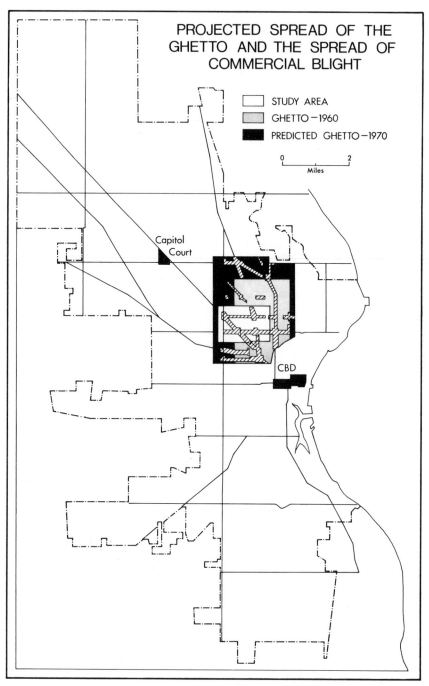

PROJECTED SPREAD OF THE
GHETTO AND THE SPREAD OF
COMMERCIAL BLIGHT

STUDY AREA
GHETTO —1960
PREDICTED GHETTO —1970

0   2
        Miles

Capitol
Court

CBD

FIGURE 4.

mercial blight unless some stabilizing forces are intentionally introduced. As the prospective Negro business operator is by custom forced to operate within Negro neighborhoods,[11] and has access to only limited risk capital, one could hardly expect him to alter this condition. If the process of commercial change which was observed within a very limited area is permitted to continue unaltered, then the problem of predicting certain kinds of commercial landscape changes, especially the intensity of blight, is a task that can be readily conducted within the context of predicting the spatial pattern of the Negro ghetto (Figure 4).

Literature Cited

1. Alexis, M. "Some Negro-White Differences in Consumption," *American Journal of Economics and Sociology,* 21 (1962), 11.

2. Bauer, R. A., S. M. Cunningham, and L. H. Wortzel. "The Marketing Dilemma of Negroes," *Journal of Marketing,* 29 (1965), 1–6.

3. Berry, B. J. L. *Commercial Structure and Commercial Blight,* Research Paper 85, Department of Geography, University of Chicago, Chicago (1963). Pp. 173–76.

4. ———. "The Retail Component of the Urban Model," *Journal of the American Institute of Planners,* 31 (1965), 151.

5. ———. "Comparative Mortality Experience of Small Business in Four Chicago Communities," Background Paper No. 4, *Small Business Reloca-tion Study,* Center for Urban Studies, The University of Chicago (1966), 19–20.

6. Boal, F. W. and D. B. Johnson. "The Functions of Retail and Service Establishments on Commercial Ribbons," *The Canadian Geographer,* 9 (1965), 157.

7. Bucklin, L. P. "The Concept of Mass in Intra-urban Shopping." *Journal of Marketing,* 31 (1967), 41–42.

8. Bullock, H. A. "Consumer Motivations in Black and White," *Harvard Business Review,* 39 (1961), 89–124.

9. Clark, W. A. V. "Markov Chain Analysis in Geography: An Application to the Movement of Rental Housing Areas," *Annals,* The Association of American Geographers, 55 (1965), 351–59.

10. Downs, A. and J. McClean. "Many are Sick, Many are Dying—What Can be Done?" *Journal of Property Management,* 28 (1963), 132–42.

11. Foley, E. P. "The Negro Businessman: In Search of a Tradition," *Daedalus,* 95 (1966), 113.

12. Galloway, L. E. "The Negro and Poverty," *The Journal of Business,* 40 (1967), 29–31.

13. Goodman, C. S. "Do the Poor Pay More?" *Journal of Marketing* (Jan. 1968), 23.

14. Marble, D. F. "A Simple Markovian Model of Trip Structures in a Metropolitan Region," *Papers, Regional Science Assoc. Western Section* (1964), 150–56.

15. Pred, A. "Business Thoroughfares as Expressions of Urban Negro Culture." *Economic Geography,* 39 (1963), 217–33.

16. Rolph, I. K. "The Population Pattern

in Relation to Retail Buying." *The American Journal of Sociology*, 38 (1932), 368.

17. Sengstock, M. C. "The Corporation and the Ghetto: An Analysis of the Effects of Corporate Retail Grocery Sales on Ghetto Life." *Journal of* *Urban Law*, 45 (1968), 673–703.

18. *The Wall Street Journal* (July 28, 1967), 5.

19. Tien, Y. *Milwaukee Metropolitan Area Fact Book—1940, 1950 and 1960.* Madison, Wisconsin: The University of Wisconsin Press, 1962.

◆ ◆ ◆ ◆ ◆ ◆ ◆ ◆ ◆ ◆ ◆ ◆ ◆ ◆ nineteen

JAMES O. WHEELER ◆

Social Interaction and Urban Space

Man has organized his cities for particular social objectives. Viewed in this sense, his cities exist to facilitate social communications or interaction. At the same time, however, diverse social goals and group frictions create barriers to the smooth flow of information among urban dwellers, as communications take place within a spatially and socially restrictive network of interpersonal contact. This paper (1) introduces the theme of urban social interaction, (2) outlines the structure of social ties in cities, and (3) examines two major urban problems relating explicitly to social interaction: the urban freeway and the ghetto. As such, this paper seeks more to provide a broad geographical perspective of social interaction and its role in urban problems than to present hard analytic data based on empirical case study. The ideas put forth here are intended to give an increased insight into one way in which the geographer may usefully view the city and its social problems.

Spatial Structure of Social Connections

Many definitions have been advanced to explain what constitutes a city. Perhaps too many of these have given emphasis to the visible features of the urban landscape, such as land use, housing density, or the extent of sewerage lines. Too often it is overlooked that these are only the more obvious manifestations of a simple desire of man to live with other men for mutual benefits. People increasingly live in cities to achieve social and economic objectives which can not as easily be obtained in a nonurban environment. Economists and others have viewed the city as a magnet attracting rural to urban migrants wishing to improve their economic level by living near desired employment opportunities. Implicit in such migration are the benefits accruing from accessibility to job locations. Concomitant with this increased economic interaction is a whole set of

◆ **SOURCE.** Reprinted by permission from *The Journal of Geography*, Vol. 70, April 1971, pp. 200–203.

social interactions necessitated by the urban life style. The tremendous variety and opportunities for social contact within the city have given rise to a social structure that sets the urban area apart from the rapidly contracting traditional agrarian social system.[1] In this context, one writer describes urbanity "as a property of the amount and the variety of one's participation in the cultural life of a world of creative specialists, of the amount and the variety of information received."[2] Since such participation and information receipt are maximized in the urban area via social interaction, one meaningful conceptualization of the city involves the nature, intensity, and extent of social interactions.

Although the city may be seen as a mechanism for facilitating information exchange through social communications, it is an imperfect mechanism when compared to some hypothetically optimal system of exchange. There are two principal limitations to the present-day city as it involves social interaction. Both are geographically based. The first is the inescapable and oppressive burden of space itself. Urban space imposes barriers between all its residents, but these are unequal barriers. The transportation route system itself is confined to specified portions of the city, creating spatial irregularity via circuity. The expense in time and money of crossing urban space is weighted against the anticipated advantages to be obtained at the trip's end. Much of the mobility differential between individuals or groups in the city relates to their evaluation of the trade-off between travel cost and the

extra utility or satisfaction to be achieved at a more distant location. Many of the basic problems of the city as a social environment can be traced to an inequality among its residents in their ability to overcome urban space.

A second restraint on urban social interaction is status, especially as manifest among the social neighborhoods of the urban area. Numerous studies have documented the higher probability of social contact among those of similar socioeconomic level compared to individuals of unlike status. For example, a professional worker will have a decreasing probability of social contact as one goes down the socioeconomic scale. Because of the tendency of residential clustering of similar socioeconomic groups, neighborhood barriers are created, maintained, and intensified by intervening distance. The chance of a resident from a high income neighborhood having social contact with an individual living in a low income area is even less than the distance between such households would suggest. Thus differentiated by the diversity of human activities and the inequalities of man, urban space itself is rendered unequal.[3]

Many powerful social forces exist to maintain a cohesive and functional urban environment. Fundamental among these is the complementarity of social roles. The basic social unit remains the family, in which the need for privacy, safety, and security underlies its preferences for individual dwellings. In addition to the family unit, with its desire for freedom to selectively pursue interpersonal contacts, are institutional units created to facilitate societal operation through formalized organization. These institutions are administered in large measure through a hierarchy of interpersonal contact, in part social and in part impersonal. The geographical concentration within cities of these organizations imposes a spatial clustering of interpersonal ties in which the participants normally have relatively little choice in selecting each other. Furthermore, these organizations have taken a dominant position in society relative to the family, now very small in relation to the institutional unit.[4] The net result is a pattern of interpersonal relations in which professional or job contacts, both personal and neutral, have come in part to replace emotional and intimate social ties. Social ties are thus often transitory and diffused among a large number of individuals.

In the typical small agrarian community of the past, by contrast, the probability that any individual would have contact with any other individual was fairly high, and under conditions of random connections it would not be too long until contact would be made with virtually all individuals in the small community. Everyone knew what everyone else was doing. However, social relations in the agrarian society were highly biased toward members of the extended family, and the intensity of social interaction was greatest with relatives. Due to the frequency of social contact, social barriers were erected when hostilities developed between individuals; because of the intense network of social ties, or clique development, individual antagonisms often would have group ramifications.

The spatial structure of social connections in the city may be summarized as frequent, both intimate and impersonal, and areally diffused. The role of the neighborhood remains strong, reflecting both the drop-off in contacts with distance and the status preference of its inhabitants. However, as the social network becomes more conditioned by institutional factors, the neighborhood role in social ties weakens. With increased mobility, it is possible to maintain friendships over greater distances. Status, promoted by institutional organization, is a paramount factor in social contact. The role of personality attributes, though little studied, is of particular interest within the urban context. Since the diversity of human activity in cities leads to the potential for numerous interpersonal contacts, the probability of personality complementarity occurring over a period of time between participants is relatively high, thus helping to explain the basis of intimate contact within a system of substantial impersonal ties. The large *quantity* of transitory and perfunctory contacts assists the selection process for developing *quality* social relations within cities.

Spatial Problems in Social Interaction

It is widely recognized in the literature of transportation geography that location and transportation are two sides of the same coin. For example, in selecting a residence one obtains both a site and a location. Just as no two sites are identical in amenities, no two locations will have the same accessibility because of the spatial structure of the physical city. Social interaction, dependent on the accessibility and connectivity of the social communications network, is associated with the spatial arrangement of both the physical and social structure of the metropolitan area. How does the physical and social structure of the city affect one's actual choices of social contact?

One of the most striking illustrations of the impact of changing physical arrangements on social ties is the urban freeway, at once an impetus and a barrier to movement. The urban freeway system to a considerable extent is built in response to the desire for individual accessibility to the major institutional units and activity nodes of the city. Only secondarily does it connect households to facilitate social contact. The freeway has been accused of primarily serving the mobility needs of suburban residents and thereby maintaining their neighborhood stability at the expense of destroying the stability of inner city neighborhoods, which are either physically displaced or fragmented by freeway location.[5] Moreover, since inner city areas tend to have the lowest per capita ownership of automobiles, the residents of the "old" city are least likely to effectively utilize the freeway, whether to gain access to the growing job potential in the suburbs or to move about the urban area for social travel. The transit system in most cities has been similarly criticized, as it makes accessible only restricted parts of the metropolitan area.

The urban freeway system clearly serves the mobility needs of various social groups in the city differently.

Higher income suburban residents not only have access to jobs and entertainment in the central business district but they also have ready connections to most other suburban areas, especially via circumferential freeway links. In contrast, inner city residents undertaking social travel must rely largely on the traditional street pattern in their multi-directional travel needs. The result is a more restricted area for carrying out social interaction. Even though the frequency of interpersonal contact might be similar for the high versus low status individual, the latter is more geographically confined in his choice of contacts to like social status groups. For the high status resident, his social contacts are more biased by status preferences than limited by urban space.

There has been increasing criticism and opposition in the United States to the construction of the urban freeway system, of which nearly 6,000 miles are yet to be built through urban areas. A large part of the opposition comes from minority and other inner city groups whose value system appears to be less oriented to access to activities than to access to people. Those with whom social ties are most desired live nearby in the same general part of the city and may be members of the same minority groups. Hence a proposed freeway is a threat both to one's precarious economic resources and to his valued sense of community and territorial control. Members of minority groups, such as blacks, achieve personal identity and recognition not so much through the powerful institutional units controlled by the white majority as they do through the social network within their own neighborhood. Residential displacement necessitated by freeway construction may be adversely perceived not only because of the economic gain or loss but also because of rending apart the social fabric of a neighborhood. In short, the freeway serves the important social and economic needs of the suburban resident, who strives for personal identity and recognition within an institutional framework spatially linked by the freeway system. For an inner city resident, especially if a member of a minority group, the freeway is a threat imposed by an "establishment" that does not understand his spatial needs for achieving personal satisfaction through social identity.

In addition to the role of the physical structure of the city in affecting social contact, the social structure of urban space exerts a fundamental influence. Members of a social group, because of intra-group communication and access to common channels of information, tend to hold similar values which may be manifest in like behavior patterns. Such information flow through social interaction is basic to group formation and maintenance. Common problems and pressures of a racial or socioeconomic status group affect its receptivity to certain kinds of information. Whereas different social status groups may generate disparate value systems, other mechanisms maintain broad patterns of similarities among groups. For example, to the extent that one participates in a variety of roles, he will have multiple channels of information through different kinds of inter-

personal contact. Thus people are basically the same, except that they are members of different social, racial, or ethnic groups, perform varied roles, live in different parts of the metropolitan area, are at various stages of the family life cycle, and therefore tend to hold values consistent with the social communication network of which they are a part.

The role of social structure in interpersonal contact and information receipt is best described by the problem of racial discrimination, which results in the spatial segregation of residence and other activities. Most of all in this case, the social interaction of the racial minority is directed inward and largely blocked from outside influences. A geographically closed system of social interaction operates. Likewise, the suburban majority may have virtually no contact with members of the minority. Not only may values between these groups become divergent, but there is little mechanism for mutual understanding to develop. Although the racial minority has a spatial awareness of a large portion of the city, the group is significantly limited in its normal area of contact within urban space by discriminatory attitudes. A black's lack of interaction with an all-white suburb may not be because he has no information as to its existence or location.

In response to white hostility, black ghettos have also developed their own institutional structure, in which the church has played a prominent role.[6] The location of the black churches within the ghetto has fostered a further areal concentration of social interaction. The various churches, often reflecting a degree of social stratification within the black community, serve as an institution for maintaining social differentiation within a group whose preferences for residential status can not always be achieved throughout the metropolitan area. In this context, it is a serious error to regard the black ghetto as homogeneous socially: in fact status barriers, as well as distance, impose a considerable influence on the patterns of social interaction.

Conclusions

Just as land use in the city is differentiated by economic function and dependent upon accessibility, urban social units are also spread over the city and functionally tied by patterns of social communications. The city, an agglomeration of people and organizational points, is a "derivative of the communications patterns of the individuals and groups that inhabit it."[7] The savings in communication costs resulting from population clustering are the modern city's greatest social asset; the inequality of social interaction associated with the spatially articulated network of communications is related to the basic social frictions and hostilities in the modern city. Since the city functions as a spatial complex, it is hoped that an appreciation of the geography of social communications gains insights into some of the uses and misuses of urban space.

Footnotes

1. Charles P. Loomis and J. Allan Beegle, *Rural Social Systems* (New York: Prentice-Hall, 1950), pp. 133–203.
2. Melvin M. Webber, *et al.*, *Explorations into Urban Structure* (Philadelphia: University of Pennsylvania Press, 1964), p. 88.
3. Jean Canaux, "Social Aspects of the City," *Ekistics*, XXVII (March 1969), 178–180.
4. C. A. Doxiadis, "Social Synthesis in Human Settlement," *Ekistics*, XXVII (October 1969), 236–240.
5. Alan Altshuler, "The Values of Urban Transportation Policy," in *Transportation and Community Values*, Special Report 105, Highway Research Board (Washington, D.C.: Government Printing Office, 1969), pp. 75–86.
6. Allan H. Spear, *Black Chicago: The Making of a Negro Ghetto, 1890–1920* (Chicago: University of Chicago Press, 1967).
7. Melvin M. Webber, "Order in Diversity: Community without Propinquity," in Lowdon Wingo, Jr. (ed.), *Cities and Space: The Future Use of Urban Land* (Baltimore: The Johns Hopkins Press, 1963), p. 31.

◆ ◆ ◆ ◆ ◆ ◆ ◆ ◆ ◆ ◆ ◆ ◆ ◆ ◆ ◆ ◆ ◆ ◆ **twenty**

ROBERT GOLD ◆

Urban Violence and Contemporary Defensive Cities

Violent crime has been increasing at an alarming pace in large metropolitan areas of the United States[1] at a time when efforts are being made to renew entire neighborhoods in central cities and new suburban communities and new towns are being built to accommodate our growing national population. Some of the causes of violent behavior may stem from the physical environment. For these reasons, it is timely to inquire whether the design and form of our cities are related to urban violence, and whether violence can be controlled or prevented by planning the physical environment. Whatever the causes of violence, it is now a hard fact of American life that violence has consequences of its own and is causing changes in the urban environment. Therefore, it is important to determine what these changes are, why and how they are occurring, and what they por-

tend for the future of urban society in America. Historical precedents and the warning of the Kerner Commission that America "is moving toward two societies, one black, one white—separate and unequal"[2] compel us to consider the dangers of violence in our cities.

Few definite relationships between the design and form of the urban environment and violent behavior have been defined in the past. The purpose of this article is to summarize available knowledge, report different ideas, and describe some conclusions about these relationships.

Urban Environment and Violent Behavior

Three possible relationships between the design and form of the urban en-

◆ **SOURCE.** Reprinted in modified version by permission of the *Journal of the American Institute of Planners*, Vol. 36, 1970, pp. 146–159.

vironment and violent behavior can be
suggested:

1. Design and form of the urban
   environment may directly *control*
   violence. Residential areas, for
   example, may be selected by a
   criterion of distance from populations with real or assumed tendencies to commit violence, or
   individual buildings or entire
   communities may be "fortified" by
   crime control features with social
   and aesthetic values subordinated
   or entirely eliminated.
2. Design and form of the urban
   environment may encourage positive forms of behavior by such
   means as participation in the process of planning, building, and
   managing the environment. To
   the extent positive behavior is promoted, negative behavior—including violence—is *prevented.*
3. Design and form of the urban
   environment may *invite* violence.
   Because people may consider
   buildings or open spaces as negative symbols or may attribute sufficiently neutral or negative
   values to certain places, they are
   willing to destroy or deface
   buildings or to commit violent
   acts in these areas.

If violent crime continues to increase, the very character of our cities
may depend on which of the relationships between design and behavior are
emphasized by urban designers, public
officials, and to an even greater extent,
urban consumers. If all three relationships are valid and if urban design or

consumer choices are primarily oriented
toward crime control, our cities will be
caught in a cycle of increasing violence
in which crime control features of the
urban environment will generate more
violence and create other economically
and socially undesirable conditions.

The following environmental variables are factors in the three relationships mentioned above:

1. *Space and location* can permit or
   limit behavior.
2. *Distance* and *access to space* can
   separate potential victims from
   potential offenders.
3. *Visibility* can enable observation,
   a deterrent to violence.
4. *Scale* can control types and
   amounts of violence. The absolute
   size of a design feature can im-
   pede entry, while overall size
   relative to the population groups
   who may commit or act to control violence can constrain their
   participation. A garden wall and
   a city wall are similar means of
   restricting access to space, differing only in scale; yet the protection afforded by setting a house
   apart from others and setting a
   city apart from its surroundings
   are quite different.
5. *Mastery, control, and ownership
   of property* may influence the values people impute to the urban
   environment and thereby affect
   behavior.
6. *High residential densities, poor
   physical condition, and low general quality of the urban environment,* usually associated with
   other features of poverty and de-

privation, may be casually related to violent behavior.

It is important to ask: What role has the urban environment played in the past in preventing or controlling violence, what present trends can be observed, and what are the consequences likely to be if urban violence continues to increase? During many periods in history, urban populations were exposed to violence committed by individuals or small groups against other persons and property; civil rebellion, riots, and commotions in opposition to political leadership or conditions in society; and military attack from outside the society. We are mainly concerned with the first type of violence, although civil rebellion is indirectly of interest because, at times, individual violence became so widespread in cities that it had the characteristics of riots. Although fortifications built to prevent invasion had secondary uses in maintaining public order, military attack is wholly outside our scope. . . .

CONCLUSIONS FROM HISTORY[3]

Although there is little uniform historical evidence about relationships between design and form of the urban environment and violent crime, some generalizations can be made to obtain a perspective on problems in contemporary American cities.

1. The *level* of urban violence has not been the same throughout the history of western civilization. During some periods, urban violence was so widespread that protection was exceptionally im-

portant in the design and form of the urban environment. When medieval cities were established, urban violence was exceptionally low. During other periods, safety in cities was imposed by repressive police tactics. Urban violence was so uncontrolled in some cases that it was the single most important fact of city life.

2. The actual or potential *targets* of crime are not apparent from historical evidence. The information available implies that a man who could afford to arm himself and fortify his house had something to defend, and hence was the actual or potential victim.

3. There is some historical evidence about violent *offenders,* but the portraits are strangely depersonalized. The clearest picture is suggested by the *cours des miracles* in Paris, where pools of criminals lived in the same districts and victimized city residents for more than a century. These areas may have been entirely criminal districts in which all or most of the inhabitants made a living through illegal activities. However, there is no evidence that all Parisian criminals of the time lived in the *cours des miracles,* and many residents of these districts may have simply been impoverished.

4. Historically, three environmental approaches to crime control can be distinguished:

   A. *Arrangement of urban form and activity.* Most people in most societies have opposed violence. The arrangement of urban form and activity suggests that when enough people who disapproved of crime were brought together, their presence *generally* deterred crime.

B. *Use of protective devices.* These have included all physical devices for the safety or protection of people and property, such as walls, moats, doors, and particularly door locks and entryway designs. They were widely used to control access to space, that is, to seal off or insulate particular areas from trespass.

C. *Management of the environment.* Control of the environment to prevent crime has been the principal objective of law enforcers throughout history. The razing of the *cours des miracles,* the Chinese block surveillance systems, and the Incan police organization are only a few of many examples of environmental management.

Current Trends of Urban Violence

Although many questions are unanswered and many refinements are needed in reporting crime and violence, particularly by types of geographic areas, it is important to summarize available findings on violence in America that are pertinent to the design and form of the urban environment.[4]

Rates of arrest vary considerably by economic status, race, and age of offenders. It is necessary to conclude from the admittedly imperfect data that the true rates of the four major violent crimes—criminal homicide, forcible rape, robbery, and aggravated assault—are many times higher for poor than for affluent populations, for Negroes than for whites, and for younger age groups (especially those eighteen to twenty-four years old) than for older age groups. The racial difference is particularly relevant to the urban environment. In 1967, the reported Negro arrest rate was about seventeen times the white rate for homicide, eleven times the white rate for forcible rape, and ten times the white arrest rate for robbery and aggravated assault. Socioeconomic differences and numerous biases in arrest data—for example, poor Negroes may be disproportionately arrested on suspicion—cannot be overlooked, but neither can Negro-white differences in arrest rates be fully explained by these features.

To a considerable extent, the characteristics of persons who most frequently commit violent crimes are the same as those of the population group residing in central cities of large metropolitan areas. Consequently, the combined reported arrest rate for the major violent offenses in 1967 was about eight times greater in cities with populations of 250,000 or more than in those with populations between 10,000 and 25,000 and ten times greater than in rural areas. Six cities of more than one million population, representing about 12 percent of the population of all reporting areas, contributed about 33 percent of all major violent crimes reported in the United States. Twenty-six cities of 500,000 or more population, whose residents totaled about one-fifth of those in the reporting areas, contributed nearly half of all major violent crimes reported. Suburbs have generally reported lower crime rates, except for forcible rape, than all but the smallest cities. The same relationships are generally true for nonviolent property crimes.[5]

The true offense rates for homicide, robbery, and aggravated assault have probably increased significantly during recent years in the nation as a whole and particularly in larger cities.[6] In cities with populations of more than 250,000 persons, the reported offense rate for robbery per 100,000 population increased 90 percent between 1963 and 1967. In the same four years, the reported homicide rate increased 51 percent, and the reported aggravated assault rate increased 46 percent. It must also be concluded that the true rates and volumes for the same violent crimes have increased rapidly in suburban areas during recent years, although they started from a much lower level. Thus, while the reported rates for all four violent crimes increased significantly in both central cities and suburban areas, the gaps between the two sets of rates and volumes widened considerably, making even greater geographic differences.

The statistical portrait of victims resembles that of offenders. The National Opinion Research Center Study for the President's Crime Commission showed the probability of being a victim of forcible rape, robbery, and aggravated assault is many times greater for central city residents than for suburban residents, for people twenty to twenty-nine years of age than for people of older ages, for males than for females, for Negroes than for whites, and for poor than for affluent populations. A recent survey in Chicago concluded than the chances of physical assault for a Negro ghetto dweller were 1 in 77, while the odds were 1 in 10,000 for an upper middle class suburbanite.[7]

When victims were related to offenders, homicide, forcible rape, and aggravated assault were found to be principally intraracial crimes, committed mainly by Negroes against Negroes and whites against whites. The only exception was robbery, where over 40 percent of all interactions involved Negro offenders and white victims.[8]

Thus, while the middle class white taxpayer often bears a disproportionate share of the cost of crime control and perhaps of robbery, the low-income Negro living in the central city pays disproportionately in the pain caused by other types of violence. Although the rate and volume of crime is increasing in suburban areas, much more violence today is committed in central cities.

Current Practices in Environmental Protection

Urban environments have always been designed to some extent for protection. Yet, despite historical precedent, professional planners, urban designers, and architects in America have paid little attention to violence. There are some fragmentary references in the professional literature, and there have been practical applications in a few cities. However, there is no well-founded body of information on protection in the design professions today.

There are a number of reasons for this apparent neglect. Comparatively little empirical study has been undertaken to relate physical design to the behavioral sciences. Theories of violent behavior have presented few, if any, practical guidelines for urban design.[9] The philosophy and proposals of the Utopian Socialists who called for and attempted reform during the nineteenth century had a profound influence on the work of important twentieth century urban design thinkers, such as Le Corbusier and Ebenezer Howard. Much of our physical planning even today is based on the behavioral assumption that if the quality of the urban environment were good enough, crime and violence would disappear. This implies that, since the goal of the design professions is to improve the urban environment, violence per se need not be considered. This tradition explains, in part, why few contemporary design proposals specifically acknowledge or consider crime or other social pathologies as major problems.

Yet some writers have considered relationships between design and crime. Also, increasing numbers of urban consumers have illustrated design possibilities in seeking to control crime by "hardening targets," and some neighborhood groups have adopted techniques of environmental management to make their communities safer.

Modern architectural features, such as elevators, enclosed stairways, pedestrian underpasses, and underground parking garages, offer seclusion and screening from public view and are often settings for violent behavior. This problem can be overcome. For example, the stairways of one public housing project were built on the exterior of buildings, enclosed in glass, and lighted well. Crime in these stairways virtually ceased. Visibility has also been improved by selection, placement, and trimming of trees and shrubbery, better street lighting, use of closed-circuit television systems, and elimination of places of concealment.

Improved safety devices, including locks, safety chains, and inexpensive alarms have recently been developed and are being utilized more and more. A simple alarm buzzer that can be easily carried or attached to handbags, doors, or windows is now available. Electrified fences are being used in suburban neighborhoods to protect residential properties. Increasing numbers of people are purchasing sophisticated intruder alarm systems, clock devices that turn lights and radios on and off in unoccupied dwellings at set hours, firearms, chemical weapons for personal protection, and watchdogs. Neighbors are more watchful of each other's dwellings, and guards, doormen, attendants, and closed-circuit television systems are becoming increasingly common.

One new subdivision under construction outside Washington, D.C., offers maximum security for all residents.[10] The sixty-seven high-cost residences in this 167-acre project will be individually guarded by electronic alarms and closed-circuit television units. The entire development will be surrounded by two fences, broken for entry at only two points, both with guardhouses. Residents will be telephoned to approve visitors. The two miles of fencing will be surveyed by a closed-circuit television system and fortified by hidden electronic sensors. All residents will carry special credentials for identification.

Bricked-in, boarded-up, barred, and shielded windows are observed with increasing frequency in some cities. In some cases, no windows or evidence of occupancy at all has been observed on ground floors of buildings. In the future, retail establishments and perhaps residences may find it desirable to use new kinds of glass that take ten to twenty-five minutes to break. The cost is at least four times that of conventional glass, but insurance premiums are reduced on the contents of display windows and other merchandise.[11] Other features of building construction can also affect protection. "Soft" interior walls and unpartitioned ceilings allow burglars to move easily between adjoining establishments. Floors, roofs, skylights, and elevators can be designed to reduce vulnerability.[12]

Address numbers are frequently obscured, especially in suburban areas. It has been shown in one city that police response time can be shortened, with increased apprehension of criminals, simply by uniform placement of address numbers so they are plainly visible to police day and night.

Since 1965, South San Francisco has had a municipal ordinance for crime control requiring the police to submit recommendations on zoning and other land use applications. Local standards for lighting and other features have shown positive results in crime reduction. Because design and relatively inexpensive equipment can contribute to crime control, it has been suggested that every local police department should consult with architects and property owners on protective features, particularly at the early stages of building design and construction.

Examples of environmental management by citizen groups in the New York City area have been reported recently. Residents of the Castlehill Complex on Seward Avenue formed a volunteer Tenants' Patrol. Members are on duty in the evenings and carry no guns or night sticks. Their duties include escorting women and children to apartments, discouraging excessive noise, and keeping the public areas of the buildings free of drug addicts who tended to congregate there. Women representing about 480 families in Marian Gardens (Jersey City) formed a Mothers' Patrol. Members patrol the neighborhood in cars to control vandalism and delinquency among children and adolescents.

More than 3,000 citizen volunteers with limited powers assist the police in New York City, especially during evening hours. One such group, the Electchester Auxiliary Police in Flushing, Queens, patrols its own neighborhood. Each member works three or four evenings a week. Members check the security of buildings and perform services such as escorting people from bus stops to their homes. Since the auxiliary began its work last year, the crime rate in Electchester has fallen 35 percent.

Several writers concerned with environmental relationships of crime have pointed out that places where large numbers of people congregate and spaces that are well lighted and visible from the interiors of surrounding buildings tend to have less crime because of the criminal's fear of apprehension. Concentrations of people in particular places depend on activities people engage in during different times of the day or night, land use patterns, and modes of transportation. Jane Jacobs believes that mixtures of land uses are needed to achieve greater safety and that safe streets are those frequented at all times of the day and night. Such streets have commercial and other activities at the ground level, some of which go on during evening hours, with residences on upper floors.[13] The difficulty in this idea for planning contemporary cities has been illustrated by a study of Oakland, California. Establishments open during evening hours occupy only four miles of the city's 2,400 total miles of street frontage.[14]

Another author believes that three kinds of urban areas should be distinguished to explain relationships between personal safety and activity patterns during evening hours when most crimes are committed: (a) areas of solely daytime activity that are safe in the evening because they are virtually deserted and therefore unattractive to criminals; (b) areas that are safe because the intensity of evening activity makes the risk of being seen committing a crime too great; and (c) areas between the extremes that are unsafe.[15] To discourage crime, the author proposes that theaters, bars, restaurants, and other establishments open during the evening hours be grouped together in a small number of "evening squares" which would be safe because of the number of people present and because good design would eliminate poorly lit places and those screened from the view of many people. Parking lots, for example, where crimes often take place, should be near the center of these safe areas, not at the periphery. Industrial, commercial, and other daytime activities should be located in areas where there would be no need to enter or pass through them during nighttime hours. Low density suburban residential areas, which are relatively free of violent crime, would be linked to other safe areas by automobile corridors that would be comparatively safe because people driving on expressways or arterial streets are rarely the victims of crime.

Contemporary Defensive Cities

There is little doubt that large American cities are currently being fortified against crime. Historically, when political institutions have failed to protect the public, individuals have taken steps to safeguard themselves, their families, and their property. The present period is no different in this respect. The urban environment is being fortified today, not primarily by public decisions, but mainly through the multiplicity of private choices and decisions individuals make in our decentralized society. The private market is responding to growing demand for an increasing range of crime control devices and other means of safety. In some cases, safety has already become a commodity that is explicitly sold or rented with real estate.

It is important to consider how Americans will live in our large cities in the future, because if urban crime continues to increase, it is likely that the urban environment will increasingly reflect this condition. Five geographic elements of a modern defensive urban environment based on safety can be suggested:

1. An economically declining central business district in the inner city would primarily serve central city residents and be protected by comparatively large numbers of people shopping or working in buildings during daytime hours. During evening and nighttime hours, the central area would be largely deserted and "sealed off" to protect properties and tax base. Anyone on the streets would attract police attention. Modern technology would enable surveillance of downtown streets by closed-circuit television units mounted on building roofs. A variety of other crime control devices, combined with methods of environmental management, would protect the interiors of individual buildings.

2. High-rise apartment buildings and residential "compounds" of other types would be fortified "cells" for upper middle and high income populations living at prime locations in the inner city, their residents protected by various expensive methods.

3. Suburban neighborhoods, geographically removed from the central city, would be "safe areas," protected mainly by racial and economic homogeneity and by distance from population groups with the greatest propensities to commit crimes.

4. Expressways would be "sanitized corridors" connecting other safe areas and would be safe themselves because they permit movement by comparatively high-speed automobile transportation. Other modes of transportation would be safe or unsafe in different degrees during day and nighttime hours.

5. Other residential neighborhoods in the central city would be unsafe in differing degrees during day and nighttime hours. At the extreme, some residential neighborhoods would be human jungles. Crime in these areas would be frequent, widespread, and perhaps entirely out of police control, even during the daytime. These neighborhoods would be modern counterparts of seventeenth century Parisian *cours des miracles* and various districts of London during the eighteenth century. Subcultures of violence would be localized in these areas

of even more homogeneous lower class populations than today.

This model assumes that if violence in our large cities continues to increase, the future urban environment would not be abandoned, but would be lived in defensively as during the violent times in the past. Individual structures and groups of buildings would be the basic units of environmental defense, constructed or altered to resist unauthorized entry. More efforts would be made to increase visibility and eliminate "blind spots" in the environment. People would avoid areas known or believed to be dangerous. A basic strategy, again as in the past, would be to exclude those regarded as potential criminals from certain areas of the city. Other areas would be perceived as "no-man's-land" to be avoided by all outsiders except the police.

The model is based on defensive features found today to some extent in almost every large American city. These rudiments can be vastly intensified, enlarged, or extended. It is also based on historical considerations. The urban environment has always been designed in part for protection, and it is noteworthy that many environmental responses to urban violence have not differed greatly under different political systems.

Although current uses of the urban environment to obtain safety are not fundamentally different from those used in the past, the underlying social factors along with the economic and social consequences that defensive cities portend for the future—especially in light of the values of our democratic society—are very different today.

RACE AND PHYSICAL DISTANCE

However sensitive we are to present inequalities and historical injustice, our findings show that: (1) Negro crime rates are higher and in some types of crimes are rising more than white rates; (2) increasingly more Negroes are living in central cities of our large metropolitan areas; (3) the volume of crime committed in central cities is greater and is increasing more than in suburban areas; (4) victimization risks for both whites and Negroes are far greater for central city than suburban residents; (5) violent crime generally diminishes proportionately with physical distance from the inner core of central cities; and (6) physical distance of residential neighborhoods from low-income Negro populations in central cities is a variable in obtaining greater safety.

The historical trends of suburbanization, involving residential movements of whites from central cities to suburbs of large U.S. metropolitan areas, began even before World War II. These trends are likely to continue in the future for many reasons unrelated to crime. Nevertheless, it must be concluded that crime during recent years has been an important factor in suburbanization and a cause of white population losses in central cities. As a consequence, central city populations have recently diminished in total size.[16] In this sense, Negro crime has not changed the direction but simply accelerated the trends of white suburbanization.

The physical distance of suburban neighborhoods from central cities is the principal way that suburban residents are protected against crime. Distance substitutes for and is more effective than other deterrent features in central cities. Single-family houses, typical of most suburban communities today, are more vulnerable structures from the viewpoint of design than multifamily apartment buildings and urban row houses. An apartment building or urban row house has more residents and fewer doors and windows at ground level to use for forcible entry. The view from upper floors overlooking fewer entrances allows less concealment and makes it much less practical for criminals to attempt entry.

The purchase of guns by large numbers of white suburbanites during and following Negro riots of the last few years may be explained by a number of factors, including the greater vulnerability of suburban areas. However, this behavior also suggests two additional features. First, many whites overreact to Negro crime and violence, even when not threatened, although the degree of reaction does not change the conclusion that white population movements from central cities to suburban areas have a rational basis. Second, many Negroes perceive urban violence differently than many whites, and this difference has other significant implications.

SUBCULTURES OF VIOLENCE AND THE "VALVE" THEORY

Urban subcultures of violence in America[17] have major implications for contemporary defensive cities. These subcultures consist of particular population groups that favor and accept violence as normal behavior, not as an illicit activity. The values and attitudes of the subcultures need not be shared by everyone living in particular neighborhoods, but they are most prevalent among lower class Negro males, ranging from late adolescence to late middle age, living in central cities. Failure to commit violence, "to prove oneself a man," for example, is most likely to result in social ostracism, although all persons belonging to the subcultures do not commit violence in all situations.

Few studies distinguish differences among poor Negro or white populations living in large American cities. Nevertheless, there are reasons to believe that both the Negro and white poor are heterogeneous populations in many ways. Evidence suggests that only a small proportion of all Negroes living in large cities and only some of the Negro poor belong to subcultures of violence. These populations have other attitudes and features differentiating them from the larger white and Negro urban society and from the other poor.

It is likely that Negro in-migrants to northern cities from southern rural areas did not bring the values and attitudes characteristic of the subcultures with them. Instead, the subcultures are an urban phenomenon that has emerged indigenously among those born and raised in large American cities. Bringing together large numbers of Negro poor for a substantial time in racially segregated and economically deprived neighborhoods has bred a modern counterpart of the violent subcultures of past centuries.

Members of the subcultures are

not "professional" criminals who minimize risks, but angry young men who have no stake in society. They have "heroes" only in their own neighborhoods to imitate, and they commit crimes haphazardly and dangerously, victimizing Negroes more than whites. It is likely that criminal activity does pay off for these subcultures. They have the same material aspirations as the larger Negro and white society, but they have a separate economy of livelihoods and monetary profit made possible by urban living. For these people, the subcultures offer substitute incentives and values for those of the larger society. Once established, attitudes toward violence are learned from life in the subcultures. In this way, as during past centuries, the subcultures of violence can be self-perpetuating for long periods.

Although there are no statistical measurements, the violent subcultures probably account for most crimes committed in central cities today, and contemporary defensive cities may result, in large part, from their existence and growth. In turn, the increasing fragmentation of the urban environment and the specialization of geographic "cells" of defensive cities would institutionalize and perpetuate the subcultures of violence even more. The traditional "valve" theory of crime shifts asserts that the volume of crime is not reduced by "hardening targets." If one type of crime, such as robbing busses, is "shut off," crime will shift to other targets, such as robbing taxicabs or stores. Applying this theory to defensive cities, those population groups who flee from the central city to suburban areas or who can afford housing in the

fortified "cells" within the central city would obtain protection. Crime would be shifted to unprotected neighborhoods inhabited by the poor, who even now are usually the victims of crime. Crime would be intensified in the neighborhoods where the subcultures of violence are localized, accentuating the values and attitudes distinguishing them.

ECONOMIC EFFECTS

Crime is likely to have far-reaching consequences for the future economic health and tax base of central cities. It is axiomatic in economic development programs in the United States that private enterprises avoid or move away from areas of crime or violence. For many reasons, commercial and industrial development does not flourish in areas where public safety is not assured. If crime continues to increase, central cities are likely to become economically depressed—the holes in the donuts of prosperous metropolitan economies. The economies of many cities are likely to function at lower levels of development than today—in volumes and types of economic activity, levels of productivity, and types of occupations and earning levels of central city residents. Tax rates are likely to be high with lower levels of services. Growth of employment opportunities and tax bases as well as investment of private capital to improve the urban environment of central cities are likely to be impaired.

FRAGMENTATION OF THE URBAN ENVIRONMENT

As metropolitan cities in America have exploded horizontally and as metropolitan populations have increased in size, larger geographic areas have come to serve increasingly specialized residential functions. From the beginning of this century, large northern cities functioned as specialized residential places for ethnic minorities in American society. There are two main differences between the present day and the first half of the twentieth century: (1) Negroes now comprise the dominant unassimilated minority in American society; and (2) Negro populations in central cities are much larger now than any other single ethnic minority was in most large northern cities during past decades. As a consequence, the relative scale of specialization now applies to much larger neighborhoods in central cities. Similarly, the economic and social homogeneity of white populations residing in suburban communities and in some central city neighborhoods are features of geographic specialization.

In this way, the urban environment of large American cities has been increasingly socially fragmented since the end of World War II. A concern for protection has probably always been associated to some extent with other more obvious features of increasingly specialized residential functions. However, contemporary defensive cities would create even more fragmentation with even greater social consequences within comparatively limited geographic areas.

The Kerner Commission warned America of the danger of being split into two separate and unequal societies. It is important to describe one of the ways this can happen in the urban environment of large American cities— as a response to crime.

Using *distance* and *access to space* to separate groups of potential victims from potential offenders requires an implicit recognition that some social groups have members who are likely to commit criminal acts. Denying access to space usually involves a more explicit recognition of social groups associated with crime on the basis of such obvious or visible human features as race. In both cases, there must be social expectations about what groups are likely to contain criminals and where crimes are likely to be committed.

Except for fugitives from justice, there are no criminals at large, by legal definition, in contemporary American society. We do not condone the medieval method of banishment or outlawry. The concept of the criminal has changed as legal rights have been expanded. Consequently, it is not possible now to formally or informally recognize potential offenders as individuals, but only as members of social groups.

Greater safety would be obtained by using distance and denying access to space. Yet, as we have seen, the other consequences of contemporary defensive cities are socially destructive— further fragmentation of the urban environment, formation of excessively parochial communities, greater segregation of racial groups and economic classes, imposition of presumptive definitions of criminality on the poor and on racial minorities, increasing chances of vigilantism, and polarization of attitudes on many issues. The use of space in this manner would inevitably limit the freedom of law-abiding citizens of all races and economic classes to move safely through large sections of the urban environment, to enjoy the diversity of urban life, to choose living accommodations among many safe residential neighborhoods, and to understand and communicate directly with other social groups in our pluralistic society.

Other Behavioral Relationships

Not all crime is committed by strangers. A significant proportion of all murders, assaults, and rapes are committed against friends or intimates.[18] In these cases, the physical environment is irrelevant, except perhaps in individual psychological ways.

Nor does historical evidence support the premise of environmental determinism that there are simple or direct causal relationships between the physical environment and positive or negative forms of behavior, including crime. Cities have differed during past centuries in amounts of violence, but not because some had particular designs or urban forms conducive to violence and others did not. Indeed, it is likely that the physical environment is more a result than a cause of human behavior. This is consistent with the traditional view prevalent among humanists that the architecture and urban design of any era are the products of the total social and technological milieu in which they were created so they reflect the paramount values of a particular society or culture. This view emphasizes the physical environment as a cultural achievement and a reflection of society, but does not admit that

the environment may have a hand in causing human behavior.

CONTROLLING VIOLENCE DIRECTLY

The discussion of contemporary defensive cities supports the conclusion that the design and form of the urban environment can control violence through use of distance and by protecting parts of the urban environment. In this relationship, the urban environment operates directly to control crime. However, this does not say that the urban environment can operate directly to create positive forms of behavior. The "valve" theory suggests that defensive cities would not eliminate or attack the roots of crime, but simply determine its types and locations. Theoretically, people might be shifted out of crime by creating a totally fortified environment to "shut off" all types of crime in all areas. In this case, people would shift to positive forms of behavior. This possibility calls for an extremely repressive closed system of the urban environment, one that would be very difficult or impossible to create.

The "valve" theory, of course, implies that there is a given quantity of criminal behavior or a propensity to commit crime in particular populations. This view is consistent with the existence of violent subcultures, but raises strong objections from some behavioral scientists who believe it creates a totally false perspective of human behavior.

ENCOURAGING POSITIVE BEHAVIOR

The idea that design and form of the urban environment can be used to encourage positive behavior has historical roots in the philosophy of the Utopian Socialists during the eighteenth and nineteenth centuries in England and America and is accepted today in many ways. The legal powers of local governments to regulate or redevelop the physical environment by zoning or urban renewal, for example, rest on court interpretations of the Fourteenth Amendment, which specify the ". . . reasonable tendency to protect the public health, safety, morality or general welfare . . . ." Yet, whatever other purposes have been served, public programs in our large cities during the past two decades have failed to enhance public safety by controlling or reducing crime. There are few, if any, documented cases where urban environments have been consciously designed for low-income populations who have responded favorably by changing from negative to positive forms of behavior. To be sure, crime and other social pathologies are associated to a considerable extent with poverty, high residential densities, and deteriorated physical conditions, but all the poor living in deteriorated neighborhoods are not criminals. Even our slum environments in major cities are vastly improved from what they were at the beginning of this century. Many examples can be cited to show how our affluent society has raised its standards of what poverty is at the same time that we have made vast improvements. Poverty in the physical environment today is a matter of absolute standards, but according to some views it has also become a matter of the relative difference between the levels at which the poor and the affluent live.

Some recent experience holds promise for the future, but much more evidence seems to indicate that violence can continue independently of whatever changes are made in the design, form, density, or quality of the urban environment. Increasing crime in white middle class suburban areas refutes the hypothesis that the quality of the urban environment associated with affluence is sufficient to prevent crime in all population groups. Indeed, in many instances, the physical environment may simply be a stage on which individuals and social groups act out their lives. The actors and the play, not the stage, may actually create positive or negative forms of behavior.

Although every major explanation of violence suggests that the urban environment plays some role in creating or preventing crime, social science theories do not suggest that the urban environment directly creates positive forms of behavior.[19] Instead, various theories assert that there are intervening variables between the environment and behavior, that people impute values to the environment that are essentially independent of any particular environmental design or form, that human behavior can be a response to the environment in terms of an individual's psychological needs, or that social variables, rather than operating directly, operate in consonance with the physical environment to encourage positive or negative forms of behavior.

Two possibilities are especially worth considering from this perspective. The first is that some means of controlling crime may have other desirable effects on human behavior. For instance, increasing visibility on comparatively small scales of architectural design may not only control crime but also further social contacts among residents of a building. Concentrating activities to improve visibility may also encourage social contacts when numbers of people congregate in "evening squares" or along streets with mixtures of land uses. Concern about crime may bring members of a community closer together and increase social cohesion.

The second possibility is that people may be motivated to endow the urban environment with social values, and in this process change behavior patterns. "Homelike" and "communitylike" qualities are general terms lacking precise meaning in the physical environment. Instead, they are little more than metaphors for values that people subjectively attribute to what they like or identify with in the environment. The present emphasis on different forms of community participation is based on the premise that the entire process of planning, building, and managing the urban environment can be used to create identity between people and physical features so that individuals and social groups will contribute constructively and attribute positive values to the homes and communities in which they live. The idea that the urban environment should be designed more to facilitate repair rather than to resist breakage suggests that the particular design of a building or other physical feature may be less important in shaping human behavior than the process by which it is designed and built.

Some professionals believe that mastery, control, and ownership of property are critical features in using the urban environment to create positive forms of behavior. The example of a playground designed and built by children in one American city some years ago can be cited. Although no statistics were kept, there appeared to be a decrease in vandalism in the neighborhood as work on the playground progressed and the children increased their mastery over a small part of the environment. The children asked the city to build a chain-link fence around the playground to keep balls from going into the streets or nearby buildings. The city constructed the fence, but did not like the crude equipment the children had built and removed it. The next day the fence was completely destroyed by the children, and it appeared that other vandalism in the neighborhood was resumed.

Various cases of environmental management have also been observed in which gangs of hostile youths who had vandalized a neighborhood and victimized its residents changed their behavior when given the responsibility for protecting the neighborhood. Some members became increasingly eager to help and did more than simply chase rival gang members from their "turf." Public programs enabling the poor to own their own homes are based on a similar premise of endowing the urban environment with positive values.

At present, there are few, if any, behavioral studies and only limited observations that suggest but do not test these principles. Much larger experiments in community participation have been started in various cities, some of which may ultimately show whether or not the process of building the urban environment, rather than the particular design or end result of the urban environment, can influence social behavior. But it is too early to tell whether these experiments will be successful, and, even if they are successful in other ways, whether they will reduce crime.

Conclusions

If urban crime continues to increase and is not abated by other means, defensive cities are likely to become a reality in America, even though they would be a retreat to earlier periods in history. The consequences are foreboding and would be economically and socially destructive. Unquestionably, our major cities are being fortified now, and defensive cities may become a reality, not necessarily by public decisions, but through mass choices of urban consumers in our decentralized society. Distance and the ways the urban environment can be changed to control crime are means that individuals will understandably use to protect themselves, their families, and their property. Such defensive use of the urban environment will not attack the causes or roots of crime, and may add to them, but it is unclear whether the environment can be used positively to reduce the overall volume of crime. Even if positive uses of the urban environment are found, they are likely to require time, public decisions, large

public investments, and the consensus of many people. Decisions by individuals to obtain protection can be made more rapidly. Moreover, criminal behavior, once established, can be expected to change slowly, however the urban environment is changed. Consequently, there is an urgent need to find other ways to reduce urban violence.

Footnotes

1.   This article is mainly concerned with violence committed by individuals and small groups of persons against other persons in large American cities. Major violent crimes are criminal homicide, forcible rape, robbery, and aggravated assault. Major nonviolent property crimes—larceny, burglary, and auto theft—are incidentally of interest.

2.   *Report of the National Advisory Commission on Civil Disorders* (New York: Bantam Books, 1968), p. 1.

3.   Chapter 16 published by the National Commission on the Causes and Prevention of Violence contains a more comprehensive summary of historical responses to violence in cities and more amply supports the conclusion that urban environments have always been designed in part for protection.

4.   Chapters 3 and 5 in Volume I, *Crimes of Violence,* Task Force on Individual Acts of Violence, Report to the National Commission on the Causes and Prevention of Violence (Washington: Government Printing Office, 1970), describe the characteristics and trends of violent crimes in America. This section summarizes the findings which are most pertinent to the urban environment.

5.   See, Federal Bureau of Investigation, U.S. Department of Justice, *Uniform*

Crime Reports-1967 (Washington, D.C.: Government Printing Office, 1967), Appendix 5, Table 1E.

6. Although the reported rate of forcible rape also increased greatly, studies for the Violence Commission were unable to reach conclusions about the true rate because of many reporting problems.

7. Norval Morris and Gordon Hawkins, *The Honest Politician's Guide to Crime Control* (Chicago: University of Chicago Press, forthcoming, 1970).

8. The percentage of Negroes who robbed other Negroes was almost as great.

9. Chapter 16 published by the National Commission contains a summary of psychological, anthropological, ethological, and sociological explanations of violence related to the urban environment, which is omitted entirely in this article but supports the conclusion stated in the text. The summary in the original chapter is based on Chapters 7 through 11 in Volume II, *Crimes of Violence.*

10. *Washington Post,* March 16, 1969, p. A8, and *The Wall Street Journal,* June 19, 1969, p. 1.

11. Small Business Administration Report on Crime Against Small Business, Appendix D, Architectural Task Force.

12. *Ibid.*

13. Jane Jacobs, *The Death and Life of Great American Cities* (New York: Random House, 1961).

14. Shlomo Angel, "Discouraging Crime Through City Planning" (Working Paper No. 75, Center for Planning and Development Research, University of California at Berkeley, 1968), p. 2.

15. *Ibid.,* pp. 15–19.

16. Recent population changes in central cities are described in: "Statement by Conrad Taeuber, Associate Director, Bureau of the Census, Before the House Committee on Banking and Currency, June 3, 1969."

17. Chapter 5 in Volume I and Chapters 11 and 14 in Volume II, *Crimes of Violence,* discuss the subcultures of violence in America in detail. This section defines and describes the relevance of the subcultures to the urban environment.

18. Chapter 5, *Ibid.*

19. See Note 9.

• • • • • • • • • • • • • • twenty-one

GEORGE W. CAREY •

Urban Ecology, Geography, and Health Problems

The urban ecologist is interested in the nature of the city as a life-supporting system for man, while the urban geographer is concerned primarily with the processes of spatial growth and development of the city. Since both of these emphases are closely related to concerns of the health field, it may prove helpful to sketch briefly a theoretical framework for interpreting them before passing to a consideration of our metropolitan ecology in the past, and to make some suggestions for researching its state in the present.

The Spatial Structure of an Urban Ecological System

Otis D. Duncan and Leo Schnore,[1] among others, have provided us with a theoretical model of the relation between man and his environment, which may be applied to the study of cities with good effect. As we see from the diagram in Figure 1, the growth of a population and its level of living is closely related to four other interlinked factors. T is the state of technology, SO represents the organization of society, SP represents the social psychology—the operational world view, so to speak—of the populace, and E represents the environment.

The point is that if change is initiated in one or several of these factors, interactions will occur which will induce changes in all. Indeed, several cycles of changes may well occur before a new equilibrium is reached, and the synergistic effects may be such that the aggregate changes may be much larger than anticipated. In a rapidly changing society, only transient tendencies toward equilibrium may be noted, while in a relatively static society the ecolog-

◆ SOURCE.   Reprinted by permission from *Bulletin of the New York Academy of Medicine,* Vol. 46, February 1970.

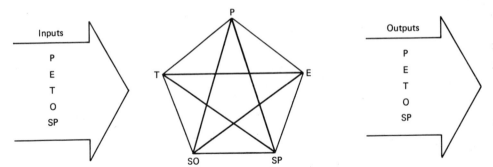

FIGURE 1.   Metropolitan Systems.

ical system may remain in rough equilibrium for a long time—the city system of the M'zab in Algeria comes to mind as an example often used by geographers.[2]

But the modern metropolis is an open system rather than a closed one. Matter and energy flow into it and leave it, and these flows may be classified in the same fashion as the other dimensions of the system. Thus migration in and out of the city is the dynamic aspect of the P factor. Technological flows ranging from goods and skills to manufactured forms of kinetic energy also enter and leave the system. In the area of social organization, managerial decisions made in far-flung capitals, in Federal Reserve Board conference rooms, or in national institutional headquarters may constitute inputs of grave consequence to the metropolis borne into it by the electromagnetic media of modern communication. Social psychological inputs and outputs ranging from patterns of prejudice to culture-conditioned preferences and ephemeral fads can also change the landscape and level of life of the region —thereby helping to create ghettos on

the one hand and acres of ranch-style or, more recently, split-level suburbs on the other. And we become even more conscious of environmental flows as they threaten us: air, water, wastes, and pollutants.

As an example of the implications of this framework of reference, consider the accompanying table. Most of these activities, which actually comprise but a small fraction of all which might have been listed, would not have been present in even the largest of cities in 1900, and the rest would have been found in a form which would scarcely reflect the relative sophistication of technology in 1967. "Trucking," for example, in 1900 had quite a different connotation than it has today. Indeed, the very existence of a sufficiently developed telephone network to justify a sizeable modern directory depended on switching inventions beginning with the Strowger switch of 1891.[3] Yet every single activity listed in the table has had its effect, great or small, upon metropolitan land-use patterns. In the case of such categories as airports, earth-moving equipment, gasoline stations, motion picture theaters, parking stations, and

TABLE 1. A Partial Listing of Classification Categories:
Quick Reference Index—Manhattan Yellow Pages

Acetate fabrics	Circuits—printed &	Mobile homes
Acetate scrap	etched	Motion picture theaters
Acoustical ceilings	Data-processing system	Motorcycles
Adding and calculating	Duplicating machines	Neon lighting equipment
machines	& supplies	Oceanographers
Advertising:	Earth-moving equipment	Oil burners
Radio	Electrical appliances	Outboard motors
Sound truck	Foods—frozen—packers	Parking meters
Subway	& distributors	Parking stations
Television	Gasoline stations	and garages
Aerial photographers	Germanium	Phonograph records—
Aeronautical engineers	High-fidelity sound	retail
Air conditioners	equipment	Plastics—research
Airline companies	Infrared equipment	and consulting
Air-pollution control	Inventories computing	Radio audience analysis
Airports	service	Radium preparations
Automobile dealers	Lamps—fluorescent	Shavers, electric
Buses	Laundries—self-service	Silicones
Business machines	Liquid air	Swimming pools
Butane gas	Loud speakers	Television stations
Cadmium plating	Magnesium and	Trucking
Camping trailer	magnesium products	Vacuum cleaners
Capacitors	Missile & rocket—	Water heater
Cathode-ray tubes	components manufacturers	X-ray equipment
Chlorophyll		
Chromium plating		

garages, the land-use effects of technological change have clearly been enormous. In the case of other activities, the separate impacts of such activities upon the use of urban land have been small or moderate, but the cumulative effect of clusters of activities has been great. In this category are the electrical and electronic goods-retailing complexes which, together with their supportive services, occupy such a prominent place both in central business districts and in satellite shopping centers throughout metropolitan America. Again, some technological innovations seem to be ubiquitous, and extremely visible wherever urban business enterprise occurs, like neon lighting, air conditioning, and various kinds of central heating. Perhaps the effects of such devices are to be understood more in the social-psychological sphere of how we sense the city than in terms of their effects upon urban use of land.

Yet whether the effects of technological change are to be appreciated in terms of our changed perceptions of the city through new visual stimuli and new media of communication, or whether the use of land itself is altered, or whether—as in the case of innovations in data processing and inventory control—the socioeconomic city is reorganized as a flow center, one fact stands out. Virtually all of the technological changes which have so profoundly altered the nature of the city in the twentieth century—whether innovations in metallurgical, chemical, manufacturing and process, transportation, or health and medical technology—have been inextricably interrelated with major social and demographic changes. And the health-services sector is part and parcel of the changing system. Merely consider the number of problems in safety and health on the one hand, and treatments and supportive services on the other which are related to the list of the table shown. The revolutionary transformation of Manhattan's East River waterfront into an agglomerated subsystem of medical care and research which straddles the midtown central business district on both sides in some of the real estate valued highest in the world testifies to the environmental impact of this metropolitan subsystem.

The urban geographer needs, in addition to an ecological framework, a theoretical structure by means of which he may understand the spatial growth of the metropolis. One very useful approach makes use of the crucial property of the metropolis as a center of flows and communications. It is, as it were, a center of access. Karl W. Deutsch enunciates some of these views in a graphic way:

Any metropolis can be thought of as a huge engine of communica-

tion, a device to enlarge the range and reduce the cost of individual and social choices. In the familiar telephone switchboard, the choices consist of many different lines. Plugging in the wires to connect any two lines is an act of commitment, since it implies foregoing the making of other connections. The concentration of available outlets on the switchboard permits a wider range of alternative choices than would prevail under any more dispersed arrangement. . . . The limits of the potentially useful size of a switchboard are fixed by the capacity of the type of switching and control equipment available. The facilities of the metropolis for transport and communication are the equivalent of the switchboard.[4]

In this quotation, lines of thought ranging from human ecology to systems theory converge in the metaphor of the engine of communication—a system metaphor. But Deutsch extends the range and scope of his analysis by pointing out that the *effectiveness* of a metropolis may be defined as its performance measured in terms of the number of contact choices which it offers to a person in one hour of round-trip commuting time, while its *efficiency* might be measured in terms of the ratio of the effectiveness to some cost unit: how many choices could a given sum make available to a person in the city?

Given the distribution of the population and the pattern of transportation in New York in 1900 the center of access was, no doubt, central Manhattan. The structure of commercial and service activities (including medical services) which arose subsequent to that time probably did reflect the Deutsch criteria of effectiveness and efficiency. Recently intraregional demographic shifts and the revolution in commuter transportation, accompanied by diseconomies of congestion at the core, have considerably diffused the foci of greatest access—a fact reflected in the regional shopping-center movement.

Peter Haggett has gone into finer detail than Deutsch in specifying the spatial elements which relate to the networks which support the metropolitan flow system. He points out that open flow systems (such as metropolitan regions) are organized into five general spatial components: (1) *movements* occur along channels which together form a (2) *network*; the network is characterized by intersections of (3) *nodes*, which vary in importance and form a (4) *hierarchy*; the interstitial areas between branches of the network can be interpreted as (5) *surfaces* which may be organized into zones of similar characteristics.[5]

Suppose there is a large lawn behind the main building of a university. Across the lawn other buildings are built. In their passage among these edifices, students, in their haste choose not to use the walkway around the lawn, cut across it without regard to damaging the grass. Eventually, to the despair of the grounds keepers, dirt paths are created. Hoping to restrict the flow, and save at least part of the lawn,

asphalt is laid along the paths, forming a network. At one place, where four paths intersect, an ice-cream vendor positions himself during the warm months and forms a major node, while at minor nodes near the specific buildings students from the schools of journalism, law, medicine, and engineering arrange to meet and gather. Thus a hierarchy of nodes manifests itself, and the lawns around the central node fill up with reclining ice-cream eaters, while those around the minor nodes are less densely occupied by chatting students. If the university accepts as many new students as it graduates, and if the curricular organization is not changed, so that the buildings in the environment do not change, an equilibrium in the pattern may result.

The parable may easily be extended to the case of the growth of a suburb. Consider the pattern of change in the use of land in Staten Island attendant upon the building of the Verrazano-Narrows Bridge and its interlinked highway network. New nodes that manifest an extended range of retailing, service, and other commercial functions and thus occupy a high hierarchical level in the set of all retailing nodes are developing on plazas oriented toward crucial intersections of the new channels. Old nodes eccentric to the new network are relatively—and sometimes absolutely—diminished in hierarchial ranking. Many geographers, by utilizing the mathematics of networks and flows, have done much toward developing quantitative models of the changes in such systems.[6]

In the New York Metropolitan Re-

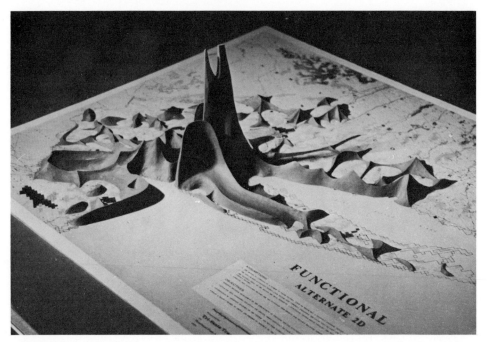

FIGURE 2.   Commercial activity concentration model: the New York Metropolitan Region. The height of the clay above the map surface is proportional to the commercial activity at the location. Reproduced by permission of Thomas J. Thomas, formerly of the Tri-State Transportation Commission.

gional System, the principal node has been the central business district of Manhattan. Figure 2 shows a clay-model conceptualization of the major activity centers in the region developed by T. Thomas. The height of the clay is proportional to the amount of activity at the locus. Variations in the value of land in general follow the patterns of centers of access and activity and, in turn, are of the greatest influence in allocating patterns of the use of land.

In the interstitial areas of the model, the "sags" in the clay, we find land surfaces primarily devoted to residential uses. These form the "flesh"— to use the terminology of Berry[7]—

which grows around the flow network or commercial "skeleton," which "is determined by broader regional and supra-regional forces."[8]

In the intricate pattern of change and variation of life quality in the "residential flesh," we find concomitant variations in health problems. The pattern of access, land-value determination, and nodal hierarchy established by the skeleton is intimately related to the question of placement of service facilities—including health services. Before considering techniques for studying these, let us glance at the ecology of the nineteenth-century city in order to provide us with a benchmark for analyzing the contemporary metropolis.

The Changing Metropolitan Environment

The media assault us on all sides with stories concerning the urban crisis. The themes are familiar. The city of today is becoming uninhabitable because densities are increasing; congestion is increasing; crime and violence, health hazards, and environmental pollution are all increasing.

It is not difficult to show that the core of New York City, at least, has been decreasing in density since 1890. The density of that year, calculated by Weber[9] for Ward 10 (the vicinity southeast of Rivington Street and the Bowery) was in excess of 523 persons per acre—or 335,000 persons per square mile. That census tract of Manhattan with the highest density in 1960 was in Harlem, south of 155th Street, with a density of 247,000 persons per square mile (386 persons per acre), or about 74% of the 1890 figure. This is not an atypical instance in American cities. As the ecosystem responds to transportation advantage, the suburbs extend and the core densities diminish.

When we consider that the 1890 densities in the old Russian-Jewish ghetto were developed on a housing technology of four- or five-story old-law tenement walk-ups, with inadequate sanitation, inefficient garbage removal, and a sewage system which, at best, discharged into the adjacent East River, we may well be appalled at the crowding—in terms of number of per-

sons per room—which the density implies. Modern sites with high-rise apartments can sustain comparable densities without crowding owing to the advancement of technology.

As books such as that of Asbury[10] show, crime and vice were rampant in the nineteenth-century New York, gaslight nostalgia notwithstanding. Gang warfare and semiorganized street violence can be traced back at least to the cockney gangs which formed after disadvantaged immigrant families came to New York from England following the Napoleonic Wars and the War of 1812.

As to transportation (in 1867) the arrangements were so inconvenient and congested and the pavements so bad that: ". . . a considerable part of the working population . . . spend a sixth part of their working days on the street cars or omnibuses, and the upper part of the city is made almost useless to persons engaged in any daily business of any kind . . ."[11] Chinitz remarks that already by World War I, pier traffic in New York had slowed to a crawl.[12]

And the inevitable concomitant of congestion in a city relying on animal-powered transportation was an accumulation of urine and manure, not to mention dead animals and offal in the principal streets: a condition that staggers the mind.[13] Mandelbaum tells us that these factors, combined with inadequate sanitary drainage, resulted in a situation in which sewers in the district south of 14th Street clogged and broke, spewing their contents into the streets and turning avenues such as Broadway into sluggish streams of dark brown mud.[14] In the 1850's, cellar dwellings (prone to flooding with street effluvium) housed 29,000 persons.[15] Consumption, typhus, typhoid fever, and cholera were frequent pestilences and, before 1823, yellow fever. The death rate per 1,000 in 1865 was 34.2; in 1853, 41.0; in 1849, 60.9,[16] compared to an estimated 1964 rate of 11.0—in an older population. Bearing in mind that these rates were citywide, surely the rates specific to the immigrant wards were much higher. One can conclude that the environment of New York City has improved remarkably in the last 100 years.

This is not to contradict the view that city conditions in many respects—because of neglect—are deteriorating, but rather to put the deterioration in long-term perspective. I find grounds for cautious optimism. Considering how the city as a system for supporting life has improved in the past century in the absence of over-all comprehensive planning from a health standpoint, we have every reason to hope that, with diligent application of invested time and money, enough progress may be made not only to reverse the slippage but to score further net advances.

Health institutions which arose in the nineteenth century, and—to a certain extent—in the early twentieth century, were oriented toward the control of plague and pestilence in epidemic situations. Since these diseases have been brought under control the emphasis in health problems has shifted to new patterns which have been "unmasked," so to speak, by progress, and which—like urban health problems for hundreds of years—bear more heavily on the poor than the affluent. Many studies correlate the illnesses included

in the following diagnostic groups with poverty: heart disease, arthritis and rheumatism, mental and nervous conditions, high blood pressure, visual impairments, orthopedic impairments, mental disorders (including schizophrenia), cancer, and infant mortality. The environment—particularly housing—seems to play an important part in a fivefold classification of complaints developed by Wilner and cited by Schorr:

1. Acute respiratory infections (colds, bronchitis, grippe), related to multiple use of toilet and water facilities, inadequate heating or ventilation, inadequate and crowded sleeping arrangements.
2. Certain infectious diseases of childhood (measles, chicken-pox, and whooping cough) related to similar causal factors.
3. Minor digestive diseases and enteritis (typhoid, dysentery, diarrhea), related to poor facilities for the cold storage of food and to inadequate washing and toilet facilities.
4. Injuries resulting from home accidents, related to crowded or inadequate kitchens, poor electrical connections, and poorly lighted and unstable stairs.
5. Infectious and noninfectious diseases of the skin, related to crowding and facilities for washing.[17]

Schorr also discusses studies which link pneumonia, tuberculosis, and lead poisoning directly to the effects of poor housing, and argues persuasively that stresses arising from crowding and the lack of personal satisfactions in a poverty-stricken environment pose mental and physical health hazards.[18] In animal populations Calhoun and Deevey have called attention to the pathologically self-destructive tendencies of animal populations when exposed to crowding stresses.[19]

But these effects—of crowding, interpersonal tension, stress, environmental hazards, and malnutrition as well—are not independent of each other. As Roemer and Kish point out,

> . . . the aggregate impact of the physical and social environment of the poor, including their housing, nutrition, occupations, and whole style of life, contributed to a burden of disease and death that blights their lives much more than among the well-to-do.

The health handicaps of poverty apply to all places, rural and urban. In the urban slum, however, congested living, air pollution, lack of recreational space, and the general squalor are not mitigated even by sunshine and grass. It is true that access to medical care for rich and poor alike is greater in the cities than in rural areas. The urban poor, however, receive much less medical treatment for their illness than the well-to-do, so that a given sickness is more likely to become advanced, disabling, and even fatal. For the Negro and other ethnic minorities, the problems of poverty and ignorance are compounded by the barriers of prejudice and discrimination.[20]

The foregoing sets the task for the urban geographer interested in health. How is one to sort out—to map, as it were—the variations of these health-associated environmental, demographic, social, and psychological elements of our urban ecology, so that the spatial pattern of the need for health services may be understood? For if that can be done, there is reason to suppose that it may cast light on the problem of deploying medical technology to meet the need.

The mapping and interpretation of complexly related areal data that bear on urban populations is an area of concern to urban and medical geography.[21] The multivariate statistical technique of principal-components analysis is one such tool which I have used in studies on Manhattan and Washington, D.C.[22] It is possible to subdivide an area of study into numerous small subareas (perhaps utilizing the census-tract divisions) and prepare a data matrix of as many as 40 or 60 variables based upon elements of the environment, the population structure, the social structure, and the subcultural outlook of the residents. One may then cluster these individual variables into syndromes of association by the principal-components technique. Each syndrome has the valuable property of statistical independence from the others and can be mapped separately.

The mapped ecological regions might then be used as a guide to the probable incidence of various health problems. This would constitute, as it were, an inquiry into the variation of health needs (in contrast to demands) as they are estimated to vary within the "residential flesh" of the metropolis.

There is no real reason, by the way, why mental as well as physical health needs might not be included in the same analysis.

Referring back to the model of Figure 2: these areas of varying need would constitute surfaces on the flanks and in the depressions of the clay model. It is appropriate next, having raised the question of the location of health needs, to ask where health facilities should be located to supply them most effectively.

In studying the nodes, channels, and networks of access which serve the retailing, service, and commercial demands of the metropolis, urban geographers have evolved a body of theory called Central Place Theory, which helps to interpret the spatial arrangement of tertiary activity in general and may be specifically applicable to health planning.

Briefly, every kind of commercial establishment (such as grocery stores, furniture stores, department stores, theaters, etc.) which satisfies the demands of the urban population for goods and services may be characterized in terms of its range and threshold. The range of a good or service is the distance—often expressed in units of elapsed travel time—which a consumer is willing to travel in order to avail himself of the commodity. Frequently purchased articles and very inexpensive articles tend to have smaller ranges than those which are expensive or infrequently consumed. The small grocery outlet is typical of a small-range establishment, while an opera house has a very large range.

The threshold is defined as the minimum amount of disposable income which suffices to support an establishment selling the good or service in question. Obviously if the circle described by the range of an establishment encloses a market area which possesses an amount of purchasing power less than the threshold, then that establishment cannot survive there.

High-range and high-threshold establishments need to locate at the principal intersections of access in the commercial and transportation "skeleton" of the metropolis by bidding for and securing location at these prized sites in the real estate market. Lower-scale activities seek out less central locations that lead to a differentiation of commercial nodes by a hierarchical level of activity after the manner implied by the model of Haggett. In Figure 2 we discern this effect in the varying heights of the activity peaks and ridges above the plain.

As the central city diminishes in the socioeconomic status of its population the disposable income per acre which provides the thresholds of commercial activity decreases. Low-order, local activities which are not at metropolitan wide-access nodes have their thresholds undercut, and often relocate where the more affluent population has moved.[23] Medical practitioners are typical, in many ways, of small-business entrepreneurs who, as providers of a service, are subject to these stresses. Their movement to the suburbs is akin to the movement of other local tertiary establishments.

Since the density of medical practitioners forms, in turn, the threshold for ancillary and supportive services such as laboratories, pharmacies, and the like, these too will follow; they thereby generate an over-all metropolitan shift toward a geographical pattern resembling an outer ring richer in local medical services that surrounds an inner ring poorer in local services which, in turn, surrounds a core of major medical institutional facilities whose mobility is limited by fixed investment and inertia. How can major treatment facilities be made available to the perimeter? How can local medical services be made available to the inner ring? These questions imply the need for metropolitan area-wide planning.

Kerr White, in an excellent paper, has elaborated on some of these health-facility supply problems.[24] He criticizes, among other things, the lack of coordination of efforts in the allocation of human medical resources, the inadequate communications which exist between different sources and levels in the hierarchy of personal health services, and the failure of previous attempts to regionalize health services on traditional categorical bases—whether by disease, geography, methods of financing, or traditional functional emphasis. In my view these telling points are reflected in the process sketched above. Berry raises a question which particularly bears on the last point. He finds that the traditional gross categories of tertiary activity often utilized for urban economic study break down when the air of analysis is to study the fine structure of commercial location, and that "multiple shades of specialization" must be recognized.[25]

We might suggest that—for planning purposes—a major effort be made to catalogue the separate activities—the multiple shades of specialization of activity—that go to make up the body of "health care," and that these activities be studied so as to discover which of them most need to be located together in interdependent clusters. What, then, is the mean range and threshold of each cluster? If this were ascertained, then it might be possible to plan the location and spacing of medical facilities in a more rational manner. This kind of study can be done for other types of activities, for instance, in planning the location and makeup of regional shopping centers. Recently, in fact, the Regional Planning Association has published a volume in which commercial employment centers are located in connection with transportation development in Manhattan in a manner consonant with many of the views expressed here.[26]

I feel that Kerr White is probably correct in *principle* when he suggests a regionalization of health facilities in a manner resembling that of the United States airlines network, but I prefer to use as a model the network of urban tertiary activity because of its similarities in structure and trend to the health-care network. This also seems to be suggested by the papers of Cherkasky and Pellegrino, which provide interesting insights into the feasibility of the approach suggested here.[27]

In summary, then, it seems to be that urban geography may possibly offer two methodological models applicable to planning for health-care centers. The first would utilize ecological methods to study the distribution of the various differential areas of health needs essential to the estimate of specific-need thresholds. The second might apply some of the approaches of Central Place Theory to the problem of analyzing the supply side of the question. In this regard it might be useful to study the activity structure of the health industry in order to establish activity clusters. These might then be located according to the relations that exist between the surfaces of need and the transportation network in the light of considerations of range and threshold.

References

1. Duncan, O. D., Human Ecology and Population Studies. In: Hauser, P. M. and Duncan, O. D., *The Study of Population*. Chicago, Univ. of Chicago Press, 1959. Schnore, L. F., *The Urban Scene*. New York, Free Press, 1965.

2. Carey, G. W. and Schwartzberg, J., *Teaching Population Geography*. New York, Teachers College Press, 1969.

3. Feder, H. W. and Spencer, A. E., "Telephone switching." *Scient. Amer.* 207: 133–143, 1962.

4. Deutsch, K. W., "On social communication and the metropolis." *Daedalus* 90: 99–110, 1961.

5. Haggett, P., *Locational Analysis in Human Geography*. New York, St. Martin's Press, 1966.

6. Chorley, R. J., and Haggett, P., eds., *Socio-Economic Models in Geography*. New York, Univ. Paperbacks, 1967, p. 34.

7. Berry, B. J. L., "Internal structure of the city." *Law Contemp. Problems* 30: 111–119, 1965.

8. *Ibid.*, p. 119.

9. Weber, A. F., *The Growth of Cities in the Nineteenth Century*. Ithaca, N. Y., Cornell Univ. Press, 1965. Originally published 1899.

10. Asbury, H., *The Gangs of New York*. New York, Knopf, 1928.

11. Mandelbaum, S. J., *Boss Tweed's New York*. New York, Wiley, 1965, p. 15.

12. Chinitz, B., *Freight and the Metropolis*. Cambridge, Mass., Harvard Univ. Press, 1960, pp. 37–40.

13. Mandelbaum, op. cit., p. 65. Duffy, J., *A History of Public Health in New York City, 1625–1866*. New York, Russell Sage Foundation, 1968.

14. Mandelbaum, *op. cit.*, p. 14.

15. Handlin, O., *The Newcomers*. Cambridge, Mass., Harvard Univ. Press, 1959, p. 16.

16. Duffy, *op. cit.*, pp. 575–77.

17. Schorr, A. L., *Slums and Social Insecurity*. Washington, D.C., Govt. Print. Off., 1966, p. 14.

18. *Ibid.*, pp. 14–25.

19. Calhoun, J. B., "Population density and social pathology." *Scient. Amer.* 206:139–148, 1962. Deevey, E. S., "The hare and the haruspex: A cautionary tale." *Amer. Scient.* 50: 339–53, 1962.

20. Roemer, M. I. and Kish, A. I., "Health, Poverty and the Medical Mainstream." In: Bloomberg, W., Jr. and Schmandt, H. J., *Power, Poverty and Urban Policy*. Berkeley, Calif., Sage Publications, 1968, p. 183–84.

21. Armstrong, R. W., Computer Graphics in Medical Geography. *Proceedings IGU* 6:69–7, 1966. Hopps,

H. C., et al. *The Mapping of Disease Project*. Washington, D.C., U.S. Armed Forces Institute of Pathology. Harvard Univ. Institute of Computer Graphics, *SYMAP Program*.

22. Carey, G. W., The Regional Interpretation of Manhattan Population and Housing Patterns through Factor Analysis. *Geog. Rev.*, pp. 551–569, 1966. Carey, G. W., Macomber, L., and Greenberg, M., Educational and Demographic Factors in the Urban Geography of Washington, D.C., *Geog. Rev.*, pp. 515–537, 1968. Murdie, R. A., *Factorial Ecology of Metropolitan Toronto, 1951–1961*. Univ. of Chicago, Dept. of Geog. Research Paper 116, 1969. Simmons, J. W., *Toronto's Changing Retail Complex*. Univ. of Chicago, Dept. of Geog., Research Paper 104, 1966.

23. Berry, B. J. L., *Commercial Structure and Commercial Blight*. University of Chicago, Department of Geography Research Paper 85, 1963.

24. White, K. L., "Personal Health Services: Defects, Dilemmas, and New Directions." In: *Social Policy for Health Care*. New York, New York Acad. Med., 1969.

25. Berry, B. J. L., *Geography of Market Centers and Retail Distribution*. West Englewood Cliffs, N.J., Prentice-Hall, 1967, p. 46.

26. Regional Plan Association, *Urban Design Manhattan*. New York, Viking Press, 1968.

27. Cherkasky, M., "Resources Needed to Meet Effectively Expected Demands for Service," and Pellegrino, E. D., "Regionalization: An Integrated Effort of Medical School, Community and Practicing Physician." In: *New Directions in Public Policy for Health Care*. New York, New York Acad. Med., 1966.

4444444444444

ENVIRONMENTAL DETERIORATION, HAZARDS, AND STRESS

4444444444444

PHILIP A. LEIGHTON ◆

Geographical Aspects of Air Pollution

It is reasonable to suppose that man originally evolved with few if any inhibitions regarding the use of that part of his environment which he was able to capture and hold from his competitors. Only with experience, as his knowledge and numbers increased, did he come to realize that the physical requirements of life are limited and that their use must be regulated. Since earliest history he has been devising systems for the ownership, protection, and use of land and food, and, more recently, of water. Last of all to become subject to this realization and regulation is air. Here the tradition of free use is still dominant. We respect rights of ownership in land, food, and water, but except as a medium of transportation we recognize none for air.

Curiously, this divergence in attitude, or in the stage of modification of

attitude, does not parallel either the urgency of man's needs or his ability to adapt his surroundings to meet those needs. He can live indefinitely away from land, he can go several weeks without food and several days without water, awake he normally eats and drinks only at intervals, and asleep he does neither, but awake or asleep his need for air is never further away than his next breath. As for ability to adapt, he can when he so wishes improve the land, he can improve and transport food and water, but except on a small scale, as in air conditioning in dwellings and other buildings or the use of wind machines in orchards, he cannot yet improve or transport air. Outdoor air in the main he only contaminates. . . .

As a result of such prodigal uses of air for waste disposal, the employment of technology has contributed far more

◆ SOURCE. Reprinted in modified version by permission from the *Geographical Review*, Vol. 61, 1966, pp. 151–174, copyrighted by the American Geographical Society of New York.

343

to the production of air pollution than to its abatement, and it is clear that the ratio must be reversed if man as a breathing organism is to retain a compatible environment. But to define the extent to which the uses of air must be regulated, we must first know something about how much is available. As with man's other needs, it is a simple matter of supply and demand.

The Supply of Air

The height of the troposphere in the middle latitudes, 10–14 km, is about one five-hundredth of the earth's radius. This is a thin skin indeed, yet it contains about four-fifths of all the air in the atmosphere, and to man on the surface of the earth the layer of air available for waste disposal is usually only a fraction—and sometimes only a very small fraction—of the troposphere. The air supply at the surface is limited

to an extent that varies with place and time, and the factors contributing to the limited surface ventilation are both meteorological and topographic.

The most common meteorological factors are inversions that limit vertical mixing of air and low winds that limit its lateral transport. An inversion is a reversal of the normal tropospheric lapse rate, or decrease in air temperature with increasing altitude above the surface, which for the United States and international standard atmospheres is 0.65° C per 100 meters (Fig. 1). A parcel of air ascending in the atmosphere expands with the decreasing pressure and is thereby cooled, and when this process occurs adiabatically, the rate of cooling, or the adiabatic lapse rate, in unsaturated air is about 1° C per 100 meters. When the atmospheric lapse rate is less than this, as it is in the standard atmosphere, an ascending air parcel becomes cooler, and hence denser, than the surrounding

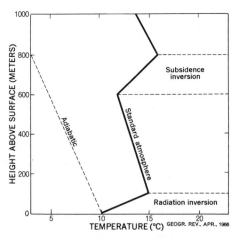

FIGURE 1. Temperature profile through two inversion layers.

air, and work is required to lift it against the downward force produced by the density difference. Similarly, a parcel of air being lowered in a subadiabatic temperature gradient becomes warmer and less dense than the surrounding air, producing an upward force against which work is again required. When the temperature gradient is inverted, the amount of work required to move a parcel of air across the inversion layer usually exceeds the supply available through turbulence and other atmospheric processes, and there is, in consequence, little or no mixing through the layer.

Inversions occur both at the surface and aloft. Surface inversions are most commonly produced by cooling of the ground by radiation loss, which in turn cools the surface air, and their depth, intensity, and duration are functions of the wind velocity, the nature of the surface, the transparency of the air above the surface to the emitted radiation, and the amount of insolation during the following day. The chief absorbers, in air, of the long-wave infrared emitted by a surface at ordinary temperatures are water and carbon dioxide. Hence radiative cooling is most marked when the air is dry and pure, and it increases with altitude as the amount of air overhead is reduced.

The commonest source of inversions aloft is the subsidence that normally accompanies high-pressure systems, but overhead inversions may also be produced, both on a local scale and on an air-mass or frontal scale, by the intrusion of cold air under warm or by the overrunning of cold air by warm. In the middle latitudes subsidence inversions are most marked in the anticyclonic gradients on the easterly sides of high-pressure cells and approach closer to the surface with increasing distance from the cell center.[1] For this reason the west coasts of the continents are subject to relatively low overhead inversions from the semipermanent marine highs, and these inversions may last for many days. Along the Southern California coast, for example, inversions below 762 m (2500 ft), mostly due to subsidence associated with the Pacific high, exist 90 percent or more of the time during the summer months. . . .

Topographic Effects

Perhaps the most important effects of topography in limiting the supply of surface air are produced by drainage. Just as water drains down slopes and gullies to form rivers in valleys and lakes in basins, so the air, cooled by radiation loss, drains down those slopes at night. And like flowing water, these density or gravity flows of cold air tend to follow regular channels, which may be marked out almost as definitely as the course of a stream. The volume of air drainage, however, is much larger than that of water drainage; hence the aircourses are broader, and if the valley or basin is not too wide the flows soon collect to reach across it. The layers thus formed, further cooled by radiation loss in the valley or basin itself, becomes so stable that they often completely control the surface wind direction and velocity and thus control the air supply; the gradient wind is blocked out, and even the gravity flows from

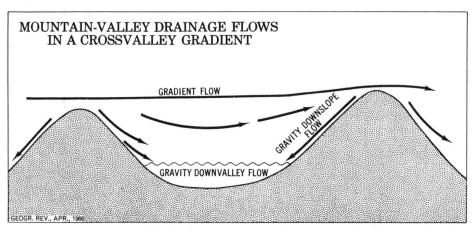

MOUNTAIN-VALLEY DRAINAGE FLOWS
IN A CROSSVALLEY GRADIENT

FIGURE 2. In the case diagramed, the gradient wind is blocked out of the valley by the bordering mountains, and the air supply on the valley floor is limited to that in the lower part of the gravity downvalley flow.

the surrounding slopes tend to overrun the air in the bottom (Fig. 2). After sunrise thermal upslope flow soon sets in on slopes exposed to the sun, but gravity flow may continue until late morning on shady slopes, and even all day on steep northern slopes.[2]

The cold layers accumulated by this process during the long nights of winter may become so deep, with inversions so intense, that they are not broken up by insolation during the short days; and when this happens, severely limited ventilation will persist until a change in weather produces gradient winds high enough, or a cold wedge strong enough, to sweep out the valley or basin. For any particular combination of topography there is usually a fairly critical gradient or synoptic wind velocity below which the local flows are dominant and above which the gradient wind is dominant. The smaller the relief, the lower is this critical velocity; for relief differences

of 300–600 m it is of the order of 10–15 knots. . . .[3]

In coastal areas diurnal warming and cooling of the land, while the water temperature remains fairly constant, produce the familiar pattern of land-sea breezes, which are usually thought of as improving ventilation but which may under certain conditions restrict it. An example is found in the Los Angeles basin, where the Santa Monica Mountains to the northwest and the Sierra Madre to the north furnish shelter to the extent that local airflow is usually dominant under the subsidence inversion. This local flow consists chiefly of a gentle seaward drainage at night and a more rapid landward movement by day. But the mountains rising above the inversion layer retard the sweeping out of the basin by the landward movement, and the diurnal reversal in direction tends to move air back and forth in the basin. As a result of this entrapment, there is often some carry-over of pollutants from the day before, and pollutants emitted at night move toward or out over the sea, only to be swept back over the land the next morning. On occasion this polluted air is carried back over a neighboring area, even a fairly distant one; thus eye irritation came to Santa Barbara for the first time in January, 1965, partly as the result of this process.

These effects are enhanced by a cold upwelling in the ocean along most of the California coast, which produces surface-water temperatures lower than the temperatures farther out to sea. As the surface layer of air moves over this cold water it also is cooled. One result is the familiar coastal fog of California, but a more important result, with respect to air pollution, is the additional stability the cooling imparts to the landward-moving air.

The airflow patterns in the San Francisco Bay Area illustrate another mechanism by which water may limit the air supply. During the extensive season of the semipermanent Pacific high, air cooled by the offshore ocean upwelling flows through the Golden Gate and between the hills of San Francisco to the inner bay (Fig. 3). Part of this air crosses the bay and is deflected to the north and south by the east-bay hills, and part travels south and southeast over the bay itself. Meanwhile, another flow of air reaches the south-bay area by moving inland across the mountains to the west. This air, having traveled farther over land, is warmer than the air that comes down the bay, and when the two flows intersect, the warmer overrides the cooler and produces a local overhead inversion that

around Palo Alto may be less than 100 m above the ground. Although the existence of this effect was demonstrated twenty years ago, its contribution to the severity of air pollution in the south-bay area remains to be determined. . . .

As urbanization and industrialization expand over the world it is interesting, and possibly beneficial, to attempt some assessment of the local air supply in areas that are still relatively empty. Although aerogeographical surveys would be required for an adequate assessment, tentative indications may be obtained merely by consulting maps and weather data. For instance, topography alone suggests that the Granby basin in Colorado would be a poor location in which to build a smelter, and both topography and weather data suggest that such places as the Santa Ynez valley in California and the Sous plain in Morocco should certainly be surveyed before any large industrial or urban development is undertaken. But one does not have to go far in this search to find that most of the unfavorable locations are already occupied. The factors that limit local ventilation are also factors conducive to habitation, and it is ironic that the areas of the world in which the air supply is on occasion most limited are often the areas in which man has chosen to build his cities.

Fortunately, poor ventilation, whether produced by general inversions and low winds or by local conditions, does not exist all the time. The sparkling clarity still enjoyed on days of good ventilation, even over large urban areas, serves to emphasize the great effect of

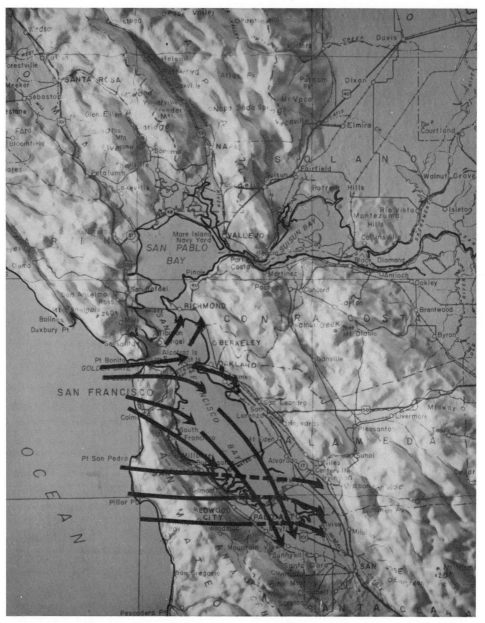

FIGURE 3. Daytime airflow patterns in the San Francisco Bay Area. In the southern part of the Bay Area wind coming over the mountains to the west overrides the colder air coming down the bay, producing an overhead inversion that may contribute to the severity of air pollution in the Palo Alto-San Jose area.

limited air supply on the poor days, and the extent to which it increases the problems of air pollution. . . .

A more difficult group of problems, most of which remain for future solution, arise when the sources of pollution, although specific, are not fixed or for other reasons cannot be easily controlled. In this category are such things as agricultural dust, smoke from agricultural burning, airborne insecticides, and hydrogen sulfide and other obnoxious gases from sewage and organic industrial wastes.

The most difficult problems occur when the effects result from a general merging of pollutants from many diverse sources. Historically, the combustion of coal has been a major cause of general air pollution, but in the United States since World War II the overall contribution of coal to air pollution has diminished with its decreasing use, while the contributions of the hydrocarbon fuels have grown with their increasing use (Fig. 4). Outstanding among the new problems created by the shift in fossil fuels is photo-

chemical air pollution. The emissions chiefly responsible for this form of pollution are nitric oxide, together with some nitrogen dioxide, and hydrocarbons. The nitrogen oxides come from virtually every operation using fire, including internal-combustion engines, steam boilers, various industrial operations, and even home water heaters and gas stoves.

Not all the hydrocarbons emitted to the air take part in the photochemical reactions. Methane, the chief component of natural gas, is inactive. Acetylene, benzene, and the simple paraffins such as propane and butane are nearly inactive. On the other hand, all the olefins, the more complex aromatics, and the higher paraffins are reactive, though they differ widely both in rate and in products. These reactive hydrocarbons come from motor vehicles, from the production, refining, and marketing[4] of petroleum and petroleum products, and from the evaporation of solvents. Other emissions that may play some part in photochemical air pollution are aldehydes, which come

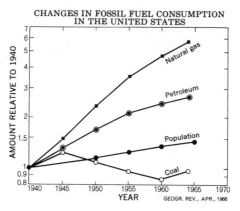

CHANGES IN FOSSIL FUEL CONSUMPTION
IN THE UNITED STATES

FIGURE 4.

chiefly from the incomplete combustion of organic materials, and sulfur dioxide. When these emissions are mixed, diluted in air, and exposed to sunlight, they undergo photochemical reactions that lead to the conversion of the nitric oxide to nitrogen dioxide, which has a brown color and may have adverse effects on plants and animals if its concentration becomes high enough. This is followed, and sometimes accompanied, by the formation of particulates that reduce visibility, of ozone and peroxyacyl nitrates (PAN) that damage plants, and of formaldehyde and other products that, along with the peroxyacyl nitrates, cause eye irritation.

An increasing intensity of pollution is required to produce these symptoms of photochemical air pollution, lowest for visibility reduction, intermediate for plant damage, and highest for eye irritation. Accordingly, the first symptom to appear in any particular area is visibility reduction, the next is plant damage, then follows eye irritation. Similarly, the areas affected are largest for visibility reduction, intermediate for plant damage, and smallest for eye irritation. An estimate of these areas in California is shown in Figure 5. The magnitude of the problem is emphasized by the fact that the eye irritation areas comprise about 70 percent of the people of California, the plant damage areas 80 percent, the areas of general visibility reduction about 97 percent.

One of the most challenging aspects of photochemical air pollution is the rate at which it has grown and is growing. . . . Photochemical pollution has now been observed in more than half the states in the United States and in an increasing number of other countries.[5]

This remarkable spread may be traced to two factors, the first of which is that nitrogen oxide and hydrocarbon emissions have increased faster than the population. The largest source of both nitrogen oxides and hydrocarbons is the automobile; in California at the present time about 60 percent of the nitrogen oxides and 75 to 85 percent of the reactive hydrocarbons, depending on how these are estimated, come from motor vehicles. Between 1940 and 1965 the population of California increased 2.7 times and gasoline use by motor vehicles in the state increased 4.3 times (Fig. 6). The growth in electric-power generation, now 9.2 times what it was in 1940, has been another contributor to increasing nitrogen oxide emissions; roughly 16 percent of the present nitrogen oxide emissions in California come from steam-electric power plants. Hydrocarbon emissions, on the other hand, over the state as a whole have probably increased more in accordance with gasoline use.

The second factor contributing to the growth of photochemical air pollution is the relation between emission rate and the area covered by a given concentration as the pollutants are carried by the wind. This may be illustrated, for idealized conditions, by use of the box model, which assumes uniform mixing to a constant height such as an overhead inversion base, with dilution by lateral diffusion beneath that ceiling. The isopleths for a given concentration, calculated from this model[6] for various emission rates in a uniform square source (that is, an

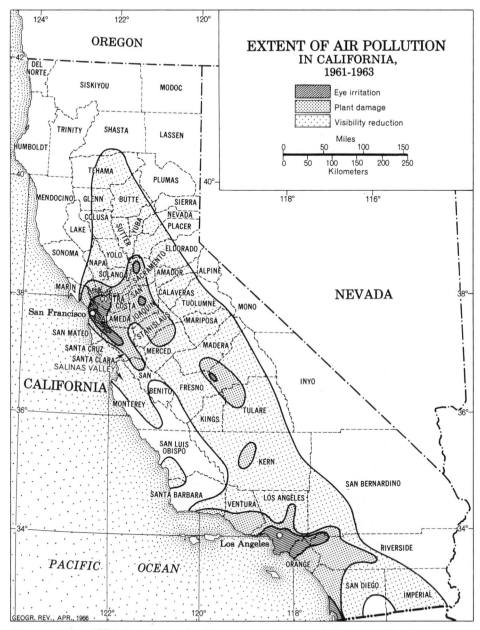

FIGURE 5. Extent of general air pollution in California, 1961–1963. The plant-damage areas are specific, but the eye irritation and visibility reduction may be due in part to forms of general pollution other than photochemical. Sources: for plant damage, J. T. Middleton: California against Air Pollution (California Department of Public Health, Sacramento, 1961); for eye irritation and visibility reduction, local reports and personal observations up to December, 1963.

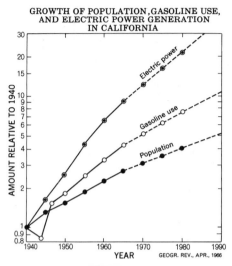

FIGURE 6. With the exception of the war years, the increase in gasoline use and, to a smaller extent, that of electric power generation relative to population have followed the exponential relation $A/A_{1940} = P/P_{1940}{}^n$, where A/A_{1940} is the amount of gasoline use or power production relative to 1940 and P/P_{1940} is the corresponding ratio for population. The indicated average values of n are 1.5 for gasoline use and about 2.2 for electric power, and the projections were made on this basis. Source, population projection to 1980, Financial and Population Research Section, California State Department of Finance.

idealized city), under constant wind direction and velocity are shown in Figure 7. Starting, by definition, with the given concentration appearing at only a single point when the emission rate is unity, the areas within the isopleths are seen to increase much faster than the corresponding emission rates.

When a specific symptom of pollution has expanded to fill a geographical area, as is the case with plant

damage in the Los Angeles basin and the San Francisco Bay Area, further increase may be expected to be in intensity rather than in extent. However, the movement of pollutants from one airshed to another is not excluded (Fig. 5); the fingers of plant damage extending north and east from the Los Angeles region and southeast and east from the Bay region show that these areas are still growing, and if photochemical air pollution is not abated it may be assumed that the present visibility-reduction area is a shadow of the coming plant-damage area, and the present plant-damage area a forecast of the coming eye-irritation area.

· · ·

The Prospects for Control

Although photochemical air pollution is well on its way to becoming the number one form of general air pollution in the United States, a broad attack against it has thus far been mounted only in California. However, the passage by Congress on October 1, 1965, of a bill requiring the installation after September, 1967, of exhaust control devices on new automobiles of domestic manufacture will expand this attack to a national scale, and in view of this prospect the California program merits examination in some detail.

In an assessment of the prospects for the abatement of photochemical air pollution by automobile controls, three factors are pertinent: the time delay or lead time; the growth in emissions over that lead time; and the degree of control likely to be achieved. To go

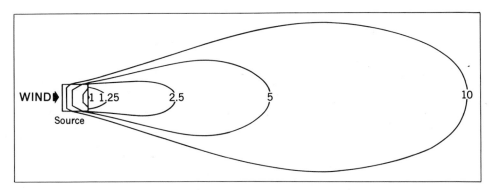

FIGURE 7. Area coverage by a pollutant as a function of emission rate. The figures are relative emission rates, and the curves are the corresponding isopleths of given concentration. Estimated for a uniform square source with constant wind direction and velocity under an overhead inversion at constant height.

back in time, we may now say that the visibility reduction which had become widespread in the Los Angeles basin as early as 1920 was due, in part at least, to photochemical air pollution. Reduction in the sizes of oranges and the cracking of rubber products, now known to be due to photochemical air pollution, were reported at least as early as 1930, specific plant damage was first observed in 1942, and eye irritation had appeared by 1945. The first step toward control was taken in 1948 with a California legislative act establishing air pollution control districts, and the control program in Los Angeles County was initiated shortly thereafter. Not until 1952 was the first evidence obtained that what was then known as "smog" was primarily photochemical and that the emissions chiefly responsible for it were nitrogen oxides and hydrocarbons.

The first control steps directed specifically at photochemical air pollution were applied to hydrocarbon emissions from stationary sources in the Los Angeles basin, and by 1960 these sources were about 60 percent controlled. In 1957–1958 the elimination of home incinerators and the restriction of fuel-oil burning during the smog season achieved about a 45 percent control of nitrogen oxide emissions from stationary sources in the basin. The attack on hydrocarbon emissions from motor vehicles was initiated on a statewide basis in 1959. Roughly 75–80 percent of the reactive hydrocarbons emitted by automobiles come from the exhaust, 14–17 percent from the crankcase, and 7–8 percent from carburetor and fuel-tank evaporation. Installation of crankcase control devices on new cars began in 1961, but their installation on used cars has encountered complex difficulties and delays. Moreover, experience has shown that in the hands of individual owners the actual control achieved by these devices falls considerably short of the theoretical, and judgments of the degree of crankcase hydrocarbon control that will eventually be achieved range from less than 70 percent to about 90 percent.

A standard for exhaust hydrocarbons and carbon monoxide, which specifies that the hydrocarbon content under a given cycle of operation shall not exceed an average of 275 ppm, was adopted in 1960, and the installation on new automobiles of devices intended to meet this standard is beginning with the 1966 models of domestic makes. Revised standards now scheduled to take effect in 1970 will reduce the allowed exhaust hydrocarbon content to 180 ppm and will also require a reduction in evaporation losses. If the installation of devices to meet these 1970 standards is limited to new cars it will be at least 1980 before the exhaust control program as it now stands is fully effective, and judgments of the degree of exhaust hydrocarbon control that may be achieved range from 50 percent to 80 percent, the latter being the theoretical value. A standard of 350 ppm for exhaust nitrogen oxides, which is now in process of adoption, will require devices that produce a theoretical 65 percent control of these emissions.

What this attack has accomplished and may be expected to accomplish must be assessed in relation to the growth in sources and emissions that has occurred and may be expected over the time periods concerned.[7] An assessment on this basis for Los Angeles County is shown in Figure 8. Examination of the hydrocarbon curve indicates that neither the controls of emissions from stationary sources initiated after 1950 nor the crankcase

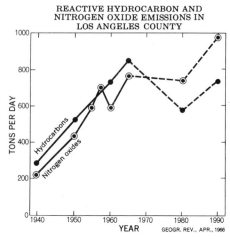

REACTIVE HYDROCARBON AND NITROGEN OXIDE EMISSIONS IN LOS ANGELES COUNTY

FIGURE 8. The projections assume that the population predictions of the California State Department of Finance will be realized; that emissions will continue to increase relative to population as they have since 1940; that motor vehicle crankcase emissions will be 80 percent controlled, exhaust and evaporation hydrocarbons 70 percent controlled, and exhaust nitrogen oxides 60 percent controlled by 1980; and that no other controls will be adopted. Source for emissions to 1965, P. A. Leighton (see text footnote 7 for reference).

controls initiated in 1961 have been sufficient to counteract the overall increase in emissions that accompanied population growth in the county. It would appear that the automobile exhaust and evaporation controls now scheduled will indeed reduce hydrocarbon emissions, even in the face of prospective growth, but if no further steps are taken, the upward climb will be resumed after the program is completed. According to the nitrogen oxide curve the controls of stationary sources initiated in 1957–1958 achieved some reduction, but by about 1963 the gains had been wiped out by the process of growth. The projection indicates that the prospective control of nitrogen oxides from motor vehicles will reduce the overall emissions slightly between 1965 and 1980, but the growth after 1980, if no further steps are taken, will soon carry these emissions to new highs.

The level of emissions in 1940 has often been taken as the value that should be regained to eliminate photochemical plant damage and eye irritation in the Los Angeles basin. To the extent that the projections in Figure 8 are valid, it would appear that unless supplemented by other measures the California motor-vehicle control program as it now stands offers little hope of returning photochemical air pollu-

compounds until it is now about a thousand times what it probably was when our physiological responses to lead were evolved.[8] The carbon dioxide content of the atmosphere has increased 9 percent since 1890, and is reported to be currently increasing by about 0.2 percent a year; and it has been estimated that by the time the known reserves of fossil fuel have been burned the resultant temperature increase on earth, due to the absorption of infrared radiation by atmospheric carbon dioxide, will be sufficient to melt the polar icecaps, inundate present coastal areas, and annihilate many life forms.[9]

In essence these ultimate problems of general air pollution may be stated in simple terms. Whether applied to a local area or to the entire atmosphere it is a matter of maintaining the relation

$$\frac{\text{Emissions per capita} \times \text{number of persons}}{\text{Air supply}} < X,$$

tion to its 1940 level in the basin. The program will gain some ground, but further steps will be required to hold the gain, and if such steps are not taken the situation will again deteriorate. . . .

In its broader aspects, the challenge is not limited to the air supply in specific geographical areas; it extends to the pollution of the entire atmosphere. Here the outstanding problem is the possibility of self-destruction through atmospheric radioactive contamination as the result of nuclear explosions. However, other problems also loom. There are indications, for example, that the atmospheric lead content in the Northern Hemisphere has increased with man's use of lead and its

where X is the maximum value to which we can accommodate. The means of maintaining this relation, however, are another matter. There is little prospect of increasing the local supply of air and none of increasing the overall supply. The per capita emissions may be reduced by controls, but, as we have seen, with increasing population the steps required become successively more severe, and the end of the process is the elimination of the sources. The accommodation coefficient X, as far as direct physiological effects are concerned, could be increased by the use of protective methods through which we breathed only purified air, but this would not help unprotected life forms or retard the other effects that must be taken into account. The remaining factor in the equation is the number of persons, and it may well be that the resource which eventually forces man to adopt population control as a requirement for survival will not be land, food, or water, but air.

Footnotes

1. M. Neiburger, D. S. Johnson, and Chen-wu Chien: Studies of the Structure of the Atmosphere over the Eastern Pacific Ocean in Summer, *Univ. of California Publs. in Meteorol.*, Vol. 1, No. 1, 1961, pp. 1–94.
2. Rudolf Geiger: The Climate near the Ground (translated by Milroy N. Stewart and others; Cambridge, Mass., 1950), pp. 204–230; Friedrich Defant: Local Winds, *in* Compendium of Meteorology (edited by T. F. Malone; American Meteorological Society, Boston, 1951), pp. 655–672; P. A. Leighton: Cloud Travel in Mountainous Terrain, *Quart. Repts. 111–3 and 111–4*, Department of Chemistry, Stanford University, 1954–1955 (Defense Documentation Center AD Numbers 96571, 96486, 96487).
3. Leighton, *op. cit.* [see footnote 2 above], *Quart. Rept. 111–3*, pp. 115–118.

4. Marketing emissions include such things as losses from tank trucks and service stations, evaporation losses during the filling of automobiles, and so on. In Los Angeles County alone it is estimated that these losses contributed an average of 120 tons of hydrocarbons a day to the air during the year 1963.
5. J. T. Middleton and A. J. Haagen-Smit: The Occurrence, Distribution, and Significance of Photochemical Air Pollution in the United States, Canada, and Mexico, *Journ. Air Pollution Control Assn.*, Vol. 11, 1961, pp. 129–134; J. T. Middleton: Air Conservation and the Protection of Our Natural Resources, *in* Proceedings, National Conference on Air Pollution (United States Department of Health, Education, and Welfare, Washington, D.C., 1963) pp. 166–172.
6. Personal communication, R. W. McMullen, Metronics Associates, Inc., Palo Alto, Calif.
7. P. A. Leighton: Man and Air in California, *in* Proceedings of Statewide Conference on Man in California, 1980's (University of California Extension Division, Berkeley, 1964), pp. 44–77.
8. C. C. Patterson: Contaminated and Natural Lead Environments of Man, *Archives of Environmental Health*, Vol. 11, 1965, pp. 344–360.
9. "Implications of Rising Carbon Dioxide Content of the Atmosphere" (Conservation Foundation, New York, 1963).

• • • • • • • • • • • • • twenty-three

PETER F. MASON ◆

Spatial Variability of Atmospheric Radioactivity in the United States

One of the problems of environmental pollution is its accurate and objective documentation. Atmospheric pollution has been poorly understood and imprecisely discussed because it has been considered in largely qualitative terms based on incomplete data. For example, atmospheric radioactivity, one of several atmospheric pollutants measured in the United States by the Public Health Service, is believed to be concentrated in high amounts in Nevada, the testing site of nuclear devices over the past two decades. Beyond a vague understanding of some spatial relationship between atmospheric radioactivity and nuclear tests, very little can be offered definitively regarding the pattern of distribution throughout the United States. The purpose of this paper is to (1) suggest an air pollution mapping method given limited data,

and (2) document and describe the pattern of atmospheric radioactivity in the United States.

Data for this study were atmospheric beta radioactivity in picocuries per cubic meter collected in 1966 and published in 1968 (*Air Quality Data*, 1966, 51–54). From a relatively uneven air sampling network, average monthly values were available and converted to state averages (Table 1). These were mapped for the 48 conterminous United States using graduated circles in proportion to the average state values (Figure 1).

Characteristics and Sources of Atmospheric Radioactivity

Atmospheric radioactivity originates naturally and artificially (Stern, 1968,

◆ **SOURCE.** Reproduced by permission from the *Proceedings* of the Association of American Geographers, Vol. 2, 1970, pp. 92–97.

TABLE 1.   Beta Radioactivity in the United States

Rank	State	Total (pCi/m^3)	Rank	State	Total (pCi/m^3)
1	Nevada	0.55	24	Utah	0.23
2	Arizona	0.53	25	Kansas	0.22
3	Texas	0.42	26	Washington, D.C.	0.21
4	Colorado	0.40	27	South Dakota	0.21
5	Wyoming	0.38	28	West Virginia	0.21
6	Michigan	0.35	29	California	0.20
7	Missouri	0.35	30	Nebraska	0.20
8	New Mexico	0.33	31	New Hampshire	0.20
9	Wisconsin	0.33	32	North Carolina	0.20
10	Illinois	0.30	33	Rhode Island	0.20
11	Ohio	0.30	34	South Carolina	0.20
12	Oregon	0.30	35	Virginia	0.20
13	Kentucky	0.29	36	Iowa	0.19
14	Oklahoma	0.29	37	Pennsylvania	0.19
15	Arkansas	0.28	38	Maryland	0.17
16	Louisiana	0.28	39	Montana	0.17
17	Idaho	0.26	40	New Jersey	0.17
18	Tennessee	0.26	41	Vermont	0.17
19	Delaware	0.25	42	Connecticut	0.16
20	Mississippi	0.25	43	Maine	0.16
21	New York	0.25	44	Minnesota	0.15
22	Alabama	0.23	45	Georgia	0.13
23	Indiana	0.23	46	Washington	0.13

Source: U.S. Department of Health, Education, and Welfare, Public Health Service, *Air Quality Data,* National Air Pollution Control Administration Publication No. APTD 68-9 (1966), Table 15, pp. 51–54.

121). The former, often referred to as "background" radiation, is considered to be a normal level with which man has established a steady-state relationship and beyond which measured artificial radioactivity becomes potentially hazardous. Natural radioactivity originates from both terrestrial and cosmic sources. Radioactive minerals in rocks and soils of the earth's crust have varying radioactivity potentials, decay rates, and radiation emissivity (Rankama, 1954). The daughter products of radon and thoron decay attach themselves to atmospheric dust and charge these particulates with apparent radioactivity.

Release of natural atmospheric radioactivity also normally accompanies the combustion of the fossil fuels, coal and fuel oil.

Cosmic radiation results from the interaction of cosmic rays with atmospheric gases to produce several radioactive species including Carbon 14 and Tritium (Gold *et al.,* 1964). Since 1954 the atmospheric content of Carbon 14 is believed to have increased due to thermonuclear explosions (U.N. *Report,* 1964). The spatial variability of natural radioactivity is incompletely understood. Acceptance of natural radioactivity as the norm against which

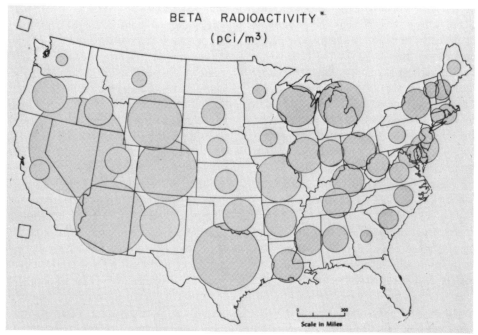

BETA   RADIOACTIVITY *
(pCi/m³)

Source: U.S. Department of Health, Education, and Welfare,
Public Health Service, Air Quality Data, National
Air Pollution Control Administration Publication No. 68-9,
(1966), Table 15, pp. 51-54.

* State yearly average, 1966

FIGURE. 1.   Beta Radioactivity, state yearly average, 1966.

artificial radioactivity is measured, however, carelessly assumes that (1) natural radioactivity is uniformly distributed both spatially and temporally, (2) natural radioactivity is physiologically safe, and (3) human intake in measured safe doses above background radioactivity provides sufficient environmental health protection which has no medical foundation for the progeny of the presently affected generation.

Artificial radionuclides are similar regardless of source whether they be nuclear reactors, nuclear or thermonuclear bombs, or plants processing spent reactor fuel (Stern, 1968, 127). Artificially produced radionuclides are

of two types: fission products and activation products. Most fission products are radioactive fragments produced from the fissioning of uranium or plutonium, and their importance stems from their emission capabilities. The three important fission products are Strontium 90, Cesium 137, and several isotopes of Iodine (Stern, 1968, 127). Strontium 90, the most dangerous because it is formed abundantly by fission, is long-lived (28 years) and chemically similar to calcium and is thus readily absorbed by living things and passed to man through the food chain. Like calcium, S 90 is deposited in bone and can bring possible injury to blood-forming tissue. Cesium 137, formed by fission in slightly greater amounts than S 90, has a thirty year half-life and chemically resembles potassium. Less hazardous than S 90, C 137 fails to fix in the skeleton. Some research now indicates, however, that C 137 may concentrate in gonadal tissue. Iodine tends to concentrate in thyroid glands. Because of its basic volatility, radioactive iodine escapes to the atmosphere to a greater degree than most radionuclides and is thus subject to increased inhalation and foliar deposition and can enter the food chain much like S 90.

Activation products are produced by the interaction of neutrons on substances in the vicinity of fission or fusion reactions. Explosions from nuclear weapons, or controlled fusion reactions whereby neutrons react with materials of construction, produce a diverse variety of activation products. Activation products may also include pollution from uranium mines, mills, or refineries mainly in the form of mildly radioactive dust and fumes. Mines and mills are relatively safe in contrast to chemical refineries where uranium salts are produced.

Nuclear reactors, an increasingly important source of atmospheric radioactivity, provide sources of heat, and neutron and gamma rays (U.S. Atomic Energy Commission, 1963). Reactors now in widespread use are air-cooled, boiling water, and pressurized water reactors. Air-cooled reactors discharge gaseous radioactivity by (1) production of Argon 41 from neutron capture by Argon 40 normally present in the cooling air, (2) neutron activation of inert dust in the cooling air, and (3) release of fission products caused by defective

cladding of the fuel in the reactor core. Atmospheric pollution from boiling water reactors results from either (1) radioactive gases in the steam, (2) noble gases diffused through fuel element cladding and carried by the steam to the turbines, (3) other fission products escaping into the water through defects in the fuel cladding, and (4) small amounts of uranium containing reactor component surfaces. This most commonly used reactor allows a 30 minute interval for radioactivity to escape through an air ejector tower after which the bulk of the radioactivity disappears. Pressurized water reactors, used in submarine and surface vessels, release relatively small amounts of atmospheric radioactivity. Gaseous pollutants increase very slowly and once neutralized can be periodically discharged. Reactors are subject to failure (H.M. Stationery Office, 1957). The most serious accidents occur when the heat production rate exceeds the capacity of the system to cool the reactor core, the results of which would be the release of unusually high amounts of radionuclides into the atmosphere and disassemblage of the unit. Rapid heat rise is due to either (1) nuclear excursion (a sudden rise in the rate of fission), (2) chemical reactions among the materials of reactor construction, or (3) loss of coolant due to a rupture in primary piping systems.

Reprocessing spent fuel is an increasingly important source of atmospheric radioactivity. After removal from the reactor fuel is taken to a chemical processing plant where it is dissolved and the solution processed. In the United States this has been undertaken at government facilities in Washington, Idaho, Tennessee, and South Carolina. The amount of radioactivity contained in spent fuel is extremely large. Hazards are related to the storage of liquid and solid wastes, including the two most important, Iodine 131 and Krypton 85. Iodine 131 is an important radioactive atmospheric pollutant and may easily penetrate the food chain like S 90. Krypton 85 cannot be removed by practical or mechanical means and will be present in the atmosphere in increasing amounts as the nuclear reactor becomes a major source of electricity (Lieberman and Belter, 1967, 474).

Shortly after a nuclear detonation, fission products are easily detected throughout the atmosphere (U.S. Atomic Energy Commission, 1962). Until 1954, nuclear devices were small and their emissions were confined to the troposphere within which radioactive dust would diffuse after a few weeks. After 1954, nuclear detonations had larger explosive yields and at this time the upper atmosphere became a reservoir of fission products from which continuous deposition has occurred subsequently. The results have been the permanent pollution of the atmosphere, subsequent deposition of radionuclides into the soil, and ingestion and concentration of fission products in all biological material formed since the middle-1950's. Intense heat results in the volatilization of the fission products and allows particles of fumes and dust to diffuse throughout the atmosphere to deposit as "fallout." The amount of radioactivity produced in nuclear detonation is enormous. Shortly after an explosion the relatively large particles of radioactive dust are deposited 100 or more miles downwind. A large radioactive cloud is distributed within the troposphere and it circulates globally several times before finally depositing completely. Finally, portions of the blast puncture the tropopause and inject radioactive material into the stratosphere within which the cloud slowly diffuses (United Nations, 1964).

Spatial Characteristics of Atmospheric Radioactivity

The many sources of atmospheric radioactivity leave open to speculation the question of accurate definition and determination of the bases for the pattern of atmospheric radioactivity in the United States. Unusually high concentrations are found in the West and Southwest with 6 of the 10 leading states found within these regions. Secondary high concentrations are noted in the Midwest and Border South states of Michigan, Wisconsin, Illinois, Ohio, and Tennessee and Kentucky. Uneven to low amounts are found in the Southeast and Northeast, and lowest concentrations in the northern Great Plains.

Western sources of atmospheric radioactivity are numerous and widespread. A combination of several sources contributes to the high concentration, including (1) surface and subsurface nuclear weapons tests, (2) uranium mining and processing, and (3) radioactive waste disposal. The types and amounts of atmospheric radioactivity emitted from these sources are not accurately known as these activities are subject to both industrial and governmental security review. In accord with the nuclear test ban treaty of 1963, atmospheric nuclear testing has ceased in the United States. Pursuant to the Atomic Energy Commission (AEC) goal toward peaceful use of a basically violent and destructive technology, nuclear detonation has taken two major forms including (1) subsurface testing, and (2) near-surface testing of nuclear excavating and cratering devices. In all likelihood the desert environment, although preferred as a test site for reasons of seclusion, may not be the ideal site because of high particulate concentration and the potential for the radioactive charging of the particles. Also important is the seasonal stagnation of the atmosphere during the summer that concentrates rather than disperses atmospheric pollution.

Uranium mining and milling, activities primarily confined to Utah, Colorado, Arizona, and Wyoming, provide a highly variable source of atmospheric radioactivity. Dry uranium tailings subject to deflation increase the number of suspended particulates for the area and increase the normal complement of background radioactivity already endemically high for the region due to cosmic and terrestrial sources of radioactivity. Insufficient information presently exists regarding the storage and maintenance of radioactive waste in Idaho and Washington either to cast suspicion on or to absolve the AEC for contributing to the high amounts of atmospheric radioactivity recorded for the region. For the West, the main sources of atmospheric radioactivity

may therefore be related to past and present nuclear testing, and secondarily related to uranium mining and processing and the storage of radioactive wastes. The high amounts of atmospheric radioactivity found in Texas at this point remain open to question.

For the remainder of the United States high and low values of atmospheric radioactivity appear to be related to climato-topographic factors. Radionuclides can become incorporated into the atmosphere and transported varying distances until they are precipitated in adjacent regions. In this sense the West may be an important source region for radionuclides, and once incorporated into the air they may be subsequently precipitated in the Midwest, Border South, Northeast, and Southeast. High amounts of atmospheric radioactivity recorded for Wyoming and Colorado may be due in large part to this same climato-topographic relationship. Additional modes by which high levels are noted in the Midwest and Border South may relate to an increasing number of nuclear power plants, and to radioactive waste processing, storage, and maintenance activity in these areas. Moreover, like the West, the eastern one-third of the United States suffers from stagnating anticyclones that reinforce atmospheric stagnation and concentrate normally high quantities of regional atmospheric pollution from other sources. Areas of low concentration require more sophisticated data to be described accurately. Within the rainshadow of the Rocky Mountains the Great Plains exhibit noticeably low levels. In general, the distribution of atmospheric radioactivity appears to be both source- and climate-dependent.

Conclusions and Consequences

In general, the major sources of atmospheric radioactivity include nuclear tests, uranium mining and processing, radioactive waste disposal, and nuclear power plants, and most of these are situated in Nevada and adjacent states to the west, southeast, and south. Atmospheric radioactivity varies spatially in the United States with highest concentrations occuring in Nevada and adjacent states, and secondary concentrations in Missouri, Wisconsin, Michigan, Illinois, Ohio, Tennessee, and Kentucky, and Oregon, and lowest values in the northern Great Plains. The high amounts recorded for Wyoming and Colorado and for both the Midwest and Border South to the east are probably due to the precipitation of radionuclides acquired over the West. The high value of Oregon is due possibly to the same process wherein radionuclides from French and Chinese nuclear tests are precipitated along the Pacific Coast mountain system.

Atmospheric radioactivity is but one part of the total environmental radioactivity. Provided here is a preliminary view, a point of departure, for the consideration of the larger questions of environmental radioactivity. The hazard from atmospheric radioactivity may be due not necessarily to the concentration or total amount of radioactive debris in the atmosphere, but from the deposited fallout that ultimately affects the foodchain. For this reason, the geographer can make substantive contributions by establishing techniques for accurately documenting the spatial character and associations of an increasingly important atmospheric and environmental pollutant.

References

1. Gold, S., Barkhan, H. W., Shleien, B., and Kahn, B., in *The Natural Radiation Environment,* J. A. S. Adams and W. M. Lowder, eds. (Chicago: University of Chicago Press, 1964), pp. 369–382.

2. H. M. Stationery Office, *Accident at Windscale No. 1 Pile on 10th October, 1957* (London, 1957).

3. Lieberman, J. A., and Belter, W. G., "Waste Management and Environmental Aspects of Nuclear Power," *Environmental Science and Technology,* Vol. 1 (1967).

4. Rankama, K., *Isotope Geology* (New York: McGraw-Hill, 1954).

5. Stern, A. C. (ed.) *Air Pollution* (New York: Academic Press, 1968).

6. United Nations, *Report of the United Nations Science Committe on the Effects of Atomic Radiation* (New York, 1964).

7. United States Atomic Energy Commission, *The Effects of Nuclear Weapons* (Washington, 1962).

8. United States Atomic Energy Commission, *United States Atomic Energy Commission Code of Federal Regulations,* Title 10, Part 20 (Washington, 1963).

9. United States Department of Health, Education, and Welfare, Public Health Service, *Air Quality Data,* National Air Pollution Control Administration Publication No. APTD 68-9 (1966), Table 15, pp. 51–54.

twenty-four • • • • • • • • • • • •

• IAN BURTON
• ROBERT W. KATES

The Perception of Natural Hazards in Resource Management

To the Englishman on his island, earthquakes are disasters that happen to others. It is recognized that "while the ground is liable to open up at any moment beneath the feet of foreigners, the English are safe because 'it can't happen here.' "[1] Thus is described a not uncommon attitude to natural hazards in England; its parallels are universal.

Notwithstanding this human incapacity to imagine natural disasters in a familiar environment, considerable disruption is frequently caused by hazards. The management of affairs is not only affected by the impact of the calamities themselves, but also by the degree of awareness, or perception of the hazard, that is shared by those subject to its uncertain threat. Where disbelief in the possibility of an earthquake, a tornado, or a flood is strong, the resultant damages from the event are likely to be greater than where awareness of the danger leads to effective precautionary action.

In this article we attempt to set down our imperfect understanding of variations in the perception of natural hazard, and to suggest some ways in which it affects the management of resource use. In so doing we are extending the notion that resources are best regarded for management purposes as culturally defined variables, by consideration of the cultural appraisal of natural hazard.

◆ **SOURCE.** Reprinted with permission from *Natural Resources Journal,* Vol. 3, 1964, pp. 412–441, published by the University of New Mexico School of Law, Albuquerque, N. M.

It may be argued that the uncertainties of natural hazards in resource management are only a special case of the more general problem of risk in any economic activity. Certainly there are many similarities. But it is only when man seeks to wrest from nature that which he perceives as useful to him that he is strongly challenged by the vagaries of natural phenomena acting over and above the usual uncertainties of economic activity. In other words, the management of resource use brings men into a closer contact with nature (be it viewed as friendly, malevolent, or neutral) where the extreme variations of the environment exercise a much more profound effect than in other economic activities.

The Definition of Natural Hazards

For a working definition of "natural hazards" we propose the following: Natural hazards are those elements in the physical environment, harmful to man and caused by forces extraneous to him. According to Zimmerman's view, the physical environment or nature is "neutral stuff," but it is human culture which determines which elements are considered to be "resources" or "resistances."[2] Considerable cultural variation exists in the conception of natural hazards; change occurs both in time and space.

In time, our notion of specific hazards and their causal agents frequently change. Consider, for example, the insurance concept of an "act of God." To judge by the volume of litigation, this concept is under constant challenge and is constantly undergoing redefinition. The "acts of God" of today are often tomorrow's acts of criminal negligence. Such changes usually stem from a greater potential to control the environment, although the potential is frequently not made actual until after God has shown His hand.

In space a varied concept of hazard is that of drought. A recent report adequately describes the variation as follows:

> There is a clue from prevailing usage that the term 'drought' reflects the relative insecurity of mankind in the face of a natural phenomenon that he does not understand thoroughly and for which, therefore, he has not devised adequate protective measures. A Westerner does not call a rainless month a 'drought,' and a Californian does not use the term even for an entire growing season that is devoid of rain, because these are usual occurrences and the developed water economy is well bolstered against them. Similarly, a dry period lasting several years, or even several decades, would not qualify as a drought if it caused no hardship among water users.[3]

This may be contrasted with the official British definition of an "absolute drought" which is "a period of at least 15 consecutive days to none of which is credited .01 inches of rain or more."[4]

Even such seemingly scientifically defined hazards as infective diseases seem to be subject to changes in interpretation, especially when applied to the assignment of the cause of death. Each decennial revision of the International Lists of Causes of Death has brought important changes to some classes of natural hazards. Thus, the change from the fifth to the sixth revision found a decrease of approximately twenty-five per cent in deaths identified as caused by syphilis and its sequelae as a result of the new definition arising from ostensibly improved medical knowledge.[5]

The definability of hazard is a more sophisticated form of perceiving a hazard. It is more than mere awareness and often requires high scientific knowledge, *i.e.*, we must understand in order to define precisely. But regardless of whether we describe definitions of drought by western water users or the careful restatement of definitions by public health officials, all types of hazard are subject to wide variation in their definition—a function of the changing pace of man's knowledge and technology.

To complicate the problem further, the rise of urban-industrial societies has been coincident with a rapid increase in a type of hazard which may be described as quasi-natural. These hazards are created by man, but their harmful effects are transmitted through natural processes. Thus, man-made pollutants are carried downstream, radioactive fallout is borne by air currents, and pesticides are absorbed by plants, leaving residues in foods. The intricacies of the man-nature relationship are such that it is frequently not possible to ascribe a hazard exclusively to one class or the other (natural or quasi-

natural). A case in point is the question of when fog (a natural hazard) becomes smog (quasi-natural).[6] Presumably some more or less arbitrary standard of smoke content could be developed.

In the discussion that follows, we specifically exclude quasi-natural hazards while recognizing the difficulty of distinguishing them in all cases. Our guide for exclusion is the consideration of principal causal agent.

A Classification of Natural Hazards

Table 1 is an attempt to classify common natural hazards by their principal causal agent. It is but one of many ways that natural hazards might be ordered, but it is convenient for our purposes. The variety of academic disciplines that study aspects of these hazards is only matched by the number of governmental basic data collection agencies which amass information on these hazards. The most cohesive group is the climatic and meteorological hazards. The most diverse is the floral group which includes the doctor's concern with a minor fungal infection, the botanist's concern with a variety of plant diseases, and the hydrologist's concern with the effect of phreatophytes on the flow of water in streams and irrigation channels.

In a fundamental way, we sense a distinction between the causal agents of geophysical and biologic hazards. This distinction does not lie in their effects, for both hazards work directly and indirectly on man and are found in both

TABLE 1. Common Natural Hazards by Principal Causal Agent

Geophysical		Biological	
Climatic and Meteorological	Geological and Geomorphic	Floral	Faunal
Blizzards & Snow	Avalanches	Fungal Diseases *For example:*	Bacterial & Viral Diseases *For example:*
Droughts	Earthquakes	Athletes' foot	
	Erosion (including	Dutch elm	Influenza
Floods	soil erosion &	Wheat stem rust	Malaria
	soil and beach	Blister rust	Typhus
Fog	erosion)		Bubonic Plague
		Infestations	Venereal
Frost	Landslides	*For example:*	Disease
			Rabies
Hailstorms	Shifting Sand	Weeds	Hoof & Mouth
		Phreatophytes	Disease
Heat Waves	Tsunamis	Water hyacinth	Tobacco Mosaic
Hurricanes	Volcanic Eruptions	Hay Fever	Infestations *For example:*
Lightning Strokes & Fires		Poison Ivy	Rabbits Termites Locusts
Tornadoes			Grasshoppers
			Venomous Animal Bites

large and small scales. Rather, our distinction lies in the notion of preventability, *i.e.*, the prevention of the occurrence of the natural phenomenon of hazardous potential as opposed to mere control of hazardous effects. A rough rule of thumb is that changes in nature are to be classed as prevention, but changes in man or his works are control.

Given this rule of thumb, it is clear that few hazards are completely preventable. Prevention has been most successful in the area of floral and faunal hazards. Some such hazards (*e.g.*, malaria) have been virtually eliminated in the United States by preventive measures, but they are still common in other parts of the world.

At the present levels of technology, geophysical hazards cannot be prevented, while biological hazards can be prevented in most cases, subject only to economic and budgetary constraints.

We suggest that this is a basic distinction and directly related to the areal dimensions and the character and quantities of energy involved in these natural phenomena. While much encouraging work has been done, we still cannot prevent a hurricane, identify and destroy an incipient tornado, prevent the special concentration of precipitation that often induces floods, or even on a modest scale alter the pattern of winds that shift sand, or prevent the over-steepening and sub-soil saturation that induces landslides. We might again note the distinction between prevention and control: we can and do build landslide barriers to keep rock off highways, and we can and do attempt to stabilize shifting sand dunes.

Despite much loose discussion in popular journals, repeated surveys of progress in weather modification have not changed substantially from the verdict of the American Meteorological Society in 1957, which was that:

Present knowledge of atmospheric processes offers no real basis for the belief that the weather or climate of a large portion of the country can be significantly modified by cloud seeding. It is not intended to rule out the possibility of large-scale modifications of the weather at some future time, but it is believed that, if possible at all, this will require methods that alter the large-scale atmospheric circulations, possibly through changes in the radiation balance.[7]

The non-preventability of the class of geophysical hazards has existed throughout the history of man and will apparently continue to do so for some time to come. Our training, interest, and experience has been confined to this class of hazards. Moreover, as geographers we are more comfortable when operating in the field of geophysical phenomena than biological. However, we do not know whether the tentative generalizations we propose apply only to geophysical hazards or to the whole spectrum of natural hazards. A priori speculation might suggest the hypothesis that men react to the non-preventable hazard, the true "act of God," in a special way, distinct from preventable hazards. Our observations to date incline us toward the belief that there is an orderly or systematic difference in the perception of preventable and non-preventable natural hazards.

This arises from the hiatus between popular perception of hazard and the technical-scientific perception. To many flood-plain users, floods are preventable, *i.e.*, flood control can completely eliminate the hazard. Yet the technical expert knows that except for very small drainage areas no flood control works known can effectively prevent the flood-inducing concentration of precipitation, nor can they effectively control extremely large floods of very rare occurrence. On the other hand, in some parts of the world hoof and mouth disease is not considered preventable, although there is considerable evidence that it is preventable when there is a widespread willingness to suffer large economic losses by massive eradication of diseased cattle combined with vigorous control measures of vaccination.

The hiatus between the popular perception of hazard and the perception of the technician scientist is considered below in greater detail.

The Magnitude and Frequency of Hazards

There is a considerable volume of scientific data on the magnitude and frequency of various hazards. The official publications of the agencies of the federal government contain much of it. Examples of frequency data are shown in Figures 1, 2, and 3. In general, these show spatial variations in the degree of hazard in terms of frequency occurrence. The measurement of magnitude is more difficult to portray in graphic form, but in general it is directly related to frequency. For example, areas with higher frequency of hailstorms are also likely to experience the most severe hailstorms. The magnitude

of floods is more complex, and attempts to portray variations in magnitude of floods graphically have generally not been successful.[8] We have attempted to show variation in magnitude of floods for New York (Figure 4).

It is our finding that the variations in attitude to natural hazard cannot be explained directly in terms of magnitude and frequency. Differences in perception mean that the same degree of hazard is viewed differently. Part of this variation is due, no doubt, to differences in damage experienced, or in damage potential. In Tables 2 and 3 we have attempted to set out some examples of damage caused by natural hazards. These tables give some idea of the order of magnitude of damages

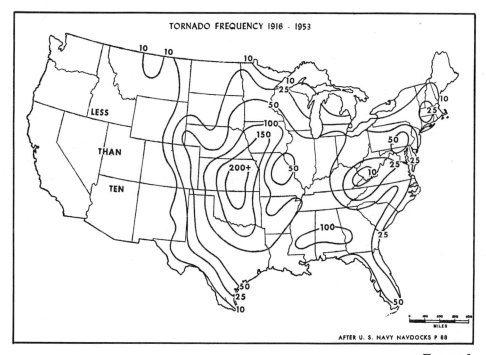

TORNADO FREQUENCY 1916 - 1953

AFTER U. S. NAVY NAVDOCKS P 88

FIGURE 1.

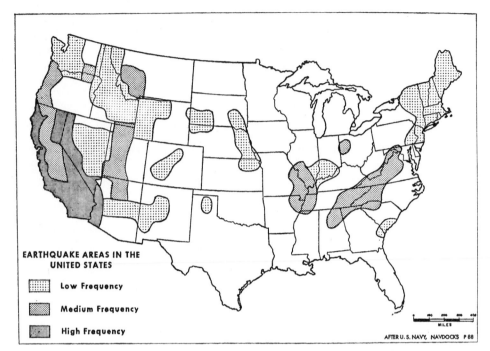

EARTHQUAKE AREAS IN THE UNITED STATES

Low Frequency

Medium Frequency

High Frequency

AFTER U. S. NAVY, NAVDOCKS P 88

FIGURE 2.

to life and property. The estimates are in most cases crude. The loss figures given in Table 2 amount to about $12 billion. If we add to this the $25 billion which are spent annually for health care,[9] and the large amounts spent for control and prevention of other natural hazards, then it is clear that our struggle against natural hazards is of the same order of magnitude as the defense budget!

That these estimates are not highly reliable is demonstrated in the wide variation of some of them. Flood damages, for example, are placed at $350 million by the United States Weather Bureau,[32] over $900 million by the United States Army Corps of Engineers,[33] and $1,200 million by the

United States Department of Agriculture.[34]

There are partial explanations for the wide discrepancies in these and other similar data. These usually include such questions as definitions used, time period employed, methods of computation, accuracy and completeness of reporting, changing dollar values, and so on. However, even when all these differences are taken into account the perception of natural hazards still varies greatly. There is variation in the resource manager's perception of hazard. Managers as a group differ in their view as opposed to scientific and technical personnel, and the experts, in turn, differ among themselves. These differences persist even when all the

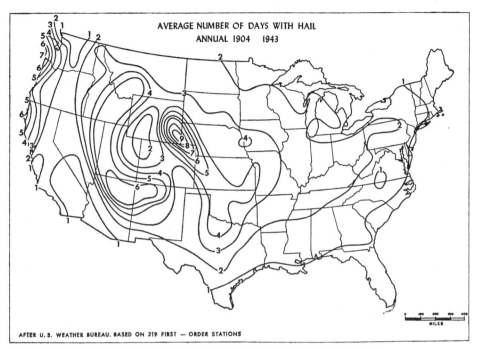

AVERAGE NUMBER OF DAYS WITH HAIL
ANNUAL 1904 1943

AFTER U. S. WEATHER BUREAU. BASED ON 219 FIRST — ORDER STATIONS

FIGURE 3.

scientific evidence upon which conclusions are based is identical. It is to this complex problem of differing perceptions that we now turn.

Variations in Perception

It is well established that men view differently the challenges and hazards of their natural environment. In this section we will consider some of the variations in view or perception of natural hazard. In so doing we will raise more questions than we shall answer; this is a reflection of the immaturity and youth of this line of research.

Our scheme will be to consider the *within group* and *between group* variation in perception of two well-defined groups: resource users, who are the managers of natural resources directly affected by natural hazards (including of course their own persons),[35] and technical and scientific personnel—individuals with specialized training and directly charged with study or control of natural hazards.

VARIATION IN THE PERCEPTION OF NATURAL HAZARD AMONG SCIENTIFIC PERSONNEL

The specialized literature is replete with examples of differences in hazard perception among experts. They fail to perceive the actual nature of the hazard, its magnitude, and its location in

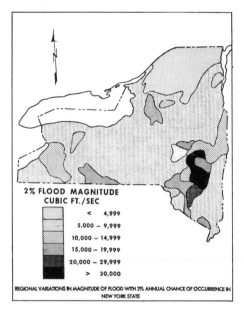

2% FLOOD MAGNITUDE
CUBIC FT./SEC

< 4,999
5,000 − 9,999
10,000 − 14,999
15,000 − 19,999
20,000 − 29,999
> 30,000

REGIONAL VARIATIONS IN MAGNITUDE OF FLOOD WITH 2% ANNUAL CHANCE OF OCCURRENCE IN
NEW YORK STATE

FIGURE 4.

time and space. Technical personnel differ among each other, and the use of reputable methods often provides estimates of hazards of great variance from one another.

Such variation is due in small part to differences in experience and training, vested organizational interest, and even personality. But in a profound and fundamental way, such variation is a product of human ignorance.

The Epistemology of Natural Hazard. We have emphasized the nature of natural hazard as phenomena of nature with varying effects on man, ranging from harmless to catastrophic. To know and to fully understand these natural phenomena is to give to man the opportunity of avoiding or circumventing the hazard. To know fully, in this sense, is

TABLE 2. Average Annual Losses from Selected Natural Hazards

Floods	$350 M (Million) to $1 Billion[10]
Hail	$53 M[11]
Hurricanes	$100 M[12]
Insects	$3,000 M[13]
Lightning Strokes	$100 M[14]
Plant Disease	$3,000 M[15]
Rats and Rodents	$1,000 M to $2,000 M[16]
Tornadoes	$45 M[17]
Weeds	$4,000 M[18]
TOTAL	$11,648 M to $13,268 M

TABLE 3. Loss of Life from Selected Natural Hazards

Cold Waves	242[19]	(1959)
Floods	83.4[20]	Average annual, 1950–1959
Hay Fever	30[21]	(1959)
Heat Waves	207[22]	(1959)
Hurricanes	84.8[23]	Average annual, 1950–1959
Influenza	2,845[24]	(1959)
Lightning Strokes	600[25]	Average annual, Years not specified
Malaria	7[26]	(1959)
Plague	1[27]	(1959)
Tornadoes	204.3[28]	Average annual, 1950–1959
Tuberculosis	11,456[29]	(1959)
Venomous Bites & Stings	62[30]	(1959)
Venereal Disease	3,069[31]	(1959)

to be able to predict the location in time and space and the size or duration of the natural phenomenon potentially harmful to man. Despite the sophistication of modern science or our ability to state the requirements for such a knowledge system, there seems little hope that basic geophysical phenomena will ever be fully predictable. No foreseeable system of data gathering and sensing equipment seems likely to pinpoint the discharge of a lightning bolt or the precise path of a tornado.

Given this inherent limitation, almost all estimation of hazard is probabilistic in content, and these probabilities may be computed either by counting (relative frequency) or by believing in some underlying descriptive frequency distribution. The probability of most hazardous events is determined by counting the observed occurrence of similar events. In so doing we are manipulating three variables: the magnitude of the event, its occurrence in time, and its occurrence in space.

For some hazards the spatial variable might fortunately be fixed. Volcanic eruptions often take place at a fixed point, and rivers in humid areas follow well-defined stream courses. For other hazards there may be broadly defined belts such as storm paths or earthquake regions (see Figure 2). There are no geophysical hazards that are apparently evenly or randomly distributed over the earth's surface, but some, such as lightning, approach being ubiquitous over large regions.

The size or magnitude of the hazard varies, and, given the long-term human adjustment to many hazards,

this can be quite important. Blizzards are common on the Great Plains, but a protracted blizzard can bring disaster to a large region.[36] On great alluvial flood plains small hummocks provide dry sites for settlement, but such hummocks are overwhelmed by a flood event of great magnitude.

Magnitude can be thought of as a function of time based on the apparent truism of extreme events: if one waits long enough, there will always be an event larger than that previously experienced. In the case of geophysical events, waiting may involve several thousand years. Graphically, this is presented for fifty years in Figure 5 for two common hazards.

Most harmful natural phenomena are rare events; if they were not, we humans would probably have been decimated before we became entrenched on this planet. Since the counting of events is the major method of determining probabilities, rare events by their nature are not easily counted. Equally disturbing is the possibility that by climatic change, or improved scientific knowledge, or human interference, the class of natural events may change and create further uncertainties in the process of observing and recording.

Faced with a high degree of uncertainty, but pressed by the requirements of a technical society for judgments and decisions, scientific and technical personnel make daily estimates of hazard with varying degrees of success.

An example of unsuccessful estimating is seen in the case of the San Carlos Reservoir on the Gila River in

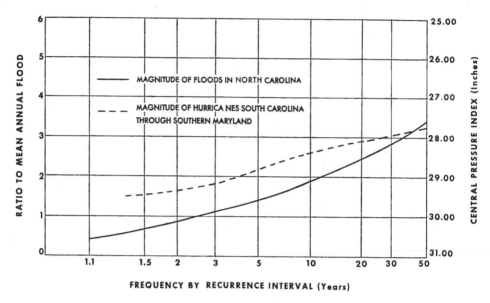

SOURCE: NATIONAL HURRICA NE RESEARCH PROJECT REPORT NO. 33; FLOODS IN NORTH CAROLINA; MAGNITUDE AND FREQUENCY

FIGURE 5.

Arizona. Completed in 1928, this reservoir has never been filled to more than sixty-eight per cent of its capacity and has been empty on several occasions.[37] The length of stream flow record on which the design of the dam was based was short (approximately thirty years), but it was not necessarily too short. The considerable overbuilding of this dam, according to Langbein and Hoyt, was due in part to the failure to take into account the increasing variability of annual flows as indicated in the coefficient of variation. In their view, the San Carlos Reservoir is "a victim of a deficiency in research to develop the underlying patterns of fluctuations in river flow."[38] To our knowledge, this deficiency still exists, and we have doubts as to whether such patterns can actually be determined.

Until recent years, that highly reputable practitioner of actuarial precision, the insurance industry, charged rates for hail insurance that were largely a matter of guesswork.[39] Flora notes that

often in widely level areas, where we now know that the hail risk varies but little over a distance of a hundred miles or more, one county might have several damaging hailstorms while the adjacent counties might escape entirely. In such instances, the county which had suffered severe damage would be given a much higher insurance rate than others.[40]

With regard to flood insurance, the industry has long apologized for its unwillingness to even enter the fray, using words similar to these:

[The insurance company underwriters believe that] specific flood insurance covering fixed location properties in areas subject to recurrent floods cannot feasibly be written because of the virtual certainty of loss, its catastrophic nature and the reluctance or inability of the public to pay the premium charge required to make the insurance self sustaining.[41]

Some hazards have been only belatedly recognized. Langbein and Hoyt cite the fact that in the American Civil Engineers Handbook, published in 1930, there are no instructions about reservoir sedimentation.[42]

Public agencies charged with flood control responsibilities have had to make estimates of the long run recurrence of these phenomena. Despite a great deal of work and ingenuity, results are not overly impressive. Three highly respected methods of flood frequency analysis place the long run average return period of the largest flood of record in the Lehigh Valley as either twenty-seven, forty-five, or seventy-five years.[43]

The disparate views and perceptions of technical and scientific personnel are a reflection of our ignorance of the chance occurrence of events, and more fundamentally of our lack of understanding of the physical forces themselves. There is little hope of eliminating this uncertainty, and the technical-scientific community follows the course of recognizing it, defining it, and finally learning to live with it.

VARIATIONS IN THE PERCEPTION OF NATURAL HAZARD AMONG RESOURCE MANAGERS

Resource users or managers do not display uniformity in their perception of natural hazard any more than do scientific and technical personnel. Not being experts, they have less knowledge or understanding of the various possible interpretations or data and are often amazed at the lack of agreement among the professionals. Their views may be expected to coincide insofar as the lay managers subscribe to the various popular myths of hazard perception (whether "it can't happen here," or "after great droughts come great rains," or "a little rain stills a great wind"). But in this age of enlightenment, perception is not easily limited to such aphorisms. Differences in perception arise both among users of the same resource and between users of different resources.

Perception Among Users of the Same Resource. Urban and rural flood-plain users display differences in the perception of flood hazard. Our own studies of urban[44] and agricultural[45] flood-plain users suggest a greater hazard sensitivity in terms of awareness on the part of agricultural land users. However, the frequency of hazard that encourages certain responses on the part of resource users is approximately equal for both urban and agricultural land users.[46]

The limited work on flood plains in variation of perception between users suggests three explanatory factors: (1) the relation of the hazard to the dominant resource use, including in agriculture the ratio between area subject to flooding and the total size of the management unit, (2) the frequency of occurrence of floods, and (3) variations in degree of personal experience. Interestingly, there seems to be little or no significant effect in hazard perception by the few generalized indicators of level of social class or education that have been tested against hazard perception.

The first factor is essentially a reflection of an ends-means scheme of resource use. We would expect to find a heightened hazard perception in those cases, such as drought in an agricultural region or beach erosion on a waterfront cottage, where the hazard is directly related to the resource use. Where it is incidental, such as lightning or tornadoes, the perception of hazard is variant, vague, and often whimsical.

The second factor suggests that the frequency of natural events is related to the perception of hazard. Where the events in question are frequent, there is little variation among users in their perception. The same holds true where the event is infrequent, for here the failure to perceive a significant hazard is widely shared. It is in the situation of moderate frequency that one expects to find (and does find) considerable variation among resource users.

The third factor is also related to frequency. One would expect that when personally experienced a natural event would be more meaningful and lead to heightened perception. The limited evidence to date does not clearly bear this out. There is a pronounced ability to share in the common experience, and newcomers often take on the shared or dominant perception of the community.

Also given a unique or cyclical interpretation of natural events, the experience of an event often tends to allay future anxiety; this is in keeping with the old adage about lightning not striking in the same place twice. Thus the effect of experience as a determinant of hazard perception is considerably blurred.

Perception Between Different Resource Users. Differences in perception are found between coastal and flood-plain land resource users in areas subject to storm damage or erosion. Unfortunately, we cannot say more about hazard perception differences between resource users. To our knowledge, they have never been carefully explored, although such study would undoubtedly throw much light on the problem of comparing the resource management policies of different groups and nations.[47] Some historical comment provides suggestions for the direction that such differences might take.

In a recent article, David Lowenthal notes the changes in our attitude towards wilderness. Once viewed as awesome and tyranical, nature in the wild is now wonderful and brings us close to the spirit of the Creator. "Our forefathers mastered a continent; today we celebrate the virtues of the vanquished foe."[48] Nature itself has become synonymous with virtue.[49] This subject has been examined in some detail by Hans Huth in his study of the attitudes that led to the establishment of the conservation movement.[50]

The rapid expansion of agriculture in the Great Plains during a relatively humid period by settlers from areas with different environmental experience and background is well known. Unprepared for the climatic hazards they encountered, many settlers "were predisposed to believe that the climate was becoming permanently more humid. In fact, many thought that it was the spread of cultivation that brought about an increase in rainfall."[51]

Study of other hazards suggests that there is considerable difference in the social acceptance of personal injury depending on the kind of hazard that was the causal agent. Edward Suchman notes that "a report of a few cases of polio will empty the beaches, but reports of many more deaths by automobile accidents on the roads to the beaches will have little effect." He suggests that one explanation may lie "in the greater popular acceptance of accidents as inevitable and uncontrollable."[52]

A contrast in awareness of natural hazards is exemplified by a warning sign observed in a coastal location on the Island of Hawaii. Affixed to a palm tree in an area subject to *tsunamis* at the front door and the hazard of volcanic eruptions and lava flows at the back door (Mauna Loa volcano), this sign merely advises the reader: "Beware of falling coconuts!"

VARIATION IN NATURAL HAZARD PERCEPTION BETWEEN TECHNICAL-SCIENTIFIC PERSONNEL AND RESOURCE USERS

It is our impression that there is considerable divergence between the perception of natural hazard of technical-scientific personnel and resource users.

In the case of floods such divergence is widespread.

Although we have emphasized in the previous section the variation in probability that technical people might assign to a given flood event, these are essentially differences in estimation. Over the past several years we have interviewed or spoken with well over one-hundred technical people concerned with floods, and we have never met one who discounted the possibility of a flood occurring again in a valley that had been previously flooded. By contrast, out of 216 flood-plain dwellers interviewed in a variety of small urban places between 1960 and 1962, all of whom had a measurable flood hazard, some 84 categorically did not expect to be flooded in the future.[53]

Another example of the disparity between the technical and resource user perception is found in the occasional experience of the rejection of plans for protective works by at least part of the resource users, even when the cost of such works directly to the users in monetary terms was nominal or nonexistent. In Fairfield, Connecticut some users of waterfront property opposed the construction of a protective dike along the shore, principally on the contention that such protection "would seriously interfere with their view and result in loss of breeze."[54] Similarly, dune-levelling which is universally condemned by technical personnel as destructive of nature's main protection against the ravages of the sea, is widely practiced (as at West Dennis, Massachusetts) to improve the scenic view or to make room for more buildings.

Is such behavior adopted out of

ignorance of the hazard; is it symptomatic of the irrationality of resource users in hazard situations; or is there some other explanation? While there are resource users who act in total ignorance of natural hazards, their number is relatively small. Nor can the difference simply be explained away in terms of irrationality. In our view, the difference arises primarily out of the evaluation of the hazard. We offer the following explanation for divergence in hazard evaluation:

1. For some resource users, the differences in perceiving a natural hazard may be a reflection of those existing among scientific and technical personnel themselves. Given the great uncertainty that surrounds the formulation of an "objective" estimate of hazard, the estimate made by a resource user may be no more divergent than that supplied by the use of a different formula or the addition of more data.

2. For some resource users we suspect the divergence in hazard perception may be as fundamental as basic attitudes towards nature. Technical-scientific estimates of hazard assume the neutrality of nature. There are resource users who perceive otherwise, conceiving of nature as malevolent or benevolent. Our language is full of metaphors and descriptions of "Mother nature," "bountiful nature," or, conversely, of "angry storms." Besides attributing motivation to nature, there is also the distinction of man's relation to nature. One recent anthropological study, using a cross-cultural approach, developed a man-nature classification comprising man over nature, man with nature, and man under nature.[55] Each of these three divergent points of view is represented by the following statement:

Man Subject to Nature. *'My people have never controlled the rain, wind, and other natural conditions, and probably never will. There have always been good years and bad years. That is the way it is, and if you are wise you will take it as it comes and do the best you can.'*

Man With Nature. *'My people help conditions and keep things going by working to keep in close touch with all the forces which make the rain, the snow, and other conditions. It is when we do the right things—live in the proper way—and keep all that we have— the land, the stock and the water —in good condition, that all goes along well.'*

Man Over Nature. *'My people believe that it is man's job to find ways to overcome weather and other conditions just as they have overcome so many things. They believe they will one day succeed in doing this and may even overcome droughts and floods.'*[56]

Samples of respondents were selected from five different cultural groups in an area of western New Mexico, and their responses were distributed as shown in Table 4.

The wide divergence of human views of nature, as illustrated in Table 4, is strong testimony to support our contention that variations in perception

TABLE 4.   Views of Man and Nature by Cultural Groups (in percentages)

Cultural Group	View of Nature	Man Subject to Nature	Man with Nature	Man over Nature	Number Interviewed
Spanish-Americans		71.7	10.9	17.4	23
Texans		30.0	22.5	47.5	20
Mormons		25.0	55.0	20.0	20
Zuni Indians		19.0	62.0	19.0	21
Rimrock Navaho Indians		18.2	68.2	13.6	22

Source: Variations in Value Orientations, Appendix 4.

are significant and are likely to affect management policies. A society in which belief in the dominance of nature is strong, such as among the Spanish-Americans, is less likely to be conscious of the possibilities of environment control than one in which belief in the dominance of man over nature is more pronounced, as among the Texans.

The belief in technical engineering solutions to problems of hazard is widespread in American society. This belief in the efficacy of man's control over nature is frequently encountered in studies of hazard perception. Thus, it is no longer surprising to find protective powers ascribed to flood control works far beyond their designed capacity. Notable examples are seen in those persons who consider themselves protected by dams downstream from their floodplain location, or who are satisfied that floods will not occur in the future because a government agency has been established to study the problem.[57]

3. How much of the divergence in hazard perception can be ascribed to fundamental views of nature is speculative. Much more of the divergence is explicable in terms of basic attitudes towards uncertainty.

We are convinced that there is a fundamental difference between the attitudes or values of technical-scientific personnel and resource users towards uncertainty. Increasingly the orientation and formal training of scientific personnel emphasizes an indeterminate and probabilistic view of the world. Common research techniques involve the use of estimates that reflect imperfect knowledge, and stress is placed on extracting the full value of partial knowledge.

We have considerable social science and psychological theory and some evidence that resource users are unwilling or unable to adopt this probabilistic view of the world and are not able to live with uncertainty in such a manner as to extract full value from partial knowledge.

Malinowsky held that every human culture possesses both sound scientific knowledge for coping with the natural environment and a set of magical practices for coping with problems that are beyond rational-empirical control.[58] Festinger describes the role of the concept of "cognitive dissonance" as a motivating force, which may lead to actions or beliefs concerning the state of nature that do not accord with rational or logical expectations.[59] For example, he cites the case of a severe earthquake in India in 1934, in which some people experienced the earthquake but saw no evidence of damage which was quite localized. This situation apparently led to the circulation of rumors which helped to reduce the dissonance created by the fear generated by the earthquake and the absence of signs of damage. People were left in a state of fear but no longer saw reason to be afraid. The rumors that circulated in such a situation have been described by Prasad[60] and include the following:

> There will be a severe cyclone at Patna between January 18th and January 19th. [The earthquake occurred on January 15th.]
>
> There will be a severe earthquake on the lunar eclipse day.
>
> January 23rd will be a fatal day. Unforeseeable calamities will arise.

In our experience resource users appear to behave in ways that suggest an individual effort to dispel uncertainty. Among flood-plain users and in coastal areas, the most common variant is to view floods and storms as a repetitive or even cyclical phenomenon. Thus the essential randomness that characterizes the uncertain pattern of the hazard is replaced by a determinate order in which history is seen as repeating itself at regular intervals. Some experiments in the perception of independent events and probability distributions have been conducted by psychologists. The results of such rigorous tests are interesting but are not yet at the level that affords

useful generalizations about the real world.[61] Where the hazard is made repetitive, the past becomes a guide to the approximate timing and magnitude of future hazardous events. An historical example of this is documented by Niddrie.[62] A mild earthquake was recorded in London on February 8, 1750. A somewhat more severe earthquake occurred exactly one lunar month (twenty-eight days) later on March 8th. Predictions were made that a third and more terrible earthquake would occur on April 5th. Niddrie describes the events which followed:

> A contagious panic spreading through every district of the town required only the slightest indication that those who could afford to leave the town unobtrusively were doing so, for a wholesale evacuation to begin. The gullible who could not leave bought pills 'which were very good against the earthquake.' As Doomsday came nearer whole families moved to places of safety . . . . By April 3rd it was impossible to obtain lodgings in any neighboring town or village.[63]

When no earthquake occurred on April 5th the prophesies changed to April 8th as though the number eight had some special connotations for earthquakes. Niddrie reports that in fact few of the gentry and well-to-do returned to London until April 9th.

Another view, which is less common, is the act of "wishing it away" by denigrating the quality of the rare natural event to the level of the commonplace, or conversely of elevating it to a unique position and ascribing its occurrence to a freak combination of circumstances incapable of repetition. Either variant has the advantage of eliminating the uncertainty which surrounds hazardous natural phenomenon.

The last alternative view that we can suggest is the completely indeterminate position that denies completely the knowability of natural phenomena. For this group, all is in the hands of God or the gods. Convinced of the utter inscrutability of Divine Providence, the resource users have no need to trouble themselves about the vagaries of an uncertain nature, for it can serve no useful purpose to do so.

These viewpoints are summarized in Table 5.

Divergence of values. Natural hazards are not perceived in a vacuum. They are seen as having certain effects or consequences, and it is rather the consequences that are feared than the hazard phenomenon per se. Another source of divergence in the perception of natural hazard between technical-scientific personnel and resource users is related to the perceived consequences of the hazard. For very good and sound reasons the set of probabilities related to the occurrence of a natural phenomenon at a given place is not the same as the set of probabilities of hazard for an individual. Given the high level of mobility in our society, the nature of the personal hazard is constantly changing, while the probabilities for a given place remain fixed (although not precisely known).

Thus, the soil erosion that concerns the technicians in Western Iowa, reported in a recent study,[64] is an ongoing continuous long-term hazard. The carefully calculated long-term rates of erosion, however, do not have the same meaning for farmers who averaged only nine years as individual farm managers, or where ownership itself changes hands every fourteen years on the average. Soil losses arise from a series of discrete physical events with intensive rains and high winds acting as the major erosional force. The long-term average of these erosional events may have meaning for the continued occupancy of the agriculture of this area.

TABLE 5. **Common Responses to the Uncertainty of Natural Hazards**

Eliminate the Hazard		Eliminate the Uncertainty	
DENY OR DENIGRATE ITS EXISTENCE	DENY OR DENIGRATE ITS RECURRENCE	MAKING IT DETERMINATE AND KNOWABLE	TRANSFER UNCERTAINTY TO A HIGHER POWER
"We have no floods here, only high water."	"Lightning never strikes twice in the same place."	"Seven years of great plenty . . . . After them seven years of famine."	
			"It's in the hands of God."
"It can't happen here."	"It's a freak of nature."		
		"Floods come every five years."	"The government is taking care of it."

Hence, the technician's concern for the cumulative soil loss. But given the short average managerial period, the cumulative soil loss seems hardly worth the cost and effort involved in its control for the individual manager.

The Case of the Modern Homesteaders.
Evan Vogt's study of the "Modern Homesteader"[65] provides a case study that exemplifies the types of divergence that we have been describing.

Homestead, the site of Vogt's studies during 1951–1952, is in his own words "a small dry-land, bean-farming community" of 200 people in western New Mexico.[66] It was founded in the early 1930's by families from the South Plains Region of western Texas and Oklahoma, but prior to the deep drought of 1934–1936. While spurred by low agricultural prices, Vogt felt they migrated for primarily what they perceived as a good farming opportunity, a chance to receive 640 acres for sixty-eight dollars in fees and residential and improvement investments.[67]

By 1932 eighty-one families had obtained sections under what was objectively governmental encouragement to agricultural settlement in an area with an average rainfall of about twelve inches. By 1935 the official perception of the suitability of the natural environment for agriculture had changed drastically. Under the Taylor Grazing Act,[68] all the land in the area which was still in the public domain was classified for grazing, and no additional homestead applications were accepted. The official estimate had changed, but that of the local citizens had not. To this day they perceive of their submarginal farming area as one quite suitable for dry land farming. In so doing, their perception is at considerable variance with that of the governmental technicians in a variety of ways.

As we suggested before, total ignorance of natural hazards is uncommon. While drought and frost are perennial hazards (two decades have provided seven good years, seven average years, and six crop failures), these were not ignorant city folk lured to the Plains by free land. They came from agricultural families in an area of less than twenty inches average rainfall. They do, however, perceive the marginality of the area in their own fashion. So marked is the divergence of this perception that Vogt reports the following:

> But through the critical days of 'battle' with the government, which had defined their community as 'submarginal' and unsuitable for agriculture, there emerged in the Homesteaders a sense of mission in life: To demonstrate to the experts in the Departments of Agriculture and Interior that the Homestead area is farming country and that they can 'make a go of it' in this semi-arid land. They point to the fact that Pueblo Indians made a living by farming in the area long before the white man arrived. There is a general feeling that somehow the surveys and investigations made by the experts must be wrong. They insist that the Weather Bureau has falsified the rainfall figures that were submitted by the Homestead Weather station in the 1930's, and

indeed they stopped maintaining a weather station because they felt that 'the figures were being used against us.'[69]

Vogt mentions in passing another divergence in hazard perception. Homesteaders appear alert to the high westerly wind hazard that erodes the top soil, and they strip crop and plow across the line of this prevailing wind. In so doing, they look askance at the elaborate terraces constructed by the Soil Conservation Service in the 1930's because these terraces are on the contour, and contour plowing itself inevitably results in some of the rows lying in the direct path of the westerly winds.[70]

Faced with continued drought, sandstorms, and killing frosts, the "Homesteaders" exemplify much of what has been discussed in this paper. Vogt finds the predominant attitude as that of nature being something to be mastered and, arising from this, a heady optimism in the face of continued vicissitudes. He finds the strong need to eliminate uncertainty to the point of not collecting weather data as reported above, or through the widespread resort to agricultural magic, involving signs of the zodiac, planting by the moon, and water witching. It is in this last act, the use of water witching, that we find direct parallels with the behavior of flood-plain users. The geology of the Homestead area as it relates to ground water supply is one of considerable uncertainty. The geological structure generates an uncertainty as to the depth and amount of water available at a particular point. Faced with such

uncertainty, there was a strong-felt need to hire the local water witch to dowse the wells. While the performance ratio of successful wells to dry holes appeared equal whether they were witched or not, Vogt gives a convincing explanation that witching provides a determinate response to uncertainty where the best that the local soil conservation geologists could provide was a generalized description of the ground water situation. Whether, as in Vogt's terms, the motive is to reduce anxiety, or in Festinger's, to reduce cognitive dissonance, or as we would put it, to eliminate uncertainty, there is the apparently strong drive to make the indeterminate determinate.

In conclusion, Vogt emphasizes

that despite more secure economic alternatives elsewhere, most 'Homesteaders' choose to remain in the community and assume the climatic risks rather than abandon the independence of action they cherish and the leisure they enjoy for the more routinized and subordinate roles they would occupy elsewhere.[71]

Levels of Significance in Hazard Perception. There are men who plow up semi-arid steppes, who build villages on the flanks of volcanoes, and who lose one crop in three to floods. Are they irrational? Or, to put it another way, having looked at the variation in hazard perception and speculated on the causes of variation, what can be concluded about the rationality of hazard perception? In general, we find absent from almost every natural phenomenon a standard for the objective (*i.e.*, true) probability of an event's occurrence. Even if such existed, we are not sure that man can assimilate such probabilities sufficiently to be motivated to act upon them. If decisions are made in a prohibilistic framework, what level of probability is sufficient for action? In the terms of statistics, what level of significance is appropriate? What amount of hazard or error is tolerable? Science is of little help here, since levels of statistical significance are chosen at ninety-five per cent or ninety-nine per cent primarily by convention.

Despite the impressive growth of game theory, the growing literature of decision-strategies, and some psychological experimentation with perceived probabilities, the artificiality of the game or laboratory seems to provide at best only limited insights into this complex phenomenon. On the other hand, the derivation of empirical observations, *i.e.*, estimates of the perceived frequency of events or perceived probabilities at which decisions are actually made, provides almost insuperable research difficulties.

In the last analysis, we seem destined to judge the rationality of man's actions vis-à-vis natural hazard out of a mixture of hindsight and prejudice. For the successful gambler in the game against nature there are but a few lonely voices crying that the odds will overtake him. The unsuccessful is clearly judged as foolhardy, ignorant, or irrational. Our prejudice expresses itself in our attitudes towards uncertainty, our preferences for certain types of risk, and how we feel about the objects of resource management.

Conclusion

There is a wide variation in the day-to-day management practices of resource users, even within culturally homogeneous groups. We believe that the variations in hazard perception reported in this article are an important explanatory variable. Unfortunately, careful studies of variation in resource management practices are few and far between. Some of the recent studies of innovation[72] and the study of farm practices in western Iowa, already cited,[73] approach what we have in mind. To our knowledge there have been no studies which adequately describe variations in management practice and rigorously attempt to assess the role of differing perception.

We can say that there is good reason to believe that variations in perception of hazard among resource managers tends to diminish over time. Those who are unwilling or unable to make the necessary adjustments in a hazardous situation are eliminated, either because disaster overtakes them or because they voluntarily depart. Those who remain tend to share in a uniformity of outlook.

Long-term occupancy of high hazard areas is never really stable, even where it has persisted over time. A catastrophe, a long run of bad years, a rising level of aspiration marked by the unwillingness to pay the high costs of survival—each provides stimulants to change. The "Modern Homesteaders," while determined to stay put and exhibiting a high degree of uniformity in their assessment of the environment and its hazards, may yet yield to a combination of an extended run of drought and frost and the lure of a more affluent society. Long-term occupancy, while potentially unstable, is still marked by a tenacity to persist, reinforced, we think, by the uniformity of hazard perception that develops over time. Thus all of the homesteaders who took jobs elsewhere in the bad drought of 1950 returned to the community. More dramatic is the return of the residents of Tristan da Cunha to their volcanic island home.

We have no evidence of a similar growth in accord between resource users and scientific-technical personnel. Clearly, variations in perception may profoundly affect the chances of success of a new management proposal developed by the experts. Such new programs are constantly being devised, but assessments of past programs are seldom found. George Macinko's review of the Columbia Basin project is a recent welcome exception.[74] Rarely do such studies review programs in terms of divergence of perception. L. Schuyler Fonaroff's article on differences in view between the Navajo and the Indian Service is another exception which proves the rule.[75]

While lacking many detailed statements of this divergence, we can nevertheless state the implication of our findings to date. The divergence in perception implies limits on the ability of resource managers to absorb certain types of technical advice regardless of how well written or explained. Thus, to expect farmers to maintain conservation practices for long periods of time may be wishful thinking if such practices do not accord with the farmer's view of his resource and the hazards to which it is exposed. Similarly, to expect radical changes in the pattern of human adjustments to floods simply by providing detailed and precise flood hazard information is unduly optimistic. Yet another example is seen in the upper Trinity River area in Texas.[76] To expect farmers to convert flood-plain land from pasture to cotton or other high value cash crops simply because flood frequency is reduced is to assume that he shares the perception of the Soil Conservation Service. Nor is it a strong argument to claim that such changes in land use were indicated as possible by the farmers themselves, if the question was put to them in terms of the technologist's evaluation of the problem. Good predictions of the future choices of resource managers are likely to be based on an understanding of their perception and the ways in which it differs from that of the technologists.

It seems likely that the hiatus between technical and managerial perception is nowhere greater than in the underdeveloped countries.[77] There is good reason, therefore, for further research into this topic and for attempts to harmonize the discrepancies in technical programs wherever possible.

While the study of natural hazard perception provides clues to the ways in which men manage uncertain natural environments, it also helps to provide a background to understanding our national resource policy. Despite the self-image of the conservation movement as a conscious and rational attempt to develop policies to meet long term needs, more of the major commitments of public policy in the field of resource management have arisen out of crises generated by catastrophic natural hazards (albeit at times aided and abetted by human improvidence) than out of a need to curb man's misuse and abuse of his natural environment. Some years ago this was recognized by White: "National catastrophes have led to insistent demands for national action, and the timing of the legislative process has been set by the tempo of destructive floods."[78] It has also been documented in some detail by Henry Hart.[79] The Soil Erosion Service of the Department of Agriculture was established as an emergency agency in 1933 following the severe drought and subsequent dust bowl early in the decade. The Service became a permanent agency called the Soil Conservation Service in 1935.[80]

Just as flood control legislation has followed hard upon the heels of major flood disasters, so the present high degree of interest in coastal protection, development, and preservation has been in part stimulated by recent severe storms on the east coast.[81] Such a fundamental public policy as the provision of water supply for urban areas was created partly in response to needs for controlling such natural hazards as typhus and cholera and the danger of fire, as well as for meeting urban water demands.[82] Agricultural and forestry research programs were fostered as much by insect infestations and plant diseases as by the long-range goals of increased production.

Unusual events in nature have long been associated with a state of crisis in human affairs. The decline of such superstitions and the continued growth of the control over nature will not necessarily be accompanied by a reduction of the role of crisis in resource policy. Natural hazards are likely to continue to play a significant role, although their occurrence as well as their effects may be increasingly difficult to separate from man-induced hazards of the quasi-natural variety. The smog of Donora may replace the Johnstown flood in our lexicon of major hazards, and *The Grapes of Wrath* may yield pride of place to *The Silent Spring* in the literature of the effects of environmental hazard, but there will continue to be a pattern of response to crisis in human relations to an uncertain environment. Under these circumstances, understandings of the variations of perception such as we have attempted here are likely to remain significant.

Footnotes

1. Niddrie, When the Earth Shook 36 (1962).
2. Zimmermann, World Resources and Industries (1951); see also Zimmermann's diagram, *id.* at 13.
3. Thomas, The *Meteorological Phenomenon of Drought in the Southwest, 1942–1956,* at A8 (United States Geological Survey Prof. Paper No. 372-A, 1962).
4. Meteorological Office, United Kingdom Air Ministry, British Rainfall, 1958, at 10 (1963). This definition was introduced in British rainfall research in 1887.
5. DHEW, Public Health Service, I Vital Statistics of the United States, 1950, at 31 (*Interpretation of Cause-of-Death Statis-*

tics), 169 (*Mortality by Cause of Death*) (1954).

6. Glossary of Meteorology 516 (Huschke ed. 1959), defines "smog" as follows: A natural fog contaminated by industrial pollutants; a mixture of smoke and fog. This term coined in 1905 by Des Voeux, has experienced a recent rapid rise in acceptance but so far it has not been given precise definition.

7. Senate Select Comm. on Nat'l Water Resources, 86th Cong., 2d Sess., *Weather Modification* 3 (Comm. Print No. 22, 1960); see also Batton & Kassander, *Randomized Seeding of Orographic Cumulus* (Univ. Chi. Meteorology Dep't Tech. Bull. No. 12, 1958); Greenfield, *A New Rational Approach to Weather-Control Research* (Rand Corp. Memo. No. RM-3205-NSF, 1962).

8. See, *e.g.*, the maps prepared by M. Maurice Pardé in Comité National de Géographie, Atlas de France, Sheets 20, 22 (1934).

9. Mushkin, *Health as an Investment*, 70 J. Political Economy 129, 137 (1962); see also Merriam, *Social Welfare Expenditures, 1960–1961*, 25 Social Security Bull. 3 (No. 11, 1962).

10. See notes 32–34 *infra*.

11. Flora, Hailstorms of the United States 3 (1956).

12. Our estimate.

13. Byerly, *Why We Need Loss Data*, Nat'l Academy of Science, Nat'l Research Council, *Losses Due to Agricultural Pests* 3 (Summary of Conference of the Agricultural Bd. Comm. on Agriculture Pests, Nov. 4–5, 1959).

14. Bureau of Yards & Docks, United States Navy, *Natural Disasters* 24 (Navdocks P-88, 1961).

15. Byerly, *op. cit. supra* note 13.

16. *Ibid.*

17. Flora, *op. cit. supra* note 11.

18. Byerly, *op. cit. supra* note 13.

19. DHEW, Public Health Service, II Vital Statistics of the United States 18–36 (1959).

20. Metropolitan Life Ins. Co., Statistical Bulletin, vol. 41, at 9 (April, 1960).

21. DHEW, Public Health Service, *op. cit. supra* note 19.

22. *Ibid.*

23. Metropolitan Life Ins. Co., *op. cit. supra* note 20.

24. DHEW, Public Health Service, *op. cit. supra* note 19.

25. Bureau of Yards & Docks, *op. cit. supra* note 14.

26. DHEW, Public Health Service, *op. cit. supra* note 19.

27. *Ibid.*

28. Metropolitan Life Ins. Co., *op. cit. supra* note 20.

29. DHEW, Public Health Service, *op. cit. supra* note 19.

30. *Ibid.*

31. *Ibid.*

32. Weather Bureau, Dep't of Commerce, Climatological Data, National Summary, Annual 1961, at 85 (1962).

33. Senate Select Comm. on Nat'l Water Resources, 86th Cong., 2d Sess., *Floods and Flood Control* 5–7 (Comm. Print No. 15, 1960).

34. Senate Comm. on Banking and Currency, *Federal Disaster Insurance*, S. Rep. No. 1313, 84th Cong., 2d Sess., 69–71 (1956).

35. A definition of "resource manager," as we use the term, is found in White, *The Choice of Use in Resource Management*, 1 Natural Resources J. 23, 24 (1961).

36. Calef, *The Winter of 1948–49 in the Great Plains*, 40 Ass'n Am. Geographers, Annals 267 (1950).

37. Langbein & Hoyt, Water Facts for the Nation's Future 229 (1959).

38. *Id.* at 230.

39. Flora, Hailstorms of the United States

56 (1956).

40. *Ibid.*

41. American Ins. Ass'n, Studies of Floods and Flood Damage 3 (1956).

42. Langbein & Hoyt, *op. cit. supra* note 37, at 232.

43. *Delaware River Basin, New York, New Jersey, Pennsylvania, and Delaware,* H.R. Doc. No. 522, 87th Cong., 2d Sess., VI, Plate 42 (1962).

44. Kates, *Hazard and Choice Perception in Flood Plain Management* (Univ. Chi. Dep't of Geography Research Paper No. 78, 1962).

45. Burton, *Types of Agricultural Occupance of Flood Plains in the United States* (Univ. Chi. Dep't of Geography Research Paper No. 75, 1962).

46. Kates, *Perceptual Regions and Regional Perception in Flood Plain Management,* Papers of the Regional Science Ass'n (1963). [Ed. note: A volume number has not been assigned to this set of papers.]

47. For one such attempt see Comparisons in Resources Management (Jarrett ed. 1961).

48. Lowenthal, *Not Every Prospect Pleases—What Is Our Criterion for Scenic Beauty?,* 12 Landscape 19 (Winter, 1962–1963).

49. Lowenthal, *Nature and the American Creed of Virtue,* 9 Landscape 24 (Winter, 1959–1960).

50. Huth, Nature and the American (1957).

51. Thornthwaite, *Climate and Settlement in the Great Plains, Climate and Man,* USDA Yearbook 177, 184 (1941).

52. Suchman, *A Conceptual Analysis of the Accident Phenomenon,* Ass'n for Aid of Crippled Children, Behavioral Approaches to Accident Research 40 (1961).

53. Kates, *op. cit. supra* note 46.

54. *An Interim Hurricane Survey of Fairfield, Connecticut,* H.R. Doc. No. 600, 87th Cong., 2d Sess., 14 (1962).

55. Kluckholm & Strodtbeck, Variations in Value Orientations (1961).

56. *Id.* at 86–87.

57. Such a response was given to Burton during recent field work in Belleville, Ontario. There, two respondents considered that the establishment of the Moira Valley Conservation Authority meant that no more floods would occur. Such is, in fact, far from the case. The Authority has not been successful in its attempts to have protective works constructed.

58. Malinowsky, Magic, Science, and Religion in Science, Religion, and Reality (Needham ed. 1925).

59. Festinger, The Motivating Effect of Cognitive Dissonance in Assessment of Human Motives (Lindzey ed. 1960); Festinger, A Theory of Cognitive Dissonance (1947).

60. Prasad, *A Comparative Study of Rumors and Reports in Earthquakes,* 41 British J. Psychology 129 (1950).

61. Hake & Hyman, *Perception of the Statistical Structure of a Random Series of Binary Symbols,* 45 J. Experimental Psychology 64 (1953); Cohen & Hansel, *The Idea of a Distribution,* 46 British J. Psychology 111 (1955); Cohen & Hansel, *The Idea of Independence,* 46 British J. Psychology 178 (1955); Hyman & Jenkin, *Involvement and Set as Determinants of Behavioral Stereotypy,* 2 Psychological Rep. 131 (1956).

62. Niddrie, When the Earth Shook 20–34 (1962).

63. *Id.* at 29–30.

64. Held, Blase & Timmons, *Soil Erosion and Some Means for Its Control* (Iowa State Univ. Agri. and Home Econ. Experiment Sta. Special Rep. No. 29, 1962).

65. Vogt, Modern Homesteaders (1955).

66. *Id.* at 1.

67. *Id.* at 17–18.

68. 48 Stat. 1269 (1934), as amended, 43 U.S.C. §§ 315–315r (1958).

69. Vogt, *op. cit. supra* note 65, at 68.

70. *Id.* at 70.

71. *Id.* at 176.

72. See the bibliography in Lionberger, Adoption of New Ideas and Practices (1960).

73. Held, Blase & Timmons, *op. cit. supra* note 64.

74. Macinko, *The Columbia Basin Project, Expectations, Realizations, Implications,* 53 Geography Rev. 185 (1963).

75. Fonaroff, *Conservation and Stock Reduction on the Navajo Tribal Range,* 53 Geography Rev. 200 (1963).

76. Burton, *op. cit. supra* note 45, at 59–73.

77. The results of a recent effort to improve communication between technical experts and resource managers are reported in Central Treaty Organization, Traveling Seminar for Increased Agricultural Production, Region Tour (1962).

78. White, *Human Adjustments to Floods* 24 (Univ. Chi. Dep't of Geography Research Paper No. 29, 1945).

79. Hart, *Crises, Community, and Consent in Water Politics,* 22 Law & Contemp. Prob. 510 (1957).

80. Buie, *Ill Fared the Land,* USDA Yearbook 155 (1962).

81. Burton & Kates, *The Flood Plain and the Sea Shore: A Comparative Analysis of Hazard Zone Occupance* (Unpublished manuscript, 1963), scheduled for publication in July, 1964 issue of Geographical Review.

82. Blake, Water for the Cities (1956).

twenty-five ◆ ◆ ◆ ◆ ◆ ◆ ◆ ◆ ◆ ◆ ◆ ◆

◆ IAN BURTON
◆ ROBERT W. KATES

The Floodplain and the Seashore: A Comparative Analysis of Hazard-Zone Occupance

The United States is in danger today of embarking on a large-scale and costly program of coastal defense against storm hazard comparable with the program of flood control that has been operating in river valleys for the past quarter of a century. Federal legislation passed in 1936, and subsequently, has been largely the reason for the heavy investment in flood-control engineering works, to the neglect of possible alternatives. Yet appraisals of the flood-control program are in general agreement that despite federal expenditures of about five billion dollars, average annual damages from floods have continued to rise.[1] Nor is a brighter prospect held for the future. The Chief of Engineers stated in 1960 that at the present rate of expenditure flood protection will "just about keep up with the increase in flood damage that may be anticipated by 1980 as a result of flood plain development over the next two decades."[2]

A repetition of the same course of action with respect to coastal flood problems seems likely. The storm of March 5–8, 1962,[3] on the east coast of the United States (Fig. 1) focused attention on coastal storm damage. One informed official recently remarked that it seems unlikely Congress will be satisfied that it has done its duty by coastal constituents until an Atlantic Wall has been built from Maine to Mexico!

It is feared that more than one billion dollars could be spent on coastal

◆ SOURCE. Reprinted by permission from the *Geographical Review*, Vol. 54, 1964, pp. 366–385, copyrighted by the American Geographical Society of New York.

FIGURE 1.   Storm damage at Point O'Woods, Fire Island, N.Y., on March 7, 1962. (Photograph by United Press International.)

protection by the federal government alone in the next fifteen to twenty years without any assurance that storm damage would be reduced; in fact, it might well be that average annual damages resulting from storms and saltwater flooding would be increasing by the 1980's. Because of long-term sea-level fluctuations and other factors, a program to "contain" the sea would seem to have as little chance for success as King Canute's attempt to command the waves.

Human Adjustments

A variety of human adjustments[4] have evolved in response to flood hazards in river valleys, of which engineering works are the most prominent. Others are permanent or emergency evacuation of population and property; bearing the losses with or without public relief; rescheduling of production so as to have low inventories at times of highest hazard; elevation of land; alteration of structures to make them flood-resistant; insurance; regulation and change of land use.[5] For prevention of flood damage a framework of human adjustments may be arranged as in Figure 2, a presentation widely used by the Tennessee Valley Authority.

Adjustments are also possible in coastal areas. The Chief of Engineers has declared that "in most cases, . . . on exposed reaches of shoreline, the

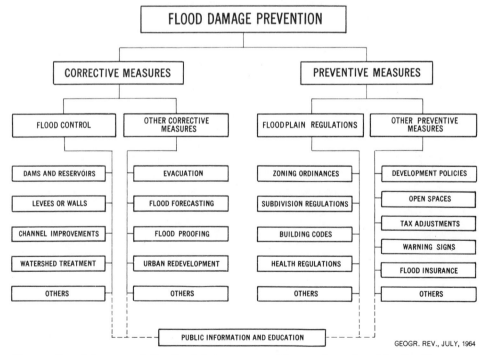

GEOGR. REV., JULY, 1964

FIGURE 2.   A framework for flood-damage prevention, as formulated by the Tennessee Valley Authority, 1962.

principal reliance for reduction of damage from hurricane floods will probably have to rest with adequate warning service, proper building codes, evacuation plans and routes, and with the zoning of more hazardous areas."[6]

Thus there would appear to be a clear need for careful guidance in the human occupance of hazardous coastal areas. Such guidance will be more effective if based on studies of the rate of coastal development and the processes by which this development is advanced. The need for study applies to much of the United States coastal zone,[7] though public interest usually centers on areas of spectacular damage, such as the New Jersey coast, or on areas of controversy, such as Fire Island, New York, and Assateague Island, Maryland-Virginia, for which highway and bridge construction is being debated.

The writers have recently turned their attention to problems of coastal areas,[8] beginning with a reconnaissance of parts of the east coast of the United States from Boston to Cape May, New Jersey. A major conclusion emerging from this work is that new damage potential is being created at an accelerating rate, by occupance of coastal areas subject to high winds, wave action, and saltwater flooding associated with storms. This occupance, however, is uneven and diverse. It appears to be influenced by a variety of factors, physical and cultural, but the relationships are poorly understood.

Basic to a better understanding of coastal occupance is some assessment of the rate of development in hazard areas. Indications may thus be obtained

regarding rates of expansion over the next twenty to twenty-five years and the locations of areas of most rapid growth. A partial answer to the second of these questions is available. It seems reasonable to assume that the most rapid coastal development is occurring on the northeast coast in the urbanized area from Massachusetts Bay to the Potomac Valley, which Jean Gottmann has called Megalopolis.[9] Therefore, the need for better understanding of coastal occupance is probably nowhere greater than on the shores of this giant conurbation. It is not clear, for example, whether the rates of coastal development exceed those which might be expected elsewhere in Megalopolis or whether they are merely what might be expected in view of the rates of urban expansion being recorded in the conurbation as a whole.

Definition of Hazard Areas

In order that rates of encroachment may be established, the complex problem of defining the areas of hazard must be solved. As an interim measure, an arbitrary contour level may be selected, but a more satisfactory definition could be gained from a careful study of the factors that determined the height of surge in recorded storms. It may ultimately become possible to calculate theoretically the probable maximum elevation of tidal damage for given stretches of coast.

Storm-surge elevations at a given level of probability may be derived from empirical relationships established by the National Hurricane Research

FIGURE 3. Relative storm-surge potential of different coastal sections. Adapted from *National Hurricane Research Project Rept. No. 32*, U. S. Weather Bureau, Washington, 1959, Fig. 4 (p. 8).

Project of the United States Weather Bureau (Figs. 3–5). Figure 3 represents the distribution of a topographic variable of storm surge O, which is based on the distance of the fifty-fathom depth contour from the shore. This variable O when related to the central pressure of a hurricane at the point of coastal entry provides an estimate of storm surge in feet (Fig. 4). Figure 5 introduces a probabilistic element by relating central pressure to frequency of occurrence. Thus the hurricane experience of 1900–1956 would suggest that there is a probability of 0.01 of receiving a hurricane with a central pressure as low as 931 millibars or lower, and such a hurricane would generate maximum storm surges ranging from 12.5 feet to 14.5 feet, depending on where it

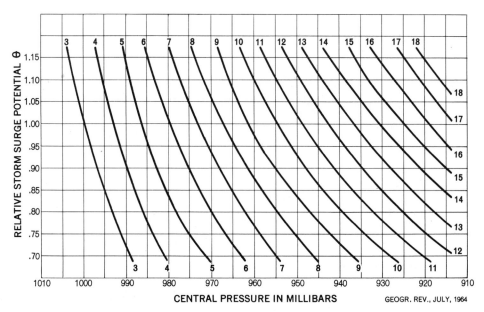

FIGURE 4. Storm-surge prediction chart. Adapted from *National Hurricane Research Project Rept. No. 32*, U. S. Weather Bureau, Washington, 1959, Fig. 3 (p. 7).

crossed the coast from Maine to Maryland (Figs. 2 and 4). However, in view of the considerable local variability in depth of inundation, it is desirable to produce maps showing areas of hazard and other technical information similar to that now being issued by the United States Geological Survey, the Army Corps of Engineers, and the Tennessee Valley Authority.[10]

The Processes of Development

The definition of hazard areas and the establishment of rates of development are only preliminary. The greater need is for knowledge of the processes. The role of private, public, and corporate bodies in the creation of new damage potential is little understood; so is their

role in urging expensive protection policies on government agencies after major catastrophes. Understanding is lacking of the attitudes and the perception of hazard prevalent among coastal developers, businessmen, and residents.[11] Hopefully, studies directed toward increased knowledge of the problems would provide the basis for more intelligent use of the nation's coastal resources, and would also provide guidelines for the formulation of sound public policy and planning in areas with regulations for shore protection and coastal land use.

In order to establish a body of concepts dealing with development processes and possible adjustments in areas of high hazard, a systematic comparison has here been attempted between the characteristics of floodplains

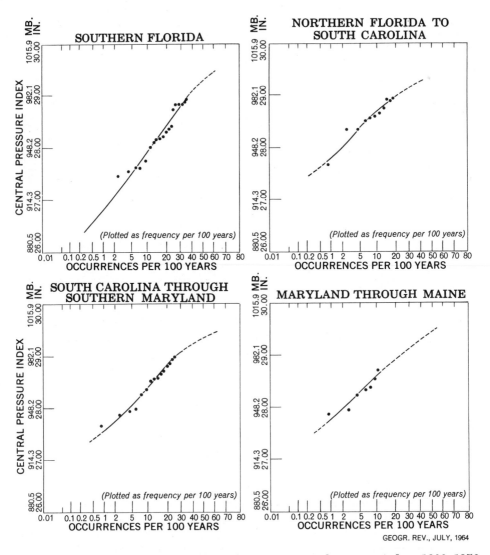

GEOGR. REV., JULY, 1964

FIGURE 5. Cumulative frequencies of hurricane central-pressure index, 1900–1956, plotted as frequency per 100 years. Adapted from *National Hurricane Research Project Rept. No. 33*, U. S. Weather Bureau, Washington, 1959, Fig. 4 (p. 23).

and those of coastal areas with reference to their suitability for human occupance.[12] The comparison is made largely on a priori grounds, supplemented by the coastal reconnaissance described above.

Hydrologic Features

The causes of coastal and riverine floods are dissimilar. Rivers flood by the addition of water through excessive runoff from the drainage basin or blockage in the channel. In coastal flooding the effect of precipitation is negligible, there is no equivalent of the ice-jam flood, and the main factor is wind-driven water, which rarely enters the riverine flooding pattern.

Although causally unlike, river and coastal floods have some similar or analogous characteristics. The *height* (or depth) of flooding, as measured by stream or tidal gauges, is a useful measure in both. Height of flooding can be more easily compared from place to place in coastal areas because mean sea level provides a uniform frame of reference; in riverine areas height is relative to an arbitrary local datum. Among the factors affecting height, length of fetch is in part analogous to size of drainage basin. A number of characteristics of flooding and occupance are related to size of drainage basin,[13] and similar analysis can be made of coastal areas, using length of fetch.

For any given storm pattern over a drainage basin or a coast, height of flooding varies with the set of prior or associated conditions. Just as saturated or frozen ground increases runoff and produces a greater depth of inundation, so the coincidence of storms with high tides increases coastal flooding. Tidal fluctuations can be predicted with greater precision than associated or prior conditions related to riverine flooding, but both need careful consideration in any estimate of maximum hazard. Estimates of height have assumed great importance in river flooding because of their value in the construction of stage-damage curves. As study of coast protection develops, height of storm tides is likely to be recognized as one of the more important variables.

In addition to height, six other measures have been found useful in describing river floods: (1) velocity (the average speed of flow of floodwaters); (2) discharge (the volume of water per unit of time); (3) range (the maximum variation in the height of a stream at a given point); (4) duration (the length of time that the river exceeds flood stage); (5) seasonality (the concentration of flood events within a part of the calendar year); and (6) flood-to-peak interval (the time lapse between flood stage and the maximum peak or crest).

Velocity can also be measured in coastal floods, and in both types it is an important variable, to which the amount of damage is directly related. *Discharge* has had more limited use, with reference to tidal inlets and the measurement of littoral currents.

Range varies considerably both in river and in coastal floods, but it is our impression that extreme ranges are more frequent along major rivers. Associated with the range is the extent of the area subject to flood. Floodplains several miles in width may be inundated, and analogous to such flooding is the inundation of extensive flat coastal areas. An outstanding example of a great saltwater flood occurred on the north European coast and in eastern England in February, 1953.[14] More commonly, however, flooding is limited to a narrow strip of land along the river or the seacoast. Where the hazard area is a narrow strip, and where similar land resources are available close by without the attendant hazard, there seems little reason to place residential or industrial property in the path of possible future floods. Yet this has frequently happened, both in river valleys and, as examination of new communities on the south shore of Cape Cod suggests, in coastal areas. Some purchasers of such property have been ignorant of the risk or have underestimated it.

Duration of flooding on floodplains is related to size of drainage basin and may be several days or even weeks, as in the backwater flooding in the delta of the Mississippi River. In a coastal area, "duration" may have the same meaning as in riverine areas with respect to slow-draining tidal marshes or a somewhat different meaning with respect to tide changes. Since a storm tide represents an increment over normal high tide (storm surge), maximum damage and inundation accompany high tides. Storms that persist through several tidal changes are exponentially more severe than those of shorter duration. The duration is shortest with hurricanes and longest with extratropical storms. Thus it was the duration of the

storm of March 5–8, 1962, through three successive high tides rather than the height of the storm surge that was the major damage factor.[15]

The duration of a flood affects occupance in a variety of ways. In urban areas prolonged floods increase indirect losses, such as the loss of business and wages resulting from delays, and the loss due to continued submersion, which weakens structures, warps floors, and the like. Duration is of even greater importance in agricultural areas, since crops that might have been partly salvaged after a short flood become total losses if the floodwater does not drain rapidly away.

The recoverability of losses due to the duration of a flood is a matter of considerable dispute. The business of a retail store in an urban area on the floodplain may be interrupted for several days, but when the flood has receded, the lost business may be recovered, since sales may be above normal for a period. But the manager of a business in a coastal resort who is forced by flood damage to close early in the season cannot recover his losses in the same way. "Purchase" of the commodity he supplies has been diverted elsewhere or prevented, and not merely postponed.[16]

Seasonality of floods permits adjustments, which may reduce damages, provided the seasonality is recognized and understood. For example, some farmers make deliberate adjustments by late planting or early harvesting to avoid having valuable crops in the ground during known periods of high hazard. A similar opportunity is provided by a well-defined season of hurricanes on the east coast, from August 1 to September 15, which contained 60 percent of the recorded occurrences from 1887 to 1956.[17] For example, those who wish to have a summer cottage on the beach in an exposed part of the coast could use a trailer or mobile dwelling, which would be removed to a safer place with the onset of the hurricane season or with early warning of an approaching hurricane. The danger lies in the unexpected, out-of-season storm, which may increase damage by catching floodplain or coastal residents unaware. However, improved forecasts and their dissemination seem to be reducing this danger.

A long *flood-to-peak interval* provides the time needed for pressing into action a variety of emergency adjustments to river floods. It also permits extended measurement and observation, leading to greater accuracy and dissemination of flood forecasts. Conversely, flash floods give little or no warning, and damage may be correspondingly increased, with possible loss of life. In coastal areas the growing threat of an offshore hurricane compares with a rising flood in major rivers, and an extended period of observation permits hurricane warnings to be widely disseminated well in advance. In some coastal areas, however, especially where storms may develop quickly and unexpectedly, tidal inundations occur much more rapidly and may in effect be almost instantaneous, a situation comparable with flash flooding.

Geomorphic Factors

The hydrologic characteristics of floods are affected by the configuration of the land surface. It is helpful, therefore, in examining flood-hazard areas to be able to classify them according to their geomorphic characteristics. Ohya and others working at the Ministry of Construction in Japan have developed a classification of flood types on this basis.[18] A classification of types of agricultural floodplain occupance in the United States has also been formulated.[19] Here we have attempted to classify coastal types and to relate them to their floodplain equivalents or analogues (Fig. 6). The typology is unlike other coastal classifications in that it is based on those characteristics which seem to us to be important for human occupance. To the coastal geomorphologist it will probably appear meaningless. Nor is the comparison with river floodplains intended to have genetic or morphological implications. This is a purely anthropocentric typology believed to have significance for present and potential occupance. It is not comprehensive, but merely representative of some of the more common kinds of floodplain and coastal terrain. It is based mainly on width and slope of the flood-prone area and presence or absence of natural protection, such as levees and dunes or terraces and raised beaches. Each main type can be subdivided by size-class of material (boulders, gravel, shingle, and so on) or susceptibility to erosion, factors that have important implications for occupance.

WIDE TYPE

In an analysis of data from 104 cities with flood problems it was found that width of floodplain was directly related

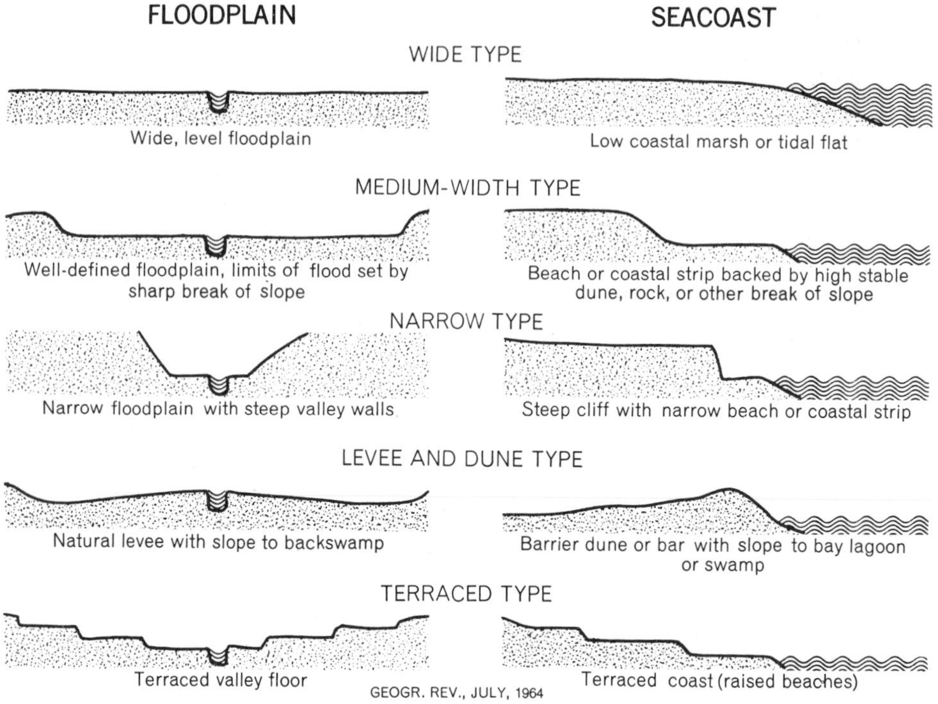

FLOODPLAIN   SEACOAST

WIDE TYPE

Wide, level floodplain   Low coastal marsh or tidal flat

MEDIUM-WIDTH TYPE

Well-defined floodplain, limits of flood set by   Beach or coastal strip backed by high stable
sharp break of slope   dune, rock, or other break of slope

NARROW TYPE

Narrow floodplain with steep valley walls   Steep cliff with narrow beach or coastal strip

LEVEE AND DUNE TYPE

Natural levee with slope to backswamp   Barrier dune or bar with slope to bay lagoon
                                                       or swamp

TERRACED TYPE

Terraced valley floor   Terraced coast (raised beaches)

GEOGR. REV., JULY, 1964

FIGURE 6.   A comparative typology of floodplains and seacoasts.

to size of city but inversely related to frequency of flooding.[20] It seems likely that the reverse obtains in coastal areas; that is, where the coast is low and flat and the area subject to flooding is extensive, floods may be expected to occur more frequently, and large cities are noticeably absent. Floodplains and seacoasts of the wide type may be expected to share problems of high water table and poor drainage.

MEDIUM-WIDTH TYPE

Where hazard zones are smaller and well defined, it is surprising to find their use expanding and little concern apparent. Such, however, has been the case on urban floodplains and, though

not yet observed, could conceivably be in process in coastal areas also. An example of the medium-width type is the stretch of coast included in the Cape Cod National Seashore. The high stable dunes provide a splendid view for the residents who live on top of them, without flood hazard. However, no evidence has been observed of expansion down the front face of the dune in such areas or onto the beach itself.

NARROW TYPE

The narrow floodplain in the steep-sided valley is difficult of access and often remains free from dense settlement. When settlement does take place

FIGURE 7. Hazard, Kentucky, lying in the narrow valley of the North Fork of the Kentucky River, was inundated by floodwaters in March, 1963. (Photograph by Billy Davis, courtesy of *The Courier-Journal*, Louisville.)

under the press of local circumstances, buildings are crowded on the floodplain, and the potential for a devastating flood is created (Fig. 7). An example is the village of Lynmouth in north Devon, England, a small community crowded into the mouth of a narrow valley, which was virtually wiped out in August, 1952, by the rapid rise of a small stream following a torrential storm concentrated over its small watershed. Settlement is normally absent from the analogous coastal type, though the village of Hallsands is situated in such a position on the south

Devon coast, and has suffered severe storm and flood damage, perhaps associated with increased hazard due to offshore dredging.[21]

LEVEE AND DUNE TYPE

Levees, dunes, and bars afford a degree of protection against high water levels, but they are not invulnerable, and severe damage may result when they are breached by man or nature. Property on the crest is destroyed in the area of the breach, and considerable volumes of water may flow through and inundate large areas. One characteristic of coastal occupance appears to be unique: there is no riverine analogue to the prevalent and continued destruction of coastal dunes to provide improved scenic views or building sites.

TERRACED TYPE

Terraced river valleys are common and provide safe sites for human occupance. Only the lowest terraces are subject to flooding, and that infrequently. Less common, but equally valuable as safe sites, are marine terraces, which may command a view of the ocean without undue exposure to its dangers.

The Role of Engineering

In certain river and coastal situations engineering works can be constructed to protect vulnerable areas. Where earth or sand can be used, artificial levees and dunes can be constructed. Floodwalls in some cities, and seawalls on some coasts, protect high-value property against damage. The dam has no exact equivalent in coastal engineering, though a hurricane dam is under construction at the mouth of the Providence River to protect the city of Providence, Rhode Island, and a plan is under study to build such a dam at the mouth of Narragansett Bay.[22] Coastal harbor walls and jetties are more common, but they do not strictly compare with dams.

It is worth stressing that there are great technical unknowns in both riverine and coastal engineering. The effects of a dam on a downstream river channel, or of a groin on a beach from which the littoral current is being deflected, are only partly understood. However, there appears to be greater uncertainty in coastal engineering, related in some fundamental way to the magnitudes of energy that can be dissipated on the coasts.

One conclusion emerging from studies of river floods is that protection against floods of a low order of magnitude but high frequency of occurrence may encourage more rapid development in hazardous areas and thus increase the damage potential for less frequent but higher-order floods. It is possible, therefore, that where protection in coastal areas is not accompanied by new zoning laws or building codes, further encroachment may be stimulated there also.

However, our coastal reconnaissance leads us to suggest that the reverse may likewise be true. If removal of a barrier dune (levee and dune type) increases the amenity of a coastal site by giving more houses a view of the ocean, further development may take place, with a resultant increase in the frequency of damage. Conversely, the obliteration of an ocean view by construction of an artificial dune may reduce amenity value and slow up development.

Construction of levees in agricultural areas may have what has been described as the "levee effect." Managers of farms severed by the levee may be tempted to farm the land between the levee and the river on a speculative basis, and may be better able to do so because of more secure farming behind the protection of the levee (Fig. 8).

FIGURE 8.   A levee successfully holds back floodwaters of the Mississippi River on the wide floodplain of the Yazoo Basin, May 29, 1961. (Photograph by the U. S. Army Corps of Engineers.)

A coastal analogue is the construction of a house on the sea slope of a barrier dune, especially where this is a speculative venture in the hope of quick returns from high rents during a few storm-free seasons.

Watercourses are canalized in both coastal and riverine areas. Ditches pierce natural levees to provide improved drainage for backswamp areas, but they may also act as inlets for water from the main river, which flows into the backwaters and accentuates the flood problem. A coastal analogue is the construction of canals to provide water-

front sites for dwellings that may be hundreds of yards or even several miles from the open ocean; in this manner many more coast dwellers are able to keep a boat close to the house and sail out to sea. These same canals, however, provide avenues up which seawater can be wind-driven far inland and cause severe flood damage in previously safe localities.

Cultural Features

In an assessment of what adjustments should be made in floodplain settlement

FIGURE 9.   The value of deep-piling construction is well illustrated in the case of this $80,000 home, which before the storm of March 5–8, 1962, was firmly sited atop a sand dune. (Photograph courtesy *Eastern Shore Times*, Berlin, Md.)

to minimize flood damage, the factors must be considered that induce men to settle on floodplains and remain there in spite of a demonstrated hazard. It is helpful, therefore, to compare the locational advantages of floodplain sites and coastal sites.

River valleys have played a traditional role as corridors, particularly through dissected terrain. They provide low-incline routes for highways and railroads as well as the medium for waterborne transport. Installations associated with these transport arteries, and activities benefiting from nearness to them, have tended to locate close to the river, and often on flood-prone land.

Coastal margins rarely provide such convenient paths. More normally, coastal settlements serve as termini. Coastwise movement of people and

goods may result in the development of ports, but these are isolated settlements, and their sites are often selected for shelter from the ocean, so that storm damage is low. So far as transport utility is concerned, coastal settlements have a greater opportunity for judicious selection of sites, and by virtue of the nature of their business and their high degree of awareness of the potential force of the sea, they have a strong motive for seeking out places where they are protected from its full force.

The association with transport is only one of the locational advantages of rivers and coasts. In the case of rivers, easy disposal of waste, the supply of water, the opportunity to develop power, and the comparative advantage of level land for building have historically influenced settlement. With the

FIGURE 10. Branches and boards protect a clay dike at Bethany Beach, Delaware, and help hold the accumulation of sand. The dike was built by the State Highway Department. (Photograph by Robert W. Kates.)

deterioration in the quality of river water, the reduction in the adequacy of waterpower for modern industrial needs, the substitution of other modes of transport, and the advent of earth-moving machinery, much of the historical motivation for floodplain settlement has declined or even disappeared. Settlement itself has not declined, however, and continues, by inertia, to expand from its original foci.

Coasts possess some of the same advantages. Easy disposal of waste is an increasingly important asset of coastal location. The waste products from human activity, though still small in relation to the capacity of the ocean, present a growing problem, especially in estuaries and bays that provide a terminus for river-borne waste.

In most places the ocean is not considered a source of water supplies. Continuing technical advances in the process of desalinization, and the rising

cost of "fresh" water, suggest circumstances in which coastal locations could become highly favored, though not in the near future. Opportunity to develop power has also been absent in coastal areas. Modern technology, however, is changing this assessment of coastal resources. In the Rance estuary of northern France power stations are under construction that will use tidal fluctuations to turn the turbines.[23] Similar plans have been developed for Passamaquoddy Bay, on the Maine-New Brunswick border.[24]

The comparative advantage of level land cannot be said to exist to any great extent in coastal areas. But two other inducements are of great significance—access to the resources of the sea, and recreation. Fishing is of paramount importance and leads to the settlement of coastal areas that would otherwise be devoid of human habita-

FIGURE 11. Sand fences erected by the National Park Service at Cape Hatteras National Seashore, North Carolina. This view shows a six months' accumulation of sand. (Photograph by Robert W. Kates.)

tion. As in the location of coastal settlements directed primarily to trade, sites were formerly selected that would minimize the effect of storms. Advances in coastal engineering now permit greater flexibility and attention to markets in the construction and expansion of port facilities.

Undoubtedly the main attraction of coastal areas today lies in their opportunities for recreational use.[25] This is a relatively minor factor in riverine situations, but on the coast it is the dominant reason for the rapid expansion of settlement in the past decade. An important aspect of the recreational amenity is proximity to the sea. The most favored sites overlook a fine sandy beach, with easy access to warm, calm water. There is a large extent of such seacoast in the eastern United States, and a thin ribbon of settlement (only in specially favored places is coastal settlement dense, and rarely does it extend far inland) tends to spread out along it. A situation is rapidly being reached, therefore, in which all seafront lots suitable for recreational use will be developed to some degree, so that wherever a storm or an exceptionally high tide strikes, some damage will result.

In both riverine and coastal locations the particular damage patterns we have observed appear somewhat random. There is a systematic variation in some of the factors at a particular place, but when all factors are considered, a random pattern is perhaps the most accurate description of the resulting damage.

The effect of flood damage on property values and on the social and economic status of the communities affected is complex. There is evidence to indicate that after heavy damage a community may never completely recover its former status. Examples are the decline of Narragansett Pier, which is attributed to the hurricane damage in 1938, and the more rapid decline of floodplain neighborhoods reported by Roder in his study of Topeka, Kansas.[26] On the other hand, rather poorly constructed buildings or sea defenses may be replaced by more substantial structures after a storm. Evidence of high-quality reconstruction after the March, 1962, storm was seen along the New Jersey coast in August from Cape May to the Barnegat Light.

It has been observed[27] that on river floodplains awareness of flood hazard is, in part, a function of the number of floods experienced. Also, farmers are known to have a keener awareness of hazard than city dwellers.[28] Our impression, after interviews with a number of managers of coastal property, is that they too have a greater awareness of the hazards of storms than is common among city dwellers on river floodplains. Even the seasonal coast dwellers, who see the sea only in its usually more placid summer mood, seem to share this heightened awareness. The presence of the sea, the impact of the tide on the imagination, the increasingly widespread ownership of boats, and the minimal knowledge of the weather that may be associated with such ownership all contribute to this awareness. The city floodplain dweller with no knowledge of flood hazard is common.

The coast dweller without a little knowledge of storm potential has not been found.

Nevertheless, coast dwellers, while showing a more realistic appreciation of what is possible, tend to be optimistic in their assessments of the frequency, likelihood, or probability of storm damage. They also tend to underestimate the possible severity of such damage. It might be safe to forecast that increased coastal protection will develop an even greater sense of confidence, without a corresponding increase in security.

If our appraisal of the coastal flood problem is correct, it follows that there is urgent need for further research and for greater understanding not only of the nature and degree of the hazard itself but, especially, of the process and rate of settlement in hazard areas. Such understanding may help to promote a more rational approach to the management of coastal lands.

Footnotes

This paper constitutes a first report on a study of coastal occupance and hazards being conducted by C. W. Thornthwaite Associates with support from the Office of Naval Research under contract Nonr 4043 (00). The authors are consultants on the study. Grateful acknowledgement is due Gilbert F. White, Rodman E. Snead, and William F. Tanner, who made valuable comments on the draft of the paper.

1. William G. Hoyt and Walter B. Langbein: Floods (Princeton, N.J., 1955), pp. 77–90; Gilbert F. White and others: Changes in Urban Occupance of Flood Plains in the United States, *Univ. of Chicago, Dept. of Geogr., Research Paper No. 57*, 1958, pp. 1–11; "Water Resources Activities in the United States: Floods and Flood Control," *Committee Print No. 15*, Select Committee on National Water Resources, U.S. Senate, 86th Congress, 2nd Session, 1960, p. 18.

2. "Water Resources Activities" [see footnote 1 above], p. 29.

3. For details of the storm see John Q. Stewart: The Great Atlantic Coast Tides of 5–8 March 1962, *Weatherwise*, Vol. 15, 1962, pp. 116–120. See also D. L. Harris: Coastal Flooding by the Storm of March 5–7, 1962 (U. S. Weather Bureau, unpublished manuscript).

4. The concept of human adjustment was first clearly proposed and developed in geographic literature by Harlan H. Barrows in his presidential address before the Association of American Geographers: Geography as Human Ecology, *Annals Assn. of Amer. Geogrs.*, Vol. 13, 1923, pp. 1–14.

5. The classic statement of the range of human adjustments to flood hazard is Gilbert Fowler White's "Human Adjustment to Floods" (Dissertation, Ph.D., The University of Chicago, 1942; Chicago, 1945), pp. 128–204. Also published as *Univ. of Chicago, Dept. of Geogr., Research Paper No. 29*.

6. "Water Resources Activities" [see footnote 1 above], p. 10.

7. The Coast and Geodetic Survey estimates the total length of the tidal shoreline of the United States at 53,627 miles, exclusive of Alaska and Hawaii. If these states are included, the total is 88,633 miles.

8. For a guide to such study, the writers have drawn heavily on similar studies of flood-prone riverine areas. Two recent contributions are Ian Burton: Types of Agricultural Occupance of Flood Plains in the United States, *Univ. of Chicago, Dept. of*

Geogr., Research Paper No. 75, 1962; and Robert William Kates: Hazard and Choice Perception in Flood Plain Management, *ibid., Research Paper No. 78,* 1962.

9. Jean Gottmann: Mégalopolis: The Urbanized Northeastern Seaboard of the United States (New York, 1961).

10. See, for example, "Tidal Floods, Atlantic City and Vicinity, N.J.," *U. S. Geol. Survey Hydrologic Investigations Atlas HA–65,* 1962; "Farmington, Michigan, Flood Plain Information Report on the Upper River Rouge" (U. S. Army Corps of Engineers, Detroit, 1963); "A Program for Reducing the National Flood Damage Potential" [this describes the work of the TVA] (Committee on Public Works, U. S. Senate, 86th Congress, 1st Session, 1959). Such a map has recently been completed by Donald Crane for the Massachusetts Water Resources Commission (Donald A. Crane: Coastal Flooding in Barnstable County, Cape Cod, Massachusetts [Massachusetts Water Resources Commission, Boston, 1962]).

11. A discussion of the present state of knowledge may be found in Ian Burton and Robert W. Kates: The Perception of Natural Hazards in Resource Management, *Natural Resources Journ.,* Vol. 3, Albuquerque, 1964, pp. 412–441.

12. A selected bibliography of floodplain literature is included in Gilbert F. White, edit.: Papers on Flood Problems, *Univ. of Chicago, Dept. of Geogr., Research Paper No. 70,* 1961, pp. 222–228.

13. See, for example, Wolf Roder and Brian J. L. Berry: Associations between Expected Flood Damages and the Characteristics of Urban Flood Plains: A Factorial Analysis, *in* Papers on Flood Problems [see footnote 12 above], pp. 46–61.

14. Hilda Grieve: The Great Tide: The Story of the 1953 Flood Disaster in Essex (Chelmsford, 1959). See also the Report of the Departmental Committee on Coastal Flooding (Waverley Report), [*British Command Paper*] *Cmd. 9165,* London, 1954.

15. "Improvement of Storm Forecasting Procedures, Hearing before the Subcommittee on Oceanography of the Committee on Merchant Marine and Fisheries" (U. S. House of Representatives, 87th Congress, 2nd Session, 1962), pp. 2–3 and 22.

16. From the national view many indirect losses are simply transfer payments from flooded to non-flooded areas, rather than actual losses of goods and services. However, when no alternative amenity is available to recreation seekers, a real loss of the amenity is experienced for a time.

17. "Survey of Meteorological Factors Pertinent to Reduction of Loss of Life and Property in Hurricane Situations," *National Hurricane Research Project Rept. No. 5,* U. S. Weather Bureau, 1957, p. 16.

18. Fumio Tada and Masahiko Ohya: The Flood-Type and the Classification of the Topography, *in* Proceedings of IGU Regional Conference in Japan 1957 (Tokyo, 1959), pp. 192–196.

19. Burton, *op. cit.* [see footnote 8 above].

20. Roder and Berry, *op. cit.* [see footnote 13 above], p. 48.

21. See also Thomas Sheppard: The Lost Towns of the Yorkshire Coast (London, 1912).

22. John B. McAleer: Hurricane Protection of Narragansett Bay, *Military Engineer,* Vol. 54, 1962, pp. 112–115.

23. Information on the Rance Tidal Power Station may be found in the French *Technical Bulletin No. 2,* 1962, pp. 1–11, issued by the French Embassy, Ottawa. See also R. Gibrat: L'exploitation d'une usine marémotrice en régime d'économie de charbon, *Bull. Soc. Français des Électriciens,* Vol. 2, 1962, pp. 136–143.

24. "The International Passamaquoddy Tidal Power Project and Upper Saint John River Hydroelectric Power Development: Report to President John F. Kennedy . . .

[by the Passamaquoddy-Saint John River Study Committee]" (U. S. Department of the Interior, 1963).

25. The coastline of England and Wales has been thoroughly studied and classified according to quality of scenery, character of the coastal morphology, and patterns and type of human occupance. See the reports by J. A. Steers: Coastal Preservation and Planning, *Geogr. Journ.*, Vol. 104, 1944, pp. 7–27, and Vol. 107, 1946, pp. 57–60. See also "Seashore Preservation: Recreation Opportunities and Storm Damage" (U. S. Department of the Interior, National Park Service, Region 5, 1962).

26. Wolf Roder: Attitudes and Knowledge on the Topeka Flood Plain, *in* Papers on Flood Problems [see footnote 12 above], pp. 62–83.

27. Kates, *op. cit.* [see footnote 8 above].

28. Burton, *op. cit.* [see footnote 8 above].

twenty-six ◆ ◆ ◆ ◆ ◆ ◆ ◆ ◆ ◆ ◆ ◆ ◆

◆ JOSEPH SONNENFELD

Personality and Behavior in Environment

It has been apparent for some time that the environmental behavior of individuals and of groups is too variable to be accounted for simply by reference to different kinds of physiology or culture or environmental experience. Within any population there may be found risk-takers and risk-avoiders, those who are sensitive to environment and those who are insensitive to it, those who seek out the exotic and those who prefer the conventional, those who are mobile and migratory by disposition, and those who appear wedded to place. The population in which these types are found may be quite homogeneous in racial physiology; all may have been equally exposed to the traditional group culture; and all may have had equivalent experience with environment. Yet individuals will differ one from the other, and similar differences may be found among populations who

differ in race or culture or environmental experience. The behaviors may be differently manifest in different populations, but these will still be recognizable as involving risk, or sensitivity, or a restlessness which causes one to seek out the different in environment.

This tendency to behave in certain ways is a function of personality which is specific to behavior in the physical environment, and which implies a behavioral potential, a predisposition to behave in a certain and consistent fashion in environment.

The significance of personality for understanding variation in environmental behavior relates to the fact that environmental users and managers are in all cases behaving individuals liable to a variety of behavioral controls and influences. They are responsible for decisions concerning the allocation of

◆ SOURCE. Reproduced by permission from the *Proceedings* of the Association of American Geographers, Vol. 1, 1969, pp. 136–140.

limited spaces and resources, whether operating as individuals with designated decision-making authority, or as integral members of a group of interacting individuals collectively charged with the responsibility of making decisions, in critical or complex situations. At the extreme, whole community groups may also be involved in the decision-making process, if only as voters who are required to approve appropriations or elect officials to whom they subsequently relinquish part of their decision-making powers.

The significance of the individual was recognized by the Sprouts, who have been studying issues of environmentalism in politics and international relations. In their discussion of cognitive behavioralism, they described geopolitical decision-makers as basing their decisions ultimately on what was known or believed to exist in environment, with success being determined by the extent to which the cognitive or psychological environment of the decision-maker coincided with the operational environment representing the real world. But this is only a partial analysis of the geopolitical decision-maker, for his psychological environment is made up of more than a variably limited or complete knowledge of the real world. It is made up of a set of attitudes and expectations and predispositions to behavior which are a function of the individual's personality, a personality that predicts for environmental behavior within the context of the geographical environment as much as social personality predicts for social behavior within the context of the social environment.

The Nature of Environmental Personality

In a recent paper on the concept of the behavioral environment, I made a distinction between the geographic and non-geographic environment in behavioral terms. Neither the human/non-human distinction, nor the natural/artificial distinction was seen to have any functional relevance when behavior in environment was at issue. The only clear difference between the environments that geographers are concerned about, and that which most other social and behavioral scientists deal with, is the existence or non-existence of social interaction. I have defined the geographical behavioral environment as a non-interacting environment which may be physical, biotic or social. Human behavior—for example, such as results in environmental disturbance—may yield a reaction from the physical environment, but this is a reaction directed toward the disturbance rather than to the human source of the disturbance. Social interaction, by contrast, involves a relationship between individuals who are capable of behaving and adapting to each other, generally with expectation of a behavior in return.

Environmental personality can be distinguished from social personality in equivalent terms. While social personality may be defined as a predisposition to certain kinds of behavior within the context of the interacting social environment, environmental personality can be defined as a predisposition to behavior within the context of the non-interacting environment—the geographic environment of space, resources, and landscape. Making such a distinction implies differences in the behaviors directed toward the social environment by contrast with those directed toward the geographic environment. For example, an individual's reaction to risk inherent in people may be quite different from his reaction to risk inherent in the non-interacting environment; his sensitivity to beauty in people may be quite different from his sensitivity to beauty in nature; his submissiveness toward dominating people may have no equivalence in the behavior he directs toward "overpowering" elements of environment. In fact, there may or may not be consistency in social and environmental personalities: this remains to be tested.

Personality Measurement

A major problem in the study of personality is to get measures of its existence. Personality as such is not seen; it is inferred; it implies a potential to behave; it exists as a predisposition or predictor of behavior which must be inferred from actual behavior. Thus, personality exists as a hypothetical construct, the measure of which rests ultimately with behavior. Developing a measure of behavior potential which is amenable to testing against real world behaviors is therefore basic to the personality characterization of individuals and groups. Efforts over the last several months have been directed toward developing such a measure, more in the nature of an inventory, of certain basic personality attributes potentially predictive of behavior in environment.

The personality inventory which was finally put to test focuses on four categories of behavior or of personal characteristics which have implications for behavior: (1) *sensitivity to environment* based on a measure of complexity of perceptions; (2) *mobility in environment* based on preferences for certain environments, and the characterization of these in terms of "exoticness" and risk; (3) *control over environment* based on beliefs concerning the control exerted by environment over the human situation, as applied both to self and to others in a cognitive and prescriptive sense; and (4) *risk-taking in environment* as a function of attribution of risk to a systematic set of situations and activities involving some degree of hazard, which yields, in addition, a measure of the individual as risk-taker.

Briefly, the sensitivity measure is made up of a check list of terms descriptive of environment—positive, negative, and neutral in their connotations (e.g., annoying, artificial, attractive, barren, changing, etc.)—by which the respondent is asked to characterize his home environment. The number of items checked is not so much a measure of the complexity of the environment occupied as it is a measure of the complexity of perceptions and the level of sensitivity to environment. Preliminary results do, in fact, indicate that the number of items checked is *not* a function of the areal extent or "objective complexity" of the home environment being characterized; the consistency in number of items checked by individuals who base their ratings on quite different environments, and, similarly, the inconsistency in the number of items checked by those who occupy essentially similar environments, is striking.

The mobility measure suggesting a tourist and possibly migration potential gives indications of being one of the more productive of measures. This measure is obtained by contrasting the respondent's rankings of a set of ten real world locations (Alaska, East Africa, Florida, Greenwich Village, Mediterranean Coast, Mexico, Paris, Russia, Swiss Alps, Tahiti) according to those the respondent would most and least like to visit, in the one case, and those he would most and least prefer to live in on a long-term basis in the other. In addition, these same locations are ranked in terms of risk and exotic character. These rankings are then compared with the preference rankings in order to get indications of the importance of the exotic and environmental risk as motivations—positive and negative—for travel and residential choices. Using each respondent's own risk and exotic rankings eliminates the problem of differences in the exotic and risk characterizations of locations by different individuals, the existence of which has been separately verified.

Attitudes relating to the control exerted by environment over individual and group behavior is determined by choices from a set of possible reactions to the occurrence of natural hazard in environment: suggesting, alternately, that it is best (a) to avoid areas containing natural hazards; (b) to work harder to reduce the risks; (c) to learn to live with natural hazards; (d) or to be thankful for the excitement and challenge that hazards in environment

provide. Not only does the individual indicate which of these most accurately describes his own position, but also that which he thinks others consider to be their position, as well as what he thinks ought to be the "proper" attitude toward natural hazards in environment.

Finally, risk-taking potential is determined by a variety of measures, including: (a) an index based on risk attributed to certain residential situations, occupations, sports activities, and military specialties, together with an indication of which of the activities or situations the respondent would like to participate in, as well as those he would definitely prefer to avoid; and (b) an index based on risk attributed to a set of normal experiences (traffic, recreational, and medical contexts, for the most part) in which the respondent has previously been involved. The extent to which individuals engage in these behaviors is also scaled, to provide a measure of actual risk-taking behavior. Implicit is the assumption that a measure of risk-taking potential requires not only an indication of what risks the individual normally takes, but also whether or not he is aware that he is taking risks.

Inventories have been completed by a mixed sample of some 350 respondents and data analysis is now in progress. Populations are initially being compared by age, sex, education, environmental experience, residence, occupation, and marital status. Following this, rankings on the various indices (sensitivity, mobility, risk) will be used to establish quartile populations. These will be treated as representing behavior or personality types, and analyzed for characteristics distinguishing the quartile extremes: the more and less sensitive to environment, the risk-takers and risk-avoiders, the stimulus seekers and stimulus avoiders, and so on.

The results so far suggest that the measures are distinguishing what they are supposed to be distinguishing, in the sense that population differences that one might have predicted are being verified. However, a number of less obvious kinds of differences are also becoming apparent.

Thus, the mobility index in which locations are ranked according to residential and visiting preferences and then compared with exotic and risk attributes, showed group differences in practically all dimensions of population analysis. The females, for example, were more consistent than the males in their ranking of locations for both visiting and longer-term residence, as well as more conventional by indicating that they would avoid those places they characterized as risky and as exotic to a greater extent than did the males.

Among age groups, there was no consistent difference between the places most preferred for visiting and those preferred for longer-term residence, but it was clear that the more exotic and more risky places became less attractive with increasing age.

Preferences also differed according to level of schooling completed. Those with the least schooling preferred places less exotic and risky and were more consistent in wanting to live in the kinds of places they would also like to visit; the more educated by contrast were much less consistent in their preference for visiting and longer-term

residences, and much more attracted to risk and the exotic in environment.

Occupational groups also varied, though not always in obvious ways. Those classified in creative occupations were apparently the most exotic-preferring, while the medical types were the most risk-preferring in terms of the places they most wanted to visit. The group of research scientists and engineers (actual and potential) had the most contrasting set of rankings for visiting and residential locations (high tourist potential), but their preference for the exotic and risky environments varied about the norm; if they were the most curious in terms of a desire to see places different from those in which they wanted to reside permanently, the source of the curiosity was a stimulus or differentness not necessarily exotic or risky in nature. Interestingly, business, engineering, and military types were—next to the creative group—the most exotic preferring in terms of the places they ranked as most desirable for visiting; but they were also the most risk avoiding in their preferences.

The results obtained from different residential groups were also rather interesting. Those currently living in the denser urban areas were the most preferring of places to visit different from those which they preferred to live in on a long-term basis; they were also the most preferring of exotic locations for their visiting. This was especially the case for those who listed the megalopolis or city (in apartment houses) as the place of current residence. Those who listed childhood residences in cities had essentially similar tastes, but with a striking preference for visiting the more exotic and risky locations. When groups were distinguished according to preferred residence, the city types stood out again as preferring the more exotic environments for visiting. That group which chose farms as the preferred residence were closest of all other groups to the megalopolis types in wanting to visit what they characterized as the more exotic and risky environments. Yet those who lived on farms during their childhood and those who currently were living on farms, were among the least interested in visiting places different from those they wanted for long-term residence, and about average in their desire to see the riskier and more exotic environments.

Residential groups also proved distinctive on the "environmental sensitivity" index. Those who either were residing or who would prefer residing in urban areas, scored the highest on this index; i.e. they checked off more descriptive terms to characterize their home environment than did other residential groups. Those who preferred farms for living also scored relatively high on this index. Surprisingly, however, those who derived from megalopolis or city apartment environments during childhood, though relatively few in number (10), ranked the lowest on the sensitivity index. Since this group also ranked high in wanting to see places different from those they preferred for residence, their lesser sensitivity may be the result of a sensory adaptation to their own environment. Yet the much higher rating on the sensitivity scale of those who currently live in urban settings and/or who prefer such settings is striking, and suggests

that more than adaptation to local conditions is at issue. Actually, rural types did not fare so badly on the sensitivity scale, but small town as well as large town living seemed to yield individuals ranking low on the sensitivity scale.

Analysis of the risk scale is only partially completed, but differences again are apparent. For example, with the exception of recreational activities, the males generally seem less aware of risk than the females. In addition, the young differ from the older groups in attributing less risk to the variably hazardous occupations and recreation activities listed. The more educated seem generally to perceive less risk in the residential settings, occupations, and military activities listed than do those with less schooling; they also were more interested in experiencing more of the situations and activities than were those with less schooling. At the other extreme, the older groups indicated that they definitely would avoid more of the risk situations and activities than did the young; and similarly, the less schooled were more risk-avoiding than those with more schooling.

The only data on risk-potential at the time of writing, based on the attribution of risk to normally experienced situations and activities, and respondents' behaviors in respect to these, suggest that the older groups both perceive greater risk and behave consistently by taking fewer risks than is the case with the younger age groups. Less consistently, the females are much more apprehensive of risk than males, but appear to be equal to the males as risk-takers. Only partial data are available on the risk-taking behavior of the various occupation groups. These suggest that production workers (factory, agricultural types) take the greatest risks, with the military and creative types close behind; the technical-engineer and medical types appear to be the least risk-taking of occupational types.

None of the above represents final conclusions, since data analysis is far from complete. However, the data clearly are suggestive of the existence of real group differences in environmental behavior. And while differences appear as a function of age, sex, and other group characteristics, each of these groups contains individuals who differ from the norm at more and less extreme levels. There is clearly need to inquire into the nature of the extreme types; at this stage, these represent potential personality types, which, I am predicting, will be found to occur among most populations. This is central to the concept of environmental personality as a source of both within and between group differences as well as of between group similarities. Yet the existence of age and residential group differences suggest an important dynamic dimension to personality development that begs of further examination and testing.

twenty-seven

JULIAN WOLPERT ◆

Migration as an Adjustment to Environmental Stress

Introduction

Each year, one out of five American families change their place of residence. Common explanations for these movements revolve around the attractions of new economic and social opportunities, climes, or landscapes and repulsion from areas of limited opportunity or negative milieus (7). Yet the migration record is filled with cases of reshuffling exchanges between similar environments. Thus deterministic hypotheses based upon economic, climatic, aesthetic, and other causes are only partial and do not correspond to any inherent determinism in migration behavior.

The usual procedures in migration analysis have been to either: (1) assume a constant environment and to observe migration behavior by individuals distributed among demographic subgroups—the study of migration dif-ferentials which focus usually upon one attribute at a time (age, race, sex, education, et cetera), or (2) assume a constant population and observe variations in migration between places which differ in terms of intervening distance, economic characteristics or amenities. A third procedure is very rare—relating migration behavior simultaneously to variations in people and places.

Relatively few of the crucial behavior issues have been examined or noted in most of the research in this area, which appears to be directed solely at obtaining the maximum possible "explanation" in a regression sense. This analysis returns to primitive notions in examining the evaluation process which precedes the decision to move or stay. The model which is suggested reflects an attempt to structure the ecological relationship between individuals and their social and physical

◆ **SOURCE.** Reprinted by permission from *Journal of Social Issues*, Vol. 22, 1966, pp. 92–102.

environment on a "continuum of *harmony*" in the matching of individuals to sites. Emphasis in the model is given to the urban environment and most especially to situations of urban threat and stress.

Stress and Strain

Perhaps all of man's *creative* efforts occur under moderate degrees of stress. We shall limit our notion of stress, however, to "noxious" or potentially "noxious" environmental forces pressing upon the individual.[1] *Strain*, on the other hand, refers to the individual's reaction to the stress. More precisely then, we shall be dealing with the implications of locational decisions by individuals and groups under strain which has been caused by noxious environmental forces.

Langner cites a good operational definition of stress which is given by Engel:

> *a stress may be any influence, whether it arises from the internal environment or the external environment, which interferes with the satisfaction of basic needs or which disturbs or threatens to disturb the stable equilibrium.*

Langner also notes Engel's emphasis on the relative impact of stress, which depends upon the strength of the organism, or its capacity to deal with a particular force at a particular time. Thus, mediating between stress and strain are personality factors, such as the cumulative physical, emotional and social experiences of the individual combined with his endowment.

The stress-strain relationship may be considered in terms of stress tolerance models (4, pp. 229–232). In linear form strain is a function of stress with the slope parameter describing the degree of stress tolerance and the intercept a minimal threshold. The concept may be broadened to incorporate the positive counterpart to stress and strain, which may be termed respectively positive forces and slack. Positive forces and stressors are analogous in this discussion respectively to environmental amenities and disamenities. The simplest linear case without a threshold is illustrated in Figure 1a as Line A which could represent a clean-polluted dimension for an individual's environment. Slack and strain are seen as directly proportional to the magnitude of pollution or its positive counterpart, cleanliness. Line B could illustrate a danger-security dimension in which a danger threshold must be exceeded before strain is induced and some danger (or excitement) has a positive impact.

The notion of slack, of course, has its physical counterpart in terms of a cushion or buffer, a prerequisite for flexibility which must be taken up before stress may induce a strain effect. The concept has been used, also, in the literature of organizational theory by Cyert and March (1, pp. 36–38) to refer to "resources in excess of demands." Slack is then the consequence of an amenity—the simple linear form with positive slope is an indication that the individual is further cushioned by a reservoir of slack with increments of amenity levels.

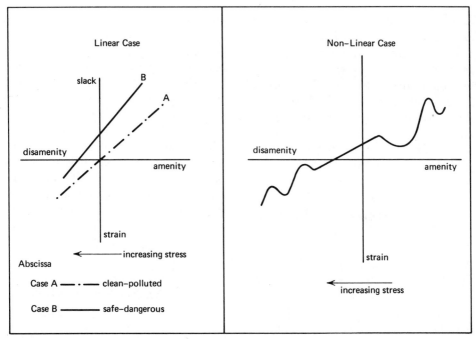

FIGURE 1a.   FIGURE 1b.

Extending the notion to a long run analysis requires the replacement of the linear form by a step function, which may also be nonlinear, to incorporate the functioning of coping mechanisms (4, pp. 232 ff.). (Fig. 1b). Here the person copes with the stress with some success and his strain level is actually reduced until a further threshold is reached requiring a new coping procedure. The coping mechanism for amenities appears not to have received attention in the literature, but coping behavior for stresses is quite well documented. Kahn, *et al.* (4, p. 234), suggest that:

The person who confronts an environmental stress may be viewed as having three interrelated tasks to accomplish: (1) to deal with objective situation so as to reduce or eliminate its stressful characteristics, that is, to resolve the core problem, (2) to deal with the tension and negative emotions which the stress arouses in him, and (3) to deal with secondary or derivative problems which may be created by his efforts to cope with the stress or its emotional consequences.

Environmental stress, whether generated by inter-personal relations or by uncontrollable fluctuations in the physical world, is always present in the action space of individuals and its

420   ENVIRONMENTAL DETERIORATION   ♦ ♦ ♦ ♦ ♦ ♦ ♦ ♦ ♦ ♦ ♦ ♦ ♦ ♦ ♦ ♦ ♦ ♦ ♦

effect plays some role in decision behavior. The omnipresence of moderate stress is hardly noticeable in man's action; and it has even been suggested that some stress may be conducive to relatively higher performance levels and innovative behavior. The concern, in this analysis, is not with these minor doses of pressure, but with the noxious environmental influences which are far-reaching in terms of the potential strain placed upon decision makers.

The Mover-Stayer Problem Under Stress

In an earlier paper the individual's search for alternative courses of action was characterized as involving essentially a sampling process. This process may be expected to exhibit significant spatial bias in favor of more prominent or conspicuous alternatives but typically the search for places to move to involves sequential probing, then evaluation, followed by additional probing, etc. A moderate degree of stress is usually helpful in encouraging such search behavior—uncertainty without anxiety is perhaps the most conducive environment to productive work. Under conditions of abnormal stress, however, during periods of crisis decision-making, evidence suggests that there is a construction of perceived choices, increased rate of error, stereotyped responses, disorganized activity, problem-solving rigidity, reduction in the focus of attention in both time and space, and distortion of time and space perspectives (cf. 3), (2). In the absence of strain, the nature of effectiveness of an

individual's evaluation of his own habitat as opposed to alternative sites may be considered as the baseline for observing crisis situations.

Strain may induce additional bias into the migration decision by (perhaps) triggering off a hasty decision to move, encouraging a disorganized search for other places to go, or fixation on a single destination place when closer examination of several alternatives is more beneficial. It is suggested, therefore, in addition to the push and pull forces which may be latent in the migrational decision, the triggering off of *that* decision may frequently be associated with a stress impetus.

An Ecological Model of Migration Decision

We shall begin with an ecological model describing relationships of individuals to elements of their immediate environmental habitat and other conspicuous places. At critical points of the life cycle, hypothetical stressors will be introduced and an attempt will be made to trace out the consequences of the resulting strain on adjustment processes with respect to that action space. The adjustment mechanisms will be analysed in terms of the mover-stayer problem. Implied (constantly) in the analysis is that individuals' social and physical needs are expressed as a set of demands from the environment mixing with positive and/or stressful impulses from a set of places in the individual's action space. These together generate the fulfillment of needs and/or generation of frustration with respect to individual places which sparks the mover-stayer decision.

It does not appear unreasonable to suggest that this process tends toward equilibrium in the matching of individuals to neighborhoods. Thus, we may talk about a middle-class neighborhood, and there is considerable agreement about the structure and attributes of such a neighborhood, that is quite separate and apart from its inhabitants. Or neighborhoods may reflect the qualities of upwardly rising but lower status individuals. A not unfamiliar sight on certain blocks of lower status metropolitan areas is the rather unreal collection of very well tended homes accompanied by a series of signs with the plea "keep our block beautiful." In this case, individuals and the neighborhood environment may develop over time in a parallel fashion, so that a harmony of consensus is maintained between the aspirations of individuals and the image attainments of their block. To a large extent, the harmony creates fertile ground for attachments and the desire to stay. The downwardly mobile or impatient risers would be more likely to feel ill at ease with the consensus and seek environments which match their own aspirations. Movers, therefore, may be found predominantly among those who are undergoing a change in status or who anticipate disharmony with the implied status of their present residence.

Assuming that the purpose of the locational decision is to alter the future in some way, stayers may be said to reject the anticipated consequences of moving to another environment. Movers, on the other hand, wish to alter the anticipated consequences of not moving. Of course, in a normative analysis, i.e., based upon the assumption of perfect knowledge, no uncertainty and a single-valued goal function of maximizing place utility, an optimal residence distribution may be specified, one that would tend to locate persons in the best possible matching system with given sites, subject, of course, to constraints upon cost, accessibility, et cetera. The matching construct is still relevant in a non-normative behavioral analysis, although other constraints become relevant, the same tendency toward an equilibrium of harmony will occur, but perhaps after a longer time delay.

The Ecological Model

In the highly simplified ecological situation to which we turn, the individual born in place A continues to dwell there throughout his entire life span. There is one other neighboring place, B, with which he had some contact but A is always more prominent than B in his action space.

To his biological inheritance or genetic endowment, there are added early positive and stressful elements from his social and nonsocial environment which shape his personality and which help to mold his actions and attitudes at later times. He also contributes positive elements as well as stress to his environment and feedback cycles are generated. A filtering process, highly related to age and Socio-Economic Status, translates the environmental stress into strain impact and positive forces into slack (6).

As development through the life cycle takes place, potentially noxious elements of places A and B become more conspicuous. The individual may attempt to minimize his exposure to these noxious elements or disamenities and maximize exposure to the positive factors to reduce strain. He may be able to reduce the stress to more moderate proportions or eliminate it entirely.

Individuals vary in their ability to control, eliminate or reduce noxious influences in their environment. For example, the city fathers may act to reduce blight, pollution and reduce noise levels, but the slum dwellers will have little impact on his attempts. Or the individual may accept a negative environment of relative stability rather than face the stress which may be associated with unpredictable change (1, pp. 119 ff.). For the individual under study, the positive factors continually dwarf the stressful elements and there is little incentive for moving to B where, upon closer examination, the grass may not be greener.

The composite environment at A is partitioned into separate components while B is known in less detail. Thus, the intertwining, but distinct strands of environmental components at A are more likely perceived in terms of their individual or combinatory stressful or positive influences. The strands at A each become prominent at various life cycle stages and produce complex reactions affecting the personality and decision behavior.

Certain examples of noxious environmental forces appear to be omnipresent in major urban centers. Among those which have been most commonly suggested are: traffic congestion, blight, air and water pollution, lawlessness, lack of open spaces, and noise levels. As is readily apparent, each of these sources of possible stress to urban dwellers would vary in their magnitude for different profile groups, as would the responses, as well. The flight to the suburbs of families with young children is perhaps illustrative of a common response. At a period of the life cycle marked by relative vulnerability to stressful elements which can be avoided, the relative attractiveness of place B (in a suburb in this case) becomes more prominent.

Implied by the ecological model is that mismatching between the individual and his habitat may induce an escalation of stress and strain, a locking in on a process which accentuates the disharmony. The converse process may also occur, whose consequences are to strengthen the attachments to places that may be far from suitable. Demographic and other dimensions play an extremely important role here in affecting tolerance levels for various environmental influences. Not only do stresses vary in their susceptibility to control by the individual, but individuals themselves vary in terms of their ability to remove or lessen the pressure from sources of stress. As Srole points out (8), midtown Manhattan is viewed alternatively as a place for the ambitious and the social climbers, and as a slum environment, a home for the poor which breeds further poverty and delinquency. The tensions of city life, the physical crowdedness, the emotional isolation, the breakneck speed, the tough and fierce competition act so as to force anxiety upon all life.

The suburbanization process does have as its consequence the removal of individual and family units from the pressures which have been mentioned. This is true also for the high-rise apartment houses, the vertical suburbs which appear to be growing relatively in importance in the cores of metropolitan areas. The horizontal and the vertical suburbs compete with one another and in a parallel manner to assure prospective residents of relief from the blatant city core pressures. Faced with urban pressures, one common reaction is a reduction of alternatives to the position that "one is forced to move." That is, stress may induce an underestimation of available alternatives and fixation on the prominent alternative of a move to the vertical or horizontal suburbs. As has frequently been noted, those whose position and status would permit reducing or eliminating noxious urban influences or preventing their escalation are the same groups whose perceived choices are the most constricted.

A preliminary investigation has been made of *block busting,* i.e., attempts by Negroes to move into previously all-white neighborhoods. This phenomenon was studied within two rather similar neighborhoods of a large metropolitan area. A more complete documentation of findings and conclusions will be published shortly, but some tentative conclusions may be noted here. Both neighborhoods consist of rather substantial single family and semi-detached homes with 1950 median values approximating $15,000 in both areas. Classic block busting attempts were enormously successful in neighborhood A which witnessed an almost complete population turnover within

three years. Lacking effective organization, homeowners narrowed their perceived choice of alternatives to the dissonant situation of "having to move." A sample of those displaced were interviewed within the vertical and horizontal suburbs where they had relocated. The decision to move had been accompanied by stress and reinforced by the consensus of neighbors. When asked about the attributes of their new housing, the overwhelming pattern of response focused upon relief from a noxious environment.

In the control neighborhood, effective homeowner organization actively countermanded block busting attempts. In place of the reduction to the single alternative of the dissonant situation, a range of several choices were investigated and maintained as prominent. The potential stress was met objectively—relatively little relocation occurred and proportional integration was introduced inhibiting a consensus perception of mismatching of the residents to their immediate environment. Additional inferences could be drawn from our ecological model and its further elaborations but because of the extraordinary complexity of the functional relationships which may be introduced, we prefer instead to incorporate the major dimensions of the processes within a simplified system model.

Outline of the Ecological System Model

Some preliminary attempt may be made to place the contents and latent implications of the analysis into a systems context (5). In this first trial, there are merely two components: the individual and the place, with the interaction confined to points of contact or interfaces which are called terminals. The initial problem is that of establishing the component models, which may be expressed in this simplified general case in the form of linear difference equations of the format:

$$
\begin{bmatrix} x_1(n+1) \\ x_2(n+1) \\ x_3(n+1) \end{bmatrix} = \begin{bmatrix} P_{11} P_{12} P_{13} \\ P_{21} P_{22} P_{23} \\ P_{31} P_{32} P_{33} \end{bmatrix} \begin{bmatrix} x_1(n) \\ x_2(n) \\ x_3(n) \end{bmatrix} + \begin{bmatrix} q_{11} q_{12} q_{13} \\ q_{21} q_{22} q_{23} \\ q_{31} q_{32} q_{33} \end{bmatrix} \begin{bmatrix} y_1(n) \\ y_1(n) \\ y_1(n) \end{bmatrix}
$$

where $x_1(n)$ and $y_1(n)$ represent the values of the propensity variables and flow variables, respectively at the discrete points in time $t = nT$. The state vector, of the component $X(n+1)$ at time $t = nT$, is then shown as a function of the previous state $X(n)$ and the flows $Y(n)$. The P and Q matrices represent respectively the transition and excitation matrices. The expression, in matrix format, may then be written as:

$$X(n+1) = PX(n) + QY(n)$$

The diagramatic presentation of the ecological model may be translated into the concise set of equivalent matrix operations

$$A_t = L \cdot A_{t-1} + P_1 S_r + \cdots$$

where the vector A_t is a listing of the attributes of individual i, the matrix L specifies the life cycles coefficients as they modify the set of n attributes during one time interval, the A_{t-1} vector lists the attributes at the previous time period, the matrix P_r, indicates the coefficients of potential susceptibility of the individual to positive and stressful environmental elements at place r, depending upon his set of n attributes,

and S_r, is a vector of positive and/or stressful environmental forces acting on the individual with his set of n attributes. Then the product of $L \cdot A$ indicates the development forces which modify the individuals' attributes between time increments and the product of $P \cdot S$ refers to the additive influence on attributes which occur as a result of positive or stressful effects from the environment. Environmental effects will be felt that occur in all r places which are conspicuous to him. Only the effect of these elements will be of less consequence to him in proportion to their generalized distance from him.

The convenience of the operations of matrix multiplication and addition provide a suitable vehicle for structuring the developmental changes over time. The format also illustrates what operations occur once the proper coefficients, which have been estimated from empirical study, are inserted. Let us assume, for example, that the attribute set (A_{t-1}) contains such elements as status and status consistency, n achievement, power, etc., which have been scaled, relatively. These individual characteristics may undergo change over time purely in a developmental sense (implied by zeros in the off-diagonals of the matrix L) or may be modified by the interaction of single or groups of the other characteristics as they are modified over time (non-zero coefficients in the off-diagonals of L). Similarly, in the incremental portion of the model, the matrix format provides a convenient shorthand for specifying data needs as well as manipulation of independent or interacting elements.

In order to specify the complement in feedback relationship, the state model of the environment may also be reduced to a corresponding set of matrix operations

$$A_{r_t} = L_r \cdot A_{r_{t-1}} + P_{ri} \cdot S_i$$

where the A vectors indicate a set of place attributes as an environment for individuals with given attributes for the two time periods, the matrix L specifies the life cycle coefficients of place r which are time-dependent modifiers, the S_i vector is a listing of the positive and/or stressful influences generated by individuals in the community and acting upon the n attributes of the place, the P_{ri} matrix contains the coefficients of potential susceptibility or tolerance of the place to positive and stressful forces from the individuals in the community.

The state models provide a convenient and concise method of illustrating the interacting elements of the ecological framework and of identifying the required data for an empirical test. In this simplified preliminary statement, a linear format has been used but a non-linear form may be justifiable.

The state vector or attribute set for individuals at any time must be considered as a cumulative resultant of all prior environmental influences plus the genetic endowment that will govern the method by which stress is translated into strain or positive forces into slack. The attribute set, may, of course, not be exhaustive but ideally the elements must be independent, as analogous to

"factors." Identification and measurement of relevant parameters are the major problems here.

In the absence of pronounced stress, that is, if the S vector values cluster about zero, the elements in the L matrix will govern the change in attributes over time. The set of positive and stressful factors could be measured and specified in the S vector as plus or minus intensity levels; a relative scale for sets of places could be most helpful here. Again, empirical study would be necessary to identify prominent environmental influences (amenities and disamenities) which are independent and to specify the relevant intensities. Some suggestions for possible environmental dimensions relevant to large metropolitan areas are factors such as:

1. noisy-tranquil
2. danger-security
3. green-gray
4. exciting-dull
5. open-congested
6. information overload-underload

As indicated, clustering of these influences near zero denotes a relatively passive environment. Moderate negative levels may have a beneficial effect upon certain of the attribute elements. Of primary concern here are the extreme situations of highly positive or negative values on single entries or combinations. Separate vectors of environmental influences may be specified for each of the r places with which the individual has contact, i.e., different neighborhoods, cities or other areal units characterized by distinct patterns of stress and/or positive environmental influences.

The magnitude of environmental impact on the attribute set or the personality is governed not only by the environment intensity as specified in the S vector but by the filter coefficients in the P matrix. These determine the susceptibility to or tolerances for stress or positive influences, while the $P \cdot S$ product may be regarded as a black box whose output is strain and/or slack which is added to the $L \cdot A_{t-1}$ product to provide the cumulative attribute set. Again, different P matrices must be assigned for each place so as to reflect the variations in tolerances for different places which are relatively more or less conspicuous in the individual's action space. A simplification which may have some validity is that the tolerance entries vary as some function of the attribute set. The measurement problem is severe here and workable estimations would require substantial empirical probing.

The complementary place model has obvious parallels with the model for the individual. The system generates place attribute levels which may be compared with the output of the individual model to check for ecological harmony. In this case, the A vectors specify those cumulative attribute sets for places for the two periods. The L matrix contains the development coefficients in the absence of pronounced stress or positive influence from individuals, i.e., with mainly low values in the S vector. The coefficients in the P matrix describe the susceptibility or tolerances of the place attributes to the influence of individuals. Individuals will vary in terms of their relative impact on the various place attributes.

Hopefully, a reasonable basis may be found for classifying the individuals into relatively homogeneous categories in order to aggregate the micro-impacts.

It is premature to suggest a mathematical model of the interconnection pattern between components. The models for the components are still sufficiently unstructured and important gaps exist in the measurement and estimation of coefficients so as to preclude a full statement of the system model at this time. But the systems approach offers many advantages by providing a more disciplined framework within which to study the complex set of dynamic and interacting forces that can only be inadequately treated in the more common push-pull hypotheses of migration behavior.

Footnotes

1. An excellent discussion of the literature on stress, strain and related concepts which is only partly summarized here may be found in the volumes of the Midtown Manhattan Study.

References

1. Cyert, R. M. and J. G. March. *A Behavioral Theory of the Firm*. Englewood Cliffs, New Jersey: Prentice-Hall, 1963, 36–38.
2. Holsti, O. R. Perceptions of time, perceptions of alternatives and pattern communication as factors in crises decision-making. *Papers of the Peace Research Society*, 1965, 3, 79–120.
3. Horvath, F. E. Psychological stress: a review of definitions and experimental research. *General Systems Yearbook*, 1959, **IV**, 203–230.

4. Kahn, R. L., *et al. Organizational stress.* New York: John Wiley, 1964, 229–232.

5. Koenig, H. E. Mathematical models of socio-economic systems. *IEEE Trans. on System Science and Cybernetics,* in press.

6. Langner, T. S. and S. T. Michael. *Life Stress and Mental Health,* Vol. II. New York: Macmillan, 1963.

7. Shryock, H. S., Jr. *Population mobility within the United States.* Community and Family Study Center, University of Chicago, 1964.

8. Srole, L., T. S. Langner, *et al. Mental Health in the Metropolis,* Vol. I. New York: McGraw-Hill, 1962.

9. Wolpert, J. Behavioral aspects of the decision to migrate. *Papers, Regional Science Association,* XV, 1965.

twenty-eight ◆ ◆ ◆ ◆ ◆ ◆ ◆ ◆ ◆ ◆

◆ WILLIAM M. ROSS

The Management of International Common Property Resources

The exploitation of international common property resources[1] is almost universally regarded by national governments in the light of potential contributions to their economies. Exploitation of these resources by noncontiguous nations has brought about a need for international management. However, most of the international political institutions that manage common property resources are restricted in scope. They have developed only when unrestricted exploitation would ultimately have lowered the quality or threatened the survival of the resource. Nations have not been able to maximize exploitation of resources by cooperating with other countries, but they have been able to minimize losses through international management.

A consideration of common property resources can be approached in two ways. The exploitation of such products as oil and fish represents *extraction* of resources from the environment. On the other hand, some industrial processes contribute to the deterioration of environmental quality by the *addition* of pollutants to the environment. The critical difference between them is that the extractive use, though at times uneconomical, adds directly to man's betterment, whereas the addition of pollutants contributes only to a decline in the quality of the environment and to an increase in treatment costs for subsequent users of the resource. These contrasting activities, however, present similar management difficulties.

Common property resources are shared by many individuals or nations; they are not legally alienated to individuals, firms, or nations, for several reasons. Often a national desire to claim rights to a resource is compli-

◆ SOURCE.   Reprinted by permission from the *Geographical Review*, Vol. 61, 1971, pp. 325–338, copyrighted by the American Geographical Society of New York.

cated or deterred by international conventions designed to prevent individual ownership, by the mobility and fluidity of the resource, or by the anticipation of returns from exploitation that are lower than the social, political, and economic costs of alienating the rights. Four fundamental problems arise when rights are not alienated and when "freedom in the commons" is condoned.[2] The resource tends to be used too quickly and is often depleted. Exploitation may be inefficient, employing more labor and capital than is required or justified by the economic rent that is derived. Frequently, there is congestion among users of the resource. Finally, the economic and legal systems have no way of accounting for externalities or "extra-party" costs.[3]

International agreements, whether bilateral or multilateral, have seldom attacked or solved more than one of the problems created by free access to a common property resource. Treaties limiting international organizations to data collection and research while failing to provide enforcement procedures have made the organizations impotent to deal with problems created by free access. These agreements attempt to maintain maximum sustained physical yield or to prevent depletion. International institutions that oversee world fisheries demonstrate the limited success of such management and may provide insights into dealing with air and water resources that are the transferring agents of destructive environmental pollutants. Disagreements over resources of the deep ocean floor illustrate the difficulties of instituting international management when nation-

states have not agreed on a legal framework to delineate jurisdiction over a common property resource. Yet improved management of the commons depends on the ability to formulate aims, to designate those responsible for overuse or misuse, to select the individuals to be restricted, and to develop the means of restriction and enforcement.

International Fisheries Management

International fisheries have long been controlled. Many treaties clarify fishing rights and privileges, provide research coordination, regulate stocks, set catch quotas, and establish regional management pacts. However, no group has direct control over fishery stocks and methods of exploitation. Most international organizations can only advise national governments, which must approve changes in management regulations. The most successful treaties have had a limited number of participating nations, and the problems have been clearly specified.

Most treaties clarify the rights of citizens of one state to fish in the waters contiguous to other states. The pacts may acknowledge historic rights in the area, provide for bait-storage facilities, permit landings for replacement of supplies, and deal with other associated rights. The treaties have encouraged exploitation by noncontiguous states, though these nations do not assume responsibility for managing the resource. Such treaties seldom allow for additional entrants, and their international application is therefore limited. They do not really help solve the depletion problem typical of many fisheries, nor do they provide for improving economic efficiency in the industry.[4]

Research treaties designed to investigate fishery habits are a logical prelude to more formal arrangements for management; for insufficient knowledge about life cycles of fishery species can cause numerous difficulties if management procedures are instituted before data are acquired. For example, under the North Pacific Fisheries Convention among Canada, Japan, and the United States, Japan was compelled to abstain from salmon fishing west of 175° W. When the agreement was signed, scientists believed that North American salmon could not possibly migrate west of the abstention line. Later research proved the assumption false, but since Japan refuses to accept the United States contention that Japanese fishing is one cause of declining salmon runs in Alaska, the treaty has not been altered.[5] And without the unanimous consent of the three contracting parties the abstention line cannot be changed.

Although most fishery research has been undertaken by national governments, the United Nations has contributed a great deal by organizing international research. The Food and Agriculture Organization (FAO) has sponsored meetings such as the 1955 International Technical Conference on the Conservation of the Living Resources of the Sea. It has also helped developing nations in Asia and Africa to formulate research programs. Through regional councils[6] such as those for the Indo-Pacific, the Mediterranean, and the West African and Southeast African Atlantic coasts, the FAO has attempted to avoid duplica-

tion by providing a framework in which several developing countries with similar fisheries can undertake research. The pooling of research has been moderately successful, but like many pacts limited to research coordination, it has not yet resulted in many multilateral management pacts.

Stock and quota treaties have not been as numerous as those that clarify rights or coordinate research, though they have been useful in arresting the depletion of threatened stocks. Often treaties have been signed only when it became apparent that continued free entry would result in species extinction. The tortuous deliberations over the North Pacific Fur Seal Convention in the early twentieth century demonstrate these difficulties. Proposals for the complete restriction of sealing were rejected in favor of delegating the harvesting rights to the United States and the Soviet Union who shared the returns with Japan, Great Britain, and, later, Canada as well.[7] The Soviet Union and the United States undertook to exploit the fishery under rules laid down by the regulatory commission. Exploitation methods were left to the signatories, but restrictions were placed on the number of seals caught. The treaty has operated successfully since 1911, and stocks have increased, though they are still below nineteenth-century levels. This pact has not been an international prototype, however; it is still the only agreement whereby the conservation efforts of two nations are shared with others.

INTERNATIONAL AGREEMENTS

The International Pacific Halibut Commission has tacit power to regulate layoffs (periods when fishing is prohibited) and quotas for United States and Canadian halibut vessels. As a result of the commission's detailed research, sound physical management, and care to consult industry representatives before issuing regulations, both governments now merely endorse its recommendations. Each year the commission sets an upper limit on the number of halibut to be taken from different areas of the North Pacific, but it does not apportion the catch. Nationals of both countries are free to take as many halibut as possible within the limits set for the fishery. Since ratification of the treaty neither nation has dominated the fishery. If one became dominant, the treaty might be abrogated.

Prior agreements on quotas or on the division of the catch among nations have not guaranteed successful protection of stocks. The International Whaling Commission has attempted to allocate the total catch among member nations, but disagreements have arisen. In most cases, the commission's recommendations for the total allowable catch have been ignored. As a result, whale stocks are more depleted now than when the commission was first established in 1948.

Divisions of the catch between two nations on an equal basis are primarily political allocations based on mutual self-interest. For example, the International Pacific Salmon Fisheries Commission, first organized to protect sockeye, and later pink, salmon of the Fraser River system, regulates the fishing periods of Canadian and United States fishermen. The spawning areas are all in Canada, but the runs migrate through United States waters in Puget Sound. Since both nations had the capability to destroy the runs, some agreement was needed. No scientific information or economic rationale was advanced in favor of the present catch division, but an unequal apportionment would have created an unwanted source of friction between the two countries.

The creation of regional commissions is an encouraging step toward international fisheries management. This effort complements, and is an extension of, FAO attempts to organize fishery research among the developing nations. The regional commissions typically encompass more than two countries and are responsible for all species in a designated area. Research is organized by national governments, but recommendations for fishing periods are made by the commission. Organizations such as the Northwest Atlantic Commission lack the power of such bodies as the International Pacific Halibut Commission, which has tacit power to make recommendations that are binding on national governments. To be effective, regional commissions must be able to enforce management recommendations. Present obstructions, however, are likely to continue.

CONSERVATION AND POLITICAL WILL

International fishery problems are seldom debated on their relative merits, since most nations place these issues in the broader context of foreign relations. In many countries of Western Europe and North America, fishing is generally left to private companies, and governments do not participate directly. Those states have not been zealous in protecting fishing interests, since fishery conservation is seldom a national priority in foreign affairs. However, in some major fishing nations—for example, the Soviet Union—the industry is state controlled, and the government is responsible for its economic success. Yet these countries have also not shown great interest in stock preservation. Japan and the Soviet Union feel that participation in the deliberations of the regional commissions will protect their historic rights to fish and their share of the regional catch, but they are not particularly interested in measures to preserve the fishery.

The absence of international accord on fishery problems is not dependent solely on the lack of agreement with respect to fisheries but more on the lack of political will and on the reluctance of many nations to surrender domestic powers to an international organization. Existing international fishery organizations mirror the frustrations that face many international agencies; they will remain relatively impotent so long as states place primary emphasis on national interests.

The present condition of world affairs does not encourage optimism for international fisheries management. Many treaty organizations lack the necessary research capabilities, few have arrested the decrease of stocks, and still fewer have attacked the problems of congestion and extended effort. But this does not mean that improvements cannot be made. Regional commissions could be established in all areas where no pacts exist, thus ensur-

ing management agencies in all parts of the world. Where present commissions have jurisdiction over one or two species, the mandate might be expanded to encompass all species. Regional commissions could also provide a framework for formal international management of stocks at some future time. In the interval, joint management agreements might be made among commissions for species whose life cycles cause them to migrate within the ocean. Increasing integration of regional commissions might facilitate subsequent movements toward international control.

As we have noted, United Nations agencies such as the FAO have made considerable progress in organizing fishing industries in the developing nations. With additional funds, FAO could assume responsibility for a research program in world fisheries. Initially such a program might be restricted to biological research on threatened species, but later steps should be taken to improve the economic efficiency of the fisheries. FAO needs to expand the amount of assistance given to countries that are just beginning to develop their fishing industries so that these nations can avoid the mistakes of the developed nations.

Interim improvements, short of international control, have been suggested for the economic ills that plague world fisheries. One is the "manager nation" concept,[8] under which one nation would have exclusive management rights over the fish that frequent its contiguous continental shelf. If some species were not being utilized fully by the manager nation, it could lease exploitation rights. Such a plan might improve efficiency, but it leaves resources of the high seas unprotected by any organization or commission, except for those that are already operating.

Air and Water Management

Pollution of the environment is increasingly becoming a global problem; yet little can be achieved in pollution control until nations recognize its global nature.[9] International management remains even more restricted than in the case of fisheries. Nuclear testing in the atmosphere by the Soviet Union, the United States, France, and China has demonstrated the rapidity with which nuclear fallout can pollute the earth. Before nuclear testing, pollution was regarded as a localized problem, which could be controlled through such limited institutions as river-basin authorities.

Unlike fish, pollution is neither a desired product nor a marketable commodity. Nations gain little economic benefit from controlling pollution because they are able to pass treatment costs on to other states. At the same time international agreements to limit pollution can increase costs for the polluter, and many nations have chosen to ignore the damages rather than to accept the higher costs. This reluctance has meant that agreements have been limited to cases in which nations clearly recognized that the political and social costs of nontreatment exceeded those of control.

Pulp mills discharge untreated waste into bays or rivers. Ore smelters emit untreated sulfide gases into the atmosphere which damage vegetation. Each polluter contributes to a general decline in the quality of the world environment. Nations, however, have jurisdiction over pollution control. Unless the actions of one state directly interfere with another's use of a resource, there have been no international controls. Even then no agency can compel a state to appear before an international court on a pollution charge or to desist from polluting if it is judged liable for damages.

INTERNATIONAL CONTROL OF POLLUTION

The major obstacles in controlling global pollution have been traditional use and sovereignty rights, the cost of control, and the differing perception of pollution by various cultural groups. Since industrialization contributes heavily to pollution, the problem of assigning responsibility becomes more difficult. The degree of pollution is greatest at the point of discharge into the commons and decreases as the commons dilute the waste products. If in the case of a river basin, for example, four nations are discharging pollutants into a stream, it is virtually impossible to determine who is legally responsible for polluting the water that is used by a fifth state.

Thus the success of treaties to control international pollution is predicated on each nation's acceptance of responsibility for pollution within its own borders. This acceptance is complicated by economics and by a lack of international law, but it remains fundamentally a question of political will. Most treaties regulating pollution have been signed by nations with a long history of cordial relations and with substantial degrees of industrial development. Bilateral treaties are most common, though some multilateral treaties have recently been reached. Abatement of river pollution has been the target of most efforts; air and ocean pollution have received only scant attention until the last decade.

Commissions designed to protect international waterways have formed the basis for cooperation to control river pollution. The International Commission for the Protection of the Rhine against Pollution, the International Joint Commission (Canada and the United States), and the International Boundary and Water Commission (Mexico and the United States) are three examples. Each has the power to investigate pollution problems and to make recommendations but has no power to implement them.[10] Commissions that involve only two countries have been more successful than larger groups in gaining political approval for their recommendations. For example, a recent International Joint Commission report on the control of pollution on the Red River of the North was accepted by Canada and the United States. The report called for strict enforcement of standards established by the Minnesota and North Dakota legislatures to prevent injury to property and health downstream in Canada. A similar agreement was signed by the United States and Mexico when the quality of water delivered to Mexico from the Colorado River deteriorated. The saline waters from the Colorado basin could

not be used in Mexican irrigation works. To solve the problem the United States agreed to build, at its own expense, a bypass around the Mexican diversion works.

Multilateral commissions have made studies of water quality, but they have lacked authority to determine who is responsible and who will pay for control. The International Commission for the Protection of the Rhine against Pollution was formed in 1950 by Switzerland, France, Luxembourg, the Federal Republic of Germany, and the Netherlands, but until recently its work was limited to testing water quality. The commission has done little to control pollution, and increasing industrial development on the lower Rhine has only intensified the problem. A petrochemical executive commented, "Yes we draw a lot from the Rhine and we put plenty back."[11] Faced with a barrage of complaints, some chemical industries increased their efforts to reduce effluent discharge. In 1965 the mandate of the Rhine Commission was extended, giving it power (1) to prepare studies to determine the nature, extent, and origin of pollution and to draw conclusions from the results of such studies; (2) to recommend to the signatory governments appropriate measures for the protection of the Rhine against pollution; and (3) to prepare studies which may serve as a basis for future international agreements or arrangements. Standardized measurements and data collection are prerequisites of international control, but commissions limited to such functions cannot achieve rapid progress in reducing or preventing pollution.

The fallout from testing of nuclear

weapons in the atmosphere demonstrates the global nature of the pollution problem and the importance of political will in solving it. Fallout from nuclear devices is distributed throughout the world in a matter of days. Scientists have argued that continued fallout can seriously endanger human health and result in infant mortality.[12] In response to public outcry, two nuclear nations, the Soviet Union and the United States, agreed to stop atmospheric testing, but two other nations, France and China, chose to ignore the health hazard and to continue tests, placing their own political and defense objectives above the concern for world health.

Agreements for controlling ocean pollution have focused on oil discharges. Ships commonly pump their bilges into the oceans, and oil tankers drain their holds at sea. Under the 1954 International Convention for the Prevention of Pollution of the Seas by Oil, ships were forbidden to discharge oil within fifty miles of a coastline. A 1962 amendment to the convention completely prohibited discharge, but so far it has been ratified by only thirty-nine countries. In anticipation of stricter regulations, Shell, British Petroleum, and Esso have begun to pump out the oil at refineries.[13]

INDUSTRIAL SOURCES OF POLLUTION

Industrial products cause international pollution. Automobiles and other motor vehicles are good examples. Gas engines emit incombustible materials into the atmosphere, creating serious problems in major cities. Although automobile pollution is limited spatially, there is considerable international trade, and automobiles made in one country can contribute to pollution in another. Modelski has discussed the spread of corporations, including automobile manufacturers, and argues that technology and production will become increasingly international.[14] Much of the technology emanates from the Western industrial countries, and many international pollution problems therefore stem from the products of these countries.

Since most of the technological advances in the twentieth century have taken place in the Western industrialized countries and have then been adopted elsewhere, the actions of international corporations such as the three oil companies mentioned above could have a significant effect on future global pollution levels. Large corporations could escalate the spread of industrial pollution, especially in the developing countries. Many of these nations desire economic growth and are reluctant to impose stringent antipollution regulations on potential investors. Through research these same corporations may well contribute, however, to a decline in pollution. The shift from coal to other energy sources, for example, has contributed to a decrease in local pollution. If similar improvements can be made in several other industrial processes, the quality of the global environment could be enhanced.

Corporations may be unwilling to control pollution unilaterally because of the cost and competition from other companies. In this case, the action of one nation to curb domestic pollution might have beneficial effects in others. Under the United States Clean Air Act of 1963, for instance, all new automobiles—domestic and imported—sold in the United States must now be equipped with emission-control devices. In the wake of these regulations, several other countries are designing standards comparable to those of the United States. In addition, recent efforts have been made in California to outlaw the internal combustion engine, replacing it with other means of power generation such as steam. If such a law were adopted by the United States Congress, there would be a considerable decline in global pollution. Similar regulations for other products and processes in one nation might in effect create a world standard without the benefit of a regulating international agency.

RESPONSIBILITY FOR POLLUTION CONTROL

Little research has been conducted to determine who is responsible for pollution. The 1968 International Conference on the Biosphere pointed out that lack of knowledge of pollution sources was the most critical problem to be solved before controls could be implemented.[15] In codifying the sources, the conference recognized that both social and technical solutions would have to be investigated. Regional councils that bring together more than two countries have traditionally been research and data-gathering organizations. A practical first step toward greater international control would be to extend the councils' mandates and give each power to make management recommendations. Bilateral commissions might have

their mandates extended to include all pollution problems. If each commission were able to acquire competent staff, recommendations would probably receive more attention from national governments.

Complete international control of global pollution is obviously neither practical nor politically possible at this time. However, international agencies such as UNESCO could play an important role as clearing houses for all research on pollution. Research by Western nations on various industrial processes could be made available to assist developing nations in avoiding many pollution problems now faced by the industrial countries. On the basis of this research, international agencies could suggest global standards for each process.

Ocean Floor Management

The current controversy over the ownership of ocean-floor resources demonstrates the difficulties in instituting international control, even when national vested interests are minimal. At present, most of the ocean floor cannot be exploited, but technology is rapidly being created that will enable nations to exploit previously undeveloped undersea areas. Present technology permits recovery of most mineral deposits down to depths of 300 feet. This has been accomplished by conventional methods of drilling, dredging, and underground mining. The use of deep-sea vehicles has increased, and though most development has been restricted to the continental shelf, exploration in waters below the 200-meter (656-foot) contour line has begun.[16]

No legal-political framework presently defines property rights in these deep-sea areas, and the laws governing the ocean floor are inadequate. The 1958 Geneva Convention on the Continental Shelf does not establish a clear standard for determining areas beyond the 200-meter line subject to national jurisdiction. In the Geneva Convention, which came into force in 1964, the continental shelf is defined as the sea adjacent to the coast "to a depth of 200 meters or, beyond that limit, to where the depth of the superjacent waters admits of the exploitation of the natural resources of the said areas." The convention further states that "the coastal state exercises over the continental shelf sovereign rights for the purposes of exploring it and exploiting its natural resources." In other words, a nation is able to extend its jurisdiction as far as technology permits. Within such a framework, there are no restrictions on developing the ocean floor, which could be subjected to conflicts not unlike those that characterized the opening of many land frontiers.[17]

Concern about possible conflict over the ocean floor and a desire for the wealth that exploitation of deep-sea resources might produce has stimulated interest in control of exploitation beyond national jurisdiction and in sharing revenues derived from exploitation. In 1967 Arvid Pardo, the ambassador to the United Nations from Malta, proposed that the United Nations consider measures to control uses of the ocean floor. In the memorandum that accompanied the proposal, he sug-

gested that any treaty should embody four principles: that those areas of the sea not presently under national jurisdiction not be subject to national appropriation; that exploitation of the sea-floor be undertaken in a manner consistent with the United Nations charter; that any financial benefits derived from the use of the sea floor beyond present limits of national jurisdiction be used to assist developing countries; and that use of the sea floor beyond present national limits be reserved exclusively for peaceful use.

This proposal has been challenged in some developed nations. In the United States twenty-four resolutions were introduced in the Congress condemning the Maltese proposal and instructing the President to oppose any action in the United Nations General Assembly. Some opposition was based on lack of knowledge and on the absence of a United States policy on the matter of ocean-floor development. Further opposition came from military and marine research oriented industries, which feared cuts in government financing of their activities if the Congress supported the proposal, and from such groups as the American Legion, which argued that the United Nations should have no source of income independent of the contributions of member states.[18] But Philip S. Kelley, who analyzed the reaction of Congress, concludes that another significant factor in the reactions against the Maltese proposal was a desire for economic benefit.[19]

There is now an opportunity for nations to develop a global commons where no state has jurisdiction over any part of the deep ocean floor. If internationalizing the commons is to be successful, nations will have to agree on precise boundaries for the areas of seabed beyond national jurisdiction. Any agreement should also provide for preservation of unique ecological areas, for orderly development that reflects the interests of the international community, for conditions conducive to investment, and for allocation of part of the recovered resources to international-community purposes.

The success of international common property resource management in world fisheries, air and water resources, and resources of the ocean floor is closely related to the willingness of nations to surrender parts of their sovereignty to international institutions. Many of the problems in fishery management, pollution abatement, and control of the ocean floor could be solved if nations had the political motivation. But for many states international resource management has a lower priority than national economic and defense objectives. However, we do not have time to wait for the political will of nations to change. While international organizations investigate abuses of the commons, large numbers of fish are killed in the Rhine, Lake Erie degenerates into a sewer, and oil imperils coastlines throughout the world. The need to foster an international ecological conscience and to develop institutions that have the power to implement this viewpoint is imperative.

However, international common property resource management can be upgraded through existing states and organizations. These improvements would not require major adjustments in national attitudes, since they represent an extension and broadening of current programs to manage world resources. Greater efforts at the national level to limit abuses of the commons would also contribute to better international management. The scope of regional commissions should be extended to give them greater powers to implement controls of local resource problems. International agencies could become a clearing house for the exchange of national research and could begin to undertake research programs on a global scale. These are currently the most practical means of developing global standards for managing international common property resources.

Acknowledgments

Grateful acknowledgment is made to Dr. Richard A. Cooley, Chairman, Environmental Studies, University of California at Santa Cruz; to Dr. James A. Crutchfield of the Department of Economics and School of Public Affairs, University of Washington, and to fellow students in geography at the University of Washington for their comments and criticisms of earlier drafts of this paper.

Footnotes

1. Barbara Ward has argued that all resources, even those within national borders, should be regarded as part of the common resources of this "spaceship earth" (Barbara Ward: Spaceship Earth [New York and London, 1966]). In the present paper

"common property resources" are defined as those found outside the jurisdiction of nation-states or as those whose fluidity and mobility bring them under the jurisdiction and control of several nations. Compare these definitions with Dales's analysis of unrestricted common property resources (John Harkness Dales: Pollution, Property and Prices [Toronto, 1968], pp. 58–76).

2. Francis T. Christy, Jr.: Efficiency in the Use of Marine Resources (Resources for the Future, Inc., Reprint No. 49, Washington, 1964), pp. 1–5. See also James A. Crutchfield: An Economic Evaluation of Alternative Methods of Fishery Regulation, *Journ. of Law and Economics*, Vol. 4, 1961, pp. 131–143; *idem:* Common Property Resources and Factor Allocation, *Canadian Journ. of Econ. and Polit. Sci.*, Vol. 22, 1956, pp. 292–300; Garrett Hardin: The Tragedy of the Commons, *Science*, Vol. 162, 1968, pp. 1243–1248. Hardin uses the term "commons" to define resources that are not appropriated to individuals. Each man is locked into a system that compels him to increase his use of the commons in a world that is limited. In Hardin's view "ruin is the destination toward which all men rush, each pursuing his own best interest in a society that believes in the freedom of the commons."

3. N. Wollman: The New Economics of Resources, *Daedalus*, Vol. 96, 1967, pp. 1099–1104.

4. Much of the data on fishery treaties comes from Francis T. Christy, Jr., and Anthony Scott: The Comon Wealth in Ocean Fisheries (Baltimore, 1965), pp. 158–174.

5. Richard A. Cooley: Politics and Conservation: The Decline of the Alaska Salmon (New York, Evanston, and London, 1963), pp. 184–192. Cooley argues that overfishing in Alaska and mismanagement by federal and territorial authorities have been the major cause of the declining salmon runs. See also Julian V. Minghi: The Conflict of Salmon Fishing Policies in the North Pacific, *Pacific Viewpoint*, Vol. 2, 1961, pp. 59–84.

6. Regional councils are groups of nations that have banded together through treaties for the purpose of organizing research on fisheries.

7. Peter Neary: Grey, Bryce, and the Settlement of Canadian-American Differences, 1905–1911, *Canadian Hist. Rev.*, Vol. 49, 1968, pp. 357–380. Neary points out that many of the early fishery treaties between Canada and the United States were not debated on merits of the fishery problem alone. Most of the fishery questions were negotiated in the context of external affairs between the two countries. Britain had earlier signed the North Pacific Fur Seal Convention on Canada's behalf, since Canada did not exercise full control over her foreign affairs until 1932.

8. S. Patty: Canada Has Plan to Save World Fisheries, *Seattle Times*, Feb. 10, 1969, p. 7.

9. Abel Wolman: Pollution as an International Issue, *Foreign Affairs*, Vol. 47, 1968–1969, pp. 164–175. This article is an excellent summary of international efforts to control pollution.

10. Kenneth J. Langran: The Political and Administrative Control of Water Pollution in International River Basins (unpublished M.A. thesis, Department of Geography, University of Washington, 1968).

11. "Not So Silent Spring," *Economist*, Vol. 210, January 25, 1964, p. 305.

12. Ernest J. Sternglass: Infant Mortality and Nuclear Tests, *Bull. of the Atomic Scientists*, Vol. 25, No. 4, 1969, pp. 18–20.

13. C. L. Boyle: Oil Pollution of the Sea: Is the End in Sight? *Biological Conservation*, Vol. 1, 1969, pp. 319–328.

14. George Modelski: The Corporation in World Society, *Yearbook of World Affairs*, Vol. 22, 1968, pp. 64–79.

15. As reported in *Nature and Resources* [UNESCO], Vol. 4, 1968, pp. 2–11.

16. "Panel Reports of the Commission on Marine Science, Engineering, and Resources: Vol. 3: Marine Resources and Legal-Political Arrangements for Their Development" (Washington, D.C., 1969), p. VII–91.

17. Lewis M. Alexander: Geography and the Law of the Sea, *Annals Assn. of Amer. Geogrs.*, Vol. 58, 1968, pp. 177–197.

18. "Governing the Use of Ocean Space," U. S. Senate Committee on Foreign Relations, Hearings, 90th Congr., 1st Sess., 1967.

19. Philip S. Kelley: International Control of the Ocean Floor, *in* Congress and the Environment (edited by Richard A. Cooley and Geoffrey Wandesforde-Smith; Seattle and London, 1970), pp. 188–204.

5 5 5 5 5 5 5 5 5 5 5 5 5

POPULATION GROWTH AND PRESSURE

5 5 5 5 5 5 5 5 5 5 5 5 5

• • • • • • • • • • • • • •twenty-nine

IRENE B. TAEUBER •

Demographic Transitions and Population Problems in the United States

The increase, expansion, and transformation of the population of the United States are unique in the annals of world development. No other modernizing population had available to it a continental area so superbly supplied with the resources for agriculture and industry and so sparsely utilized. Our problems of population are not rooted in the antiquity of history, the intensity of land use, or the paucity of resources for the industrial economy. They are, rather, products of unbalanced or ill-advised interplays of demographic factors with political, economic, and social developments or their absences.

The experience of the United States in the past does not forecast the future elsewhere, nor indeed is our own future simply forecast. The singular

aspects of the increase, the geographic expansion, and the metropolitan concentration are a distinctive laboratory for the assessment of many processes and interrelations. Here, perhaps, the inherent forces in growth and modernization may be separated from the coincidental. Here immigrants and their descendants formed a population that was American, but acculturation did not preclude ethnic problems defined mainly in terms of African ancestry.

The timing of the American epic is critical to its wider relevance. The centuries of development spanned the transition from animate to inanimate power, from tradition and folklore to science and technology, from rural settlement to metropolis, from pervasive

◆ SOURCE. Reprinted by permission from *Annals of the American Academy of Political and Social Science*, Vol. 369, January 1967, pp. 131–140.

deaths and abundant births to postponed deaths and controlled births.

Dimensions

In 1790, the population of the newly formed United States of America was 3.9 million. Ninety-five per cent of the people were rural, and some 85 per cent were agricultural. Birth rates were above 50 per 1,000 total population, and more than half the people were less than sixteen years of age. Increase was 35 per cent or more a decade.

This is not prelude to a Malthusian tale, though Malthus cited early America as indicative of man's potential to reproduce and the statesmen of the time were concerned with land for the multiplying people. The epic of the first century, the years from 1790 to 1890, was increase and expansion. The population was less than 4 million in 1790. It reached 25 million in 1850, 50 million in 1880, 75 million in 1900. Fertility was declining along with mortality, and rates of natural increase were slowing. The economic problem was labor sparsity; millions of immigrants contributed to economic development and cultural diversity. The land area was extended from the Atlantic to the Pacific, from the Great Lakes to the Rio Grande. Hawaii and Alaska added Pacific dimensions to production and trade, communication and exchange, political responsibility, and military decisions.

The years from 1890 to 1900 were transitional in economic growth and population dynamics. The nation had developed the most productive agricultural population the world had yet seen;

that population declined as the youth of the agricultural areas moved to more abundant living in urban areas and non-agricultural occupations. Urbanization was continuing. By 1900, 40 per cent of the population lived in places of 2,500 or more, and more than 60 per cent of the economically active population labored outside agriculture. Thirteen per cent of the young adults had finished high school; almost 3 per cent were college graduates. Birth rates were declining along with economic and social change. The birth rate had been perhaps 55 in 1820; in 1900 it was 32. Numbers of children below 5 years of age per 1,000 women aged 15 to 44 were 1,295 in 1820; in 1900 they were 666.[1]

The decades from 1900 to 1960 were ones of rapid and generally quickening change. The major process in distribution was the concentration in metropolitan areas. The major process in occupational transformation was the growth in professional, technical, and managerial workers. The major process in education was the advance to a high school graduation as median level and the increasing orientation to college education. The demographic response to this evolving world of the twentieth century was traditional for the first four decades. Death rates declined rapidly; birth rates declined precipitantly. Millions of immigrants had entered the metropolitan areas prior to the restrictions of the quota system; they, too, participated in the demographic transition. The childbearing of the foreign-born women may have buoyed fertility, but the maximum postponement of marriage, the maximum childlessness, and the minimum marital fertility were those of the upwardly mobile population of foreign or mixed parentage. By the 1930's birth rates had fallen to 19 per 1,000 total population. In 1935 the gross reproduction rate was 1,091, the net rate 975. Declining fertility characterized rural as well as urban populations; it prevailed among Chinese, Japanese, and Negroes, as well as Caucasians. Projections of the trends of the then present indicated a maximum population within a generation. The outlook was gloomy—and the assessment of that outlook was based on analyses of declines in fertility and mortality that had been in process for a century and a half.

The projections of the 1930's were enormously erroneous.[2] Economic growth, rural depopulation, metropolitan increase, educational pushes of men to higher and higher levels, an affluence that defined family incomes of less than $3000 as poverty—these were the characteristics of the 1940's and 1950's. Age at marriage and the proportions who never married declined. Voluntary childlessness almost vanished. The fertility of the married increased. There were projections of continuing growth to massive numbers at future periods. Demographic pessimism prevailed again. But again projection of a present into an indefinite future seems to be proving erroneous. The birth rate that had been 25.3 in 1957 declined to 22.4 in 1962 and to 19.4 in 1965.[3]

The economic and social consequences of the changing rates of growth are inherent in the future. Today's population will carry its irregularities in age dynamics and age structures over

time until those now infants become the aged. The critical question is the duration and the magnitude of future growth. Projection of the levels of the recent period show the population of 195 million in 1965 reaching 300 million in 1990, 400 million in 2010. No sophisticated person assumes that the population of the United States has to reach 300 million within a quarter century; 400 million within a half century.[4] But what numbers will it reach? Where will the people of the future live? How will they vary by color, by education, by residence in and outside the central cities of metropolitan areas? Will the future evolve without essential problems of numbers? Or will the slowing of growth that must come sooner or later proceed through pressures generated by the growth itself?

Urbanization and Metropolis

Growth in numbers and in proportions urban characterized the population of the United States from 1790 to the present. The urban population increased almost 40 per cent from 1900 to 1910, more than 20 per cent each decade thereafter except in the 1930's. Rural increase was less than 10 per cent from 1900 to 1910, negative from 1950 to 1960. The population of the United States was 76.2 million in 1900, 179.3 million in 1960. The urban population increased from 30.2 million in 1910 to 125.3 million in 1960, the rural from 46.0 million in 1900 to 54.1 million in 1960. In the latter year, only 7.5 per cent of the population lived on farms in rural areas.

Urban transformation involved the growth of metropolitan areas on the one hand, the depopulation of the countryside on the other. In 1960, the 70 per cent of the population that was urban occupied one per cent of the land area, whereas the 30 per cent that was rural occupied 99 per cent. Half the counties declined in population from 1950 to 1960; many of them had also declined from 1940 to 1950.

The major areas of concentration were the counties in the Standard Metropolitan Statistical Areas (SMSA's) of 1960 (Table 1). They included 42 per cent of the total population in 1900,

63 per cent in 1960. Perhaps the most incisive index of metropolitan concentration is the proportion of the total national increase that occurred in these metropolitan counties. That proportion was almost two-thirds in the first decade of the century, more than three-fourths in the second, more than four-fifths in all other decades except the 1930's, when it was two-thirds. The metropolitan concentration of the Negro population was continuing and spectacular; in the last three decades the rate of increase has been twice that for whites.

The formation of the metropolitan population differed increasingly from

TABLE 1.   Per Cent Population by Ethnic Group, and Metropolitan Residence by Ethnic Group, Selected Dates, 1900 to 1960

Group and Area	1900	1920	1940	1950	1960
Ethnic group	100.0	100.0	100.0	100.0	100.0
White	87.9	89.7	89.8	89.5	88.8
Negro	11.6	9.9	9.8	10.0	10.6
Total population	100.0	100.0	100.0	100.0	100.0
SMSA	41.9	49.7	55.1	59.2	63.0
Central City	26.0	32.8	34.5	34.7	32.3
Outside	15.9	16.9	20.6	24.5	30.6
Outside SMSA	58.1	50.3	44.9	40.8	37.0
White population	100.0	100.0	100.0	100.0	100.0
SMSA	44.0	51.6	56.2	59.7	62.8
Central City	27.6	33.9	34.9	33.8	30.0
Outside	16.3	17.6	21.3	25.9	32.8
Outside SMSA	56.0	48.2	43.8	40.3	37.2
Negro population	100.0	100.0	100.0	100.0	100.0
SMSA	26.6	33.9	45.4	55.6	64.7
Central City	14.5	22.8	33.9	43.0	51.5
Outside	12.1	11.1	11.5	12.6	13.2
Outside SMSA	73.4	66.1	54.6	44.4	35.3

Source: Irene B. Taeuber, *Population Trends in the United States, 1900–1960*, U. S. Bureau of the Census, Technical Paper No. 10 (Washington, D. C.: United States Government Printing Office, 1964), Table 2: Population in the areas defined as SMSA (Standard Metropolitan Statistical Area) in 1960, with central city populations as of the dates of enumeration, Conterminous United States.

simple growth across a hierarchy of places from hamlet to great city. Until the 1920's, rates of increase were associated positively with size of place. In recent decades, modern means of transportation, rising incomes, and general affluence have been associated with dispersion from central cities to peripheries. In the twenty years from 1900 to 1920, metropolitan population increased 65 per cent. The increase was 75 per cent in the central cities, 48 per cent outside them. In the twenty years from 1940 to 1960, the metropolitan population increased 55 per cent. The increase was 27 per cent in central cities, 102 per cent outside them.

There are distinctive concentrations of whites and Negroes within metropolitan areas. Between 1950 and 1960, the white population increased 5 per cent in central cities, 49 per cent outside them, while the Negro population increased 50 per cent in central cities, 31 per cent outside them (Table 2). In 1960, more than half the white population of SMSA's lived outside central cities, while almost four-fifths of the Negro population lived within them. In 1900, Negroes constituted 6 per cent of the population in central cities, 9 per cent outside them. In 1940, the percentages were 10 and 6. In 1960, they were 17 and 5.

Thus, the economic difficulties and the social tensions of demographic change involve both growth and distribution. The increasing cohorts of those born in the years of declining but still sufficient fertility were followed by the declining cohorts of those born in the years of very low fertility. Then there were the larger cohorts of those born in the years of increased fertility. Now

TABLE 2.   Per Cent Change in Population by Ethnic Group and in Metropolitan Residence by Ethnic Group, 1900 to 1960

Group and Area	1900– 1910	1910– 1920	1920– 1930	1930– 1940	1940– 1950	1950– 1960
Total population	21.0	14.9	16.1	7.2	14.1	18.8
SMSA	32.0	24.9	27.1	8.8	22.6	26.3
Central City	37.1	27.7	24.3	5.6	14.7	10.7
Outside	23.7	19.9	32.3	14.6	35.9	48.5
Outside SMSA	13.1	6.5	5.4	5.4	3.7	7.9
White population	22.3	16.0	16.3	7.2	13.8	17.8
SMSA	32.6	25.4	25.7	8.2	20.7	24.0
Central City	36.9	27.2	22.9	4.4	10.2	4.7
Outside	25.4	22.2	31.1	15.0	38.0	49.2
Outside SMSA	14.2	7.4	6.3	6.0	4.8	8.7
Negro population	11.3	6.5	13.6	8.2	16.8	25.4
SMSA	19.9	25.8	40.7	17.0	43.2	45.9
Central City	32.6	40.0	52.4	19.9	48.1	50.3
Outside	4.6	4.2	16.7	9.2	28.5	30.8
Outside SMSA	8.1	−1.3	−0.2	1.8	−5.1	−0.3

Source: See Reference, Table 1.

TABLE 3. Per Cent Population Change, by Age, Enumerated and Estimated Populations, Selected Decades, 1890 to 1980

Age	Enumerated Populations			Projected Populations	
	1890–1900	1930–1940	1950–1960	1960–1970	1970–1980
Total	21.4	7.6	18.8	15.6	19.4
0–4	20.1	−7.2	24.4	5.9	41.0
5–14	16.1	−8.4	44.6	15.4	17.6
15–24	16.8	6.9	8.4	47.9	15.2
25–44	26.3	10.1	3.9	2.4	29.2
45–64	27.0	22.3	19.3	15.5	3.2
65 and over	27.4	36.4	32.0	17.6	17.8

Sources: 1890–1960—processed from decennial census reports; 1970 and 1980—U. S. Bureau of the Census, "Revised Projections of the Population of the United States by Age and Sex to 1985," *Current Population Reports, Population Estimates,* Series P-25, No. 329, March 10, 1966. Estimate 3—assumptions of increasing life expectancy, a net immigration of 400,000 a year, and a fertility moving toward a terminal level of 2.755 births per woman, the average level of 1945–1946.

births are again declining, but numbers may increase again as youth now maturing reach the childbearing ages. Gyrations in rates of change by age introduce major problems of adjustment, whatever the views as to the relations of over-all growth to economic functioning, resources sufficiency, and the quality of living (Table 3).

The problems of distribution are also severe. Adjustments were difficult as depopulation characterized the open country and the small towns. The swift growth of metropolitan areas and regions outpaced man's effective ingenuity. Perhaps the most intricate of the problems concern the economic, social, and ethnic differentiations in central cities and in dispersion from them.

Transformation and Migration

Major changes in occupations and in education underlie changing rates of population growth and altered migra-

tions. In 1900, more than half the economically active population was in agriculture; in 1960, the proportion was one-sixth.[5] In 1900, 4.3 per cent were in professional, technical, or related occupations; in 1960, the percentage was 11.4. Today, persons in professional and technical occupations are more numerous than those in farm occupations; they are also more numerous than laborers outside agriculture. Professional, technical, and managerial workers outnumber farm operators, farm managers, and all laborers, farm or nonfarm.

The upward educational movement was as astounding as the occupational transformation. In 1900, almost 25 per cent of the population aged 25 to 29 had only a fourth-grade education or less; in 1960, the percentage was less than three.[6] In 1900, only 2.6 per cent of those aged 25 to 29 had completed college; in 1960 the percentage was 11. Upward progression in educational level was fairly consistent from 1900 to 1940 for men and women, but then the educational attainments of men moved upward swiftly while those of women lagged. Early marriage and more abundant childbearing influenced not alone the labor force participation of women but the capabilities for functioning at higher levels.

The educational advance, as the occupational transformation, was the path to full participation for those youth who achieved high levels. The limitation to education was a basic barrier. Education was related directly to age; each cohort was potentially more productive than those that preceded it, less productive than those that followed it. But educational level, which was an enduring capability of the adult, placed enduring handicaps on those who came from remote rural areas, lowly economic backgrounds, or disadvantaged ethnic status. The demographic relevance was and remains major. Given earlier marriage and higher fertility among the less educated, the persistence of deprivation is accentuated.

The development of the metropolitan population involved diverse, massive, and continuing migration. In recent decades the predominant regional movements have been westward and southward. Florida, the Southwest, and California were the major areas of gain. The Deep South, Appalachia, the Mississippi-Missouri valley, and the high plains were the major areas of loss. The process is apparent if attention is focused on the movements of youth in the 1950's. In the age group that was 15 to 19 in 1950, 25 to 29 in 1960, all regions lost native whites except the

West, all regions gained Negroes except the South.

The urbanward movement dwarfed the regional and subregional ones, for they occurred alike within regions and in regional interchanges. There were also expansions of urban areas, contractions of rural areas. Again in the decade of the 1950's, and again for youth, the percentage gains in urban population through net migration and area expansion amounted to 8 for the Northeast, 23 for the North Central Division, 33 for the South, and 69 for the West. The percentage losses in the rural population amounted to 12 per cent in the Northeast, 27 per cent in the North Central Region, 25 in the South, and 23 in the West.

The changes were accentuated in the nonwhite population. The percentage increase of young adults through net migration was 82 in the Northeast, 78 in the North Central Region, 17 in the South, and 171 in the West. In the decade of the 1950's, the rural South lost 57 per cent of the Negroes aged 25 to 29 who would have been there had there been neither net migration nor urban expansion.

Given the depletion of the rural farm population, the massive departures from such areas as Appalachia, and the exodus of Negroes from the Deep South, the migrations and redistributions of youth will be increasingly intermetropolitan. The problems of absorbing the severely disadvantaged will decline progressively if the metropolitan areas themselves provide educational and other opportunities for the youth who will be involved in the metropolitan interchanges of the future.

Demographic Transitions

If the demographic transitions in the United States are examined in comparative focus, the queries are more numerous than the answers. The earliest transition was doubtless increase in fertility along with decline in mortality among the colonists as contrasted with the European peoples of origin. The national transition to declining fertility was already in process when the thirteen states formed a federal union. That decline accompanied industrial and social advance; it probably preceded the decline in mortality. Decennial rates of natural increase declined continually from the late eighteenth and early nineteenth centuries through the 1930's of this century.

Mortality declined as medical attention became more available, the store of science and technology relevant to health and longevity larger. The critical questions concern the declines in fertility. The forces that would seem to stimulate early marriage and large families long remained operative. If America was the land of opportunity in the late eighteenth century, it certainly remained so throughout the nineteenth century. Homesteads were available until 1890, even thereafter. Millions of immigrants confirm the fact of labor sparsity in the development of the industrial economy. The explanation of the declines in fertility must lie in aspirations and opportunities. Perhaps individualism and the democratic concept were critical. There was faith in an ever-moving future whose limits were fixed by an almost boundless nature rather than by man. Parents be-

lieved that children should move upward from the parental position, whatever that position was. The path to mobility was education. Schools were local institutions, available to girls as to boys. The upward extension of public education was a major innovation in the American development. With the establishment of the land grant colleges and the universities, public education was available from the elementary school to the post-graduate and professional levels.

The interpretation of fertility changes in the past, the explanation of current levels and differentials, and the estimation of the future are alike complex. The birth rate per 1,000 population is precise but difficult to interpret. The rate declined from 30.1 in 1910 to 18.4 in 1936, then rose to 25.3 in 1957. It has now been declining for nine years; it was 19.4 in 1965. Some refinement is introduced if births are related to the numbers of women in the reproductive ages of 15 to 44. The fertility rate was 127 in 1910. It declined to 76 in 1936, rose to 123 in 1957, declined to 97 in 1965.

The conclusion of rapid movement toward the lower fertility of the 1930's would be premature, for the births of given periods may be deflated or inflated by changes in the age at marriage and in the timing of those births that are desired. The age at marriage decreased sharply in the war and postwar years; it is now increasing. The prevalent pattern became one of early childbearing; this too may be changing. Perhaps people now young will have smaller families. Recent studies of ideals, expectations and performance suggest that this may occur. If so, final size of family may decline when those now young complete their childbearing years.[7]

The larger relevance of the recent American transition to higher fertility is not dependent on the still conjectural answers as to the behavior of fertility in the coming decade. The decline of fertility, as the decline of mortality, was an aspect of modernization. The terminus of decline was not in depopulation and disappearance. Rather, marriage, family, and children were enduring values.

Present and Future

Population problems are a natural component in change. This is apparent in the less developed countries, where declines in death rates, aspirations beyond realities, and the complicated problems of economic and social development make the traditional high birth rates that were once essential to continuity a hazard to development and a threat to continuity itself. It is equally true in the United States. If the severe limitations to childbearing had continued, the population would now be aging and declining. If the high rates of reproduction of the early postwar years had continued, severe pressures of population on agricultural and other resources would have developed. Three essential facts should be emphasized. (1) The alternative of decline and disappearance did not occur. (2) Current trends make the alternative of continuity at the relatively high levels of the recent past dubious. (3) Since

fertility now depends on the motivations and decisions of the couples in a dynamic economic, social and political milieu, it is changeable.

The population growth implicit in the future is substantial, in part because of the enlarged age groups now entering childbearing years, in part because marriage, family, and children beyond two remain ideals for young Americans. What, then, is the range of the future? Population is now more than 195 million. If mortality declines further, if immigration is slightly above present levels, and if fertility moves toward the annual level of 1953, the population will be 273 million in 1985.[8] The birth rate will be 25.2, the death rate, 8.8, the annual growth, 1.8 per cent. If other changes remain the same but fertility declines to the annual level of 1941–1942, the population will reach 239 million in 1985. The birth rate will be 20, the death rate, 9.7, the annual rate of growth, 1.2 per cent. If the difference between the populations that result from these variant fertility assumptions seems limited, it need only be noted that all persons who will be aged twenty and over in 1985 were already alive in 1965. The differences in projected numbers below age twenty are large. The implications of the alternate trends for the responsibilities of parents, the needs for educational and other facilities, the expansion needed in the labor market, and the formation of new families differ widely. In 1965, there were 77 million youth below age twenty in the population. Given continuation of fertility at the 1953 level, the number would increase to 112 million in 1985. Given decline in fertility to the 1941–1942 average level, the number would increase only to 79 million.

The population problems of the United States involve the numbers of the population, over-all and in the various age groups. This is only initial base for the complicated problems of movement within and toward a society that meets the needs and aspirations of its members. There are problems of flexibility in the dynamics of a population whose age groups change at varying rates in different times (Table 3). There are all the problems of developing proper amenities, more equalitarian distribution, and more democratic opportunities in metropolitan areas. There are the continuing problems of transition for the disadvantaged who are moving from places of lesser to places of greater opportunity. There are the problems of ethnic and nativity groups whose access to the potentialities of the society is limited by color of skin or place of origin.

The most intricate of population problems is posed by the changing population trends of recent decades. Those problems of numbers that we now have or may have are product of the decisions of many families to have three or more children. Most of the families who so decided accepted the parental responsibilities that were involved and had sufficient resources to do so. Yet, given today's low mortality, along with the early and almost universal marriage and the virtual absence of voluntary childlessness, the three-child family yields substantial population increase. The actions of couples in accord with their ideals as to family size and the family-oriented life yield the relatively high rates of growth that may be deterrents to economic development and social advance. The decisions as to parenthood that are the inalienable rights of the couple thus present a democratic society with its greatest challenge in public education.

Footnotes

This article utilizes analysis in process for a volume on *The Changing Population of the United States: 1900 to 1960*, jointly with Conrad Taeuber, in the series of monographs on the 1960 census, sponsored by the Social Science Research Council in co-operation with the Bureau of the Census. Three reports from the study have been published by the Bureau of the Census: *United States Census of Population, 1960: Selected Area Reports: Standard Metropolitan Statistical Areas*, Final Report PC(3)-1D (Washington, D.C.: U.S. Government Printing Office, 1963); *United States Census of Population, 1960: Selected Area Reports: Type of Place*, Final Report PC(3)-1E (Washington, D.C.: U.S. Government Printing Office, 1964); *Population Trends in the United States: 1900 to 1960*, Technical Paper No. 10 (Washington, D.C.: U.S. Government Printing Office, 1964).

1.   Summaries of census and vital statistical data from 1790 to the time of report are presented in: U.S., Bureau of the Census, *Historical Statistics of the United States: Colonial Times to 1957* (Washington, D.C.: U.S. Government Printing Office, 1960). For current data: *Statistical Abstract of the United States, 1965* (86th ed.; Washington, D.C.: U.S. Government Printing Office, 1965).

2.   For summaries of population dynamics,

projections, and assessments: Conrad Taeuber and Irene B. Taeuber, *The Changing Population of the United States* (Census Monograph Series; New York: John Wiley and Sons, 1958).

3. U.S., National Center for Health Statistics, "Births, Marriages, Divorces and Deaths for 1965," *Monthly Vital Statistics*, Report 14(12), February 28, 1966.

4. U.S. Bureau of the Census, "Projections of the Population of the United States, by Age and Sex: 1964 to 1985," *Current Population Reports, Population Estimates*, Series P-25, No. 286 (July 1964).

5. David L. Kaplan and M. Claire Casey, *Occupational Trends in the United States, 1900 to 1950*, U.S. Bureau of the Census, Working Paper No. 5 (Washington, D.C., 1958).

6. These percentages are approximations, based on an analysis of the data on years of school completed by age in 1940 on the assumption that education was a relatively unchanging characteristic of individuals, and that survivors in specified years represented the total cohort at earlier years.

7. Ronald Freedman, Pascal K. Whelpton, and Arthur A. Campbell, *Family Planning, Sterility and Population Growth* (New York: McGraw-Hill, 1959). Pascal K. Whelpton, Arthur A. Campbell, and John E. Patterson, *Fertility and Family Planning in the United States* (Princeton, N.J.: Princeton University Press, 1966). Charles F. Westoff, Robert G. Potter, Jr., Philip C. Sagi, and Elliott G. Mishler, *Family Growth in Metropolitan America* (Princeton, N.J.: Princeton University Press, 1961). Charles F. Westoff, Robert G. Potter, Jr., and Philip C. Sagi, *The Third Child: A Study in the Prediction of Fertility* (Princeton, N.J.: Princeton University Press, 1963).

8. U.S. Bureau of the Census, "Revised Projections of the Population of the United States by Age and Sex to 1985," *Current Population Reports, Population Estimates*, Series P-25, No. 329, March 10, 1966.

thirty •••••••••••••••••••

◆ EUGENE P. ODOM

Optimum Population and Environment: A Georgian Microcosm

The world seems to be getting smaller and more limited in its capacity to support human beings because the per capita use of resources in developed countries, and the per capita expectations in undeveloped countries, keep going up. Thoughtful persons everywhere are agreeing, perhaps reluctantly in many cases, that if a high quality human existence is to be achieved man must now "manage" his own population as well as the natural resources on which he depends.

To the ecologist, this means first and foremost that the population growth rate must be drastically reduced so that an equilibrium can be reached in the very near future if we are to avoid the very high risk of excessive population, reduction in the per capita availability of resources and a loss in the individual's freedom of action. If this is indeed the case, then the question of what constitutes an optimum population density for man becomes a key issue. An ecological approach to this problem involves considering the total demands that an individual makes on his environment, and how these demands can be met without degrading or destroying his living space or *lebensraum*.

Since the environment is both a "supply depot" and a "house" for man, the concept of the integrated system, the "ecosystem," is the basis for the relevant ecology of today. In the conduct of human affairs in the past, these two functions of the environment have been considered as separate and unre-

◆ **SOURCE.** Reprinted by permission from *Current History*, Vol. 59, 1970, pp. 355–359, published by Current History, Inc.

lated problems, as many writers are now pointing out.[1] The dramatic change in peoples' attitude towards their environment and the rise of a sort of "populist" ecology in the 1970's stem from a general recognition that the quality of the *lebensraum* is so intimately interrelated with the rate of production and consumption of resources that the total "man-in-nature" ecosystem must now be the basis for intelligent management. Lewis Mumford places this concept in more general terms when he says that "Ideological misconceptions have impelled us to promote the expansion of knowledge, power, productivity, without inventing any adequate systems of controls," and that therefore "the problem of our age" is how to use quality to control quantity.[2] In actual fact, it will be much easier to "invent" controls than to agree on a "set point," or optimum level, for the "population-stat."

The Georgian Microcosm

In the fall of 1969, my class in advanced ecology at the University of Georgia elected to tackle the question of "the optimum population for Georgia" on the assumption that this state was large enough and typical enough to be a sort of "microcosm" for the nation and the world. The basic question asked was: How many people can Georgia support at a reasonably high standard of living on a continuing, self-contained equilibrium basis, in the sense that imports and exports of food and resources would be balanced. As it turned out, Georgia is a good microcosm for the

United States because its present density and growth rate, and the distribution of its human and domestic animal population are close to the mean for the whole nation. Likewise, food production and land use patterns in Georgia are average. Furthermore, since pollution, overcrowding and loss of non-renewable resources have not yet reached very serious proportions, the state, like most of the nation, has the opportunity to plan ahead for a new kind of "progress," based on the right of the individual to have a quality environment and to share in the economic benefits of wise use and recycling of resources.

It is self-evident that such planning must start at the local and state level. The ecological and population situation is so varied in the nation as a whole that it is not likely that a nationwide plan for optimum population and environment can be initiated until states and regions take their inventories and set tentative standards. For example, the impetus to redesign the internal combustion engine to reduce air pollution started in California where the problem was locally acute. And once California sets rigorous control standards the nation must quickly follow, because manufacturers have to meet maximum, not minimum, standards, since they cannot (for long, at least) build one kind of car for California and another for other states.

As background for the Georgia inventory, two general principles were adopted. The first principle can be stated as follows: "The optimum is almost always less than the maximum." In terms of human population density, the number of people in a given area that would be optimum from the standpoint of the quality of the individual's life and his environment is considerably fewer than the maximum number of people that might be supported, that is, merely fed, housed and clothed as dehumanized robots or "domestic animals." The same principle can be applied to automobiles; certainly the greatest number of cars that can be accommodated bumper-to-bumper on a freeway is not optimum for the forward progress of the individual automobile. Perhaps, then, the idea of the "greatest good for the greatest number" is not really a tenable principle. Maybe Dr. George Wald's slogan, "a better world for fewer babies" is more relevant to our times.

A second principle is that affluence actually reduces the number of people who can be supported by a given resource base. Thus, the optimum population for a highly developed, industrialized nation with a high per capita G.N.P. (gross national product) is very much lower than the population that can be supported at a subsistence level in an undeveloped nation, because the *per capita* consumption of resources and the production of wastes are so much greater in the developed countries. Thus, if one person in the United States exerts 50 times more demand on his environment than does an Asian, then it is obvious that no environment can support as many Americans as Asians without disastrous deterioration in the quality of that environment. Table 1 illustrates how sharply our world is divided into "developed" and "undeveloped" nations. The distribution

TABLE 1.   World Distribution of Per Capita G.N.P.

Per capita G.N.P. ($)	Number of countries	% world population
40–149	31	56.5
150–299	25	8.8
300–599	15	4.7
600–2400	16	30.0

Source: Revelle in *Prospects of the World Food Supply* (Washington, D.C.: National Academy of Science, 1966) Table 1, p. 24.

of G.N.P. is strongly bimodal, with very few people living in intermediate (so called "developing") nations. Shocking as it may seem, the United States is now in as much danger of overpopulation at its level of per capita living as is India at her present standard of living. Population control must be an overriding issue in both the developed and undeveloped worlds, but the levels that are critical, the limiting factors and the strategy of control are quite different.

Minimum American Per Capita Acreage Requirements

Table 2 is the consensus estimate made by the students of the minimum acreage necessary to support one person at a standard of living now enjoyed by Americans, including a pollution-free living space, room for outdoor recreation and adequate biological capacity to recycle air, water and other vital resources. The per capita area required for food was obtained by taking the diet recommended by the President's Council on Physical Fitness and determin-

TABLE 2. Minimum Per Capita Acreage Requirements for a Quality Environment

Food-producing land	1.5 acres
Fiber-producing land	1 acre
Natural use areas (watershed, airshed, greenbelt, recreation, waste disposal, etc.)	2 acres
Artificial systems (urban, industrial, highways, waste treatment facilities, etc.)	0.5 acre
TOTAL	5.0 acres

ing how much crop and grazing land is required to supply the annual requirement for each item. If Americans would be satisfied with merely getting enough calories and greatly reducing their consumption of meat, as little as a third of an acre per person would be adequate, but the kind of diet Americans now enjoy including orange juice, bacon and eggs for breakfast and steaks for dinner —all of which require a great deal of land space to produce—takes at least 1.5 acres per capita. Thus, the American "demands" from his agricultural environment 10 times the space that is required to produce the rice diet of the Oriental (assuming equally efficient crop production in both cases). The one-acre requirement for "fibers" is based on present per capita use of paper, wood, cotton and so forth, that equals the average annual production of one acre of forest and other fiber-producing land. The two acres for "natural area use" are based on the minimum space needs for watersheds, airsheds, green belt zones in urban areas, recreation areas (state golf courses) as estimated by recent land use surveys. Again, we could do with

less by designing more artificial waste recycling systems and doing away with outdoor recreation, but at a high cost to society as a whole.

In considering the five-acre per capita estimate, two points must be emphasized: (1) If the per capita use goes up in the future, either more land is needed or greater production per acre must be forced by increased use of chemical controls that, in turn, tend to pollute the total environment, creating a cost in taxes that would reduce the individual's "take home" pay. (2) The five-acre estimate is relevant only to an area such as Georgia that has a favorable climate (adequate rainfall and moderate temperature). The per capita area requirement would be much greater in regions with large areas of deserts, steep mountains or other extreme ecosystems.

The inventory of Georgia is summarized in Tables 3–6. The per capita density (Table 3) of 1 in 8 acres com-

TABLE 3. Georgia: Area and Density, People and Domestic Animals

Total area	37.7 million acres
Total people	4.8 million
Per capita density	1 in 8 acres
Population density—¼ (31% Atlanta met. area.: 60% urban, 56% under 30 yrs. of age.)	
Domestic Animals Population equivalent*	21 million
Total Man-Animal	26 million
Population equivalent*	1 in 1.5 acres

* Population equivalent is a unit of animal weight equivalent in metabolism to one adult person.

TABLE 4. Georgia—Land Use in 1968

	(per cent)
Crops	
food	7.5
fiber	.8
idle (rotated)	3.7
Pasture	7.4
Forest	
private	66.3
public	4.5*
Recreation (public)	1.8*
Coastal wetlands	1.3*
Urban, etc.	4.5

* Total of these 3 categories or 7.6% is all land now set aside for "natural use" only (i.e., protected from exploitation).

pares with the national average of 1 in 10 acres. The urban-rural distribution is comparable to the national average. A domestic animal population 5 times that of people is also close to the national average, as is the 10 per cent of land devoted to agriculture (see Table 4). In considering the impact of man on his environment, the importance of the domestic animal is too often overlooked; yet such animals are actually consuming more "primary production" (i.e., photosynthetic conversion of sun energy to organic matter) than man,

TABLE 5. Food Production in Georgia —1969

	Kcal/year $\times 10^{12}$*
Corn	8.5
Grain	0.6
Sweet Potatoes	0.03
Soy Beans	1.8
Peanuts	1.4
Vegetables	0.05
Total	$\pm 12 \times 10^{12}$

* 10^6 Kcal will support one person one year.

and they require huge amounts of land. Also, in this country, pets such as dogs and cats are estimated to consume enough food to support five million people. We could do away with all domestic animals, of course, and substitute people, but to the ecologist that would mean not only giving up meat in the diet, but also dehumanizing man to the level of a domestic animal. It is interesting that Georgia now produces enough food to feed 12 million people, provided that people actually consumed the crops directly. A diet of corn, other grains, soy beans, peanuts and vegetables could supply adequate calories and protein. In actual practice, of course, very little of Georgia's crop production is consumed directly; most of it is fed to animals or shipped out of state in exchange for food from elsewhere.

If we consider for the moment that one person in five acres is a reasonable per capita density, then Georgia is rapidly approaching that level. As shown in Table 6, the net growth rate is two per cent which, if continued, would mean a doubling of the population (leaving only four acres per capita) in 35 years. Almost before we realize it Georgia is moving from what was considered essentially a sparsely populated state to one that is beginning to feel

TABLE 6. 1970 Estimates of Population Growth Rate in Georgia

	(per year)
Birth rate	2.4%
Immigration	0.4%
Death rate	0.8%
Net growth rate	2.0%

the adverse effects of population pressure. As emphasized, this pressure is due not so much to the number of people, but to the great increase in per capita demands on space and resources. It comes as a shock to everyone that Georgia and the nation could be badly overpopulated by the year 2000.

Natural Regulators

It is possible to prepare graphic models for population growth and stabilization to show how animal populations in nature normally regulate their density well below the limit that would be imposed by the food supply.[3] In this event the quality of both the individual and the environment is insured, since the individual is neither likely to run out of food (or other resources) nor to "overgraze" or otherwise permanently damage his habitat in his effort to obtain the necessities of life. In some populations, death controlled by predators, disease or parasites is the regulator; in other populations, birth control is the mechanism. In some of the best regulated species of the most highly evolved animals, namely the birds and the mammals, the essential control is behavior that restricts the use of space.

This sort of "territorial control" would seem to be relevant to the human population problem. Best of all, planned and controlled land use mutually agreed upon through the democratic process can be accomplished at the local and state level right now, while we continue the discussions

about birth control and abortion in an effort to reach some kind of national and international consensus that can make these approaches effective nationwide and worldwide. Consequently, it certainly will be worthwhile to consider what we might accomplish along the lines of territorial control through land use planning.

Land Use Planning

In actual fact, Georgia is extremely vulnerable to overpopulation for two reasons: (1) the immigration rate is high and can be expected to increase as people flee from the crowded, polluted and deteriorated part of our country and (2) land is open to immediate exploitation on a huge scale because there are so few protective laws and so little land in public ownership. Many of these factors apply to other areas of the nation. Even if the birth rate drops in Georgia and other less crowded states, population growth rate would remain high because of immigration that will come as people discover the relatively cheap and quickly available "open spaces." As already indicated, a growth rate of two per cent per year means that Georgians would be down to one man in 4 acres in 35 years.

A land speculation spiral that is economically ruinous to all but a few speculators could well result unless plans are made now, and control legislation is enacted. Georgia has a lot of open land now but very little has been set aside to remain so. Only about seven per cent of Georgia (see Table

4) is reserved in national, state or city parks, refuges, greenbelts or other protected categories; even our best farmland is vulnerable to real estate exploitation.

As citizens, what can Georgians do? First, they can instigate and support drives, both at the local and state levels, to get more land into public ownership (parks, state and national forests, greenbelts) and can work to have an "open space" bill passed that will enable private owners to establish scenic easements and other restrictions on the use of land that is valuable in its natural state. Second, they can work towards the establishment of metro-commissions and state-wide environmental commissions with strong zoning powers. The passage by the Georgia legislature of the marshlands protection bill early in 1970 was a step in this direction because almost half a million acres were put into a protective category with an agency empowered to insure the best and highest use of a natural resource that otherwise is very vulnerable to destructive types of exploitation.

If about one-third of the area of Georgia were in a protected category, then we would be well protected against overpopulation, and we would have a big buffer that would make the technical problems of pollution control much easier. It is important to note that Western states are fortunate in that 40–50 percent of their land is already in public ownership. The battle there will be to mobilize public opinion to prevent overdevelopment and degradation of these lands.

The third function that citizens can perform is to be more selective about the type and location of new industry. Citizens will be doing industry and society a favor by establishing tough pollution standards and requiring advance waste treatment because it is much cheaper to engineer and internalize the costs of complete waste treatment, water and air recycling at the beginning than to take action later and also pay for repairing a damaged environment. There is no longer a need nor excuse for "dirty" industries that pollute and pay low wages. Any state can now attract industries that have the resources to pay good wages and the public conscience to do what is necessary in waste management.

In summary, our microcosm study makes a case for basing the optimum population on total space requirement and not on food as such. The world can feed more "warm bodies" than it can support high quality human beings.

Footnotes

This article is based on the sixth and final presentation in a public lecture series: "Ecology 1970—Principles for Action," sponsored by the Institute of Ecology, University of Georgia, Winter Quarter, 1970. Copyright held by the author.
1. See, for example, historian Lynn White's essay entitled "The Historical Roots of Our Ecological Crisis," originally published in SCIENCE, 115: 1203, 1967, and widely reprinted in paperback.
2. See *Natural Resources: Quality and Quantity* (Berkeley: University of California Press, 1967), pp. 7–18.
3. Several such models were prepared for the University of Georgia lecture series. See footnote* Table 3.

•••••••••••••• thirty-one

CALVIN L. BEALE ◆

Rural Depopulation in the United States: Some Demographic Consequences of Agricultural Adjustments

The fact that the number of farm people in the United States is steadily decreasing is no longer news. It was news fifteen—even ten—years ago, but the decline has become so prolonged, so deep and so common that it has been widely noted and accepted as a fact of life. Indeed, the Department of Agriculture itself has repeatedly emphasized in very recent years the fact that only a small proportion of all farm youth can expect to find careers as operators of adequate-sized commercial farms. Nevertheless, despite recognition of a decline in the farm segment of the population and knowledge that a similar trend characterizes other advanced nations, the existence of a widespread overall depopulation in rural areas re-mains a paradoxical phenomenon when one considers that the nation as a whole has been in a period of unparalleled population growth.

An annual average of 2.8 million persons has been added to our population since 1950. With two-thirds of the United States population now concentrated in a little more than 200 metropolitan centers, and with the equivalent of 85 percent of our growth taking place in these metro centers, it is not surprising that the bulk of demographic attention has been focused on the growth aspects and metropolitan character of our development. Meanwhile, back at the ranch and down on the farm, some demographic consequences of agricultural adjustments are evident which

◆ **SOURCE.** Reprinted by permission from *Demography*, Vol. 1, 1964, pp. 264–272.

both reflect and foster a different set of problems from those of most metro areas. Whereas rural life has become increasingly similar to urban life in many respects—such as material possessions, educational levels, and life styles—the demographic situation of many rural areas has never been more divergent from that of the cities or metro areas than it is today.

It is not the principal purpose of this paper to discuss the factors producing rural population change but rather to delineate broadly the scope of depopulation resulting from loss in rural areas and to point to some of the structural changes brought about in the residual population.

Migration from the Farm

In considering the process of agricultural adjustment as it affects population, it is well for perspective's sake to note that the trend from the land to the cities is not new.

During the last quarter of a century farm machinery, inventive genius, and new discoveries . . . have made it possible for one man to produce four times as much of many farm products as formerly. If a greater percent of the farm boys did not find some other occupation . . . it is evident that there would not be employment for all. . . .

[They see] . . . that three-fourths of the labor formerly required for harvesting . . . crops annually (is) being performed in the

cities . . . [that is in] the construction of binders, mowers, harvesting machines, thrashers. . . .

The exodus from the farm was inevitable and justified. . . .[1]

These excerpts are not from a speech made yesterday by a rural sociologist. They are taken from an address by the Director of the Cornell Agricultural Experiment Station in 1896. What is new today is the rate of the agricultural exodus and its widespread nature.

Depopulation resulting from agricultural changes has taken place in some part of the nation at practically every stage of our national history, although the total farm population did not reach its peak of 32,530,000 persons until 1916. Under the migration-inhibiting conditions of the Depression Era, the farm population remained as high as 30,547,000 in 1940, with some areas still gaining farm people.[2]

In this situation the effect of World War II was electrifying. Five million people of labor force age alone left the farms in four years (April 1940 to April 1944), the great majority for civilian work rather than for military service.[3] The policy of federal encouragement of subsistence farming ceased and agriculture began an accelerated progress toward use of advanced techniques and specialized production for the commercial market. Since the war the number of farms has declined everywhere except in a few newly irrigated localities. The 30,547,000 farm population of 1940 has become the 13,367,000 of 1963.[4] Not all this loss has involved migration. Some of it has resulted from reclassification of places as nonfarm when operations ceased or definitions changed. But the great majority of the decline does represent outmovement. It is estimated that net migration (and reclassification) from farms amounted to about 11,390,000 persons in the 1940's and 10,130,000 in the 1950's. Inasmuch as the base farm population was lower in the 1950's than in the 1940's, maintenance of nearly the same absolute level of net loss in the 1950's required a higher rate of migration than in the 1940's. The average annual net migration from farms is estimated at 4.4 percent in the 1940's and 5.5 percent in the 1950's. In the three years since 1960, the rate appears to have risen to 6.3 per 100 annually.[5] The current rate is fully as high as that prevailing during the peak of outmovement in World War II.

The factors permitting such a reduction in farm people are numerous and reasonably well known. Mechanization, improved seeds, better breeds and animal nutrition, good management, and advances in fertilizer, pest control, and weed control have all combined to raise productivity and reduce manpower. In addition, the generally high operating level of the nonfarm economy, the ease of physical access to the cities, and the dominant stylistic position of metropolitan life have attracted people away from farming areas. Some federal agricultural programs such as acreage restrictions and conservation reserves (the "soil bank") also have tended to reduce manpower needs in agriculture.

In addition to agricultural outmigration, other factors lowered the level of rural population, such as the decline in coal mining employment and the reclassification of territory from rural to urban through suburbanization, annexation, or census definitional changes.

Rural Population Change

Total U.S. rural population remained almost stationary between 1950 and 1960, dropping from 54,479,000 to 54,054,000, as gains nearly offset losses. The gains, however, tended to be larger per county and more concentrated than the losses. Thus, more than five-eighths of all counties lost rural population as a substantial redistribution took place.

Rural population change in the 1950's by state economic areas is shown on the accompanying map (Fig. 1). Heavy rural loss (more than 10 percent) characterized the interior coastal plain of the Lower South from Georgia through Texas. This was also true of contiguous areas of the Great Plains, especially from Texas to Nebraska. Other prominent zones of heavy loss were sections of the Allegheny Plateau (particularly the coal fields), much of the Ozark and other upland country of Arkansas, Oklahoma, and Missouri, and marginal Corn Belt areas of Iowa and Missouri. For the most part these areas are bordered by others that had rural losses of up to 10 percent.

At the other extreme are areas of sizable rural increase (10 percent gain or more), which often grew from net migration as well as from natural increase. These were noticeable in Florida, California, and Nevada, as might be anticipated from the boom

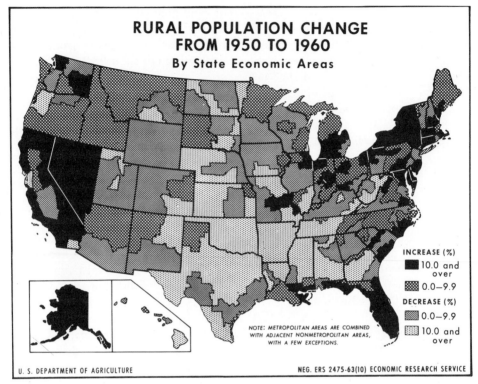

RURAL POPULATION CHANGE
FROM 1950 TO 1960
By State Economic Areas

INCREASE (%)
■ 10.0 and over
▨ 0.0–9.9

DECREASE (%)
▨ 0.0–9.9
▨ 10.0 and over

NOTE: METROPOLITAN AREAS ARE COMBINED
WITH ADJACENT NONMETROPOLITAN AREAS,
WITH A FEW EXCEPTIONS.

U. S. DEPARTMENT OF AGRICULTURE   NEG. ERS 2475-63(10) ECONOMIC RESEARCH SERVICE

FIGURE 1.

character of those states. They were also widespread in the hinterlands of the large industrial centers of the Lower Great Lakes and the Atlantic Seaboard. For the most part areas of growing rural population have had large farm population losses, but agriculture has not been the principal rural activity in them and gains of rural non-farm people have more than offset farm losses. Many of the areas of recent rural population growth in the Northeast and the East North Central States earlier passed through a period of mild rural population losses based on agricultural changes. The revival of rural growth here is associated with factors seldom

related to the traditional rural primary industries of farming, mining, and lumbering. Zelinsky has aptly referred to this population as the "neorural society."[6]

County Changes in Total Population

In all, 1532 counties or a little less than half of the nation's total of 3,081 dropped in total population during the 1950's. Of the 1,060 counties that were entirely rural three-fourths declined, of the 1355 that were primarily rural one-half declined, and of the 662 that were

TABLE 1. Population Growth Trend of Counties in the United States, 1950–1960, by Whether Predominantly Urban or Rural in Residence of Population in 1950

Residence type	Number of Counties (a)			Percent losing
	Total	Gaining	Losing	
Total	3,081	1,549	1,532	49.7
Urban	662	556	106	16.0
Rural	2,419	993	1,426	58.9
Partly urban	1,358	701	657	48.4
Entirely rural	1,061	292	769	72.5

Source: Bureau of the Census, 1960 Census of Population, Volume 1.

(a) Independent cities consolidated with counties in Virginia, Alaskan Election Districts combined to 1950 Judicial Division boundaries. County with no change treated as gaining.

primarily urban only one-sixth declined (see Table 1). Thus, the overwhelming majority of instances of total population loss stemmed from events in the rural population. And the rural economy of most of the declining counties was dominated by agriculture.

A major effect of widespread population declines in the midst of national population growth has been to increase the variation in size and density among counties—the basic political geographical units of the nation. This is a demographic exception to general reduction of group differences within the United States population—such as in education, income, and fertility—which I believe it fair to say has been widely considered a dominant trend of our generation.

The fact that many more counties have lost population during a period of high national growth (the 1950's) than did so during the period of lowest national growth (the 1930's) is reasonably well known, at least among demographers. What may have escaped notice, however, is the circumstance

that in each of the last four decades the proportion of losing counties that have been heavy losers has grown (see Table 2). For example, in the 1920's, little more than a fourth of the declining counties fell in population by more than 10 percent. But by the 1950's the proportion of losers in this class exceeded one-half. Concurrently, the proportion of gaining counties that have had sizable rates of gain has grown since the 1930's and the proportion with only modest gains has been reduced. Therefore, at the same period when more counties are faced with problems associated with rapid population growth than heretofore in this century, more counties than ever before are also confronted with the dilemmas posed by rapid loss.

The effect of this pattern of change on the distribution of counties by size can be seen in Table 3. Since 1940 the number of counties in the modal class —from 10,000 to 50,000 inhabitants— has diminished, while the number at both extremes—more than 50,000 people or less than 10,000—has in-

TABLE 2.   Distribution of Counties in the United States by Population Change, 1950–1960, 1940–1950, and 1930–1940

Population change	Number of counties			
	1950–60 (a)	1940–50	1930–40 (b)	1920–30 (b)
Total	3,114	3,111	3,089	(c)
Gain:				
10 percent or more	957	888	929	(c)
0–10 percent	621	702	1,196	(c)
Loss:				
0–10 percent	754	811	650	934
10 percent or more	782	710	314	324
Distribution of losing counties by amount of loss				
0–10 percent	49.1	53.3	67.4	74.2
10 percent or more	50.9	46.7	32.6	25.8

Source: Bureau of the Census, 1930, 1940, 1950, and 1960 Censuses of Population, Volume I for each year.

(a) 1960 Election Districts of Alaska consolidated to Judicial Divisions for 1950–60 comparison.
(b) Independent cities of Virginia consolidated with counties of origin in 1930–40 and 1920–30.
(c) Not computed.

creased. Conceptions of traditional levels of rural settlement density have to be altered. There are Corn Belt parts of Missouri and Iowa today that have only 15 persons per square mile, including all townspeople, whereas at one time densities of less than 25 or 30 per square mile were unheard of. And the density is still falling. The same changes are true of old Cotton Belt counties in Georgia. In varied areas of Arkansas and Oklahoma, county densities have been reduced to 10 per square mile where once they were 20 or 25. In the Plains, areas which may once have aspired to an over-all density of 10 are now lucky to have 5 per square mile.

Age Selectivity of Migration

Migration other than enforced transfers rarely is nonselective by age, and the movement from farms is no exception. Although some established young or middle-aged farmers have sold out and moved away in the past decade, most of the reduction in farm population is taking place now through the heavy outmovement of young people who have decided not to enter agriculture. Thus, as many older farmers die or retire, their manpower is not replaced, although their land may be absorbed by another farm. Gladys K. Bowles has estimated that of all net migrants from the farm in the 1950's, at least 60 percent was less than 20 years old or reached age 20 some time during the decade.[7] By contrast, it can be shown that decade outmigration rates for middle-aged groups seldom exceed 10 percent even in rapidly declining counties.

The existence of a significant amount of migration from an area usually stimulates questions about the social and economic selectivity of the migrants. One demographic aspect of rural migration that is often overlooked when the question of selectivity is raised is the fact that in areas where the total rural population has declined by as little as 5 to 10 percent in a decade, the net outmigration of young adults is typically more than 50 percent in the decade. There were about 1,500 counties in the United States in 1960 where this was true.[8] To the extent that the term "selectivity" is generally employed to connote the characteristics of a minority coming from a mass, it is the nonmigrants at

prime labor force ages 25 to 45 or 50 in the counties just mentioned who are in effect the "selected" minority. The majority of the original population that grew up in such rural areas has gone. The pertinent research question in such cases would seem to be "Who has remained?" rather than "Who has left?"

The Emergence of Natural Decrease

As a result of the prolonged and increasingly high net outmigration of young rural adults in many counties, a condition has now been reached in a number of areas in which births occurring to the depleted population of childbearing age are exceeded by the number of deaths taking place in the numerically larger older population. In other words, sections of the nation are experiencing a natural decrease in the midst of the more widely heralded population explosion.

TABLE 3.   Number of Counties in the United States, Classified by Population Size, 1940–1960

(Includes county equivalents such as independent cities, Louisiana parishes, Alaska election districts and judicial divisions)

Population size of county	1960		1950		1940	
	Number	Percent of total	Number	Percent of total	Number	Percent of total
Total	3,134	100.0	3,112	100.0	3,109	100.0
100,000 or more	303	9.7	242	7.8	187	6.0
50,000–100,000	293	9.3	259	8.3	258	8.3
25,000–50,000	589	18.8	651	20.9	680	21.9
10,000–25,000	1,094	34.9	1,182	38.0	1,265	40.7
5,000–10,000	561	17.9	516	16.6	475	15.3
Under 5,000	294	9.4	262	8.4	244	7.8

Source: Bureau of the Census, 1950 and 1960 Censuses of Population, Volume I for each year.

This is not the first time such cases have occurred. During the Depression of the 1930's some counties showed a natural decrease. This fact attracted little attention however, apparently being mentioned first by Harold Dorn in a brief note in 1939, when the Depression Era with its accompanying low fertility was nearing its close.[9]

A total of 143 different counties showed an excess of deaths in either 1937 or 1938. A majority of these had a conventional net reproduction rate for the white population of less than 1,000 for the period 1935–1940, indicating the dominant role that low age-specific fertility played in producing the natural decrease. Some of the counties were farming counties in the Midwest or small rural mining counties in the mountain West, but many were in the industrial Northeast, where every state was represented, or in California.[10]

In recent years, the practically unnoticed occurrence of natural decrease has been almost entirely rural and heavily agricultural. In contrast to the 1930's, it has without exception occurred in counties where the level of fertility of women of childbearing age is more than adequate for generational replacement. The excess of deaths has occurred solely because of the distorted age structure, the cohorts from which most deaths occur being large compared with the migration-depleted childbearing groups.

The extent to which the current pattern is new may be judged from the fact that all except one of the 98 counties showing a natural decrease in some year from 1955 to 1961 had a natural *increase* in 1950. With the revival of the birth rate during and immediately after World War II, the Depression-born instances of natural decrease had disappeared almost entirely.

Two principal concentrations of naturally declining counties now have emerged. One is the southern fringe of the Corn Belt, in southern Iowa, northern and western Missouri, and eastern Kansas. In most of these counties population started to drop from outmigration as early as 1890 or 1900, but farms today are still too small or marginally productive to maintain even the reduced level of population, and industrial alternatives have not developed. In addition, age-specific fertility, although adequate for replacement, has long been about the lowest of any farming region.

The second clustering of counties with an excess of deaths is in Texas and part of Oklahoma. Several economic subregions are involved, but with very few exceptions the counties have in common the heritage of a former commitment to cotton under rather marginal climatic and competitive conditions. For a generation they have been subject to a drastic reorganization of land use into more extensive forms (grazing and forestry) and to a flight of people to cities or to the West.

Other types of counties represented elsewhere are small relict Western mining counties, dating from the gold and silver rushes of the last century, and a few widely scattered resort and retirement counties. Whereas counties of the latter type have a distorted age structure, they usually differ from all other types by being areas of inmigration of older people rather than outmigration of young persons.

Perhaps just as meaningful in a

discussion of natural decrease is a notation of the predominantly rural areas that have *not* experienced the phenomenon. The condition is entirely absent from the northern half of the Great Plains. This seems in part to derive from the higher than average fertility of the population in this region. The relative recency of farming settlement in the northwestern plains may be a second factor, for it contributes to a younger population and fewer deaths.

The southeastern states, too, are conspicuous for the absence of natural decrease, except for two retirement counties. The essential reason is fertility, which has always been high enough to keep the age structure young despite heavy outmigration. The general picture does conceal the fact, however, that in the Lower South the demographic structure of rural population is usually radically different between whites and Negroes. Both groups have moved out in large numbers. The median age of the white rural population has risen, and in some counties white deaths have come to exceed births (17 counties in 1961). In the Negro population, however, an increased fertility since 1950 and a pattern of higher outmigration at middle ages than is true for white have been instrumental in producing many more births than deaths. Thus where Negroes are a significant element in the population, an over-all natural decrease has not occurred and is not likely to occur in the foreseeable future.

Should employment opportunities stabilize in counties having a natural decrease, the more normal relationship of births and deaths would reassert itself as the outmigration of the young was considerably reduced or halted. In many areas natural decrease or the near approach of such a condition is most likely to be a temporary stage during the transition of rural sections to forms of agriculture or other land use that directly support fewer people than were present in the past. Temporary may mean a generation, however. The phenomenon of natural decrease has been dwelt on here at some length because it is so counter to cherished American themes of youth, growth, and progress. The very existence of depopulation through migration that is so severe it begets further loss by natural decline epitomizes the magnitude and rapidity of present day change in rural society. But, the basic problems and prospects of the natural decrease counties are little different from those of hundreds of other essentially rural areas that are groping for antidotes to the demographic and other consequences of agricultural adjustment.

Future Considerations

With respect to the future, one point that can be made with certainty is that in the United States as a whole the bulk of the demographic adjustment stemming from agricultural changes has now taken place, for the farm population has already declined by more than one-half. The rate of change from a reduced base can remain high for another decade or two, however. This seems probable from the fact that there are still hundreds of thousands of small-sized farms in the hands of late middle-aged or elderly operators, who have some years of activity remaining before retirement or death.[11] Under foreseeable trends few of these operators are likely to migrate at their stage of life, but in the future most of their farms are likely to be absorbed by other farmers through lease or purchase, or in many upland areas even removed from agriculture altogether and returned to woodland.[12] In addition, the advance of labor-reducing equipment and techniques continues apace. For example, technical advances are permitting the replacement of most cotton and peanut tenants with smaller numbers of wage workers, and threaten in the coming decade to reduce the still heavy inputs of tenant and family manpower used in tobacco culture.[13] The forms of agricultural change are usually not as radical in the northern states as in the South, but the trend toward larger and fewer farms continues without slackening, both in the dairy belts and in the grain and livestock country. In addition, mining employment in the rural coal fields is expected to drift lower.

Modifying factors of a growth nature for presently depopulating areas are (1) the spreading peripheries of metropolitan centers, which bring more rural districts into urban commuting distance, and (2) the decision of the federal government since 1961 to promote the nonagricultural development of rural areas through such instruments as the Area Redevelopment Act.

The nation has never been free of the social costs of space associated with low settlement densities. They have always been present in the Great Plains and the Mountain West. But, when the combination of a small total population

in the county or other local government unit with (in many areas) a low density is aggravated by a steady downward trend of population and is extended over much greater areas of the nation, the problems arising in almost every field of social and economic life become severe and perplexing.[14]

The demography and sociology of decline are not attractive subjects for most researchers.[15] The power and the glory and the action are in megalopolis. But if 70 percent of the United States population is urban, 99 percent of the land area is rural, then the need for additional attention to the demography of depopulating rural areas and for the insights that such research can provide seems to be rising.

Footnotes

This paper was presented at the annual meeting of the American Association for the Advancement of Science, Cleveland, December 27, 1963.

1. I. P. Roberts, "The Exodus from the Farm," *Proceedings of the Tenth Annual Convention of the Association of American Agricultural Colleges and Experimental Stations* (Washington, 1897), pp. 80–82.
2. Except as otherwise stated, all farm population and migration figures cited are taken from Vera J. Banks, Calvin L. Beale, and Gladys K. Bowles *Farm Population— Estimates for* 1910–62 (Economic Research Service, October, 1963).
3. *Net Movement away from Farms in the United States, by Age and Sex: 1940 to 1944* (Series Census-BAE No. 4, Bureau of the Census and Bureau of Agricultural Economics, June, 1945).
4. Figure for 1963 from *Estimates of the Farm Population of the United States:*

April 1963 (Series Census-ERS (P-27), No. 34, Bureau of the Census and Economic Research Service, March, 1964).

5. Rate for 1960–63 period from forthcoming release of the Economic Research Service.

6. See Wilbur Zelinsky, "Changes in the Geographic Patterns of Rural Population in the United States 1950–1960," *Geographical Review* LII, No. 4 (October, 1962), 523. This study, with the monumental amount of work that it reflects, is basic to any investigation of rural population trends in the United States.

7. "Net Migration from the Farm Population, 1950–1960" (paper presented to 1961 annual meeting of the Population Association of America).

8. Estimated by the author.

9. "The Natural Decrease of Population in Certain American Communities," *Journal of the American Statistical Association,* XXXIV, No. 205 (March 1939), 106–9. The fact that births were not tabulated by county of residence (as well as county of occurrence) until the 1937 data year may have concealed the trend from notice.

10. Some instances of natural decrease in the 1930's may have been spurious, reflecting the poorer birth registration completeness of that period. These seem to have been few, however, for most of the natural decrease cases occurred in areas with the best registration systems.

11. In 1959 there were about 500,000 farmers aged 55 years and over who sold less than $2,500 worth of farm products and had little or no off-farm work or other sources of income.

12. The proportion of all farm real estate purchases in the United States in which the land was bought for farm enlargement, rather than use as a single farm, rose from 26 percent in 1950–54 to 46 percent in

1962. See *Farm Real Estate Market Developments* (Economic Research Service, Department of Agriculture, December 1962), p. 9.

13. The proportion of the United States cotton crop harvested by machine increased from 34 percent in 1958 to 70 percent in 1962, and the proportion of the peanut crop combined rather than stacked rose from 20 percent in 1950 to 76 percent in 1959. (Data from Economic Research Service, Department of Agriculture.)

14. Good recent discussions of some of these problems include: Clarence J. Hein, "Rural Local Government in Sparsely Populated Areas," *Journal of Farm Economics,* XLII, No. 4 (November 1960), 827–41; Frederick D. Stocker, "Local Government Costs and Services under Conditions of Sparse Population" (speech at Western Farm Economic Association, July 1963); Luther G. Tweeten and Odell L. Walker, "Estimating Socio-Economic Effects of a Declining Farm Population in a Sparse Area" (paper prepared for Workshop on Regional Development Analysis, Stillwater, Oklahoma, May 1963); Ward W. Bauder, *The Impact of Population Change on Rural Community Life: The Economic System* (Iowa State University of Science and Technology, October 1963), 52 pp.

15. Lowenthal and Comitas note that neither the term "depopulation" nor any of its equivalents is listed in the Index to the extensive survey of the field of demography by Philip M. Hauser and Otis Dudley Duncan, *The Study of Population: An Inventory and Appraisal* (Chicago, 1959; 864 pp.). See David Lowenthal and Lambros Comitas, "Emigration and Depopulation: Some Neglected Aspects of Population Geography," *Geographical Review,* III, No. 2 (April 1962), 195–210.

thirty-two ◆ ◆ ◆ ◆ ◆ ◆ ◆ ◆ ◆ ◆ ◆ ◆ ◆

◆ HALLIMAN H. WINSBOROUGH

The Social Consequences of High Population Density

The man who participates in decisions about urban affairs today seems a most unreasonably imposed-upon fellow. Not only is he called upon to be comfortable in both of C. P. Snow's two cultures (on the one hand considering engineering problems and on the other choosing among competing notions of urban esthetics), but he is frequently asked to show some familiarity with a third minor but lustily growing culture: that of the social sciences. To walk in the elegant and orderly garden of natural science and to trace subtle paths in search of taste no doubt offer some pleasure. To hack one's way through the tangled thicket of the social sciences, however, must frequently seem an imposition—especially so if one's major business lies elsewhere.

The motive of this paper is to offer some aid and comfort to the person who looks in the social sciences for assistance in making choices in urban planning.

Let us begin by arguing that most work in the social sciences can be divided into two kinds. The distinction between the two depends on taste and judgment as to how things in the social world are to be explained. One group of social scientists, who may be designated behavioralists, explain things in terms of the actions which individuals take. From the point of view of the behavioralists, if we know enough about the causes, motives for, and constraints upon individual action we can account for the behavior of groups of people, or even of whole cities, by a process of aggregation.

The second group, whom we will

◆ SOURCE. Reprinted with permission from a symposium "Urban Problems and Prospects" appearing in *Law and Contemporary Problems*, Vol. 30, No. 1, Winter 1965, published by the Duke University School of Law, Durham, N.C. Copyright, 1965, Duke University.

call the structuralists, argue that the very collection of persons into groups provides possibilities and produces characteristics which are not to be derived from a summation of the characteristics of individuals. For example, the law of a country is not easily explained in terms of the motives and actions of the persons presently resident there.

Each of these points of view can be made persuasively by their adherents. Each has been productive of exciting research and discovery. When each is on its home ground all is well. However, when both points of view seem to apply at the same time, or when one tries to take both factors into account at once, the problem becomes complex and the dogmatic statements issuing from both camps become vociferous. It is at this juncture that one must keep one's head and, recognizing the limits as well as the extent of knowledge, try to assess the balance of effects in exercising decision.

Since all of the foregoing no doubt seems fairly abstracted from the everyday decision in urban affairs, let us consider an extended example. A not uncommon problem in urban planning concerns the proper level of population density for which to plan. Certainly various levels of density have various costs and various advantages. Supposing that an intrepid man began to search the literature in sociology in hopes of finding some guidance about the nature of these costs and advantages: what might he find?

He would discover that two somewhat separate traditions in sociology argue that the level of population density in a human society has important social consequences. Each tradition is based on the writings of one of the founding fathers of modern sociology and each has fairly vigorous present-day adherents. The consequences presumed by these two traditions are, however, rather different. On the one hand, the structuralists, following a Durkheimian point of view, see high population density, along with high population size, as a prerequisite for the development of division of labor.[1] On the other hand, behaviorally-oriented followers of Simmel stress the psychological—and even physiological —strain involved in the frequent stimulation and interaction concomitant with dense living.[2]

The Durkheimian position is succinctly summarized by Halbwachs as follows:[3]

In reality, the division of labor results from the expansion of human groups and from the increase in their density. These are necessary conditions, (1) for the appearance and development . . . of a great variety of aptitudes and also of needs; (2) for bringing aptitudes and needs together in reciprocal stimulation . . . and (3) for establishing increasingly precise adaptation between the techniques of the more and more specialized producers and the needs of the more and more diversified consumers.

This point of view has received theoretical and empirical elaboration in the development of central place theory. This theory argues that a certain number of consumers are necessary within a given radius of a center for the support of a specific good or service.[4] Whether a specific good or service becomes a central one, then, depends upon the population density of the area in question, that is, upon whether it will find a sufficient number of consumers within its range. Some recent developments in this theory suggest it may apply to the distribution of services in the city as well as the distribution of cities in space.[5]

The Simmelian point of view has also received recent empirical support —a good deal of it from studies of animal behavior. In an attempt to investigate the relationship between animal behavior and population characteristics in a species living in the wild, Calhoun confined a group of wild rats to a quarter-acre enclosure.[6] He provided an abundance of food and relative freedom from predators. Population did not rise as expected because of an increase in infant mortality. This increase, Calhoun held, came about because stress from social interaction led to disruption of maternal behavior. Pursuing this hypothesis under laboratory conditions, Calhoun permitted caged populations of experimental rats to develop about twice the density which seemed to provide only moderate stress.[7] His results were dramatic. Many females became unable to carry pregnancy to full term. Many of those who did were unable to survive the delivery. Of those who survived, many subsequently fell so short in their maternal functions that infant mortality ran as high as ninety-six per cent in some experimental groups.

Males, too, exhibited strange behavior, ranging from sexual deviation to cannibalism, and from frenetic overactivity to pathological withdrawal.

Calhoun holds that these disturbances in behavior are the result of the stress from social interaction. Other investigators have found a direct relationship between density and adult animal mortality. Deevey cites some literature in support of this relationship and offers a physiological explanation of the relationship between the stimulation due to increased interaction and mortality.[8]

In summary, then, there is considerable evidence supporting both consequences of high levels of population density. Given the weight of the evidence it would seem unwise to simply disregard one or another of these effects. The problem becomes one of assessing the outcome of their joint influence. In a paper in which he speculates on the combination of these effects on human populations, Calhoun conceptualizes the problem as follows.[9] He associates the level of density which maximizes the division of labor with what he calls the economic climax state of the society. That level of density which minimizes psychological and physiological stress from interaction he associates with the social climax state. Of these he says:[10]

> *It is logical to assume that the social climax can be achieved at a lower density than the economic climax. Thus the population characteristic of the economic climax community may serve as a yardstick of value judgment at what*

*level the population should sta-
bilize. Since this level is likely to
be attained in the United States
within the next 50 to 100 years,
any individuals or groups who encourage population growth at a
rate likely to make this level to be
exceeded, draw upon themselves
the onus of contributing to the
difficulties of achieving the climax
social community.*

Although Calhoun's statement may
well be correct, it seems an oversimplification of a complex problem. First, it
seems likely that, as with the problem
of optimum city size, the optimum
level of density, taking into account
both stress and the division of labor,
may vary with the characteristic to be
optimized.[11] Further, there remains the
question of the relative magnitude of
the effects of stress and the division
of labor upon a characteristic to be
optimized. Given that the human animal is subject to the psychological and
physiological stress due to interaction
documented for other animals, it remains a question, for instance, whether
easier access to medical facilities in a
dense population may not significantly
ameliorate effects of stress on adult
human mortality.

By the time our urban decision-
maker had reached this point in his
search of the sociological literature, he
would no doubt feel that his patience
as well as the accumulated knowledge
was exhausted. Not a great deal of specific information about the problem of
the effects of various density levels
within the urban community has been
provided. In fact, about all that has

been accomplished is to suggest that
the decision about the level of population density is an important one.

Given all the foregoing information, how should a man try to influence
the decision process with respect to
population density levels? Certainly the
behavioralists' findings are impressive.
But in many circumstances the pressure of costs will argue for higher
density. Since the latter argument has
a kind of life of its own, perhaps one
should use his influence to argue for
lower density presuming that the net
result will approximate Calhoun's social
climax state.

Would such a decision be justified? Would further research on the
problem make this decision strategy
wrong? I was curious enough about
these questions to try to carry the research process along another step in the
hope of being able to make some
pertinent assessment.

To begin this investigation, I returned to the original Simmelian topic
of people living in the city. I investigated the relationships between population density and a series of variables
similar to or suggested by Calhoun's
work as they occurred in the seventy-
five Community Areas in the city of
Chicago. These Community Areas are
a partitioning of the land area of the
city which was accomplished some
years ago and are convenient for this
analysis because they demonstrate a
considerable variability in population
density.

Five variables suggested by Calhoun's writings were readily available.[12]
They are the infant death rate, an overall death rate which has been adjusted

for differences between areas in age composition, a tuberculosis rate, an overall public assistance rate adjusted for differences in age composition, and a measure of the rate of public assistance to persons under eighteen years old. Parsonian correlation was used as a measure of the association between each of these variables and the level of population density over the community areas. These correlations are given in the first column of table one. All but one of the variables showed a positive correlation with population density. That is, the higher the density the higher the rates. The exception to this rule was the overall death rate which showed no appreciable association with density.

These findings certainly suggest that increased density has a deleterious effect on the population. To assume that this effect is caused by increased stress is, however, a long logical leap. In fact, only a moderate acquaintance with cities would suggest an alternative explanation. People of lower socioeconomic status—people more likely, irrespective of density, to score higher on all of the rates investigated—tend to live closer to the center of the city than do persons of higher socioeconomic status. Further, population density declines in a regular way as one moves outward from the city center. These facts suggest that socioeconomic status may be confounding the relationships which we wish to investigate. Another variable which may confound the relationships is quality of housing, which also has association with density and with each of the rates. Finally, any effects of stress which may be present

are confounded because the number of in-migrants to each area is likely to be different.

In order to avoid these confounding variables, then, one would like to investigate the associations between population density and each of the five rates "controlling" for socioeconomic status, quality of housing, and migration.[13] We have chosen to accomplish this by partial correlation, a fairly satisfactory technique which allows one to approach the "control" of the classical experiment. A list of the variables "partialed out" can be found in note [a]-2 of table one. The values of the partial correlations are given in column two of that table.

Removing the effects of socioeconomic status, quality of housing, and migration changes the pattern of the findings considerably. The overall death rate, which had originally shown no relationship with density, changed to a strong negative association: the higher the density, the lower the rate. The infant mortality rate, however, which had originally been positively associated with density, continued virtually unchanged in its association with density. Thus, after control, one mortality rate is in the direction predicted by the behavioralists and another in the direction predicted by the structuralist argument. The tuberculosis rate, which originally had a positive association with density, becomes, under control, strong and negative. This is a very odd finding, suggesting that, *ceteris paribus,* high density leads to low tuberculosis rates. Both public assistance measures were originally positively associated with density. After control,

Table 1. Zero-Order and Partial Correlation of Gross Population Density and Stated Dependent Variable; Community Areas, City of Chicago, 1950

Dependent Variable	Variable Set Held Constant[a]	
	1	2
Infants deaths per 100 live births	.32**	.33**
Age standardized deaths per 1000 persons	.14	−.62**
Tuberculosis cases per 10,000 persons 15 years and older	.20*	−.67**
Age standardized public assistance per 1000 persons	.37**	−.39**
Quintile ranking of public assistance to persons under 18 per 1000 persons under 18	.45**	.14

[a] 1. Zero-order correlations

2. Percent of workers in professional, technical, and kindred occupations
  Median income of families
  Median years of school completed by persons 25 years and older
  Percent of population foreign born white
  Percent of population Negro
  Median age
  Percent of dwelling units owner occupied
  Median rent of renter occupied dwelling units
  Percent of dwelling units with no water, no bath, or dilapidated
  Percent of dwellings built before 1920
  Percent of dwellings with 1.5 or more persons per room
  Percent of persons one year and older living in same household, 1949 and 1950

* Significantly different from zero at the .05 level.

** Significantly different from zero at the .01 level.

each has changed but in a somewhat different way. Overall public assistance becomes negatively associated with density while assistance to persons under eighteen years of age demonstrates no appreciable association.

After control for the three confounding factors, then, we have a fairly mixed bag. One rate shows the positive association with density predicted by the behavioralists' argument.[14] Three show the negative association predicted by the structuralist argument. The final rate shows no association.

Perhaps the only order that we can bring to these heterogeneous findings is to suggest that the effects of density on the young seem to be different from the effects on the adult population. The findings certainly add weight to the previously stated guess that the optimum level of density varies with the thing to be optimized.

Before proceeding further let me insert the scholar's usual note of caution. Clearly the foregoing findings are rather tentative. Inferences from high order partial correlations is a notoriously tricky game. I have investigated the effects of density as it varies within only one city. Clearly there might be different outcomes in other cities, and variation between cities might produce still other outcomes. Despite these demurs, the results of the analysis are strong and curious enough to warrant further investigation.

Where does all this leave the man who must arrive at some policy with respect to urban planning? Not very far along, I expect. The original strategy proposed before the statistical analysis seems to fare reasonably well. It might be modified only by suggesting that lower density should be accompanied with a diminution of the catchment area for medical facilities.

If all the foregoing is taken as a cautionary tale, I suppose its moral is to take with a grain of salt dogmatic claims by either behavioralists or structuralists when good sense or the pressure of realistic constraints suggests that variables from the opposite camp should be taken into consideration. No doubt some day the social sciences will offer a larger fund of demonstrated principles to aid the decisionmaker. But it will certainly be a long time before solutions to problems in urban affairs can be spewed forth from a computer without the inclusion of a factor of good judgment.

Footnotes

This paper is based on research supported by a grant from the Duke University Council on Research. Some of the computations involved were carried out in the Duke University Computing Laboratory which is supported, in part, by the National Science Foundation.
1. Emile Durkheim, The Division of Labor in Society 256–82 (George Simpson transl. 1960).
2. Simmel, *The Metropolis and Mental Life*, in Paul K. Hatt & Albert J. Reiss (Eds.), Cities and Society 635–47 (1957).
3. Maurice Halbwachs, Population and Society 173 (Otis Dudley Duncan & Harold W. Pfauts transl., 1960).
4. A concise presentation of central place theory is given in Ullman, *A Theory of Location for Cities*, in Hatt & Reiss, *op. cit. supra* note 2, at 227–36. For a more lengthy treatment, see August Losch, The

Economics of Location (William H. Woglam & Wolfgang F. Stolper transl., 1954). Additional citations can be found in Brian J. L. Berry & Allen Pred, Central Place Studies: A Bibliography of Theory and Applications (1961).
5. Carol, *The Hierarchy of Central Functions Within the City*, 50 Annals of the Ass'n of Am. Geographers 419 (1960). Some additional pertinent discussion is found in Ludlow, *Urban Densities and Their Costs: An Exploration Into the Economics of Population Densities and Urban Patterns*, in Coleman Woodbury (Ed.), Urban Redevelopment: Problems and Practices 102–20 (1953).
6. Calhoun, *A Method for Self-Control of Population Growth Among Mammals Living in the Wild*, 109 Science 92 (1949).
7. Calhoun, *Population Density and Social Pathology*, Scientific American, Feb. 1962, pp. 139–48.
8. Deevy, *The Hare and the Haruspex: A Cautionary Tale*, 40 Yale Rev. 161 (1959).
9. Calhoun, *Social Welfare As a Variable in Population Dynamics*, 22 Cold Spring Harbor Symposia on Quantitative Biology 339–56 (1957).
10. *Id.* at 355.
11. Duncan, *Optimum Size of Cities*, in Hatt & Reiss, *op. cit. supra* note 2, at 759–72.
12. Data are taken from Philip M. Hauser & Evelyn M. Kitagawa (Eds.), Local Community Fact Book for Chicago, 1950 (1953).
13. It may be noted that one of the variables held constant, per cent of dwelling units having more than 1.51 persons per room, is related to the number of persons per room, a component of total density. This aspect of density was treated separately because of some thought that its effects might be different from those of total density. The finding was, however, that the pattern of partial correla-

tion was similar to that for total density except that all correlations except for those for assistance to juveniles were smaller and that public assistance was signed positively and assistance to juveniles was signed negatively.

14. An interesting methodological point arises in using the data in this fashion. At first blush, it appears that we are committing the "fallacy of ecological correlation" in investigating a phenomena which occurs at the individual level using aggregated data for census tracts. It seems to us, however, that our problem is rather different from that usually discussed in terms of the classical fallacy. Our problem is not to assess the existence of an individual effect of density on stress. Such an assessment can be performed with considerably greater elegance and precision in an experiment. In the main we find Calhoun's demonstration fairly compelling as to the existence of the effect. Rather, it is our aim to investigate the balance of effects, individual and aggregative, which derive from the variation in density. Thus we argue that, rather than being fallacious, an ecological correlation is a convenient device to investigate the balance of effects in the aggregate.

thirty-three ◆ ◆ ◆ ◆ ◆ ◆ ◆ ◆ ◆ ◆ ◆ ◆

◆ WILBUR ZELINSKY

The Geographer and His Crowding World: Cautionary Notes Toward the Study of Population Pressure in the Developing Lands

If anything is safely predictable for the final third of this most complex, dynamic, and crucial of mankind's many centuries, it is that the management and consequences of rapid, massive population increase will engross the attention of more and more of our best minds. Parallel with that ominously steepening arc graphing the total accumulation of human beings, there has been a recent upsurge of interest in such matters not only among social scientists but also among statesmen and the public at large. For anyone who recalls with chagrin the apathy concerning matters

demographic in places both high and low a mere twenty years ago, the current general consternation over the "Population Explosion" is scarcely credible, and even a bit disconcerting. What is implied thereby is an expectation that somehow, however late in the game it may be, the "experts" will save the day with some brilliant panacea or technical legerdemain. The main burden of this essay is that there is as yet little grounds for such faith. The enormity and uniqueness of the huge twentieth century proliferation of human numbers has caught population scientists un-

◆ SOURCE. Reprinted by permission of the author from *Revista Geografica*, Vol. 65, 1966, pp. 7–28.

aware, or at least technically and methodologically unequipped. I can say this with some assurance for the still rather underdeveloped field of population geography; but I suspect that the situation is not much better among demographers in general.

The basic argument can be stated quite simply: We are about to confront practical decisions of the utmost gravity in our social, economic, ethical, political, and ecological affairs brought about, in large part, by very great population increments in recent years in most inhabited areas and by the even greater growth forecast for the immediate future. Furthermore, theoretical problems of major interest and importance are being posed by the radically novel situations now coming into being. Unfortunately, our existing body of population doctrine was distilled from the experience of past or vanishing epochs of decreasing relevance to this strange new "crowded" world. Indeed, the inertia of ideas being what it is, we may find ourselves positively hindered in the scientific study of developing population pressures by some of our scholarly legacy or the related folk wisdom of the literate. As a contribution toward the more realistic, meaningful, and utilitarian theoretical framework still to be erected—a ground-clearing operation so to speak—I propose to examine eleven important ideas that are either explicit or implicit in recent statements and thought on population matters, and are also of some interest to geographers. It will be argued that all can be classed as either fallacies or unproved assumptions, the latter to be used with caution

awaiting the time they can be either certified or discredited. The casual reader may infer congenital pessimism or malicious mischief in this approach. In actuality, the mood is one of painful self-scrutiny and the intent that of breaking through to deeper levels of understanding and ultimately to truly constructive approaches to the long-term welfare of our species and its habitat. In this process, it is necessary to concede that a lively appreciation of one's ignorance is the beginning of true wisdom.

Attention is confined to the so-called "underdeveloped" world, or "developing lands," more for the sake of convenience than through conviction. It is quite possible that the arithmetically less alarming rates of population growth in the advanced nations, combined as they are with virtually unlimited expansion of economic production and consumption and by more mischievous manipulation of the environment, may ultimately engender crises more pernicious and insoluble than those so visibly looming over less affluent countries. It is also arguable that both the ultimate causes and cures for the population-resource afflictions of the underdeveloped world are to be found in the advanced nations. Currently, neither proposition is so nearly generally accepted as the imminence of trouble in the former class of areas. And since a separate essay would be needed to validate these theses, the question of the advanced nations is bypassed reluctantly for the time being.

Before this review of dubious propositions can be begun, two premises must be stated: that a critical situation is indeed being produced in the developing lands by the amount and rate of population growth; and that, quite aside from the sheer magnitude of this expansion, the new sets of man-earth and man-man relationships that are linked to this growth are qualitatively distinct from anything that has preceded them historically.

Scientists are obliged to be skeptical creatures, by virtue of temperament and their professional charge. The sheer raucousness of some of the Neo-Malthusian canon and the fear-mongering of various journalistic approaches to the population problems of developing lands will automatically induce some students to assume that so much sound and fury may well signify nothing. Unfortunately, though the shriller criers of havoc may be doing their cause more harm than good, the simple facts are incontrovertible.

There are many ways to indicate the severity of the approaching crisis, even though, admittedly, we are still quite uncertain as to exactly what forms it will take or what the outcome will be. One device, as effective as any, is to consider the probable change in total population of the developing lands during the expected lifetime of children already born. For the following six, randomly chosen nations, I have projected the aggregate population that will reside in each at the time the average female inhabitant born in 1964 can be expected to die. These projections, based on 1964 population figures, the most reliable estimates of annual rate of increase for the same date, and the most recent data on female expectation of life at birth, are somewhat conservative. The indicated rate of change for 1964 may understate the true rate in some instances; in addition, mortality rates are susceptible to lowering, or are actually declining in some of these countries; and almost certainly the 1964 life expectation value in every case well exceeds that given here.

Thus we must quite soberly contemplate the prospect that an Egyptian girl born in 1964 will breathe her last

	Population[1] 1964 (millions)	Annual Rate[2] of Increase 1964	Expectation of[2] Life at Birth, Female	Projected Population, Year of Death of Average Female Born 1964 (millions)
Brazil	78.8	+2.81%	45.5 (1940–50)	289.2
Costa Rica	1.4	3.82	57.0 (1949–51)	12.3
Egypt	28.9	2.73	53.8 (1960)	132.4
Jordan	1.9	4.08	50.0 (est.)	13.7
Indonesia	102.2	2.2	50.0 (est.)	302.5
South Korea	27.6	2.76	53.7 (1955–60)	125.9

[1] Population Index, 32.1 (1966).
[2] Population Index, 31.4 (1965).

in a nation containing over 132 million inhabitants. Given Egypt's present social and physical resources, I find it impossible to imagine how so many individuals could live in reasonable material comfort without some truly revolutionary remodeling of the social and economic structure of the country. Such a development is, of course, not necessarily undesirable or impossible, but would be quite a feat during the next 54 years. The same argument applies to the other nations, although the immediate environmental constraints upon demographic growth are not nearly as great in Brazil, Costa Rica, or (outer) Indonesia. The dilemmas of large populations pressing upon limited, immediately exploitable resources could be circumvented by a rapid reduction in fertility; but this too (unless implemented by brute force) would imply a rather implausible degree of skill in social engineering or incredibly good luck. The more probable alternative is a serious depression of level of living and a return to the former pattern of high mortality rates and low expectation of life. In any event, the status quo cannot be maintained; difficult, painful, and even disastrous alternatives must be pondered.

The argument that the present or impending population-resource situation of the developing lands is historically unique could be sustained quite firmly on quantitative grounds. Never before in human history has there been so rapid and persistent an increase in population involving so large a percentage of mankind; and, although there is little comfort in this fact, it seems highly unlikely that the expe-

rience can ever be repeated during a later epoch. The sheer mass and rapidity of this change would in itself induce major qualitative social and geographic innovations. But there are more fundamental reasons for the uniqueness of the developing situation. There is growing evidence that the current extraordinary demographic situation is but a single phase of a larger unique episode in human history—the phenomenon that has received the unfortunate, but probably indelible, designation "underdevelopment." Poverty, in many forms and degrees, has always been with us; and there have been earlier large, rapid, localized spurts of population. But the existence of large, impoverished masses of people undergoing rapid numerical increase for several decades is indeed quite unprecedented; and the profound disequilibrium between demographic growth and a relatively slow expansion or exploitation of physical and social resources appears to be symptomatic of some quite deep structural changes— possibly of a pathological character— in the nature and organization of human society. Thus the so-called "Population Explosion" is both a symptom of and a contributing factor to a much larger process, of which "Underdevelopment" is another relatively visible manifestation. This observation leads logically to the first of the ideas to be scrutinized:

1. The fallacy that the population-resource disequilibrium of the developing lands is an isolated phenomenon, and the unproved assumption that it constitutes

their single most important problem.

The first portion of this statement is one that few thoughtful scholars would endorse, since it collapses the moment the real world is examined. Nonetheless, it merits our attention since this is a notion that much recent non-academic literature would tend to convey. There is also the ever-present danger that the population student may unconsciously slip into this fallacy when, as he often must, he disaggregates the fearsome complexities of social reality into manageable fragments. In any event, the image of a simple, stable underdeveloped community, idyllically undisturbed and unchanging for centuries, suddenly erupting demographically with the arrival of a few physicians, nurses, wonder drugs, and DDT is patently misleading. In almost every instance, the community had, for some time, been experiencing radical changes, either under the direct impact of the advanced nations or through endogenous processes initiated by such contacts. Thus a great many new things had been going on; and the rather abrupt onset of a decidedly lower death rate (and possibly also a significantly higher birth rate) came as the culmination of a whole series of changes, not as a whimsical trick of fate. Furthermore, the new demographic regime is associated with major revisions in socioeconomic and psychological patterns and with innovations in transportation, communications, education, and many aspects of technology. The interactions among all these are real and important; and this functional interrelatedness, which may frequently find spatial expression, is a quality that should endear the study of population change to the geographer.

A major reason for belief in this fallacy—or allegiance to the unproved assumption that population-resource disequilibrium, i.e., the "Population Problem," is the most urgent of problems in the underdeveloped world—is its exceptional statistical visibility. The number of inhabitants is probably the most widely available statistic for underdeveloped countries taken as a whole. Rapid change in this index can be detected quickly and easily even by the most amateurish of observers. On the other hand, it is reasonable to suggest, at least for the sake of argument, that even more momentous upheavals have been going on in the basic socioeconomic structure, in ideas, values, and attitudes, in the nature of the relations among communities, among individuals, and between man and the land, or even in the essential psychological makeup of the people—and that, in fact, one or more of these sets of changes comprise the truly central and decisive problem. If such is the case, then we are faced with problems of observation, measurement, and analysis that will tax our most resourceful social scientists. The more radical transformations that may underlie an abrupt demographic change could involve entities not easily quantifiable and, in any case, ones not immediately rising to any statistical surface. Least of all are they likely to reveal themselves in the visible landscape; and in much of the underdeveloped world revolutionary new generations of social and economic geographies may have reached an advanced embryonic stage and be ready for hatching within the shell of old, traditional vistas.

In brief, then, recent population growth in underdeveloped countries at a pace well beyond the demonstrated capacity of social and economic systems to provide adequately for human needs is a phenomenon inextricably bound to other less well observed, or poorly understood, ongoing processes. Until we learn the true nature and interrelations of this complex of processes, the chain of causes and effects, and the hierarchy of forces among them, there is no sound basis for claiming that excessive population growth is the most crucial problem confronting these areas.

2. The fallacy that any consensus exists concerning the kind of resolution to be sought for the population-resources problems of the developing lands (disregarding the means to be employed to attain this desideratum).

The discovery that the foregoing notion is indeed a fallacious one is probably more unsettling philosophically and more suggestive of future practical difficulties than any of the other negative or cautionary statements offered in this essay. Virtually every writer and social scientist who has been responsive to the demographic distress of the underdeveloped world has instinctively adopted the idea that he, or the people concerned, clearly visualizes the sort of normalcy, the demographic or economic good health to which the community must be restored. In actual fact, almost

no methodical thinking has been done on this crucial issue.

A rough medical analogy may be in order. Imagine that some students of natural history acquire in a young, immature form the only known specimen of a rare animal species, one never before observed in its adult stage, and attempt to rear and study it in captivity. During the process, this unique creature contracts a serious chronic disease, one which finally becomes acute, produces serious malformations, and threatens its life. All the attending veterinarians agree that everything possible must be done to save it. They have succeeded in describing the symptoms and are able to diagnose intelligently the probable causes. Several possible courses of treatment suggest themselves. They have, of course, never previously been applied to this particular animal; and although it is not certain whether any of the possible therapies will be efficacious, it is agreed to try the most promising one. At this juncture, one of the more reflective veterinarians points out that during the course of his illness their patient has apparently entered the adolescent stage and may, in fact, be on the verge of full adulthood. How are they to tell just when the treatment has succeeded, i.e., when the creature begins to look and act like a healthy, normal *adult* of its species? How can they be sure that, although the therapy may save its life, it may not also produce a permanently crippled, abnormal organism and, incidentally, spoil forever their earlier plans for studying its behavior and biological characteristics?

As we leave our imaginary friends with their unresolved quandary, it must be admitted that this is a defective analogy. Strictly speaking, no discussion of either immediate action or ultimate results is absolutely necessary in the case of "runaway" population growth in the underdeveloped lands. It is simple to demonstrate mathematically that the problem is self-limiting, that within a very few generations the current rate of growth must come to an end because of the finiteness of terrestrial mass and space and the existence of certain basic physical laws. And the patient will not necessarily die if left unattended. Even though the final results may be most unpleasant, the prognoses are, in order of declining plausibility, an arresting or reversal of growth through (a) a death rate rising well above present levels, (b) a spontaneous decline in fertility, or (c) any of the many possible combinations of the two foregoing changes. The countries passing through this experience of letting their population crisis run its course may find themselves subsisting under wretched conditions; but the population will have survived somehow.

Many of the affected countries still remain at the stage where the problem is unrecognized or where, through disinterest, indecision, or positive choice, a laissez-faire policy is being followed. But more and more—and eventually possibly all—will agree that it is desirable and urgently necessary to avoid major catastrophe. And that, finally, returns us to the main point of this discussion: Is it possible to adhere to a policy that limits itself to the purely negative objective of substantially reducing rates of population growth? It seems much more intelligent, more commonsensical tactically, to recognize that, willy-nilly, such a policy will result in a country basically different from what it has been, or that the negative program is more likely to be consummated if it is combined with a positive push toward useful and desirable goals. The status quo ante cannot possibly be patched together again. And so what sort of world are we getting in its stead? Or what sort of world *can* or *should* we strive for?

We are, in fact, being coerced by the huge, inexorable mechanism of the "modernization" process into thinking seriously about which utopias, or sub-utopias, or reasonable facsimiles thereof, we can put on the drawing boards. It is even conceivable that this compulsory review of means and ends may be a blessing in disguise. Gone are the leisurely days when history took care of itself. Until recently, one could hopefully contemplate the autonomous forces of social and economic change propelling mankind forever forward and upward along the erratic, but ascending, paths of progress toward some glorious, if rather indistinct, destiny. Now it is abundantly clear that active, skillful human intervention is mandatory for survival or for the qualitative enhancement of human existence.

No agreement has been reached, and none is possible without great difficulty, over the goals—the signs of returning health—that might be striven for in any campaign to deal with extremely rapid population growth. Or perhaps the issue has already been settled tacitly. Many writers claim that the underdeveloped countries have been undergoing a "Revolution of Rising Expectations" (though without much specificity as to what is being expected). It is not really clear, and certainly has not been verified by any rigorous research, that any truly fundamental revision of material appetites or life-goals has taken place; but if it has, these new values must be reckoned with in any demographic programs. In any case, what aspirations can be proclaimed concerning the size, composition, dynamics, economic status, environmental ecology, or any of a variety of relationships between man and physical and social resources in the populations that will have survived their period of trauma? Even more basically, which (or whose) values— cultural, philosophical, or whatever— are to be preserved and strengthened? What of our obligations to other species of life or to the quality of the inanimate environment? For whose benefit are plans to be made and implemented— for that of the locality, the nation, or all of mankind? Or for which segment of the population—the business community, the military, the administrative bureaucracy, the intelligentsia, or the "common people"? And for which generation—those who are now alive, or their children or grandchildren? Or do we think in terms of perpetuity? These are profound questions of intent to be debated, questions of scale, duration, conflict of interest, and philosophic bias. I would suggest that the time has arrived when we should begin asking them.

3. The preoccupation with population numbers as items of essential importance per se.

Population scientists are so accustomed to dealing with statistics as a useful surrogate for the reality with which

they are, in fact, truly concerned that they may impute to them an importance not actually inherent in them. More specifically, scholars, and many laymen as well, may tend to view population-resource problems in the light of numerical indices rather than the grosser, and partly unmeasurable, world that underlies them. It is self-evident that for any given area or community a particular population size is not absolutely good or bad in itself as long as it stands somewhere above the minimum needed for biological and cultural survival and below that maximum where sheer physical congestion inhibits the movement or physical and mental health of individuals. This statistic is important, of course, but only takes on meaning in the context of specific conditions and specific value systems (even though, incidentally, it is extremely difficult to assign hard numerical values to the concepts of "underpopulation," "overpopulation," or "optimum" population even when all the facts and assumptions are open to inspection). In the same vein, no specific rate of population change is necessarily good or evil—unless it is prolonged to the point where the population either disappears or expands to calamitous dimensions. Thus, during a limited time span, population growth or decline, or stasis, or a complex cycle of change may be good, bad, or indifferent, depending on the character of the place and the period. An annual net reproductive increase of + 4.0 per cent or thereabouts in Kentucky in 1790 was an occasion for rejoicing; in El Salvador in 1990 it could be disastrous.

Excessive preoccupation with population counts may lead to treatment of symptoms rather than causes. We may find ourselves worrying over how to slow down the annual population increment in some area from 3 per cent to 1 per cent or less, while omitting any real concern about gains or losses in human and social values. Conversely, the absence of any perturbations on the demographic fever chart may lead to a false sense of well-being. A stable population is not necessarily a happy or a fundamentally healthy one. Just as we can delude ourselves into believing that all is well with the body politic if the citizens are not actively rioting in the streets, so too it is possible to postpone dangerously any serious investigation of the population/resource situation in a region that seems stationary in its behavior.

4. The fallacy of demographic predestination—the belief that mankind is moving teleologically toward a happy resolution of its population problems or, conversely, directly toward demographic doom.

This is a fallacy that is much more likely to be implicit, or sometimes even subconscious, rather than explicitly avowed by the student. It may be the result of belief in supernatural forces or simply a matter of temperamental outlook. The scholar is, of course, entitled to harbor his own private credo, whether it be melioristic or fatalistic, but should guard against letting it warp his judgment when attempting to deal in systematic, scientific fashion with the facts at hand. In particular, there is genuine danger that this kind of innate bias may predispose the population scientist to write as though man were either utterly impotent or else all-powerful in grappling with his demographic destiny. As it happens, no very convincing evidence is yet visible in the pattern of history or the innate logic of current facts to support belief in either brand of teleology—the inevitable ascent of mankind to higher levels of social and geographic grace or the imminence of Doomsday. Is it not the better part of wisdom for the population scholar to take nothing for granted, but rather proceed to test the limits of the necessary and the possible through careful observation and analysis and through the design of action programs that are not circumscribed by unproved, a priori assumptions?

5. The fallacy that the population-resource problem in developing lands is simply one of adequate food production.

This is a fallacy that is widely and explicitly current in both the scholarly and popular literature on demographic problems. And since food production is a favorite subject for geographic investigation, geographers may be particularly vulnerable to it. It is, of course, axiomatic that the day-to-day problem of feeding most of the low-income citizens of low-income lands is a matter of large, lasting concern. During the millennia when most communities were small, self-contained, nonmonetary economic units operating outside any large regional or world market, local food production could indeed be the paramount problem in survival; and insofar as population-resource crises appeared, food shortages might be cause or effect. But it does not follow, now that all the world's peoples are more or less integrated into the world market economy, that either the population-resource problem or the phenomenon of underdevelopment can be defined solely, or even primarily, in terms of the calories people consume or how much food they can grow. To see them as such, even at the rudimentary level of immediate human needs, is a gross distortion of reality, a sort of alimentary determinism.

For his animal survival, man everywhere requires food, potable liquids, and breathable air and, in those areas with winters or cold nights, clothing, shelter, and domestic fuel. But even the most primitive communities have other needs; and in those lands that can be realistically called "developing," there is an imposing inventory of necessities. Industrial fuel and energy requirements must be met; a wide range of industrial raw materials is called for; various services—among them, transportation, education, and administration—must be supplied; and the amenities are in ever increasing demand. Indeed, as the country climbs up the developmental scale, the problem of producing and supplying food recedes as other problems come to the fore; yet population-resource crises may still occur. Indeed, I believe it is possible for even the most advanced of nations to anticipate severe population-resource situations in which the issue of food supply may be totally irrelevant. And the irrelevance of food production as the critical element in population-resource imbalances may also be demonstrated in those various countries, past or present, that have

produced food surpluses but, nonetheless, have displayed acute symptoms of "underdevelopment" or of an incapacity to provide for the wants of rapidly increasing populations.

A country may be said to have mastered its population-resource problems when it is living within its own technical, institutional, and ecological means and at the same time offering its inhabitants the wherewithal for acquiring all the goods and services they regard as basic for a decent existence. This "wherewithal" simply means purchasing power. And money, in turn, implies the existence of reasonably well-paying jobs for all, or nearly all, the labor force, and a labor force with a reasonably high level of productivity, or, more precisely, the capacity for producing in abundance goods and services other people wish to buy. Where a market demand exists, in the form of would-be purchasers willing and able to spend money, food or any other commodity can be furnished to the inhabitants of either underdeveloped or advanced countries from either external or internal sources.

It is quite inaccurate to characterize an area as suffering from "population problems" if it does not produce all the foodstuffs it consumes. (Most advanced nations would fall into this class.) It is equally erroneous to believe that an underdeveloped land experiencing food shortages will shed its status as an area undergoing population-resource problems simply by importing or producing more food—unless the augmented production yields a marketable, transportable surplus that will generate capital for the developmental process. This is not the solving of a problem, but simply the temporary staving off of starvation or malnutrition. In any case, it is unfair to expect the underdeveloped lands to be what nearly all the advanced nations are not —self-sufficient in the basic raw materials for human existence.

Even on a planetary scale, the availability of food cannot be said to be an essential issue in present or impending population-resource crises, at least for the next few generations. If consumers in the underdeveloped areas were, through some magic, to acquire instantaneously large amounts of cash for food purchases or, better still, the negotiable goods and services which such cash represents, the nations possessing advanced agricultural techniques could probably double, or perhaps triple, their output of foodstuffs within the next few years, using currently known techniques and capital equipment already on hand or readily obtainable. And it is quite thinkable that this brisk demand might also induce farmers in the less developed countries to extend and upgrade their activities and vastly increase their output. It has been estimated that if all the world's present and potential food-producing surfaces were exploited to maximum capacity, using current technologies or those that can be reasonably anticipated for the future, it should be possible to feed as many as 50 billion persons. We are ignoring, of course, the supply of other physical and social needs or the quality of human existence that would result from such single-minded agricultural zeal.

Thus, until a genuine impasse in agricultural expansion is reached, the real problem is employment and productivity, how an underdeveloped society can rearrange and revolutionize its socioeconomic structure so that its citizens can produce enough goods (including edibles, but certainly much else besides) and services that can be exchanged with other peoples for other goods and services and thus also, one hopes, makes life comfortable, purposeful, and interesting. Unfortunately, the steps whereby these revolutionary changes are initiated are still rather mysterious; and there is no guarantee that any country can enjoy such a transformation just by wanting and struggling for it. However, anything else, including the simple expansion of food production for subsistence within the traditional economy, will not provide a way out of the economic dilemma faced by such areas; at best, it would merely postpone the crucial period. In summary, then, population-resource problems in developing lands can be neither defined nor solved solely in terms of food production.

6. The unproved assumption that processes already in operation will rid the developing countries of their population-resource problems.

Under this dubious proposition, we can group several rather different notions, but ones that all imply strong faith in some deus ex machina or in the long-term rightness and equilibrium induced by the autonomous workings of basic geographic, social, economic, and political processes. They are thus not unrelated to the teleological dogma discussed above as Item 4. Perhaps the most interesting and attractive of these various sub-assumptions is:

(a) The unproved assumption that rapid, massive population growth under contemporary conditions will of itself trigger major economic advance or, at least, contribute materially to its success.

The chief inspiration for this notion is, of course, the fact that among the advanced nations both phenomena —rapid growth and qualitative change in the economy; and a great expansion in the population—have been roughly concurrent. Furthermore, under certain conditions, within these same countries, it is clear that population growth is a positive stimulant to the economy. But it would appear that this is a dangerous analogy as applied to the underdeveloped countries. Although the two events do much overlap in time, the evidence indicates that it was significant economic innovation that tended to precede the demographic revolution, not the other way around. An even greater difficulty is the fact that the preconditions for both demographic and economic growth in the advanced nations were so strikingly different from those prevailing in the currently "developing" lands. In brief, then, there is as yet no well-authenticated instance in modern demographic history of rapid demographic growth in any sort of country preceding, or becoming one of the significant reasons for, basic improvements in the economy. It is true enough that such might seem superficially to have happened in Hong Kong, Taiwan, Puerto Rico, Jamaica, Mexico, and Venezuela; but I believe that the facts indicate quite the contrary in each case—that large population increments have been economic hindrances or, at best, of neutral value.

It is not impossible that rapid population growth may become the main instrument for significant economic advance in some underdeveloped land in the future; but for the moment we have no proof that this has ever happened or that it is likely to happen. It is, of course, also possible that an awareness of rapid population growth may precipitate a course of action leading to economic progress; but this is quite another matter.

There are persuasive arguments, as put forward by Ester Boserup (*The Conditions of Agricultural Growth: The Economics of Agrarian Change under Population Pressure*, Chicago, 1965) for a related hypothesis—that sustained, relatively slow population growth may have been the prime genetic factor in bringing about the intensification of agricultural output per unit of land and, ultimately, radical changes in land-use systems and a complex train of consequences in the spheres of social and political behavior. There may be much truth in this argument (although I suspect that the actual situation has been rather more complicated and ambiguous than such a simple one-way cause-and-effect formula would indicate); but the author is careful to refrain from any claim that her idea is valid for places currently undergoing rapid rural population increases.

(b) A mystic belief in national salvation through the more or less spontaneous development of "great, untapped natural riches."

This amounts to a visceral feeling rather than any coherent doctrine, and is simply faith in the prospect that somehow through the exploitation in some unspecified ways of natural resources, whose nature and extent are at best quite approximately surveyed, the nation will arrive at some unspecified answer to its demographic, social, and economic worries. A careful inventory of possibilities and a detailed set of working plans for their realization may or may not be necessary eventually; but they are incidental to the central article of this faith: the transcendent goodness and wonder-working nature of these as yet untouched gifts of Nature. Although this sort of feeling will not withstand logical analysis, it is influential among large sections of the general population, as well as the governing elite, at least in Indonesia, Mexico, Guatemala, Brazil, and other nations sharing the Amazon Basin, and in several African nations.

(c) Present and future pioneer settlement as the way out of the demographic dilemma.

This notion is, of course, closely related to the preceding one. And it is also a most appealing option in the diminishingly few underdeveloped countries that do still have any considerable amount of land suitable for pioneer settlement—particularly in the light of the historical experience of Anglo-America, Siberia, Australia, Argentina, and a few other areas where rapid frontier advance seems to have had a salutary effect upon the national welfare. Unfortunately, only a few realistic observations will quickly deflate one's confidence in the frontier as the great hope of underdeveloped nations suffering from population pressure upon available resources. Recent experience indicates that the supply of empty land meriting any sort of capital input under present conditions is quite finite and likely to be exhausted rapidly, that (with the one, quite temporary, exception of Costa Rica) the frontierward migration removes only a minor fraction of the redundant population from overcrowded areas, that these frontier zones contribute little, if anything at all, to the net worth of the national economy of underdeveloped lands, and that where, as so often happens, unplanned or unsupervised settlement occurs, the effects may be most deleterious to the habitat and to its agricultural and general biotic productivity. However, this is not to deny the possibility that pioneer settlement may be a most useful and profitable device as part of a larger, well-organized national development plan.

(d) The continuing export of permanent or temporary emigrants to foreign lands as a demographic "safety valve."

There is little doubt that this device has worked well to alleviate population pressures in a number of smaller nations or dependencies. Among those that come readily to mind are Jamaica, Puerto Rico, several of the Lesser Antilles, the Azores, the Canary Islands, Algeria, Malta, Syria, Lebanon, Greece, and Western Samoa. In these cases and others, there are two obvious advantages: the immediate reduction in the ranks of the unemployed or the underemployed; and the return flow of remittances from abroad. But there is one major drawback. Those most likely to leave are usually those who are also the least expendable—the skilled, well-educated, and ambitious—precisely the persons most needed to man the growth points in the national economy and infrastructure. Mass emigration is, in any case, not a valid general solution, and least of all in those countries with more than a very few million inhabitants. It is ludicrous even to think of it in connection with the Chinese, Indians, or Pakistani, or even the much smaller Egyptian population. And it is the most irresponsible, pseudoscientific sort of folly to suggest extraterrestrial outlets for potential emigrants.

Even the maintenance of the *status quo* may be difficult for the various smaller areas that are postponing a basic solution to their population-resource difficulties through vigorous emigration. The historic trends of the present century point clearly to further restrictions on international movements of migrants not to their relaxation. Even where the channels are left open for small, but crowded, lands enjoying a privileged political or economic relationship with a larger, more affluent patron, the relative demand for unskilled labor is likely

to shrink, while the flow of the skilled and semi-skilled may quicken, to the benefit of the latter and detriment of the former.

(e) The transfer of redundant population from rural tracts to urban centers as a major contribution toward the solution of population-resource problems.

The urbanization process is well begun and rapidly accelerating in nearly all underdeveloped lands. Thus, if this cityward movement does indeed offer much hope as a way of eliminating population pressures, it has the added advantage of calling for little artificial encouragement. Largely for lack of sufficient research, we know much too little about the economic and demographic consequences of rapid urbanization in the underdeveloped world. The few broad generalizations that can be offered, however, do little to support the stated assumption. In virtually every instance, the removal of migrants from countryside to town or city is much less rapid than the natural increase of rural populations. Although the availability of social services and amenities may be greater in the cities, it has yet to be demonstrated that, as a general rule, the chances for full employment are greater or that real incomes are significantly higher in an urban milieu. There may be certain cost-saving advantages for the national economy in the centralization of skills and markets; but there are also severe strains upon poorly developed supply systems. Thus we may be rapidly approaching the danger point in the logistics of water, food, fuel, and raw materials in several large metropolises, not to mention grave difficulties in waste disposal and the provision of vital social services.

Another disappointment is the finding that the depression of fertility rates has been much less in the metropolises of developing lands than in their counterparts in advanced nations. The urban birth rates, though appreciably lower than in the countryside, are still high enough so as to ensure a vigorous growth of city population even without further recruitment of rural migrants. Thus, as with pioneer settlement, the urbanization process is far from a complete answer, even though it may well play a significant role in a larger, more effective program.

(f) The belief that many demographically distressed underdeveloped lands can survive indefinitely through charitable contributions from the richer nations.

This is a doctrine seldom proclaimed publicly, but one implicit in the actions of the client countries. In a sense this notion underlies all the various aid programs in the developing lands financed by a few rich nations, but with the critical distinction that most of such programs are intended to be catalytic in effect, to furnish "seed money" for what will hopefully become self-sustaining socioeconomic processes rather than a long-term dole. The simple facts of world economic life are adequate prima facie evidence that, even with a maximum effort on the part of the donors, international alms would

suffice for only a few fleeting years to support all countries who are acquiring more inhabitants than they are able to provide for. There is little doubt, however, that for a few small, poorly equipped areas—among them, Malta, Okinawa and other Pacific islands, the Gaza Strip, the Netherlands Windward Islands, and French Guiana—present and future survival is contingent upon the uninterrupted flow of outright subsidies. It is also clear that foreign subsidy, though often in disguised form, is a large component in the economic life of many other dependent territories and nominally independent nations; and it is possible that their ranks may swell rather than dwindle during the next few decades.

(g) The fallacy that through the age-old more or less "normal" institution of warfare, a reasonable balance between people and resources can be restored.

This doctrine, one that only rarely erupts into print, but unquestionably lurks in the minds of many individuals, is shaky on some fundamental points. First, there is little evidence that, in the past, warfare has been a *major* long-range determinant of population size among human communities, except among those small, relatively primitive tribal societies for whom a rather ritualized form of battle has been the major outdoor recreation. Secondly, the extension of European economic and political control over nearly the whole of the non-European world during the past few centuries has resulted (despite some notable lapses) in the gradual imposition of a *Pax Europaea* on those areas. Furthermore, the structure of the modern world has become such, specially during the past 20 years, that general agreement seems to have been reached, however tacitly, that military conflicts within and among the underdeveloped nations will be suppressed or contained, the alternative being devastation and bloodletting on an unimaginable planetary scale. In short, as a demographic constraint, mid-twentieth century warfare appears to be a cure much worse than the disease.

The fallacy posed above is quite patently a variant of another subterranean notion, seldom uttered aloud in politer academic circles, that perhaps, after all, it is best to be "hard-boiled" and realistic about the situation and let the imbalance between people and resources take care of itself by doing nothing to avoid a rebounding of mortality to pre-modern levels in the underdeveloped areas, or by even actually encouraging the restoration of the old demographic regime. When it is objectively reviewed, however, this policy fails to make any sense on social, economic, or political grounds, quite aside from moral considerations.

(h) The fallacious hope that the traditional, approximate balance between births and deaths can be maintained in the last few areas beyond the reach of the modernization process, or that somehow the developing countries can reverse course and return to the simple, equilibrial demographic ways of the past.

This nostalgic aspiration has no basis in fact. Again what we have is

hardly a coherent, articulate doctrine but rather a set of emotions that do not altogether reach the surface of conscious deliberation. But this is an attitude that may well have affected the treatment of relatively primitive folk within certain advanced nations as well as the handling of relatively retarded communities within the developing lands. Unless another small, remote tribe or two still remains to be found in New Guinea, northern Australia, or some obscure recess of the Amazon and Orinoco basins, all of contemporary humanity has been launched upon the modernization process, with all that that implies in a demographic sense, as well as in other ways. Furthermore, there is a great mass of evidence proving beyond any reasonable doubt that this is an irreversible process. Thus there is no way of erasing the impact of the advanced nations upon the underdeveloped, to make people forget what they have learned and shun the Great World, or to declare a moratorium on change. The question is not whether the peoples of the developing lands must move forward, but rather how, at what rate, and toward what specific destinations.

7. The unproved assumption that rapid population growth per se will damage man's habitat.

This widespread idea, which is, of course, of peculiar interest to geographers, rests precariously on two technical questions: the definition of the quality of our physical environment; and the measurement of changes therein. There appears to have been confusion of three distinct items among those who have expressed concern over the human impact upon the face of the earth—the present or potential economic productivity of the affected areas; their aesthetic attractiveness; and the preservation of the ecological integrity of "wild" areas. It must be admitted immediately that no one has yet devised ways of measuring these conditions, much less any techniques for describing their dynamics. But, even assuming that we could, it is most doubtful whether there is, in general, any direct correlation between population density or rate of increase in a specific place on the one hand and its economic worth or visual beauty on the other. Per-unit area output of agricultural and other economic goods may, in fact, increase as fast or faster than population numbers (at least to that point of total, hopeless congestion that has never yet been achieved over any appreciable land surface). Indeed the argument is credible that augmented population density is a major genetic factor in bringing about major increments in soil productivity or in the discovery, creation, or more efficient exploitation of various "natural" resources. Furthermore, archaeological evidence indicates that, among other areas, portions of Mexico, Ceylon, and Iraq maintained for long periods of the past populations greater than those now resident there and without any apparent adverse effects upon the food-producing qualities of the land.

The aesthetic quality of an area is, of course, a highly subjective matter. Nevertheless, a consensus might be reached for the view that some of the loveliest landscapes in the world are to be seen in some of the most crowded, e.g. Japan, the Low Countries, or Highland Guatemala, and that further humanization of many areas, as growth proceeds, may enhance rather than detract from their aesthetic appeal. It is equally apparent that any number of very distressing, contrary examples could be cited to show that population growth has meant both environmental and aesthetic degradation. The point to be made here is that the kinds of changes induced in the appearance and economic utility of an area undergoing brisk demographic growth is most decidedly a function of the nature, structure, and operations of the specific culture or community, not of such growth per se, and that universal postulations are probably not feasible. Thus there exists a wide spectrum of situations, from the thin, nearly static or transient population that commits the most horrendous vandalism upon its surroundings to the very dense, rapidly multiplying groups that husband their physical resources with jealous devotion and constantly add to the value and beauty of their land.

There is no logical riposte to the adherents of the wilderness mystique who are so profoundly distressed by the damage being wrought by man's activities to the delicate ecological fabric of relatively empty areas. There is little doubt that the further spatial extension or intensification of the human presence will further violate much that is priceless ethically or in any ultimate economic reckoning. As it happens, however, the virginity of even the wildest tracts has already been compromised; and there, as in the more obviously humanized areas, it is urgent that some modus vivendi be contrived that metes out the maximum benefits possible to all species of living things. But this is a concern peripheral to the agenda of the population geographer and the demographer.

8. The unproved assumption that demographic salvation is possible through modern contraceptive technology and exhortation.

If one accepts the thesis that a sharp reduction in fertility is a necessary condition for solving the population-resource pressures of underdeveloped lands, then the means for effecting such a reduction become an issue of transcendent importance. Historically, the only proved method for inducing a lasting and significant lowering of the birth rate has been to raise quite substantially a population's levels of living —and aspiration for further gains. Unfortunately, this process is difficult to initiate, requires the generation and input of considerable capital, and consumes much valuable time. This time lag is a significant one, for not only does it take a number of years to push a population upwards to a higher socioeconomic stage but there is also a further, roughly equivalent period before the new fertility pattern reflects this achievement.

It is understandable, then, that ways are being sought whereby fertility reduction can be realized without waiting out the difficult passage through the "Demographic Transition." Two obvious techniques are not normally feasible either politically or financially—the physical separation of the sexes for

prolonged periods (including the enforced postponement of marriage), or massive programs of subsidies designed to limit the number of children or to encourage voluntary sterilization. Nor are any other coercive measures likely to be considered seriously in the near future.

Currently much stress is being laid on the mass distribution of new contraceptive devices and information in the underdeveloped countries. The theory behind such programs is that a number of developing countries have now reached the point where parents realize it is to their economic and social advantage to limit family size even before the inception of significant socioeconomic advances and that they need only some cheap, simple, safe, effective, and psychologically acceptable techniques and perhaps a little official encouragement and propaganda to become successful contraceptors. The two items which seem best to meet the stringent requirements for widespread acceptability among underdeveloped populations are the oral contraceptive pill and the intra-uterine device, or coil (IUD's); and field trials for both have been initiated on a rather ambitious scale.

It is still somewhat too early to have collected and analyzed enough data from Korea, Taiwan, India, Pakistan, and elsewhere to determine whether these programs have had any significant results within the test groups, whether the new fertility pattern, if any, is likely to be a lasting one, or whether the method in question can be extended to the total population of reproductive age. A further complication is the fact that some of these experimental efforts are being carried on in areas, such as Taiwan, where significant socioeconomic development may have already initiated some spontaneous declines in fertility. Organized family limitation programs may, in such cases, simply accelerate an ongoing process, as appears to have happened in Japan during the 1940's and 1950's. Demographic history tells us that possession of advanced contraceptive technology is an incidental matter, while the truly crucial question is whether the potential contraceptors genuinely wish to achieve the small-family pattern. Quite probably the ease with which each community accepts a new, lower fertility pattern will depend upon the fundamental character of its culture and other spatially variable factors. When the need for fewer children is felt, even old, rather primitive contraceptive methods will suffice. But, insofar as the present and impending population-resource impasse is a unique episode in human history, past precedents are not necessarily binding. It is not unthinkable that major, rapid declines in the birth rate can be engineered on a national scale in advance of any important socioeconomic breakthrough, however implausible this may seem in the light of earlier experience. We do not know; we must await the evidence. But, in the interim, it would be imprudent not to examine other alternatives.

9. The unproved assumption that major socioeconomic advance can somehow be achieved in every underdeveloped country that wishes to do so.

If a nation elects to strive for a more comfortable balance between population and resources—and also to achieve other social and economic ends generally deemed desirable—by initiating major socioeconomic development, there is no assurance that it will succeed. Some nations undoubtedly can and will reach their declared goal; but historical precedents are too few in number and too distinct in character from the territories in question to offer any grounds for unqualified optimism. The various European and Neo-European nations and Japan were (with a few exceptions in Southern Europe) launched upon their developmental careers in the nineteenth century or earlier. In any event, their start was made under conditions radically different from those confronting our contemporary underdeveloped countries. Economic development preceded or ran parallel with demographic expansion. Population growth was not racing ahead of economic and social capabilities so as to absorb most of the short supply of capital and physical resources.

A critical survey of the assets and liabilities for economic development of the various underdeveloped countries would indicate that the former are greatly outweighed by the latter. In addition to the severe braking effect of disproportionately rapid population growth, it is obvious that most of these territories are seriously deficient in some of the more elementary physical resources. That this is not an insuperable obstacle is shown by the attainments of such areas as Iceland, New England, Israel, Switzerland, Japan, or Finland, all of whom are at best marginal with respect to natural endowments—or perhaps best of all by the near-miracle of Hong Kong.

What is discouraging is the fact that the combination of advantages necessary to surmount physical handicaps may be lacking. Thus there may be an acute shortage of venture capital, domestic or foreign, available for developing critical components in the economy of the national infrastructure; and, in fact, much in the way of locally generated investment funds may have been exported to safer or more lucrative havens. The exploitation and export of abundant local mineral and agricultural resources can produce funds that may or may not be channeled into local growth-producing enterprises; but future problems in procuring materials needed for an advanced society may also be created thereby.

Many, perhaps most, underdeveloped countries are plagued by chronic political instability, or even military disorder, that makes it difficult to execute even the best-laid development schemes. Paradoxically, the small size of the population and market of many rapidly growing underdeveloped countries makes the formulation of valid economic plans a trying task. One's imagination strains at the prospect of any development plans that are both efficacious and primarily reliant on local resources in such "ministates" as the Maldives, Tonga, Basutoland, Bhutan, Singapore, Mauritius, Jordan, or some, such as Panama, Jordan, Malawi, or Ruanda, that are a bit ampler.

Along with the annoyances of deficiencies of physical resources, investment capital, effective government, and markets of non-economic size, there are at least two other handicaps that may prove even more frustrating: the dearth of skilled or experienced personnel, native or alien, capable of designing and managing the developmental process; and our quite limited knowledge of how best to draw up intelligent, realistic, and effective developmental blueprints to fit the peculiar needs of each individual country.

It is not even certain whether, under the best of conditions, a more or less sovereign nation can escalate itself upward to genuinely advanced socioeconomic status, and to the demographic concomitants thereof. In this connection, it will be interesting to learn whether such states as Kuwait and Bahrein, with their windfall economies—or Libya, Iraq, and Venezuela—can forcefeed themselves and buy their way quickly into advanced status. The answer should be available in a few years. One final uncertainty looming over every country (except China) that aspires to better its socioeconomic standing is the attitude of the two superpowers who monopolize so much of the world's economic and military power. Without their moral, technical, and financial support—or at least acquiescence—it would be foolish to count upon much progress.

10. The unproved assumption that the demographic consequences of major socioeconomic progress in the developing countries will replicate those experienced in the advanced nations.

Once again, we should be restrained by lack of solid historical precedent from declaring that economic development is not only a possible but is a necessary and sufficient means for achieving an efficient demographic budget, i.e. a pattern of low fertility closely approximating a low mortality rate. The assumption that the attainment of advanced socioeconomic status is *always* followed, after an interval of some years or decades, by a major reduction in fertility has not yet been fully tested in enough different countries with different historic and cultural settings. To date, the Demographic Transition and the modernization process have indeed always accompanied each other; but in every instance, development was well under way by the end of the nineteenth century (as was the case in Japan, incidentally), or the country in question is European or Sino-Japanese in culture, and, without exception, the country did not start out after it had begun to suffer the symptoms of underdevelopment. Is there not some possibility that the causal connection between socioeconomic development and fertility may be culture-specific? And may it not be possible that a nation beginning its development program in an underdeveloped condition may follow a rather separate demographic course from that previously observed? In any case, is it safe to extrapolate a universal principle to cover all countries from the experience of a limited number of rather special countries?

The answers to these questions may be forthcoming in the next few years. In addition to the oil-rich states of the Middle East, there are several situations in Latin America where sustained or increasing prosperity should test the hypothesis that family limitation is a necessary sequel to socioeconomic development. These would include por-

tions of Mexico and Venezuela, Puerto Rico, Curaçao, and possibly Jamaica, but would exclude Cuba, Argentina, Uruguay, and Southern Brazil, areas that enjoyed major influxes of European migrants during the past several decades. It may be noteworthy that substantial rises in standardized birth rates have occurred in most Latin American countries, starting in 1920 or later, even where there has been no appreciable socioeconomic progress. It must be admitted, however, that some of our difficulty in knowing just what to expect can be attributed to the fact that the earlier stages of the Demographic Transition were rarely well documented in the currently advanced nations. Thus we cannot be certain whether or not the dynamics of vital rates in the developing lands are paralleling those of earlier travelers through the Demographic Transition.

11. The unproved assumption that developing lands that succeed in attaining advanced socioeconomic status quo and then duplicate the demographic pattern of currently advanced nations will thereby have permanently solved their population-resource problems.

Entry into the charmed circle of advanced nations by no means guarantees any final, absolute resolution of imbalances between people and resources. It may simply change the terms of the problem. The advanced nations comprise a highly unstable system. Population growth does continue at a fairly brisk rate (as compared to the premodern period) in nearly all such countries; and economic product and per-capita wants and consumption are climbing an upward slope that has no visible crest. The problems being engendered by large, growing, affluent masses of people caught in the grip of an accelerating technology that seems to have no essential rationale except its own perpetuation and expansion are likely to be much more intense, perverse, and resistant to simple answers than those of the underdeveloped lands. But proper exploration of this point takes us into territory well beyond the range of this essay.

I hope it is evident from the foregoing discussion that we do not yet have enough facts, historical models, or general theory concerning the demography and population geography of the underdeveloped lands to describe, evaluate, and interpret their population-resource problems at all adequately, to predict the future course of these problems, or to prescribe infallible solutions. It should also be plain that it is urgent that much work and thinking be done and the proper research questions asked before much more time has elapsed. For the first time in human history, we are forced to take a hard look at the conditions of humanity in general and the forces that control our lives. And as the era of spontaneous change and piecemeal decisions draws to a close, we are being compelled not only to grasp what has been happening but also somehow to take our futures into our own hands. It is difficult; it is painful; it is necessary; and it is a tremendous challenge to the scholar.

For the geographer, the questions are particularly intriguing. Barring some catastrophe, the underdeveloped world will have at least twice its present population by the end of the century. And it is difficult to conceive how near-stability of numbers can be managed before these countries have three or four times the population now inhabiting them. What will be the geography of these crowding lands, with their burgeoning cities, their ever more mobile citizens, their intensifying ecological stresses, and tremendous, if still unforeseen, new social tensions? Some of the answers may be reportable soon in places such as Haiti, Egypt, El Salvador, Java, Mauritius, and South Korea, possibly even in the 1970's. In any case, we must begin to learn how to study this new geography of mounting population pressures, clearly, analytically, and without the incubus of myth or obsolete dogma. Then perhaps we can help in the effort to realize the full potential of our species and our planet, sanely, richly, and for many millennia to come.

6666666666666

CONFLICT AND CONFLICT RESOLUTION

6666666666666

KEITH D. HARRIES ◆

The Geography of American Crime, 1968

Introduction[1]

Crime is a perennial social issue and most of the research relating to it has been performed by sociologists and criminologists, in whose work the focus has been behavioral, with some explicitly spatial statements having been made from time to time; two of these (Lottier, 1938, and Shannon, 1954) are used for comparative purposes below.[2] The objective of this paper is, while acknowledging the vital importance of basic behavioral research, to present a generalized spatial interpretation of American crime which may provide a collection of raw material of some utility to geography instructors, particularly at the secondary and college levels.

What is illustrated here is actually far from a comprehensive treatment of spatial variation in crime. In the first place, the maps shown represent only state data and the resulting patterns constitute but a rough model of reality. Since crime rates tend to be highest in the largest metropolitan areas, the most heavily metropolitan states (such as Maryland, which is represented mainly by Baltimore) tend to have the balance of crime tipped in their favor (see Table 3). Furthermore, only the so-called Index crimes of the Federal Bureau of Investigation are represented, and these account for a mere twenty percent of the arrests that the F.B.I. reports.[3] These Index Crimes were selected in 1927 (and modified in 1958) on the basis of their seriousness, frequency, and the reliability of their reporting to the police.

The crimes are divisible into two broad categories—those against the person, represented by murder and nonnegligent manslaughter, rape, robbery, and aggravated assault, and those

◆ SOURCE. Reprinted by permission from *The Journal of Geography*, Vol. 70, April 1971, pp. 204–213.

505

against property which are summarized in statistics of burglary, larceny over fifty dollars, and auto theft. The last three—the property crimes—represent over eighty percent of the Index offenses in terms of numbers of reported occurrences. This observation provokes discussion of some of the weaknesses of the maps of crime. In the first place, crime is generally greatly under-reported, and it has been pointed out that "the actual amount of crime in the United States today is several times that reported in the UCR [the Uniform Crime Reports of the F.B.I.]."[4] Secondly, the maps represent the rates of crimes per 100,000 persons. This is a realistic form of measurement for crimes against the person, but somewhat less so in relation to crimes against property, which would be more appropriately measured in terms of units of property or property value.[5] The practical difficulties involved in this are perhaps insurmountable, however. A third problem is that the economic impact of crime is not explicitly represented, though one suspects that the maps may coincidentally show the pattern of the cost of crime reasonably well, in the sense that major metropolitan states such as New York and California are probably the major locations not only of Index Crimes against property, but also of non-Index activities such as fraud and embezzlement which may have a larger dollar volume than the Index property offenses. Similarly, many crimes against the person, such as kidnapping, arson, and simple assault are not included in the data mapped here, and constitute a further gap. Finally, it should be pointed

out that the data mapped represent only one year—1968 (the most recent year for which published data were available at the time of writing), so that variation is represented which may have been reduced if an average of several years had been used.

Having discussed a selection of the problems associated with this criminal geography, some observations concerning the maps themselves are appropriate.[6] They are divided into three sections. The first consists of five maps, showing the four Index Crimes against the person, plus a summary map; the second shows the three property crimes, plus a summary map; and the third consists simply of a "total crime" map which summarizes the preceding maps and is weighted in favor of the property crimes, which have the highest rates (see Table 1).

TABLE 1.   Average Crime Rates Per 100,000 Population Fifty States, 1968

Crime Category	Average
Murder and Nonnegligent Manslaughter	6.01
Forcible Rape	13.06
Robbery	77.17
Aggravated Assault	111.56
Violent Crime	207.79
Burglary	772.63
Larceny over $50	559.33
Auto Theft	312.50
Property Crime	1,640.49
Total Crime Index	1,848.26

Source: Federal Bureau of Investigation, *Uniform Crime Reports—1968* (Washington, D.C.: U. S. Government Printing Office, 1969) and calculations by author.

Violent Crimes

Figure 1 serves to point out that each map follows the same basic format—a quintile division of states based on rank-ordered crime rates (per 100,000 persons). This map, showing the distribution of murder rates, is perhaps the most striking of all. The dominance of the South is by no means a chance occurrence. Stuart Lottier, in his 1938 study of criminal geography, noted a similar pattern, as did Lyle Shannon in 1954.[7] Apparently, no simple explanation of this pattern and its persistence is adequate. Sheldon Hackney recently presented a discussion of the phenomenon in which he pointed out that the classic explanatory theories relating to such factors as the large Southern black population, allegedly lower status occupations in the South, ruralism, poverty, and modernization, do not individually seem adequate. Other possible factors, including anomy (or normlessness), the closeness of relationships, and certain aspects of childrearing also failed (according to Hackney) to provide acceptable explanations, as did guncarrying, which is more frequent in the South. Hackney implied that Southern subjugation is perhaps a more convincing root of aggression than any other single cause—"Being Southern," he wrote, "involves a feeling of persecution at times and a sense of being a passive, insignificant object of alien and impersonal forces."[8]

At the other extreme, the first example can be seen of a pattern that persists throughout these crime maps—low rates in New England (notably New Hampshire and Vermont) and several other states, including North Dakota, Minnesota, and Wisconsin.

Consideration of Figure 2, illustrating the distribution of forcible rape, shows that a block of western states—California, Arizona, New Mexico, and Colorado—constitute a "rape region" of sorts. Alaska should not be excluded, either. It may be argued that Alaskan males have some excuse for this form of deviant behavior—in 1960 there were about 132 males per 100 females in the State, or some 28 more males per 100 females than in the next most deprived state, Hawaii.[9] However, while Alaska ranked sixth in rape, Hawaii ranked forty-second, below Massachusetts, the State with the greatest proportionate surplus of females in 1960. These observations do not, of course, take into account the age structure of the population or changes in the sex ratio that may have taken place between 1960 and 1968. As in the case of homicide, it is clear that no simple explanation is forthcoming. The most extreme rates are actually found in California, Michigan, Colorado, and Maryland, in which states metropolitan rape rates include the highest in the nation. Los Angeles, indeed, was apparently the rape capital of the metropolitan United States in 1968, with a rate of 45 per 100,000, which compares with 14.7/100,000 for all U.S. metropolitan areas. However, the rates for Denver, Detroit, and Baltimore were also very high.

In the robbery pattern (Figure 3), California and Nevada are dominant in the west, while eastern states actually

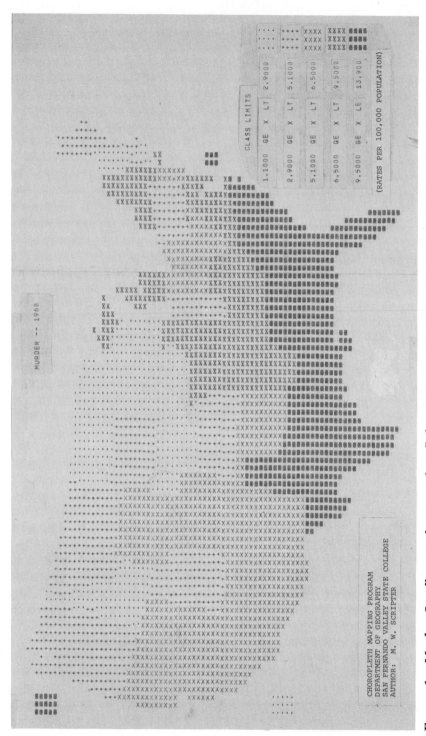

FIGURE 1. Murder. On all maps, the rectangles off the West coast represent Alaska and Hawaii, while that off the Eastern seaboard represents Washington, D.C. Rates range from 1.1 (North Dakota) to 13.9 (Georgia) and are expressed per 100,000 population.

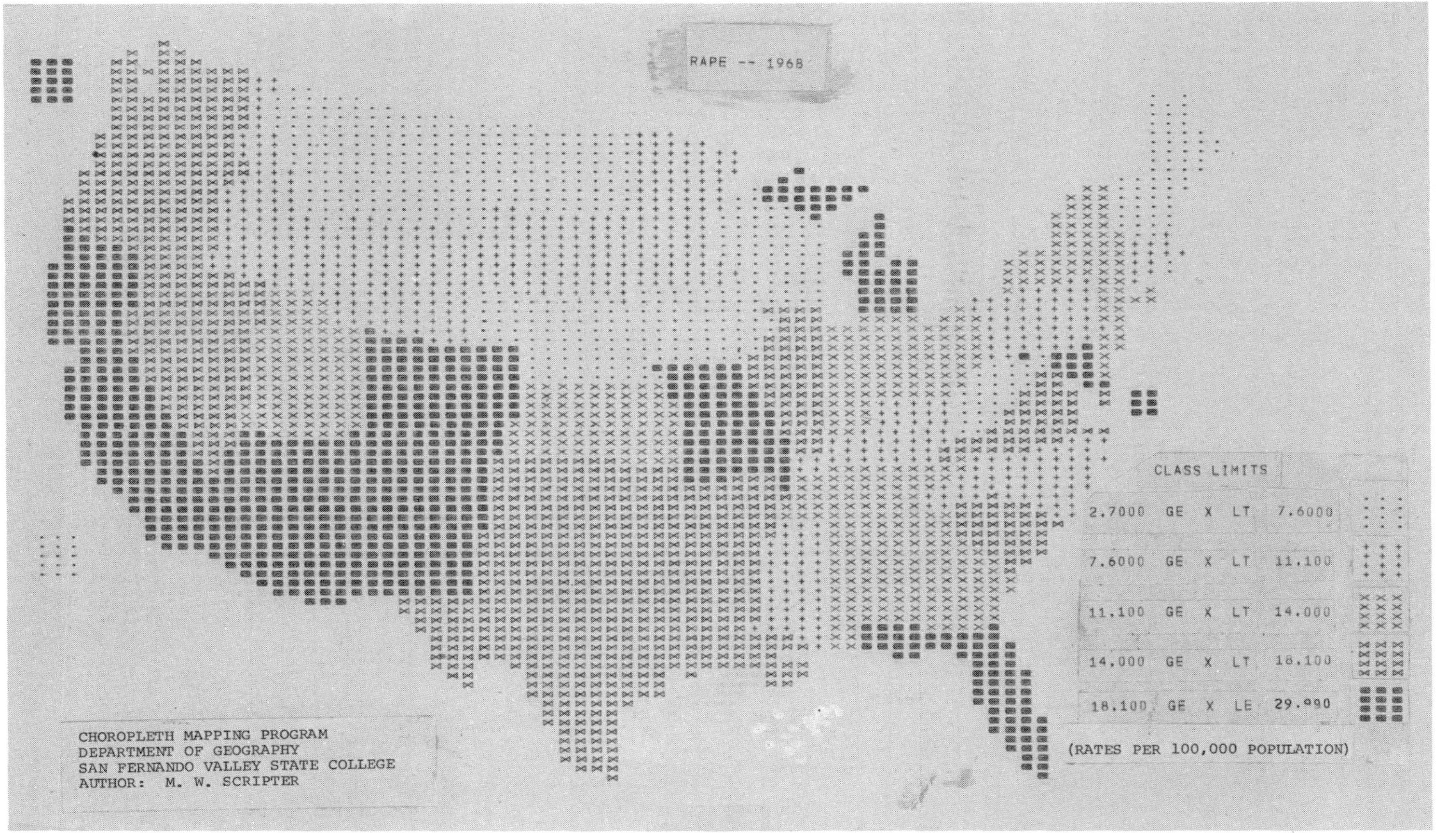

FIGURE 2.   Rape. Rate range: 2.7 (New Hampshire) to 29.9 (California).

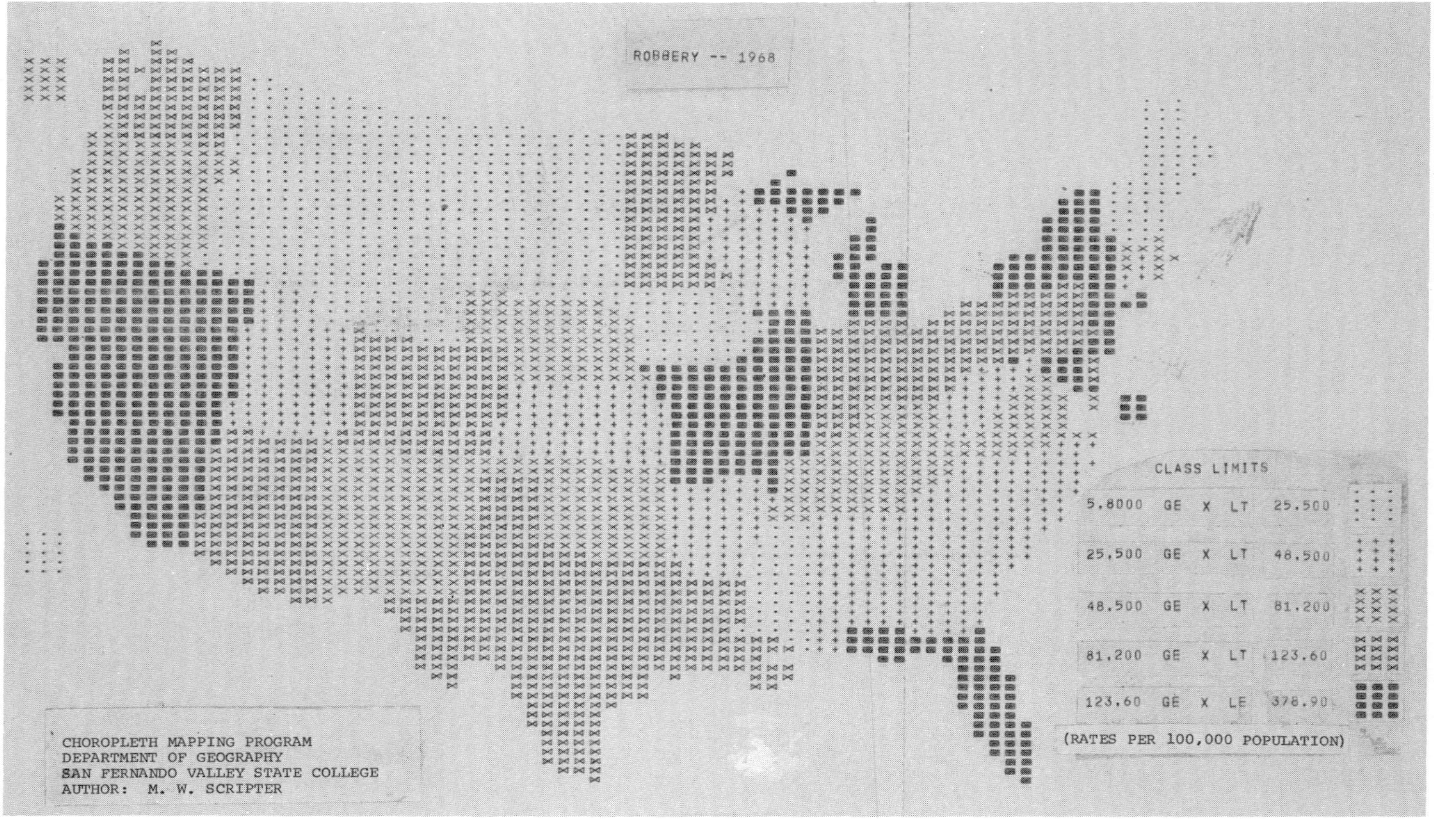

FIGURE 3. Robbery. Rate range: 5.8 (No. Dakota) to 328.4 (New York).

dominate the rank order. New York and Maryland have extremely high rates (the New York metropolitan area leads the nation) while Illinois, Michigan, Florida, and Missouri follow. Although Lottier, in 1938, felt able to describe a central axis of robbery running east-west, Shannon, in 1954, could not detect such an axis and it certainly does not seem evident here.

In relation to Figure 4, which shows aggravated assault, Lottier found a concentration of high rates in the Southeast, particularly in North Carolina, Virginia, Tennessee, Kentucky, and Florida. Shannon observed a pattern similar to Lottier's, but only one of Shannon's top five assault states—North Carolina—is in the top five in terms of the 1968 data. Such states as California, Louisiana, Florida, and Maryland (which was first in 1968), have all moved to higher ranks, while North Carolina retained first or second place in the present study as well as in Lottier's and Shannon's. Charlotte, North Carolina, contributed to this situation in 1968 with an aggravated assault rate some ninety-four points higher than its closest national rival, Baltimore. The Miami and Jacksonville rates assist Florida to third place.

In order to summarize the pattern of crimes against the person, a summary map (Figure 5) is presented, as are some of the characteristics of simple correlations between the violent crime variables. The summary map shown correlates most strongly with the robbery pattern ($r = .90$),[10] while the weakest relationship is with murder (.57). Aggravated assault shows the highest level of dependence[11] on the other three violence variables, while homicide shows the least. However, the strongest correlation between the violence patterns is found between murder and assault (.72).

Property Crimes

Each of the property crime variables are positively and quite strongly correlated and the map patterns illustrate the similarities. The burglary map (Figure 6) does not bear much resemblance to the findings of Lottier, but of Shannon's eight highest states, calculated for the period 1946–52, five were still in the top eight in 1968. California takes top place, and San Francisco-Oakland constitutes the leading metropolitan area in the U.S., though it beats Fresno, California, narrowly for this dubious distinction. Outside the West, several now-familiar states—Florida, Maryland, Michigan, and New York have the highest rates.

The distribution of larceny (Figure 7) has apparently shown appreciable temporal consistency. Lottier said that the offense was "concentrated in the western states" and Shannon mentioned that "larceny rates by states show a spatial regularity more readily than any other crime against property." That regularity involved concentration in the Pacific and Mountain states and, as may readily be seen, this has been retained. New York is actually the leading state, however, and New York City is presumably to blame for this, since it has the nation's highest metropolitan rate.

The auto theft pattern (Figure 8)

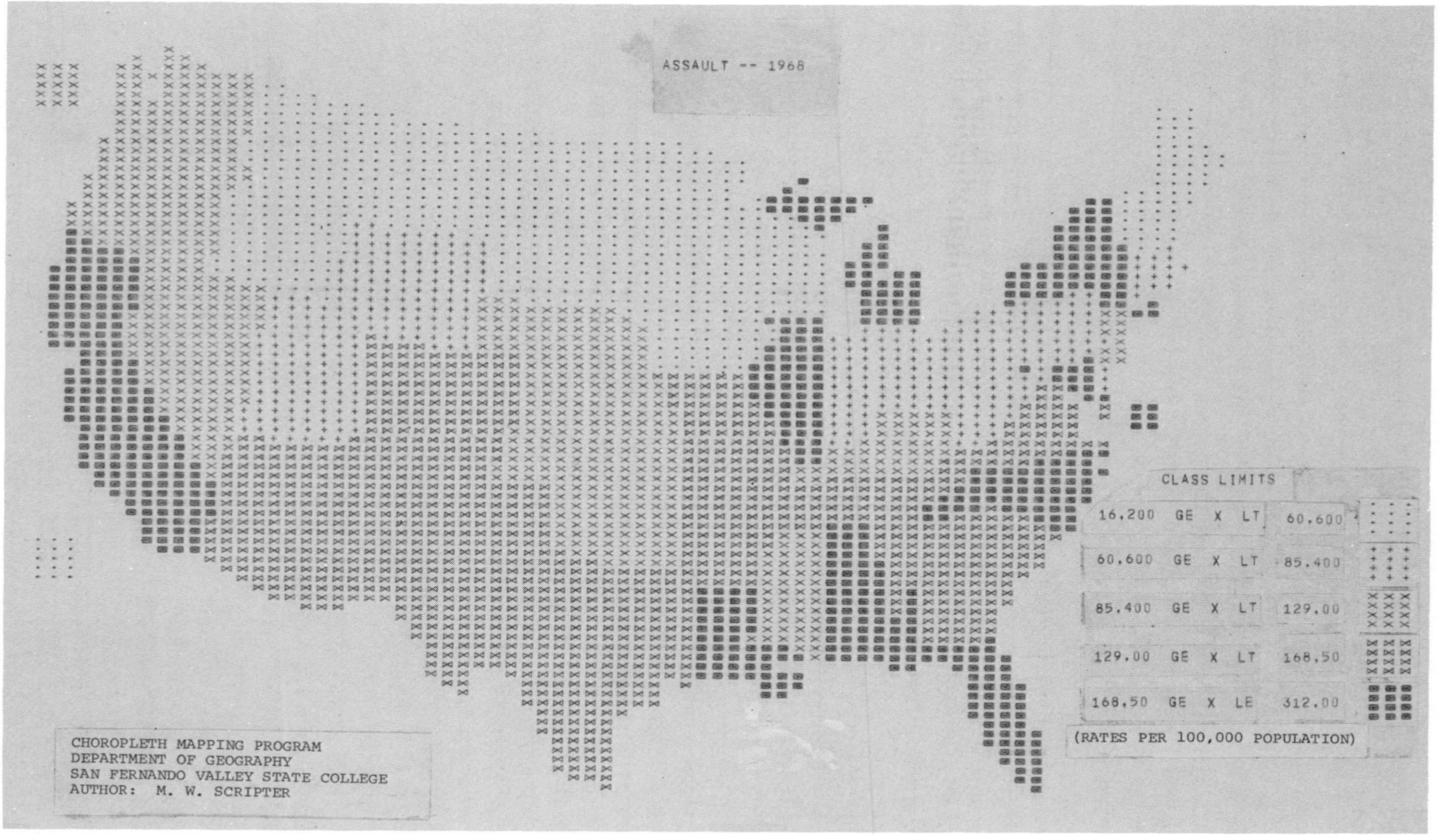

FIGURE 4. Assault. Rate range: 16.2 (No. Dakota) to 312.0 (Maryland).

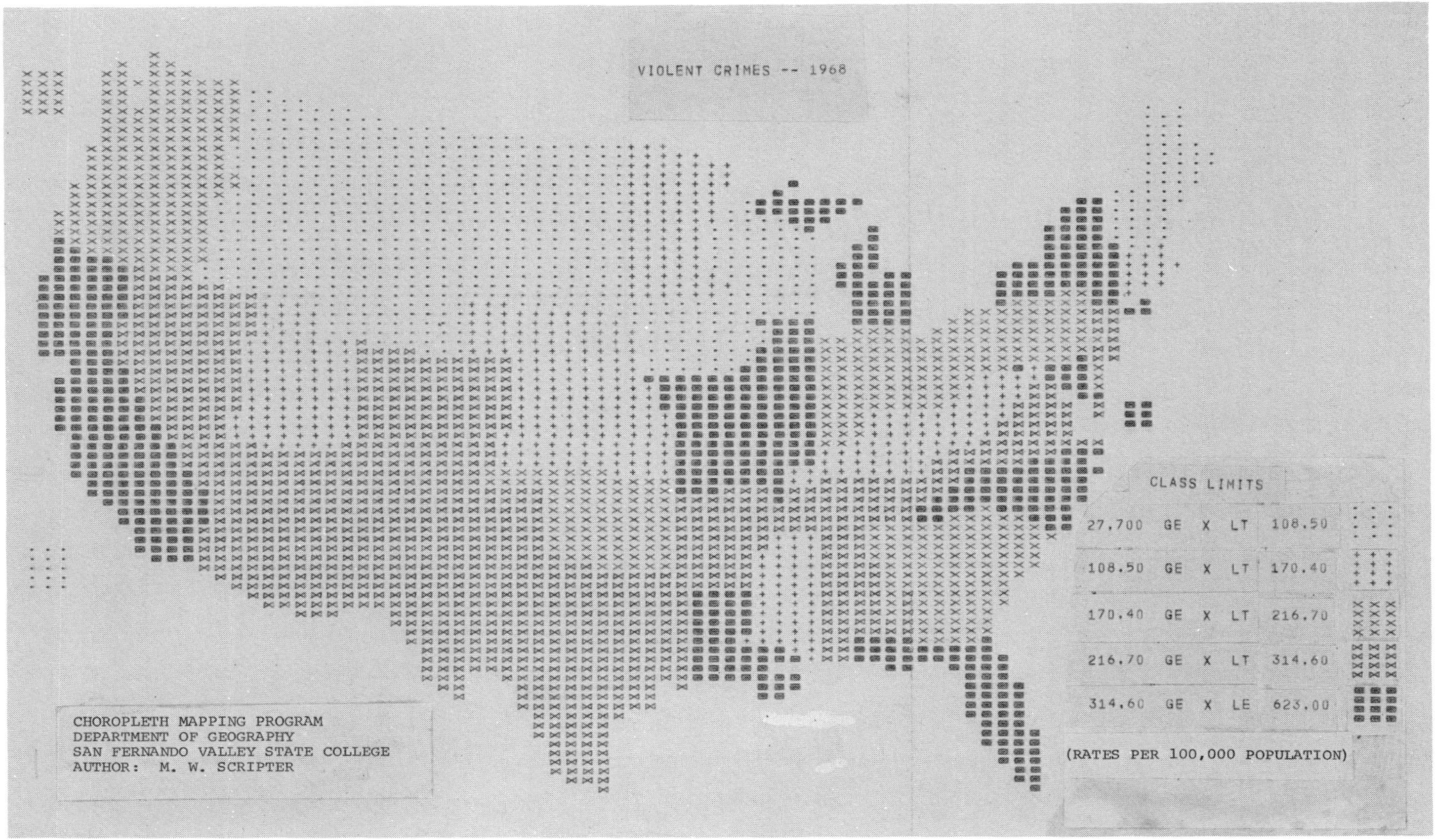

FIGURE 5. Violent crimes in summary.

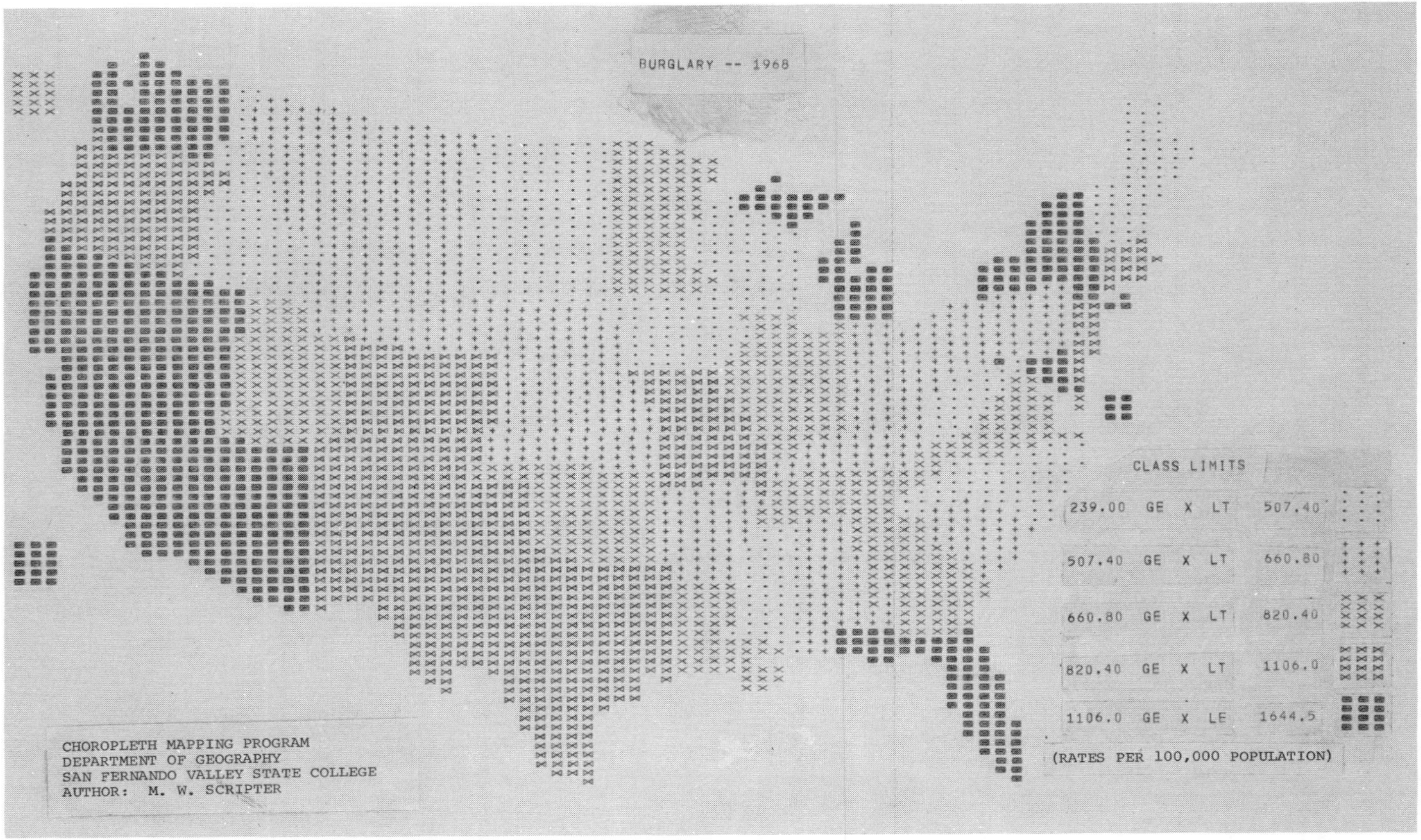

FIGURE 6.   Burglary. Rate range: 239.0 (No. Dakota) to 1644.5 (California).

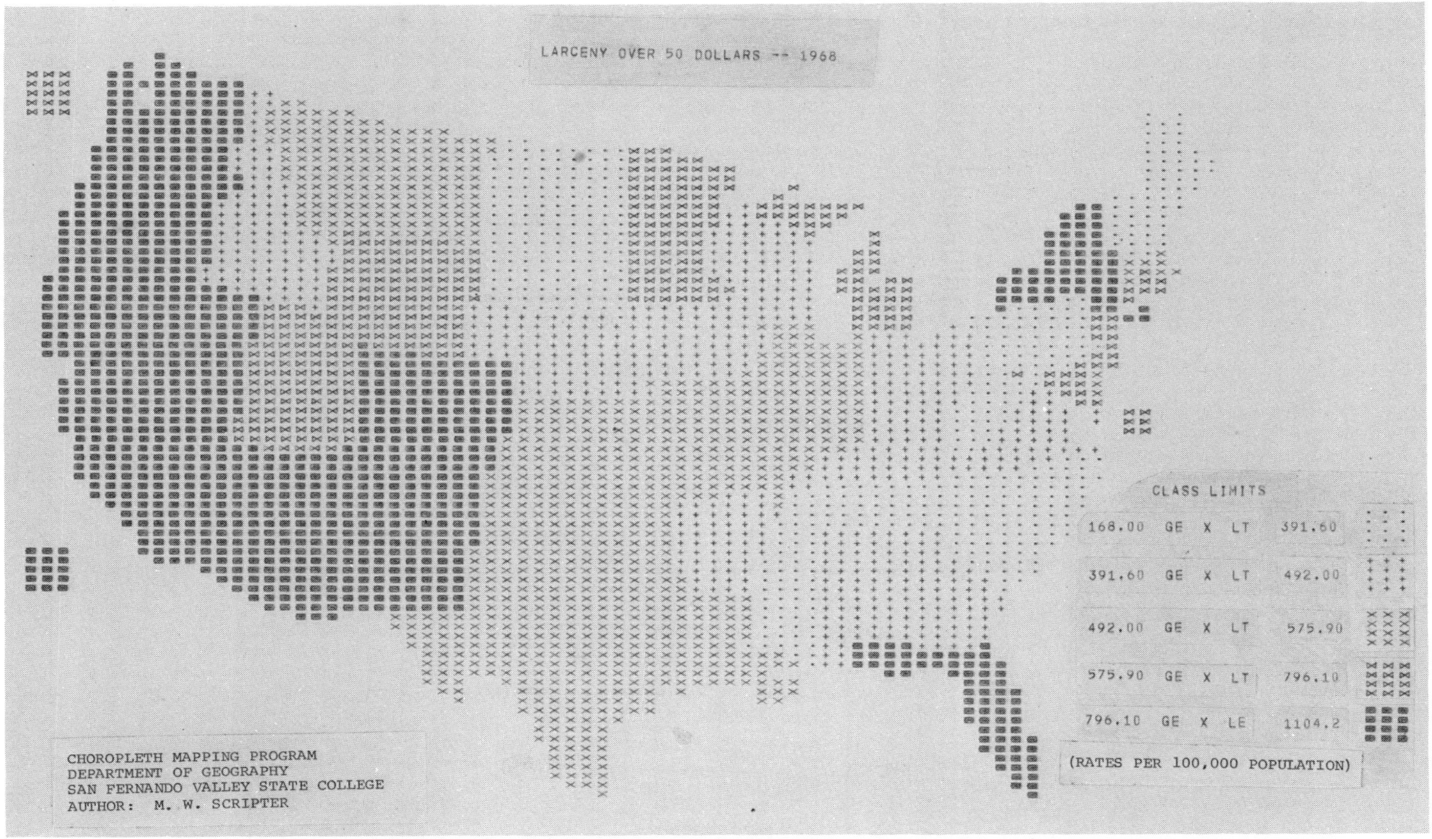

FIGURE 7. Larceny over $50. Rate range: 168.0 (Vermont) to 1104.2 (New York).

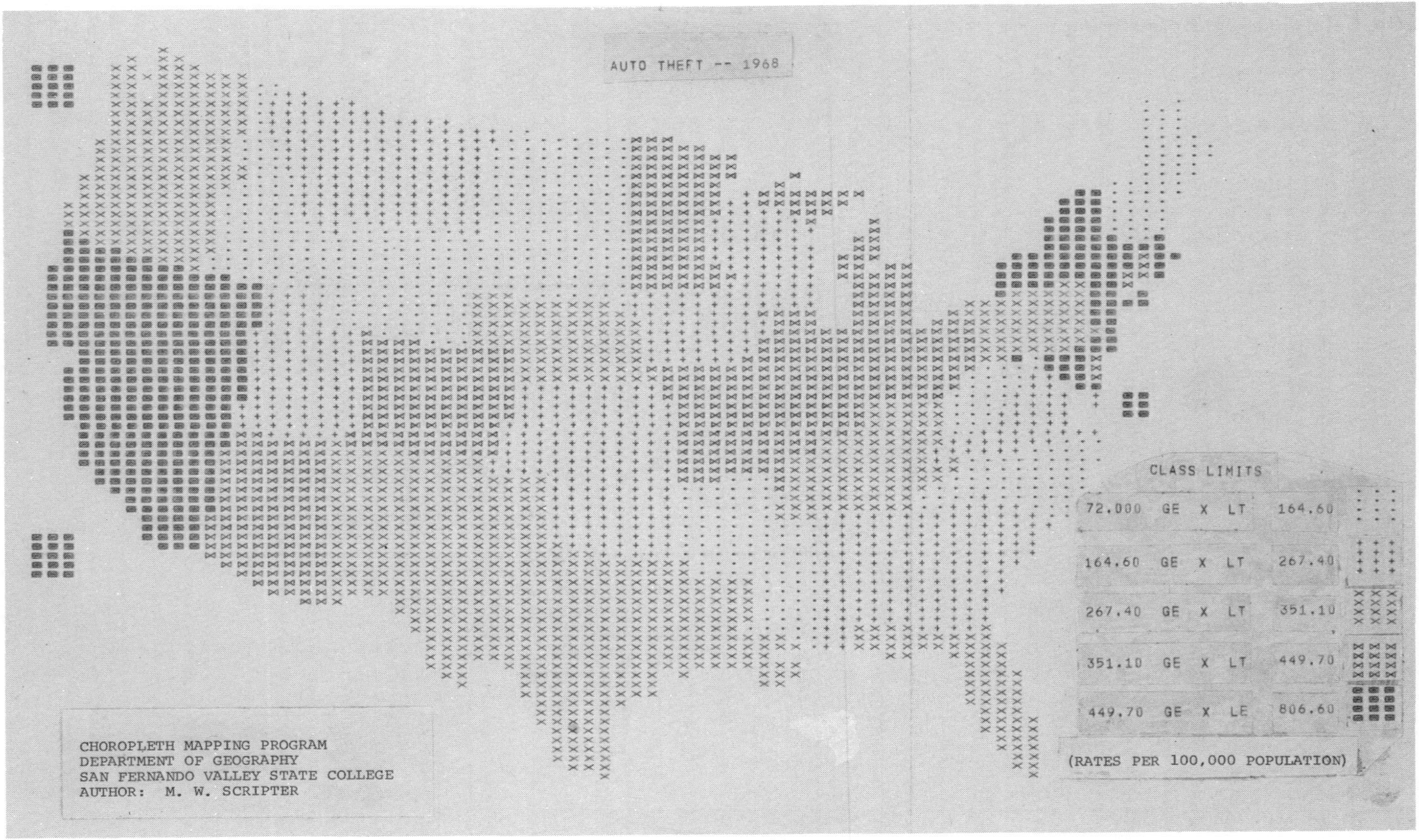

AUTO THEFT -- 1968

CHOROPLETH MAPPING PROGRAM
DEPARTMENT OF GEOGRAPHY
SAN FERNANDO VALLEY STATE COLLEGE
AUTHOR: M. W. SCRIPTER

CLASS LIMITS		
72.000 GE X LT	164.60	
164.60 GE X LT	267.40	
267.40 GE X LT	351.10	
351.10 GE X LT	449.70	
449.70 GE X LE	806.60	

(RATES PER 100,000 POPULATION)

FIGURE 8. Auto Theft. Rate range: 72.00 (Mississippi) to 806.6 (Massachusetts).

is somewhat similar, though the leading states are about equally divided between the East (Massachusetts, Rhode Island, Maryland, New York, and New Jersey) and the West (California, Hawaii, Alaska, and Nevada). This pattern does not resemble Lottier's, perhaps because his rates were expressed in terms of automobile registrations rather than population. Figure 8 is somewhat closer to Shannon's observations, though only two of the current top five states were in Shannon's top five, while the other three were ranked thirty-third, thirty-eight, and forty-first by Shannon.

The summary map of property crimes (Figure 9) generalizes the previous three maps, though correlation of this pattern is strongest to the most numerous offenses (burglary [.97] and larceny [.93]) and somewhat weaker to auto theft (.84). This is consistent with the observation that of the property crimes, auto theft shows the lowest level of dependency either on the other property crimes, or, in fact, on all seven offenses taken together.

Conclusion

The final summary map (Figure 10) shows the Total Crime Index for 1968. Sinces this represents simply the rank-ordered aggregate of the violent and property crime rates, it is not surprising that the murder pattern, or example, with its relatively small rates (a mean of 6.01 compared to 772.63 for burglary), does not emerge in this generalized arrangement, which correlates most strongly with the property crime maps.

In order to summarize some of the characteristics of the extremes of the data, Tables 2 and 3 were prepared. Table 2 shows all the states which scored among the lowest five states for any of the seven Index offenses in 1968. The rank of these states on the Total Crime Index is also indicated. Table 3 represents the opposite extreme; it lists those states which scored among the top five of the fifty states, together with the Total Crime Index ranks. These tables help to illustrate the relationship between the level of urbanization (or perhaps more accurately metropolitanization) and crime. This is not to suggest that urban development is the only significant explanatory variable—partial explanations in various studies[12] have also been derived from such factors as employment characteristics, the size and nature of minority groups, age composition, economic status, and so forth. Geographical differences in the effectiveness of law enforcement and in attitudes to crime should also be taken into account. Indeed, it is in this respect that such maps as these may have some practical value—in pointing out the clear regional differences in crime (or at least in its perception) and the desirability of territorially differentiated approaches to law enforcement.

The tables also emphasize the weight that attaches to property offenses with respect to the composition of the Total Crime Index. Thus it is most important that discussions of crime rates take into account specific offenses —as well as social and economic considerations, which vary—and change— spatially and temporally.

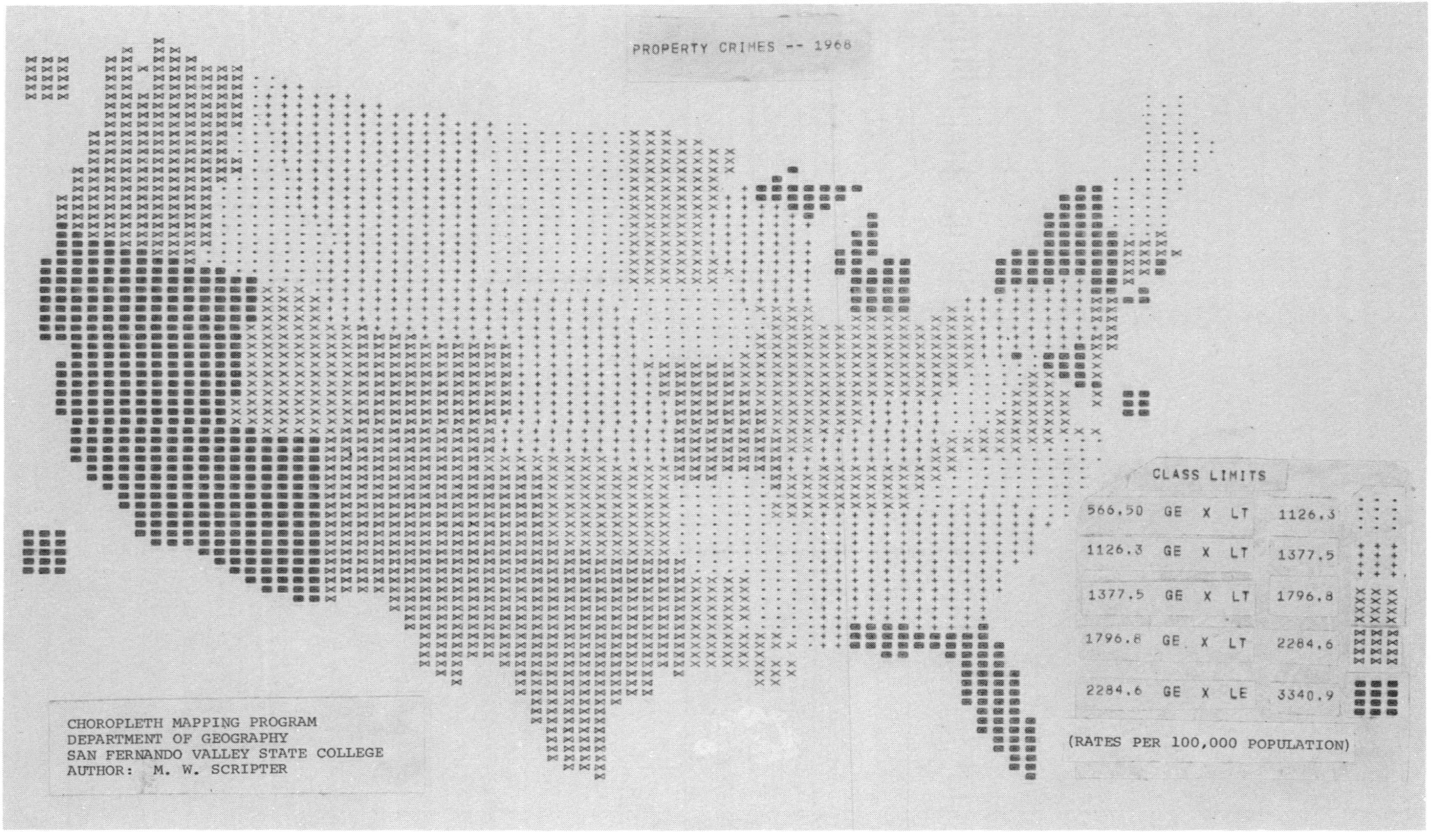

FIGURE 9. Property crimes in summary.

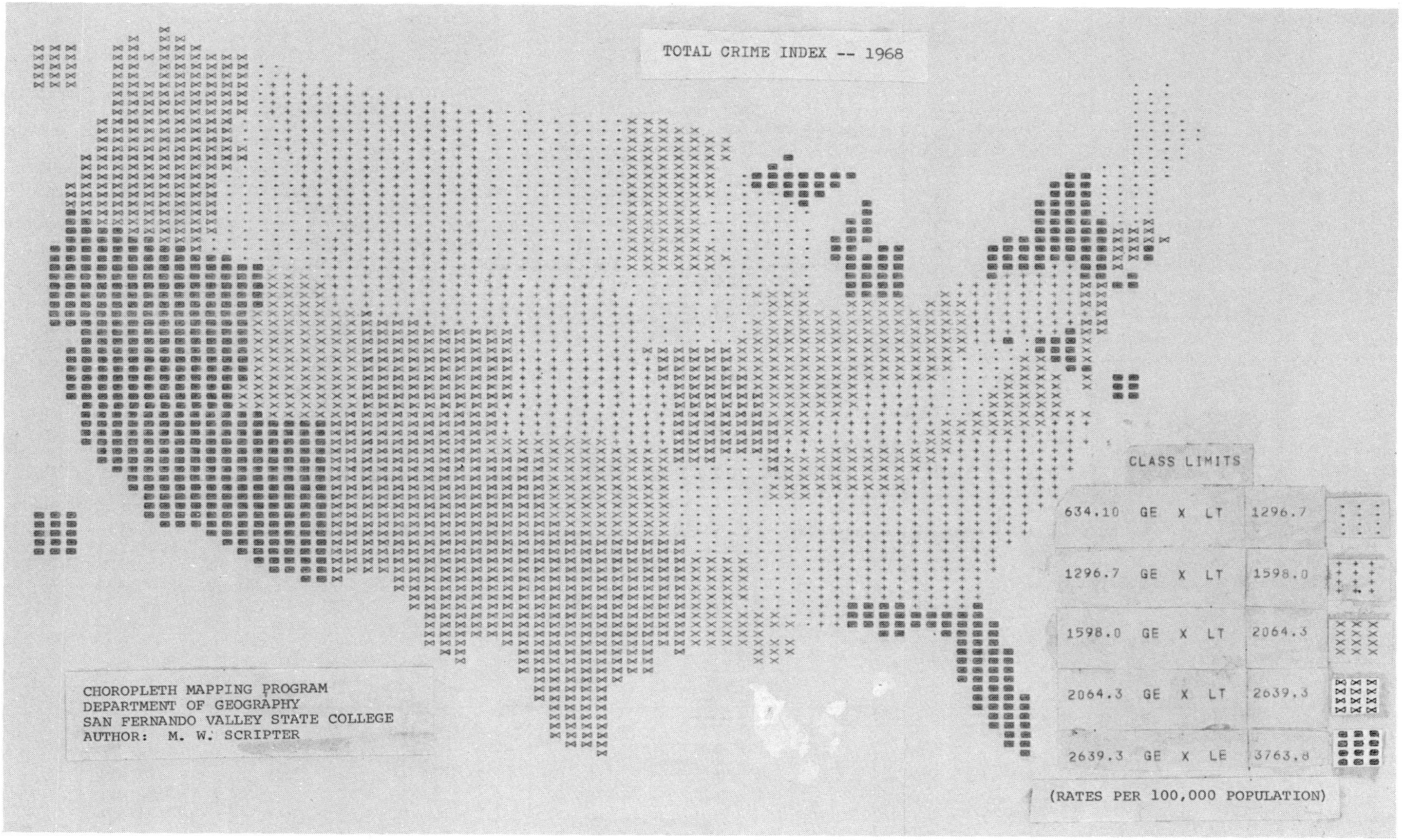

FIGURE 10. Total crime index. This index is weighted in favor of property crimes, which are most numerous.

519

TABLE 2. List of States with Crime Rates Falling in Lowest Five in at Least One Index Category

States	Rank of State on Total Crime Index	Index Crime Category in which State Fell in Lowest Five							Total Row
		Murder	Rape	Robbery	Assault	Burglary	Larceny Over $50	Auto Theft	
North Dakota	50	x	x	x	x	x		x	6
Mississippi	49					x	x	x	3
West Virginia	48		x			x	x	x	4
Vermont	47			x	x		x	x	4
New Hampshire	46	x	x	x	x	x	x		6
Maine	45			x			x		2
South Dakota	44					x			1
Iowa	43	x			x				2
Idaho	42			x					1
Arkansas	41							x	1
Wisconsin	40	x	x		x				3
Minnesota	22	x							1
Rhode Island	9		x						1

Source: Federal Bureau of Investigation, *Uniform Crime Reports—1968* (Washington, D.C.: U.S. Government Printing Office, 1969) and calculations by author.

TABLE 3. List of States with Crime Rates Falling in Highest Five in at Least One Index Category

States	Rank of State on Total Crime Index	Index Crime Category in which State Fell in Highest Five							Total Row
		Murder	Rape	Robbery	Assault	Burglary	Larceny Over $50	Auto Theft	
California	1		x	x	x	x	x	x	6
New York	2			x		x	x	x	4
Maryland	3		x	x	x	x		x	5
Nevada	4						x		1
Florida	5	x			x	x			3
Arizona	6						x		1
Hawaii	7					x			1
Michigan	8		x	x					2
Rhode Island	9							x	1
Colorado	11		x						1
Massachusetts	12							x	1
New Mexico	14						x		1
Missouri	15		x						1
Texas	19	x							1
Illinois	20			x					1
Louisiana	25				x				1
Georgia	30	x							1
Alabama	33	x							1
South Carolina	35	x							1
North Carolina	35				x				1

Source: Federal Bureau of Investigation, *Uniform Crime Reports—1968* (Washington, D.C.: U.S. Government Printing Office, 1969) and calculations by author.

Footnotes

1. This paper was first presented at the annual meeting of the California Council for Geographic Education, held at Fresno, California, in May 1970.

2. It should be noted that, strictly speaking, rigorous historical comparisons of crime distributions are not possible owing to changes in reporting procedures, including changes in the definitions of some crimes.

3. Robert W. Winslow, *Crime in a Free Society* (Belmont, California: Dickenson Publishing Co., 1968), p. 2.

4. *Ibid.*, pp. 38–42.

5. Stuart Lottier, "Distribution of Criminal Offenses in Sectional Regions," *Journal of Criminal Law and Criminology*, Vol. XXIX (1938), p. 343.

6. The initial processing and mapping of the data was performed using the computer mapping program CHORMAP, written by Dr. Morton W. Scripter of San Fernando Valley State College. The advice of graduate assistant Robert Borgstrom is also gratefully acknowledged.

7. Lyle W. Shannon, "The Spatial Distribution of Criminal Offenses by States," *Journal of Criminal Law and Criminology*, Vol. XLV (1954), pp. 268–269.

8. Sheldon Hackney, "Southern Violence," in Hugh D. Graham and T. R. Gurr (eds.), *The History of Violence in America* (New York: Frederick A. Praeger, 1969), pp. 505–527.

9. U.S. Bureau of the Census, *Pocket Data Book, U.S.A., 1967* (Washington, D.C.: U.S. Government Printing Office, 1966), p. 47.

10. The correlation coefficient (r) ranges from $+1$ to -1; values close to $+1$ indicate a strong positive relationship between the variables considered, while values approaching -1 indicate a strong inverse relationship. All coefficients mentioned here are positive.

11. Calculated by summing the correlations of each violence variable with the other violence variables.

12. See, for example: Karl Schuessler, "Components of Variation in City Crime Rates," *Social Problems*, Vol. IX (1961–62), pp. 314–323.

VIRGINIA L. SHARP •

The 1970 Postal Strikes: The Behavioral Element in Spatial Diffusion

Through an investigation of the spread of the United States postal strikes of 1970, this paper intends to assess the applicability of diffusion concepts developed largely with respect to material innovations to a "human action" type of innovation. In most previous diffusion studies, the spread of information relative to the innovation occurred primarily through interpersonal communication, with the mass media acting only as secondary agents in spreading the innovation. Distance was viewed as a prime determinant of communication intensity and, therefore, the strongest influence on the diffusion process. Studies dealing with diffusion on a regional or national scale, which regard both the mass media and interpersonal communication as significant, have demonstrated the importance of a place's position in the urban hierarchy, in addition to distance, in predicting diffusion patterns. However, in studying the spread of cultural or political beliefs and ideas, it may not be reasonable to assume that interpersonal communication is the dominant form of information flow. Similarly, diffusion of information about "human action" innovations does not necessarily pass down through the central place hierarchy. Such an innovation might originate at any level of society and spread without regard to urban scale. Therefore, this paper is concerned with a combination of not only the neighborhood and hierarchical effects on spatial diffusion, but also incorporates economic and political resistance as possible determinants of the resultant spatial pattern. The U.S. postal strikes of 1970

◆ SOURCE. Printed by permission of the author.

are examined in order to demonstrate the possible utility of such an approach for understanding the diffusion of conceptually similar ideas and items.

The Postal Strike in a Diffusion Framework

The 1970 postal strike was the first major strike against the Federal government since the signing of the Constitution and the first strike by postal workers in the 195-year history of the federal postal system. The wage protest strike began in New York on March 17th and spread rapidly across the country with individual post offices commencing to strike as late as March 25th. In most diffusion studies, acceptance serves as a present or potential reward for the adopter. However, a definite penalty was associated with the decision to strike. It is a felony for a federal worker to go on strike, with a maximum penalty of one year and one day in jail plus a one-thousand dollar fine.

The first strikers were, in a sense, testing the government to determine if, in fact, the law would be enforced. The strength in numbers adage was therefore important in a local union's decision to strike. If 5000 employees strike at once, the probability of arresting and/or fining them all is low; if only fifty employees start a strike, it would be feasible to arrest and/or fine all of them. Assuming that the percentage of postal employees interested in striking is uniform across the nation, it is reasonable to assume that post offices with many employees would be more likely to strike, and to strike sooner,

than smaller post offices. A diffusion down through the national post office hierarchy would be intuitively plausible.

The strength in numbers nature of the decision to strike may also be reflected in the channels of communication utilized. Interpersonal communication between local union leaders to gain support for the strike may have occurred. If so, a distance-decay effect may be important in explaining the actual diffusion pattern. In addition to possible interunion leader communication, the mass media flooded the nation's population with news of the postal strike by March 18th. Less than twenty-four hours after the first letter carriers struck, virtually every American knew of the postal upheaval in New York. The effect of each of these channels of communication has been well documented for material innovations. In the early stages of diffusion, innovators respond to the mass media. Later in the diffusion process, interpersonal communication is required for adoption. Assuming that such a categorization is relevant in the diffusion of "human action" innovations, we may hypothesize an increase in the relative importance of distance on the diffusion process through time.

The major issue of the postal strike was wages. Salaries for all employees in the postal department are set by Congress and are uniform across the nation. Postal employees in New York City are paid the same wages as employees in Parkersburg, West Virginia. Variations in the cost of living are not incorporated in government wage scales. Thus, it would be logical to expect that postal employees in areas with relatively high living costs would be more likely to strike for higher wages than employees in areas where the cost of living is comparatively low. Economic resistance, then, would be directly related to the cost of living.

Local social structure, in that it reflects a certain set of political values, should also affect the decision to strike. Post offices located in politically conservative areas, with their adversity to union power and challenges to the status quo, should be less likely to experience strikes than post offices located in politically liberal areas. Thus, the political disposition of an area affects the probability of acceptance of the decision to strike, serving as a socio-political resistance factor. That is, the more politically conservative an area is, the less likely are its postal employees to pass a strike vote, or even to be organized to the extent that a strike vote would be taken.

These four factors: distance, position in the postal hierarchy, economic resistance, and socio-political resistance, are incorporated into a regression model to elucidate the relative importance of each in explaining the actual spread of the U.S. postal strike in March 1970.

Formation of the Model

The dependent variable, time, was measured on an interval scale such that the time of the first strike, March 17th, was set equal to 9, March 18th = 8, etc. For the last date that a strike started, March 25th, time = 1. For post offices not experiencing strikes, time was set equal to zero. A problem arises with this representation in that striking post offices can take a range of values from 1 through 9 for time, whereas nonstriking post offices can take on only one value, zero. There is no measure of the extent to which a post office did not strike. It is assumed that all places not experiencing strikes possess the same amount of "nonstrikingness." Logically, this does not seem a legitimate assumption. Some places should be more extreme in their resistance to striking than others. However, since there are no data available which would indicate the extent of a post office's opposition to the strike, no range of values could be assigned as a measure of "nonstrikingness." Because a majority of the post offices in the sample studied did not experience strikes, and therefore have a time value of zero, and because time is measured on an interval scale while the other variables are measured on continuous real number scales, the variance explained by the regression model will remain small. This does not necessarily mean that the model cannot replicate the diffusion pattern accurately. Alternative measures of the model's accuracy will be discussed.

It is also important to note that this measure of time indicates the time at which local postal employees actually began to strike. It does not measure the time at which the employees made the decision, but the time when the physical act began.

Distance, X_1, was measured as the distance from post office i to the nearest place experiencing a postal strike during a previous time period. Thus,

X_1 changes through time. To replicate the actual diffusion process, the regression must be calculated for each time period, distance being remeasured between regressions.

The hierarchical factor, X_2, is represented in the model by the number of people employed at each post office. Thus, X_2 measures the post office's position in the postal hierarchy rather than the city's position in the central place hierarchy of the U.S.

Economic resistance to striking, X_3, is represented by the cost of living in the city where each post office is located.

As a measure of social resistance, X_4, voting behavior in the U.S. House of Representatives was used as a surrogate for the level of conservatism in each city, since "All congressmen are sensitive to the ultimate decision of the voters. Failure to take into account constituency views may result in defeat at the polls" (Nimmo and Ungs, 1967, p. 363). And Miller and Stokes found that, although district opinion had little bearing on how representatives voted in foreign-policy matters, they were influenced by constituency attitudes in civil rights, social welfare, and national internal policy matters.[4] The annual vote ratings for each congressman by the Americans for Constitutional Action are explicitly designed to test conservatism. Evans[3] attests to the essential accuracy of the ACA's "percent conservative votes" as a measure of political conservatism. The average ratings for each congressional district for the past five years was used as a surrogate for conservatism. Thus we are hypothesizing that the probability of a post office striking is directly proportional to the political liberalism of that community.

The regression model is applied to a system of 190 post offices in the United States. This sample includes the fifty largest post offices in terms of total employment and a random sample of the remaining U.S. post offices with one hundred or more employees. Since the sample is weighted toward the top of the postal hierarchy, the importance of the hierarchical effect in the model should be slightly underestimated. The inclusion of the smaller post offices tends to reinforce the general pattern of diffusion, strengthening the effect of distance. The number of striking post offices during each twenty-four hour time period predicted through the regression model was set equal to the actual number striking in the sample at each interval. Figure 1 illustrates the observed strike diffusion pattern through this sample of post offices. Notice that the overall pattern shows a general diffusion out from the hearth area, New York, during the first three days of striking. On the fourth day, postal strikes occurred in more widely separated areas: the Northeastern seaboard, the Detroit-Chicago-Milwaukee-Minneapolis corridor, and the southern Pacific coast. Notice also that no strikes occurred south of the Mason-Dixon line.

The basic regression model may now be stated

$$Y_i = a + b_1X_1 + b_2X_2 + b_3X_3 + b_4X_4 \tag{1}$$

where Y_i = time of strike at post office i

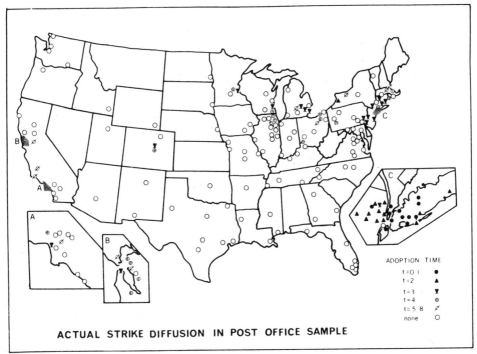

ADOPTION TIME
t = 0 1   •
t = 2   ▲
t = 3   ♈
t = 4   ⊕
t = 5 8   ⊘
none   ○

ACTUAL STRIKE DIFFUSION IN POST OFFICE SAMPLE

FIGURE 1.

X_1 = distance from post office i to the nearest previously striking post office

X_2 = post office size

X_3 = cost of living

X_4 = conservatism

The coefficients in the regression equation are estimated for each time period, with the distance variable (X_1) being remeasured following each regression.

In addition to the additive effects of these four variables, the multiplicative effects produced by the conditional effects of the resistance factors on X_1 and X_2 may also be incorporated into the model. The regression coefficients (b_1) of distance and (b_2) of hierarchy may be conditioned by the level of economic or socio-political resistance at place i. That is, in equation (1) b_1 and b_2 may be functions of X_3 or X_4. Then:

$$b_1 = a_0 + c_0 X_3 \qquad b_2 = a_2 + c_2 X_3$$
$$b_1 = a_1 + c_1 X_4 \qquad b_2 = a_3 + c_3 X_4 \tag{2}$$

The complete regression equation is formed by substituting equations (2) into (1):

$$Y_i = a + b_1 X_1 + b_2 X_2 + b_3 X_3 + b_4 X_4$$
$$+ b_5 X_1 X_3 + b_6 X_1 X_4$$
$$+ b_7 X_2 X_3 + b_8 X_2 X_4 \tag{3}$$

The coefficients may be interpreted as follows: b_3 indicates the additive effect of X_1, distance, on Y; b_5 indicates the multiplicative effect of X_3, economic resistance, on the effect of X_1, distance, on Y.

Application and Interpretation of the Model

A stepwise multiple regression was performed on equation (3) for each time period. New York City was assumed to have experienced the first strike, as in the actual data. Thus, distance in the first time period was measured as the distance between place i and New York City. Following each regression the N post offices with the highest computed Y values, where N equaled the number of places actually experiencing strikes during that time period, were taken as the places predicted to have struck by the regression model. Because of the inadequacies of the time measure noted previously, all computed Y values differed considerably from the actual measure of striking time. For this reason, and because the change in the computed values of Y through time is only indirectly affected by change in distance, post offices experiencing strikes at time t were removed from the set of observations included in the regression at time $t + 1$. Had these previously striking post offices not been deleted from the observations, the multiplicative effects of the economic and socio-political resistance factors on distance would take on values of zero, since the distance from a place to itself would be zero. Therefore, the value of the predicted Y would change relative to Y for other places. This could produce a change in the predicted time of strike at place i with each regression.

Obviously, this would be highly unsatisfactory.

Using this method of recomputing distance after each time period and deleting those post offices which are predicted to experience strikes, then running the regression for the next time period, a predicted pattern of postal strike diffusion was derived. This method predicted the actual time of strike accurately for 67.4 percent of the post offices. Whether or not a post office experienced a strike was accurately predicted for 88.4 percent of the observations. The highest multiple R^2 was .573. This does not appear to provide as meaningful a measure of the model's accuracy as the other measures. It should be noted that the predicted time of strike deviated from the actual time by more than two days for only 13.8 percent of the observations.

The residuals from the regressions show only a slight regional variation. The New England area, on the whole, is overpredicted. That is, the model predicted strikes to occur earlier than they actually did, or in cities where no strikes occurred. The model underpredicts a disproportionate number of the post offices located in suburbs of large cities. From these observations one might hypothesize that the distance factor is more important in predicting strike diffusion within a metropolitan area than over large distances. Such a relationship would be logically consistent with the previous proposition that local union leaders might tend to contact other union leaders within their metropolitan area for strike support.

The partial correlation coefficients associated with each of the variables included in the regression model serve as measures of the relative importance of each factor in explaining the actual pattern of postal strike diffusion. Table 1 contains the partial correlation coefficients for each factor and their significance, as measured by the t test, for the eight regressions computed.

Throughout the eight time periods, the economic and sociopolitical resistance factors proved to be more important in explaining the observed variation in postal strike timing. The distance and hierarchy factors, prime determinants of material innovation diffusion processes, were far less important than the two resistance factors in predicting this "human action" diffusion process. The variables representing the multiplicative effects of the factors, on the whole, were more significant than the distance and hierarchy factors, but less significant than the resistance factors.

Change in the relative importance of the variables occurs through time. Although the two resistance factors are by far the most effective in explaining the variation in the observed distribution of striking times, the percentage of the explained variation attributable to each fluctuates considerably. Economic resistance, as measured by cost of living, is most important in time periods 1, 2, and 5. Notice that the distance and multiplicative effect of cost of living on distance factors (X_1 and X_5) show patterns of change in relative importance similar to that for the cost of living alone (X_3). They are all most effective for the time periods just following those in which major cities experienced strikes. Socio-political resistance (X_4) is relatively most important during

time periods 3, 4, 7, and 8—time periods during which strikes are predicted to occur in cities widely separated in physical space.

Only two variables increase in overall importance through time: the multiplicative effect of conservatism on distance, X_6, and the multiplicative effect of cost of living on employment, X_7. This is to say that, if there were no socio-political resistance to striking, the probability of a strike occurring in a city far from previously striking post offices decreases through time. One reason for this relationship is that the maximum distance to a post office previously experiencing a strike decreases through time. Also, this relationship shows the effect of suburban post offices striking during the later time periods, after the larger metropolitan post offices struck. To a slightly lesser extent, if the cost of living were uniform across the U.S., the probability of smaller post offices striking would increase through time. This relationship lends credence to the hypothesis that the "strength in numbers" adage should be relevant in predicting strike behavior.

Thus, of the eight variables studied here, economic and socio-political resistance are the most significant for replicating the diffusion pattern of the postal strike. In fact, using only these two factors in a regression equation, it is possible to predict the timing of 64.7 percent of the sample cities accurately and whether or not a strike occurred correctly for 83.2 percent of the observations. This seems to be a rather minimal amount of accuracy lost for the amount of simplification in calculating the model. When considering only

TABLE 1. Results from Regressions

Time	No. of Observations	Partial Correlation Coefficients								Significance*							
		X_1	X_2	X_3	X_4	X_5	X_6	X_7	X_8	X_1	X_2	X_3	X_4	X_5	X_6	X_7	X_8
1	189	.173	.046	.394	−.301	−.202	.044	−.046	−.113	.98		.99	.99	.99			.50
2	178	.148	.041	.357	−.278	−.173	.026	−.040	−.118	.80		.99	.99	.95			.50
3	165	.066	−.010	.269	−.311	−.085	.062	.012	−.095	.50		.99	.99	.50	.50		.50
4	148	.038	−.062	.249	−.326	−.057	.077	.068	−.121			.99	.99		.50	.50	.50
5	130	.167	.054	.330	−.280	−.156	−.106	−.071	.092	.90		.99	.99	.90	.50	.50	.50
6	124	.130	.033	.249	−.144	−.114	−.164	−.042	.037	.50		.99	.90	.50	.90		
7	120	.088	—	.186	−.236	−.121	.141	−.074	—	.50	.50	.95	.98	.50	.50	.50	
8	119	.078	.039	.179	−.213	−.098	.061	−.059	.096	.50		.90	.95	.50	.50		.50

X_1 = distance
X_2 = post office size
X_3 = cost of living
X_4 = conservatism

X_5 = distance * cost of living
X_6 = distance * conservatism
X_7 = post office size * cost of living
X_8 = post office size * conservatism

* Significance = probability of t value of particular magnitude not being due to chance occurrence.

cost of living and conservatism in the regression equation, no distances need to be measured and only one multiple regression need be performed. Predicted time of strike is obtained simply by ranking the computed Y values and assigning observations to time classes according to their rank and the number of post offices actually experiencing strikes during each time period. Using this method the only regional inaccuracies prominent are an overprediction of large Texas cities and a slight underprediction of cities close to New York City.

Summary

In this study, it has been shown that diffusion concepts developed primarily with reference to material innovations are not necessarily generalizable to "human action" innovations. For innovations which produce an actual change in human behavior, factors logically related to that innovation are more important predictors of the diffusion pattern than the general surrogates which have previously received primary attention.

Perhaps the economic and sociopolitical resistance factors studied here can be considered measures of some form of "functional behavioral space" applicable in the study of other ideas and actions with strong cultural deterrents to acceptance. Consider, for example, the distribution of university riots. The behavioral space defined by the socio-political resistance factor previously described appears to correlate quite highly with the actual pattern of university riots. Conservative regions, most notably the entire South, experienced few riots. Those which did occur were primarily race riots at all-Black colleges. More liberal regions experienced numerous disturbances. By casting the study of university disturbances into a diffusion framework such as the one postulated in this paper, much of the variation in the spread of the riots may be understood. At present, further examination of the relationship between such a behavioral or 'social awareness' space and the distribution of various forms of social and political dissent must be completed before any meaningful generalizations can be made. A reformulation of current diffusion theory in which emphasis is diverted from surrogate measures of interaction to innovation-specific resistance factors may be in order.

Acknowledgments

The author gratefully acknowledges the assistance of the U.S. Post Office Department in providing the data used in this study. She is also indebted to Professors George J. Demko, The Ohio State University, and Peter R. Gould, The Pennsylvania State University, for assistance in the preparation of this paper.

References

1. American Chamber of Commerce, *Cost of Living Indicators*, mimeographed report, 1968.
2. Americans for Constitutional Action, *The ACA Index*, Washington, D.C.: Americans for Constitutional Action, 1965–1969.

3. Evans, M. S., *The Future of Conservatism*, New York: Holt, Rinehart, and Winston, 1968, pp. 75–79.

4. Miller, W. E. and D. Stokes, "Constituency Influence in Congress," *American Political Science Review*, Vol. 57, 1963, pp. 45–56.

5. Nimmo, D. and T. D. Ungs, *American Political Patterns*, Boston: Little, Brown and Company, 1967.

6. U.S. Post Office Department, *Employee Complements*, Washington, D.C.: U.S. Post Office Department, 1969.

thirty-six

GEORGE J. DEMKO •

VIRGINIA L. SHARP •

JACQUE L. HARPER •

CARL E. YOUNGMANN •

Student Disturbances and Campus Unrest in the United States: 1964-1970

Student disturbances, campus unrest and violence, and the general crises associated with colleges and universities in the United States are phenomena which, in recent years, have preoccupied a great many journalists, educators, politicians, and social scientists. This obviously timely topic has generated a plethora of hasty studies and comments in the press as well as in scholarly journals, but too few measured analyses of the available data related to these phenomena. Moreover, the bulk of the writing on this topic is addressed to the etiology of student dissent, even though most of the investigators focus on a single disturbance or a set of disturbances over a relatively short period of time.[1] The present study is a preliminary attempt to (1) bring together some relevant data in a concise manner; (2) examine the general spatial trends and relationships exhibited by these data; and (3) recognize patterns of spatial interaction portrayed by the data.

Some Selected Characteristics of Campus Unrest

The Berkeley disturbance in December, 1964, which represented the beginning of a new era of student activism, was

◆ SOURCE. Printed by permission of the authors.

selected as the starting point for data collection. This study encompasses all disturbances of normal university operation involving 50 or more people which occurred between 1964 and 1970 at four-year institutions of higher education with 100 or more students.[2] By viewing student disturbances over this seven-year time period, a more valid picture of the phenomenon can be derived than from a single-disturbance or single-year analyses. Furthermore, this extended time interval allows for examination of the changing character of student unrest. Specific data collected included the date and duration of the disturbance, number of participants, injuries, and arrests, and data describing the particular school (enrollment, Gourman rating,[3] city population). Additionally, disturbances were classified by types according to the major underlying motive of each (as interpreted from the printed accounts of each incident). Five types of disturbances were distinguished: *social* disturbances instigated by a victory in an athletic event or similar incident, *internal* disturbances, sparked by faculty tenure decision, non-academic personnel wage disputes or similar events, *external* disturbances which were sparked by foreign policy or related incidents, *recruiting* disturbances related directly to military or industrial recruiting on campus, and *racial* disturbances which were associated with some racially related event or incident.

Several generalizations concerning the nature of student disturbances can be made by simply organizing these data (Table 1). First, more student disturbances resulted from conflict internal to the college or university (133) than from any other source. Second, social disturbances were generally the

TABLE 1.   Selected Characteristics of Student Disturbances: 1964–1970

| Characteristics | Type of Disturbances | | | | |
	Social	Internal	Recruiting	External	Racial
Total number of disturbances	9	133	41	77	86
Mean no. of disturbances at school	1.0	2.2	2.3	3.5	2.2
Mean time period[a]	9.8	13.5	12.6	16.5	14.0
Mean no. of participants	802.2	899.4	868.9	3010.6	565.6
Mean length of disturbance	1.6	3.2	2.7	3.1	3.2
Mean no. of arrests	8.1	35.7	10.4	33.3	21.6
Mean no. injured	0.0	2.3	2.6	7.6	1.4
Mean school enrollment	19,555	14,723	17,763	16,692	12,770
Mean city population	1,314,133	2,032,945	1,126,678	1,776,946	1,426,641
Mean Gourman rating	468	466	550	522	471

[a] All disturbances were grouped into three-month time intervals. Thus all disturbances occurring in September, October, and November of 1964 were placed in time period 1 (one) and so on.

least serious type in terms of length, arrests, and injuries, while those resulting from internal and external causes were the most serious. Third, externally-caused disturbances occurred later with respect to both calendar time and the position in the school's overall disturbance pattern and mobilized far more students than did other types of unrest. This pattern is due primarily to the rash of disturbances which occurred in the spring of 1970, following the announcement of U.S. military incursion into Cambodia. Fourth, disturbances caused by occurrences outside of the university community (both recruiting and external types) were more characteristic of "better" schools, as measured by the Gourman rating, than were other types of disturbances. This may be due to a greater awareness of national and international matters by students in higher quality institutions. Fifth, disturbances induced by racial conflicts generally involved fewer participants, occurred fairly late in the overall pattern, were relatively long in

duration, involved a fairly large number of arrests (especially when compared to the number of participants), and occurred in smaller schools, on the average, than did other types of disturbances. Sixth, there appears to be a general disturbance sequence for schools. That is, "social" disturbances were, in each case, the school's first student conflict experience. Internally and racially instigated disturbances occurred next, and, finally, the students turned their attention to nonschool matters and protested national and international events. It should also be noted that the cause of these disturbances becomes more complex through time. Whereas in the first few years of this era of student activism a single banner was usually waved, by 1969 and 1970, rarely was there a clear-cut, single cause for conflict.

Sorting the disturbances with respect to month of occurrence produces an interesting pattern (Figure 1).[4] Cursory examination of this graph immediately suggests close correlations

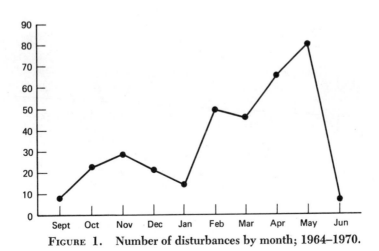

FIGURE 1.   Number of disturbances by month; 1964–1970.

between time of disturbance and climatic conditions and position in the school term. However, when the schools are divided by climatic region, this first correlation is shown to be insignificant. In addition, most of the disturbances which are shown to have occurred during Spring, 1970 were precipitated by President Nixon's announcement of the Cambodia invasion.

The Spatial Distribution of Campus Unrest

In examining the spatial patterns of intensity of student disturbances, a variety of data definitions is possible. In order to present the most accurate portrayal three different sets of data were mapped. Figure 2 depicts the total number of disturbances by state. New York and California are clearly most

prominent, though followed closely by Massachusetts. Next in importance is a cluster of states in the Midwest and Middle Atlantic regions which includes Ohio, Pennsylvania, New Jersey, Wisconsin, and Illinois. This pattern of frequent disturbances obviously corresponds spatially to the heavily populated, urban-industrial states. It is also evident in this map that there is a lesser degree of activity in the southern and border states. Among these, North Carolina is most noteworthy. It should also be mentioned that most of the activity in this region is attributable to predominantly Black Colleges. In the Southwest, only Texas stands out with respect to total number of disturbances, followed to a lesser degree by Colorado. On the Pacific coast there exists a noticeable localization of disturbances centered mainly in California. The map is also interesting in that there are large

CAMPUS UNREST 1964-1970

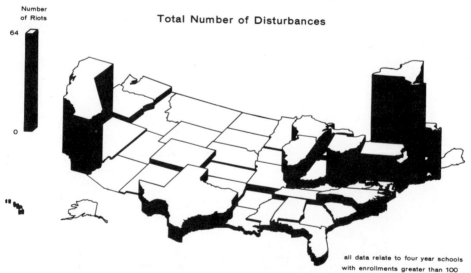

Number of Riots

Total Number of Disturbances

64

0

all data relate to four year schools
with enrollments greater than 100

FIGURE 2.

CAMPUS UNREST 1964-1970

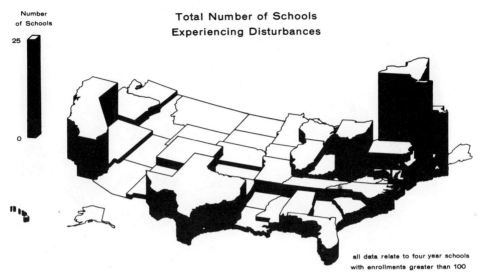

Number
of Schools

Total Number of Schools
Experiencing Disturbances

25

0

all data relate to four year schools
with enrollments greater than 100

FIGURE 3.

areas where few or no disturbances occurred, including the Great Plains states, the Mountain West, most of the Southwest, and the upper New England states.

The second definition of the intensity of unrest chosen was the number of schools in each state which experienced disturbances (Figure 3). The nation is shown in sharper relief in this cartographic representation than in Figure 2, although there is very little alteration in the order of states. New York and Massachusetts dominate the northeast quadrant of the U.S. again, although Ohio stands in a more prominent position in this portrayal. In the southern and border states, Tennessee and Florida join North Carolina in relative importance while Texas again stands out in sharp relief in the Southwest. The Pacific coast again is note-

worthy for the high intensity of activity in California. The areas of little or no activity show minor change from the pattern exhibited by the total number of disturbances.

The degree of student involvement in campus unrest may be most accurately measured by the third index of unrest, students involved in disturbances as a percentage of total enrollment in each state (Figure 4). Although the general regional patterns are similar to those in Figures 2 and 3, there are some noteworthy reshufflings of states in terms of their order of importance. Massachusetts clearly stands out as the leading state in this distribution, followed by Connecticut and New York in the Northeast, Wisconsin in the Midwest, and California on the Pacific coast. In terms of the latter region, the localization of unrest in California is most

CAMPUS UNREST 1964-1970

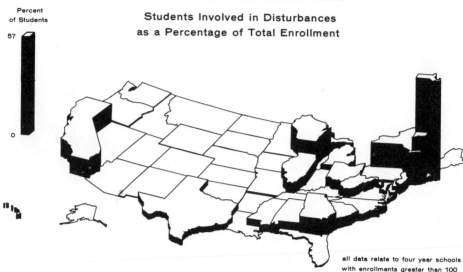

Figure 4.

noteworthy. In the southern and border states the use of this measure singles out West Virginia and Georgia as states affected relatively severely by student unrest. The areas of little or no activity are even more clearly depicted in this pattern.

In summary, all three representations of campus unrest produce similar generalizations. The northeast quadrant of the country is a focus of activity, with the states of Massachusetts, New York, Connecticut, Wisconsin, and Ohio standing out most sharply. California is an outstanding focus of unrest in the western portion of the country. As a region, the southern and border states are of some importance, although the ordering of the states varies considerably with the measure used. Outside these regions, only Texas is consistently conspicuous. The states of

upper New England, the Great Plains, and of the West are conspicuous because of their relative dearth of student activity.

Patterns of Spatial Spread of Campus Unrest

Because student disturbances have occurred at various points along a time continuum, they can exhibit not only static patterns of spatial distribution, but also dynamic patterns of spread between regions. While no such dynamic patterns were exhibited by the data describing internal disturbances, general spatial/temporal movement patterns could be discerned for external (including recruiting) type disturbances as well as racially-induced student unrest.

In general, the pattern of spread of external disturbances can be characterized as a west to east process. The first externally-induced student disturbance occurred at Berkeley, five of the next six occurred in the Midwest, and then the next four were experienced by East coast schools. This early pattern of a slow dispersion of disturbances among West coast (especially California) schools, an explosion in the Midwest, and then a slow spread down the East coast to Southern (primarily all-Black) schools was further reinforced through time. A second discernible pattern exhibited was the filtering down the hierarchy of "quality" schools. The first schools to respond to external problems with student sit-ins, marches, and rallies were generally higher on the scale of academic quality than those which experienced disturbances later. For example, Berkeley, the University of Wisconsin, UCLA, Columbia, and Princeton were among the first to experience student disturbances attributable to external causes.

The pattern of spatial/temporal spread of racially-induced student unrest is almost the opposite of that for external disturbances. While the first few schools to respond to the cries of racial injustice, most notably in terms of University admissions policies, were generally high-quality schools, they were, more specifically, East coast quality schools. However, this cause was very quickly picked up by all-Black colleges, first by those in the East, and then by those further South. Concomitant with this spatial filtering through the Black schools was an east-west pattern of spread, with schools in the Midwest responding to the outcries of racial inequality before Pacific coast schools.

While the dynamic spatial patterns discussed above are difficult to describe verbally, they can be readily observed through conversion to real-time animation.[5] However, the existence of these general spatial patterns in no way imparts any form of causation to the spread of campus unrest. One hypothesis which has been repeatedly put forward suggests that the student disturbances were diffused across the United States by radical student groups. To test this hypothesis, a number of analyses involving locations and sizes of SDS (Students for a Democratic Society) chapters were conducted. None of the tests proved statistically significant.

Thus, while general patterns which describe the spatial spread of the student disturbance phenomenon can be identified, the existence of a spatial diffusion process cannot be substantiated due to the lack of a particular "carrier" for the phenomenon.

Summary and Some Tentative Conclusions

This paper has attempted to illuminate some of the more salient, if somewhat obvious, characteristics of campus unrest which have occurred in U.S. institutions of higher education over the past seven years. With regard to the motivation for student unrest it is clear that the types of disturbances changed character during the study period, beginning with social types of protests, then internal and external types of protest, and finally racial disturbances. Toward the end of the study period it is most difficult to label disturbances by a prime motivating factor, but rather the motives blur and combine into a more complex type. Intensity of unrest as measured by the length of disturbances, number of arrests, and number injured, was greatest for internal and external types of protest, followed closely by racial protests. With regard to recruiting and external types of protests, there is an apparent hierarchical effect with the better quality schools (employing the Gourman index) experiencing this type of unrest earlier and more frequently than other schools. Conversely, protests related to internal factors are characteristic of schools which ranked lower on the Gourman scale.

The temporal pattern of unrest for the study period is noteworthy in that there is a general growth of activity throughout the academic year with the peak reached in May and two troughs evident, one at mid-year (January) and the other at year-end (June).

With regard to the spatial distribution of unrest there is an overwhelming concentration of activity in the populous northeast section of the country, particularly the states of Massachusetts, Connecticut, New York, Wisconsin, and Ohio, and on the West coast, rather neatly localized in California. Regions of the country most significant for their relative dearth of campus unrest include upper New England, the Great Plains, and most of the western and southwestern areas.

Although the spatial movement and spread of unrest are less readily evident in the data, there are some general trends to be noted. External types of protest have their origin in California and there is a general spread to the Midwest and Northeast, respectively. From the Northeast external types of protest display a tendency to spread southward along the east coast into the South. Racial types of protest appear to start in the Northeast and spread simultaneously to the Midwest and West coast as well as southward along the Atlantic coast, and particularly in predominantly Black schools of the southern and border states.

Although this study provides some insights into the phenomenon of student activism and particularly its spatial dimensions, it raises many more questions than it answers. Some of the more obvious of these questions involve the role of the mass media in the spatial spread of student unrest, the role of student leaders in precipitating unrest, and the association of ecological characteristics of location and disturbances. Clearly, student activism and campus unrest which occurred from 1964 to 1970 are indicative of behavioral patterns symptomatic of our time, and fully deserve careful attention and study.

Footnotes

1. See, for example, D. W. Leslie, *Student Unrest on the American University Campus: A Bibliography*, Center for the

Study of Higher Education, The Pennsylvania State University, November, 1969
(mimeo), for a rather comprehensive listing of recent studies of student unrest.

2. Primary data sources were *The New
York Times Index* (and specific issues) and
Facts on File. Data derived from these
sources were checked against the following additional sources: local newspapers
(where available), Lemberg Center for
the Study of Violence and the U.S. Senate
Committee on Government Operations,
Report on Riots, *Civil and Criminal Disorders*.

3. The Gourman rating is a composite
measure based on numerous criteria describing both the quality of a school's
physical plant and the individual depart-
ments in a college. See Jack Gourman,
*The Gourman Report: Ratings of Ameri-
can Colleges*, Phoenix, Arizona, 1968, and
monthly updates.

4. Data were not collected for the months
of July and August.

5. A computer movie of the spatial spread
of student disturbances has, in fact, been
made.

thirty-seven ◆ ◆ ◆ ◆ ◆ ◆ ◆ ◆ ◆ ◆ ◆ ◆

◆ JOHN S. ADAMS

The Geography of Riots and Civil Disorders in the 1960's

Alexis de Tocqueville wrote that:

The sufferings that are endured patiently, as being inevitable, become intolerable the moment it appears there might be an escape. Reform then only serves to reveal more closely what still remains oppressive and now all the more unbearable. The suffering, it is true, has been reduced, but one's sensitivity has become more acute.

This paper explores the psychological and physical environments that surrounded the riots of the 1960s. It examines why some cities had riots while others were peaceful, and presents a model proposing why some black neighborhoods exploded while others remained tense but calm. The study concludes that during the decade, urban black Americans experienced a widening gap between sharply rising

expectations and limited capabilities. This "relative deprivation" gap appears to have been greatest in neighborhoods which exploded first.

The Revolt of the Ghettos, 1964 to 1968: The Psychological Side[1]

The revolt of black America did not happen overnight; it began with an unfulfilled promise. Claude Brown, in his *Manchild in the Promised Land*, began his portrayal of Harlem with this denial of the promise:

I want to talk about the first Northern urban generation of Negroes. I want to talk about the experiences of a misplaced generation of a misplaced people in an extremely complex, confused society. . . .

◆ SOURCE. Reprinted by permission from *Economic Geography*, Vol. 67, January 1972, pp. 24–42.

These migrants were told that unlimited opportunities for prosperity existed in New York and that there was no "color problem" there. They were told that Negroes lived in houses with bathrooms, electricity, running water, and indoor toilets. To them, this was the "promised land" that Mammy had been singing about in the cotton fields for many years. . . . There was a tremendous difference in the way people lived up north. There were too many people full of hate and bitterness crowded into a dirty, stinky, uncared-for closet-sized section of a great city. . . .

The children of these disillusioned colored pioneers inherited the total lot of their parents—the disappointments, the anger. To add to their misery, they had little hope of deliverance. For where does one run to when he's already in the promised land? [7, pp. vii–viii].

One runs to one's soul brother. Sentiment and experience fused in Harlem and in ghettos across the country. Metropolitan areas grew, ghettos expanded, whites escaped to the suburbs, more blacks arrived, and ghetto life deteriorated.

Any living organism thrives at only one scale according to a "law of proper proportions," but it will collapse of its own weight if size is doubled, tripled, or quadrupled and proportions are held constant [46, pp. 15–22]. The same laws of allometric growth may apply to cities and ghettos. Let us say a city's

black neighborhood comprised a compact zone covering a tenth of the city in 1920, and by 1960 the urbanized area and its black neighborhood had both tripled in size (Figure 1). Even though the black neighborhood is segregated from white neighborhoods in both

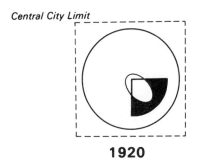

1920

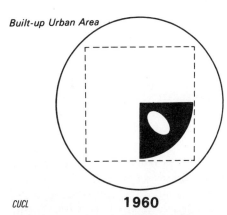

1960

FIGURE 1. As a built-up urban area (circle) and its black neighborhood (solid color) expand, the activity space of an inner city poor black resident (elipse) intersects an ever smaller fraction of not only the available urban experience, but also the available experience inside the black neighborhood. In recent decades activity spaces of the poor may even have shrunk as public transportation service has deteriorated.

cases, the "activity space" of an average black resident (schematically suggested by the elipses in Figure 1) intersects a proportionately wider spectrum of the available urban experience in 1920 than in 1960. As the metropolis and the ghetto expand, activity spaces of poor residents remain constant or shrink somewhat as public transportation deteriorates. In 1920, blacks and whites lived rather close to one another. By 1960, due partly to the geometry of human behavior and unregulated urban and ghetto expansion, the centers of gravity of each city's black and white populations were drifting farther and farther apart.

What started out as an urban experience ended as a ghetto existence for black newcomers to the northern city. From Harlem to Watts ghetto life became the common denominator, with its own life style, language, and restricted range of experience. The ghetto became a dead end for many of its residents. It became an object of loathing, a mirror of a squalid existence. Feelings of helplessness and isolation recurred in city after city. When asked what she would do if she had enough income one woman declared: "The first thing I would do myself is move out of the neighborhood. I feel the entire neighborhood is more or less a trap" [49, p. 6].

Compounding these antagonisms were the intensifying anti-urban attitudes of whites, drawn to the city of economic necessity but seizing the first opportunity to escape to the suburbs [19, pp. 187–89]. Meanwhile, the poorest citizens were not only poor, they were black and located in those sections of the city vacated by earlier immigrant

groups who had succeeded in translating upward social and economic mobility into geographic mobility [48, 51, 41]. As Kenneth Clark wrote:

The poor are always alienated from normal society, and when the poor are negro as they increasingly are in American cities, a double trauma exists—rejection on the basis of class and race is a danger to the stability of the society as a whole [11, p. 21].

The inauguration of John F. Kennedy in 1961 introduced the rhetoric and promises of the New Frontier and a significant fraction of mesmerized Americans became convinced that change was not only possible, but that rapid improvement of their lot lay just around the corner. President Kennedy's death in 1963 interrupted that dream, but even more extravagant promises accompanied the unveiling of a plan for a Great Society with full civil rights for all and a war on poverty [34, pp. 119–21].

Gradually at first, then picking up steam, a sense of betrayal of expectations brought grievances into focus. To lower class and lower middle class blacks, the visibility of an affluent and comfortable white middle class, exaggerated by mass media, induced dual feelings of emulation and smoldering resentment. After the riots, the Kerner Commission found the same complaints in city after city [40, p. 143]. The most intensely felt problems were: (1) police practices, perceived as attacks against personal dignity; (2) unemployment and underemployment, perceived as attacks against personal and family economic security; and (3) inadequate housing, perceived as an attack against the health, safety, and comfort of the family's personal environment. Such deep-seated, long-term malaise can lead to only one result in a decade of rapid change and rising expectations. Aaron Wildavsky summarized the situation in his recipe for violence:

Promise a lot; deliver a little. Lead people to believe they will be much better off, but let there be no dramatic improvement. Try a variety of small programs, each interesting but marginal in impact and severely underfinanced. Avoid any attempted solution remotely comparable in size to the dimensions of the problem you are trying to solve. . . . Get some poor people involved in local decision-making, only to discover that there is not enough at stake to be worth bothering about. Feel guilty about what has happened to black people; tell them you are surprised that they have not revolted before; express shock and dismay when they follow your advice. Go in for a little force, just enough to anger, not to discourage. Feel guilty again; say you are surprised that worse has not happened. Alternate with a little suppression. Mix well, apply a match, and run . . . [34, p. ii].

Dysfunctional Population and Housing Changes, 1950 to 1960: The Stage for Unrest

In most large cities the spatial organization of the housing supply resembles a series of distinct concentric zones around the downtown. Higher density, lower priced, and older housing is available in the inner rings; newer, lower density, higher priced units, mainly single family detached dwellings, are concentrated in the outer rings (Figure 2).

The demand for housing is expressed sectorally. As each household passes through the stages of the family life cycle its housing needs change and the household relocates, either *outward* to a larger more expensive unit, or *inward* to a smaller, cheaper dwelling. Most households try to satisfy changed housing requirements with a move as short as possible, so a city's aggregate migràtion fabric displays pronounced sectoral biases.

At the suburban edge of each sector, the addition of new housing provides upwardly mobile inner-city families with an opportunity to move outward. As they move outward they vacate older housing which then becomes available to families localized nearer to the downtown core. Within each areal sector, the invasion-succession process is the principal means by which better housing "filters down" from the prosperous to the poor [20]. In normal times housing filters smoothly, but from 1950 to the 1960s, the poor and the middle class black neighborhoods experienced a housing squeeze of alarming proportions.

Let us examine the source of the housing squeeze. Residential structures have high durability. According to the 1960 census of housing there were 58 million housing units in the United States. Thus, 1.5 million new housing starts in one year is only about 2.5

Housing Change

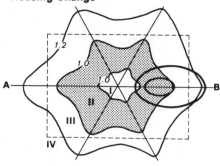

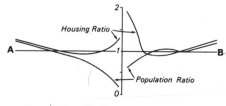

Population Change

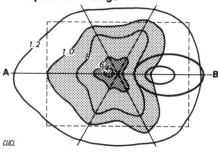

FIGURE 2. A map of housing change ratios (1960 housing units in a tract divided by 1950 units in the place) has four housing zones: zone I housing increased, zone II (stippled) housing declined, zone III was stable or had a modest housing increase, zone IV had vigorous suburban growth. The map of population change ratios (1960 tract population divided by 1950 tract population) reveals the sharpest losses (stippled) next to the downtown center and sharp increases in suburban areas. Dysfunctional change occurs when population ratios exceed housing ratios as they often did in the middle zones (small elipse) of the black neighborhood (large elipse).

percent of the housing stock, a relatively small change in the total number which is also affected by housing removals, especially in core areas of cities. In the aggregate metropolitan housing market, removals generate a replacement demand which is less important than either household formations or other influences on housing demand. In certain areal submarkets, however, demolition in one neighborhood is the principal stimulus for incremental demand in adjacent neighborhoods [32].

During the 1960s demolitions due to public and private urban land redevelopment and urban highway construction proceeded at a brisk rate, but housing starts and vacancy rates varied widely, putting a serious crunch on the most active housing sectors. Despite *increasing* demands for more housing throughout the 1960s, annual new private housing starts reached a peak of 1.6 million in 1963, then dropped to 1.2 million by 1966. By 1968, with only 1.5 million private units started, the construction industry still had not recovered to its 1962 levels of production. Just when more housing was desperately needed, less was provided; meanwhile, in some neighborhoods, housing was even being removed.

Vacancy rates are another indicator of the degree of pressure that demand is exerting on available supplies. The annual average rental vacancy rate for the United States rose from 5.1 percent in 1957 to 6.4 percent in 1959, and to 8.1 percent in the second quarter of 1961. Then, dropping as the market tightened, the rate fell to 4.9 percent at the end of 1968. Homeowner vacancy rates were more stable, but they too reached a peak in 1963 and fell to 1.0 percent in 1968. From 1960 to 1968 mobile home shipments quadrupled in response to strong demand, but this particular low income housing alternative, virtually banned from core housing areas of cities, remained largely a rural or suburban option. Thus, black households account for fewer than two percent of mobile home households [50, p. 92].

Racial and ethnic ghettos develop in the most vigorous residential sectors [44]. At the turn of the century diverse ethnic groups clustered around the downtowns of American cities. Some groups, usually white Anglo-Saxon Protestant or Jewish, prospered more rapidly than others and moved outward, as a group, with disproportionate speed. Because they moved in large numbers they vacated whole neighborhoods, which then stood ready for occupancy by the next wave of newcomers. This explains why black populations now occupy housing formerly used by the city's largest and most prosperous upwardly mobile groups [42, pp. 7–16].

The expansion of the Indo-Chinese war in the 1960s prompted major increases in the federal military budget. Increased spending coupled with deficit financing of the war produced severe inflation, which persisted and intensified until the end of the decade despite tax increases. Monetary controls were applied to the economy and tighter credit hit the home mortgage market. As government insured mortgage interest rates rose from 5 and 6 percent to 9 and 10 percent, suburban new home construction was drastically curtailed. The sectors where the black ghettos were located were hit the hardest. Filtering was sharply curtailed. Departures from middle class black neighborhoods (in the form of migration outward, or to other cities, or death) did not keep up either with arrivals or with the pressing need for additional space (immigration from core areas, from other cities, or from the South; births; infants and young children becoming young children and adolescents). Thus crowding or congestion radically increased without a safety valve during the 1960s *in certain parts* of black neighborhoods—not in the oldest core area, nor the upper middle class advancing edges, but in the middle zones where working class and lower middle class blacks saw their situation deteriorate at precisely the time when they expected their lot to improve. These middle zones were precisely the places where violence erupted.

Theories of Riot Origin

Some explanations of riot occurrence differentiate rioters from nonrioters. Other theories emphasize environmental circumstances, arguing that certain sets of conditions, if prevalent in a place, trigger violence. The most successful theories are psychological and emphasize the difference between what people think they have and what they feel they deserve.

The Riffraff Theory. The "riffraff theory" argues that "rioters are irresponsible deviants: criminals, unassimilated migrants, emotionally disturbed persons or members of an underclass. . . peripheral to organized society with no broad social or political concerns, and views the frustration that leads to rioting as simply part of a long history of personal failure" [9, p. 15]. By sampling populations in the Detroit and Newark census tracts where violence and damage occurred, Kerner Commission interviewers found no differences between rioters and nonrioters that would support the riffraff theory. Instead, occupational aspirations of the rioters in Newark were higher than among nonrioters. Moreover, the vast majority of the rioters were Northerners, either born in the riot city or immigrants from another Northern city.

Relative Deprivation. The "relative deprivation theory" was rejected by the Kerner Commission for the same reason as the riffraff theory: it failed to distinguish rioters from nonrioters in the census tracts which exploded. Relative deprivation is more complex than a simple "want-get" ratio suggests. The greater the deprivation a person perceives relative to what he feels are "justified expectations" the greater discontent. Relative deprivation is not what the outside observer thinks people ought to be dissatisfied with. It is people's perception of a discrepancy between their level of expectations and the capabilities they realize (Figure 3). People become most intensely discontented when they fail to get what they think they justly deserve, not just what they *want* in an ideal sense, and when they feel they are making inadequate progress beyond their expectations, not whether they have actually attained them or not [22].

Progressive deprivation, the third form of relative deprivation in Figure 3, seems to be often tied to revolutionary movements. Prolonged experience of increasing well-being generates intense expectations about continued increases. If changing circumstances mean that these expectations seem unsatisfiable, the likely consequence is intense discontent [12].

Applied to black populations and black neighborhoods, the relative deprivation theory can emphasize: (1) the economic gap between blacks and whites, which is a popular and somewhat invalid impression; (2) the gap between urban blacks and rural blacks, which is a discounted view and in any case fails to explain urban discontent [21]; and, (3) the perceived gap between upper middle class blacks and the blacks that rioted. The Kerner Commission found substantial and unexpected support for this third type of gap; the rioters used prosperous, successful blacks as their principal reference group [9, 43].

Black Americans in the 1960s should have benefited from the most prolonged economic expansion in the nation's history, and they apparently did. Median income of nonwhite families as a percent of white family income rose from 53 percent in 1961 to 62 percent in 1967. The percentage of nonwhite persons below the poverty line fell from 55 in 1961 to 35 in 1967 [33]. But just looking at income changes—the realizations or capabilities—misses half the point. Expectations changed too! As Boulding paraphrases Veblen: "We cannot assume that tastes are given in any dynamic theory . . . we cannot afford to neglect the processes by which cultures are created and by which preferences are learned' [6, p 2].

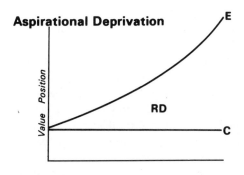

Aspirational Deprivation

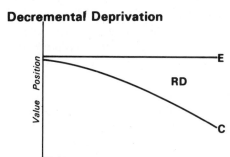

Decremental Deprivation

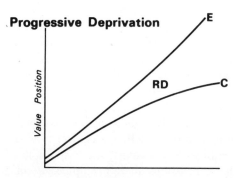

Progressive Deprivation

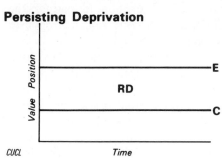

Persisting Deprivation

CUCL　　　　　*Time*

Blocked Opportunity. Another theory of riot origin stresses "blocked opportunities." It claims that black Americans have been systematically excluded from white society and white controlled economic institutions. "This theory views white discrimination as a constant barrier to occupational mobility; thus, the Negroes who are most likely to react violently are those who want to better themselves . . ."[9, p. 15].

The most useful theory of riot origin seems to be a combination of the second and third theories. The relative deprivation theory accounts for the level of intense discontent among the working class and lower middle class blacks who are neither the poorest nor the most prosperous. The blocked opportunity theory accounts for the low level of capabilities or realization of personal, economic, and environmental rewards inside the American system.

Besides overt discrimination in many places, feelings of relative deprivation and blocked opportunity were sometimes aggravated in innocent ways as well. The exclusion of blacks from many construction jobs is frequently cited as a particularly glaring form of blocked opportunity. Because such jobs are highly visible, reputed to be lucrative, and seem relatively easy to learn, "justified expectations" on the part of blacks are that a representative fraction

FIGURE 3. Relative deprivation (*RD*) is the perceived gap between justified expectations (*E*) and capabilities (*C*). If the gap increases through time, tensions and dissatisfaction mount. Progressive deprivation seems to be most often tied to revolutionary movements. Source: Gurr [22, pp. 598–601].

of all construction workers should be black. Yet many of these occupations have little if any room for newcomers, black or white [1]. Journeymen tradesmen, often anxious for their own jobs in the face of automation and declining employment, jealously guard their union membership as a birthright to pass on to whomever they choose. From the black point of view, opportunities appear to be blocked just when aspirations are rising.

The Location of Riots and Civil Disorders

Rioting black Americans can be classified in socioeconomic or locational terms. In socioeconomic terms the question "Who riots?" is answered in terms of an ambitious, hard working, but intensely dissatisfied group of working class and lower middle class blacks who feel deprived and excluded from what they feel are justified expectations. In geographical terms the question can be handled either at a macro-scale (Why did some cities explode while others were peaceful?) or at a micro-scale (Why did some black neighborhoods explode and others remain quiet?)

INTER-CITY ANALYSIS

In an analysis of 76 black-white race riots between 1913 and 1963, Lieberson and Silverman [27] found no important connection between the occurrence of violence and population growth, a city's proportion of black population, the unemployment rate, black income levels,

the proportion of blacks in good housing or other local environmental conditions.

A reanalysis of the Lieberson and Silverman data confirmed that no single factor discriminated clearly between riot and control cities, but did reveal that of the nine variables used, employment conditions discriminated better than any other single factor [4]. Reporting these results Downes agrees with Tomlinson that: "What is unacceptable about Negro life does not vary much from city to city . . . the differences in Negro life from city to city are irrelevant" [14; 47, p. 30]. Yet in his study of 239 outbursts between January 1964 and May 1968, Downes concluded that violence was somewhat more likely in cities that were densely settled, were large with little post-1950 population change, had a high and rapidly increasing fraction of black population since 1950, lower educational and income levels, higher unemployment rates, less sound housing, relatively little owner occupied housing, and high central employment. The differences turned out to be statistically significant because each municipality, whether a central city or a suburb, was treated as a "city." Thus, the conclusions merely emphasize the city-suburb distinction instead of the differences between riot metropolises and nonriot metropolises.

In a 1967 study, Maloney [28] tried to show how Standard Metropolitan Statistical Areas (SMSAs) that had riots differed from those that were peaceful in 1967. He selected 85 metropolitan areas on the basis of data availability and studied their differences in terms of 70 census and noncensus variables. A factor analysis of the 70 by 70 correlation matrix revealed eight principal dimensions of variation: metropolitanism or size, urban growth, a Southern syndrome, sporadic employment, highway spending, Negro concentration, a suburban syndrome, and density. Each metropolitan area received a separate factor score for each of the eight independent facors. Each score's magnitude depended on the metropolitan area's alignment with the corresponding factor or basic pattern of variation. The 85 by 8 matrix of factor scores provided Maloney with a set of eight measures for each SMSA. With the factor scores as independent variables, and a binary measurement of riot activity for the dependent variable (SMSAs having a riot before August 5, 1967 received a 1; others received a 0), a regression analysis produced a model arguing that riot experience (RE) varied positively with metropolitan size (M), the presence of a black population (B), and metropolitan density (D); and varied inversely with "Southernness" (S):

$$RE = -1.45 + .67M - .26S$$
$$+ .25B + .18D$$

Only four regression coefficients were statistically significant, but even with all eight variables included the coefficient of multiple determination was only .35. The 85 metropolitan areas were ranked on the basis of their "expected riot scores." Of the 24 highest scoring SMSAs, 22 had riots; of the 29 lowest scoring areas, mainly Southern cities or cities lacking black populations, 26 were peaceful. Between these extremes the regression model was a poor

predictor of riot experiences of different SMSAs.

Maloney's model is consistent with the theory that the largest SMSAs are the best known and most popular migration destinations for blacks looking for economic opportunity. Migrants expect greater rewards from the system than nonmigrants. Migration out of Southern cities has been selective; outmigrants have been more aggressive and better educated than others left behind. If a Northern or Western metropolitan area has a disproportionately high concentration of blacks, it is because the area was large and well known and perceived as a place of opportunity vis-à-vis alternative destinations. Metropolitan density is associated with riot activity because some of the largest and most attractive migration destinations in the North and Northeast are also very old cities with extensive high density central city areas.

When Maloney [29] expanded his study to include 96 metropolitan areas and additional variables he found little additional explanation, although by correlating individual variables with the occurrence or nonoccurrence of riots he made some surprising discoveries which support the combined relative-deprivation blocked-opportunity theory. The following SMSA variables were correlated with riot activity:

a. percent of adults that voted in 1964 (correlation = +.42), reflecting a basic sense of political involvement and faith in the system;

b. percent of adults with less than five years of schooling, and percent of families with less than $3,000 annual income (both − .38), reflecting that when well-educated migrants enter an area in large numbers they dilute the relative concentration of the resident poor and uneducated at the destination, and intensify the concentration in source areas;

c. percent of sound housing, and percent of families with incomes over $15,000 (both +.40), reflecting visible prosperity and the generation of high expectations; and,

d. percent of the SMSA population living in suburbs, and number of local governments (both +.35), reflecting rapid metropolitan and suburban expansion, producing further expectations about drastic change in housing environments.

The relative deprivation theory argues that a rising gap between justifiable expectations and current capabilities produces intense frustration; the blocked opportunity theory explains why capabilities rise slowly if at all. Maloney's metropolitan area model yielded patterns consistent with both constructs. A Midwestern city model linking city scores with riot scores brings patterns into even sharper focus.

RIOT EXPERIENCES OF MIDWESTERN CITIES

Berry [3] computed city scores for 1,762 legal cities with 1960 populations exceeding 10,000, using 97 standardized and normalized census variables. A factor analysis of the 1,762 by 97 data matrix identified 14 basic urban factors or dimensions accounting for 77 percent of the variation in the original data matrix. The dimensions included: functional size, socioeconomic status, family structure, nonwhite concentrations, foreign born concentrations, recent population growth, recent employment growth, females in the labor force, elderly males in the labor force, manufacturing activity, mining activity, college and university activity, military installations, and service centers or central places. Each city received fourteen scores, a separate score in terms of each factor. The city receiving top score on a certain factor is the most typical representative of the combination of traits that reflect the factor. For example, on the college and university factor, the highest scoring cities included State College, Pennsylvania, Chapel Hill, North Carolina, and Athens, Ohio. Cities with the highest socioeconomic status scores were Scarsdale, New York, and Winnetka, Illinois, and so forth. From Berry's 1,762 by 14 matrix of standardized factor scores this author selected the 212 rows representing all the Midwestern cities in the East North Central and the West North Central census divisions.

Riot scores were computed from 15 riot variables describing 166 major disturbances that occurred between 1965 and July 31, 1968 [52]. The author expected a factor analysis to reveal just one major pattern of riot activity, but three independent dimensions of civil disorder were uncovered, accounting for 59 percent of the original data variation. The first rotated factor represented the number of law officers and civilians killed and injured, arson, arrests, and property damage. The second factor emphasized the number of state police used to contain the disturbances, and the occurrence of interference with firemen. The third factor, independent of the other two, was linked to the incidence of sniping, vandalism, and the use of the national guard. Three standardized factor scores were computed for each of the 166 riots, 59 of which occurred in 37 Midwestern cities. For cities having two or more riots, a mean score was computed for each factor. For the 175 Midwestern cities which had no *major* disturbances (most of which presumably had minor unrest), dummy factor scores were provided. The lowest Riot I score among the 166 riots was −.59; thus, the 175 nonriot cities were assigned a Riot I score of −1.0. The lowest Riot II and Riot III scores (−2.56, −3.02) meant assigning scores of −3.0 and −4.0, respectively, to the nonriot cities.

The riot scores as dependent variables and city scores as independent variables were put into a step-wise multiple regression procedure whereby all statistically significant independent variables enter the regression equation one at a time in decreasing order of importance. The resulting equations are as follows:

$$\text{Riot I} = .010 + .225\,FS + .106\,NW + .063\,EG$$
$$R^2 = 0.35$$

$$\text{Riot II} = -.029 + .502\,FS + .394\,NW$$
$$R^2 = 0.25$$

$$\text{Riot III} = -.040 + .886\,FS + .478\,NW + .203\,EG$$
$$R^2 = 0.35$$

where:

FS = functional size score,

NW = nonwhite score,

EG = recent employment growth score.

The first regression equation suggests that riot deaths and injuries, arson arrests, and property damage vary directly with city size, black population concentrations, and recent employment growth. The third equation ties sniping, vandalism, and the use of the national guard with the same independent variables. The second equation relates the use of state police and interference with firemen to city size and black population.

This three-equation Midwestern cities model, like the Maloney model, is consistent with the relative-deprivation blocked-opportunity theory. Big cities with expanding job opportunities are not only the most common migration destinations for black migrants, but also the places where expectations are highest for local residents. Small stagnant areas of outmigration had low riot scores, and the large thriving cities tended to have the most serious problems. Maloney's use of SMSA data caused certain city-suburb and large-city small-city contrasts to be diluted or overlooked. Downes' use of city data identified city-suburb contrasts but because it included cities from every part of the country, it failed to reveal important regional differences. The three-equation Midwestern cities model does not escape the city-suburb bias, but by dealing with only one region's cities it

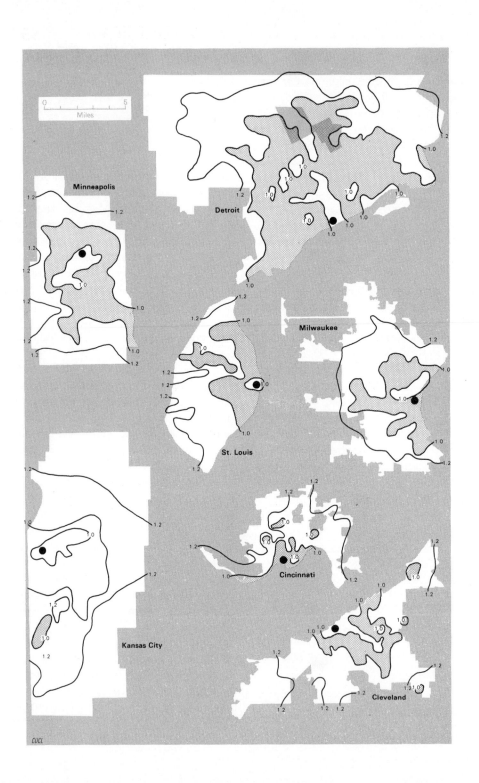

Minneapolis

Detroit

Milwaukee

St. Louis

Cincinnati

Kansas City

Cleveland

CUCL

eliminates or controls one source of data variation. Yet coefficients of determination are still low because patterns of riot occurrence are difficult to explain at the macro scale. Comparing black neighborhoods inside specific cities seems to be a much more fruitful approach.

THE EXPERIENCE INSIDE SEVEN MIDWESTERN CITIES

The people who live in cities also live in neighborhoods, and although cities differ substantially from one another, the range of neighborhood diversity is much greater. Two attributes which dramatize neighborhood diversity are census tract population change between 1950 and 1960, and the change in each tract's housing supply during the same decade.

The *population change ratio* for a census tract is computed by dividing the tract's 1960 population by its 1950 population. An isopleth map of the ratio for each of seven Midwestern cities reveals that in every case the downtown is surrounded by a zone of sharp population decline, which gives way to stability and then growth from the city edge into the suburbs. The deepest losses are concentrated in the all-white sectors (Figure 2). The black neighborhood develops in the most active housing sector (Figure 2). Housing filters down to lower income black newcomers as the previous residents prosper and move as a group toward the sub-

urbs. The faster the original residents prosper, the sooner they are able and anxious to abandon old housing for something better. New suburban housing is built wherever demand warrants; it is erected at the locations where builders expect effective purchasing power to be strongest. The large volume of old housing units that are vacated in a sector attracts newcomers. If more are attracted than can be comfortably housed, the tract population change ratios are stabilized instead of dropping as fast as they do in the more stagnant all-white sectors (Figure 4). In Cleveland, the black population is concentrated east of downtown and net population losses were highest on the west side. In Cincinnati the largest black neighborhoods lie to the northeast of downtown but the largest population decline occurred in tracts north and southeast of downtown. In St. Louis the black sector is northwest of downtown, but the tracts with the most abrupt population losses in the 1950s were in the western and southern sectors.

The *housing change ratio* equals 1960 housing units in a tract divided by the number in 1950. When mapped, each Midwestern city studied revealed four distinct housing zones (Figure 2). The number of housing units increased in zone I, which is a public and private renewal area; zone II underwent net housing losses in the 1950s; zone III was an area of stability where the few demolitions were cancelled out by mod-

FIGURE 4. Population change 1950 to 1960 in seven Midwestern cities is represented by isopleth values computed by dividing 1960 tract population by 1950 tract population. Stippled areas are zones of net population loss during the decade; compare Figure 2.

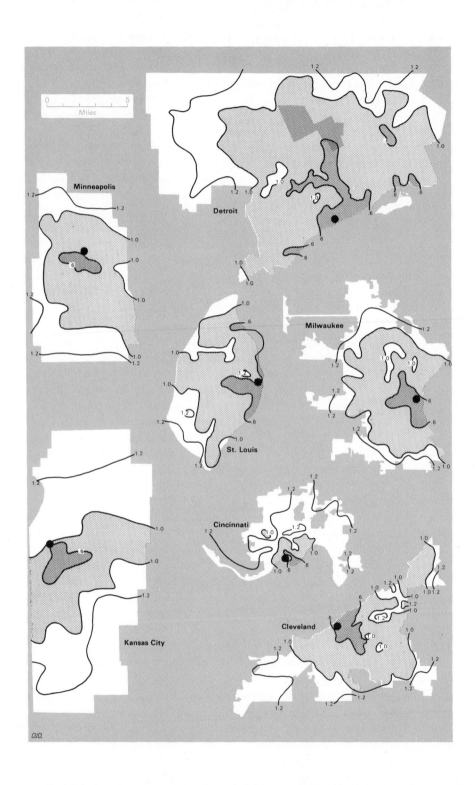

0 5
Miles

1.2   1.2
1.2   1.2
Minneapolis
1.2   1.2   Detroit
1.2   1.0   1.0
1.0   1.0
6   1.0   6   6
1.0   6
1.2   6
1.2   1.0   1.0
1.2   1.0

6   Milwaukee
1.0   1.2
1.0   1.0   1.0
1.2   1.2   1.2   1.0
1.2   1.0   6
St. Louis   1.2   6
1.2   1.0   1.2
1.2   1.2   1.0

1.2
Cincinnati   1.2   1.2
1.2   1.0   1.2   1.2
1.0   1.0   1.2
1.0   1.0   1.2
1.0   6   6   1.2
1.0   1.0   1.2   1.0 1.2
1.0   1.2   1.0
6   1.2   1.0
Cleveland   1.0   1.0   1.0
1.2   1.0   1.2
1.0   1.2
Kansas City   1.2   1.2
1.2   1.2

CUCL

est growth. Zone IV represents vigorous suburban expansion (Figure 5). Housing problems are concentrated in zones I and II of the active sectors containing black populations. Because black neighborhoods lie in the most active housing sectors, they are exceptionally visible to a substantial fraction of community economic and political leaders. Moreover, in Midwestern cities, the *center* of the downtown has migrated *from* its initial location *toward* the center of gravity of the city's purchasing power. This direction of movement approximates the location of the most active housing sector. If there are two exceptionally active sectors, the direction of displacement of the downtown center represents a resolution of forces. A consequence of all this is that today, black neighborhoods lie between the vigorous retailing and service edge of the downtown, and the mass, upper middle class clientele that downtown tries to tap as employees and customers. Thus, downtown councils in Midwestern cities have been more anxious to support public and private renewal in black neighborhoods than in poor white sectors elsewhere. Expressways also displace housing and particularly black housing for at least two reasons: black neighborhoods as we have just seen usually lie between downtown and the largest concentrations of prosperous commuters and shoppers; and, black neighborhoods, especially those close to downtown, have had practically no political punch

in city politics and are unable to get roads relocated when they threaten to cut neighborhoods in two.

In Cleveland, Cincinnati, and Detroit serious riots and civil disorders occurred midway between ancient, emptying ghetto cores, and youthful, prosperous, advancing ghetto margins (Figure 6). Trapped in the middle zones were people with intense expectations who found the relative deprivation gap widening when it should have diminished. Housing was a major problem. In these middle zones the population ratio actually exceeded the housing ratio and crowding as measured by persons per dwelling unit thereby increased. The squeeze was especially grim in Cleveland's Hough neighborhood. This "middle zone" in Cincinnati was only about 40 percent black, but the crowding got worse nevertheless. In the neighborhood at the center of the 1967 Detroit riot, population rose from 22,000 in 1956 to 38,000 in 1967 while the available housing supply was stable to declining [53, vol. 5, p. 1276]. At the ghetto margins and in white suburbs outside the city, young nuclear families live in single family dwellings. In these circumstances when the population ratio exceeds the housing ratio it is due to childbirth.

In Kansas City and Milwaukee the black neighborhood's expanding edge and its crowded midsection overlap (Figure 6). Yet when violence flared in the middle zone it was at locations

FIGURE 5. Housing change 1950 to 1960 in seven Midwestern cities is represented by isopleth values computed by dividing the number of housing units in a tract in 1960 by the number in 1950. Stippled areas indicate net housing removal; compare Figure 2.

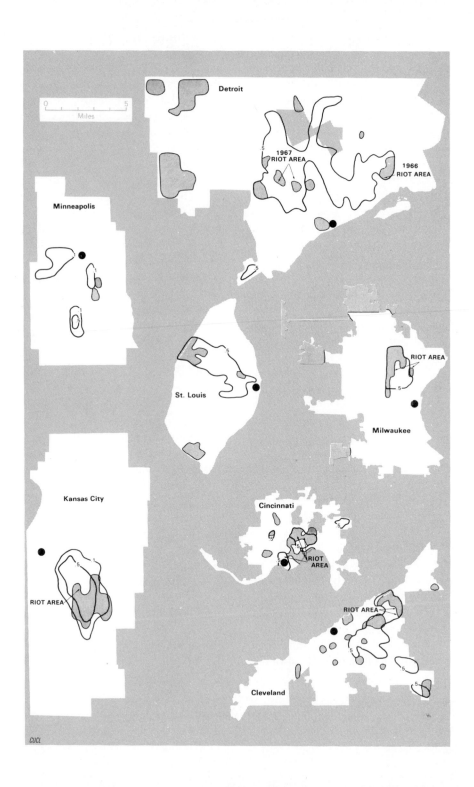

Detroit

1967 RIOT AREA

1966 RIOT AREA

Minneapolis

Miles

St. Louis

RIOT AREA

Milwaukee

Kansas City

Cincinnati

RIOT AREA

RIOT AREA

RIOT AREA

Cleveland

CUCL

analogous to those in Cleveland, Detroit, and Cincinnati.

St. Louis and Minneapolis avoided serious disturbances between 1965 and 1968 (low Riot I, II, and III scores) but were included in the analysis to see how housing and population ratios in middle zones differed from patterns in riot cities. Census data for St. Louis reveals no increased crowding problems in the middle zones, but only the evidence of typical family growth on the ghetto margins. Housing appears to have been filtering smoothly up through 1960. In the Minneapolis case, the black population was so small in 1960 that in no census tract did black population reach 75 percent of the total. Black neighborhoods west and south of downtown reflect vigorous urban expansion mainly in these directions, but in no "black" tract did the population ratio exceed the housing ratio.

Reflections on Environmental Stimulation and the Need for Personal Space

As with many social pathologies, our evidence about the riots of the 1960s resembles the tip of an iceberg—it gives only a hint of the structure that lurks below. We have barely scratched the surface in our understanding of the spatial organization of black neighborhoods, of the processes and behavior that produced them, or of the ways in which they influence learning as young people grow toward adulthood. It seems likely however that ghetto neighborhoods are a trap reinforced not only from without but from within as well. Yet, according to Dubos, in every kind of neighborhood:

Man makes himself in the very act of responding to his environment through an uninterrupted series of feedback processes. . . . Early influences are of particular importance because man's body and brain are incompletely developed at the time of birth. It is well known that various forms of deprivation impair learning ability. By acting on a child during formative years, the environment shapes him physically and mentally and influences how he will function as an adult [17, p. 153].

If children are denied the opportunity to experience early in life the kind of stimuli needed for mental development, if they fail to acquire needed mental resources, their range of free choices as adults shinks to zero. As Dubos continues:

It is not right to say that lack of culture is responsible for the behavior of slum children or for their failure to be successful in our society. The more painful truth is that these children ac-

FIGURE 6. Riot locations found inside black neighborhoods. In areas enclosed by solid lines, the fraction of the population that is black exceeds the fraction shown. This fraction declines slowly toward the suburbs. In stippled areas the population ratio exceeds the housing ratio.

quire early in life a slum culture from which escape is almost impossible. Their early surroundings and ways of life at a critical period in their development limit the range of manifestations of their innate endowment and thus destroy much of their potential freedom [17, p. 153].

Cities are created by man's need and ability to move, to interact, and to exchange. Yet, after it reaches a certain size a city unfortunately becomes a collection of functionally and spatially segregated districts. Sheer size reduces the city to an administrative abstraction. Interaction is thwarted as the number of "contact choices" (different persons, goods, services) offered to the average citizen within an hour's round trip declines. In the ideal city, each resident's activity space should produce an optimum level of stimulation and opportunity. Visual monotony has adverse psychological consequences, especially for children who need a degree of diversity in their surroundings and in the orbit of their daily wanderings [13, 16, 25, 39].

In addition to the psychological consequences of excessive residential segregation, the social and physiological consequences of increased crowding (number of persons per dwelling unit) and high density (number of persons per unit area) are only dimly understood [45]. Calhoun's [8] crowding experiments with rats and Christian's [10] studies of animal crowding revealed pathologies that may be relevant to the problem of crowding and density in cities.

Hall [24] in his work on proxemics (the perception and use of space) observes that man shares with lower life forms certain basic needs for territory. Each man has around him an invisible series of space bubbles that expand and contract, depending on his emotional state, culture, activities, and social status [15]. People from different ethnic origins need spaces of different kinds. There are those who like to touch and those who do not. There are those who like to be auditorially involved with everyone else and those who depend on architectural barriers to screen them from the world [23].

Besides ethnic differences in spatial requirements, there are variations from person to person in each culture. When Hall studied urban renewal's effects on slum dwellers he found evidence indicating "that poor uneducated people have a much lower tolerance for being displaced than people of the middle class. Even a move across the street can be traumatic because it alters the pattern of social relationships" [24, p. 182]. Nowhere does he find evidence that public housing or urban renewal plans recognize the existence of different needs for different ethnic groups.

Conclusions

If it can be shown that uncoordinated programs of tight money, urban renewal, and highway construction can have a disastrous aggregate impact on certain parts of the city, what should be done? The President's Committee on Urban Housing argued that federally assisted and public housing should be built where people want to live and where production costs are low. But it recognized that "the removal of existing constraints on freedom of location, such as racial discrimination and zoning abuses, is essential to the achievement of decent housing for all" [1, pp. 69–70]. On the subject of quality and location of government assisted housing, care must be taken that it does not become an additional "storage bin for the poor" [1, pp. 12, 71]. Instead of exclusive reliance on public housing programs around the downtown core, additional sound housing could be supplied to the inner city poor and working classes by speeding up the filtering process. Abundant new housing at the suburban margins of each residential sector stimulates outmigration from the central city portions of the sector. Vacated housing is thereby released to the poor, who can afford sound housing only when they are subsidized or when prices are stabilized or depressed by rapid expansion in the amount of new housing supplied [35, 36, 37].

Yet solving the housing quality problem is more than a supply and demand situation. The isolation of ghetto children must be dealt with. The spatial arrangement of human settlements may be the most basic item in preparing children to live and participate in diverse groups, to travel, to profit from their experiences, and to be at home in strange environments. As the metropolis and its black neighborhoods expand, ghetto youngsters become progressively more cut off from a diverse, instructive, and racially integrated urban experience [31]. Integrated

schools become segregated, then segregated schools near the ghetto core start deteriorating. The busing of young school children attempts to equalize educational opportunities that have been rendered unequal by economic and racial segregation. If busing is to succeed in overcoming ghetto isolation, care must be taken to avoid journeys which *seem* long to the child, whether they are or not, thereby affecting his perception of his accessibility to his home and mother [26, pp. 111–12].

Because of its full range of problems and promises, the metropolis is a useful model for tomorrow's world. For example, the urbanized-industrialized Northeast has been settled since the eighteenth century, and has spread since then into the Florida, Gulf, and West Coast areas. A map of net migration shows that the edges gain at the expense of the older settled interior. The metropolis with its old-style core of high density residential and business activities is adjusting in a parallel way. Concentrations at the downtown center are dropping and residential, commercial, and industrial efforts on the edges are spreading aggressively into the former agricultural countryside.

At a still more detailed scale we can consider the racial-ethnic ghetto as a metropolis in miniature. High densities at the core of the ghetto have been dropping sharply as jobs and houses have fallen into decay and ruin. The bright, the young, the successful, and the enterprising have pushed outward from the old ghetto core and have invaded adjacent residential territories on the outer edges of the ghetto territory. Looked at in this way we see the ghetto as a small expanding world, located within the metropolis, which itself comprises a larger and expanding spatial unit. As these changes occur, society must either regulate them, or society will be regulated by their consequences. Our recent national experiences with violence reflect a vacillation between an anachronistic culture of violence that surrounds us, and the perplexing culture of constant change that makes impossible demands on the ill-equipped. Violent aggression was once a useful form of coping behavior, but in today's urban and technological age it produces maladaptive and destructive results [18].

Footnotes

The author gratefully acknowledges the assistance of Roman A. Cybriwsky, Gene E. Krueger, Harold M. Rose, Anthony V. Williams, and Eugene L. Ziegler, and the financial support of the Central Fund for Research of the Pennsylvania State University.
1. The first part of this section draws heavily on Joseph Boskin's excellent essay [5].

Literature Cited

1. *A Decent Home: The Report of the President's Committee on Urban Housing.* Washington, D.C.: Government Printing Office, 1968.

2. Altman, I. "Ecological Aspects of Interpersonal Functioning." Paper presented at the annual meeting of the American Association for the Advancement of Science, Dallas, Texas, December 31, 1968. (Mimeographed.)

3. Berry, B. J. L. *American Urban Dimensions: 1960.* Chicago: Center for Urban Studies, University of Chicago. (Mimeographed.)

4. Bloombaum, M. "The Conditions Underlying Race Riots as Portrayed by Multidimensional Scalogram Analysis: A Reanalysis of the Lieberson and Silverman Data," *American Sociological Review,* 33 (February, 1968), pp. 76–91.

5. Boskin, J. "The Revolt of the Urban Ghettos," *Annals of The American Academy of Political and Social Science,* 382 (March, 1969), pp. 1–14.

6. Boulding, K. "Economics as a Moral Science," *American Economic Review,* 59 (March, 1969), pp. 151–54.

7. Brown, C. *Manchild in the Promised Land.* New York: New American Library, 1965.

8. Calhoun, J. B. "Population Density and Social Pathology," *Scientific American,* 206 (February, 1962), pp. 139–48.

9. Caplan, N. S. and J. M. Paige. "A Study of Ghetto Rioters," *Scientific American,* 219 (August, 1968), pp. 15–21.

10. Christian, J. "The Pathology of Overpopulation," *Military Medicine,* 7 (July, 1963), pp. 571–603.

11. Clark, K. *Dark Ghetto.* New York: Harper and Row, 1964.

12. Davies, J. C. "The J-Curve of Rising and Declining Satisfactions as a Cause of Some Great Revolutions and a Contained Rebellion." *The History of Violence in America.* Edited by H. D. Graham and T. R. Gurr. New York: Bantam Books, 1969.

13. Deutsch, K. "On Social Communication and the Metropolis," *Daedalus,* 90 (Winter, 1961), pp. 99–110.

14. Downes, B. T. "The Social Characteristics of Riot Cities: A Comparative Study," *Social Science Quarterly,* 49 (December, 1968), pp. 504–20.

15. Doxiadis, C. A. "A City for Human Development," *Ekistics,* 25 (June 1968), pp. 374–94.

16. Doxiadis, C. A. "Man's Movement and His City," *Science,* 162 (October, 1968), pp. 326–34.

17. Dubos, R. "The Crisis of Man in His Environment," *Ekistics,* 27 (March, 1969), pp. 151–54.

18. Gilula, M. F. and D. N. Daniels. "Violence and Man's Struggle to Adapt," *Science,* 164 (April 25, 1969), pp. 396–405.

19. Glazer, N. and D. P. Moynihan. *Beyond the Melting Pot.* Cambridge: MIT Press, 1963.

20. Grigsby, W. G. *Housing Markets and Public Policy.* Philadelphia: University of Pennsylvania Press, 1963.

21. Grindstaff, C. G. "The Negro Urbanization, and Relative Deprivation in the Deep South," *Social Problems,* 15 (Winter, 1968), pp. 342–52.

22. Gurr, T. R. "A Comparative Study of Civil Strife," *The History of Violence in America.* Edited by H. D. Graham and T. R. Gurr. New York: Bantam Books, 1969.

23. Hall, E. T. *The Hidden Dimension.* Garden City: Doubleday, 1966.

24. Hall, E. T. "Human Needs and Inhuman Cities," *Ekistics,* 160 (March, 1969), pp. 181–84.

25. Hobsbawn, E. "Cities and Insurrections," *Architectural Design,* 38 (December, 1968), pp. 581–88.

26. Lee, T. "On the Relation Between the School Journey and Social and Emotional Adjustment in Rural Infant Children," *The British Journal of Educational Psychology,* 27 (June, 1957), pp. 110–14.

27. Lieberson, E. and A. R. Silverman. "The Precipitants and Underlying Conditions of Race Riots," *American Sociological Review,* 30 (December, 1965), pp. 887–98.

28. Maloney, J. C. "Metropolitan Area Characteristics and Problems." Memorandum to: A.P.M.E. Conference Participants. Evanston: Medill School of Journalism, Northwestern University, October 19, 1967. (Mimeographed.)

29. Maloney, J. C. *Statistical Analysis of 1967 Disturbance Data.* (Letter to Anthony Downs.) Evanston: Medill School of Journalism, Northwestern University, December 14, 1967. (Mimeographed.)

30. Marx, G. T. *Protest and Prejudice: A Study of Belief in the Black Community.* New York: Harper and Row, 1967.

31. Mead, M. "Preparedness for Participation in a Highly Differentiated Society," *Ekistics,* 167 (October, 1969), p. 243.

32. Miller, G. H., Jr. "Housing in the 60s: A Survey of Some Non-Financial Factors," *Monthly Review,* Federal Reserve Bank of Kansas City (May, 1969), pp. 3–10.

33. Mooney, J. D. "Urban Poverty and Labor Force Participation: Reply," *American Economic Review,* 59 (March, 1969), pp. 194–98.

34. Moynihan, D. P. *Maximum Feasible Misunderstanding.* New York: Free Press, 1969.

35. National Commission on Urban Problems. *Housing America's Low and Moderate Income Families.* Research Report No. 7. Washington, D.C.: Government Printing Office, 1968.

36. National Commission on Urban Problems. *Housing Conditions in Urban Poverty Areas.* Research Report No. 9. Washington, D.C.: Government Printing Office, 1968.

37. National Commission on Urban Problems. *Urban Housing Needs Through the 1980s.* Research Report No. 10. Washington, D.C.: Government Printing Office, 1968.

38. Oberschall, A. "The Los Angeles Riot of August, 1966," *Social Problems,* 15 (Winter, 1968), pp. 322–41.

39. Parr, A. E. "Psychological Aspects of Urbanology," *Journal of Social Issues,* 22 (October, 1966), pp. 29–38.

40. *Report of the National Advisory Commission on Civil Disorders.* New York: Bantam Books, 1968.

41. Rodman, H. "Family and Social Pathology in the Ghetto," *Science,* 161 (August 23, 1968), pp. 756–62.

42. Rose, H. M. *Social Processes in the City: Race and Urban Residential Choice.* Resource Paper No. 9. Washington, D.C.: Association of American Geographers, 1969.

43. Sommers, M. S. and G. D. Bruce, "Blacks, Whites, and Products: Relative Deprivation and Reference Group Theory," *Social Science Quarterly,* 49 (December, 1968), pp. 631–42.

44. Taeuber, K. and A. Taeuber. *Negroes in Cities.* Chicago: Aldine Publishing Company, 1965.

45. Taylor, D. A., L. Wheeler, and I. Altman. "Stress Relations in Socially Isolated Groups," *Journal of Personality and Social Psychology,* 9 (August, 1968), pp. 369–76.

46. Thompson, D. W. *On Growth and Form.* Cambridge: Cambridge University Press, 1966.

47. Tomlinson, T. M. "Development of a Riot Ideology Among Urban Negroes," *The American Behavioral Scientist,* 2 (March–April, 1968), pp. 27–31.

48. U.S. Bureau of the Census. *Poverty Areas in the 100 Largest Metropolitan Areas.* Report PC (51)–54. Washington, D.C.: Government Printing Office, 1968.

49. U.S. Commission on Civil Rights. *A Time to Listen . . . A Time to Act.* Washington, D.C.: Government Printing Office, 1967.

50. U.S. Department of Housing and Urban Development. "Mobile Homes and the Housing Supply." Part 2, *Housing Surveys.* Washington, D.C.: Government Printing Office, 1968.

51. U.S. Office of Economic Opportunity. *Maps of Major Concentrations of Poverty in Standard Metropolitan Statistical Areas of 250,000 or More Population.* 3 vols. Washington, D.C.: Government Printing Office, 1967.

52. U.S. Senate. Permanent Subcommittee on Investigations of the Committee on Governmental Operations. *Staff Study of Major Riots and Civil Disorders—1965 Through July 31, 1968.* Washington, D.C.: Government Printing Office, 1968.

53. U.S. Senate. Permanent Subcommittee on Investigations of the Committee on Government Operations. *Riots, Civil and Criminal Disorders.* Hearings. Washington, D.C.: Government Printing Office, 1967–1969. 23 volumes.

54. Wohlwill, J. F. "The Physical Environment: A Problem for a Psychology of Stimulation," *Journal of Social Issues,* 22 (October, 1966), pp. 29–38.

• • • • • • • • • • • • • **thirty-eight**

DAVID HARVEY ◆

Social Justice and Spatial Systems

Normative thinking has an important role to play in geographical analysis. Social justice is a normative concept and it is surprising, therefore, to find that considerations of social justice have not been incorporated into geographical methods of analysis. The reason is not far to seek. The normative tools characteristically used by geographers to examine location problems are derived from classical location theory. Such theories are generally *Pareto-optimal* since they define an optimal location pattern as one in which no one individual can move without the advantages gained from such a move being offset by some loss to another individual.[1] Location theory has therefore characteristically relied upon the criterion of *efficiency* for its specification. Efficiency may be defined in a variety of ways, of course, but in location theory it usually amounts to minimizing the aggregate costs of movement (sub-ject to demand and supply constraints) within a particular spatial system. Models of this type pay no attention to the consequences of location decisions for the distribution of income. Geographers have thus followed economists into a style of thinking in which questions of distribution are laid aside (mainly because they involve unwelcome ethical and political judgments) while efficient 'optimal' location patterns are determined with a particular income distribution assumed. This approach obviously lacks something. In part the reaction away from normative thinking towards behavioral and empirical formulations may be attributed to the search for a more satisfying approach to location problems. This reaction has been healthy, of course, but partly misplaced. It is not normative modelling which is at fault but the *kind* of norms built into such models. In this paper, therefore, I want to

◆ **SOURCE.** Reprinted by permission of the author and the editor from Antipode Monographs in Social Geography, No. 1, *Geographical Perspectives on American Poverty*, 1972, pp. 87–106.

565

diverge from the usual mode of normative analysis and look at the possibility of constructing a normative theory of spatial or territorial allocation based on principles of social justice. I do not propose this as an alternative framework to that of efficiency. In the long run it will be most beneficial if efficiency and distribution are explored jointly. The reasons for so doing are not hard to state. If, in the short run, we simply pursue efficiency and ignore the social cost that may be incurred, then those individuals or groups who bear the brunt of that social cost are likely to be a source of long-run inefficiency either through a decline in what Liebenstein[2] calls 'x-efficiency' (those intangibles that motivate people to cooperate and participate in the social process of production) or through forms of anti-social behavior (such as crime and drug addiction) which will necessitate the diversion of productive investment towards their correction. The same comment can be made about the single-minded pursuit of social justice. It is counter-productive in the long-run to devise a socially just distribution if the size of the product to be distributed shrinks markedly through the inefficient use of scarce resources. In the long-long-run, therefore, social justice and efficiency are very much the same thing. But since questions of social justice have been neglected (except in political rhetoric) and there is a persistent tendency to lay them aside in short run analysis, I shall do the opposite and lay aside questions of efficiency. To lay aside these questions for the purposes of this investiga-

tion should not be taken to imply, however, that efficiency is irrelevant or unimportant.

The concept of social justice is not an all-inclusive one in which we encapsule our vision of the good society. It is a rather more limited concept. Justice is essentially to be thought of as a principle (or set of principles) for resolving conflicting claims. These conflicts may arise in many ways. Social justice is a particular application of these principles to conflicts which arise out of the necessity for social cooperation in seeking individual advancement. Through the division of labor it is possible to increase production. The question then arises as to how the fruits of that production shall be distributed among those who cooperate in the process. The principle of social justice therefore applies to the division of benefits and the allocation of burdens arising out of the process of undertaking joint labor. The principle also relates to the social and institutional arrangements associated with the activity of production and distribution. It may thus be extended to consider conflicts over the locus of power and decision-making authority, the distribution of influence, the bestowal of social status, the institutions set up to regulate and control activity, and so on. The essential characteristic in all such cases, however, is that we are seeking a principle which will allow us to evaluate the distributions arrived at as they apply to individuals, groups, organizations, and territories, as well as to evaluate the mechanisms which are used to accomplish this distribution.

We are seeking, in short, a specification of a just distribution justly arrived at.

Unfortunately there is no one generally accepted principle of social justice to which we can appeal. Yet the notion of social justice underpins social philosophical thought from Aristotle's *Ethics*[3] onwards. Its two most important forms are derivative of the social contract (initially formulated by Hume and Rousseau) and *utilitarianism* (initially formulated by Bentham and Mill). Recently, there has been a resurgence of interest in these principles resulting in modern versions of them which seem much more acceptable for a number of reasons—the work of Rawls,[4] Rescher,[5] and Runciman,[6] being outstanding in this respect. There are other strands to this thinking of course. The detailed discussion of the concept of equality by writers such as Tawney[7] and the now voluminous literature on the question of the proper distribution of income in society[8] have added their weight to the argument. I have not space to review this literature here, however, so I shall confine myself to articulating one possible argument concerning social justice and endeavour to show how it can be formulated in a manner that is geographically relevant and useful.

The principle of social justice which I shall explore starts with the skeleton concept of 'a just distribution justly arrived at'. The main task of this paper is to put flesh on this skeleton and to formulate its geographic variant. There are two preliminary questions which may be asked about it:

(1) *What is it that we are distributing?* It is easy enough to say that we are distributing the benefits to be had from social cooperation but it is very much more difficult to specify what those benefits are, particularly as they relate to individual preferences and values. For the purpose of this paper I shall leave this question unanswered and merely call whatever it is that we are distributing INCOME. This indicates a very general definition of income—such as Titmuss's[9] 'command over society's scarce resources' or an even more general one such as that proposed by Miller and Roby.[10] I hope to be more specific about this point elsewhere,[11] but for the purpose of this paper I shall assume that we can devise a socially just definition of income —for it would indeed be a net injustice to devise a socially just distribution of something defined in an unjust manner!

(2) *Among whom or what are we distributing it?* There is general agreement that the ultimate unit with which we should be concerned is the human individual. For convenience it will often be necessary to discuss distribution as it occurs among groups, organizations, territories, and so on. As geographers we are particularly interested in the territorial or regional organization of society and it will be convenient to work at that level of aggregation. But we know enough about the various forms of ecological fallacy[12] to know that a just distribution across a set of territories defined at one scale does not necessarily mean a just distribution achieved at another scale or a just distribution among individuals.

This scale or aggregation problem poses some thorny methodological difficulties. In principle, we may hold that distribution made at any scale or across any aggregates should be accountable to distribution as it occurs at the individual level of analysis. This is difficult to do, but for the purposes of this paper I shall assume that justice achieved at a territorial level of analysis implies individual justice even though I am all too aware that this is not necessarily the case.

I. "A Just Distribution"

Having assumed away two rather important questions, I shall now undertake an analysis of the principle of social justice. It can be split into two parts and here I shall seek an understanding of what is meant by a 'just distribution'. It is not possible to determine a just distribution without first establishing a basis for that distribution. This is, of course, an ethical problem which cannot be resolved without making important moral decisions. These moral decisions essentially amount to establishing what it is that justifies an individual making claims upon the product of the society in which he lives, works, and has his being. Several criteria have been suggested:[13]

(1) *Inherent equality*—all individuals have equal claims on benefits irrespective of their contribution.

(2) *Valuation of services in terms of supply and demand*—individuals who command scarce resources which society needs most have a greater claim than do others. It is perhaps important to differentiate here between situations in which scarcity arises naturally (inherent brain and muscle power) and situations in which it is artificially created (through the inheritance of resources or through socially organized restrictions on entry into certain occupations).

(3) *Need*—individuals have rights to equal benefits which means that there is an unequal allocation according to need.

(4) *Inherited rights*—individuals have claims according to the property or other rights which have been passed on to them from preceding generations.

(5) *Merit*—claims may be based on the degree of difficulty to be overcome in contributing to production (those who undertake dangerous or unpleasant tasks—such as mining—have a greater claim than do others). Likewise those who undertake long periods of training—such as surgeons—have greater claims than do others.

(6) *Contribution to common good*—those individuals whose activities benefit most people have a higher claim than do those whose activities benefit few people.

(7) *Actual productive contribution*—individuals who produce more output—measured in some ap-

propriate way—have a greater claim than do those who produce a lesser output.

(8) *Efforts and sacrifices*—individuals who make a greater effort or incur a greater sacrifice relative to their innate capacity should be rewarded more than those who make little effort and incur few sacrifices.

These eight criteria are not mutually exclusive and they obviously require much more detailed interpretation and analysis. I shall follow Runciman[14] and suggest that the essence of social justice can be embodied in a weak ordering of three of these criteria so that *need* is the most important, *contribution to common good* is the second and *merit* is the third. I shall not argue the case for this decision. It necessarily rests, however, on an appeal to certain controversial and ethical arguments. But as will become apparent in what follows, the issues raised in the detailed examination of these three criteria are sufficiently comprehensive to subsume many of the issues which could legitimately be raised under the other headings. These three criteria could be examined in detail in a variety of contexts. I choose at this juncture to introduce the geographic aspect to the argument and examine how they might be formulated in the context of a set of territories or regions. For purposes of exposition I shall mainly consider the problem as one of a central authority allocating scarce resources over a set of territories in such a way that social justice is maximized. As I have already stated, I shall assume that

territorial distributive justice automatically implies individual justice.

II. Territorial Distributive Justice

The first step in formulating a principle of territorial distributive justice lies in determining what each of the three criteria—need, contribution to common good, and merit—means in the context of a set of territories or regions. Procedures may then be devised to evaluate and measure distribution according to each of these criteria. The combination of the three measures (presumably weighted in some way) provide a hypothetical figure for the allocation of resources to regions. This figure can then be used, as happens in most normative analyses, to evaluate existing distributions or to devise policies which will improve on existing allocations. A measure of territorial justice can be devised by correlating the actual allocation of resources with the hypothetical allocations. Such a procedure allows the identification of those territories which depart most from the norms suggested by standards of social justice. This whole procedure is not, of course, easy. Bleddyn Davies, who first coined the term 'territorial justice' has published a pioneering work on the subject, a detailed study of which indicates some of the problems involved.[15]

(1) NEED

Need is a relative concept. Needs are not constant for they are categories of human consciousness and as society is transformed so the consciousness of need is transformed. The problem is to define exactly what it is that need is relative to and to obtain an understanding of how needs arise. Needs can be defined with respect to a number of different categories of activity—these categories remain fairly constant over time and we can list nine of them:

(i) food; (ii) housing; (iii) medical care; (iv) education; (v) social and environmental services; (vi) consumer goods; (vii) recreational opportunities; (viii) neighborhood amenities; (ix) transport facilities.

Within each of these categories we can set about defining those minimum quantities and qualities which we would equate with needs. This minimum will vary according to the social norms accepted at a given time. There will also be a variety of ways of fulfilling such needs. The need for housing can be met in a number of ways but at this time these would presumably not include living in shacks, mud-huts, tents, crumbling houses, and the like. This raises a whole host of issues which I can best examine in the context of a particular category—medical services.

Nobody, presumably, would deny that medical care is a legitimate form of need. Yet that need is not easily defined and measured. If we are to obtain a normative measure of social justice we have first to define and measure need in a socially just way. For example, the category 'health services' comprises a multitude of sub-categories some of which, such as cosmetic surgery and back massages, can reasonably be regarded (in our present

society at least) as non-essential. An initial decision has to be made, therefore, on which sub-categories should be regarded as 'needs' and which should not. Decisions then have to be made as to what are reasonable standards of need within each sub-category. Let us consider some of the methods for doing this.

(i) Need can be determined through looking at market demand. Wherever facilities are working very close to capacity we may take it that there is an unfulfilled need in the population and thereby justify the allocation of more resources to expand medical services. This procedure is only acceptable if we can reasonably assume that nothing is inhibiting demand (such as lack of money or lack of access to facilities). To accept market demand as a socially just measure of need required that the other conditions prevailing in society (affecting both demand and supply) are themselves socially just. This is usually not the case and this method of determining need is therefore likely to be socially unjust.

(ii) Latent demand may be arrived at through an investigation of relative deprivation as it exists among individuals in a set of regions. An individual would be relatively deprived if (a) he does not receive a service; (b) he sees other people (including himself at a previous or an expected time) receiving it; (c) he wants it; and (d) he regards it as feasible that he should receive it.[16] The concept of relative deprivation (basically similar to perceived or felt need) has been associated in the literature with the concept of a reference group (a group against which an individual measures his own expectations). The reference group may be socially determined—i.e. all blacks or all blue-collar workers—or spatially determined—i.e. everybody in a neighborhood or even in a large region. The difference between the expectations of the group for health care and actual services received provides a measure of relative deprivation. This measure can be obtained either by direct survey data, or if we know something about reference groups we can calculate likely relative deprivation by looking at variance in provision within different groups. The advantage of this approach is that it (a) incorporates a behavioral element so that legitimate differences in group preferences can be expressed and (b) provides a measure of dissatisfaction and therefore an indicator of likely political pressure. Its disadvantage is that it assumes that 'real' needs are reflected by felt needs. This is often not the case. Very poorly served groups often have very low standards of felt need. Also, all kinds of social inequities are likely to be incorporated into the measure of need if as is usually the case in class differentiated and (or) segregated societies, the reference group structure is itself a response to conditions of social injustice.

(iii) Potential demand can be evaluated by an analysis of the factors which generate particular kinds of health problems. Population totals and characteristics will have an important impact on territorial needs. Health problems can be related to age, lifecycle, amount of migration, and so on. In addition there are special problems which may relate to occupational characteristics (such as mining), to sociological and cultural circumstances, as well as to income levels. Health problems can also be related to local environmental conditions (density of population, local ecological conditions, air and water quality, and so on). If we knew enough about all of these relationships we should be able to predict from them the volume and incidence of health care problems across a set of territories. This requires a far more sophisticated understanding of relationships than we currently possess, but various attempts have been made to employ this method.[17] The attraction of it, of course, is that it does provide a reasonably objective method for measuring potential demand for health care. Unfortunately, we are still left with the problem of converting this potential demand into a measure of need. A measure of need in this case requires that we determine appropriate forms and levels of response to these statistically determined potential demands. This response usually amounts to setting standards and these are usually set with a given quantity of resources in mind.

(iv) We could also seek to determine needs through a consultation process with experts in the field. Experts tend to determine need with one eye on available resources. But those who have lived and worked in a community for a long period of time are often capable of drawing upon their experience to provide subjective assessments which are nevertheless good indicators of need. The resolution of opinions provided by judiciously selected experts in the health field (health planners, hospital administrators, physicians, community groups, social workers, welfare rights groups, and so on) may provide a socially just determination of need. It relies upon the subjective judgements of a selected set of individuals but it has the benefit of drawing directly upon the experience of those who have been most concerned with the health care problem. The wealth of experience tapped by such a process should not be lightly discounted. The disadvantage, of course, lies in the inherent possibility that the experts brought into the consultation process are selected on the basis of socially unjust criteria—to place the determination of need in the hands of a committee of the AMA would at this juncture be disastrous from the point of view of social justice.

We may select among the various methods for determining need in such a way that we maximize on the social justice of the result. In the current circumstances I would discard (i) altogether in the health field and I would only accept (ii) if I felt that legitimate variations in preference were being expressed rather than variations in a felt need arising out of a socially unjust social situation or out of ignorance or false consciousness. Both (iii) and (iv) provide possible methods for establishing needs in the health field, but neither are easy to employ and both contain within them the possibility of a socially unjust determination of need.

If need is a primary criterion for assessing the social justice of a distribution of resources across a set of territories, then we are first obligated to establish a socially just definition

and measurement system for it. The various methods (and their attendant difficulties) outlined in the medical care case can be applied to each of the categories—education, recreation, housing, consumer goods, and so on. It is not easy to decide upon a socially just definition of need within each category. The appropriate method may also vary from category to category—it may be best to determine consumer need through conventional supply and demand analysis, recreational needs through relative deprivation analysis, housing needs through statistical analysis, and medical care needs through resolution of expert opinion. These, however, are open questions. Defining social justice in terms of need thrusts onto us the whole uncomfortable question of what is meant by need and how it should be measured. It is imperative that we make socially just decisions on these issues. Otherwise our pursuit of a principle of social justice for evaluating geographic distributions will be worthless.

(2) CONTRIBUTION TO COMMON GOOD

The concept of contribution to common good can be translated into existing geographic concepts with relative ease. We are here concerned with how an allocation of resources to one territory affects conditions in another. We have an existing technology to handle some of these questions in the work on interregional multiplier analysis,[18] growth poles,[19] and externalities.[20] The spread effects may be good or bad—pollution being an example of the latter. The notion of contribution to common good (or common 'bad' in the case of pollution) suggests that our existing technology should be used to extend our understanding of interregional income transfers, interregional linkages, spatial spread effects, and so on, insofar as these have actual or potential consequences for the distribution of income in society. This is not an easy task, as is demonstrated by the problems which have plagued the attempt to evaluate the benefits of urban renewal.[21] There are two rather different aspects to this problem. We can seek to improve on existing allocations given the existing pattern of interregional multipliers or we can take a more radical approach and seek to restructure the pattern of interregional multipliers by re-organizing the spatial system itself. If we take the latter approach we seek a form of spatial organization which will make the greatest contribution to fulfilling needs through the multiplier and spread effects generated by a particular pattern of regional investment. Common good may have a second component to it, that of increasing the total aggregate product. In this case contribution to common good comes close to the usual efficiency and growth criteria with externalities and side-effects incorporated into the analysis. In the search for social justice this sense of contributing to the common good should remain subsidiary to the concern for distributive consequences.

(3) MERIT

I shall translate the concept of 'merit' into a geographical concept which relates to the degree of environmental difficulty. Such difficulties may arise out of circumstances in the physical environment. Certain hazards, such as drought, flood, earthquakes, and so on, pose extra difficulty to human activity. If there is a need for a facility (say a port facility in an area subject to hurricane damage) then extra resources should be allocated to counter this hazard. In terms of the weak ordering that I have imposed on the criteria for social justice, this works out to mean that if a facility is needed, if it contributes to the common good in some way, *then and only then* would we be justified in allocating extra resources for its support. If people live in flood plains when they have no need to live in flood plains and if they contribute nothing to the common good by living there, then under the principle of social justice they ought not to be compensated for damage incurred by living there. If, however, individuals are forced by circumstances (such as lack of alternative choice) to live there then the primary criterion of need may be used to justify compensation. The same remarks apply to problems which arise in the social environment. Hazards posed by crimes against property, fire and riot damage, and the like, vary according to the social circumstances. Individuals need adequate security if they are to be able to contribute meaningfully to the common good and if they are to be able to allocate their productive capacity to fulfill needs. Under a principle of social justice it can therefore be argued that society at large should underwrite the higher costs of insurance in areas of high social risk. To do so would be socially just. The same argument can be applied to the allocation of extra resources to reach groups who are particularly difficult to service—as Davies points out "it may be desirable to over-provide needy groups with services since they have not had access to them in the past and have not formed the habit of consuming them."[22] This issue arises particularly with respect to the education and health care facilities extended to very poor groups, recent immigrants, and the like. Merit can therefore be translated in a geographical context as an allocation of extra resources to compensate for the degree of social and national environmental difficulty.

The principles of social justice as they apply to geographical situations can be summarized as follows:

(1) The spatial organization and the pattern of regional investment should be such as to fulfill the needs of the population. This requires that we first establish socially just methods for determining and measuring needs. The difference between needs and actual allocations provides us with an initial evaluation of the degree of territorial injustice in an existing system.

(2) A spatial organization and pattern of territorial resource allocation which provides extra benefits in the form of need fulfillment (primarily) and aggregate output (secondarily) in other territories through spillover effects, multiplier effects, and the like, is a 'better' form of spatial organization and allocation.

(3) Deviations in the pattern of

territorial investment may be tolerated if they are designed to overcome specific environmental difficulties which would otherwise prevent the evolution of a system which would meet need or contribute to the common good.

These principles can be used to evaluate existing spatial distributions. They provide the beginnings of a normative theory of spatial organization based on territorial distributive justice. There will be enormous difficulties in elaborating these principles in detail and there will be even greater difficulties in translating these principles into concrete situations. We have some of the technology at hand to do this. It needs to be directed towards an understanding of just distributions in spatial systems.

III. "Justly Arriving at a Distribution"

There are those who claim that a necessary and sufficient condition for attaining a just distribution of income lies in devising socially just means for arriving at that distribution. Curiously enough this view prevails at both ends of the political spectrum. Buchanan and Tullock—conservative libertarians in viewpoint—thus suggest that in a properly organized constitutional democracy the most efficient way to organize redistribution is to do nothing about it.[23] Marx attacked those 'vulgar socialists' who thought that questions of distribution could be considered and resolved independent of the prevailing mechanisms governing production and distribution.[24] Marx and constitutional democrats have a basic assumption in common—that if socially just mechanisms can be devised then questions of achieving social justice in distribution will look after themselves. In the literature on social justice (and in the arena of practical policy determination) there is a varied emphasis on 'means' or 'ends' with liberal and some socialist opinion apparently believing that social justice in the latter can be achieved without necessarily tampering with the former. But most writers indicate that it is fool-hardy to expect socially just ends to be achieved by socially unjust means. It is instructive to follow Rawls' argument in this respect:[25]

> the basic structure of the social system affects the life prospects of typical individuals according to their initial places in society. . . . The fundamental problem of distributive justice concerns the differences in life-prospects which come about in this way. We . . . . hold that these differences are just if and only if the greater expectations of the more advantaged, when playing a part in the working of the social system, improve the expectations of the least advantaged. The basic structure is just throughout when the advantages of the more fortunate promote the well-being of the least fortunate. . . . The basic structure is perfectly just when the prospects of the least fortunate are as great as they can be. (emphasis mine).

The problem then, is to find a social, economic and political organization in which this condition is attained and maintained. Marxists would claim, with considerable justification, that the only hope for achieving Rawls' objective would be to ensure the least fortunate always has the final say. From Rawls' initial position it is not difficult by a fairly simple logical argument to arrive at a 'dictatorship of the proletariat' type of solution. Rawls tries to construct a path towards a different solution:

> if law and government act effectively to keep markets competitive, resources fully employed, property and wealth widely distributed over time, and to maintain the appropriate social minimum, then if there is equality of opportunity underwritten by education for all, the resulting distribution will be just.

To achieve this, Rawls proposes a fourfold division in government in which an allocation branch acts to keep the market working competitively while correcting for market failure where necessary, a stabilization branch maintains full employment and prevents waste in the use of resources, a transfer branch sees to it that individual needs are met, and a distribution branch looks after the provision of public goods and prevents (by proper taxation) any undue concentration of power or wealth over time. From Rawls' initial position it is possible to arrive, therefore, at a Marx or a Milton Friedman, but no way can we arrive at the liberal or socialist solutions. That this is a sensible conclusion is attested to by the fact that the socialist programs of postwar Britain appear to have had little or no impact upon the distribution of income in society while the liberal anti-poverty programs in the United States have been conspicuous for their lack of success.[26] The reason should be obvious—programs which seek to alter distribution without altering the capitalistic market structure within which income and wealth are generated and distributed are doomed to failure.

Most of the evidence we have on group decision making, bargaining, the control of central government, democracy, and bureaucracy, and the like, also indicates that *any* social, economic and political organization which attains any permanence is liable to cooptation and subversion by special interest groups. In a constitutional democracy this is usually accomplished by small well-organized interest groups who have accumulated the necessary resources to influence decision making. A dictatorship of the proletariat type solution is likewise subject to bureaucratic subversion as the Russian experience all too readily demonstrates. An awareness of this problem has led good constitutional democrats, such as Jefferson, to look favorably on an occasional revolution to keep the body politic healthy. One of the practical effects of the sequence of revolutions which have occurred in China since 1949 (and some have attributed this to Mao's conscious design) has been to prevent what Max Weber long ago called the 'routinization of charisma'.[27] The question of the appropriate form of social, economic and political orga-

nization and its maintenance for the purpose of achieving social justice is beyond the scope of this paper. Yet the way in which it is resolved effectively determines both the mode and likelihood of achieving territorial justice. I shall therefore confine my remarks to considering how considerations of the means of achieving distribution take on a specific form in the territorial context.

The geographical problem is to design a form of spatial organization which maximizes the prospects of the least fortunate region. A necessary initial condition, for example, is that we have a socially just way of determining the boundaries of territories and a just way of allocating resources among them. The former problem lies in the traditional field of 'regionalizing' in geography but in this case with the criterion of social justice put foremost. The experience of gerrymandering indicates only too well that territorial aggregates can be determined in a socially unjust way. Boundaries can be determined so that the least advantaged groups are so distributed with respect to the more advantaged groups in a set of territorial aggregates that whatever the formula devised for allocation of resources, the latter are benefited rather than the former. It should be possible to devise territorial boundaries to most benefit the least advantaged groups—in which case social justice in allocation becomes the normative criterion for regionalization.[28] In the actual allocation of resources we may take Rawls' objective to mean that the prospects for the least advantaged territory should be as great as they can be. How to determine when this condition exists is itself an intriguing problem, but the prospects for its achievement are presumably contingent upon the decision making mechanism which a central authority uses in determining the territorial disposition of the resources under its control. Since poor areas are often politically weak, we are forced to rely on the sense of social justice prevailing in *all* territories (and it takes an assumption of only mild self-interest to counter that hope), upon the existence of a benevolent dictator or a benevolent bureaucracy at the center (a condition which perhaps prevails in Scandinavia), or upon a constitutional mechanism in which the least advantaged territories have the power of veto over all decisions. Exactly what arrangements are made for arbitrating among the demands of political territories (demands which do not necessarily reflect need) and for negotiating between a central authority and its constituent territories are obviously crucial for the prospect of achieving territorial justice.[29] It is arguable for example, whether a greater centralization of decision making (which has the potential for ironing out differences between territories) should prevail over a greater decentralization (which has the merit of being able to prevent the exploitation of disadvantaged territories by the richer territories). The answer to this probably depends upon the initial conditions. When they are characterized by exploitation (as they appear to be in the United States) a tactical decentralization may be called for as an initial step; when exploitation is not so important (as in Scandinavia), centralization may be more appropriate.

Advocacy of metropolitan control or neighborhood government should be seen in this light.[30]

Similar kinds of problems arise if we examine the impact of the highly decentralized decisions over capital investment characteristic of a freely working capitalist economy. Leaving aside the problems inherent in the tendency for modern capital to congeal into monopoly forms of control,[31] it is useful to examine how an individualistic capitalist system typically operates with respect to territorial justice. Under such a system it is accepted as rational and good for capital to flow to wherever the rate of return is highest. Some argue that this process will continue until rates of return are equalized over all territories while others suggest that circular and cumulative causation will lead to growing imbalances.[32] Whatever the long term implications of this process are for growth, capital clearly will flow in a way which bears little relationship to need or to the condition of the least advantaged territory. The result will be the creation of localized pockets of high unfulfilled need, such as those now found in Appalachia or many inner city areas. Most societies accept some responsibility for diverting the natural stream of capital flow to deal with these problems. To do so without basically altering *the whole* capital flow process seems impossible however. Consider, as an example, the problems arising out of the housing situation in inner city areas of British and American cities. It is no longer profitable for private capital to flow into the inner city rental housing market. In London in 1965 a return of 9% or more would have been necessary to get private capital to return and conditions were such that there was no hope of obtaining such a return by legal means.[33] In Baltimore in 1969 a rate of 12–15% would be required but actual rates were probably nearer 6–9%.[34] It is hardly surprising that the private inner city rental housing market has collapsed in most cities as capital is withdrawn, buildings depreciated, and capital transferred to other sectors or out to the much more profitable private building market in the suburban ring. Thus arises the paradox of capital withdrawing from areas of greatest need to provide for the demands of relatively affluent suburban communities. Under capitalism this is good and rational behavior—it is what the market requires for the 'optimal' allocation of resources.

Is it possible to reverse this flow using capitalist tools? Government can (and often does) intervene to make up the difference between what is now earned in the inner city and what could be earned elsewhere. It can do this in a number of ways (rent supplements to tenants, negative income taxes, direct grants to financial institutions, etc.). But whatever the means chosen the effect is to bribe financial institutions to get back into the inner city rental market; otherwise the government must take over responsibility for provision (through public housing). The first solution at first sight appears attractive, but it has certain flaws. If we bribe financial institutions to get back into the market, one effect will be to create a greater relative scarcity of capital funds for (say) suburban development. The more advantaged suburbs will ad-

just the rate of return they offer upward to bring back the capital flow. The net effect of this process will be a rise in the overall rates of return which is obviously to the advantage of financial institutions—most of which are owned, operated and managed by people who live in the suburbs anyway! What this suggests is that there is a built-in tendency for the capitalist market system to counteract any attempt to divert the flow of funds away from the most profitable territories. More specifically, it is impossible to induce action in one sector or territory without restricting it at the same time in other sectors and territories. Nothing short of comprehensive government control can do this effectively.

What this suggests is that 'capitalist means invariably serve their own, capitalist, ends,'[35] and that these capitalist ends are not consistent with the objectives of social justice. An argument can be formulated in support of this contention. The market system functions on the basis of exchange values and exchange values can exist only if there is relative scarcity of the goods and services being exchanged. The concept of scarcity is not an easy one to comprehend although we are constantly making reference to it when we talk of the allocation of scarce resources. It is questionable, for example, whether there is any such thing as a naturally arising scarcity. Pearson thus writes:

> *the concept of scarcity will be fruitful only if the natural fact of limited means leads to a sequence of choices regarding the use of*

these means, and this situation is possible only if there is alternativity to the uses of means and there are preferentially graded ends. But these latter conditions are socially determined; they do not depend in any simple way upon the facts of nature. To postulate scarcity as an absolute condition from which all economic institutions derive is therefore to employ an abstraction which serves only to obscure the question of how economic activity is organized.[36]

The concept of scarcity, like the concept of a resource, only takes on meaning in a particular social and cultural context. It is erroneous to think that markets simply arise to deal with scarcity. In sophisticated economies scarcity is socially organized in order to permit the market to function. We thus say that jobs are scarce when there is plenty of work to do, that space is restricted when land lies empty, that food is scarce when farmers are being paid not to produce. Scarcity must be produced and controlled in society because without it price fixing markets could not function. This takes place through a fairly strict control over access to the means of production and a control over the flow of resources into the productive process. The distribution of the output has likewise to be controlled in order for scarcity to be maintained. This is achieved by appropriative arrangements which prevent the elimination of scarcity and preserve the integrity of exchange values in the market place. If it is

accepted that the maintenance of scarcity is essential for the functioning of the market system, then it follows that deprivation, appropriation, and exploitation are also necessary concomitants of the market system. In a spatial system this implies (the ecological fallacy permitting) that there will likely be a series of appropriative movements between territories which lead some territories to exploit and some to be exploited. This phenomenon is most clearly present in urban systems since urbanism, as any historian of the phenomenon will tell us, is founded on the appropriation of surplus product.[37]

Certain benefits stem from the operation of the market mechanism. The price system can successfully coordinate a vast number of decentralized decisions and it can consequently integrate a vast array of activities into a coherent social and spatial system. The competition for access to scarce resources, on which the capitalistic market system rests, also encourages and facilitates technological innovation. The market system therefore helps to increase, by immeasurably great amount, the total product available to society. It is expert at promoting overall growth. This has led some to argue that since the market mechanism successfully promotes growth it follows as a matter of course that the prospects for the least fortunate territory are naturally as great as they possibly can be. Appropriation obviously takes place but this appropriation is not to be characterized as exploitation because the appropriated product is put to good use and is the source of benefits which flow back into the territories from which it was initially exacted. Appropriative movements which occur under the price system are therefore justified because of the long-term benefits which they generate. This argument cannot be rejected out of hand. But to concede that appropriation is justifiable under certain conditions is not to concede that the appropriation achieved under the market mechanism is socially just. In any economy appropriation and the creation of a social surplus product is necessary, but the pattern achieved under the market economy is not in many respects a necessary one unless the internal logic of the market economy itself is regarded as a form of justification. Under a capitalistic market economy there occurs an enormous concentration of surplus product (at the present time this is mainly located in large corporations) which has to be absorbed in ways which do not threaten the continuance of that scarcity upon which the market economy is itself based. Hence the surplus product is consumed in socially undesirable ways (conspicuous consumption, conspicuous construction in urban areas, militarism, waste, and other unproductive ways of absorbing the surplus). The market system cannot, therefore, find ways of disposing of the socially won surplus product in socially just ways. It therefore seems necessary, from the point of view of social justice, to find ways of increasing total social product without the use of the price-fixing market mechanism. In this regard the Chinese and Cuban experiments in seeking to promote growth with social justice are probably the most significant ever undertaken. Otherwise the third world

is presumably doomed to repeat the experience of individual or state capitalism in which growth is achieved at huge social and human cost. In contemporary 'advanced' societies, however, the problem is to devise alternatives to the market mechanism which allow the transference of productive power and the distribution of surplus to sectors and territories where the social necessities are so patently obvious. Thus we need to move to a new pattern of organization in which the market is replaced (probably by a decentralized planning process), scarcity and deprivation systematically eliminated wherever possible, and a degrading wage system steadily reduced as an incentive to work, without in any way diminishing the total productive power available to society. To find such a form of organization is a great challenge, but unfortunately the enormous vested interest associated with the patterns of exploitation and privilege built up through the operation of the market mechanism, wields all of its influence to prevent the replacement of the market and even to prevent a reasoned discussion of the possible alternatives to it. Under conditions of social justice, for example, an unequal allocation of resources to territories and appropriative movements would be permissible if (and only if) those territories favored were able, through their physical and social circumstances and through their connections with other territories, to contribute to the common good of all territories. This pattern of appropriation will obviously be different to that achieved under the market mechanism, for the latter is institutionally bound to maintain patterns of appropriation, deprivation, and scarcity, and institutionally incapable of distributing according to need or contribution to common good. The social organization of scarcity and deprivation associated with price-fixing markets makes the market mechanism automatically antagonistic to any principle of social justice. Whether the market mechanism can be justified on grounds of efficiency and growth depends on how it compares with those alternatives which most are unprepared even to discuss.

IV. "A Just Distribution Justly Arrived at— Territorial Social Justice"

From this examination of the principles of social justice we can arrive at the sense of *territorial social justice* as follows:

(1) The distribution of income should be such that (a) the needs of the population within each territory are met, (b) resources are so allocated to maximize interterritorial multiplier effects, and (c) extra resources are allocated to help overcome spatial difficulties stemming from the physical and social environment.

(2) The mechanisms (institutional, organizational, political, and economic) should be such that the prospects of the least advantaged territory are as great as they possibly can be.

If these conditions are fulfilled

there will be a just distribution justly arrived at.

I recognize that this general characterization of the principles of territorial social justice leaves much to be desired and that it will take a much more detailed examination of these principles before we are in a position to build some kind of theory of location and regional allocation around them. It took many years and an incredible application of intellectual resources to get to even a satisfactory beginning point for specifying a location theory based on efficiency and there is still no general theory of location—indeed we do not even know what it means to say that we are 'maximizing the spatial organization of the city' for there is no way to maximize on the multiplicity of objectives contained in potential city forms. In the examination of distribution, therefore, we can anticipate breaking down the objectives into component parts. The component parts are as follows:

(1) How do we specify need in a set of territories in accord with socially just principles, and how do we calculate the degree of need fulfillment in an existing system with an existing allocation of resources?

(2) How can we identify interregional multipliers and spread effects (a topic which has already some theoretical base)?

(3) How do we assess social and physical environment difficulty and when is it socially just to respond to it in some way?

(4) How do we regionalize in such

a way that territories are distinguished which maximize on social justice?

(5) What kinds of allocative mechanisms exist to ensure that the prospects of the poorest region are maximized and how do the various existing mechanisms perform in this respect?

(6) What kinds of rules should govern the pattern of inter-territorial negotiation, the pattern of territorial political power, and so on, so that the prospects of the poorest area are as great as they can be?

These are the sorts of questions which we can begin to work on in some kind of single-minded way. To work on them will undoubtedly involve us in making difficult ethical and moral decisions concerning the rights and wrongs of certain principles for justifying claims upon the scarce product of society. We cannot afford to ignore these questions for to do so amounts to one of those strategic non-decisions, so prevalent in politics, by which we achieve a tacit endorsement of the status quo. Not to decide on these issues is to decide. The single minded exploration of efficiency has at best amounted to a tacit endorsement of the status quo in distribution. To criticize those who have pursued efficiency for this reason is not to deny the importance of analysis based on efficiency itself. As I indicated at the beginning of this article, we need to explore questions of efficiency and distribution jointly. But to do so we first need a detailed exploration of those questions of distribution which have for so long been left in limbo.

Footnotes

1.   The relevance of this condition to equilibrium in the housing market is explored in Muth, R. F., *Cities and Housing* (University of Chicago Press, Chicago; 1969), pp. 21–9.

2.   Liebenstein, H., "Allocative efficiency versus x-efficiency," *Amer. Econ. Rev.*, 61 (1966), 392–415.

3.   Aristotle, *Ethics*, translated by J. A. K. Thompson (Penguin Books, Harmondsworth, Middlesex; 1955).

4.   Rawls, J., "Distributive Justice," in Lanslett, P. and Runciman, W. G. (eds.), *Philosophy, Politics and Society (Series III)* (Basil Blackwell, Oxford; 1969).

5.   Rescher, N., *Distributive Justice* (Bobbs-Merrill, Indianapolis; 1966).

6.   Runciman, W. G., *Relative Deprivation and Social Justice* (Routledge and Kegan Paul, London; 1966).

7.   Tawney, R. H., *Equality* (George Allen and Unwin, London; 1931); see also Pennock, R. J. and Chapman, J. W., *Equality*, Volume IX of Nomos (Atherton Press, New York, 1967).

8.   See, for example, Titmuss, R., *Income Distribution and Social Change* (Allen and Unwin, London, 1962) and Miller, S. M. and Roby, P., *The Future of Inequality* (Basic Books, New York; 1970).

9.   Titmuss, R., *op. cit.*

10.   Miller, S. M. and Roby, P., *op. cit.*

11.   Harvey, D., *Social Justice and the City* (forthcoming monograph); I have attempted a preliminary excursion into this field in "Social processes, spatial form, and the redistribution of real income in an urban system," in Chisholm, M. (ed.)

Regional Forecasting, Proceedings of the 22nd Colston Symposium (Butterworths Scientific Publications, London; 1971).

12. Alker, H., "A typology of ecological fallacies," in Dogan, M. and Rokkan, S. (eds.), *Quantitative Ecological Analysis in the Social Sciences* (MIT Press, Cambridge, Mass.; 1969).

13. I am here largely following Rescher, N. *op. cit.* and Runciman, W. G. *op. cit.*

14. Runciman, W. G. *op. cit.*, pp. 260–74.

15. Davies, B., *Social Needs and Resources in Local Services* (Michael Joseph, London; 1968).

16. Runciman, W. G. *op. cit.*, p. 10.

17. Davies, B. *op. cit.* provides a good example of how care for the aged might be determined by this kind of method.

18. Isard, W., *Methods of Regional Analysis* (Wiley, New York; 1960).

19. See the review by Darwent, D., "Growth poles and growth centers in regional planning," *Environment and Planning*, 1 (1969), 5–32.

20. Mishan, E. J., *The Costs of Economic Growth* (Praeger, New York, 1967); *Welfare Economics: Ten Introductory Essays* (Random House, New York; 1969); Margolis, J., *The Public Economy of Urban Communities* (Resources for the Future, Washington; 1965); Harvey, D. *op. cit.*

21. Rothenberg, J., *The Economic Evaluation of Urban Renewal* (Brookings Institution, Washington; 1967).

22. Davis, B., *op. cit.*, p. 18.

23. Buchanan, K. and Tullock, G., *The Calculus of Consent* (University of Michigan, Ann Arbor; 1965), p. 192.

24. Marx, K., *Critique of the Gotha Programme* (International Publishers, New York; 1970 edition), p. 11.

25. All the following quotes are taken from Rawls, J., *op. cit.*

26. See Titmuss, R., *op. cit.*; Webb, A. L., and Sieve, J. E. B., *Income Redistribution and the Welfare State* (G. Bell, London, 1970); Miller, S. M. and Roby, P., *op. cit.*

27. Weber, M., *The Theory of Social and Economic Organization* (Free Press, New York; 1967 edition), pp. 363–85. For a fascinating account of the events in China see Buchanan, K., *The Transformation of the Chinese Earth* (Praeger, New York; 1970).

28. A noble attempt to do this is illustrated in the Detroit Geographical Expedition's "School Decentralization," *Field Notes* (Discussion Paper No. 2, Detroit Geographical Expedition, East Lansing, Michigan).

29. One of the most interesting formulations for this problem is given in Friedmann, J., "A general theory of polarized development," *mimeo* (School of Architecture and Urban Planning, University of California at Los Angeles; 1969).

30. See, for example, Kotler, M., *Neighborhood Government* (Bobbs-Merrill, Indianapolis; 1969).

31. Baran, P. A. and Sweezy, P. H., *Monopoly Capital* (Monthly Review Press, New York; 1968).

32. See Borts, G. H. and Stein, J. L. *Economic Growth in a Free Market* (Columbia University Press, New York; 1964) and Myrdal, G., *Economic Theory and Under-Developed Regions* (Duckworth, London; 1957).

33. Report of the Committee on Housing in Greater London (the Milner-Holland Report), HMSO, Cmnd.2605 (London; 1965).

34. Grigsby, W. C., Rosenburg, L., Stegman, M., and Taylor, J., *Housing and Poverty* (Institute for Environmental Studies, University of Pennsylvania, 1971).

35. Huberman, L. and Sweezy, P. M., *Socialism in Cuba* (Monthly Review Press, New York; 1969).

36. Pearson, H. W., "The economy has no surplus: Critique of a theory of develop-

ment" in Polanyi, K., Arensberg, C. M. and Pearson, H. W., *Trade and Market in the Early Empires* (Free Press, New York; 1957), p. 320.

37.   Adams, R. McC., *The Evolution of Urban Society* (Aldine, Chicago; 1967) and Wheatley, P., *The Pivot of the Four Quarters* (Aldine, Chicago; 1971).

Index ••